691-4574

WITHDRAWN
UTSA LIBRARIES

GROUP

PSYCHOTHERAPY

AND

GROUP FUNCTION

GROUP PSYCHOTHERAPY AND GROUP FUNCTION

REVISED EDITION

EDITED BY

MAX ROSENBAUM, Ph.D.

&

MILTON M. BERGER, M.D.

BASIC BOOKS, INC., PUBLISHERS

NEW YORK

LIBRARY
University of Texas
At San Antonio

Library of Congress Cataloging in Publication Data

Rosenbaum, Max, 1923-   ed.
  Group psychotherapy and group function.

  Includes bibliographical references and index.
    1.   Group psychotherapy—Addresses, essays, lectures.
I.   Berger, Milton Miles, joint ed.   II.   Title.
[DNLM: 1.   Psychology, Social.   2.   Psychotherapy,
Group.   WM430 R815g]
RC488.R66   1975   616.8'915   73-91084
ISBN 0-465-02721-0

© 1963, 1975 by Basic Books, Inc., Publishers
Manufactured in the United States of America
75 76 77 78 79   10 9 8 7 6 5 4 3 2 1

Ac ne forte roges,
quo me duce,
quo lare tuter.
(Nullius addictus iurare
in verba magistri.)
—HORACE

And do not ask, by chance,
what leader I follow
or what godhead guards me.
(I am not bound to revere
the word of any particular master.)

CONTENTS

Part 3
THEORY AND TECHNIQUE

Part 4

APPLICATIONS TO PARTICULAR DIAGNOSTIC ENTITIES

Part 5
TRAINING

Part 6
THE CURRENT SCENE:
GROUPS FOR THERAPY AND GROWTH

PREFACE

The original edition of this book has met with an enthusiastic response. It appears to have begun to answer the need and desire for practitioners of group psychotherapy and students of group process to find some common reference points. Over a decade has passed since the original volume was compiled, and many of the original questions remain unanswered. Before his untimely death, Kurt Lewin, an important figure in the fields of social psychology and group dynamics, was about to embark on a study of group psychotherapy. He was never able to achieve his goal.

In the tradition of research, this volume has sifted through the articles in the field of social psychology and group process for information which should be of value to the practitioner. In addition, we have asked some of our contributors to summarize the relevant research and practice and have attempted to move beyond articles that are testimonial in nature. Some of the contributors to the first edition have amended their articles from the vantage point of 1974.

This volume has a dual aim—first, to give some idea of the vastness and historical roots of group psychotherapy, and second, to encourage all who work with groups to begin to share with one another their experiences. Hopefully, this should lead to some conceptualizations and finally to hypotheses that may be systematically studied. There is a great deal of dogma in the field of psychotherapy. While it is not our intent to criticize assumptions or opinions, it is our hope that assumptions and opinions will not be confused with facts. Perhaps the very humanness and authenticity of intensive psychotherapy will preclude systematic research, but in the absence of data to deny the possibility of research we can still make efforts to formulate and test research hypotheses.

Many scientists in different major fields of interest share with us the common goal of seeking to know man. To the degree that we do know man we may be in a better position not only to help our fellow man and ourselves therapeutically but also to help man singly and in groups to more completely develop and fulfill his healthy potential for his own good and the good of that larger group referred to as mankind. We can influence our own evolution through the knowledge of people in groups.

We have attempted to select articles and excerpts that are truly representative. On occasion, an author of an article would feel that the work chosen was not truly representative of his effort. Our purpose was to note the historical importance of such an article at a particular point in the evolution of group psychotherapy and group function. Unfortunately, a few authors refused consent unless an article was reprinted in its entirety or was brought "up to date." Some articles have indeed been updated, but due to space limitations we were unable to reprint some articles which we believe to be valuable. Originally, the collection of readings was envisioned as a two-volume work, but practical considerations put this plan to rest. It is our hope that this edition will serve as part of a continuing effort devoted to the rapprochement between group psychotherapy and group dynamics.

There is currently an almost unbelievable profusion of approaches to psychotherapy and group psychotherapy. Many of the approaches are "hard sell," offering much in the way of testimonials and little sound conceptualizing. A recent conference on psychotherapy listed twenty-two varieties of individual and group approaches. Each new technique acquires a new following of aficionados. No school of psychotherapy agrees to disband because a more effective technique has been found.

Our culture is changing rapidly and dramatically. People who are alienated and feel threatened by the loss of familiar values or standards, or changes in geographic locations, often turn to psychotherapy as the answer to their fears and confusions. The encounter group movement, with its emphasis on instant intimacy, is an effort to cope with the loneliness of many people. Recently, there has been an enormous interest in mysticism and the occult. Some psychotherapists give up in despair and become involved in social change approaches, or question the sanity of the culture in which we live. In view of all this, our text is devoted to the task of bringing some order to the confused and confusing fields of group psychotherapy and group approaches.

We are grateful for the generous cooperation of the numerous contributors to this volume, as well as to the publishers and professional societies who granted consent for reprinting.

We are deeply appreciative to all those who participated with us in our multiple group experiences, which ranged from our own family groups to our current research, teaching, and therapy groups. All group experiences are valuable and the knowledge gained in these experiences, if shared with the "influentials" of the world, can be utilized to clarify man's relationship with his fellow man and to improve these relationships constructively.

We give special thanks to the groups we live with—our families—and to the groups we work with—our patients and colleagues.

M.R.
M.M.B.

October 1974

LIST OF AUTHORS

Nathan W. Ackerman, M.D.
H. Altmann, Ph.D.
Solomon E. Asch, Ph.D.
Kurt W. Back, Ph.D.
John Elderkin Bell, Ed.D.
Milton M. Berger, M.D.
Eric Berne, M.D.
Cornelius Beukenkamp, M.D.
Carolyn Bascom Bilodeau, R.N.
Anne L. Bloxom, M.A.
Trigant Burrow, M.D., Ph.D.
Dorwin Cartwright, Ph.D.
Bernard Casella, Ph.D.
Erika Chance, Ph.D.
Raymond J. Corsini, Ph.D.
Max Day, M.D.
Louis DeRosis, M.D.
Rudolf Dreikurs, M.D.
S. H. Foulkes, M.D.
Ruth Fox, M.D.
Jerome D. Frank, M.D., Ph.D.
Maurice Friedman, Ph.D.
William Furst, M.D.
Joseph J. Geller, M.D.
Lester H. Gliedman, M.D.
George D. Goldman, Ph.D.
Robert L. Goulding, M.D.
Hanna Grunwald, Ph.D.

Thomas P. Hackett, M.D.
Samuel B. Hadden, M.D.
Eugene L. Hartley, Ph.D.
Hans A. Illing, Ph.D.
Maxwell Jones, M.D.
Asya L. Kadis, M.A.
Edward Kaufman, M.D.
J. W. Klapman, M.D.
Irvin A. Kraft, M.D.
D. H. Lawrence
Robert Paul Liberman, M.D.
Lawson G. Lowrey, M.D.
L. Cody Marsh, M.D.
J. L. Moreno, M.D.
Hugh Mullan, M.D.
Gardner Murphy, Ph.D.
Helen T. Nash, Ph.D.
James T. Payne, Ph.D.
Joseph H. Pratt, M.D.
Max Rosenbaum, Ph.D.
Bina Rosenberg, M.D.
David Rosenthal, Ph.D.
Mathew Ross, M.D.
Uri Rueveni, Ph.D.
R. A. Sandison, M.D.
Elvin V. Semrad, M.D.
Paul Schilder, M.D.
Muzafer Sherif, Ph.D.

S. R. Slavson
Ross V. Speck, M.D.
Christopher T. Standish, M.D.
Aaron Stein, M.D.
Walter N. Stone, M.D.
Hans H. Strupp, Ph.D.
Hans Syz, M.D.
Herbert A. Thelen, Ph.D.

Murray E. Tieger, Ph.D.
Charles B. Truax, Ph.D.
John Warkentin, M.D., Ph.D.
Louis Wender, M.D.
Dorothy Stock Whitaker, Ph.D.
Martha Williams, Ph.D.
Alexander Wolf, M.D.

GROUP

PSYCHOTHERAPY

AND

GROUP FUNCTION

INTRODUCTION

Philosophic tradition in the United States stresses the ethic of individual responsibility, with, historically, little emphasis on the group and its relationship to the individual. Nevertheless, the country is in fact group oriented. Certainly, although the pioneers who settled our frontiers stressed the rights of the individual, they were dependent upon group functioning to carry out their ambitious goals of settlement. With the turbulent passage of the nation from an agrarian to an industrial life, one of the problems of American reformers during the early 1900's was that in fighting for individual values they had to use techniques of organization. As the homogeneous, rural, Protestant Yankee community felt the impact of industrialization and of new waves of immigration, individualistic forms of living were supplanted by highly organized forms of group living. The image of the independent and extremely self-reliant man was rapidly disappearing. Today the student of human behavior, however deeply concerned with the individual, must also be concerned with the individual within the group.

Symptomatic of this shift in emphasis has been the expansion of group psychotherapy since the end of World War II. Much of this growth was stimulated by the problems of the large numbers of people in need of psychiatric treatment and the limited number of professional personnel. Thus, group psychotherapy made it possible for one therapist to increase treatment facilities by seeing a group of patients at one time. However, group psychotherapy before long was seen as having intrinsic value of its own. Today many therapists prefer to prescribe group treatment even for the patient who is financially able to obtain individual psychotherapy.

Meanwhile, in settings such as universities, religious groups, labor unions, and settlement houses, the study of group dynamics was growing. With increasing awareness of the development of the individual personality within a group-cultural setting, students of human behavior became more and more interested in studying the group's impact upon the growing person. For some time these two streams—group dynamics, the study of the unique ways in which a work or recreation or family group functions, and

1

group psychotherapy, in which individual patients with emotional difficulties could meet together and clarify their personal problems in living while experiencing their problems in this group setting—have been running parallel to one another. The streams then began to converge. Some practitioners in each field began to share and profit from one another's experiences. In one instance there were ostensibly "normal" individuals working within a group framework. In another setting there was a group of neurotic or psychotic individuals led by a group psychotherapist. Were there any principles of group structure common to both settings? Could the psychotherapist who was working with a group of troubled patients apply any of the knowledge gained by the student of the so-called normal group?

Psychotherapists as a group have been remarkably ignorant of the various relevant studies by "academic" psychologists and sociologists. Not until World War II did psychologists discover that they were often talking about the same thing that interested the sociologist.* Some sociologists who study groups consider themselves social psychologists. These *sociological* social psychologists study groups from the basic orientation of the study of society, in which a society is seen as a group. The *psychological* social psychologists, coming from a tradition where the individual is studied, are oriented toward the group as a society. To further complicate matters, the psychologist has been bound by a tradition of studying the individual apart from groups. Biologically oriented psychologists, on the other hand, tend to be skeptical of the notion of the cultural impact upon personality. There are even many who question the existence of the field called "social psychology."† Inkeles writes, in the book *Sociology Today*:[1] "I find it

---

* A sociologist stated: "Doubtless there always was some misunderstanding, and there never was quite enough open debate between the two, but they were never oblivious to the nature of each others concern."

† The first modern coverage of social psychology was published in 1902, written by Charles Horton Cooley, and titled, *Human Natures and the Social Order*. The first two textbooks in the field, both titled *Social Psychology*, were published in 1908. They were written by the psychologist William McDougall and the sociologist Edward A. Ross.

Sociologists teach approximately one half of the courses in social psychology (see W. B. Cameron, P. Lasley, and R. Dewey, "Who Teaches Social Psychology?" *American Sociological Review*, 15:554, 1950). The American Sociological Association has organized a section on social psychology. One fourth of this association's membership allied themselves with social psychology (see M. W. Riley, "Membership of the American Sociological Association," *American Sociological Review*, 25:925, 1960).

It is difficult to find information after 1950. Sociologists teach courses in social psychology under the title "The Individual in Society." When sociologists teach such courses they generally emphasize role theory. Psychologists who teach social psychology courses generally emphasize more molar Gestalt theory and reinforcement theory. There are currently four major lines of approach in social psychology: the psychoanalytic; role theory; Gestalt theory; and reinforcement theory. The Gestalt and reinforcement theories are basically laboratory-based approaches.

extremely difficult to understand just what social psychology is today. . . ." This sounds like semantic bedlam. Nevertheless, there has been a constant attempt to delineate fields of study.

Gardner Murphy[2] considers the psychology of perception the keystone for modern social psychology. This research in perception followed upon the studies of viewpoints, values, and folkways carried out by sociologists and anthropologists. The work in perception was helped immeasurably in the late 1920's and early 1930's by the work of two psychologists, F. C. Bartlett,[3] who carried on research in England, and Muzafer Sherif,[4] a young Turkish scholar who came to the United States during the early 1930's. Sherif studied the autokinetic effect and the group's influence upon the individual observer of this phenomenon. In the autokinetic effect, subjects are exposed to an ambiguous stimulus situation. An individual in a totally darkened room, with no visible perceptual standards—anchorages—by which to orient himself, will perceive a fixed point of light as moving. The subject is instructed to look into a box in this darkened room. Nothing can be seen except a light from a pinhole in the box which shines briefly and then goes out. Without prompting, the subject will invariably see the light as moving. When questioned, the subject will describe how much the light moves. Each subject appears to have a certain order about his judgments. Sherif then placed his subjects in groups of two or three. Each subject was asked to give his judgment of the light while the other subjects were present. Very quickly the subject became a member of a group and a group norm began to evolve. A group pattern developed, with a leader and followers. When the group was dissolved it was found that the individual carried the group norm into the setting where he was asked to give his judgment privately. Sherif has continued his basic research schema in many complex group settings, studying the impact of membership in a group upon perception.

Murphy[5] credits Sherif* with developing the experimental and conceptual model of the *new* social psychology in contrast with the older behavioristic social psychology.[6] Murphy himself, together with his wife, Lois Murphy, had written an encyclopedic text in social psychology.[7] Six years later, a revised edition of this text could be only a synthesis, for the field had grown so rapidly that it was impossible to summarize studies.[8]

---

* The assertion of credit is debatable. The only major scholar in this area who preceded Sherif was G. H. Mead, who described himself as a behaviorist [see his book, *Mind, Self and Society*] (Chicago: University of Chicago Press, 1934). Some of the more recent work in the social psychology of perception also contains elements that stem from the behaviorism of Watson.

A BRIEF HISTORY OF GROUP PSYCHOTHERAPY

The Early Period

Group psychotherapy has been described as uniquely American. It is indeed a consequence of the pragmatism of American psychiatry, which appeared willing to explore any new and possibly helpful technique.

Viewed in perspective, group psychotherapy's historical roots go back to the beginning of recorded time. Every great religious movement from Moses on has been psychotherapeutic and has reached masses of people. The Greek dramatists of the Hellenic era were deeply concerned about family relationships. The day-long performances of the Grecian classics were a form of mass psychotherapy in that the audience watched actors interpret many of the themes of family involvement. The dramas of Shakespeare, although set in the Elizabethan era, are concerned with many of the same themes. Formal group psychotherapy as such may be traced to Anton Mesmer's group hypnotic sessions of the early 1700's.

Today, most observers credit Joseph Hersey Pratt, a Boston internist, with the beginning of group psychotherapy. It is believed that Pratt originated the technique in 1905, when he organized tuberculosis patients into groups in class-type settings.[9]

Most of these patients were seriously ill and discouraged. They were suffering from a disease that then had a poor prognosis. Pratt was interested in helping his patients establish sound practices of physical hygiene. He lectured to them and conducted group discussions. He utilized an inspirational approach as he reassured them and tried to help them to overcome their discouragement and pessimism, to relinquish secondary gains from their illness, and to develop increasing self-confidence and self-esteem.

One can doubt that Pratt was entirely clear as to what he was doing. His first theoretical awareness seemed to develop in 1913, after he had been practicing his early version of group psychotherapy for a few years. Though self-taught in the area of emotional reeducation, he maintained a limited contact with a few psychiatrists who answered some of his questions. However, the psychiatrists were for the most part uninterested. Possibly the struggle of psychiatry to develop as a specialty in the field of medicine led to an overreaction on the part of many practitioners so that they were unwilling to explore anything which was not strictly "scientific." In 1876, Beard had first publicly proposed his theory that the mind might be the cause of disease, which led to fears that psychiatry might become part of theology. In 1908, an editorial in a leading medical journal attacked the clergy who had become active in psychotherapy.[10] Pratt, who had received financial support for his work from one of these clergymen, came under criticism because of this and had to point out that he had no involvement with the work of these clergymen.

During his early group work, Pratt was largely left to his own devices. He believed that most patients with emotional difficulties should be treated by the internist and general practitioner and that the physician should treat both the inner and outer man. Psychiatrists were too busy fighting their own battle for recognition to be concerned with one busy internist and his problems. The psychiatrists gave him little encouragement, and the psychologists were involved with problems of introspection.

During this first decade of the twentieth century, Freud's new concepts were attracting the interest and attention of some very aware psychologists, but nothing in his theories related specifically to the group.

Although Moreno has stated that from 1910 to 1914 he carried on experiments with groups of children, displaced persons, and prostitutes in Vienna, and classifies this work with Pratt's class method as the beginning of modern group psychotherapy, he too has described group psychotherapy as an "American product."

Dreikurs and Corsini[11] have stated that in the early period of group psychotherapy, from 1900 to 1930, a group method called "collective counseling" was being used by German and Austrian psychotherapists to treat stammerers, neurotic patients, alcoholics, and patients with sexual disturbances. Russian and Danish psychiatrists also employed group methods.

Alfred Adler is credited with being the first European psychiatrist to use group methods. Combining his interest in intensive psychotherapy with his political philosophy of socialism, Adler was concerned with ways of bringing psychotherapy to the working class. The group method of treatment seemed to be an excellent solution to the problem, since psychoanalysis, which stemmed from the environment of the Viennese intellectual elite, had little impact upon the working people of that time.

Most traditional European psychoanalysts, bound by their own class and status needs, expressed opposition and hostility to group psychotherapy (an observation that seems to confirm later studies[12] indicating that psychotherapists are often drawn to patients who reflect their own class and status needs and mirror the psychotherapist's value system). Consequently, those European psychiatrists who used the group method worked in relative ignorance of one another. In later years, the growth of fascism in Europe discouraged the group method which seemed to flourish in a climate of political freedom.

In the United States, before World War I, there were few physicians other than Pratt who used a group method of psychological treatment, although in New England of the early 1900's some inspirational group psychotherapy was carried on by ministers, within a religious setting.[13] At the end of World War I, Edward Lazell established lecture classes for patients at the St. Elizabeth Psychiatric Hospital in Washington, D.C.[14] Aware of group influences, he was enthusiastic about the group method in his therapy, which was essentially didactic.

About ten years later, L. Cody Marsh, a minister who later became a psychiatrist, described in some detail his use of the group method of psychotherapy.[15] Marsh combined his treatment with everything that he believed might be helpful to the psychological well-being of his patients. He employed techniques such as art classes, dance classes, and so on. A good deal of this work evolved from the theory that patients could be supportive to one another. Marsh worked with psychotic patients on an active level as contrasted with Lazell's series of didactic lectures to schizophrenics. When Louis Wender practiced group therapy with borderline patients in a mental hospital, he began using psychoanalytic concepts. This work, begun in 1929, was reported in 1935.[16]

Although Jacob L. Moreno is supposed to have coined the term *group psychotherapy* in 1931, in 1920 Trigant L. Burrow had used the term *group analysis*. In the history of psychotherapy there has been little attention given to Burrow—a great and original thinker of the early years of psychoanalysis who has been oddly neglected in surveys of contemporary psychotherapy. His pioneer group analytic studies were largely ignored and only currently is he receiving some recognition.

Burrow wrote sixty-eight articles and five books which summarized much of his research and concepts. His work is today carried on by his son-in-law, Hans Syz, a physician and psychiatrist. Burrow, after he obtained his medical degree and a doctorate in psychology, began to work in psychiatry under Adolf Meyer. After meeting Freud and Jung in 1909, in the United States, Burrow went to Switzerland to study psychoanalysis with Carl Jung. He returned in 1910 and began the practice of psychoanalysis. In 1911, he was one of the founding members of the American Psychoanalytic Association. Clarence Oberndorf, in his book *History of Psychoanalysis in America* cites Burrow as one of the four most original contributors to the science of psychoanalysis before 1920. From 1923 to 1932, Burrow engaged upon research in group dynamics, which he later called phyloanalysis. This group behavioral exploration stemmed from Burrow's dissatisfaction with the psychoanalytic emphasis on the individual—an emphasis which, he felt, excluded social forces. He believed that behavioral disorders should be traced back to social relatedness and that such research could best be carried out in the group setting. Burrow believed that in a therapeutic group, the emotionally troubled person would find his distorted self-image clarified as he observed others and their reaction to him. In 1923, Burrow and some twenty other persons—associates, students, patients—lived and worked together at a summer camp in the Adirondacks. From this group, the Lifwynn (Joy of Life) Foundation was formed. As Burrow studied groups, he moved more and more to an exploration of *his underlying concept*—the biological principles of behavior underlying the "group." He finally discarded the term "group analysis" in favor of the term "phyloanalysis." Burrow's position with regard to groups was essentially exploratory, although he was concerned with psychotherapy as carried out in the group setting. His work estranged him from the psychoanalytic community, and in 1933, when the American Psychoanalytic Association was reorganized, he was dropped from membership. It has been conjectured that Burrow's impact upon D. H. Lawrence, who admired Burrow, indirectly came through to Fromm and Horney, who were familiar with Lawrence's writings. Toward the end of his life Burrow complained that Harry Stack Sullivan, whom he knew, had never properly acknowledged Burrow's contribution to Sullivanian theory. In the years prior to his death Burrow was almost solely concerned with physiological studies of human behavior.

Another American pioneer was Paul Schilder, who introduced group psychotherapy at the Bellevue Psychiatric Hospital in New York City. He based his group psychotherapy on psychoanalytic concepts, and in 1939 he described the results of his pioneering efforts.[17] In this same period Moreno was developing and refining his concepts of psychodrama.[18] During the 1930's, Samuel Slavson, an engineer who later entered group work, established activity group therapy at the Jewish Board of Guardians. He worked with emotionally disturbed youngsters and encouraged them to work out their conflicts within a controlled play setting. He used psychoanalytic concepts in exploring the difficulties of these children but did not interpret directly for the youngsters. Essentially, Slavson's method of activity group therapy was not designed for severely disturbed children. The method encourages the acting out of conflicts and behavior problems in the setting of a play group, a relatively permissive environment. The interaction of the children as well as their relationship to the activity group therapist is carefully studied. The activity group is usually composed of eight children, about the same age and same sex. The group is carefully structured to achieve some sort of balance. Thus, the withdrawn child would be a balance to the aggressive child.[19] In 1943, at a symposium meeting of the American Orthopsychiatric Association, he reported his work in detail.[20] A briefer report by him was published in 1940.[21]

Group Psychotherapy After World War II

At the end of World War II, group psychotherapy was being used in many different settings. It had received a tremendous stimulus during World War II, when, largely due to the limitations of trained personnel and the number of psychiatric casualties who could not be treated, there was a strong effort to explore newer and briefer treatment methods. By 1943, Giles Thomas was ready to compile a relatively extensive review of the literature.[22]

Every school of psychotherapy was involved in group psychotherapy by 1945. The continuum ranged from the frankly repressive-inspirational, where group psychotherapy was used supportively, to the psychoanalytic, where group psychotherapy was used reconstructively. Carl Rogers, while not directly interested in group psychotherapy, encouraged students of his "client-centered psychotherapy" to apply his techniques in the group.[23] Reports came to the United States of the English psychiatrists who had begun to use group techniques. Joshua Bierer used Adlerian concepts in organizing his social club groups in England.[24] Foulkes was using a direct psychoanalytic technique in his work with groups in England.[25]

The annual conference of the American Orthopsychiatric Association was held in February 1943 and two section meetings were devoted to group psychotherapy. Lawson Lowrey, founder of the AOA, encouraged Samuel Slavson to post a notice at the conference inviting those who were interested in group psychotherapy to attend a luncheon meeting. Fifty people attended the luncheon meeting and it was at that time decided to form a group psychotherapy association. The first organization meeting took place in June 1943. The organization was first called the American Group Therapy Association; after some years, in 1952, the name was changed to the American Group Psychotherapy Association, because it seemed important to differentiate group psychotherapy from other group methods of helping people. Today, of course, the association has become concerned with all types of group methods.

In 1949, in the United States, Alexander Wolf published a lengthy paper in which he described in much detail his work on the "psychoanalysis of groups." [26] Both in 1948 and 1949 he had reported his work at conferences of the American Group Psychotherapy Association. Wolf has directly applied the principles of individual psychoanalysis to the group setting, using the major tools of the psychoanalytic method such as the transference, free association, dreams, and historical development. Wolf describes his group as the re-creation of the original family wherein the patient works through his unresolved problems. This is similar to the primary group that the sociologist is concerned with. Wolf had begun his work in 1938, stimulated by the reports of Wender and Schilder. Within one year, he was so excited and optimistic about his results, that he telescoped most of his private practice, and in 1940 he was working with five groups of eight to ten patients each. During four years of Army service, he continued his active interest in group psychotherapy and gained more insights into his work. He has stimulated and trained many psychiatrists, psychologists, and social workers in the technique of group psychoanalysis.

By the time Wolf reported his findings, many were ready to report their clinical experiences with group psychotherapy. Since then, there has been conflict as to who is entitled to recognition as a pioneer in the field of group psychotherapy. Since World War II, the literature on group psychotherapy has grown tremendously. Through the end of 1955, there was a bibliography of 1,700 items.* There are approximately 200 items—books,

* There has been no extensive bibliography since this very comprehensive one by

articles, and so on—written each year. Bach,[27] with a background and interest in the field of group dynamics, and heavily influenced by Kurt Lewin, the social and child psychologist, attempted to graft Lewin's concepts of group dynamics to the practice of group psychotherapy. His work is provocative, but at times he seems too speculative. A major problem apparently confronting the student of human behavior who attempts to relate group psychotherapy and group dynamics is the resistance to Freud's biology-based instinct theory of human behavior. Many group dynamics researchers feel more comfortable with a concept such as Harry Stack Sullivan's theory of interpersonal relations, which is provocative but quite vague at times. Leary,[28] in a study primarily centered on clinical diagnosis, has described the types of exchanges different personality types will look for. He has developed a very elaborate schematic system where his *principle of reciprocal relationships* is charted. Leary worked with an eight-dimensional multilevel system to predict the individual's behavior in group therapy and the effectiveness of the group as a whole. Each of the eight variables covered the adaptive to pathological range:

(1) competitive—narcissistic
(2) managerial—autocratic
(3) responsible—hypernormal
(4) cooperative—overconventional
(5) docile—dependent
(6) self-effacing—masochistic
(7) rebellious—distrustful
(8) aggressive—sadistic

However, Leary's report is not specific as to data analysis, the samples of subjects for his research, or how certain conclusions are drawn from certain observations.

Group Dynamics and Group Psychotherapy

One English psychiatrist, W. R. Bion, has made significant progress in attempting to formulate a relationship between group dynamics and group psychotherapy. His work has attracted the interest of American researchers in the field of group dynamics but has been in the main ignored by most group psychotherapists in the United States. Bion, unlike most group psychotherapists, has concerned himself with an understanding of what the group context is. Most group psychotherapists, in their emphasis on the individual, have neglected the group variables at work in group psychotherapy. Bion, in a series of articles, attempted to set forth a theory of group cul-

---

Raymond J. Corsini and Lloyd J. Putzey (*Bibliography of Group Psychotherapy 1906–1955*, Psychodrama and Group Psychotherapy Monographs No. 29, Beacon House, 1957). There are some periodicals which survey the group psychotherapy literature on a yearly basis, but these surveys are often rather incomplete.

ture and social structure which would apply to group psychotherapy.[29] Bion's work has been studied by group dynamics researchers at Teachers College, Columbia University and researchers working under the direction and stimulus of Herbert Thelen at the University of Chicago. Thelen has presented an excellent summary of Bion's speculations concerning group processes which are included in our volume of readings. To evaluate Bion it is important to first note that Bion has been trained and influenced in his psychoanalytic development by Melanie Klein. She was an English psychoanalyst whose influence is apparently minimal amongst American psychoanalysts but who carries great weight in Europe and in South America. While Bion has not specifically advanced Klein's controversial theories, her thinking is imbedded in much of his conceptualizations. To summarize Klein's position we would say that Klein has modified the orthodox Freudian concept of personality. She believed that the *ego exists from birth*. Good and bad emotions come from the infant's contact with the mother, who represents the external world. The capacity to love and feelings of persecution stem from these early contacts, which in turn are influenced by constitutional and environmental forces. As the infantile ego develops, two major processes come to the fore—introjection and projection. The people and situations that the infant encounters are taken up in the inner life of the infant—thus introjection. The infant attributes to others different feelings—thus projection. The interplay of these two processes is basic to the infant's perception of the world. The ego splits, dividing objects into good and bad. This splitting occurs in the early months of living. The ego growth is accompanied by anxiety and destructive impulses which Klein labeled the paranoid-schizoid position. With healthy development, the infant is increasingly able to understand reality, but from the sixth to the twelfth month of his life, he enters a depressed period related to his guilt and anxiety about his destructive impulses. The infant never fully recovers from this depressive period, and all this plays a part in the child's concept of social relationships. Human relationships can then be interpreted, according to Klein, in terms of introjection and projection and splitting, with the individual accepting his good feelings and denying his bad impulses. This is an individual-centered concept of group phenomena.

While there are many misunderstandings of Melanie Klein's position, some theorists see it as one of the most important turning points in the theory of human development. Rather than the previous stress on organically determined processes, she has emphasized psychodynamic object relationships.

Bion has related group formations to type of leadership, but essentially he has expanded upon Freud's limited ideas concerning group psychology. Like almost all group psychotherapists, Bion has ignored the influence of group structure. There is no attention given to the new social roles that the patient may take on when he enters a group therapy situation, as the patient responds to the group interaction. Bion has been aware that there are group goals which are often not overtly expressed by group members. In this area, he draws our attention to the nonverbal aspect of group processes, which has been detailed by Berger with reference to group psychotherapy (see our collected papers). Herbert Thelen (see our collected papers), in his work with groups, became aware of how often his findings touched upon Bion's speculations. From that point, he began to use these speculations as hypotheses which could be systematically researched. For example, Stock and Thelen,[30] working with training groups, used the sentence completion test to characterize each group member as preferring one of Bion's six valences of behavior toward others. The six valences are:

pairing—counterpairing (movement toward intimacy or a desire to remain
    isolated)
dependency—counterdependency (reliance on or rejection of external
    authority)
fight—flight (fighting or fleeing from stress)

They related these individual characterizations to group behavior that was also conceptualized in these terms. The results showed a relatively weak relationship between the personal patterns as derived from the reactions to the Group Situation Test (a sentence completion test) and behavior in the group. It can be stated, therefore, that the group behavior of any individual cannot be predicted from this test. In this way, we may begin to study the relationship between group goals and group function. The clinical, subjective experience of the practitioner in the field of group psychotherapy—the one great stream—is finally joined with the other great stream—the objective researcher in group dynamics.

Before the group dynamics researcher and the group therapist practitioner join hands too firmly, they will have to include the researcher in child development. This is because the student of child development will inform us as to how the child socializes or learns "the rules of the game." The outstanding student in this area is Jean Piaget, who is largely summarized and not often read in the original in the United States.* Piaget has described the child's first orientation to learning the "rules of the game."[31] To clarify his presentation, Piaget discussed the concepts of the sociologist Emile Durkheim (one of the first students of the group) regarding the individual's relationship with the group,[32] as well as the evolution of moral realities.

* In connection with the many studies based on Piaget's work that have appeared in the literature over the past decade, Piaget himself has stated that unfortunately many of them are poor. He says that they merely add to the current confusion about his theory. (Piaget's comments are available in two forty-minute 16 mm sound films, entitled *Dialogue with Piaget and Inhelder*, Parts I and II; Richard I. Evans, producer and interviewer. The films may be obtained from CCM Films, Inc., 34 MacQuesten Parkway South, Mount Vernon, New York, 10550.)

THE HISTORY OF SMALL GROUP RESEARCH

The Primary Group

The concept of the primary group was discussed both extensively and intensively by the American sociologist Charles H. Cooley[33] in the early 1900's. He defined the primary group as the "face to face" group characterized by intimate cooperation. A basic primary group is the family. It is a primary group that some group psychotherapists attempt to recreate in clinical practice. This group is primary in the sense that it gives the individual the early and complete experience of social unity. Furthermore, the primary group does not change in the same degree as more elaborate relationships. It forms a comparatively permanent source out of which the latter are ever springing. Cooley's writing had a marked impact upon the American social philosophers of his day. At about the same time as Cooley set forth his observations, over seventy years ago, Emile Durkheim,[34] in France, was also noting the importance of the group in human behavior. In Germany during the same period, the sociologist Simmel[35] was similarly concerned about the interaction amongst individuals.

The concern for the primary group, which occupied Cooley, later found expression in the writings and teachings of George Herbert Mead,[36] the philosopher and student of human behavior who, independent of psychoanalytic thinking, expressed the view that the primary group is the group which essentially trains the individual and provides him with the emotional and psychological developments that he will need in his functioning in human society. Mead* developed in great detail Aristotle's basic premise—man is a *social* animal. Quite removed geographically from the Chicago of George Herbert Mead, Sigmund Freud had been speculating about the different aspects of the individual's functioning in the primary group called the family and about the importance of the early familial experience in the psychological and emotional development of the individual. Freud pointed out the necessity of recognizing the important figures who influenced the child in his development in the primary group. There is no evidence to indicate that either Mead or Freud was influenced by the other, although Mead knew of Freud's work. Freud pondered about the primary group in his book, "Group Psychology and the Analysis of the Ego," [37] a work which is highly speculative and influenced by the concept of Le Bon, the French sociologist who described the group as a collective entity—a distinct being.[38] Freud's speculations concerning group psychology are even today apparently highly valued by many practitioners of psychoanalytic group psychotherapy. He noted that a group is held together by a common identification with a leader, and in his book he commented upon the primary group. He stated:

* Cooley and Mead were contemporaries and close friends.

We may further emphasize, as being specially instructive, the relation that holds between the contrivance by means of which an artificial group is held together and the constitution of the primal horde. We have seen that with an army and a church this contrivance is the illusion that the leader loves all of the individuals equally and justly. But this is simply an idealistic remodelling of the state of affairs in the primal horde, where all of the sons knew that they were equally persecuted by the primal father, and feared him equally. This same recasting upon which all social duties are built up is already presupposed by the next form of human society, the totemistic clan. The indestructible strength of the family as a natural group formation rests upon the fact that this necessary presupposition of the father's equal love can have a real application in the family.

Freud's basic point, that a group is formed by the identification of group members with the leader, represents one view. Although Freud's ruminations were little more than that, many contemporary group psychoanalysts tend to base all theory of group functioning on this early text of Freud. A survey of Freud's writings, published after his book on group psychology, indicates his optimism concerning the possibilities of group treatment.

Mead's students at the University of Chicago carried his concepts into many academic settings. He made a tremendous impact upon the social sciences with his writing and teaching about the development of self and the awareness of social relationships. His writing and his apparent effectiveness as a teacher stimulated an entire generation of sociologists. His work and that of Cooley are of prime significance in the early history of group dynamics. During this period, the sociologists were apparently more aware of the impact of interpersonal relationships and social roles than the psychologists. Park,[39] with his emphasis on research, was also an outstanding teacher during this time and influenced much sociological research in the area of community interaction. A group of sociologists who were students at this time at the University of Chicago, amongst them Zorbaugh and Thrasher,[40] carried out studies of the Chicago Gold Coast and the slums of the city and during these studies observed primary group formation in boys' gangs. Thrasher in his study did not assume that primary group relations are inevitably affective or nonlogical or consistently solid. William Foote White continued studies of the gang.[41] During the late 1920's and early 1930's, a series of studies was carried out in the Hawthorne plant, located in Chicago.[42] This plant, a division of Western Electric, was the scene of continuing studies of incentives and work productivity amongst groups of employees. It was found that *increased output was very much related to the interaction of the members of a working group.* Workers in the plant would increase or restrict productivity, and this was related to group pressures. From these studies it was recognized that workers who are in close contact with one another over a period of time tend to develop a primary group organization with loyalties, codes of behavior, and value systems. The pioneer and leader in this research was Elton Mayo* and the research studies of the group in industry have continued through the years.[43] During the 1920's, Edward Sapir set forth his observations of the group and the cultural scene.[44] He observed that there are basic principles underlying the formation of a group. The casual group and the structured and more permanent group are subject to the same principles. To illustrate, he cited two groups, the crowd at an automobile accident and the Senate:

> There is in reality no definite line of division anywhere along the gamut of group forms which connect these extremes. If the automobile accident is serious and one of the members of the crowd is a doctor, the informal group may with comparatively little difficulty resolve itself into something like a medical squad with an implicitly elected leader. On the other hand, if the government is passing through a great political crisis, if there is little confidence in the representative character or honesty of the senators or if an enemy is besieging the capitol and likely at any moment to substitute entirely new forms of corporate authority for those legally recognized by the citizens of the country, the Senate may easily become an unimportant aggregation of individuals who suddenly and with unexpected poignancy feel their helplessness as mere individuals.

Sapir did not delineate the basic principles of group formation but merely stated that these could be ascertained at some future time. His observations influenced the theoretical formulations of the early cultural psychoanalysts such as Harry Stack Sullivan. However, outside of atypical occurrences such as Sapir's influence upon Sullivan, there was little intermingling of the streams of academic thinking and psychiatric practice. An example of an atypical analyst who attempted to integrate studies of the individual and the group is Trigant Burrow, discussed earlier, one of the first American psychoanalysts.

Jacob L. Moreno, the psychiatrist and group psychotherapist, has been consistently interested in the individual's relationship to the group. He welcomed the cooperation of social scientists when he arrived in the United States in the 1930's. During the late 1920's in Europe and in the early 1930's in the United States he developed the concept of sociometry. This concept is essentially a recognition of the group membership needs

---

* It is interesting to note that Elton Mayo taught Joseph Pratt, the pioneer in modern group therapy, techniques of hypnosis, modifications of which Pratt used with "classes" of patients. Most industrial psychologists and students of human behavior in industry are unaware of the "other side" of Mayo, who served as a professor at the Harvard School of Business Administration. He was friendly with Pierre Janet, the physician and psychologist who pioneered dynamic psychiatry in France. Mayo was intrigued by Janet's concepts and wrote a book, published posthumously, in which he attempted to relate Janet's concepts to problems of industrial employees (*The Psychology of Pierre Janet*, Routledge and Kegan Paul, 1952).

of the individual and is based upon a measurement of group relationships. Members of a group are asked to list which members of the group they would like best or least to engage with in given activities. Generally three to five choices are requested. For example, in a boys' club, a member may be asked: "With which three boys would you like most to go to a ball game?" The spontaneous likes and dislikes are then charted out on "sociograms," graphic representation as to who is liked most or least and by which individuals. This technique of studying to whom an individual reaches out has been related by Moreno to his theory of spontaneity. Further, Moreno has been concerned with role-playing, the capacity of an individual to take another's role. This concept is related to how individuals perceive one another. It is of interest to note that role-playing had been discussed in the writings of Mead and Cooley. Moreno integrated role-playing into the group psychotherapy technique known as psychodrama in which an individual plays the role of another person and thereby gains awareness and insight into that person's expectations and anxieties. Psychodrama is a valuable reeducative technique in clarifying interpersonal distortions.

When Moreno established his journal, *Sociometry*, which was later turned over to the American Sociological Association, he encouraged psychologists and sociologists to join him in his work. Over the years, many students of the behavioral sciences have tended to dismiss him as too strongly partisan and as a result have tended to overlook his contributions to group psychology.[45]

The Group and Individual Change

The German Gestalt psychologist, Kurt Lewin, before his arrival in the United States in the early 1930's, had, in Germany, been a psychologist in an academic and theoretic setting, interested in the analysis of the child's social behavior. The tremendous upheaval and the rise of Nazism apparently dislodged him quite thoroughly from his earlier interests. He became acutely aware of the social problems of the day and began to devote his genius to the solution of these problems from a psychologist's perspective. He died in 1947, but during the decade or more that he spent in the United States he stimulated and led the field of group dynamics and left his impact upon a generation of students and colleagues. He worked first at Cornell, then at the University of Iowa Child Welfare Research Station and stimulated students and colleagues, among them, Ronald Lippitt and Dorwin Cartright. He moved briefly to Massachusetts Institute of Technology under the sponsorship of Douglas MacGregor.[46] His influence was felt in the establishment of the Research Center for Group Dynamics at the University of Michigan. This research center carries on his work with small groups and other problems in the field of social psychology.

Lewin was active in many projects and stimulated research in a variety of problems. Prior to World War II, Lewin and two of his students, Ronald

Lippitt and Ralph K. White, carried on an experimental study of leadership and group life.[47] Both a summary of the research and a fuller report of the original study are worth reading. Although the original study has been criticized on the grounds of experimental design and ideological bias, its basic contribution remains—*the investigation of the impact of the leader upon the structure and functioning of the group as well as the climate of the group and its relationship to productivity.* Lewin was increasingly aware toward the end of his life of the impact of group decision upon social change. He wrote in some detail about this. A brief excerpt from one of his writings is pertinent at this point. Lewin stated:

> Group decision is a process of social management or self-management of groups. It is related to social channels, gates and gate keepers—to the problem of social perception and the planning and to the relation between motivation and action between individuals and the group. . . . The effect of group decision can probably best be understood by relating it to a theory of quasi-stationary social equilibria to social habits and resistance to change and to the various problems of unfreezing, changing and freezing social levels.[48]

In this same article Lewin generalized that it is "usually easier to change individuals formed into a group than to change any one of them separately." This generalization, independently derived from studies of group function, is a basic tenet of the practice of group psychotherapy. During World War II, he embarked on a series of studies in which he was interested in increasing productivity, exploring problems of prejudice, changing food habits of individuals so that in a wartime economy they would eat foods which they previously were averse to, as well as many other related areas where social and individual change were concerned. In a summary of these studies he made the following statement:

> The prevalent theory in psychology assumes action to be the direct result of motivation. I am inclined to think that we will have to modify this theory. We will have to study the particular conditions under which a motivating constellation leads or does not lead to a decision or to an equivalent process through which a state of "considerations" (indecisiveness) is changed into a state where the individual has "made up his mind" and is ready for action although he may not act at that moment. The act of decision is one of those transitions.[49]

It would appear that Lewin, if anything, overemphasized the influence of social forces, but he certainly stimulated research in the area of group processes. Toward the end of his life, Lewin became an ardent Zionist and was deeply concerned with the creation of the state of Israel. He was particularly interested in the problems of minority group identification and the relationship to the majority group. His theme was "action research"—research that could be put into use—a far cry from the very academic Gestalt psychologist who first came to the United States.

Since then, the National Education Association, as well as other groups, have stimulated further research in group functioning. The National Training Laboratories have awarded grants for study of group processes, and almost every major industrial, labor union, religious as well as educational group is interested in group processes in relationship to their particular field of interest.

Group Pressure and Individual Change

The most significant breakthrough in this regard would appear to be in the area of social perception. How an individual perceives others, in what context the percept is made and the influence of the setting upon the perceptual process, has major significance in delineating group goals and working through hostilities between antagonistic groups that are composed of individuals. This perceptual research has been largely stimulated by the work of Muzafer Sherif in the mid-1930's. Its earlier structure was also based upon the perceptual studies of the English psychologist Bartlett in the late 1920's and the early 1930's. Through the years, Sherif has stimulated his students to more and more provocative research concerning the relationship between group membership and social perception. A good deal of research along this line has been carried out by Solomon E. Asch.[50] Asch, in a series of experiments, has found that when an individual is confronted with a majority group opinion that is contrary to his own as well as to fact, he will commonly change his opinions to conform with those of the group. However, there are some individuals who do not give in to group pressure and maintain their own opinions. The study of such people —who they are and what they are or whether they find the need to be in opposition to the group or whether they are truly "independent" personalities—will reveal much that is valuable to students of human behavior.

LATER RESEARCH AND THEORY

Since World War II, small group theory and research has expanded tremendously.

A Mathematical Approach

Von Neumann and Morgenstern introduced the modern game theory approach in 1944.[51] They analyzed some fundamental questions of economic theory in terms of a mathematical theory of games. The common elements of economic behavior and such factors as strategy in games were presented. The interrelated concepts were analyzed around a more or less central problem of utility. When the theory was introduced, many economists and sociologists felt that it might aid in the development of a theory of human behavior and group function and decision. Since then, the band-wagon feeling has terminated. Modern statistical decision theory has been helpful to many researchers in conceptualizations. However, we are dealing with a *human* organism when we begin to explore the nature of rational choice. This fact apparently eludes some researchers. In 1957, the game theory was surveyed by Luce and Raiffa.[52] They were still moderately enthusiastic about its usefulness. Solomon[53] edited a readings book in 1960, titled *Mathematical Thinking in the Measurement of Behavior*. In this volume are three distinct monographs. The monograph of particular interest to the student of group function was written by James S. Coleman. It is called "The Mathematical Study of Small Groups." This 150-page monograph was prepared as part of the program of the Bureau of Applied Social Research at Columbia University. The research was initiated during the years 1952-1956. In the monograph, Coleman discusses the relative paucity of mathematical models for behavior of small groups. He then examines in great detail several models which have been proposed. His systematic analysis of the pros and cons of each model are extremely discerning.

In 1959, Thibaut and Kelley[54] wrote a book on group behavior. Although the book includes references to 314 pieces of research on small group behavior, its main value lies in its theoretical constructs. In the book, Thibaut and Kelley try very strongly to introduce the game theory approach to group dynamics. While they do deal with interaction between two or more persons, rather than simple behavior in a social context, in common with the many psychologists who are researchers in group dynamics, they pay minimal attention to personality variables as they may be related to interaction in a group. This is one of the real problems of the statistical approach.*

In 1973, Hare published a summary of the various theories of group development.[55] This covered Tuckman's first major review of studies of group development (1965),[56] and the studies by Dunphy (1964),[57] Mills (1964),[58] Slater (1966),[59] and Mann (1967).[60] Mann's is the most recent and comprehensive report on group development.

The study of groups has been rather dormant among social psychologists. The emphasis has been upon dyadic studies. There have been studies, for example, of bargaining procedures using such techniques as the prisoner's dilemma. The growth of group therapy has not been accompanied by systematic research.

Group Life and Personality Variables

Homans, in setting forth his concepts of group life, has attempted to

---

* This statement would be called unfair by strong believers in this approach.

pay attention to the personality variables. He distinguishes between the internal and external systems of a group which make up the total social system. Thus, the internal system is "group behavior that is an expression of the sentiments towards one another developed by the members of the group in the course of their life together." The external system is conditioned by the environment and is the solution to the group's problem—how to survive in the environment.[61]

In 1954, an encyclopedic handbook devoted to social psychology appeared,[62] a handbook that may be a helpful reference to the student of social groups. Before his premature death at the age of 37, Olmsted wrote an introductory text to small group theory. The text stemmed from his doctoral dissertation, which was concerned with small group interaction and social norms.[63] This work is valuable, but it is still somewhat cursory.

The Problem-Solving Approach

One of the most systematic investigators of the small group has been Robert Bales and his many associates and students. He has studied, for the most part, problem solving groups, among them several psychotherapy groups. These studies are devoted to the process of interaction and communication in the group as well as to group size. The studies depend mainly upon the spoken word, as the group observer records on a moving tape who says what to whom in terms of one of twelve types of interaction. The Bales system of categorizing group interaction involves twelve possible ratings:

(1) shows solidarity, raises other's status, gives help
(2) shows tension-release, jokes, shows satisfaction
(3) agrees, shows passive acceptance, understands
(4) gives suggestion, implying autonomy for others
(5) gives opinion, evaluation, analysis
(6) gives orientation, information, clarifies
(7) asks for orientation, information, confirmation
(8) asks for opinion, evaluation, expression of feeling
(9) asks for suggestion, direction, possible ways of action
(10) disagrees, shows passive rejection, withholds help
(11) shows tension, asks for help, withdraws out of field
(12) shows antagonism, deflates other's status, defends or asserts self

Each participant's response, whether a few words or lengthy, would be considered a unit and scored as a unit as long as the major theme and attitude expressed remained essentially the same. Within one speech, if one or more noteworthy shifts occurred, an appropriate second or third score would be indicated. The observer would rely on the inflection and modulation of speech, the words that made up the verbalization and the body and face mannerisms that accompanied each statement, in addition to the content. All this in order to evaluate a response. Gestures and movements without verbalization are not part of a scorable response.

The Bales system may be considered useful in preliminary investigations, but it is not a very adequate measure.* It conceptualizes social interaction as a problem-solving sequence and categories are overgeneralized. The rating method appears overly atomistic. There appears to be a major emphasis on a verbal approach, and the nonverbal aspects of communication are not given sufficient recognition.[64]

In April, 1960, one organization, under a U.S. Air Force contract, compiled a bibliography of small group research.† This bibliography was part of an over-all program designed to provide integration of small group research knowledge. The bibliography contains some 2,200 items and is comprehensive for the period 1950-1959 but not as complete for preceding years, since there are existing bibliographies. This bibliography included only *selected* group psychotherapy studies and omitted masters' and doctoral theses as well as studies written in languages other than English.[65] It is understandable that even the devoted student of small group research will be hard put today to keep abreast of the deluge of studies. The practitioner of group psychotherapy will probably end up reading only selected studies or summaries of research with small groups.

CURRENT TRENDS

Current approaches to small group theory may be classified in four major categories: First, the exchange theory of Thibault and Kelley, which also encompasses the concepts of Homans[66] and Blau[67] and current approaches to field theory; second, Parsons' system theory; third, Bales' interaction process analysis; fourth, unconscious processes in groups.

Parsons,[68] in developing his theory of action, has given considerable attention to specifying systems and subsystems of action and to identifying the goal states of all systems of action. He has conceptualized the goal states as four system problems which must be solved if the system is to continue to maintain its boundaries with regard to the environment. There has been criticism of Parsons' theories with specific reference to how "testable" they are.[69] The same type of criticism has been directed at Homans,[70] whose propositions *appear* very clear and specific but become ambiguous when there is an effort made to test them. Some sociologists

---

* The inventory of observational categories is derived from Bales' theoretical conception of group functions.

† No significant bibliography has appeared since. There have been isolated surveys, but none as comprehensive as the 1960 compilation.

†† The *Handbook of Leadership* "covers more than 3,000 books and articles and covers some group research." R. M. Stagdell, *Handbook of Leadership* (New York: Free Press, 1974).

then state that Homans has really been quite ambiguous in his comments.

Probably the most attractive approach for the student of small group process is Bales' book, *Personality and Interpersonal Behavior*[71]—described as a "theoretical treatise in the form of a didactic handbook"—which is to be used by group participants to help them analyze and understand the groups to which they belong. The main thrust of this book is in its presentation of a model which is three-dimensional. The model is used to classify personality and/or group roles of group members. The book and techniques in it encourage group members to engage in self-analysis as well as study of the group.

This overview of group psychotherapy and group function would be incomplete without some comment on the development of encounter, sensitivity, and growth groups, embodied in the "human potential movement." The movement has also been called bod biz, or the acidless trip. It claims to restore "the poetry of life" in an industrialized world. These approaches have rarely been considered as group psychotherapy by serious professionals, but have been used by the troubled, lonely, or alienated to obtain contact, intimacy, awareness, new directions, pseudopsychotherapy, or stimulation of their risk-taking capacities and growth potential.

The encounter movement had its roots in a number of group activities in the 1940's and 1950's, such as: a) workshops conducted by the National Training Laboratory in Group Development of the National Education Association, which later became the Institute for Applied Behavior Science; b) the annual institutes of the American Group Psychotherapy Association; c) the weekend institutes of the growing local and regional affiliate societies of the AGPA all over the country, as well as the two-day sensitivity workshops of nonaffiliated groups; d) the growing interest in T-Groups ("T" for training). The T-Group concept was that "participants have the task of constructing a group which will meet the requirements of all of its members for growth. Members have the opportunity to learn about themselves, about interpersonal relations, about groups and about larger social systems. Trainers help to establish processes of data collection, data analysis and diagnoses of the changing here-and-now experiences of the group and its members."[*][72]

In a paper by Jerome Frank on "Training and Therapy," which appears in the book by Bradford, Gibb, and Benne, he emphasizes the difficulties of comparison, since therapy groups and T-Groups have so much in common. "Both are learning situations which have the aim of bringing about changes in their members. Both stress learning to communicate accurately with others as an important means. Both value mature, group-centered, altruistic, responsible functioning of members—therapy groups because it

* Leland P. Bradford, Jack R. Gibb, and Kenneth D. Benne, three T-Group innovators, made this statement in the preface to their book, *T-Group Theory and Method*.

is a sign of improvement in individual patients; T-Groups because it improves group functioning."

In the last decade, the atmosphere of daily life in the United States was characterized by heightened individual anxiety, frustration, helplessness, and isolation. Collectively, we were involved in: a questionable war in Vietnam; increasing disillusionment and doubts about the credibility of our elected government officials; interracial riots; the assassination of three popular leaders; student revolts and disillusionment with education, which resulted in the loss of lives and property; and a marked increase in open crime in our cities. Large numbers of youth from all levels of society became school dropouts, rejected cultural and family value systems and mores, and became involved in drug experimentation.

This serious malaise throughout the fabric of our national life provided a natural focal point for the real and fancied "fruits" of the encounter and growth group movement, which centered at Esalen, California, and led to the establishment of nearly one hundred "growth" centers in this country. The popularity of these centers has crested and they appear to be in a decline. However, social psychologists must record the significant functions they serve during a period when alienated, troubled, and demoralized people are attracted to them by the promises of instant awareness, closeness, trust, release of pent-up feelings, growth, and even sexual experience as well as fantasy.

The pseudointimacy and freedom of encounter groups, ostensibly unrestricted by interpersonal restraints and boundaries, were attractive to some group psychotherapists as well as to patients and nonpatients during a time when posters, automobile bumpers, and graffiti proclaimed, "Make Love, Not War." Many therapists experimented with confrontational and cathartic encounter techniques and incorporated certain of them in their psychoanalytically oriented practices; undoubtedly the most constructive and protherapeutic of these will remain in the repertoire of responsible group psychotherapists. Historically, many of these "new" techniques are to be found in the work of pioneer psychoanalysts. The encounter movement has also provided a major impetus for serious attempts by therapists, educators, and sociologists to distinguish needs for education and stimulation toward growth from needs for clarification and resolution of intrapsychic and interpersonal psychopathology.*

The members of the Association for Group Psychoanalysis and Process published a new journal in 1968, which included in its first issue a significant appraisal of "Similarities and Differences between Group Psychotherapy and Intensive Short Term Group Process Experiences."[73] In

---

* There is an increasing interest in further identifying the educational aspects of the psychotherapeutic process, and for efforts to be made to use the psychotherapeutic method or process in educational settings at all levels from kindergarten to college.

its continued examination of the encounter movement, the Association later published a special issue of *Group Process* on "Use and Misuse of Group Techniques."[74]

The concern of responsible professionals led the American Psychiatric Association, the American Psychological Association, and the American Group Psychotherapy Association to publish statements of caution concerning encounter group involvement when reports of disastrous consequences to participants appeared in the late 1960's and early 1970's. The official statement of the American Psychological Association appears in Chapter 62 of this book. The areas of major concern to responsible professionals were: (1) lack of adequate selection criteria; (2) lack of training and supervision of many "leaders"; (3) lack of preparation for post-encounter "reentry"; and (4) lack of professional personnel to care for those involved in potentially destructive afterreactions.

However, many participants were stimulated by their encounter experience to seek psychotherapy afterward. Many became better able to take risks emotionally and behaviorally than they would have otherwise, and many were in fact started on a road to introspective and interpersonal sensitivity and awareness previously not available to them. Encounter groups have been defined as an "experiment in psychological community. It is a shared opportunity for personal learning."[75]

While there are some advocates of a gentle approach in the encounter group, the majority of encounter group experiences are oriented toward goading participants toward an emotional explosion, such as intense weeping, with hoped-for comforting from other group members. All of this is supposed to produce self-awareness and self-understanding. The claim is made that the encounter method accomplishes a great deal in a short time. Today, there is no denial that encounter is considered a form of psychotherapy by its exponents, and, indeed, its adherents stress that it is a "stronger method" than the more common forms of psychotherapy.

However, most participants in encounter groups revert to their earlier behavior after a passage of less than a year, although some encounter group leaders conduct "follow-up" meetings or try to maintain contact with former participants in the encounter group. Carl Rogers, at his Western Behavioral Science Institute, conducted a three-year study, using the encounter techniques he endorses so strongly, in various colleges and schools in California. His experiment may fairly be considered a failure.

THE MEETING POINTS

Every piece of research on the conforming or nonconforming member of the group studied by the academic psychologist or sociologist can find its counterpart in the clinical experiences of the group psychotherapist who describes the resistant or compliant group patient. We may not always see the immediate impact of academic research, but the practitioner of group therapy does finally and hopefully look for some plausible reason as to *why*. He observes that an intensive psychotherapy group should optimally be composed of not more than eight or nine members. He cannot merely decree that the reason is because it works best. Why do some patients improve in a group while others do not? Is it all to be found in the dynamics of the individual, or can modification of group structure make the difference? Hopefully the hypotheses will come from the clinical hunches and inferences that are capable of operational testing.

It is necessary for the practitioner to have a frame of reference. Otherwise he cannot deal with his patients. He cannot afford to be insensitive to their needs, whether he functions in private practice or in an outpatient clinic. He has to have some way of getting started. However, he should conceive of his principles in psychotherapy as a sort of hypothesis. There should not be rigidity. There should be a willingness to orient toward research, toward the possibility of alternative theories giving a reasonable accounting of a particular clinical phenomenon. This may perhaps help him to improve his practice. He cannot take a complete research orientation toward his practice; but there is research, and it is increasing in quantity, quality, and scope. Researchers do not talk quite the same language as therapy practitioners or therapy theoreticians do. That does not mean that any one is wrong. It doesn't mean that there is trouble. It simply means that some way has to be found for these things to be reconciled—what goes on and what is found on the couch or in the group with what is found in the laboratory. If the psychotherapists do not interest themselves in research, the research workers may waste a lot of time. They may go along on a lot of problems that are of no earthly use to the psychotherapist. If, however, the therapist keeps alert and keeps communication open with the line of research, the possibility of having the research relate to the therapeutic question is increased. In our introduction we have reviewed development and changes in group psychotherapy, and we have reviewed re search. These are two independent quests. A few people have come ahead and attempted to reconcile these two quests. There is more to be done, and we believe that every therapist should try his own system of reconciliation.

A major problem that will confront the researcher is that the psychotherapy group is not a laboratory problem-solving group. There is no neat problem set up for a solution which has to be reached by the end of the meeting. The free, spontaneous discussion of the psychotherapy group is still quite different from the task-directed laboratory group. There is a difference between the transient involvement of the group member in the laboratory problem-solving group and the deep emotional involvement of patients who are in the same psychotherapy group, where they expose their deepest fantasies and feelings about themselves and toward one another, session after session, over a prolonged period.[76] While the goal of the group psychotherapist is individual psychological change, and he is concerned about maintaining a shifting and ever-changing group to achieve that goal, he does use group relationships to change the personalities of group members. The therapeutic group is one example of a group in which the therapist or leader uses principles of group dynamics—in this case group influence and interaction to induce individual change.

We offer to the practicing psychotherapist a positive philosophy of openmindedness, nonrigidity and nondoctrinairism. For the practice of psychotherapy, we present material about the practice of group psychotherapy. But for the sake of the psychotherapist's insight and understanding we offer research findings so that there may be new emergence. Do the research findings concerning cohesiveness and leadership or other processes jibe with what goes on in the therapy group? Can we extrapolate what we have learned about the psychodynamics of family structure as we observe it in the therapy group (see the Alexander Wolf article) and translate this into observations of all social behavior?

The reader may state, "Is this a series of questions?" Yes, this is what we suggest—that therapists transform doctrine into questions. Remember that Freud's individual psychology started with his patients and in a short time was extrapolated to all of mankind, all cultures, all ages. Some therapists speak of schizophrenic nations. While the soundness of this statement may be questioned, the statement is nevertheless made. It is as good a hypothesis and a way of beginning to structure the complex data that we have on social groups as any that we know about from other points of view.

The present writers are sympathetic with the work of Sherif, but once you have the concept of frames of reference, what does the therapist do with it? Does the group therapy experience and its norms change the patient because he responds to group pressure? Does he really change? The phrase "ego involvement" is often used, but what do you do with it? We must go beyond phrases and explore ways of applying or extending them. (See Stock and Thelen's research with Bion's concepts.)

Sapir's comments on the group function and Freud's belief that the leader was the crucial factor in group function are speculations. Consider the following. When nine young men meet to play baseball they are drawn together by a common goal. This serves to regulate the behavior and structure the group. When nine young men are brought together by a psychotherapist, there is no common goal other than the therapist's opinion that the group experience will be beneficial for each patient and the patient's hope that this opinion is valid. In this situation, does the group psychotherapist set this goal? Is this absurd, or are there common principles at work? Many therapists have observed that in psychotherapy we largely explore the patient's fantasy about reality. What brings the person to psychotherapy is mainly fantasy. Does fantasy bring together the nine young men who play baseball? The exploration of group fantasy may conceivably be a research problem that concerns the student of group function.

As practicing psychotherapists, we make our approach to our groups and our patients as we see fit. However, at this point, a true synthesis of the approaches that we make in a therapeutic setting with the approaches that are made in the laboratory is premature. There are many directions in which the research people have moved and had interesting findings. There are many areas where psychotherapists do not know the answers. We have many questions, and each therapist can raise questions. There will not always be the same questions because therapists obtain their patients from different sources, and they work with them in different ways. However, unless the questions are asked, will we ever get answers?

This, therefore, is a book to stimulate therapists to ask questions and to stimulate social psychologists to be aware of the many questions that therapists are asking them. It is also a book that reviews the approaches that have been made to the findings of answers. The section on social psychology gives some picture of social psychology that is particularly meaningful to psychotherapists—convergence, group pressure on the individual, status, productivity in different kinds of groups, and the beginning of research in social psychology and group psychotherapy. As the reader goes on, he may at different points have many questions. For example, when there is convergence in the group, status problems come up. If you have a relatively unsophisticated and naïve subject in an experiment, the convergence will be from the naïve to the high prestige position. Perhaps we are dealing with a situation which is somewhat comparable in the psychotherapy group. The group therapist may serve as an anchorage and get convergence, if not to what he says, at least to the value system which he represents. Is ᵗhe group an extension of these values?

Group psychotherapy offers a unique and important setting for the student of small groups. While the line-judging group of college sophomores is artificially created and somewhat unreal, the therapy group becomes very real to the patient who is deeply involved in it. It might be reasonable to ask why the academician cannot be involved in the study of therapy groups. Until recently there were few students of small groups who had sufficient therapeutic awareness or clinical experience to be aware of the complexities of psychotherapy. The patient must be consistently seen as an individual in distress and not as an experimental subject. Therefore the patient's interest must always come first, no matter how much this upsets the usual research patterns.

The practicing group psychotherapist has fumbled along with the little established theory of group functioning to guide him. He has generally learned through experience to solve such problems as the optimal size of a therapy group and the various clinical entities with whom he can best work.

The various theories of psychoanalytic psychology have been helpful as the group psychotherapist gropes along. For the most part, the language of psychoanalysis has been used as a framework for group psychotherapy theory and in the formulation of hypotheses. Until recently, there has been little systematic attention paid to the *group* variables which operate specifically in the group psychotherapy setting.

Some twenty-five years ago, Murphy, in an introduction to Sherif's text on social psychology, wrote:

> What a society does when it molds the individual into membership in the group is first of all to insist upon his learning to see the world in one way rather than another.[77]

Murphy further noted:

> . . . a sound psychological analysis will discover in laboratory situations and in life situations the same fundamental dynamics of human life and conduct, because being human, one cannot ever function without displaying these basic principles from which every sound interpretation proceeds. It is the task of the laboratory to discover the essentials of the "real life" situations, and to throw light upon them, just as it is the task of the study of life situations to see where a given principle may be systematically explored in laboratory terms.[78]

It is to this theme that these collected papers are dedicated.

REFERENCES

1. A. Inkeles, "Personality and Social Structure," in R. K. Merton, L. Broom, L. S. Cottrell (eds.), *Sociology Today* (New York: Basic Books, 1959), p. 274.
2. G. Murphy, "Social Psychology," in *American Handbook of Psychiatry*, Vol. 2 (New York: Basic Books, 1959), pp. 1738-1739.
3. F. C. Bartlett, *Remembering* (Cambridge: Cambridge University Press, 1932).
4. M. Sherif, *The Psychology of Social Norms* (New York: Harper & Brothers, 1936).
5. Murphy, *loc. cit.*
6. F. H. Allport, *Social Psychology* (Boston: Houghton Mifflin Company, 1924).
7. G. Murphy and Lois B. Murphy, *Experimental Social Psychology* (New York: Harper & Brothers, 1931).
8. G. Murphy, Lois B. Murphy, and T. M. Newcomb, *Experimental Social Psychology* (revised ed.; New York: Harper & Brothers, 1937).
9. J. H. Pratt, "The Class Method of Treating Consumption in the Homes of the Poor," *J. A. M. A.*, 49:755-759, 1907.
10. Editorial, "The Emmanuel Church Movement in Boston," *N. Y. Med. J.*, 87:947-1048, 1908.

11. R. Dreikurs and R. Corsini, "Twenty Years of Group Psychotherapy," *Am. J. Psychiat.*, 8:567-575, 1954.
12. A. B. Hollingshead and F. C. Redlich, *Social Class and Mental Illness* (New York: John Wiley & Sons, 1958).
13. Editorial, "The Emmanuel Church Movement in Boston," *loc. cit.*
14. E. W. Lazell, "The Group Treatment of Dementia Praecox," *Psychoanalyt. Rev.*, Vol. 8, pp. 168-179, April 1921.
15. L. C. Marsh, "Group Therapy and the Psychiatric Clinic," *J. Nerv. & Ment. Dis.*, Vol. 82, pp. 381-392, 1935.
16. L. Wender, "Current Trends in Group Psychotherapy," *Am. J. Psychother.*, 3:381-404, 1951.
17. P. Schilder, "Results and Problems of Group Psychotherapy in Severe Neurosis," *Ment. Hyg.*, Vol. 23, pp. 87-98, 1939.
18. J. L. Moreno, "Psychodrama and Group Therapy," *Sociometry*, Vol. 9, pp. 249-253, 1946.
19. S. R. Slavson, *An Introduction to Group Therapy* (New York: International Universities Press, 1954).
20. L. Lowrey (Chairman), S. R. Slavson, Dorothy Spiker, H. B. Peck, Mrs. Helen Glauber, N. W. Ackerman, "Group Therapy Special Section Meeting, 1943," *Am. J. Orthopsychiat.*, Vol. Xiii, No. 4, 1943.
21. S. R. Slavson, "Group Therapy," *Ment. Hyg.*, Vol. 24, pp. 36-49, January 1940.
22. G. W. Thomas, "Group Psychotherapy. A Review of the Recent Literature," *Psychosomat. Med.*, Vol. V, pp. 166-180, 1943.
23. N. Hobbs, "Group Centered Psychotherapy," in C. R. Rogers (ed.), *Client Centered Psychotherapy* (Boston: Houghton Mifflin Company, 1951).
24. J. Bierer (ed.), *Therapeutic Social Clubs* (London: H. K. Lewis, 1948).
25. S. H. Foulkes, *Introduction to Group-Analytic Psychotherapy* (London: Wm. Heineman Medical Books Limited, 1948).
26. A. Wolf, "The Psychoanalysis of Groups," *Am. J. Psychother.*, 4:16-50, 1949; 1:525-558, 1950.
27. G. R. Bach, *Intensive Group Psychotherapy* (New York: Ronald Press, 1954).
28. T. Leary, *Interpersonal Diagnosis of Personality* (New York: Ronald Press, 1957).
29. W. R. Bion, "Experiences in Groups, I-VII," *Hum. Relat.*, 1:314-320, 487-496, 1948; 2:13-22, 295-303, 1949; 3:3-14, 395-402, 1950; 4:221-227, 1951; "Group Dynamics: A Re-View." *Int. J. Psychoanal.*, Vol. 33, pp. 235-247, 1952.
30. Dorothy Stock and H. A. Thelen, *Emotional Dynamics and Group Culture*, No. 2 of Research Training Series of the National Training Laboratories, National Education Association of the U.S. (New York: New York University Press, 1958).
31. J. Piaget, *The Moral Judgment of the Child* (New York: Harcourt, Brace & Company, 1932; Glencoe, Ill.: Free Press, 1952).
32. E. Durkheim, *The Division of Labor in Society* (Glencoe, Ill.: Free Press, 1947).

33. C. Cooley, *Social Organization* (New York: Charles Scribner's Sons, 1909).
34. Durkheim, *op. cit.*
35. G. Simmel, *Soziologie* (Leipzig: Duncker and Humblot, 1908).
36. G. H. Mead, *Mind, Self and Society* (Chicago: University of Chicago Press, 1934).
37. S. Freud, *Group Psychology and the Analysis of the Ego* (London: Hogarth Press, 1948), p. 80.
38. G. Le Bon, *The Crowd: A Study of the Popular Mind* (*La Psychologie des Foules*) (New edition; London: T. Fisher Unwin, 1922).
39. R. E. Park, E. W. Burgess, and R. D. McKenzie, *The City* (Chicago: University of Chicago Press, 1925); R. E. Park, *Human Communities* (Glencoe, Ill.: Free Press, 1952).
40. F. Thrasher, *The Gang* (Chicago: University of Chicago Press, 1927).
41. W. F. White, *The Streetcorner Society* (Chicago: University of Chicago Press, 1943).
42. F. J. Roethlisberger and W. J. Dickson, *Management and the Worker* (Hawthorne Studies; Cambridge, Mass.: Harvard University Press, 1939)
43. E. Mayo, *Human Problems of Industrial Civilization* (Cambridge, Mass.: Harvard University Press, 1933).
44. E. Sapir, "Group," in E. R. A. Seligman and A. Johnson (eds.), *Encyclopedia of the Social Sciences*, Vol. VII-VIII (New York: The Macmillan Company, 1932).
45. J. L. Moreno, *Who Shall Survive? A New Approach to the Problems of Human Interrelations* (Washington, D.C.: Nervous and Mental Disease Publishing Company, 1934); "Psychodrama and Group Therapy," *Sociometry*, Vol. 9, pp. 249-253, 1946; Helen H. Jennings, *Leadership and Isolation* (2nd ed.; New York: Longmans, Green & Company, 1950).
46. K. Lewin, "The Research Center for Group Dynamics at Massachusetts Institute of Technology," *Sociometry*, Vol. VIII, pp. 126-136, 1945.
47. K. Lewin, R. Lippitt, and R. K. White, "Patterns of Aggressive Behavior in Experimentally Created Social 'Climate,'" *J. Soc. Psychol.*, Vol. 10, pp. 271-299, 1939; R. Lippit and R. K. White, "An Experimental Study of Leadership and Group Life," in T. M. Newcomb and E. L. Hartley (eds.), *Readings in Social Psychology* (New York: Henry Holt & Co., 1947), pp. 315-330.
48. K. Lewin, "Group Decision and Social Change," in T. M. Newcomb and E. L. Hartley (eds.), *Readings in Social Psychology* (New York: Henry Holt & Co., 1947), p. 344.
49. Lewin, *ibid.*, p. 336.
50. S. E. Asch, *Social Psychology* (New York: Prentice-Hall, 1952).
51. J. Von Neumann and O. Morgenstern, *Theory of Games and Economic Behavior* (Princeton, N.J.: Princeton University Press, 1944).
52. R. D. Luce and H. Raiffa, *Games and Decisions: Introduction and Critical Survey* (New York: John Wiley & Sons, 1957).
53. H. Solomon (ed.), *Mathematical Thinking in the Measurement of Behavior* (Glencoe, Ill.: Free Press, 1960), pp. 314.
54. J. W. Thibaut and H. H. Kelley, *The Social Psychology of Groups* (New York: John Wiley & Sons, 1959).

55. A. P. Hare, "Theories of Group Development and Categories for Interactional Analysis," *Small Group Behavior*, 4:259-304, August 1973.

56. B. W. Tuckman, "Developmental Sequence in Small Groups," *Psychol. Bulletin*, 63:384-399.

57. D. C. Dunphy, "Social Change in Self-Analytic Groups," Ph.D. dissertation, unpublished, Harvard University.

58. T. M. Mill, *Group Transformation: Analysis of a Learning Group* (Englewood Cliffs, N.J.: Prentice-Hall, 1964).

59. P. E. Slater, *Microcosm: Structural, Psychological, and Religious Evolution in Groups* (New York: John Wiley, 1966).

60. R. D. Mann, *Interpersonal Styles and Group Development* (New York: John Wiley, 1967).

61. G. Homans, *The Human Group* (New York: Harcourt, Brace & Company, 1950).

62. G. Lindzey (ed.), *Handbook of Social Psychology*, Vols. I and II (Reading, Mass.: Addison-Wesley Publishing Company, 1954).

63. M. S. Olmsted, *The Small Group* (New York: Random House, 1959).

64. R. F. Bales, *Interaction Process Analysis* (Cambridge, Mass.: Addison-Wesley Publishing Company, 1950).

65. A. Terauds, I. Altman, and J. E. McGrath, A *Bibliography of Small Group Research* (Arlington, Va.: Human Sciences Research, 1960).

66. G. C. Homans, *Social Behavior: Its Elementary Forms* (New York: Harcourt, Brace & Jovanovich, 1961).

67. P. Blau, *Exchange and Power in Social Life* (New York: John Wiley & Sons, 1964).

68. T. Parsons, *The Structure of Social Action* (New York: Free Press, 1968).

69. C. D. Shearing, "How to Make Theories Untestable: A Guide to Theorists," *The American Sociologist*, Vol. 8, pp. 33-37, February 1973.

70. G. C. Homans, *The Nature of Social Science* (New York: Harcourt, Brace & Jovanovich, 1967).

71. R. F. Bales, *Personality and Interpersonal Behavior* (New York: Holt, Rinehart & Winston, 1970).

72. L. P. Bradford, J. R. Gibb, and K. D. Benne, *T-Group Theory and Method* (New York: John Wiley & Sons, 1964).

73. M. M. Berger, "Similarities and Differences Between Group Psychotherapy and Intensive Short Term Group Process Experiences," *J. Group Psychoanal. & Process*, Vol. 1, pp. 11-30, Spring 1968.

74. M. Rosenbaum (ed.), "Use and Misuse of Group Techniques," *Group Process*, Vol. 3, pp. 1-112, Winter 1970-71.

75. W. R. Coulson, *Groups, Gimmicks and Instant Gurus* (New York: Harper & Row, 1972).

76. G. A. Talland, "Task and Interaction Process: Some Characteristics of Therapeutic Group Discussion," *J. Abnorm. and Soc. Psychol.*, 1:105-109, 1955.

77. M. Sherif, *An Outline of Social Psychology* (New York: Harper and Brothers, 1948), p. ix.

78. *Ibid.*, p. x.

Part 1

SOCIAL PSYCHOLOGY AND SMALL GROUP THEORY

THIS SECTION INCLUDES PAPERS that relate social psychology to group process. According to the classical psychoanalytic approach, all of the social values, as well as ego values, which remain primary are derivatives of basic drives. This appears to be a denial of the emergences in group interaction. People associate and interact primarily to secure satisfaction of their basic psychobiogenic needs. After this original interaction has occurred and continued, there emerge values and norms which, in turn, begin to have a validity of their own and act as primary factors in the determination of individual or group behavior. This important issue is often overlooked by students of human behavior who are entirely motivational in their approach to group function. The philosopher Ralph Barton Perry has referred to the classical psychoanalytic concept as the atavistic fallacy. He states that psychoanalysis is founded on this fallacy and quotes Freud, "This oldest portion of the mental apparatus [the id] remains the most important throughout life." * "The fallacy [according to Perry] consists in supposing that despite his racial evolution and personal history man remains at heart a fetus or a rat." † Perry points out that through the process of conditioning and learning the individual's behavior is varied, and new motivations are engrafted, and he states that supporters of the atavistic fallacy believe these new motivations remain on the original stem of human behavior. Perry believes that later experiences and influences may count far more than the earlier ones in mature behavior, the primary drives having been succeeded by secondary drives and psychogenic drives. Perry's position and his concern with the influence of the atavistic fallacy in the behavioral sciences is highly relevant.‡ When individuals begin to be to-

* From *Outline of Psychoanalysis*, trans. by J. Strachey (New York: W. W. Norton & Co., 1949), p. 14.
† Perry, *Realms of Value* (Cambridge, Mass.: Harvard University Press, 1954), p. 21.
‡ We do not deny the importance of instinctive behavior; the behavior of man cannot be understood without study of instinct and evolution. See in this regard K. Breland and M. Breland, "The Misbehavior of Organisms," *Am. Psychol.*, Vol. 16, No. 11, November 1961.

gether within a group structure, new configurations become apparent. Some students of group process criticize advocates of motivational theory and state that these people have consistently ignored the intellective processes that are at work in group formation. For example, Asch, one of the authors we have included in the papers in this section, stresses the cognitive or intellective approach in his study of social interaction and group function. He has criticized many social psychologists for stressing the emotional in their studies of social interaction.

In the early days of social psychology, as far back as the 1920's, there were great debates over the concept of the group mind. This concept, briefly stated, is that a group continues to exist even if there has been a complete change in membership; that a group has properties such as a system of values and a certain structure which cannot be conceived of as being properties of individuals and that there are specific laws governing this group functioning. Some contemporary psychotherapists still perceive the student of group process as working along this concept of the group mind. That is to say, they are suspicious of any feelings of students of group dynamics that these people are postulating a group mind and are therefore denying any individual approach to group behavior.

On the other extreme of this controversy is the position that only individuals are real and that groups are repeated in each individual mind and exist only in these minds. Groups are conceived of as abstractions from collections of individuals, and the group mind is considered fallacious, since it is nothing but the similarities among individual minds. Therefore, a group exists only in the minds of men. The studies of social interaction which are presented in this group of papers touch this area but relate specifically to the concepts of the social norm. Murphy notes the interplay between the work of social psychologist and student of group behavior and the work of the group psychotherapist when he discusses the question of group thinking. Asch questions what happens when groups of individuals get together. How important is it for individuals to conform in a group? Is there really individual difference? Is the prime motivation of the individual to be liked and to be accepted by the group? Could this conceivably play a part in the thinking of patients who come for a therapeutic experience within a group structure?

Asch, in his paper, stresses the cognitive aspect. A paper that would be more toward the frame of reference of the individual psychotherapist is the paper by Sherif, which is a summary of some of his studies of group process and group conflict. Sherif, for years, as noted in the introduction, has worked on the feasibility of subjecting group behavior to experimental investigation. He first started by forming groups in laboratory settings and observing how these groups begin to set up artificial but, for them, valid social norms. By subjecting this concept of a social norm to psychological analysis, he helped to break down the barrier that existed, the artificial categorization and separation of the individual and the group. His research was instrumental in establishing among psychologists the belief that groups may have certain properties, including the development of social norms. He suggested that there may be a valid psychological basis in the contention of some social psychologists that new and supra-individual qualities arise in group situations. In the research that is reported in this collection of readings, Sherif has moved on to studying the natural history of groups. He expresses great enthusiasm for changing human behavior within group structure and feels that group therapy is more effective than the one-to-one psychotherapeutic relationship.*

The articles that we have selected in this section are in keeping with our position as editors in terms of an approach to group behavior. When we speak of the group here, we do not speak of a collection of individuals. For example, a collection of advertising men may not be considered a group. They may properly be referred to as a class of people. When we speak of a group, we refer to two or more people who bear a definite psychological relationship to one another. This means that for each member of the group, the other group members exist in some psychological way, so that the behavior and the characteristics of the other members of the group influence a particular member of a group. One of the problems that plagues many students of group behavior is that, in doing away with the concept of the group mind, the concept that many lay people still accept, the social psychologist is left with the individual as the unit of analysis. Yet he gropes for a unit that is larger than that of the individual. He begins to speak in terms of a series of social behaviors, and he exchanges the word "group" for the word "individual" in setting up what he believes to be certain valid psychological laws. From this he deduces what he feels are valid laws of group dynamics. This does not appear to be either fair or possible. Sherif and the workers who have followed him appear to be more systematic in their treatment. They explore the social variable and demonstrate the group influence on personality functioning.

This is relevant to the rather lengthy presentation in this section of the abstract from the carefully reported study by Stock and Thelen. Thelen is a student of child development and personality development, and primarily an educational psychologist. Though he was influenced by the work of the social psychologists at the University of Michigan, he attempted in his own work at the University of Chicago to do systematic studies of group formation and group structure. He became aware of the work of Bion, the English psychiatrist and psychoanalyst, who was formulating an approach to group behavior along analytic lines. Bion feels that his psychoanalytic approach through the individual and his approach through the group are essentially facets of the same phenomena. Bion attempted to apply psychoanalytic principles to the study of natural groups.

* Personal communication.

The paper by Stock and Thelen is the beginning of a bridge between group function and group psychotherapy. They describe the results of research which had tested the culture, or what Bion and others have called the "work-emotionality" of specific groups. It is a valuable study for the group psychotherapist because it indicates how certain approaches to individual behavior can be subjected to systematic research. It is a valuable study for the student of group dynamics and the social psychologist and sociologist because it indicates the direction they may turn to if they begin to systematically test or research the particular clinical experiences and concepts of psychotherapists who practice both individually and in the group setting.

Stock, now called Stock Whitaker, later became interested in group psychotherapy. She has added some comments developed from a fifteen-year passage of time. Thelen stated that he was quite content with the article as it is printed.

Back, a sociologist and social psychologist, and a strong, but perceptive, critic of the encounter movement, has written in detail about various approaches to groups. His article, included in this section, approaches the problems of social change in a unique fashion. He has defined specific social processes derived from the biological level, and then integrated all this with a systems analysis approach. In view of current questioning of such basic concepts as the nuclear family, his approach is valuable. As Kurt Lewin wrote: "There is nothing so practical as a good theory."

Cartwright, one of the early leaders in the field of group dynamics, reviews in his article the literature on group decision making and some of the central theoretical problems—the complicated effects of group decision and how this relates to risk taking by individuals and groups. All of us who work with groups are concerned with conceptualization of group discussion and group decision.

Eugene Hartley's treatment of the field of group psychotherapy from the viewpoint of an active researcher and social psychologist should properly be read after most of these readings have been studied. However, the reader may want to jump immediately to Hartley's postscript to this collection of readings to study more the interrelationship between group psychotherapy and group function.

1

GROUP PSYCHOTHERAPY IN OUR SOCIETY

Gardner Murphy

There is not, I suppose, anything essentially new about small groups which exert fundamental directive influences on their members in educational and therapeutic directions.

In many periods like that of the "mystery religions" of the Greeks or the guilds of the Medieval Period, special interests and skills permitted a strongly inculcated sense of identification. The informal groups that gathered at a bridge on the river Cam in the thirteenth century developed a fellow feeling and gave strength and discipline to individual members. We can readily imagine that the therapeutic and the educational tended to coalesce. I should not, therefore, urge that there is anything absolutely new about the use of groups, led or unled, in the service of therapy and personal reeducation. The two things that are new are first the *secular*, rather than the religious, spirit in which individual aims are redirected, and secondly the sense of *skill* or technique. This emphasis on skill is a part of the scientific, technological movement which began in the seventeenth and eighteenth centuries, underlying the growth of science on the one hand and the Industrial Revolution on the other. From this point of view we move away from "Mark Hopkins on a log," conveying personal inspiration to a student, all the way to the modern teacher armed with many years of formal educational theory and "practice teaching" under supervision, which gives a sense of professional identity and professional competence. Many students speak of such experiences as therapeutic.

Along with this the point has often been made that a group can convey at least three things which the individual therapist cannot accomplish:

This article is based upon a speech delivered at the Seventeenth Annual Conference of the American Group Psychotherapy Association, New York City, January, 1960.

37

It can supply the warmth and cohesion of a sort of family solidarity, with which the suffering individual can identify; without any change of role the individual patient can immerse himself in and become deeply identified with the other group members. This is in itself a form of support, characteristic of men and women of all periods but refurbished with the sense of professional identity which pervades all who lead in such movements. Secondly, the group can sometimes prepare for life by giving opportunities in the group itself to exemplify forms of social adaptation, such as love and friendly competition, which can perhaps be directly carried over to other and larger groups. The process of transfer from the polarized situation of individual psychotherapy to living one's daily life in the group may perhaps, in some cases, be simplified and its sharp edges rounded off and made bearable; in other cases, of course, this is not true. Third, groups can make possible for the individual, from the very beginning, the experience of giving as well as receiving help. There is therefore a direct and fundamental ego fulfillment in being capable of directed love and support, controlled by the individual for the benefit of other group members.

It is fundamental in our modern way of living, let us say in the growth of America since the disappearance of the frontier, that we have preferred to solve our problems in a group rather than individually. This is the theme of David Riesman's impelling analyses of Western culture, and of American life in particular, in his volume on *The Lonely Crowd*; it is the theme of Holly Whyte's *The Organization Man* and of many studies of "suburbia," of families of young executives, and of the lost quality of those who must find solidarity in groups, however tenuous, because they are no one by themselves alone. There is, however, a tremendous difference between the group in which one is *lost* and the group in which one is *found*. It is partly a question of the size of the group, partly a question of its aim, its organization, and its leadership. We have been groping for a century or more in our churches, fraternal orders, college fraternities, and sororities for something to keep going the spirit of brotherhood and of sisterhood which the Roman Catholic Church maintained and today so vigorously maintains as a way of building a bridge between the isolated individual and the vast community of the Church as a whole. The Church has needed familylike small groups built into scattered groups known as Orders. The development of groups for therapeutic and educational purposes can, within definite limits, reflect this response to loneliness, helplessness in the face of the vastness of today, and at the same time the use of a somewhat familylike organization, with a leader in the role of father or mother, or big brother or sister. The psychoanalytic conception of the family is rich in thoughts for the understanding of group therapy. Let us now use our psychoanalytic approach against the backdrop of a broad sociocultural definition of group life.

THE SOCIOCULTURAL APPROACH TO
GROUP PSYCHOTHERAPY

Viewing the situation in terms of a psychoanalytic model, we may certainly assume that the child who has *all* of the father's attention has something very precious which cannot be equaled in a *diffuse* family situation,
no matter how strong and well knit the family group may be. It is something to have the priest's full attention in absolution, to have the attorney's full attention in consultation, to be one who seeks out and gets a
chance to communicate with the teacher on a personal basis. These are
valuable and fundamental in themselves. They do not in themselves have
anything to do with economic considerations as such. If, however, it proves
to be economical as well as expedient and practical to work with patients
in groups, there is a further factor enormously enhancing the difference between individual therapy and group therapy. But the very fact that one
does not pay as much may sometimes mean that the therapy is not regarded as having the same value. Everyone knows that classes with just a
few members are expensive for colleges to organize and that a highly focused group-person situation, as in the Sarah Lawrence classes of ten, can
do something personally, educationally, emotionally, and spiritually, which
it is very difficult to do with even the most brilliant of classes where there
are 35 to 40 students. In a society so quick to assign monetary value to social relationships, it is not surprising that group psychotherapy should be
regarded as cheaper both in the direct economic sense and in the sense in
which we say that anything that belongs to the market place is vulgar or
cheap.

Here, however, is a basic contradiction. What we want is not just the
support of the father figure, but the support of the family as a whole. This
is true not only of the extended family, as in India or China or Japan; it is
also true of the small biological family. It is wonderfully precious to have
mother's and father's full attention, but there are many times when it is
even more precious to have the family participation and support in one's
deepest intellectual and emotional ventures, as when one starts a new and
difficult task, assuming responsibilities and emotional ties with which one
would wish to weave together all the family members so that one remains
a part of their collective unity and has their corporate support. Group psychotherapy against this background becomes for some persons a symbol of
a kind of family support. It is suggested that it offers father and mother,
big brother and big sister relationships yet maintains the collectivity, the
esprit de corps, without which we should feel isolated, lonely, polarized in
the presence of the superior or austere therapist. Not only is it easier, we
are sometimes reminded, to communicate one's intimate problems when
others are communicating their own intimate problems and getting dispas-

sionate and friendly understanding and support; one also has the sense of being important to each member and to the group in its entirety. Consequently, the feeling of intimate exchange with the strong and beloved leader might be compared with another kind of intimate exchange in which the sharing of problems makes the group almost religious in its merging of individuals in a network of interpersonal realities. But this parallel may be challenged, and in general we must study the wide range of individual differences.

Ansbacher has reminded us that the appeal of psychoanalysis from the very beginning was largely to the elite, economically, intellectually, and socially. Psychoanalysis was a rich, intricate, and demanding conceptual system. Individual psychology, on the other hand, was simple, crude, rough-and-ready. Adler's slouching, or even slovenly, manner, his delight in working-class associations and socialist affiliations, his establishment of lower middle-class kinds of clinics in the Vienna schools led Ansbacher to paraphrase the old cliché "What this country needs is a good five-cent cigar" with the phrase that what this country needs is a good five-dollar psychiatrist. There can be no doubt at all that these factors even among the very democratic and very conscientious can lead to many confused ideas about group psychotherapy, interfering with the factual examination of the situation which is so urgently necessary both for the welfare of the patient and for the long-run evaluation of what is really sound and effective in our culture. Let us prejudge no issues.

EXPERIMENTS IN GROUP THINKING

Another type of co-working group that may have some relevance to our problem is the group which has been asked to find the answer to an experimentally posed problem or to find a creative solution of a difficulty. These experiments which have been under way now for some forty years have yielded a very considerable fund of information about the kind of thinking which the group situation permits and encourages. It is a waste of time to ask abstractly whether groups think more effectively than the individuals who compose the groups, by the classical method of working with matched problems and having some of them solved by the individual method and others by the group method. The trouble with the traditional question as to superiority of the groups is that it ignores all the particulars which make the problem significant and meaningful. In some situations, one individual has the necessary information or skill or both and can do better than any other individual or than any arrangement of individuals in the group. Under other circumstances there are scattered bits of information and potential insight which can become integrated in the group setting, so that the group thinks a good deal more efficiently than any other individual members.

In some cases the beneficial result of the group setting lies not so much in the creative accumulation of potential contributions scattered in the mind of the various members, but rather in the enhancement of a critical capacity; a capacity to see the false assumptions and blind alleys which have arisen in the early attempts to solve the problem. A can criticize B and C for omitting essential issues, and if the group atmosphere is at all congenial for serious work, other individuals, let us say, D and E, see where the implications lie and develop out of the criticisms a constructive possibility. But the individual himself may actually see his own mistakes in the situation, because, as George Herbert Mead never tired of pointing out, the individual sees himself reflected in the awareness of the others. There is a "looking-glass" personality, an awareness of the "generalized other" and the way in which the "generalized other" perceives one. These kinds of experiences profoundly recast our notion that the group is merely an additive collection of fragmentary bits of information. The group experience may recast our images of ourselves and enable us to think more effectively. How much of all this is directly relevant to group psychotherapy will, I think, be clear if one refers to the writings in the twenties and thirties, in which the influence of Mead was beginning to be clear. What began as a normal part of the social science analysis of group life was taken over by the therapist.

These studies were not unrelated to the comparable studies of propaganda and resistance to propaganda which likewise made their first great advent during the 1920's. It became clear that the resistance offered to vigorously formulated public communications lay very largely in the group support which each individual shared with others when an authoritative figure went further than the psychological structure of the situation permitted. Individual resistance to propaganda, as we are led to understand it by reference to the study of psychoanalysis, and particularly the theory of ego structures, may overlook the *shared* nature of social resistance. This, despite the fact that Freud's *Group Psychology and the Analysis of the Ego* made clear that the affective bonds which tie the group together are in some ways similar to a system of affective bonds in the family and should make us ready for awareness of the fact that the resistance of the group to the strong leader is of an utterly different order from the cumulative resistances of separate individuals. The public-opinion poller neglects (to his peril) the relation of the individual response of acceptance or rejection to public communication, as if each individual were bottled up within a separate cell. Even the brilliant studies of Richard S. Crutchfield on the conformity responses seem to begin with the assumption that the individual, pocketed off and made immune to communication from others, except through a highly artificial and channelized system of beamed communications, could give us a picture of social cohesion and the act of resisting. Studies by John French and others in laboratory situations in which experimental panic has been induced through a realistic simulation of a fire with smoke, alarm, and so on, and studies by Grinker and Spiegel of the mass response of bombing crews in World War II to strong or weak leadership in their commanding officer, have taught us to see how intensely social is the response of the individual to the abuse of confidence or the inappropriate utilization of authority. One responds not to panic in general, but concretely to companions whose strength and weaknesses one knows and to leaders whose strengths and weaknesses one knows.

EXPERIMENTS IN CLASSROOM ATMOSPHERES

There is an experiment of Everett Bovard at the University of Michigan which I believe has enormous theoretical and practical value for us who are interested in group psychotherapy. I shall take the liberty of streamlining the account from various scattered publications. Bovard and a colleague at the University of Michigan undertook to teach elementary psychology to equated classes by two fundamentally different methods, each instructor utilizing each of the two methods with separate groups. One method, which we would ordinarily call the individual-centered method, involved the usual teacher-student interaction through question and answer; that is, assuming that the students had familiarized themselves with the basic required material, each student had his chance to ask questions. The instructor answered him as well as he could. In this way each student had his turn. This sounds democratic and effective. The other method, however, called the group-centered method, involved the instructor's standing back and taking as little part as possible in the proceedings. He started the ball rolling but then encouraged the various members of the class to pitch their problems at one another in a process of continuous cross fires. In this way there was no polarization of the individual student toward the instructor. Rather, there was a network of constantly shifting polarizations, all of which were fluid, unstable, and susceptible of constant redefinition. There was, moreover, a group morale which was easily observed, a collective learning process.

Now when the time came for an examination the students were tested not at all in terms of true-false or multiple choice propositions covering the content of the class work. On the contrary, they were shown motion pictures prepared by the Canadian mental health authorities. The *Feeling of Rejection* is a particularly well-known one. In these films the emotional problems of disturbed, anxious, and lonely persons are depicted, so that those with some degree of empathy and sympathy latch on, understand, and have a glimmering of possible ways of helping. We find now that when tested by their understanding and their practical remedial responses to these films, the group-centered students did substantially better. They had, in other words, learned what was emotionally significant from these films depicting a social situation, because they had learned something about empathy and social interaction in the classroom teaching situation. This, at least, is Bovard's aim and the gist of his report.

Such studies, of course, require replication. My theme is not to offer final and dogmatic evidence regarding a teaching method; rather, my aim is to arouse you to a number of important research and practical issues regarding how we actually learn in group settings. These are experiences of the sort which Daniel Prescott at the University of Maryland has emphasized for many years; experiences described by T. M. Newcomb in his Bennington College Study; by Lois Murphy and Henry Ladd in the Sarah Lawrence Study; and paralleled in some respects by J. L. Moreno's early studies at the New York State Training School at Hudson, New York. We seem to encounter here many experiences in which there is a realignment, reorganization of the affective ties of each person with his fellow, so that as the subject matter becomes meaningful to him, his social relationships to those who are coping with the same subject matter become more precious to him, and he himself, as a learner, identifies with others who are learning at the same time.

I believe that the group psychotherapy situation has much in common with this kind of educational practice, which has been going on, of course, since the laboratory school of John Dewey in 1902 and since the progressive school research efforts of George A. Coe and others before and after World War I. The whole vast field of group dynamics as defined by Kurt Lewin, especially at the University of Iowa in the mid-thirties, was an expression of this conception of the social definition of the *learning process*. This is as fresh today as it was in the time of John Dewey and in this Dewey centennial year may again be emphasized.

The work of Kurt Lewin's students on authoritarian and democratic groups are likewise relevant here. Group psychotherapy may at times involve a redefinition of the group learning situation in the best progressive educational setup. Instead of asking whether group psychotherapy is derived from the group method as used in education or derived from Kurt Lewin's group dynamics, I should be inclined, rather, to ask whether all of these are not expressions of a Whitman-like fellow feeling, a need of comradeship, which took shape as a reaction against the excessive individualism of American pioneer and frontiersman life and as a way of blunting the shock of an impersonal industrialization which swept over our country from east to west during the nineteenth and early twentieth centuries. I would ask, in other words, whether group psychotherapy is a form of sharing of personal experiences which arose as individualism and whether its counterpart—loneliness—proved to need some sort of counterpart or balance wheel. Are these not *three* trends, one toward impersonal group life, the second toward a protesting individualism, the third toward small group efforts to find companionship free of the difficulties both of mass living and of solitary living? This emotional craving joined with the technical progress of psychotherapy itself in the formulation of the very natural question: "If we have here two good things, namely, solidarity on the one hand and, on the other hand, high professional competence in dealing with people's personal difficulties, is it not possible to fuse at high temperature the best of the two movements?"

This focuses the issue where it belongs, namely, on the question of what is best in the two movements. I think we have here a good historical model for the rise of group psychotherapy as a way of carrying out one of the healing arts. I think, however, that from this point on the question is the objective evaluation of the kinds of personal and social goals which can best be reached by this kind of psychotherapy in comparison with the others now available.

SOME FINAL REFLECTIONS

1. Society itself is a "therapeutic community," making and breaking us all the time. We have become aware of the breaking function and only slowly the making function.

2. A fundanental principle in therapy enunciated by Freud—namely, that of transference—means inevitably that basic transference models established by the child in growing up are carried into the community. It also means, however, that there is a transfer from the community into the home. Hereford, at the University of Texas, has some interesting observations regarding the role of P.T.A.'s in implementing community decisions and of families in influencing children's behavior in such a way that this carries back into school.

3. The much-discussed issue whether fundamental group or personal psychotherapy can be done with an individual person in a direction which is opposed by the basic values and life rules of the society around him has to be reconsidered. In this connection, how deep into unconscious personality dynamics can we go if we really believe that there is a fundamental opposition between the therapeutic and the daily given cultural values? Is it realistic to believe that a small number of persons in therapy can in some real way change the larger society in which they are members? Are there perhaps palliative or compromise solutions? Are we perhaps involved in a sort of third step toward social reconstruction every time we carry out group psychotherapy?

4. For myself, I believe in the very fundamental possibilities for the remaking of personality, as I have tried to define this in a volume on *Human Potentialities*. My own feeling is that realistic thinking through of the way in which group therapy can modify deeper cultural interactions is fundamental before effective therapy can be done. Mere day by day or

even year by year "adjustment" will not do the job. Perhaps, being an outsider, I can go much further with this than your own professional conscience could let you go. But I shall claim this privilege and conclude by claiming a belief of group therapy, that it offers principles and modes truly prophetic for other types of group structures in a society to which small groups will have massive importance in competition with the impersonal forces of a technological society.

I have already hinted a few directions in which group psychotherapy research might move:

(1) It might emphasize the kinds of personality changes that occur in group psychotherapy as such, as contrasted with those which are concerned simply with group dynamics, group cohesion, and effective learning in group situations.

(2) It might emphasize the economic, political, and cultural contrasts in which the public image of psychotherapy is developing today, with attention to economic, cultural, and other factors which, whether rational or irrational, predispose toward acceptance or resistance.

(3) It might emphasize the potential impacts of today's group psychotherapy upon larger cultural phenomena in a lonely yet impersonal world.

2

OPINIONS AND SOCIAL PRESSURE

Solomon E. Asch

That social influences shape every person's practices, judgments, and beliefs is a truism to which anyone will readily assent. A child masters his "native" dialect down to the finest nuances; a member of a tribe of cannibals accepts cannibalism as altogether fitting and proper. All the social sciences take their departure from the observation of the profound effects that groups exert on their members. For psychologists, group pressure upon the minds of individuals raises a host of questions they would like to investigate in detail.

How, and to what extent, do social forces constrain people's opinions and attitudes? This question is especially pertinent in our day. The same epoch that has witnessed the unprecedented technical extension of communication has also brought into existence the deliberate manipulation of opinion and the "engineering of consent." There are many good reasons why, as citizens and as scientists, we should be concerned with studying the ways in which human beings form their opinions and the role that social conditions play.

Studies of these questions began with the interest in hypnosis aroused by the French physician Jean Martin Charcot (a teacher of Sigmund Freud) toward the end of the nineteenth century. Charcot believed that only hysterical patients could be fully hypnotized, but this view was soon challenged by two other physicians, Hyppolyte Bernheim and A. A. Liébault, who demonstrated that they could put most people under the hypnotic spell. Bernheim proposed that hypnosis was but an extreme form of a normal psychological process which became known as "suggestibility." It was shown that monotonous reiteration of instructions could induce in normal persons in the waking state involuntary bodily changes such as swaying or rigidity of the arms and sensations such as warmth and odor.

From *Scientific American*, Vol. 193, No. 5, November 1955, pp. 31-35. Reprinted with permission. Copyright © 1955 by Scientific American, Inc. All rights reserved.

It was not long before social thinkers seized upon these discoveries as a basis for explaining numerous social phenomena, from the spread of opinion to the formation of crowds and the following of leaders. The sociologist Gabriel Tarde summed it all up in the aphorism: "Social man is a somnambulist."

When the new discipline of social psychology was born at the beginning of this century, its first experiments were essentially adaptations of the suggestion demonstration. The technique generally followed a simple plan. The subjects, usually college students, were asked to give their opinions or preferences concerning various matters; some time later they were again asked to state their choices, but now they were also informed of the opinions held by authorities or large groups of their peers on the same matters. (Often the alleged consensus was fictitious.) Most of these studies had substantially the same result: Confronted with opinions contrary to their own, many subjects apparently shifted their judgments in the direction of the views of the majorities or the experts. The late psychologist Edward L. Thorndike reported that he had succeeded in modifying the esthetic preferences of adults by this procedure. Other psychologists reported that people's evaluations of the merit of a literary passage could be raised or lowered by ascribing the passage to different authors. Apparently the sheer weight of numbers or authority sufficed to change opinions, even when no arguments for the opinions themselves were provided.

Now the very ease of success in these experiments arouses suspicion. Did the subjects actually change their opinions, or were the experimental victories scored only on paper? On grounds of common sense, one must question whether opinions are generally as watery as these studies indicate. There is some reason to wonder whether it was not the investigators who, in their enthusiasm for a theory, were suggestible, and whether the ostensibly gullible subjects were not providing answers which they thought good subjects were expected to give.

The investigations were guided by certain underlying assumptions, which today are common currency and account for much that is thought and said about the operations of propaganda and public opinion. The assumptions are that people submit uncritically and painlessly to external manipulation by suggestion or prestige and that any given idea or value can be "sold" or "unsold" without reference to its merits. We should be skeptical, however, of the supposition that the power of social pressure necessarily implies uncritical submission to it: Independence and the capacity to rise above group passion are also open to human beings. Further, one may question on psychological grounds whether it is possible as a rule to change a person's judgment of a situation or an object without first changing his knowledge or assumptions about it.

In what follows I shall describe some experiments in an investigation of the effects of group pressure which was carried out recently with the

help of a number of my associates. The tests not only demonstrate the operations of group pressure upon individuals but also illustrate a new kind of attack on the problem and some of the more subtle questions that it raises.

A group of seven to nine young men, all college students, are assembled in a classroom for a "psychological experiment" in visual judgment. The experimenter informs them that they will be comparing the lengths of lines. He shows two large white cards. On one is a single vertical black line—the standard whose length is to be matched. On the other card are three vertical lines of various lengths. The subjects are to choose the one that is of the same length as the line on the other card. One of the three actually is of the same length; the other two are substantially different, the difference ranging from three quarters of an inch to an inch and three quarters.

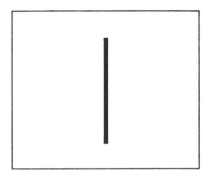 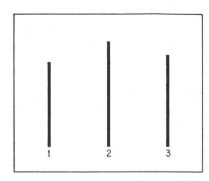

Fig. 2–1. Subjects were shown two cards. One bore a standard line. The other bore three lines, one of which was the same length as the standard. The subjects were asked to choose this line.

The experiment opens uneventfully. The subjects announce their answers in the order in which they have been seated in the room, and on the first round every person chooses the same matching line. Then a second set of cards is exposed; again the group is unanimous. The members appear ready to endure politely another boring experiment. On the third trial there is an unexpected disturbance. One person near the end of the group disagrees with all the others in his selection of the matching line. He looks surprised, indeed incredulous, about the disagreement. On the following trial he disagrees again, while the others remain unanimous in their choice. The dissenter becomes more and more worried and hesitant as the disagreement continues in succeeding trials; he may pause before announcing his answer and speak in a low voice, or he may smile in an embarrassed way.

What the dissenter does not know is that all the other members of the group were instructed by the experimenter beforehand to give incorrect

answers in unanimity at certain points. The single individual who is not a party to this prearrangement is the focal subject of our experiment. He is placed in a position in which, while he is actually giving the correct answers, he finds himself unexpectedly in a minority of one, opposed by a unanimous and arbitrary majority with respect to a clear and simple fact. Upon him we have brought to bear two opposed forces: the evidence of his senses and the unanimous opinion of a group of his peers. Also, he must declare his judgments in public, before a majority which has also stated its position publicly.

The instructed majority occasionally reports correctly in order to reduce the possibility that the naïve subject will suspect collusion against him. (In only a few cases did the subject actually show suspicion; when this happened, the experiment was stopped and the results were not

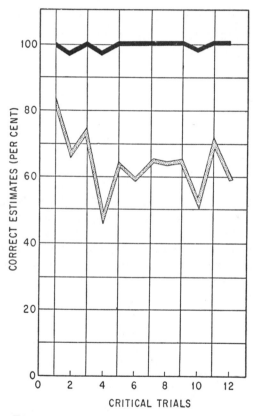

Fig. 2–2. *Error of 123 subjects, each of whom compared lines in the presence of six to eight opponents, is plotted in the shaded curve. The accuracy of judgments not under pressure is indicated in black.*

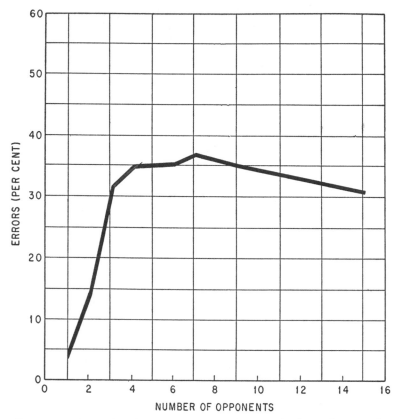

Fig. 2–3. Size of majority which opposed them had an effect on the subjects. With a single opponent the subject erred only 3.6 per cent of the time; with two opponents he erred 13.6 per cent; three, 31.8 per cent; four, 35.1 per cent; six, 35.2 per cent; seven, 37.1 per cent; nine, 35.1 per cent; 15, 31.2 per cent.

counted.) There are 18 trials in each series, and on 12 of these the majority responds erroneously.

How do people respond to group pressure in this situation? I shall report first the statistical results of a series in which a total of 123 subjects from three institutions of higher learning (not including my own, Swarthmore College) were placed in the minority situation described above.

Two alternatives were open to the subject: he could act independently, repudiating the majority, or he could go along with the majority, repudiating the evidence of his senses. Of the 123 put to the test, a considerable percentage yielded to the majority. Whereas in ordinary circumstances individuals matching the lines will make mistakes less than 1 per cent of the time, under group pressure the minority subjects swung to acceptance of the misleading majority's wrong judgments in 36.8 per cent of the selections.

Of course individuals differed in response. At one extreme, about one quarter of the subjects were completely independent and never agreed with the erroneous judgments of the majority. At the other extreme, some individuals went with the majority nearly all the time. The performances of individuals in this experiment tend to be highly consistent. Those who strike out on the path of independence do not, as a rule, succumb to the majority even over an extended series of trials, while those who choose the path of compliance are unable to free themselves as the ordeal is prolonged.

The reasons for the startling individual differences have not yet been investigated in detail. At this point we can only report some tentative generalizations from talks with the subjects, each of whom was interviewed at the end of the experiment. Among the independent individuals were many who held fast because of staunch confidence in their own judgment. The most significant fact about them was not absence of responsiveness to the majority but a capacity to recover from doubt and to re-establish their equilibrium. Others who acted independently came to believe that the majority was correct in its answers, but they continued their dissent on the simple ground that it was their obligation to call the play as they saw it.

Among the extremely yielding persons we found a group who quickly reached the conclusion: "I am wrong, they are right." Others yielded in order "not to spoil your results." Many of the individuals who went along suspected that the majority were "sheep" following the first responder or that the majority were victims of an optical illusion; nevertheless, these suspicions failed to free them at the moment of decision. More disquieting were the reactions of subjects who construed their difference from the majority as a sign of some general deficiency in themselves, which at all costs they must hide. On this basis they desperately tried to merge with the majority, not realizing the longer-range consequences to themselves. All the yielding subjects underestimated the frequency with which they conformed.

Which aspect of the influence of a majority is more important—the size of the majority or its unanimity? The experiment was modified to examine this question. In one series the size of the opposition was varied from one to 15 persons. The results showed a clear trend. When a subject was confronted with only a single individual who contradicted his answers, he was swayed little: He continued to answer independently and correctly in nearly all trials. When the opposition was increased to two, the pressure became substantial: Minority subjects now accepted the wrong answer 13.6 per cent of the time. Under the pressure of a majority of three, the subjects' errors jumped to 31.8 per cent. But further increases in the size of the majority apparently did not increase the weight of the pressure sub-stantially. Clearly the size of the opposition is important only up to a point.

Disturbance of the majority's unanimity had a striking effect. In this experiment the subject was given the support of a truthful partner—either another individual who did not know of the prearranged agreement among the rest of the group or a person who was instructed to give correct answers throughout.

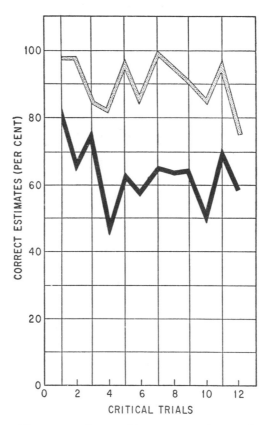

Fig. 2–4. Two subjects supporting each other against a majority made fewer errors (shaded curve) than one subject did against a majority (black curve).

The presence of a supporting partner depleted the majority of much of its power. Its pressure on the dissenting individual was reduced to one fourth: That is, subjects answered incorrectly only one fourth as often as under the pressure of a unanimous majority. (See Figure 4.) The weakest persons did not yield as readily. Most interesting were the reactions to the

partner. Generally the feeling toward him was one of warmth and closeness; he was credited with inspiring confidence. However, the subjects repudiated the suggestion that the partner decided them to be independent.

Was the partner's effect a consequence of his dissent, or was it related
to his accuracy? We now introduced into the experimental group a person
who was instructed to dissent from the majority but also to disagree with
the subject. In some experiments the majority was always to choose the
worst of the comparison lines and the instructed dissenter to pick the line
that was closer to the length of the standard one; in others the majority
was consistently intermediate and the dissenter most in error. In this manner we were able to study the relative influence of "compromising" and
"extremist" dissenters.

Again the results are clear. When a moderate dissenter is present, the
effect of the majority on the subject decreases by approximately one third,
and extremes of yielding disappear. Moreover, most of the errors the subjects do make are moderate, rather than flagrant. In short, the dissenter
largely controls the choice of errors. To this extent the subjects broke away
from the majority even while bending to it.

On the other hand, when the dissenter always chose the line that was
more flagrantly different from the standard, the results were of quite a different kind. The extremist dissenter produced a remarkable freeing of the
subjects; their errors dropped to only 9 per cent. Furthermore, all the errors were of the moderate variety. We were able to conclude that dissent
per se increased independence and moderated the errors that occurred,
and that the direction of dissent exerted consistent effects.

In all the foregoing experiments each subject was observed only in a
single setting. We now turned to studying the effects upon a given individual of a change in the situation to which he was exposed. The first experiment examined the consequences of losing or gaining a partner. The
instructed partner began by answering correctly on the first six trials. With
his support the subject usually resisted pressure from the majority: 18 of
27 subjects were completely independent. But after six trials the partner
joined the majority. As soon as he did so, there was an abrupt rise in the
subjects' errors. Their submission to the majority was just about as frequent as when the minority subject was opposed by a unanimous majority
throughout.

It was surprising to find that the experience of having had a partner
and of having braved the majority opposition with him had failed to
strengthen the individuals' independence. Questioning at the conclusion
of the experiment suggested that we had overlooked an important circumstance; namely, the strong specific effect of "desertion" by the partner
to the other side. We therefore changed the conditions so that the partner
would simply leave the group at the proper point. (To allay suspicion it
was announced in advance that he had an appointment with the dean.)

In this form of the experiment, the partner's effect outlasted his presence. The errors increased after his departure, but less markedly than after a partner switched to the majority.

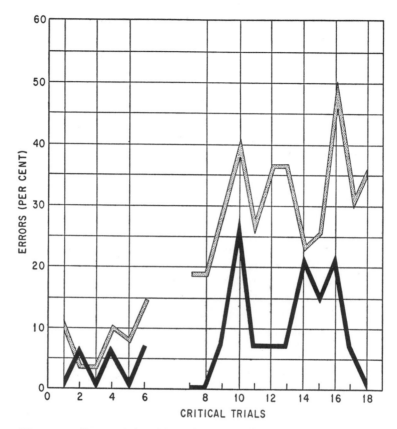

Fig. 2–5. Partner left subject after six trials in a single experiment. The shaded curve shows the error of the subject when the partner "deserted" to the majority. Black curve shows error when partner merely left the room.

In a variant of this procedure the trials began with the majority unanimously giving correct answers. Then they gradually broke away until on the sixth trial the naïve subject was alone and the group unanimously against him. As long as the subject had anyone on his side, he was almost invariably independent, but as soon as he found himself alone, the tendency to conform to the majority rose abruptly.

As might be expected, an individual's resistance to group pressure in these experiments depends to a considerable degree on how wrong the majority is. We varied the discrepancy between the standard line and the other lines systematically with the hope of reaching a point where the error of the majority would be so glaring that every subject would repudiate it and choose independently. In this we regretfully did not succeed. Even when the difference between the lines was seven inches, there were still some who yielded to the error of the majority.

The study provides clear answers to a few relatively simple questions, and it raises many others that await investigation. We would like to know the degree of consistency of persons in situations which differ in content and structure. If consistency of independence or conformity in behavior is shown to be a fact, how is it functionally related to qualities of character and personality? In what ways is independence related to sociological or cultural conditions? Are leaders more independent than other people, or are they adept at following their followers? These and many other questions may perhaps be answerable by investigations of the type described here.

Life in society requires consensus as an indispensable condition. But consensus, to be productive, requires that each individual contribute independently out of his experience and insight. When consensus comes under the dominance of conformity, the social process is polluted and the individual at the same time surrenders the powers on which his functioning as a feeling and thinking being depends. That we have found the tendency to conformity in our society so strong that reasonably intelligent and well-meaning young people are willing to call white black is a matter of concern. It raises questions about our ways of education and about the values that guide our conduct.

Yet anyone inclined to draw too pessimistic conclusions from this report would do well to remind himself that the capacities for independence are not to be underestimated. He may also draw some consolation from a further observation: Those who participated in this challenging experiment agreed nearly without exception that independence was preferable to conformity.

3

EXPERIMENTS IN GROUP CONFLICT

Muzafer Sherif

Conflict between groups—whether between boys' gangs, social classes, "races," or nations—has no simple cause, nor is mankind yet in sight of a cure. It is often rooted deep in personal, social, economic, religious, and historical forces. Nevertheless it is possible to identify certain general factors which have a crucial influence on the attitude of any group toward others. Social scientists have long sought to bring these factors to light by studying what might be called the "natural history" of groups and group relations. Intergroup conflict and harmony is not a subject that lends itself easily to laboratory experiments. But in recent years there has been a beginning of attempts to investigate the problem under controlled yet life-like conditions, and I shall report here the results of a program of experimental studies of groups which I started in 1948. Among the persons working with me were Marvin B. Sussman, Robert Huntington, O. J. Harvey, B. Jack White, William R. Hood, and Carolyn W. Sherif. The experiments were conducted in 1949, 1953, and 1954; this article gives a composite of the findings.

We wanted to conduct our study with groups of the informal type, where group organization and attitudes would evolve naturally and spontaneously, without formal direction or external pressures. For this purpose we conceived that an isolated summer camp would make a good experimental setting, and that decision led us to choose as subjects boys about 11 or 12 years old, who would find camping natural and fascinating. Since our aim was to study the development of group relations among these boys under carefully controlled conditions, with as little interference as possible from personal neuroses, background influences or prior experiences, we selected normal boys of homogeneous background who did not know one another before they came to the camp.

From *Scientific American*, Vol. 195, No. 5, November 1956, pp. 54-58. Reprinted with permission. Copyright © 1956 by Scientific American, Inc. All rights reserved.

They were picked by a long and thorough procedure. We interviewed each boy's family, teachers, and school officials, studied his school and medical records, obtained his scores on personality tests, and observed him in his classes and at play with his schoolmates. With all this information we were able to assure ourselves that the boys chosen were of like kind and background: All were healthy, socially well-adjusted, somewhat above average in intelligence and from stable, white, Protestant, middle-class homes.

None of the boys was aware that he was part of an experiment on group relations. The investigators appeared as a regular camp staff—camp directors, counselors, and so on. The boys met one another for the first time in buses that took them to the camp, and so far as they knew it was a normal summer of camping. To keep the situation as lifelike as possible, we conducted all our experiments within the framework of regular camp activities and games. We set up projects which were so interesting and attractive that the boys plunged into them enthusiastically without suspecting that they might be test situations. Unobtrusively we made records of their behavior, even using "candid" cameras and microphones when feasible.

We began by observing how the boys became a coherent group. The first of our camps was conducted in the hills of northern Connecticut in the summer of 1949. When the boys arrived, they were all housed at first in one large bunkhouse. As was to be expected, they quickly formed particular friendships and chose buddies. We had deliberately put all the boys together in this expectation, because we wanted to see what would happen later after the boys were separated into different groups. Our object was to reduce the factor of personal attraction in the formation of groups. In a few days we divided the boys into two groups and put them in different cabins. Before doing so, we asked each boy informally who his best friends were and then took pains to place the "best friends" in different groups so far as possible. (The pain of separation was assuaged by allowing each group to go at once on a hike and camp-out.)

As everyone knows, a group of strangers brought together in some common activity soon acquires an informal and spontaneous kind of organization. It comes to look upon some members as leaders, divides up duties, adopts unwritten norms of behavior, develops an *esprit de corps*. Our boys followed this pattern as they shared a series of experiences. In each group the boys pooled their efforts, organized duties, and divided up tasks in work and play. Different individuals assumed different responsibilities. One boy excelled in cooking. Another led in athletics. Others, though not outstanding in any one skill, could be counted on to pitch in and do their level best in anything the group attempted. One or two seemed to disrupt activities, to start teasing at the wrong moment, or to offer useless suggestions. A few boys consistently had good suggestions and showed ability to coordinate the efforts of others in carrying them through. Within a few days one person had proved himself more resourceful and skillful than the rest. Thus, rather quickly, a leader and lieutenants emerged. Some boys sifted toward the bottom of the heap, while others jockeyed for higher positions.

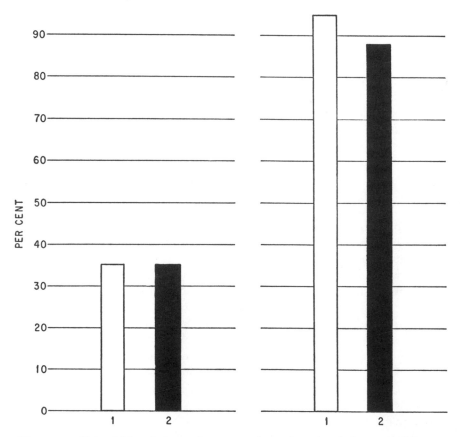

Fig. 3–1. *Friendship choices of campers for others in their own cabin are shown for Red Devils (white) and Bulldogs (black). At first a low percentage of friendships were in the cabin group (left). After five days, most friendship choices were within the group (right).*

We watched these developments closely and rated the boys' relative positions in the group, not only on the basis of our own observations, but also by informal sounding of the boys' opinions as to who got things started, who got things done, who could be counted on to support group activities.

As the group became an organization, the boys coined nicknames. The big, blond, hardy leader of one group was dubbed "Baby Face" by his admiring followers. A boy with a rather long head became "Lemon Head." Each group developed its own jargon, special jokes, secrets, and special ways of performing tasks. One group, after killing a snake near a place where it had gone to swim, named the place "Moccasin Creek" and thereafter preferred this swimming hole to any other, though there were better ones nearby.

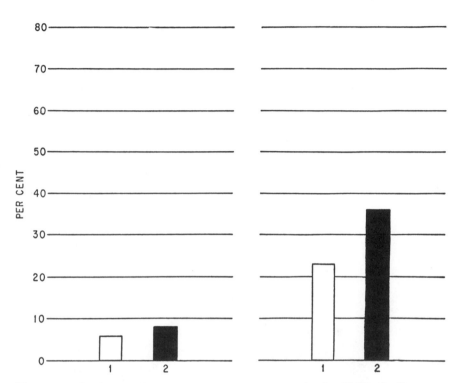

Fig. 3-2. *During conflict between the two groups in the Robber's Cave experiment there were few friendships between cabins (left). After cooperation toward common goals had restored good feelings, the number of friendships between groups rose significantly (right).*

Wayward members who failed to do things "right" or who did not contribute their bit to the common effort found themselves receiving the "silent treatment," ridicule, or even threats. Each group selected symbols and a name, and they had these put on their caps and T shirts. The 1954 camp was conducted in Oklahoma, near a famous hideaway of Jesse James called Robber's Cave. The two groups of boys at this camp named themselves the Rattlers and the Eagles.

Our conclusions on every phase of the study were based on a variety of observations, rather than on any single method. For example, we de-

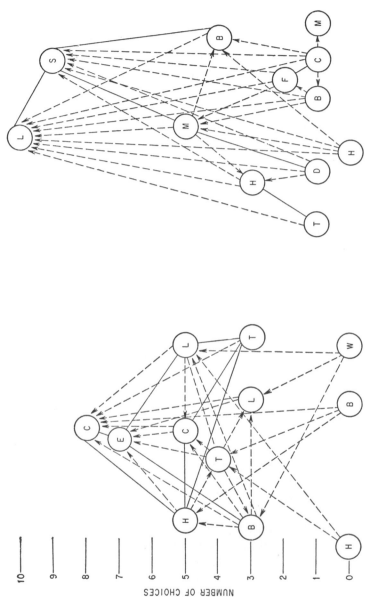

NUMBER OF CHOICES

Fig. 3–3. Sociograms represent patterns of friendship choices within the fully developed groups. One-way friendships are indicated by broken arrows; reciprocal friendships, by solid lines. Leaders were among those highest in the popularity scale. Bulldogs (left) had a close-knit organization with good group spirit. Low-ranking members participated less in the life of the group but were not rejected. Red Devils (right) lost the tournament of games between the groups. They had less group unity and were sharply stratified.

vised a game to test the boys' evaluations of one another. Before an important baseball game, we set up a target board for the boys to throw at, on the pretense of making practice for the game more interesting. There were no marks on the front of the board for the boys to judge objectively how close the ball came to a bull's-eye, but, unknown to them, the board was wired to flashing lights behind so that an observer could see exactly where the ball hit. We found that the boys consistently overestimated the performances by the most highly regarded members of their group and underestimated the scores of those of low social standing.

The attitudes of group members were even more dramatically illustrated during a cookout in the woods. The staff supplied the boys with unprepared food and let them cook it themselves. One boy promptly started to build a fire, asking for help in getting wood. Another attacked the raw hamburger to make patties. Others prepared a place to put buns, relishes, and the like. Two mixed soft drinks from flavoring and sugar. One boy who stood around without helping was told by the others to "get to it." Shortly the fire was blazing and the cook had hamburgers sizzling. Two boys distributed them as rapidly as they became edible. Soon it was time for the watermelon. A low-ranking member of the group took a knife and started toward the melon. Some of the boys protested. The most highly regarded boy in the group took over the knife, saying, "You guys who yell the loudest get yours last."

When the two groups in the camp had developed group organization and spirit, we proceeded to the experimental studies of intergroup relations. The groups had had no previous encounters; indeed, in the 1954 camp at Robber's Cave the two groups came in separate buses and were kept apart while each acquired a group feeling.

Our working hypothesis was that when two groups have conflicting aims—i.e. when one can achieve its ends only at the expense of the other —their members will become hostile to each other even though the groups are composed of normal well-adjusted individuals. There is a corollary to this assumption which we shall consider later. To produce friction between the groups of boys we arranged a tournament of games: baseball, touch football, a tug-of-war, a treasure hunt, and so on. The tournament started in a spirit of good sportsmanship. But as it progressed good feeling soon evaporated. The members of each group began to call their rivals "stinkers," "sneaks," and "cheaters." They refused to have anything more to do with individuals in the opposing group. The boys in the 1949 camp turned against buddies whom they had chosen as "best friends" when they first arrived at the camp. A large proportion of the boys in each group gave negative ratings to all the boys in the other. The rival groups made threatening posters and planned raids, collecting secret hoards of green apples for ammunition. In the Robber's Cave camp the Eagles, after a defeat in a tournament game, burned a banner left behind by the Rattlers;

the next morning the Rattlers seized the Eagles' flag when they arrived on the athletic field. From that time on name-calling, scuffles, and raids were the rule of the day.

Within each group, of course, solidarity increased. There were changes: One group deposed its leader because he could not "take it" in the contests with the adversary; another group overnight made something of a hero of a big boy who had previously been regarded as a bully. But morale and cooperativeness within the group became stronger. It is noteworthy that this heightening of cooperativeness and generally democratic behavior did not carry over to the group's relations with other groups.

We now turned to the other side of the problem: How can two groups in conflict be brought into harmony? We first undertook to test the theory that pleasant social contacts between members of conflicting groups will reduce friction between them. In the 1954 camp we brought the hostile Rattlers and Eagles together for social events: going to the movies, eating in the same dining room, and so on. But far from reducing conflict, these situations only served as opportunities for the rival groups to berate and attack each other. In the dining hall line they shoved each other aside, and the group that lost the contest for the head of the line shouted "Ladies first!" at the winner. They threw paper, food, and vile names at each other at the tables. An Eagle bumped by a Rattler was admonished by his fellow Eagles to brush "the dirt" off his clothes.

We then returned to the corollary of our assumption about the creation of conflict. Just as competition generates friction, working in a common endeavor should promote harmony. It seemed to us, considering group relations in the everyday world, that where harmony between groups is established, the most decisive factor is the existence of "superordinate" goals which have a compelling appeal for both but which neither could achieve without the other. To test this hypothesis experimentally, we created a series of urgent, and natural, situations which challenged our boys.

One was a breakdown in the water supply. Water came to our camp in pipes from a tank about a mile away. We arranged to interrupt it and then called the boys together to inform them of the crisis. Both groups promptly volunteered to search the water line for the trouble. They worked together harmoniously, and before the end of the afternoon they had located and corrected the difficulty.

A similar opportunity offered itself when the boys requested a movie. We told them that the camp could not afford to rent one. The two groups then got together, figured out how much each group would have to contribute, chose the film by a vote, and enjoyed the showing together.

One day the two groups went on an outing at a lake some distance away. A large truck was to go to town for food. But when everyone was hungry and ready to eat, it developed that the truck would not start (we had taken care of that). The boys got a rope—the same rope they had used in their acrimonious tug-of-war—and all pulled together to start the truck.

These joint efforts did not immediately dispel hostility. At first the groups returned to the old bickering and name-calling as soon as the job in hand was finished. But gradually the series of cooperative acts reduced friction and conflict. The members of the two groups began to feel more friendly to each other. For example, a Rattler whom the Eagles disliked for his sharp tongue and skill in defeating them became a "good egg." The boys stopped shoving in the meal line. They no longer called each other names, and sat together at the table. New friendships developed between individuals in the two groups.

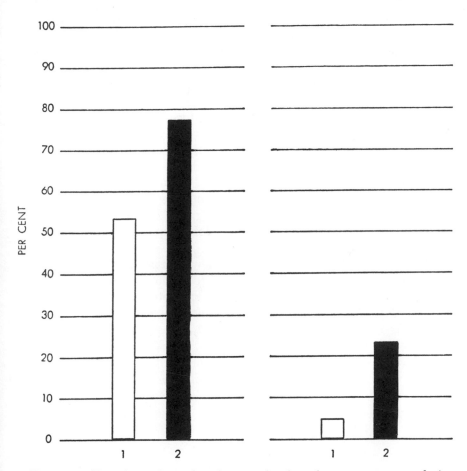

Fig. 3–4. *Negative ratings of each group by the other were common during the period of conflict (left) but decreased when harmony was restored (right). The graphs show per cent who thought that* all *(rather than* some *or* none*) of the other group were cheaters, sneaks, etc.*

In the end the groups were actively seeking opportunities to mingle, to entertain, and to "treat" each other. They decided to hold a joint camp fire. They took turns presenting skits and songs. Members of both groups requested that they go home together on the same bus, rather than on the separate buses in which they had come. On the way the bus stopped for refreshments. One group still had five dollars which they had won as a prize in a contest. They decided to spend this sum on refreshments. On their own initiative they invited their former rivals to be their guests for malted milks.

Our interviews with the boys confirmed this change. From choosing their "best friends" almost exclusively in their own group, many of them shifted to listing boys in the other group as best friends (See Figure 2). They were glad to have a second chance to rate boys in the other group, some of them remarking that they had changed their minds since the first rating made after the tournament. Indeed they had. The new ratings were largely favorable (See Figure 4).

Efforts to reduce friction and prejudice between groups in our society have usually followed rather different methods. Much attention has been given to bringing members of hostile groups together socially, to communicating accurate and favorable information about one group to the other, and to bringing the leaders of groups together to enlist their influence. But as everyone knows, such measures sometimes reduce intergroup tensions and sometimes do not. Social contacts, as our experiments demonstrated, may only serve as occasions for intensifying conflict. Favorable information about a disliked group may be ignored or reinterpreted to fit stereotyped notions about the group. Leaders cannot act without regard for the prevailing temper in their own groups.

What our limited experiments have shown is that the possibilities for achieving harmony are greatly enhanced when groups are brought together to work toward common ends. Then favorable information about a disliked group is seen in a new light, and leaders are in a position to take bolder steps toward cooperation. In short, hostility gives way when groups pull together to achieve overriding goals which are real and compelling to all concerned.

4

EMOTIONAL DYNAMICS
AND GROUP CULTURE[*]

Dorothy Stock Whitaker
Herbert A. Thelen

The theoretical position described here is the product of a series of investigations into the functioning of small groups carried on at the Human Dynamics Laboratory of the University of Chicago during the years 1947 to 1955. Under the direction of Herbert A. Thelen a number of investigators conducted studies on such group issues as composition, subgroup formation, developmental phases, sociometric choice, group culture, and individual learning and change.[1] Much effort was devoted to developing appropriate methodology for studying sequential group interaction, group-relevant aspects of personality, and member perceptions of self and others.[2] Especially composed work-groups and training-groups were utilized as settings for the research.[3]

In the course of its work the research team became interested in the theoretical writings of W. R. Bion, which seemed to fit its thinking about group interaction as a functional process, about the relevance of cognitive and emotional factors in group life, and about relationships between individual personality and group culture. Thus, at about 1950 or 1951, research became focused around attempts to understand various aspects of group functioning in terms of this theoretical approach. As substantive findings accumulated and progress was made on methodological issues, a theoretical position emerged which was based heavily on Bion's work, but included some modifications and extensions.

This chapter presents, first, an overview of Bion's theoretical approach, and then discusses implications for individual behavior and per-

Reprinted from *Emotional Dynamics and Group Culture* by Dorothy Stock and Herbert A. Thelen, No. 2 of the Research Training Series, National Training Laboratories, Division of Adult Education Service, National Education Association of the United States, Washington, D.C. (New York: New York University Press, 1958).

* As amended by D. S. Whitaker, September 1973.

sonality, sociometric choice and subgroup operation, group composition, group development, and individual change.

OVERVIEW OF BION'S THEORETICAL CONCEPTS

W. R. Bion[4] dealt with small groups of neurotic patients. As therapist, he provided the group with no direction or structure. The patients' reactions to this lack of structure constituted the initial material for therapy. As the group moved along, its content might derive from personal experiences of members or from group events, including members' feelings about the therapist or one another. The therapist's interpretations focused on two kinds of phenomena: the group's mood and individual members' reactions to the group situation. For example, Bion might indicate to the group that the members were banding together to misunderstand his comments or that Member X wanted to speak but felt he would be rejected by the rest of the group if he did so. One has the impression, from his articles, that Bion interpreted to the group its emotional state immediately as he became aware of it. The two major and perhaps distinguishing characteristics of Bion's approach as therapist are thus (1) an emphasis on the interpretation of group rather than individual phenomena and (2) a rather immediate interpretation of the group situation to the group.

As Bion observed his groups of patients, he noticed certain massive emotional reactions in the group. At times, for example, the group appeared to be *unanimously* expressing a need to run away from the group situation or to demand that the therapist provide more direction. From this kind of observation Bion developed the idea that a group could be thought of in terms of a series of emotional states or basic assumption cultures in which some affective need was inextricably associated with the work the group was trying to do. He saw individuals as contributing toward, acquiescing in, or reacting against, these cultures. Members also formed relationships with one another on the basis of their affinities for the various cultures. The particular relationship between the individual and the culture is accounted for by what Bion called "valency."

These two concepts—the basic assumption culture and valency—are fundamental in this theoretical approach. The first pertains to the situation in the group as a whole; the second refers to the individual member and his tendencies toward interaction in the total group.

In developing his concept of the basic assumption culture, Bion perceived that work and emotional components of group life are so interrelated that one never occurs without the other and that an understanding of group experience can come about only when both are studied in their dynamic and changing relationships to each other. The work aspects of group operation are the consciously determined, deliberative, reality-bound, goal-seeking aspects of the group's activities. While task activity can always be perceived in the group, there are times when an analysis of this kind of activity alone cannot explain what is happening. At times, for example, although the group may say it is interested in solving some problem, all its behavior seems to lead it farther and farther away from coming to grips with it. Or a group may seem to engage in apparently illogical activity, which becomes understandable only if one sees that it is preoccupied with (for example) its relation to its leader. As a result of this kind of observation, Bion came to see that the work activity of a group is always influenced to some extent by certain emotional states or concerns. In contrast to work, the emotional preoccupations of the group are nonpurposive, "instinctual," and not under conscious control. He felt that the emotional aspect of group operation could be described in terms of three rather comprehensively defined emotional states, which he called "cultures." These are dependency, pairing, and fight-flight. That is, a group can be described at any given time as operating in a work-dependency culture, a work-pairing culture, a work-fight-flight culture, or as being in some transitional phase. In each case the work aspects of the group's activities are suffused and influenced by the emotional state or concern.

In defining these group cultures, Bion[4] says that when the group is operating in a dependency-work culture it is acting "as if" (that is, on the basic assumption that) the group exists in order to find support and direction from something outside itself—the leader, external standards, or its own history. When it is operating in pairing-work it acts "as if" its function is to find strength from within its own peer group. When it is operating in fight-flight-work it is operating "as if" its purpose is to avoid something by fighting or running away from it. The "as if's" in these definitions are important, since they indicate what Bion does *not* mean when he describes a group as operating in a certain work-emotionality culture. He does not mean that when a group is operating in dependency-work, for example, nothing but dependency is expressed, or that the group is consciously aware of its preoccupation with dependency, or that the dependency can necessarily be directly observed. What he does mean is that if one makes the assumption that the group is acting as if it needs support and direction from something outside itself, then the diverse and apparently illogical and contradictory behaviors of the members of the group can be understood and will take on a certain coherence and order.

The concept of group culture is one that is applied globally to the total group process. It provides a means for understanding such problems as climate, group development, and overt and covert aspects of group functioning. It illuminates aspects of group operation that refer to the group as a whole rather than those involving the individual member.

Bion developed the concept of "valency" to pertain particularly to the relation between the individual and the group culture. He defines valency as ". . . a capacity for instantaneous and involuntary combination of one individual with another for sharing and acting on a basic assumption." [5] Thus valency is an inherent property of the individual that accounts for the nature of his participation in the emotional aspects of group life. It refers to the particular way in which the individual interacts with the group culture and appears to involve two interrelated aspects: expressive behavior and combining with others. Expressive behavior refers to the kind of affect the individual is most likely to express behaviorally in the group.

By "combining with others" Bion means the capacity of individuals to support or cooperate with others in developing, maintaining, or moving away from the various work-emotionality cultures. He uses the possibly obscure term "combining" because he does not want to imply that such activity is at all purposive, conscious, or planned in character. That is, the individual contributions to the affectual aspects of the group's life are in keeping with the nature of emotionality in the total group and are also essentially nonpurposive in character. Taken together, the two concepts of group culture and valency form a theoretical frame within which many problems of group operation can be described and studied.

INDIVIDUAL BEHAVIOR AND PERSONALITY

In his original formulation, Bion suggested that at any given time the group-as-a-whole acts as if it were operating on one of three basic assumptions: that it will maintain itself through developing intimacy (pairing), through reliance on external authority (dependency), or through fighting or fleeing from stress (fight-flight). During each phase members can be seen either as accepting and expressing the basic assumption or as reacting in some other way to its existence in the culture of the group. It was supposed that these individual ways of reacting to the various basic assumptions operating in the group culture might reveal basic tendencies in personality. Thus, when the group appeared to have the purpose of establishing dependency on the leader, one individual might respond with hostility (fight) and another with efforts to deepen his relationships to other individuals (pairing). Thus the question arose as to whether these basic assumption categories of modalities, meaningful for studying the group as a whole, might also be applicable to individual behavior.

Successful characterization of individual behavior in these terms should permit one to describe the individual's over-all pattern of behavior expected in group situations and to identify the way in which the individual would behave when the group was in different kinds of emotional or basic assumption situations. It should open the way to description of such roles as spokesmen for the various emotionality cultures and to identification of specific ways in which individuals respond affectively to the group situation. In short, it should help to identify the particular ways in which each group member would contribute to the development, maintenance, and dissolution of a variety of work-emotion cultures of the group.

We assume that the actual behavior observable in a group is a product of an individual's "valency pattern" plus the character of the group situation in which he finds himself. The concept of valency implies that each individual has differentiated preferences for participating with others who express the various emotional modalities and that he himself has predispositions to express these modalities in overt action. These differentiated preferences would constitute the individual's valency pattern and would throw light on his expressive behavior and his relationships with other members.

In its most simple terms, an individual who has a strong valency for fight tends to express hostility freely in the group; a strong valency for pairing indicates a tendency to express warmth freely and to wish to establish close relationships with others; a strong valency for dependency indicates a tendency to rely on others for support and direction; and a strong valency for flight indicates a tendency to avoid, in some way, the interactive situation. Every person possesses some valency, in varying degrees, for each of these emotional modalities. Such tendencies reside in the individual and form part of an habitual or stable approach to group interaction.

In applying this idea of valency pattern to a characterization of a specific individual, we find that valencies for fight, flight, pairing, and dependency are often very complexly related. (For example, an individual may pair in order to satisfy dependency needs; or he may take refuge in flight because he is so concerned about his own impulses to fight.) In order to help deal with these complexities it has seemed to us that valency—as an organized set of emotional predispositions residing in the individual—can profitably be differentiated into three related but distinguishable elements: area of concern, culture preference, and affective approach.

Area of concern is the most basic of these, yet it is most elusive and most difficult to observe directly. By area of concern we mean an affect-laden problem that, on some internal, possibly unconscious, level is felt to be significant by the individual and mobilizes his psychic energies. For example, a certain group member may be particularly sensitive to problems concerning dependency—any problem of relating to an authority figure lies within this area of concern. Another member's particular sensitivities may lie in the area of pairing—establishing close relationships with others; another may be concerned with handling his own hostility. Additional areas of concern may be important for other members. Clues to these basic or underlying concerns *may* be found in the person's behavior—either directly or as a break in his more typical pattern. But oftentimes the underlying concern is so deeply hidden or so well defended that behavioral clues are obscured. For the moment, however, let us assume that such areas of concern do exist for many individuals. In some cases they correspond somewhat to the emotional categories we have used in defining the group culture; in other cases these concerns either emphasize some one aspect of these emotionalities, cut across our categories, or fall outside them entirely.

Culture preference refers to the fact that a group member seems to prefer certain work-emotionality cultures to others. This preference may be indicated in a number of ways. He is more comfortable, more free, more relevant, more spontaneously and less compulsively active, more able to work in certain specific group-cultural environments. Some persons may express this preference directly ("I don't like it when everyone is fighting." "Why do we always have to ask the leader what to do next?"); while in other cases the preference must be inferred. The individual may or may not be aware of his own preferences.

Affective approach refers to the ways in which the individual responds expressively to the various group cultures: that is, the ways in which he behaves and does not behave. To illustrate: A certain individual may typically express fight more readily than any other affect, but when the group as a whole is in a dependency culture, he is likely to flight. He may find it easiest to express warmth toward individuals who are themselves rather withdrawn. Such a pattern can become complex, but when it is thoroughly defined for an individual it can provide a comprehensive picture of his affective approach under a variety of conditions in the group.

These three aspects of total valency pattern may, for different individuals, be related to each other in a variety of ways. For some persons the same emotionality may be dominant in all three aspects. For example, the area of concern may be dependency—that is, the individual is most alerted to dependency conditions. He is ambivalent and anxious about accepting or rejecting dependency, and he puts proportionately more of his energies into this area. At the same time he is most comfortable when the group as a whole is in a dependency state—that is, when the responsibility for group activity lies in the leader or in some external element. His habitual approach to interaction is one of appeal—a need for external limitation and goal-setting, willingness to comply with the wishes of others, and so on. This kind of uniformity is rare. Usually area of concern involves more conflict than this would imply, and the other two aspects of valency pattern are likely to be organized at least partially as a defense. There always will be a relationship among the three, such that each becomes understandable in terms of the others, but the particular relationship will be unique for each person. The total pattern may vary in the specificity of the area of concern, the extent of conflict, the character and degree of organization of the defense, and the person's awareness of his own pattern.

It should be pointed out that delineating a group member's valency pattern does not provide a complete picture of the individual's personality structure. It does, however, define in an organized way aspects of personality particularly relevant to behavior in groups.[6]

SOCIOMETRIC CHOICE AND SUBGROUP OPERATION

In addition to its relevance for individual personality, the concept of valency suggests a basis for understanding the positive and negative feelings group members develop about one another and subgroup interaction within the total group.

If an individual perceives another member as having similar needs and interests and as working toward establishing group conditions congenial to him, he is likely to feel friendly toward that person. If, on the other hand, he perceives someone else as interfering with his interests in the group and as working to establish group conditions that he finds uncongenial, he is likely to dislike that person. To illustrate: An individual who characteristically withdraws from close personal contact with others is likely to prefer others with similar needs, since these members together can meet one another's needs in this respect. The same person is likely to reject those members who are constantly urging the group to become more intimate and reveal more personal material, since these are the members who are, in effect, forcing him to enter into a kind of relationship distasteful to him.

To translate this common-sense illustration into our theoretical terms, we would say that this flight member (who flees intimacy) is likely to prefer other flight members and to reject pairing members. It is possible to imagine other flight members who might reject flight persons as well as pairing persons. This might happen, for example, when the member is so disturbed or conflicted about his own flight needs that he is equally threatened by members who wish to escape close contact with others, since these would keep his conflict in the foreground. Counterdependency members might be expected to reject (rather than accept) one another, since each member can satisfy his own needs to control the group only by competing against others with similar needs.

Several studies were conducted which taken together suggest some of the dynamic bases of sociometric choice.[7] For example, certain affective approach types do not simply or necessarily make choices among their own membership; nor do they necessarily choose specific other types. Whether a member's active participation is elicited by conditions of warmth and friendliness or by conditions of conflict influences his participation or non-participation with the persons he chooses sociometrically. Choice is influenced *both* by considerations of who will provide support in creating a need-satisfying milieu *and* by considerations of who can help support or maintain defensive needs. Total group composition and emotional state are also influencing factors, since preoccupations of the group as a whole may focus the attention of members on certain individuals.

Our current hypothesis is that group composition has a limiting or focusing influence on the choices made, but that within this context individual valency characteristics are operative.

A related assumption is that individuals with similar needs form a special kind of subgroup within the total group. That is, individuals who have in common a need (let us say) for fight are likely to act together to establish conditions in the group that will permit hostile interchanges, aggressive approaches to problem solving, and so on. Or, to state this more generally, a group can be seen as being made up of a limited number of subgroups, each of which shares certain need characteristics and may act together to establish group conditions which are congenial, comfortable, and nonthreatening.

When the members of a subtype are described as "acting together" we do not mean that they *consciously* cooperate or that they are necessarily aware of common needs. We simply mean that because they do share certain needs they can be expected (at least under interactive conditions) to express similar attitudes and to attempt to influence the group toward similar emotionality-work states.

When groups are viewed as an interacting collection of subtypes they may be seen to vary in several ways: A group might be composed of subtypes whose needs are compatible or incompatible with one another. There may be much or little communality among the subtypes. Certain needs and approaches characteristic of a particular subtype may be present in one group and not in another. The designated leader may, by his personal characteristics, reinforce one subtype and not the others. A specific member may be part of the majority subtype in one group and isolated in another. These possibilities illustrate ways in which groups may be differentiated by knowledge of subtype composition. These and other conditions may be useful in accounting for the kinds of learning opportunities the group offers its members, the extent and nature of conflict in the group, and its course of development.[8]

VALENCY COMPOSITION AND GROUP PROBLEM-SOLVING

As is implied in the previous section, the concept of "individual valency pattern" seems to offer a profitable conceptual approach to group composition.

To illustrate: Suppose an individual is reluctant to become involved in a group's activities and, more particularly, tries to avoid involvement in disagreements and feels uncomfortable when others become involved. Clinical analysis shows that he has impulses to fight, but that he attempts to suppress them. Suppose further that this general approach to group interaction is habitual with this person. In our terminology, such a person would be described as having a strong valency for flight and a weak valency for fight. He would be expected to behave in certain ways in the group: When the group is fighting he may be one of the members who tries (possibly ineffectually) to urge the group toward some other mode of emotional expression. When the group is in flight he may take the lead and act to prolong the flight situation. He is likely to go along with others who express similar needs to avoid fight and express flight. Because these members support his own inclinations and needs he may feel more friendliness toward them than toward others.

A group in which most of the members can be described in this way will take on a certain character that is an expression of the interaction of members with strong valencies for flight. Groups composed differently with respect to the valency characteristics of the members can be expected to show different over-all characteristics that are, in turn, an expression of the interaction among the valency types included in *their* composition.

The valency pattern of an individual is likely to involve very intricate relationships between tendencies to act (affective approach), preferences for pairing, fight, flight, dependency, and work (culture preference), and area of concern. All three levels of valency are important to an understanding of a particular individual's interaction in a group. When discussing a collection of individuals, however, affective approach may be the most relevant. For purposes, then, of studying the group as a whole, each member can be generally characterized as having a predominant valency for expressing one or two of the modalities.

The possibility of describing each individual in valency terms makes it possible to consider the group-as-a-whole in terms of (1) the valency type or types predominantly represented in the group and/or (2) the range of valency types present in the group.

Let us now consider the kinds of information that can be deduced from knowledge of the two aspects of group valency composition indicated above.

1. Groups may differ with respect to the valency type preponderantly represented in the group composition. Depending on the dominant modality, groups should differ in the kind of work-emotionality culture they most often establish, in the way they operate within the various work-emotionality cultures, and in their characteristic attack on task problems. To make this a little more concrete, consider two groups: one having a preponderance of members who express fight readily and who act together to maintain a fight culture in the group; and one which can similarly be characterized as predominantly "pairing." We might expect such differences as the following to exist between these two groups:

a. The groups will differ in their efficiencies when dealing with any particular task problem. Each will be more efficient than the other with respect to different kinds of problems.

b. Both groups will be able to deal adequately with certain task problems but will show differences in the way they attack these problems.

c. The two groups will have different capabilities for dealing with "process" or interpersonal problems. In the second group, ambiguities in the limits to expression and/or management of hostility might never be dealt with, since when fight situations arise the pairing members will tend to move the group out of the fight modality.

d. Considering the individual member, a person with strong predispositions toward pairing will be somewhat isolated in the first group and find little support for his needs. The same will be true of a fight person in the second group.

e. The two groups will differ in the standards they develop with respect to the tolerance and encouragement of fight and pairing. In the first group the limits imposed on fight will be much broader than in the second group. The second group will show higher tolerance for pairing than will the first group.

One would not generally expect to find compositions in which *all* members show strong predispositions for fight or for dependency, etc. Yet it is not unusual for a group to tend toward a preponderance of one or another of the emotional modalities; and such a tendency will have a significant influence on the course of group operation.

2. Groups may differ with respect to the range of valency types included in their composition. A group whose composition includes a wide range of valency types would presumably be able to deal explicitly with a wide range of emotional issues. The theoretical rationale for this may be formulated as follows: An individual whose valency pattern leads him to express a certain emotional modality readily and to feel most comfortable when this modality is predominant in the group culture may be thought of as a spokesman for that particular modality. As spokesman he might be expected to introduce that affective mode into the group and to attempt to influence the group as a whole to move into or to maintain this culture or to terminate cultures that may be antithetical to it. If the group includes spokesmen for emotional cultures opposed to each other, for example dependency and counterdependency, then both these needs are likely to be expressed overtly in the group. Moreover, the way in which this problem is eventually dealt with is likely to be settled by means of interaction between these spokesmen. If spokesmen for only one end of the dependency-counterdependency continuum appear in the group, then only that affective mode would be expressed overtly, and since there is no one to express opposition to it, the group is likely to accept this mode implicitly as its standard.

Our prediction, then, is that a group that includes a wide range of valency types will deal more explicitly with a wider range of emotional issues. A group whose range of valency types is narrower will deal with a

more restricted range of emotional issues, and it will tend to dea
them in a less explicit way. If this is true, it follows that a group of the
type will provide opportunities for a wider range of learning than wr.
group of the second type.[9]

DYNAMICS OF GROUP GROWTH

Our theoretical position states that a group can be seen as operating
successively in a series of work-emotionality cultures, each differing from
the one preceding or succeeding it in the relative dominance of the work
or the emotional aspects of the culture and/or in the particular emotional
state with which the work is associated. A group may operate in a work-
pairing culture (work-dominant) for a time, then shift to a work-dependency culture (work-dominant), and then to a fight-flight-work culture
(fight-flight-dominant), and so on. This is, of course, a stylized view and
provides only a generalized model for the characterization of a group's development. There may be many times when the group is operating in
some mixed or transitional state or when the situation is so confused that
the basic assumptions on which the group is operating cannot be identified. A particular work-emotionality state or culture may last only a few
minutes, or it may go on over several meetings or even dominate a group's
entire existence.

In considering the problem of how a group moves from one work-
emotionality culture to another, Bion suggests that unique satisfactions and
anxieties may be associated with each emotional state. For example, group
members operating in work-dependency may find satisfaction in the fact
that they can relax, rely on someone else for direction, and not have to
assume responsibility for their own operation. At the same time they may
feel anxious because of the implied immaturity, lack of control over their
own interaction, and, perhaps, denial of many individual needs.

The second of the two basic concepts, individual valency, seems operative here. For example, when a group is operating in a fight culture, certain individuals in the group who are particularly sensitive to the threats
and anxieties involved in this culture (i.e. for whom fight is an area of
concern) may so act as to communicate these anxieties to others or to attempt to move the group into some other work-emotionality culture. Presumably, when these anxieties build up to some crucial level for the group
as a whole, a shift will occur. The new culture will be maintained for a
while because of the particular satisfactions associated with it and because
of relief from the anxieties associated with the previous culture. As time
goes on, other members, particularly sensitive to the anxieties associated
with the new culture, may be expected to initiate another shift. Similarly,
one can expect certain members to fight a kind of rear guard action. Just
as some members are especially threatened by a particular work-emotional-

.ation, some others may be especially rewarded by it and can be ex-
.d to influence the group to remain in that culture. It is through the
.eraction of these kinds of forces that shifts from culture to culture oc-
.ar.

This approach to group development leads to speculations about the probable sequence of development and about the work-emotionality characteristics of the "mature" and the "immature" group. One possibility is that preoccupation with one kind of emotional issue is followed by preoccupation with another in some predictable sequence. For example, groups may typically operate in a work-dependency culture during their first meetings and move toward work-pairing or work-fight cultures during later meetings. Another possibility is that the particular way in which work and emotionality are related within a culture changes over time. For example, in early work-dependency cultures the preoccupation with dependency might disrupt the work efforts of the group, while in later work-dependency cultures the group may use its preoccupation with dependency more constructively. It is our impression that the latter is a more accurate statement of what is likely to occur. In general, we do not expect the particular sequence of work-emotionality cultures to be constant from group to group, but to depend on such factors as the particular valency characteristics of the members, the leader's personal needs and leadership approach, and the task demands to which the group is subject. Rather than a fixed sequence, the same underlying emotional preoccupations may recur from time to time in the same group, but the manner in which work and emotionality are integrated may shift. Movement toward maturity involves an increased integration of emotionality with work such that the emotional needs of the group are progressively more stimulating to and supportive of the work needs.

This view of group development includes the possibility that changes may occur in the group without, necessarily, having changes occur in the valency characteristics of individual members. That is, group growth may be a matter of a more strategic activation or use of members of particular valency types, such that specific kinds of contributions are introduced more appropriately into the discussion.

To summarize this view of group development:

1. Group interaction can be described in terms of two aspects: work and emotionality.

2. The significant emotional categories of group interaction are dependency, pairing, and fight-flight.

3. At any given time a group is operating in a work-emotionality culture in which work is associated with one or another of the above emotional states.

4. The development of a group can be described in terms of successive phases of varying duration in which one work-emotionality culture

gives way to another. Successive work-emotionality states or cultures differ in the particular emotionality associated with the work and/or in the relative dominance of work over emotionality or vice versa.

5. Anxiety and need gratification account for the shift from one work-emotionality culture to another.

6. As the group develops, there is a trend toward integration of work and emotional activity such that neither is denied and both are mutually supportive.[10]

READINESS FOR AND CHARACTERISTICS OF INDIVIDUAL CHANGE

Research at the Human Dynamics Laboratory has been done principally with training groups, and we have therefore been particularly concerned with the sorts of individual changes ordinarily expected from such groups. Thus the kinds of changes we have studied represent only a limited sampling of the many kinds of changes possible as a result of experiences in groups.

At the time the research was undertaken, training groups had a form and character different from that which obtains today, some fifteen to twenty years later. During the period 1947 to 1955, training groups tended to be larger than at present (fifteen to twenty members). Most typically, they met once a day over a period of two or three weeks with other activities of a more cognitive character interspersed; their explicit goals were to increase the members' understanding of how groups function and their understanding of themselves as group members or leaders. The encounter group, and the often more personally oriented training group of today, had not yet evolved. One more frequently found leaders who adopted a relatively nonchallenging and nondirective approach to the group. It was assumed that participants came to training groups in order to increase their skills in working in and through groups in some work context. The idea of groups whose goal is to help any individual, regardless of professional or work role, toward greater self-fulfillment did not yet exist.

Then, as now, variations could be found both in groups and in leaders. However, the following can be taken as a fair description of the groups studied: Discussion is exploratory, informal, and relatively free. The curriculum emerges from diagnosis of concerns revealed during discussion. The role of the leader is usually to suggest and interpret rather than to direct. These groups ordinarily deal with such problems as the identification of authority in the group, the nature of limits to expression of feeling, the manner of organization of efforts toward problem solving or decision making, etc. These kinds of problems are dealt with much more explicitly than in a group upon which specific task demands are imposed. For the training group-as-a-whole, the major purpose is to establish, through study of its problems, a set of agreements that will enable discussion to be profitable. For the individual, goals include increased understanding of group operation; increased awareness of one's own roles, needs, and effects on others; and increased personal effectiveness in a group situation. It is assumed that these changes or learnings will lead to increased effectivness in the back-home work situation; and this, rather than change per se, is the *raison d'être* for the training group.

The concepts of "individual valency" and "group culture," of central importance to the understanding of group phenomena, were applied to the problem of individual change. The following postulates seem most pertinent:

1. Individual change can be described in terms of shifts in valency pattern.

2. The group culture can be seen as the context within which change takes place.

3. The nature of change is determined by the particular interaction between the individual's valency characteristics and the nature of the group culture.

1. *Individual Change in Relation to Shifts in Valency Pattern*

Valency, as a property of the individual, includes the three related aspects of affective approach, culture preference, and area of concern. These three aspects of valency may be diagnosed by an observer or clinician. To some extent they are also available to the subject himself as the content of self-perceptions.

It is possible to imagine the independent occurrence of each of four kinds of change: affective approach (the way the individual behaves), culture preference (the kinds of group situations in which he prefers to operate), area of concern (the affective areas with which he is concerned or preoccupied or in conflict), or self-percept (the ways in which he thinks of his own operation in a group situation). More commonly, however, one would expect concurrent changes: change in affective approach accompanied by change in self-percept; change in area of concern accompanied by shifts in the preferred culture; and so on.

The most rigorous and thorough understanding of change would take into account all four factors. For example, a change in affective approach (behavior) in one individual might reflect a strengthening of defenses against the awareness of some more basic conflict. A change in affective approach in another member might indicate an increased freedom to express certain affective needs. A change in self-percept might indicate temporary conformity to the standards of the training group, or it might represent a shift that is also reflected in complementary modifications in behavior and culture preferences.

The "real meaning" of change is communicated as an interpretation of relationships among the four factors. Problems can be defined in such a way that one is interested in only one of these factors: only behavior or only self-percept. But it is our feeling that a consideration of the dynamic relationship among all four factors is required, first to clarify the kind of change one really is talking about and second to interpret the psychological meaning of the change for the individual.

2. The Group Culture as the Context Within Which Individual Change Takes Place

According to our conceptual approach, the continuity of interaction in the total group can be described as a series of constantly shifting and alternating work-emotionality cultures. We assume that a training group is always engaged in work: That is, it is always engaged in some rationally definable activity involving planning, making, or acting on decisions, or the like. At the same time we assume that the group is moving through a succession of emotional phases in which the atmosphere may be dominated in turn by fight (hostility, attack), by flight (withdrawal, silliness, irrelevance), by pairing (warmth, feelings of relatedness), by dependency (a wish to be led or directed), by certain combinations of these, or by transitional phases leading from one to another. At any given time the emotional aspects of the group's life have specific relationships to the work aspects of its operation. At times work may seem to be almost completely in abeyance and the group largely engulfed by its emotional preoccupations. At other times the emotional atmosphere and the affect expressed may seem to fit in constructively with the work activities and support and further the task goals of the group.

These various phases, combinations, and sequences of phases constitute a way of characterizing the ongoing group situation. Whatever change takes place in the individual results from the impact of these phases on him—the ways in which he participates in them and reacts to them.

3. Change as an Effect of Interaction Between the Individual's Valency Characteristics and the Nature of the Group-Cultural Context

It is possible that certain kinds of group environments are more conducive to change than others. We would imagine, for example, that in general more members are likely to have an opportunity to learn in a group that offers a wide variety of experiences to its members. In contrast, in a group where discussion is limited to one or a few issues, the possible learnings are more likely to be restricted. Another general characteristic of groups that may influence learning is the relative clarity or confusion of the group situation. It seems reasonable that under very confused conditions members would be less likely to learn because of the difficulty in understanding either what is going on or their own reactions to the situation.

Turning to the individual, it is likely that some persons are more ready to make use of a training experience for personal change than are others. In our terms, it is possible that certain affective approach types are more likely to change than others. It is also possible that affective approach type is not as relevant as the interrelations among affective approach, culture preference, and basic concern within the individual's total valency pattern. In the latter case we would expect such factors as extent of conflict, adequacy of defenses, rigidity or flexibility, and so on, to be influential.

To understand change thoroughly in the case of any one individual, it is probably necessary to consider the *interaction* between total valency pattern and the nature of the group situation. A group-cultural situation that is a good learning environment for one individual may not be equally effective for another. For example, an individual whose valency pattern shows a strong need for external control or reliance on an authority figure (dependency) might simply be immobilized or driven into unproductive defensive maneuvers in a group where the leader denies or rejects his own authority. This same member might be very responsive to a group in which the designated leader supplies more structure and direction. What is meaningful and insight-producing to one member may be irrelevant or disturbing to another. It is possible to imagine the probable conduciveness to learning of many combinations of individual valency and group conditions.

In considering the problem of how and why change takes place for a particular individual, it appears that the interaction between individual valency and group culture can be viewed either macroscopically or microscopically.

The macroscopic or general approach involves assessing the over-all valency characteristics of the individual and the over-all work-emotionality characteristics of the group and then predicting change in terms of the relationship between these two factors. Thus a group might be considered a potentially profitable experience for a certain member if it offers a range of experiences relevant to his problems, if it provides an atmosphere sufficiently permissive or protected (whatever he needs) to permit the member to experiment freely in his behavior, and if it offers opportunity for the member to look clearly at what he is doing and at the effects of his behavior on others. In contrast, a group is likely to provide an unprofitable learning experience if the situations that develop in the group are essentially irrelevant to the member's needs, or if they do not cover a sufficient range, or if they are so threatening that they preclude any experimentation or looking at the self.

A more microscopic and specific approach is required to trace the specific experiences and interactions that account for change in the individ-

ual. One is required to look more concretely into the group e
identifying those situations in which the individual was active a
those in which he did not participate but which can be assumed to .
portant to him. These psychologically meaningful situations must the.
examined systematically for the ways in which he responded, the range
his responses, his feelings of anxiety or adequacy communicated in his be
havior, and any tendencies for his responses to change through time.[11]

SOME MAJOR UNANSWERED QUESTIONS

The relation of the designated leader to other members and his influence on group events is both a theoretical and a practical problem. In a
training group, the two most relevant factors may well be his approach to
training and certain personal characteristics. Training approach includes
his image of what the group "should be like," the directions in which he
would like it to move, his assumptions about appropriate limits, the direc-
tiveness or nondirectiveness of his leadership, and the extent to which he
acts as an authority or assumes responsibility for group events. By personal
characteristics we mean his valency pattern: the interrelationships of affective approach, culture preference, and basic concern. His valency pattern
may not have a direct relationship with his behavior as leader because the
expectations of that office impose their own performance criteria. Even so,
it is more than likely that his training approach is subtly influenced by his
personal needs. If he is rendered uncomfortable by close contact with
others, he may in subtle ways impose on his group barriers to contact; and
he may incorporate this personal need within a training approach emphasizing strict work orientation and focus on theoretical issues. A group
characteristic which is intolerable on a personal level becomes intolerable
on a level of training philosophy.

If the designated leader influences the group through interpretation
of process, the character and timing of his interpretations are crucial. It
seems reasonable to study the *character* of interpretation in terms of the
leader's valency pattern in relation to the current group culture. The *timing* of an interpretation might be studied in terms of its location within an
established work-emotionality culture or at some point in a transitional
phase. It is proposed that the effect of leader interventions in delaying or
facilitating shifts may be due to their alleviation or reinforcement of anxieties inherent in the cultural alternatives.

Further *study of the operation of "natural" leadership* would extend
the applicability of our concepts. Bion proposed that at certain times particular individuals may "speak for" the prevailing group culture. At another
point he suggests that a particular kind of leader may be associated with
each of the work-emotionality cultures. For example, when a group is in a
fight culture one of its characteristics is that it needs to attack something

ie. Bion has observed that at such times the group may "follow" , pay special attention to, encourage to talk) a member with para- endencies, because such a member can justify the fight tendencies by ring the group that it is beset by "enemies"; or a group wishing to oid meaningful discussion may listen with rapt attention for consider- able periods of time to a member who is dull, irrelevant, or incoherent. If challenged, the group will claim that they were completely interested and absorbed. In Bion's terms, such a member is leading the group in flight.

EVALUATION OF THE THEORY

On the whole the theory described here lends itself best to concep- tualizing and spelling out the dynamics of certain total-group phenomena. Bion's fundamental insight—that the group as a whole can be seen to operate on certain shared assumptions which lie outside awareness— remains viable and transcends the specifics of his theory. The same can be said of the basic idea that group events can be seen as the varying and fluid interaction between affective and cognitive aspects of group life.

The concepts of dependency, pairing, and fight-flight seem viable but somewhat subject to oversimplification. In order to apply these concepts to real events, one has to bear in mind that group cultures which are similarly labeled can in fact take quite different forms, and that no two are exactly alike. One also needs to be aware that there are times when the group situation is confused and cannot be described clearly in terms of a single basic assumption culture. A conceptual problem arises when one notices episodes in a group in which one emotional modality may be used to express concern over another. For example, warmth and friendliness may be used to avoid getting at real issues. In other words, pairing is used to express flight. Or, to put it another way, pairing (behavior) and flight (unconscious motivation) are both present, but at different levels of awareness and expression, and in a particular relationship to one another. Such observations suggest that it is important to avoid any tendency to oversimplify, and to bear in mind that any of the emotional modalities can constitute an "as if" culture, a vehicle for expressing something quite different, a defensive maneuver, and so on.

The theoretical framework has been useful in exploring both composi- tion and development. The composition of a group, defined in valency terms, has something to do with its working style, with the range of affective issues explored, and with the sort of context it provides for indi- vidual growth and change. This line of thinking could be taken farther in identifying group compositions likely to produce effective or less effective work groups, groups which can be expected to make quick decisions, groups which can be expected to tolerate the infighting necessary for accomplishing certain tasks, and the like.

Research already undertaken with regard to development suggests that this theoretical framework can describe groups in terms of their prevailing group culture and the succession of group cultures. The idea that groups vary in how far they move toward the effective integration of work and emotionality suggests criteria for differentiating more effective or mature groups from less effective or immature groups. This latter possibility is promising but has not been tested definitively.

A further point concerning development has to do with how and why it is that a group may shift from one work-emotionality culture to another. Bion suggested that each basic assumption culture carries its own rewards and threats, and that when the threats associated with a particular culture accumulate, a shift occurs. That such shifts do occur has been demonstrated in our research, but the question of just which anxieties are specific to each of the cultures, and how individual members may contribute to the shift, has yet to be explored.

All of the above has to do with total group phenomena. The theory has also been applied to subgrouping. Subgrouping can mean at least two things: pairs or small groups within the total group which collaborate, collude, or in general support one another's efforts; or pairs or small groups within the total group which choose one another sociometrically and may form friendship groups or cliques. Ben-Zeev's work showed that subgrouping in the first sense can be shown to occur, and that certain subgroups become active and "carry" certain basic assumption cultures. As one basic assumption culture gives way to another, certain subgroups who have been dominant give way to others, who emerge as relatively more active in their turn. This relationship was so consistent that Ben-Zeev was able to develop a formula for dividing a group session into successive phases on the basis of participation patterns. Applying the concepts of valency to subgrouping in the second sense—that of sociometric choice—proved to be more complex. An attempt to predict sociometric choice from modality preference showed that such predictions held for some members but not for others, depending on the nature of the underlying conflict. It was found that choice was not specifically related to affective approach type. To remain within the terms of the theory and at the same time satisfactorily account for sociometric choice patterns, one has to attend to all three aspects of valency and to the dynamic relationships among them. Sociometric choice can be explained in these terms, but these concepts may not prove to be the most economic for this purpose. A more direct approach to unconsciously experienced conflict, for example, might be more useful.

It is with regard to individual dynamics and the relationship of the individual to the group that the theory may prove cumbersome and incomplete. In order to identify personal change in valency terms—a plausible idea—it was necessary to differentiate the concept into the three aspects of affective approach, culture preference, and area of concern, and then to add the concept of self-percept. Further, it was necessary to identify the dynamic relationships among these. To illustrate the problems which arose: one might find that two individuals had changed with regard to dependency in that both had shifted their affective approach. While true as far as it went, one might find that the change was quite different in the two instances. One person, for example, might have utilized dependency as a vehicle for expressing pairing and establishing close relationships with others. As his capacity for intimacy developed and he had less need for displaying dependent behaviors, these dropped out of his repertoire. Another individual might have displayed dependency behaviors because he censored out from his behavior all hostility, including anything remotely like assertiveness. As his capacity to tolerate his own hostile feelings developed, and as his fears of the consequences of expressing hostility diminished, counterdependent or independent behaviors began more frequently to replace dependent ones. To say that both changed with respect to dependency would be true, but insufficiently specific and precise. The example also serves to illustrate a second problem. In order to describe the uniqueness of the individual and the way in which he changed, it was necessary to spell out the dynamic relationship among the various aspects of valency, and to invoke concepts of conflict and defense. If conflict and defense are essential to an understanding of change, then it may be more economical to make use of a theory in which these concepts play a more central role.

It is also likely that for exploring some issues having to do with change and with the relationship of the individual to the group, this set of concepts is incomplete. Certain leaders, for example, may be dominated by narcissistic needs which lead them to press their members to change in their image. Much of their behavior can be understood in these terms. Such a person, and such a relationship among personal need, behavior, and impact on group cannot easily be explained in the terms of this theory.

To sum up: Bion's basic ideas remain profoundly insightful, particularly in calling attention to shared unconscious aspects of group life. The attempts of the research group to extend and operationalize his concepts proved useful for some purposes, and deserving of further attention. These purposes include studying group composition, group development, and the more microscopic flow of group events, particularly with regard to the relationship between cognitive and rational aspects of group functioning and the shifts from certain shared preoccupations to others; the relationship between composition and development; the relationship between composition and problem-solving approach; and subgrouping in the sense of combinations of persons supporting one another to establish, maintain, or dissolve particular emotional cultures. The conceptual framework is useful for describing certain forms of individual change but less useful for *explaining* individual change. Certain relationships between the individual and the group cannot be dealt with conveniently by the theory either because it is cumbersome or does not cope with the full range of possible relationships.

REFERENCES

1. Substantive findings are summarized in Dorothy Stock and H. A. Thelen, *Emotional Dynamics and Group Culture*, No. 2 of the Research Training Series, National Training Laboratories, Washington, D.C. (New York: New York University Press, 1958). Specific studies are reported in: S. Ben-Zeev, "The Formulation and Validation of a Method for Unitizing Group Interaction." Unpublished Ph.D. dissertation, Department of Education, University of Chicago, 1951; R. DeHaan, "Graphic Analysis of Group Process." Unpublished Ph.D. dissertation, Committee on Human Development, University of Chicago, 1951; J. C. Glidewell, "Group Emotionality and Productivity." Unpublished Ph.D. dissertation, Department of Psychology, University of Chicago, 1953; Bettie Belk Sarchet, "Prediction of Individual Work Role in Two Adult Learning Groups." Unpublished Ph.D. dissertation, Committee on Human Development, University of Chicago, 1952; W. F. Hill, "The Influence of Subgroups on Participation in Human Relations Training Groups." Unpublished Ph.D. dissertation, Committee on Human Development, University of Chicago, 1955; M. A. Lieberman, "The Relationship Between Group Emotional Culture and Individual Change." Unpublished research, Department of Psychology, University of Chicago, June 1957; A. G. Mathis, "Development and Validation of a Trainability Index for Laboratory Training Groups." Unpublished Ph.D. dissertation, Department of Education, University of Chicago, 1955; Dorothy McPherson, "An Investigation into the Nature of Role Consistency." Unpublished Ph.D. dissertation, Department of Education, University of Chicago, 1951; J. McPherson, "A Method for Describing the Emotional Life of a Group and the Emotional Needs of Group Members." Unpublished Ph.D. dissertation, Department of Education, University of Chicago, 1951.
2. Methodology is summarized in Stock and Thelen, *op. cit.*, and described in greater detail in S. Ben-Zeev, Ida Heintz Gradolph, P. Gradolph, W. F. Hill, Dorothy Stock, and H. A. Thelen, "Methods for Studying Work and Emotionality in Group Operation" (planographed) (Human Dynamics Laboratory, University of Chicago, 1954), p. 208.
3. The training group is a special educational opportunity for adults which has been developing over a period of years in Human Relations Workshops conducted by the National Training Laboratories of the N.E.A. It was regarded as an especially appropriate setting for the study of many issues related to group development and functioning because of its initial lack of structure and the absence of a previous history or externally imposed

goals. See L. P. Bradford and J. Gibb (eds.), *Theory of T-Group Training.* In Press.

4. W. R. Bion, "Experiences in Groups, I," *Hum. Relat.*, I:314-320, 1948; "Experiences in Groups, II," *Hum. Relat.*, I:487-496, 1948; "Experiences in Groups, III," *Hum. Relat.*, II:13-22, 1949; "Experiences in Groups, IV," *Hum. Relat.*, II:295-304, 1949; "Experiences in Groups, V," *Hum. Relat.*, III:3-14, 1950; "Experiences in Groups, VI," *Hum. Relat.*, III:395-402, 1950; "Experiences in Groups, VII," *Hum. Relat.*, IV:221-228, 1951; "Group Dynamics: A Re-View," *Int. J. Psychoanal.*, 33:235-247, 1952.

5. W. R. Bion, "Group Dynamics: A Re-View," *Int. J. Psychoanal.*, 33:235-247, 1952.

6. The elaboration of valency pattern into the three elements of affective approach, culture preference, and area of concern developed in response to some early research efforts and were then utilized in later work. A sentence completion test (the Reactions to Group Situations Test) was developed to identify an individual's valency pattern. It has been used as a clinical instrument to assess individual learning and change. Ben-Zeev used it as an objective instrument in a study relating valency tendencies to behavior. Lieberman studied relationships between the emotionality predominant in the members' valency patterns and their perceptions of their own roles and of the character of the total group. Lieberman also related valency pattern to sociometric choice. These studies, as well as others to be referred to later are reported in Stock and Thelen, *op. cit.*

7. In separate studies, Morton A. Lieberman and Dorothy Stock explored the relation between valency pattern and sociometric choice. Lieberman found that group composition and culture were mediating factors. Ben-Zeev related sociometric choice and the extent to which members participated in the group, showing that a mediating factor was individual valency pattern.

8. Studies by William F. Hill examined subtype formation in training groups, exploring their relation to behavior, intermember perception, and group development.

9. John C. Glidewell conducted research on the relation between the valency composition of small groups and their problem-solving styles. Ida Heintz Gradolph studied the problem-solving and interactive characteristics of groups which were homogeneously composed with reference to the predominant affective approach of members. Lieberman compared a group composed of a wide range of valency types with a group composed of a narrower range.

10. Dorothy Stock and Saul Ben-Zeev traced the development of a single training group in work-emotionality terms. Stock and William F. Hill related the developmental characteristics of this and a second group to compositional factors.

11. Studies of individual change have been conducted by Andrew G. Mathis and Dorothy Stock. Mathis developed a "trainability index" which incorporated personality factors found to be conducive to and inhibitory of change. Stock studied changes in self-percept and valency pattern which occurred during the course of a training group experience.

5

BIOLOGICAL MODELS OF SOCIAL CHANGE

Kurt W. Back

Social theory embraced early in its history primitive evolutionism, and the indiscriminate application of this theory in Social Darwinism has brought this analogy to biological models into disrepute. Modern biological theory does not assume the ruthless unidirectional change which the primitive interpretation of Darwinism postulated, but investigates mechanisms through which changes in the adaptive system occur. In addition, other mechanisms have been identified which show the possibility of adaptation for varying ranges. From short to long, they are: perception, learning, immunity, maturation, heredity, and evolution. By identifying the essential properties of each process, types of mechanisms can be proposed which relate to different problems of change within any system, including the social system. Those indicating the ways in which mechanisms of this kind could work in social systems can help in locating and understanding these processes in social change.

The analogy of society as an organism is old, attractive, and disreputable. It has been used to justify existing schemes of hierarchical structures, sometimes with telling effect if legend is to be believed. According to Livy, Menenius Agrippa, a patrician, settled an incipient revolt by the plebeians by telling them a story about the usefulness of the stomach. Although the stomach apparently does not do any work but gets all the food which the other parts of the body make a great effort to obtain, a strike against the stomach by the rest of the body is obviously self-defeating. Hence, the necessity for an analogous group in society or, as we may say today, a leisure class. Similar facile applications have recurred, using new insights into the biological process. Thus when organic evolution showed itself to be a workable theory, Social Darwinism tried to adapt this theory

Reprinted from *American Sociological Review*, Vol. 36, No. 4, August 1971, pp. 660-667.

to explain the current social and economic system. Again the data on biological organisms were used to justify an existing state of affairs, and the deficiencies of this approach soon became apparent. In the development of scientific sociology, grand developmental theories treating society like an organism have become extremely suspect.

Even with all these setbacks, the idea of a social unit as a kind of organism dies slowly. Common language, from the "body politic" to "heads of state," bears witness to man's inclination to find organic traits in societies. Over the years these have ranged from the analogy comparing human life to the life of a culture to theories explaining the structure of small groups in terms of the psychoanalytic organization of the psyche. There is, after all, an intuitive similarity between the organization of the human body and the kinds of organizations men create. And so, undaunted by the failures of the human-social analogy through time, new theorists try afresh in each epoch.

With the revived interest in large-scale models of social change and development, this approach has also come in for renewed criticism. Robert Nisbet (1970) has given some of the most incisive critiques; his strictures against developmentalism can be grouped into two headings: (1) in general, there is more permanence than change, therefore any model should account more for stability than for change, especially the even rarer, abrupt changes; (2) changes in society do not occur in a vacuum—depending only on intrinsic features—but in history, and they cannot be understood without reference to historical events. In this sense changes are unique and cannot be fitted into a general developmental scheme. Nisbet shows the challenges of any analogy between organisms and society which have to be overcome in any serious effort. The difficulties rest on the great obvious differences between organisms and societies. The shapes of organic configurations and societies are determined by particular circumstances. An organism owes many of its peculiar characteristics to its particular survival situation. And societies are formed in great part by historical accidents; looking at them, one finds that they look very different. If we take societies as a whole, we can consider only such a small number that each exception must be dealt with separately, and most of the theory will look like ad hoc reasoning. On the other hand, the wealth of detailed information on living organisms and the abundance of animal species have made possible detailed biological theories. Thus the stress on history in discussing social systems as compared to biological systems rests largely on the larger size and smaller number of social systems. However, the same difficulty with intrinsic theories which Nisbet discusses also plagues theories of organisms, if we substitute biographical for historical idiosyncrasies. Thus the disengagement theory of aging (Cummings and Henry, 1961) has been criticized as depending overly on intrinsic factors while overlooking influences of personal history analogous to Nisbet's strictures on developmentalism (Lowenthal and Boler, 1963; Maddox, 1965). The usual effort of the analogists has been to assimilate societies to the biological theories of the development of species and individuals and to fit in a few selected examples of social change. Thus in Western history the unique occurrences of the fall of the Roman Empire and the French Revolution have led to the expectation of regularity in falls of empires and courses of revolutions.

Any model which purports to display general features of development must be able to face Nisbet's two strictures. It must attempt to show similarities in mechanism beyond historical accidents and account for persistence as well as for change.

If the study of biological organisms can help in understanding society, it has to go beyond the accidents of biological and social conformation. Both societies and organisms are organized in such a way that they are self-maintaining; they react to preserve their organizations, and they maintain a certain stability or identity while changing some of their parts. These are characteristics which all living systems have in common, which make them "open systems." Allport (1960) states four conditions for an open system. They are input and output of matter and energy, maintenance of steady states, increase in complexity, and active interaction with the environment. Thus any living organism or complex of organisms can be considered to be an open system.

The first two conditions relate to the maintenance of the system; the last two, however, make change part of the definition of the system. This seeming contradiction—that the nature of systems is both preservation and change—makes it possible to describe both stability and change. The biologist has distinguished mechanisms, some of which maintain equilibrium under changing conditions, some of which create change in the system, and some of which are indicators of breakdown of adaptation. Study of the essential characteristics of these processes can help the sociologist in understanding stability and change in social systems.

There are several ways in which the model of the biological open system can be related to models of society. One distinction is between material and formal relationships. The former refers to the fact that man is a physiological organism and a separate species which has to obey the general laws of biology. Thus Duncan's (1964) paper on ecology treats population processes from the point of view of a species living in an ecosystem. Work of social psychologists in sociobiology (Shapiro and Crider, 1969) has shown the importance of physiological processes in social interaction. The other mode of extension, which we shall be using here, is the formal mode; here the emphasis is on the equivalence of processes which occur in all living systems, biological as well as social. We shall pursue here a theoretical, logical analysis of the importance of biological concepts in understanding social change and equilibrium, not an application of the biological characteristics of man to social processes.

The formal approach has been used productively by the general system theorists (Bertalanffy, 1968; Buckley, 1967; Miller, 1965). However, in the main they have been working on the principles which characterize *all* system processes, starting with such concepts as information, communication, organization, or decision. This approach has lost some of its power by being too general, by the difficulty in translating these general concepts into specifics. We shall here attempt to overcome this obstacle by concentrating not on general system characteristics but on distinct processes which have been identified in biological systems and show their explanation in social systems. Presumably other concepts are more conveniently identified first in social systems and may help in understanding biological events; concepts which come to mind are stratification, organization, or power. We shall attempt to understand the functioning of six processes which have been studied in detail in biological organisms and determine their meaning in social systems.

THE TYPES OF TRANSACTION

The six processes which biologists have used in characterizing living systems (Quarton, 1967) are commonly identified in biological organisms as perception, learning, maturation or growth, immunity, heredity, and evolution. These processes differ according to four characteristics: the manner in which organisms process information, the time span over which they operate, the feedback mechanisms they employ, and the source of their motive power.

Interaction Process

One of the conditions which distinguishes living systems is their use of communication and transmission of information instead of the transport of matter and energy. The basic feature of the communication process is the translation of available facts into a composite code which can be stored and transmitted easily. The form of the code and its storage depend on the particular transmitting system used. The code carries the information, which can be retrieved at a later time. However, the original input and output may be quite different from each other. The retranslation from the code will depend on the context, the conditions under which retrieval occurs. The retrieved information will be decoded and become a new body of facts influenced by the new situation. These facts may be coded again if new transmission is needed. The newly coded information may be the same in spite of a change by the organism during adaptation to the current situation. Thus coded information will be constant over time, but the interpretation will determine whether transmission occurs at all. For instance, in the case of genetics, the coded information is called genotype, or basic state, and the interpretation, phenotype, or seeming state. The genotype persists over time, depending on the viability of the phenotype.

In looking at biological systems, we find three ways of dealing with information. One is the processing of information and acting on it directly by the system. An example of this would be the reflex arc. A second way is the storage of information for use at a later time, such as use of memory. The third is the alternation of the above two systems—one phase which interacts with the environment and the other which transmits the information. This is the mechanism of genetics which implies growth, decline, and death of the single organism.

There are several ways in which organisms can use these three information-processing mechanisms in their interaction with the environment. In identifying these processes in organisms, we find two kinds of mechanisms for each of the ways of dealing with information, and the six resulting combinations are those previously mentioned as being characteristics of living systems. For the direct reaction we have perception and evolution. For memory we have learning and immunity. For genetics we have maturation, or growth, and heredity.

Time Span

The second of the four characteristics used to describe the processes by which the organism establishes its dynamic equilibrium is that of the time dimension. The processes are, from shortest to longest duration: perception, learning, maturation, immunity, heredity, and evolution. The first three—perception, learning, and maturation—refer to the life span of one organism; the last two—heredity and evolution—refer to the continuity between organisms. The immunity mechanism is a peculiar development of higher organisms. It consists of the creation of specific proteins which become defenses against invasion by foreign bodies; its ability to conduct the defenses is partly genetically determined, and partly formed through encounter with particular invaders. After one experience the protein keeps the shape adapted to this invasion and in a way learns to recognize the specific danger. The immunity process is thus a specific learning ability to defend the integrity of the organism and to maintain its boundaries. It may apply to individuals as well as to the whole species and is thus intermediate in time span.

We shall not look for direct analogies to these processes in societies. At this point we may only take notice of the importance of the time range of these processes and how different durations lead to quite different types of maintenance processes.

The time span is the most easily noticeable characteristic, and the differences have been discussed usually under the heading of the cultural and biological evolution. Thus Campbell (1965) has contrasted two pairs in our scheme, perception and learning on one side and heredity and evolution on the other, to demonstrate that biological principles do not lead necessarily to a theory of unilinear progress. He then shows how selective retention can operate on shorter and longer time spans.

Feedback

One of the most discussed features of living systems is the feedback mechanism which is the third characteristic given above (Watzlawick *et al.*, 1967). Some part of the output of a transmission is channeled back toward the input to the same transmission, creating in this way a kind of loop. Feedback can be of two types, positive and negative. In positive feedback the new input increases the outside stimulation and therefore makes the reaction stronger. Negative feedback counteracts the ongoing transaction and therefore keeps the resultant output on an even keel. In general, interest has centered on negative feedback, as this is the mechanism through which equilibrium or balance is maintained. However, positive feedback may have equal importance. This process works against stability, but it can result in increased power of the transaction, and on an individual level, in emotion and excitement. As it is a one-sided incremental process, it cannot go on unchecked. Therefore, it has been considered to be pathological, as the vicious circle. Unchecked growth due to hormonal imbalance in the individual organism can be compared on the interpersonal level with the pathological conditions leading to schizophrenia (Bateson, 1956) or with Richardson's (1960) theory of arms races. Rapoport (1968) has noted that the same process may be beneficial and lead, say, to better understanding and disarmament. There is no term, however, denoting this beneficial effect. We may classify the six processes listed above according to their affinity for negative or positive feedback.

Perception, learning, and heredity seem to be mainly dependent on negative feedback; they are the equilibrium-maintaining processes. The organism's perceptual apparatus has developed to give it a stable view of its surroundings, giving constancy to an ever-changing world of phenomena. The same may be said of learning and memory over a somewhat longer time span. Similarly, the mechanisms of heredity insure the stability of transmission of the organism's characteristics to its offspring. On the other hand, maturation and evolution as mechanisms of change are especially open to positive feedback. Maturation of a single organism typically implies growth which depends on positive feedback; if the organs which are changing work well, they will be more and more stimulated and will keep growing and functioning even more as time passes. What is true for the growth of the individual is true for evolution between generations. Success in adaptation will encourage more survivors to breed, and drift in a certain direction will become established as continuous. In this way new species are formed.

Immunity is ambiguous with regard to feedback as well as to time. It is self-limiting, restricting itself to eliminating noxious intruders, but positive feedback occurs frequently and leads to the generalization of immunity and frequently to exaggeration or allergies. Again, the boundary-maintaining function is sometimes ambiguous.

Motive Power

The fourth distinguishing characteristic of the six processes is the source of the motive power for the transaction. Here we find that the clearest distinction lies in the fact that perception and evolution are dependent mainly on external factors, stimulation and survival respectively, whereas maturation and heredity are dependent mainly on endogenous factors. Learning and immunity are dependent on both factors, both of them consisting of a kind of memory which changes the organism to benefit from previous experience. In fact, we find a correspondence between the source of motive power and the manner of dealing with information. The externally motivated processes deal with information in a direct way. The internally motivated ones are the basis of the alternation principle, and memory (i.e., learning and immunity) can use internal as well as external motive power.

Fig. 5–1.　　*Transaction of systems.*

Transaction	Perception	Learning	Growth	Immunity	Heredity	Evolution
Information Processing	Direct	Memory	Genetics	Memory	Genetics	Direct
Feedback	Negative	Negative	Positive	Both	Negative	Positive
Source of Motive	External	Both	Internal	Both	Internal	External
Time Span		Individual				Species

SHORT ————————————————➤　　————————➤ LONG

PATTERNS OF TRANSACTION

Figure 1 shows schematically the different types of transactions according to the categories which we have discussed; each transaction is characterized by a particular combination of the four categories. Thus we can find the equivalent transaction in a different kind of system by looking for the same combination of information handling, time span, feedback, and motive power.

The figure can show us more. The four characteristics can have several categories each. Thus we have distinguished two kinds of feedback, three kinds of information handling, and so on. Mathematically there is a great number of possible combinations, but we find only the six transactions discussed above existing in an organism. The nature of the particular combinations gives us an idea of the correlation between the characteristics and the joint conditions necessary for stability and change in open systems.

The first feature which we can glean from the figure is a certain symmetry. If we omit for the moment the two memory activities (learning and immunity), we find that the two externally motivated processes (perception and evolution) reflect the shortest and the longest durations, with the internally motivated ones (maturation and heredity) lying between them. However, there is an important difference in feedback. If there is an external disturbance for the externally motivated transactions, then in the short run (i.e., perception) the tendency of the system is to reestablish equilibrium; in the long run (i.e., evolution) the system will establish a gradual drift to a new adaptive mode.

In the internally motivated transactions the situation is the opposite. Maturation or growth of one individual has positive feedback and no specified equilibrium; this is compensated for by the equilibrium positions of heredity-connecting generations. Thus the alternation principle is maintained by the system itself. This contrast results then in a wavelike pattern: growth and decay over the short range (i.e., maturation) and repetition of the pattern (i.e., heredity) over the long range.

Learning has a different position. We have distinguished two types of learning: cognitive learning or memory processes, and immunity, which is learning of identity. In both cases there is a question of how far internal or external motives prove to be present, or whether there is selection or instruction. Learning in any case is the most "living" of all the processes discussed. It determines the individuality of the organism and society, its peculiar abilities and its identity. Basically it is probably an equilibrium-producing transaction, but it can easily upset the equilibrium; cognitive learning may lead to strengthened activity, and in the long-range immunity process the transaction may lead to overrejection and upset of equilibrium with the environment.

For memory, the figure shows three pairs of processes of information transmission. One set (perception and evolution) regulates the adaptation to environment; the system will either immediately react to a disturbance of its equilibrium, or over the long range will change its whole equilibrium condition. The second pair of processes (growth and heredity) is the mechanism of internal development corresponding to the alternation of phenotypical configuration and the coded genotype. The transcription will result in cumulative change, adapting the particular phenotype to the life situation of the organism. The stability of the message itself is guaranteed through a longer-range process which reduces the basic message and transmits it.

Finally there are the learning processes which are both active and passive. They are ambiguous as well in whether they establish an equilibrium or destroy it, and are, in the main, what Allport meant by activities in active interaction with the environment which keep the system open.

CATASTROPHIC CHANGES AND SYSTEM BOUNDARIES

The regular workings of living systems are carried on by the fore-named six processes. In these cases, the systems work in a stable manner and show adaptation to the environment. However, in addition to this slow kind of change, we find some abrupt, creative, or catastrophic kinds of change which occur when the processes function differently from the normal situation. For instance, positive feedback occurring in perception will lead to the organism's seeking more and more intense stimulation and experiences. Further, if perception is internally stimulated, then the organism is subject to illusory-wrong information about its environment and may act in a nonadaptive manner. These experiences may produce strong emotions in an individual, leading to abrupt personal changes. The conditions for peak experiences in the individual are the reversal of normal conditions of short-term stimulation of the organisms, making their reactions destitute of equilibrium and adjustment but reaching new states with potentially deep effect.

A similar effect can occur in the long-range transactions which maintain equilibrium. Under some conditions coding is defective and does not create the equilibrium and adjustment of the original gene-pool. Mutation of genes produces changes which are not framed in relation to the environment, but which upset the state through positive feedback, increasing quickly some tendency which may have no relation to the current surroundings. These spontaneous changes are frequently detrimental, but they provide an important avenue for completely novel ventures.

The fact that a comprehensive system theory has to provide for maintenance of equilibrium and gradual adaptation and catastrophic change has led to many difficulties in sociological system theories. Functional theories, such as Parsons', stress the maintenance of equilibrium, while conflict theories from Marx on have concentrated on revolution, i.e., catastrophic change. It is necessary to specify the functioning and breakdown of each type of mechanism to be able to study the conditions under which each kind of stability and change occurs.

Catastrophic changes lead to major changes, sometimes making the original unit unrecognizable. This brings up the question of the definition of the system, of its limits and boundaries. Admittedly, the definition of the system and its boundary is a difficult problem for systems analysis. Definition of a system is to some degree arbitrary, a decision of the investigator, and to some degree derived from measurable distinctions between what is included in and what is excluded from the system. Here, the biologist has the advantage over the sociologist; organisms are generally well defined. But even with biological systems the boundaries are not always obvious. The single organism is in effect an abstraction (Back,

1971) as it functions only within an ecological context; controversy on the point where an embryo is an independent organism also points to the ambiguity of the definition.

In compensation, the sociologist has his own advantage, namely one of the most effective measures distinguishing membership within the system. In effect, there are two ways to determine the boundaries of a social system: one through identification of the members themselves, the other through other indicators, such as internal similarity or networks. All of these measures can be used to determine whether an abrupt dislocation produced change in the same system or destroyed the system completely.

An example of this problem is the definition of region as social units. The question whether the "South" has persisted as a meaningful system can be answered partly by the affective meaning of "Southerner" as identification, and it is also possible through a series of demographic, economic, and ecological measures (Winsborough, 1965). Contrast between these two positions has persisted since Odum (1936), and is represented in two recent articles (McKinney and Boueque, 1971; Gastil, 1971).

GENERAL PRINCIPLES OF CHANGE IN LIVING SYSTEMS

We have tried to organize the modes of a system's transactions with its environment. In doing so, we have used the individual organism as a model, because on this level the mechanisms are distinct and have been studied in detail. This feature has led sometimes to the erroneous organic analogy with society which has brought this whole procedure into disrepute. We have attempted to avoid this pitfall and have identified some general principles which may be applicable to systems in general, both organic and social, and can be tested on each level. In particular, we introduced four dimensions whose combination could lead to some general principles. They are time span, mode of information processing, feedback, and sources of motive power. We can now state some principles, based on the interaction of these four dimensions on the organic level, which are relevant to social change.

1. Maintenance of internal equilibrium is one of the functions of every system. Equilibrium is maintained in two ways. At any time there is one ideal equilibrium point (set point) which the system tries to maintain; one of the important mechanisms here is negative feedback. Minor deviations are corrected and compensated for quickly. If the situation persists and stress occurs, the system can change completely through cumulative effects, and a new equilibrium condition, a new set point, may be reached. Thus different mechanisms will exist for immediate reestablishment of equilibrium, and there are those which allow for long-term drift. There will also be mechanisms for the balance of internal conditions. Within the

system itself there will be mechanisms for rhythmical growth and those which assure that their rhythm will have a stable base line.

Thus work groups will maintain a constant output using sanctions on those group members who produce below the normal level as well as on those who produce above it. Change of productivity will occur only when a new group norm is set, and this level is again used as a standard to be enforced. A similar analysis can be made of other normative behavior; the concept of quasi-stationary equilibrium has been employed to distinguish temporary and long-range changes (Lewin, 1947).

2. Besides maintenance of equilibrium, a system has mechanisms for maintaining identity. It has some mechanisms which maintain boundaries and those which reject intrusions even if they pass the boundaries. The specific definition of hostile intrusions will depend on the experience of the system, but the system is so organized that some definition will be reached. In terms of societies, ethnocentrism is not inborn, but the tendency to obtain some social identity and to defend it is.

The processes by which identity of a social system is defended can be better understood by considering their structural analogy to immunity processes. The ambiguity of immunity with regard to time span is duplicated by these defenses. Social identity is maintained by cultural tradition, but its expression is learned fresh by each member of the society through his own experiences inside and outside the system. Language is one of the mechanisms of maintaining social identity. The tenacity of clinging to languages and conflicts over the adoption of another language is a process closely analogous to maintenance of immunity (Fishman, 1966; Deutsch, 1953). We can also trace the beneficial effects for maintaining cohesion and in-group functions as well as potentially harmful results, such as overreaction (analogous to allergy) and rejection of new ideas (analogous to transplant rejection).

3. The previous point has alerted us to the importance of learning processes. Identity learning is so important that it frequently has separate mechanisms, but cognitive learning is also as important for stability and change. Both types of learning are intrinsically neutral about stability and change and can have effects in each direction. They are the mechanisms which lead to the understanding of the particular system and to general differentiation, the antientropy states of open systems. Thus development of technology in general has been in one direction, giving societies some control over nature.

They are the mechanisms which lead to the understanding of the particular system by its members, and in this sense they enhance stability. But in interaction with the environment, they lead to better understanding of the environment, to the accumulation of knowledge within the society. This trend toward differentiation of perception is a function of the antientropy states of open systems and is essentially unidirectional. The development of science and technology has been essentially in one direction in those societies which have embarked on this course, giving them more control of nature.

4. The previous points have described what can be called normal gradual changes. Abrupt changes may occur when the negative feedback mechanism turns to positive feedback. In the short range this may lead to sudden excitement and great eruption. Breakdown of the long-range adaptive mechanisms will result in novel expressions which will be put to the test of survival. Although most of these expressions are not viable, the surviving ones are the most potent instigation for social change. In the social sphere we call this creativity, the condition of science, art, and the humanities. In the long range these abrupt changes occur if there are sudden changes in the environment, national or social catastrophes, or if the cumulation of the long-term trend makes a social structure not viable any more. In the intellectual sphere Kuhn (1962) has shown how this divergence leads to scientific revolutions; revolutions in the political, economic, and religious sphere spring from similar development. These are the rare occurrences which have fascinated so many investigators. We must agree with Nisbet that developmental theory should not exist exclusively for these events, but it should account for them, their rarity as well as their far-reaching effects.

CONCLUSION

The use of biological models via the general systems approach leads to new perspectives on social stability and change. Systems analysis has two aspects. One tries to show the general principles to which all systems, both organic and social, conform. The other characterizes the applicability and expressions of the systems at each level. The principles enumerated here define specific social processes derived from the biological level. They remain hypotheses to be tested at the social level. They give guidelines to further investigation as well as a framework for integrating much existing knowledge.

BIBLIOGRAPHY

Allport, G., "The Open System in Personality Theory," *J. Abnorm. and Soc. Psychol.*, 61:301-311, 1960.

Back, K. W., "Epidemiology versus Cartesian Dualism," *Social Science and Medicine*, Vol. 5, no. 5 (Oxford: Pergamon Press, October 1971), 461-468.

Bateson, G., Jackson, D. D., Haldy, S. and Weakland, J., "Toward a Theory of Schizophrenia," *Behav. Sci.*, 1:251-264, 1956.

Bertalanffy, L. von, *General Systems Theory* (New York: George Braziller, 1968).

Buckley, W., *Sociology and Modern Systems Theory* (Englewood Cliffs, N.J.: Prentice-Hall, 1967).

Campbell, Q., "Variation and Selective Retention in Sociocultural Tradition," in H. R. Barringer, G. L. Blankston, and R. W. Mack, eds., *Social Change in Developing Areas* (Cambridge: Schenkman, 1965), pp. 19-49.

Cummings, E., and Henry, W., *Growing Old* (New York: Basic Books, 1961).

Deutsch, K. W., *Nationalism and Social Communication* (New York: John Wiley & Sons, 1953).

Duncan, O. D., "Social Organization and the Ecosystem," in R. E. L. Faris, ed., *Handbook of Modern Sociology* (Chicago: Rand McNally, 1964).

Fishman, J. A., Nahirny, V. C., Hoffman, J. E., and Hayden, R. G., *Language Loyalty in the United States* (The Hague: Mouton, 1966).

Gastil, R. D., "Homicide and a Regional Culture of Violence," *Am. Soc. Rev.*, 36:412-427, 1971.

Kuhn, T. S., *The Structure of Scientific Revolutions* (Chicago: University of Chicago Press, 1962).

Lewin, K., "Frontiers in Group Dynamics: Concept, Method and Reality in Social Science; Social Equilibrium and Social Change," *Hum. Relat.*, 1: 5-41, 1947.

Lowenthal, M. F., and Boler, D., "Voluntary vs. Unvoluntary Social Withdrawal," *J. Geront.*, 20:363-371, 1963.

Maddox, G. L. "Fact from Artifact: Evidence Bearing on Disengagement Theory from the Duke Geriatrics Projects," *Hum. Devel.*, 8:117-130, 1965.

McKinney, J. C., and Boueque, L. B., "The Changing South: National Incorporation of a Region," *Am. Soc. Rev.*, 36:399-412, 1971.

Miller, J. G., "Living Systems, Basic Concepts, Structure and Process: Cross-Level Hypotheses," *Behav. Sci.*, 10:197-237, 337-379, 380-411, 1965.

Nisbet, R. A., "Developmentalism, A Critical Analysis," in J. C. McKinney and E. A. Tiryakian, eds., *Theoretical Sociology* (New York: Appleton-Century Crofts, 1970), pp. 167-204.

Odum, H., *Southern Regions of the United States* (Chapel Hill: University of North Carolina Press, 1930).

Quarton, G. C., Melnechuk, T., and Schmitt, F. O., *The Neurosciences* (New York: Rockefeller University Press, 1967).

Rapoport, A., "A Philosophical View," in J. H. Milsum, ed., *Positive Feedback* (Oxford: Pergamon, 1968), pp. 1-8.

Richardson, L. F., *Arms and Insecurity: A Mathematical Study of the Causes and Origins of War*, Nicolas Rashevsky and Ernesto Trucco, eds. (Pittsburgh: Boxwood Press, 1960).

Shapiro, D., and Crider, A., "Psychophysiological Approaches in Social Psychology," in G. Lindzey and E. Aronson, eds., *The Handbook of Social Psychology*, vol. III (2nd ed.; Reading, Mass.: Addison-Wesley, 1969).

Watzlawick, P., Beavin, J. H., and Jackson, D. D., *Pragmatics of Human Communication* (New York: Norton, 1967).

Winsborough, H. H. "The Changing Regional Character of the South," in John C. McKinney and E. T. Thompson, *The South in Continuity and Change* (Durham, N.C.: Duke University Press, 1965), pp. 34-52.

6

RISK TAKING BY INDIVIDUALS AND GROUPS: AN ASSESSMENT OF RESEARCH EMPLOYING CHOICE DILEMMAS

Dorwin Cartwright

The research of the past decade has established a number of firm findings concerning the effects of group discussion on decisions involving risk. An examination of these findings, however, raises certain questions about the basic assumptions that have guided research. Evidence that the items of the Choice Dilemmas Questionnaire (CDQ) produce systematically different responses both before and after group discussion casts serious doubt on the propriety of using CDQ scores as measures of a unitary disposition to take risks. And the conclusion that groups are invariably riskier than individuals is no longer justified. The risky-shift paradigm has generated an impressive body of facts, but these facts reveal the inadequacy of the paradigm itself. The field therefore faces a theoretical crisis. The central task for theory is not to explain "the risky shift," but to account for the much more complicated effects of group discussion. The attainment of a proper understanding of these effects will require the use of theoretical orientations and the collection of data that focus much more closely than in the past on the concrete properties of the decision-making process and the exact way in which group discussion affects them.*

Rarely in the history of social psychology has a single study stimulated as much research as the master's thesis by Stoner (1961) which reported the discovery of "the risky shift." Its conclusion that groups are riskier than

Reprinted from the *Journal of Personality and Social Psychology*, Vol. 20, No. 3, 1971, pp. 361-378.

* The preparation of this paper was supported by Contract HSM-42-69-55 with the National Institute of Mental Health. It is based on a review of the literature on group decision making and on interviews and correspondence with a number of investigators who have contributed to this area of research. The author is greatly indebted to many people for the ideas contained in the paper, but he is solely responsible for its content.

individuals was widely interpreted as being contrary to the findings of previous research on the effects of groups on individuals. It challenged conventional wisdom, and it appeared to have implications for those responsible for making important decisions involving risk. As findings began to accumulate, certain other attractive features of the research became apparent. The Choice Dilemmas Questionnaire (CDQ), which was used by Stoner to measure the risk-taking disposition of individuals and groups, is easy to administer, permits a comparison of findings from different studies, and, most important, produces replicable results. A risky shift in CDQ scores has been found by numerous investigators in several different countries and with a variety of subjects.

The popularity of research employing the CDQ is especially interesting, since studies by Atthowe (1961), Hunt and Rowe (1960), and Lonergan and McClintock (1961), which appeared at about the same time as Stoner's thesis but used different measures of risk, did not find significant differences between individuals and groups. Several investigators have continued to use these alternative measures of risk, but their results have not led to simple general conclusions. Since the CDQ has produced the more dramatic findings, it has had greater appeal, and the choice-dilemma paradigm has continued to dominate the field.

A major reason for the great interest in the risky shift is that it has stimulated theoretical controversy. Several competing hypotheses have been advanced to explain why groups are riskier than individuals. And attempts to test these hypotheses have produced a large body of data about the effects of various experimental treatments on responses to the CDQ. It is quite apparent, however, from reviews of the literature prepared by Clark (1971), Dion, Baron, and Miller (1970), Mackenzie (1971), and Vinokur (1971b), that the theoretical issues are far from settled. Since the failure to find a convincing explanation of the risky shift can hardly be attributed to a lack of effort or ingenuity, the possibility should be considered that the effect itself is improperly conceived. The purpose of the present paper is to investigate this possibility. Toward this end, we shall review the literature to ascertain what is now known about the nature of the risky shift. Our objective is not to evaluate explanations, but to identify the facts that require explanation.

FIRM FINDINGS

What findings from the past decade of research have been sufficiently established to require theoretical explanation? What are the facts? The awarding of factual status to a finding is, of course, to some degree a matter of subjective judgment. Has it been sufficiently replicated? Is it properly stated? Can it be obtained with conceptually equivalent methods? Does it generalize to populations not previously studied? Such questions can rarely be answered with great confidence. In constructing the following list of firm findings, primary weight has been given to actual replication. Some findings, however, have been taken to be facts, even though their replicability has not been fully demonstrated, simply because they seem to fit well with other established findings. And some replicated findings have not been treated as facts because of questions concerning their interpretation. An effort has been made to be cautious but not too cautious. Perhaps a committee would have arrived at a different listing.

Effects of Treatments

A repeated-measures design has been employed in nearly all of the research. The CDQ, or some modified version of it, is first used to obtain pretreatment measures for the subjects of the experiment. Then, after the administration of some experimental treatment, the same instrument is employed to yield one or more posttreatment measures for the same subjects. The effects of experimental manipulations are usually assessed by ascertaining whether the means of the pretreatment and posttreatment measures are significantly different. If they are, a shift in risk taking is said to exist. Efforts to account for the effect of a given treatment have commonly relied upon a comparison of results obtained from it with those produced by one or more other treatments which differ in some particular way.

The standard procedure for getting pretreatment measures has been to ask subjects to fill out the CDQ as individuals and without knowledge of the nature of the subsequent treatment. Their decisions thus reflect personal preferences which are presumably unaffected by any systematic anticipation of subsequent events in the experiment. The conditions under which these measures are taken have varied somewhat from one experiment to the next. Sometimes subjects complete the CDQ in the presence of others and sometimes in isolation. The time interval between the pretreatment measures and the treatment has also varied considerably. It does not appear, however, that these differences have any substantial effect on the basic findings.

Two kinds of posttreatment measures have been used, depending on the nature of the treatment. One procedure is simply to have subjects again complete the CDQ as individuals. In asking them to take the CDQ a second time, an attempt is usually made to make subjects feel free to alter their initial decisions without suggesting that they should do so. A second procedure is to have each group complete the CDQ by means of unanimous group decisions. Often, subjects are told that the initial administration of the CDQ was intended merely to familiarize them with the nature of the problems. It should be noted that these two types of posttreatment measures, when compared with pretreatment ones, reveal conceptually different effects of a treatment. The first reflects the treatment's effects on the personal preferences of individuals, whereas the second compares the preferences of individuals and groups. In some studies, both types of measures have been taken, but group measures have always come first.

Let us now examine the dependable effects of various treatments. We consider first the results when responses to the items of the CDQ are summed to give a single score for each individual or group.

1. *Group discussion to consensus.* The most frequently replicated treatment is one in which small groups, usually containing from two to seven members, are formed and simply asked to discuss each item in order to reach a unanimous group decision concerning the lowest acceptable odds of success for the uncertain alternative. No constraints are imposed upon the content of the discussion or upon the way the group organizes itself to perform the task. The results of this treatment are remarkably consistent. The mean of CDQ scores for groups is dependably less than the mean for individuals. Group decisions, following free group discussion, are riskier on the average than personal decisions of the same individuals made prior to the discussion. It is this phenomenon to which the term risky shift was originally applied.

In several studies subjects have been asked to indicate their final personal choices, whether or not they agree with the group decisions, by completing the CDQ once again as individuals. The mean of these scores is regularly found to be close to the mean of the groups' scores. Thus, both group decisions and individual choices are riskier after group discussion to consensus than before. Although the effect of the time interval following this experimental treatment upon the shift in individual scores has not been investigated systematically, Wallach, Kogan, and Bem (1962) reported that it endures for a period of two to six weeks.

2. *Free discussion without group decision.* Another frequently used treatment is one in which groups are asked to discuss the items of the CDQ but not asked to reach an explicit decision. Here the mean of CDQ scores for individuals is significantly smaller after discussion without group decision than before. It should be noted that these results taken alone do not demonstrate that the shift for group decisions can be attributed to changes in individual preferences resulting from discussion. They do show, however, that an explicit group decision is not required for the occurrence of shifts in the choices of individuals.

3. *Observing free discussion without group decision.* A few experiments have employed a treatment in which subjects are merely exposed to a group discussion of the CDQ items without themselves participating in the discussion. They may watch or listen to an actual discussion or read a transcript of it. Studies reported by Bell and Jamieson (1970), Kogan

and Wallach (1967), Lamm (1967), and St. Jean (1970) have consistently found a risky shift in the personal preferences of observers, but its magnitude tends to be smaller than for participants. Although this research demonstrates that mere exposure to the content of a group discussion can produce a shift, it does not reveal what features of the discussion are responsible for its occurrence. Perhaps some of the arguments are found to be persuasive. Perhaps the observer learns that others are riskier than he is. Or it may be that observers are able to discern the drift of the discussion and simply make changes which they believe will match the modal choices of the participants. Actually, there is some evidence from other studies suggesting that when subjects are given information about the modal choices of others they do tend to conform to these "norms." It would be useful to know how well observers are able to predict how the discussants actually complete the CDQ.

4. *Discussion without revealing initial choices.* According to the value hypothesis proposed by Brown (1965), there is a pervasive cultural value favoring risk which makes each person want to be at least as risky as others. When subjects participate in a group discussion, some of them will discover that their initial choices were less risky than those of some others, and they will be motivated to shift toward greater risk. Thus, shifts resulting from group discussion are attributed to the information it provides about the initial preferences of the participants. If this information were withheld from the discussion, then it might be expected that no shifts would occur. Several investigators have employed such a treatment, in which subjects are requested to discuss the content of the dilemma without revealing their personal choice of odds. The results for this treatment, as reported by Clark, Crockett, and Archer (1971) and St. Jean (1970), show significant and substantial shifts. Similar findings have been obtained by Burnstein et al. (1971) and Vinokur (1970, 1971a). These investigators asked subjects to discuss the values, or utilities, involved in each dilemma, rather than preferred odds, and to reach a unanimous decision as to how to rate these utilities on a scale. These discussions were found to yield significant shifts both in utilities and odds. The results from this treatment cannot, however, be taken as a definitive test of the value hypothesis, since subjects may infer the risk preferences of others from the discussion and base their posttreatment choices on these inferences. It does appear, though, that an explicit statement of initial choices is not required for a shift to occur.

5. *Providing information about initial choices of others.* A more direct test of the value hypothesis has been attempted by constructing a treatment in which subjects are simply given information about the initial choices of others. In this research there has been considerable variation in the wording of instructions, the items used, and the ways in which the information about the choices of others is presented. It is not surprising,

therefore, that the results have not been entirely consistent. Nevertheless, the findings reported by Bell and Jamieson (1970), Clark et al. (1971), Murdoch, Myers, and Smith (1971), St. Jean (1970), Stokes (1971), Teger and Pruitt (1967), and Wallach and Kogan (1965) justify the conclusion that the mere exchange of information about initial choices does not dependably produce shifts as large as those generated by free discussion with or without group discussion.

6. *Familiarization.* One consequence of a group discussion is undoubtedly that it permits subjects to become more familiar with the choice dilemmas. It is possible, therefore, that familiarization by itself will produce shifts comparable to those resulting from discussion. Bateson (1966) first tested this possibility by constructing a treatment in which individual subjects engaged in several activities designed to familiarize themselves with the nature of each dilemma. Flanders and Thistlethwaite (1967) subsequently designed a somewhat different familiarization treatment. Both studies found a significant risky shift. Attempts to replicate these findings, however, have met with universal failure. No significant shifts following familiarization have been obtained in studies reported by Bell and Jamieson (1970), Miller and Dion (1970), Rule and Evans (1971), Stokes (1971), and Teger, Pruitt, and St. Jean (1970). The weight of evidence now strongly supports the conclusion that familiarization does not dependably produce significant shifts. The concept of "familiarization," however, has not been clearly defined, and no convincing explanation has yet been advanced to account for the differences between the two sets of findings.

7. *Irrelevant group discussion.* It is conceivable that the effects of group discussion are independent of its content. The mere occurrence of a discussion might change interpersonal relationships or personal motivation in some way that makes subjects more willing to take risks. The available evidence, however, gives little support for this possibility. Clark and Willems (1970) found no significant shift following discussion of an "irrelevant" discussion. And Alker and Kogan (1968) obtained none following a discussion of women's fashions. Nor did Lamm, Trommsdorff, and Kogan (1970) find one when they had subjects discuss the actual probability of success for each dilemma rather than the minimum acceptable odds. Inconsistent results have been obtained, however, by Madaras and Bem (1968) and Graham and Harris (1969). In both of these studies, subjects discussed only half of the items of the CDQ but gave responses to all of them. The items not discussed showed no significant shifts in the first study but significant risky shifts in the second. The situation is further complicated by findings reported by Alker and Kogan (1968). These investigators used two forms of the CDQ, one for initial choices and the other for choices after discussion, and obtained a significant shift toward risk in total scores. In another condition, they even found a cautious shift

following a discussion of certain problems of ethics. It is possible, then, that a discussion of topics other than the dilemma problems themselves may produce a change in choices, but it remains to be determined what features of a discussion make it "relevant" to preferences on the CDQ.

8. *Irrelevant activities.* Numerous investigators have employed a basic control treatment in which subjects engage in a presumably "neutral" activity between two administrations of the CDQ. In some experiments the questionnaire is completed at two different sessions which are separated by a period of naturalistic "free activity." In others, it is given twice in the same session with some standard intervening activity. Despite these procedural variations, the results uniformly show no significant differences in means between the first and second set of scores. Shifts cannot be attributed simply to repeated experience with the CDQ.

In considering the practical or theoretical implications of these results, it is important to be quite clear about the statistical properties of the risky shift. Research has demonstrated the existence of a dependable shift in the sense that mean scores on the CDQ are significantly smaller after group discussion than before, but few details about the microstructure of the data can be found in the published literature. Little attention has been paid to the magnitude of the shift, the number of groups which show it, or to the distribution of shifts made by each group on each item. Most investigators have been content with testing the null hypothesis. From the data that are readily available, however, it is evident that the average trends are made up of a great variety of specific effects.

How big is the risky shift? A review of the literature reveals that the mean initial scores on the CDQ tend to be about 70, and that mean shifts resulting from the strongest treatment approximate 10. Since the CDQ contains 12 items, the average shift per item, expressed as odds, is roughly from 6 in 10 to 5 in 10. Groups may be riskier than individuals on the average, but they are not strikingly so.

As to frequency of occurrence, the evidence indicates that the great majority of groups do display a shift toward risk in CDQ scores. But since each score combines choices for twelve items, it does not follow that a majority of the particular decisions made by groups show such a shift. In fact, there is good reason to believe that they do not. When Burns (1967) examined the entire set of group decisions in the original Stoner study, he found that 51 per cent of them deviate by one unit or less from the group's mean of initial choices. Since Stoner's scale contained only the discrete points 1, 3, 5, 7, 9, and 10, these group decisions actually fall at the point closest to the initial mean and cannot be considered genuine shifts. Only 35 per cent of the decisions give risky shifts larger than one unit, and 14 per cent show cautious shifts of this magnitude. Belovicz and Finch (1971) have made a similar analysis for three separate experiments involving a total of 564 group decisions. Of these, 40 per cent are at the point closest to the group mean, 39 per cent deviate in a risky direction, and 21 per cent in a cautious one. Thus, it appears that most group decisions are not riskier than individual ones, and that a substantial minority is actually more cautious. The most frequent outcome may actually be no shift at all. These results cast serious doubt on the adequacy of any explanation of the risky shift which assumes that the typical group decision shows a shift toward risk.

Effects of Items

Even in the earliest research it was evident that the twelve items of the CDQ contribute to the over-all shift in quite different ways. Although the mean shift was toward risk for most items, its magnitude varied considerably. There were, moreover, two items which repeatedly produced cautious shifts. The response of investigators to this discovery may be of interest to the historian of science. Some essentially ignored it and continued to deal with total scores. Others removed the two deviant items from the CDQ, apparently assuming that they would thereby improve the reliability of the instrument as a measure of risk taking. A few were motivated to discover whether they could design new items in the same format which would also display cautious shifts. On the whole, however, the magic of the risky shift was so powerful that few seriously questioned whether its existence depends upon the particular set of items that happened to be contained in the original version of the CDQ. And most theoretical efforts continued to be directed to accounting for the shift toward risk.

9. *Mean shifts for items.* There can now be no doubt that different items generate distinctively different mean shifts. Although data are still not always given separately for items, the "typical" shift for each item can be estimated from a tabulation of the mean shifts reported in the literature. For this purpose, we consider the median of the mean shifts resulting from discussion to consensus. For Items 1, 4, and 7, these medians, expressed as odds, range from 1.0 to 1.6. For Items 6, 8, and 9, they all approximate .8. And for Items 3, 10, and 11, they lie between .6 and .7. These nine items, then, consistently yield risky shifts, but their magnitudes vary substantially. On the other hand, Item 2, with a median of .3, yields small shifts which are predominantly, but not uniformly, risky. And Items 5 and 12 typically give cautious shifts, with medians of −.1 and −.6, respectively.

The attempt by Nordhøy (1962), Rabow et al. (1966), Stoner (1968), and others to construct choice dilemmas that will dependably yield cautious shifts has been generally successful. Stoner found, however, that it is more difficult to write cautious-shift items than risky-shift ones. This fact, together with the relatively small magnitude of shifts for the two cautious-shift items of the original CDQ, has sometimes been interpreted as indicating that the "natural" shift is toward risk. But such a conclusion seems unjustified, since several of the newly constructed items give larger cautious shifts than the risky shifts produced by several of the CDQ items. The difficulty in constructing cautious-shift items may merely indicate a lack of understanding of the determinants of shifts in general rather than some peculiarity of the cautious shifts.

10. *Means of initial choices.* It is now clearly established that each item also generates a characteristic distribution of initial individual choices. Three items, 4, 7, and 11, tend to produce relatively risky choices. The medians of their means lie between 4.1 and 4.5. Items 2, 5, and 12, on the other hand, yield relatively cautious choices, with medians between 6.8 and 7.5. The remaining six items may be considered "neutral," since their medians lie near the midpoint of the scale, ranging between 5.0 and 5.9. In view of the diverse conditions of testing and scoring employed in different studies, the variation in means for a given item is remarkably small. For all but two items, half of the reported means deviate from the median by less than one-third of a unit.

11. *Relation between initial means and mean shifts.* As first explicitly noted by Teger and Pruitt (1967), items with larger risky shifts tend to have riskier initial means, and those producing cautious shifts tend to have relatively cautious initial means. When Teger and Pruitt combined data from several studies to generate "national norms," they obtained a correlation of .81 between initial means and mean shifts for the items of the CDQ. Correlations of similar magnitude have since been reported by other investigators both for the original items and for newly constructed ones.

The proper interpretation of this well-established relationship is not at all obvious. It is possible that the content of each item suggests a characteristic set of persuasive arguments which influence both initial choices and the content of group discussion. Or an item may activate a cultural value favoring risk or caution which affects initial choices and is then reinforced by group discussion. It may be, however, that an entirely different causal process is involved. The correlation in question refers to properties of the total population of individuals or groups studied and only indirectly the concrete situations in which shifts occur. Since the distribution of initial choices in the population at large determines their distributions within randomly composed groups, the correlation may simply reflect the effects of these within-group distributions on shifts. Indeed, we would find such a correlation if the mean of initial choices in the general population were systematically related to other properties of the distribution, such as skewness or variance, and if shifts were dependent upon these properties of within-group distributions. No confident choice among these interpretations can be made in the absence of evidence directly relevant to them.

12. *Other responses to items.* In one of the earliest studies, Hinds (1962) asked subjects to indicate how they thought similar others would

respond to some of the choice dilemmas, and found that they tended to believe that others would make riskier choices than they. More extensive data collected by Wallach and Wing (1968) and by Levinger and Schneider (1969) have confirmed the finding for those items of the CDQ that yield consistent risky shifts. The results of this and other research justify the conclusion that for risky-shift items, subjects tend to believe that their initial choices are riskier than those of others.

There is also evidence that for risky-shift items, subjects favorably evaluate riskier choices and people who take greater risks. Levinger and Schneider had subjects specify which choice they would most admire and found that these choices were riskier on the average than their own. When Madaras and Bem (1968) and Jellison and Riskind (1970) asked subjects to attribute personal traits to people who had allegedly made risky or cautious choices, they found that these traits were generally more favorable when others were viewed as favoring risk rather than caution.

Since interest has been directed primarily to explaining the risky shift, less attention has been paid to cautious-shift items, but data provided by Levinger and Schneider (1969), Stoner (1968), and Vidmar and Burdeny (1969) indicate that for such items subjects tend to believe that their initial choices are more cautious than those of others. Evidence concerning the evaluations of the choices made to cautious-shift items is sparse and inconclusive.

On the whole, these findings are consistent with some version of the value hypothesis advanced by Brown (1965), but they do not, in themselves, demonstrate that the beliefs and values associated with choices are causally related to the shifts made by particular individuals on particular items. Evidence that they may be is provided by Clark et al. (1971), who found a larger shift toward risk among subjects who believed that their own choices were at least as risky as others than among those who believed that they were less risky than others. The findings reported by several investigators, that estimates of others' choices change as a consequence of group discussion, are also consistent with this interpretation. Further research, which relates shifts to the beliefs and values of specific individuals for specific items, is required before the issue can be settled. Such research should, of course, investigate both risky-shift and cautious-shift items. The analyses undertaken by Ferguson and Vidmar (1971) make an excellent start toward providing the kind of detailed information required.

SIGNIFICANCE OF BASIC FINDINGS

The research of the past decade has clearly established that a relevant group discussion yields a reduction in mean CDQ scores. And if it is assumed that these scores measure a readiness to take risks, the conclusion is justified that there is, indeed, a risky shift. But the significance of this shift for theory and practice is far from evident. The findings show that the shift is not large, that most choices made after group discussion are not riskier than before, and that the shifts obtained for different choice dilemmas differ in direction and magnitude. There are, moreover, serious questions yet unanswered concerning the meaning of CDQ scores, the nature of the specific choices which are combined to give total scores, and the characteristics of the concrete processes that bring about changes in the choices made by particular individuals or groups on particular items. We turn now to an examination of the more important of these issues.

Differences Among Items

Use of the CDQ in research on group decision making was originally based on the assumption that it is an instrument for measuring the risk-taking dispositions of individuals or groups. Since responses to its twelve items were conceived as being determined by this unitary disposition, they were summed to give a single score. And the reduction in the mean of these scores following group discussion was taken as evidence that groups are "riskier" than individual members when acting alone. This psychometric orientation has had a pervasive influence on most of the subsequent research.

Confidence in the propriety of this approach has been seriously undermined by the findings concerning differences among items. It is now clear that the items contained in the original CDQ are in no sense a representative sample of the universe of all possible items. Instruments similar to the CDQ could readily be constructed whose scores would display risky shifts, cautious ones, or none at all. Since there is no basis now known for selecting any one of these as the true measure of a risk-taking disposition, the argument that group discussion heightens this disposition is hardly compelling.

If the CDQ score does not measure a unitary disposition, then it has no clear referent, for it merely summarizes the choices made to a particular set of twelve choice dilemmas. There is evidence, moreover, that its use may be quite misleading. Thus, for example, when Hoyt and Stoner (1968) attempted to create "homogeneous" groups by selecting subjects on the basis of their initial CDQ scores, they found that the groups were actually heterogeneous on many of the items. Similar difficulties arise in studies of the effects of the relative riskiness of individuals within a group, since a person's rank on CDQ scores does not necessarily correspond to his rank on even a majority of items. Clearly, great care must be exercised in interpreting results based on these scores and in evaluating their implications for theory.

Meaning of Choices on Choice Dilemmas

The concrete events which generate the basic data to be explained are the choices made by individuals or groups on each choice dilemma. The significance of findings from this research therefore depends upon the meaning that can be attributed to these choices. It has commonly been assumed that they reflect a "readiness" to take risk, but the way in which they do so has not been clearly specified. If the meaning of these choices is to be clarified, it is necessary first of all to understand the nature of the dilemmas themselves. What is the structure of the problem that they present to subjects? An examination of the dilemmas reveals that each contains two alternative courses of action. One of these, R, is risky in the sense that its outcome is uncertain; it may lead either to success or failure. The other, C, is cautious in that its outcome is described as certain. Let us denote the values of success and failure on R, as assessed by a given subject, by V and $-K$, respectively, and the value of the certain outcome by v. The dilemma consists in the fact that v is assumed to be less than V and greater than K. The assigned task is to specify the minimum probability of success on R that would justify undertaking it, and this probability constitutes the choice for each dilemma.

When a subject faces such a dilemma, what determines his choice? Although little empirical work has been aimed directly at answering this fundamental question, it is possible to identify some of the possible determinants. First, it is clear that the relative magnitudes of the values of outcomes must have some effect on choices. If, for example, a person places a relatively high value on the successful outcome of R, he would be expected to recommend undertaking it even though the probability of success were small. If he believes that the costs of failure are great, he would be expected to require a higher probability of success. And if he finds the certain outcome attractive, he should be willing to recommend the risky alternative only when its probability of success is relatively high. There would seem to be little doubt, then, that the relative magnitudes of the values v, V, and $-K$ at least partially determine the choices made to dilemmas.

It should be noted that these determinants have nothing directly to do with a "value for risk," since they are concerned only with the values of outcomes. If they are the only determinants, then it is clearly not appropriate to consider choices as measures of the value for risk. It is possible, of course, that such a value also exerts an influence on choices, that a person who values risk itself will favor riskier choices. But even if this is true, it is clear that choices cannot be taken as a measure of the value for risk unless the values of outcomes are held constant. Since the requirement is obviously not met in the usual formulation of choice dilemmas, the conceptual meaning of choices remains ambiguous. And theories which account for shifts in choices by invoking some mechanism that modifies the value for risk rest on a shaky empirical base.

Miller (1970) has proposed that subjects actually understand the task presented in the dilemmas to be one of selecting the probability of success on the risky alternative such that the subjective expected utilities of the two alternatives are equal. If they do and if we consider the values v, V, and $-K$ as utilities, then it follows that they should choose a probability, p, for which $p = v + K/V + K$. According to this view, items differ in mean initial choices because they set up characteristic distributions of subjective utilities, and subjects differ because their assessments of the utilities differ. Data collected by Miller (1970), Burnstein et al. (1971), and Vinokur (1970, 1971a) are generally consistent with this interpretation. In these studies, subjects were asked to make the usual choices of minimum probability, but also to give ratings of the utilities involved. When the ratings were converted into "predicted" probabilities in accordance with the equation given above, a substantial correlation between predicted and actual probabilities was obtained.

If subjects do not respond directly to risk but instead solve the problem in terms of utilities (or values of outcomes), then the main function of group discussion is to reconcile interpersonal differences in the assessment of these utilities. Miller has shown mathematically that if a group discussion causes these assessments to converge to the mean, there will be predictable shifts in probability choices, the direction and magnitude of which will depend upon certain properties of the initial within-group distributions of utilities (and hence probabilities). It has yet to be ascertained how well actual data on shifts conform to the predictions derived from this model, but it has been shown that group discussion results in regular changes in the ratings of utilities.

Although it is clear that choices are influenced by the values (or utilities) v, V, and $-K$, the available findings do not justify the conclusion that they are completely determined by them. It is still possible that they are also influenced by a value (or utility) for risk itself. A formal model, known as *portfolio theory*, would appear to be especially well suited for dealing with this complex of determinants. As described by Coombs and Huang (1970), this theory has three critical elements: perceived risk, ideal risk, and expected value. From the perspective of portfolio theory, a choice dilemma presents a set of available choices (undertaking the risky alternative at a particular probability of success), each of which has an expected value and a degree of perceived risk. When a subject is asked to select one of these, he evaluates each in terms of its expected value and how closely it approximates his ideal level of risk. He then compares this evaluation with a similar one for the cautious alternative. A group discussion will bring about shifts in choices if it causes a change in the perceived riskiness of the choices, a heightening or lowering of the ideal level of risk, or a reassessment of the values of outcomes.

The immediate value of portfolio theory for research on choice dilemmas is its identification of separate potential influences on both initial choices and shifts. Research on the risky shift, by concentrating on a poorly defined cultural value of risk, has provided little information about the way subjects perceive the riskiness of choices, their initial levels of risk, or their assessment of the values of outcomes. A beginning has been made toward an understanding of these determinants by Pruitt (1969) and Higbee (1971) in their research on labeling of choices as risky or cautious, by Levinger and Schneider (1969) in their study of most admired choices, and by Burnstein et al. (1971) and Vinokur (1970, 1971a) in their investigations of the assessed values of outcomes. Studies are needed, however, which examine more closely the ways in which these determinants jointly affect choices. Until such research is completed, the meaning of choices on choice dilemmas will remain ambiguous.

Nature of Group Processes

Since it has been firmly established that group discussion is essential for the occurrence of shifts, it is remarkable how little attention has been paid to its content and to the function it serves. When a group discusses a particular item, are the members mainly concerned with reconciling the differences among them in their initial choices? Do they merely seek an acceptable compromise, or do they attempt to change the choices of others? Does the discussion focus mainly on the values of outcomes, the ideal level of risk, or on the amount of risk actually involved? Are particular arguments commonly advanced in support of certain choices? Are some of these especially persuasive? How does the distribution of initial choices within the group affect these processes? Unfortunately, research has not yet provided clear answers to these questions. Fascination with the analysis of variance paradigm has led investigators to look almost exclusively at differences between treatments rather than at the process directly involved. The black-box approach has unnecessarily dominated research, for these processes can be directly observed. Surely it is time to pry the lid off the box to see what goes on inside.

In order to gain a proper understanding of how group processes bring about shifts in choices, it is necessary to examine the within-group distributions of choices on specific items before and after group discussion. Although these distributions have rarely been reported, it is clear that the choice dilemmas generate a wide distribution of initial choices. Detailed data presented by Cecil (1967) from a sample of 238 subjects show that each item of the CDQ yields a remarkably flat distribution of initial choices. For each item, there are some choices at both ends of the probability scale. This finding implies that randomly composed groups will normally contain members with a diversity of choices on most items. If these members are asked to reach a unanimous group decision, they must somehow reconcile their differences. And even if they are requested merely to discuss the item, they face a similar task since they are likely to seek a single "correct" choice.

A detailed comparison of the choices made by individuals before and after discussion would greatly clarify the meaning of shifts even in the absence of information about the nature of the discussion itself. Although such an analysis was reported by Marquis (1962) in one of the earliest studies of the risky shift, the significance of his findings has not been sufficiently recognized. It is evident in the data presented by Marquis that group discussion has the effect of reducing the within-group variance of choices on each item and that when a risky shift occurs, initially cautious subjects change more than initially risky ones. Since these findings have recently been confirmed by Ferguson and Vidmar (1971) and Vidmar and Burdeny (1969), we may safely conclude that convergence is a major consequence of group discussion and that shifts in mean scores result from systematic differences in changes made by individuals who are relatively more risky or cautious than others in a particular group on a particular item. If those holding different initial opinions change in systematically different ways, it would appear that the within-group distributions of initial choices is an important determinant of shifts. It is not obvious, however, exactly which properties of this distribution are critical.

Burns (1967) has proposed an extremity-variance theory in which it is assumed that the deviation of the mean of initial choices from the midpoint of the scale and their variance jointly affect the magnitude and direction of shifts. He has tested two slightly different models based on this assumption against several sets of unanimous group decisions and has found that they successfully predict from 49 per cent to 62 per cent of the decisions. Although these results are rather impressive, it must be noted that both models contain two parameters not derivable from the initial distributions. And Haley and Rule (1971) have obtained data which they interpret as being inconsistent with Burns' theory. Whatever the ultimate evaluation of these models, the attempt to make specific predictions is commendable, and Burns' percentage of success provides a base line against which to compare alternative models.

The assumption that the extremity of a group's mean of initial choices affects the direction of shifts has also been made by theorists who interpret shifts as instances of a more general "polarization effect." Data collected by Doise (1969), Fraser, Gouge, and Billig (1971), McCauley (1970), Moscovici and Zavalloni (1969), and Myers and Bishop (1970) are generally consistent with this assumption, but there are some statistical problems in interpreting the results of several of the studies.

The possibility that the skewness of the within-group distribution of initial choices is a determinant of shifts has been examined by Vinokur (1969). From an analysis of his own data and a reanalysis of data obtained by others, he concluded that skewness does have an effect on shifts but that it cannot, by itself, account for the general tendency to find risky shifts in total scores on the CDQ. The effects appear to be different, moreover, for risky and cautious shifts. A more intensive investigation of the effects of skewness should be informative.

Since the basic question motivating this entire line of investigation is whether the decisions of groups are riskier than those of individuals, it is surprising that theories of group decision making have rarely been employed in the analysis and interpretation of data on choice dilemmas. From the perspective of these theories, the initial choice of each individual represents his preference for the group decision, and the group's task is to employ some decision rule for combining these preferences into a single choice for the group as a whole. In order to predict a particular group decision, it is necessary to know: *a*) the set of possible choices; *b*) the distribution of individual preferences over this set; and *c*) the decision rule employed by the group.

As an illustration of this type of approach, we present a reanalysis of data presented by Cecil (1967) for forty-three three-person groups who were required to make unanimous group decisions for each of four items of the CDQ. The set of possible choices provided in this study, as in many others, can be conceived as forming an odds scale with discrete points: 1, 3, 5, 7, 9, and 10. Let us examine the within-group distributions of initial choices on this scale to see whether there are decision rules that might account for the resulting group decisions.

Majority rule. In ninety (52 per cent) of the distributions, at least two of the initial choices are the same. The most natural procedure for these groups would be to select the points on the odds scale preferred by the majority. Actually, 79 per cent of them do. And it is interesting to note that essentially the same results are obtained whether the majority is relatively risky or cautious. For the entire set of 172 decisions, we thus find that 41 per cent can be successfully predicted simply by assuming that they conform to a principle of majority rule.

Coalition rule. In the remaining distributions, each choice is unique, so that the principle of majority rule cannot apply. For sixty (35 per cent) of these, however, it is meaningful to conceive of a principle of coalition rule. To do so, two types of distributions must be distinguished. First, in thirty-six of the distributions, two of the choices are adjacent on the scale, whereas a third is separated from them by at least one point (e.g., 1-3-7). Here it is reasonable to assume that the pair of adjacent members form a coalition on the basis of their relative similarity of preferences. Second, for twenty-four distributions, all three choices are adjacent, but the distribution is not symmetric around Point 5 (e.g., 1-3-5, 5-7-9, 7-9-10). Since there is good reason to believe that more extreme choices are made with greater confidence or commitment, we may assume here that the two more extreme members form a coalition on the basis of their greater involvement in relatively similar preferences. If a group adopts the principle of coalition rule, we might expect its choice to coincide with the mean of the choices of the members of the coalition. But since the two members are adjacent on the odds scale, we can predict only that the group will select one of their choices, presumably with equal frequency over a large number of cases. Cecil's data show that in fact 80 per cent of these group decisions are consistent with this principle. Separate analyses for relatively risky and cautious coalitions reveal that both conform to the decision rule quite well, but there is a tendency for risky coalitions to do so more than cautious ones.*

Mean rule. For the remaining twenty-two distributions (13 per cent), there is no obvious basis for forming coalitions. Either the choices are all adjacent but symmetric around Point 5 (3-5-7), or no two are adjacent (e.g., 1-5-10). Here the simplest procedure might be for the group to select a choice closest to the mean of the distribution. Actually, 50 per cent of these groups do so. Clearly, this principle does not predict decisions as well as the other two. It is possible that coalitions do form under these relatively rare conditions, but there are no apparent regularities in the data.

In summary, the principles of majority or coalition rule permit predictions for 87 per cent of the decisions, and 79 per cent of these are correct. The principle of mean rule applies to 13 per cent and successfully predicts 50 per cent of them. Taken together, they accurately predict 75 per cent of all group decisions.

Although the results of a single study can hardly be considered conclusive, they are sufficiently promising to encourage further exploration of decision-making models of this sort. Since the model employed here applies only to three-person groups operating with a small number of available choices, the first step would be to extend the theory of coalition formation to larger groups with a larger set of choices. But even if this problem is solved, several questions remain as to whether such a model could deal with the full array of basic findings concerning choice dilemmas. Let us look briefly at some of these questions.

---

* It should be noted that several of the cautious coalitions involve choices of 10. There is some question as to whether these choices should be considered as lying on the scale since, from the point of view of decision theory, they violate the assumption that v is less than V. In future research, special attention should be directed to the behavior of subjects who make these choices.

First, it is clear that according to this model a group will display a risky shift on a particular dilemma if and only if it has a relatively risky majority or coalition. This prediction, it might be argued, is inconsistent with findings reported by Wallach and Mabli (1970), who obtained a risky shift when they created three-person groups so that each would have a relatively cautious majority. Actually, however, this study does not provide an adequate test of the model, since the groups were formed on the basis of total scores for ten items of the CDQ, and shifts refer to changes in means of these scores. A reanalysis of these data separately for items might lead to a rather different interpretation of their theoretical significance. The results of the analysis of the effects of skewness reported by Vinokur (1969) may appear to present a more serious difficulty for the model, since this analysis was conducted on an item-by-item basis. But, again, the test cannot be taken as definitive, since the model makes no simple predictions about the effects of skewness. Although the principle of majority rule does have direct implications for these effects, the principles of coalition rule and mean rule do not. It is quite possible for coalitions to form even when the distribution of initial choices is symmetrical.

It might also be argued that no model of group decision making can appropriately be employed to account for those changes in individual choices that result from discussions where there is no requirement for an explicit group decision. But this argument is not compelling. The finding that individual choices tend to converge to the same choice as that selected by an explicit group decision suggests that group discussion eventuates in an implicit group decision as to which choice is "correct." If this conclusion is justified, then both kinds of shifts could be treated as effects of decision making, and a single model could be applied to both.

Finally, there is the problem of how to deal with the finding that substantial shifts in individual choices occur when subjects simply observe a group discussion. Since these choices are not part of a decision-making process, it is clear that shifts cannot be accounted for by our model. It must be noted, however, that the inability of the model to account for these shifts in no way implies that it cannot explain shifts resulting from actual participation in group discussion. The determinants of the two effects need not be the same.

Since these problems do not appear to be insurmountable, efforts to account for the effects of group discussion by means of some decision-making model should be encouraged. Even if these efforts eventually prove to be unsuccessful, they will serve to focus attention on the concrete processes that actually determine the basic findings which we seek to explain.

PROBLEMS IN GENERALIZING FINDINGS

One basic question remains to be considered: What do the findings for choice dilemmas tell us about the relative riskiness of individuals and groups in the real world? Clearly, they do not justify the proposition that groups are invariably riskier than individuals, for the effects of group discussion depend upon the content of the dilemmas and probably upon the distribution of initial choices within groups. A proper statement of the findings will have to recognize these and possibly other dependencies. But even if these influences are taken into account, the implications of the research for natural groups are not immediately obvious. The question of generalization requires careful consideration of the conditions under which the results have been obtained.

It is important, first of all, to recall that nearly all research on choice dilemmas has used a repeated-measures design. Strictly speaking, the results refer to *shifts* in choices and not to *differences* between the choices of individuals and groups who are considering the dilemmas for the first time. It is possible, therefore, that individuals and groups who make choices *de novo* on the same dilemma would not differ in their choices. Data presented by McCauley, Teger, and Kogan (1971) suggest that this may actually be the case. If this finding were to be confirmed, the results of research on choice dilemmas could be generalized only to natural settings in which group members formulate personal preferences prior to group discussion.

The problem is further complicated by the fact that the groups studied have certain "unnatural" properties. They are created for experimental purposes and consequently have no history, future, established structure, or significant enduring relationships with a surrounding social system. Results derived from such groups can be extended to groups in general only if it is assumed that they are not dependent upon these unusual properties. Unfortunately, almost nothing is known about the effects of group properties on the basic findings. One might expect that in a group with a status hierarchy, higher status members would have more influence on group decisions, but Mackenzie (1970) and Siegel and Zajonc (1967) found little support for this assumption. On the other hand, Dion, Miller, and Magnan (1971) have obtained data indicating that shifts in CDQ scores may be quite different in groups with different levels of cohesiveness. Further investigation of the effects of these and other group properties is clearly needed.

The question as to whether results can be generalized from ad hoc experimental groups to natural groups with an extended history is especially interesting. If, as is maintained by one version of value theory, the critical feature of group discussion is to inform subjects of the risk-taking dispositions of others, then groups with a history of decisions involving risk would not be expected to show shifts. The confirmation of this hypothesis would seriously limit the applicability of findings to the real world.

The properties of choice dilemmas also pose problems of generalization. Each dilemma refers to a hypothetical situation and calls for a recommendation to be given to an imaginary person who is not a member of the group. The assigned task is to select the minimum of odds of success that would justify undertaking the uncertain alternative rather than to recommend simply whether it should be undertaken. And the consequences of abiding by the recommendation do not directly affect the members of the group. Few groups, if any, have ever faced a decision with this combination of properties.

Since it can no longer be assumed that choice dilemmas measure a general disposition to take risks, an understanding of the effects of these unnatural properties of choices becomes critical. A few investigators have rewritten the choice dilemmas so as to alter the relationship between the subject and the hypothetical person described in the dilemma. Results reported by Dion et al. (1970), Fraser et al. (1971), Graham and Harris (1969), and Rabow et al. (1966) suggest that this relationship may affect shifts in scores, but the findings are not entirely consistent. Several investigators have also attempted to assess the importance of the hypothetical nature of outcomes by comparing individual and group decisions in situations where the outcome of the decision has direct and tangible consequences for the participants. But the experiments reported by Bem, Wallach, and Kogan (1965), Kogan and Zaleska (1969), Marquis and Rietz (1969), Pruitt and Teger (1969), and Zajonc et al. (1968, 1969) produce quite heterogeneous results. Sometimes groups are riskier than individuals, sometimes more cautious, and sometimes there is no difference. A great deal more research is required before we can confidently generalize from choice dilemmas to the kinds of decisions faced by natural groups.

The experimental conditions employed in research on choice dilemmas certainly cannot be conceived as simulating any typical natural setting. Nor can they be considered a representative sample of any known universe of such situations. How then can the findings from this research be generalized to the real world? The only feasible way would seem to be through the use of theory. If the findings can be given theoretical meaning, then they can be applied to any empirical situation that satisfies the requirements specified by the theory. Thus, for example, if there were a clearly defined theoretical concept of risk, it could then be applied to both artificial and natural settings despite any phenotypic differences between them. A major reason for hesitation in generalizing findings from CDQ scores is the ambiguity concerning the theoretical meaning of these scores.

The problem of generalization, then, cannot be solved until the theoretical significance of the experimental findings is clearly understood. There would appear to be no shortcut to relevance.

Conclusions

The research of the past decade has produced a number of firm findings and several ingenious "explanations." One is left, however, with the uncomfortable feeling that theoretical thinking has not kept pace with the discovery of facts. Most publications still refer to the risky shift as if it were a well-established phenomenon. And until quite recently most theoretical efforts have been directed to the task of accounting for the "fact" that groups make riskier decisions than individuals. But the facts are not so simple. The assumption that CDQ scores measure a unitary disposition to take risks is no longer tenable, and it is now clear that shifts in means of these scores reflect poorly the concrete changes in specific choices brought about by group discussion. Explanations of the risky shift which postulate some mechanism that uniformly moves choices toward greater risk are unable to account for the total body of findings.

As so often happens in science, a paradigm has served to stimulate the discovery of facts which reveal the inadequacy of the paradigm itself. Research employing the risky-shift paradigm has cast serious doubt on the existence of the risky shift and on the usefulness of CDQ scores in the analysis of risk taking. The findings even suggest the possibility that the basic phenomena may have been mislabeled and that they have nothing specifically to do with risk at all. It would be unfortunate, however, if dissatisfaction with the original paradigm were to diminish interest in the findings that have been established. The critical problem is to find a conceptual framework capable of dealing with phenomena that have proved to be more complex than first anticipated.

Much of the uncertainty about the relevance of the research on choice dilemmas to the concept of risk might be reduced with the help of mathematical decision theory. As noted above, portfolio theory (Coombs and Huang, 1970) is well suited to the analysis of choice dilemmas and provides a means for clarifying the role of risk in both initial choices and shifts. The model proposed by Miller (1970) approaches the problem in a somewhat different way. Both of these conceptualizations should be carefully examined to discover how well they can deal with the total set of findings.

A curious feature of the history of research on choice dilemmas is the early rejection of theories of conformity and social influence as explanatory orientations. The risky shift was interpreted from the beginning as being inconsistent with previous findings from research on conformity. The argument against conformity theory has relied mainly on the assertion that it implies a convergence of postdiscussion choices toward the *mean* of initial choices. Actually, however, conformity theory provides no clear basis for making any predictions about the location, or content, of an emergent norm from the beliefs or preferences of group members, since it has concentrated primarily on processes arising after group norms have been established. To the extent that it makes use of theories of social influence, it would predict that an emergent norm will coincide with the mean of initial choices only under rather special circumstances, as for example when all members have equal weight in the influence process. The model developed by Miller (1970) assumes convergence but predicts shifts in means as a consequence of differential weights among group members. This model, together with those of French (1956) and Harary (1959), might well provide a way to relate the findings on choice dilemmas to theories of conformity and social influence.

Since it is not yet clear how risk enters into the choices made by subjects, it is possible that shifts would best be conceived as instances of the effects of group discussion on attitudes. Such a view has been advocated by Moscovici and Zavalloni (1969), and its plausibility has been enhanced by results reported by Fraser et al. (1971). These investigators asked subjects to respond to each dilemma by means of a Likert scale on which they were to indicate how strongly they favored one or the other of the two alternative courses of action. When these responses were compared with the usual probability choices, there was a remarkable similarity between the two kinds of responses both before and after group discussion. If responses to choice dilemmas are in fact indicators of attitudes, then theories of attitude change should help to improve our understanding of the processes that bring about changes in these responses.

There is a real possibility, however, that the attitudes related to choice dilemmas have certain special characteristics which influence the way in which group discussion affects them. The findings concerning subjects' expectations about the choices of others, the choices they most admire, and their evaluations of people who make various choices suggest that the dilemmas generate a conflict between ideals and reality. Several interesting suggestions have been advanced by Higbee (1971), Jellison and Riskind (1970), Levinger and Schneider (1969), and Pruitt (1969) concerning the nature of this conflict and the role of group discussion in resolving it. It may turn out that such a conflict is critical for the occurrence of shifts and that group discussion does not affect all attitudes alike. Since so little is known about the effects of group discussion on attitudes of any sort, the findings for choice dilemmas may contribute valuable information about this form of attitude change.

Perhaps the greatest uncertainty surrounds the question of how best to conceptualize the processes of group discussion and group decision. Should group discussion be conceived as providing persuasive arguments concerning the correct answer to a problem or as a mechanism for combin-

individual preferences into a single group decision? Despite the demonstrated importance of group discussion for the occurrence of shifts, almost nothing is known about its nature. It is clear that discussion serves in some way to reconcile differences in initial choices and brings about a reduction in their variance, but it is not clear how this is accomplished. A direct examination of the content of group discussion is needed to identify the immediate determinants of shifts in choices.

The search for a suitable theoretical home for the findings established by the research on choice dilemmas will require careful attention to the concrete processes that determine both initial choices and changes in these choices. Unless these processes are clearly identified and placed in an appropriate theoretical context, the work on the risky shift may well become nothing more than an interesting episode in the history of social psychology.

BIBLIOGRAPHY

Alker, H. A., and Kogan, N., "Effects of Norm-oriented Group Discussion on Individual Verbal Risk Taking and Conservatism," *Hum. Relat.*, 21: 393-405, 1968.

Atthowe, J. M., Jr., "Interpersonal Decision Making: The Resolution of a Dyadic Conflict," *J. Abnorm. Soc. Psychol.*, 62:114-119, 1961.

Bateson, N., "Familiarization, Group Discussion, and Risk Taking," *J. Exp. Soc. Psychol.*, 2:119-129, 1966.

Bell, P. R., and B. D. Jamieson, "Publicity of Initial Decisions and the Risky Shift Phenomenon," *J. Exp. Soc. Psychol.*, 6:329-345, 1970.

Belovicz, M. W., and Finch, F. E., "A Critical Analysis of the 'Risky Shift' Phenomenon," *Org. Behav. and Hum. Perform.*, 6:150-168, 1971.

Bem, D. J., Wallach, M. A., and Kogan, N., "Group Decision Making Under Risk of Aversive Consequences," *J. Pers. Soc. Psychol.*, 1:453-460, 1965.

Brown, R., *Social Psychology* (New York: Free Press, 1965).

Burns, J. F., "An Extremity-variance Analysis of Group Decisions Involving Risk," Ph.D. dissertation, Massachusetts Institute of Technology, Sloan School of Management, 1967.

Burnstein, E., Miller, H., Vinokur, A., Katz, S., and Crowley, J., "Risky Shift is Eminently Rational," *J. Pers. Soc. Psychol.*, 20:462-471, 1971.

Cecil, E. A., "The Effect of Group Composition on the Level of Risk in Group Decisions," Ph.D. dissertation, Indiana University, Graduate School of Business, 1967.

Clark, R. D., III, "Group-induced Shift Toward Risk: A Critical Appraisal," *Psychol. Bull.*, 76:251-270, 1971.

Clark, R. D., III and Willems, E. P., "The Risky-shift Phenomenon: The Diffusion-of-responsibility Hypothesis or the Risk-as-value Hypothesis," paper presented at the meeting of the Southwestern Psychological Association, St. Louis, April 1970.

Coombs, C. H., and Huang, L. C., "Tests of a Portfolio Theory of Risk Preference," *J. Exp. Psychol.*, 85:23-29, 1970.

Crockett, W. H., and Archer, R. L., "Is Knowledge of Others' Specific Risk Levels Necessary for the Risky Shift to Occur?," *J. Pers. Soc. Psychol.*, 20:425-429, 1971.

Dion, K. L., Baron, R. S., and Miller, N., "Why do Groups Make Riskier Decisions Than Individuals?," in L. Berkowitz, ed., *Advances in Experimental Social Psychology*, vol. 5 (New York: Academic Press, 1970).

Dion, K. L., Miller, N., and Magnan, M. A., "Cohesiveness and Social Responsibility as Determinants of Group Risk-taking," *J. Pers. Soc. Psychol.*, 20:400-406, 1971.

Doise, W., "Intergroup Relations and Polarization of Individual and Collective Judgments," *J. Pers. Soc. Psychol.*, 12:136-143, 1969.

Ferguson, D. A. and Vidmar, N., "Effects of Group Discussion on Estimates of Culturally Appropriate Risk Levels," *J. Pers. Soc. Psychol.*, 20:436-445, 1971.

Flanders, J. P., and Thistlethwaite, D. L. "Effects of Familiarization and Group Discussion Upon Risk Taking," *J. Pers. Soc. Psychol.*, 5:91-97, 1969.

Fraser, C., Gouge, C., and Billig, M., "Risky Shifts, Cautious Shifts, and Group Polarization," *Eur. J. Soc. Psychol.*, 1:7-29, 1971.

French, J. R. P., Jr., "A Formal Theory of Social Power," *Psychol. Rev.*, 63: 181-194, 1956.

Graham, W. K., and Harris, S. G., "Effects of Group Discussion on Accepting Risk and on Advising Others to be Risky," paper presented at the meeting of the Western Psychological Association, Vancouver, June 1969.

Haley, H. J., and Rule, B. G., "Group Composition Effects on Risk Taking," *J. Pers.*, 39:150-161, 1971.

Harary, F., "A Criterion for Unanimity in French's Theory of Social Power," in D. Cartwright, ed., *Studies in Social Power* (Ann Arbor, Mich.: Institute for Social Research, 1959).

Higbee, K. L., "The Expression of 'Walter Mitty-ness' in Actual Behavior," *J. Pers. Soc. Psychol.*, 20:416-422, 1971.

Hinds, W. C., Jr., *Individual and Group Decisions in Gambling Situations*, Master's thesis, Massachusetts Institute of Technology, Sloan School of Management, 1962.

Hoyt, G. C., and Stoner, J. A. F., "Leadership and Group Decisions Involving Risk," *J. Exp. Soc. Psychol.*, 4:275-284, 1968.

Hunt, E. B., and Rowe, R. R., "Group and Individual Economic Decision Making in Risk Conditions," in D. W. Taylor, ed., *Experiments on Decision Making and Other Studies* (Arlington, Va.: Armed Services Technical Information Agency, 1960).

Jellison, J. M. and Riskind, J., "A Social Comparison of Abilities Interpretation of Risk-taking Behavior," *J. Pers. Soc. Psychol.*, 15:375-390, 1970.

Kogan, N., and Wallach, M. A., "The Risky-shift Phenomenon in Small Decision-making Groups: A Test of the Information-exchange Hypothesis," *J. Exp. Soc. Psychol.*, 3:75-85, 1967.

Kogan, N., and Zaleska, M., "Level of Risk Selected by Individuals and Groups When Deciding for Self and Others," *Proceedings of the 77th Annual Convention of the American Psychological Association*, 4:423-424 (summary), 1969.

Lamm, H., "Will an Isolated Individual Advise Higher Risk-Taking After Hearing a Discussion of the Decision Problem?," *J. Pers. Soc. Psychol.*, 6:467-471, 1967.

———, Trommsdorff, G., and Kogan, N., "Pessimism-optimism and Risk Taking in Individual and Group Contexts," *J. Pers. Soc. Psychol.*, 15:366-374, 1970.

Levinger, G., and Schneider, D. J., "A Test of the 'Risk as a Value' Hypothesis," *J. Pers. Soc. Psychol.*, 11:165-169, 1969.

Lonergan, B. G., and McClintock, C. G., "Effects of Group Membership on Risk Taking Behavior," *Psychol. Rep.*, 8:447-455, 1961.

Mackenzie, J. D., "The Effects of Status upon Group Risk Taking," *Org. Behav. and Hum. Perf.*, 5:517-571, 1970.

———, "An Analysis of Risky Shift Experiments," *Org. Behav. and Hum. Perf.*, 6:249-266, 1971.

Madaras, G. R., and Bem, D. J., "Risk and Conservatism in Group Decision Making," *J. Exp. Soc. Psychol.*, 4:350-365, 1968.

Marquis, D. G., "Individual Responsibility and Group Decisions Involving Risk," *Industrial Management Rev.*, 3:8-23, 1962.

———, and Reitz, H. J., "Effect of Uncertainty on Risk Taking in Individual and Group Decisions," *Behav. Sci.*, 14:281-288, 1969.

McCauley, C. R., Jr., "Risk and Attitude Shifts After Group Discussion," Ph.D. dissertation, University of Pennsylvania, 1970.

———, Teger, A. I., and Kogan, N., "Effect of the Pretest in the Risky Shift Paradigm," *J. Pers. Soc. Psychol.*, 20:379-381, 1971.

Miller, H., "Is the Risky Shift the Result of a Rational Group Decision?," *Proceedings of the 78th Annual Convention of the American Psychological Association*, 5:333-334 (summary), 1970.

Miller, N., and Dion, K. L., "An Analysis of the Familiarization Explanation of the Risky-shift," *Proceedings of the 78th Annual Convention of the American Psychological Association*, 5:337-338 (summary), 1970.

Moscovici, S., and Zavalloni, M., "The Group as a Polarizer of Attitudes," *J. Pers. Soc. Psychol.*, 12:125-135, 1969.

Murdock, P., Myers, D. G., and Smith, G. F., "Information Effects on Cautious and Risky Shift Items," *Psychon. Sci.*, 20:97-98, 1971.

Myers, D. G., and Bishop, G. D. "Discussion Effects on Racial Attitudes," *Science*, 169:778-789, 1970.

Nordhøy, F., "Group Interaction in Decision-making Under Risk," Master's thesis, Massachusetts Institute of Technology, Sloan School of Management, 1962.

Pruitt, D. G., "The 'Walter Mitty' Effect in Individual and Group Risk Taking," *Proceedings of the 77th Annual Convention of the American Psychological Association*, 4:425-426 (summary), 1969.

———, and Teger, A. I., "The Risky Shift in Group Betting," *J. Exp. Soc. Psychol.*, 5:115-126, 1969.

Rabow, J., Fowler, F. J., Bradford, D. J., Hofeller, N. A., and Shibuya, Y., "The Role of Social Norms and Leadership in Risk Taking," *Sociometry*, 29:16-27, 1966.

Rule, B. G., and Evans, J. I. F., "Familiarization, the Presence of Others and

Group Discussion Effects," *Rep. Res. in Soc. Psychol.*, 1971. (Chapel Hill: University of North Carolina).

St. Jean, R., "Reformulation of the Value Hypothesis in Group Risk Taking," *Proceedings of the 78th Annual Convention of the American Psychological Association*, 5:339-340 (summary), 1970.

Siegel, S., and Zajonc, R. B., "Group Risk Taking in Professional Decisions," *Sociometry*, 30:339-349, 1967.

Stokes, J. P., "Effects of Familiarization and Knowledge of Others' Odds Choices on Shifts to Risk and Caution," *J. Pers. Soc. Psychol.*, 20:407-412, 1971.

Stoner, J. A. F., "A Comparison of Individual and Group Decisions Involving Risk," Master's thesis, Massachusetts Institute of Technology, Sloan School of Management, 1961.

———, "Risky and Cautious Shifts in Group Decisions: The Influence of Widely Held Values," *J. Exp. Soc. Psychol.*, 4:442-459, 1968.

Teger, A. I., and Pruitt, D. G., "Components of Group Risk Taking," *J. Exp. Soc. Psychol.*, 3:189-205, 1967.

———, St. Jean, R., and Haaland, G. A., "A Re-examination of the Familiarization Hypothesis in Group Risk Taking," *J. Exp. Soc. Psychol.*, 6:346-350, 1970.

Vidmar, N., and Burdeny, T. C., *Interaction Effects of Group Size and Relative Risk Position with Item Type in the "Group Shift" Effect*, Res. Bull. No. 128, Department of Psychology (Waterloo, Ontario: University of Western Ontario, 1969).

Vinokur, A., "Distribution of Initial Risk Levels and Group Decisions Involving Risk," *J. Pers. Soc. Psychol.*, 13:207-204, 1969.

———, "Effects of Group Process upon Individual and Group Decisions Involving Risk," Ph.D. dissertation, University of Michigan, 1970.

———, "Cognitive and Affective Processes Influencing Risk-taking in Groups: An Expected Utility Approach," *J. Pers. Soc. Psychol.*, 20:472-486, 1971.

———, "Review and Theoretical Analysis of the Effects of Group Processes upon Individual and Group Decisions Involving Risk," *Psychol. Bull.*, 76:231-250, 1971.

Wallach, M. A., and Kogan, N., "The Roles of Information, Discussion and Consensus in Group Risk-Taking," *J. Exp. Soc. Psychol.*, 1:1-19, 1965.

———, and Bem, D. J., "Group Influence on Individual Risk Taking," *J. Abnorm. Soc. Psychol.*, 65:75-86, 1962.

Wallach, M. A., and Mabli, J., "Information versus Conformity in the Effects of Group Discussion or Risk Taking," *J. Pers. Soc. Psychol.*, 14:149-156, 1970.

Wallach, M. A., and Wing, C., "Is Risk a Value?," *J. Pers. Soc. Psychol.*, 9:101-106, 1968.

Zajonc, R. B., Wolosin, R. J., Wolosin, M. A., and Sherman, S. J. "Individual and Group Risk-taking in a Two-choice Situation," *J. Exp. Soc. Psychol.*, 4:89-106, 1968.

———, "Group Risk-taking in a Two-choice Situation: Replication, Extension, and a Model," *J. Exp. Soc. Psychol.*, 5:127-140, 1969.

Part 2

HISTORICAL SURVEY

THIS PART IS an historical survey for the reader and an overview of most of the theoretical positions to be found in group psychotherapy. Joseph Pratt is presented here as the founder of group psychotherapy in the United States. Because his original article announcing his findings is not particularly specific in terms of what he actually did with the groups he formed for his tuberculosis classes, the editors have selected for this collection an article which we believe to be a more detailed statement of his work at that time. The second article was written by Pratt toward the end of his life. It is a statement of his later experiences and how he ventured into the field of psychotherapy. It is a much clearer overview of Pratt's thinking.

Marsh's article is a statement by one of the pioneers in the field of group psychotherapy. It is an interesting example of a revival-inspirational approach to group psychotherapy, and very much "in tune" with some current methods of group therapy. We have dealt at some length in this historical survey with the work of Trigant Burrow, whom we feel to have been a significant figure in the entire development of psychotherapy in the United States. Unfortunately, Burrow has written in such complex and often esoteric language that it is "tough sledding" for the reader. His son-in-law, Hans Syz, who carries on Burrow's tradition, has written a detailed statement of Burrow's work and an excellent summary of Burrow's philosophy and approach to psychotherapy which he states is up-to-date. One of the clearest statements of Burrow's own approach to psychotherapy in the group treatment of the individual is the article on the group method of analysis which we have included. It is a rare article because it is specific as a statement and not couched in the often obscure language that Burrow later used to describe his work.

We have included a review of Burrow, written by D. H. Lawrence, for three major reasons. First, it is a precursor to much of what is currently called "existential psychotherapy." Second, it shows the many currents that were at work during the early years of psychoanalytic psychotherapy and awareness of the group by some major figures in the culture. Third, it

beautiful statement of the importance of the group experience for the individual, as perceived by one of the great novelists of contemporary culture who was also a gifted psychologist.

The remaining articles in this section are statements of the theoretic positions of group psychotherapists who stem from various analytic persuasions. They seem to confirm what Fred Fiedler has concluded in his research at the University of Chicago. Experienced therapists apparently are much more similar to one another in clinical practice than they are aware. They often find a good deal of difficulty in fitting their everyday clinical practice to the theoretical persuasions by which they were originally influenced and which they attempt to hold on to in the course of their professional development. DeRosis has commented on Horney's views in his article, which is newly included in this collection.

The series of letters that Illing exchanged with Jung are interesting, as they are a specific statement of a pioneer psychoanalyst's approach to the group method of treatment.

7

THE TUBERCULOSIS CLASS:
AN EXPERIMENT
IN HOME TREATMENT

Joseph H. Pratt

The topic assigned to me is the Convalescent Care of Tuberculosis Patients, but the term "convalescence" cannot properly be applied to tuberculosis as it can be to such diseases as pneumonia and typhoid fever. I accepted the invitation to speak, because I appreciated greatly the honor of coming here, to a city that has taken the lead in so much good work along the lines of public health, and, although I cannot talk to you about convalescent care, in speaking of my experiments in the home treatment of tuberculosis I shall lay special reference on the after care.

The after care of tuberculosis depends a good deal upon the treatment the patient has had during the active stage of the disease. As I just said, we cannot speak of a patient with tuberculosis as being convalescent any more than we can speak of a patient who has syphilis as being convalescent. Those of you who are social workers among tuberculosis individuals must realize the truth of this. A man may appear perfectly well who a short time before presented symptoms of tuberculosis. The disease may show no signs of activity, the temperature and pulse may be normal, and yet, a day after some trifling overexertion he may have a hemorrhage and a return of symptoms. Recently I saw a patient who had been free from symptoms for several months, with no fever, no cough, and yet such slight exertion as dressing and going down one flight of stairs to dinner was followed by a return of cough, elevation of temperature, and a feeling of general malaise. Therefore, it is very important in dealing with tuberculosis to remember the distinction between this disease and such diseases as

Reprinted from *Proceedings*, New York Conference on Hospital Social Service, Vol. IV, 1917, pp. 49-68. Some statistical tables accompanying this article were omitted for reasons of space.

typhoid fever and pneumonia, for example, which have definite convalescent stages.

In the spring of 1905 I formulated a plan for the treatment of consumption in the homes of poor patients. The organization was called a tuberculosis class. Sanatorium methods were to be employed and supervision obtained (1) by visits to the home by the class nurse; (2) a record book in which the details of the daily life were noted down by the patient—the value of this I had learned from Dr. Charles L. Minor of Asheville—and (3) weekly meetings of the patients.

It was the intention from the outset to give a great deal of care to a small number of patients. My project did not find favor with the existing organizations to which I appealed for financial support, but finally I obtained from Dr. Elwood Worcester, the rector of Emmanuel Church, the sum of $500 with which to begin the experiment.

In organizing the class I had the able assistance of Dr. John B. Hawes and of Miss Isabel Strong, a graduate nurse of unusual ability and well suited to carry on work along original lines. Miss Strong became the first class visitor and gave her entire time without pay.

Before the class started on July 1, I spent a week with Dr. Lawrason Brown, at that time resident physician of the Adirondack Cottage Sanatorium at Trudeau. From him I learned much of value. From the monograph of Moeller, which had recently appeared in the Deutsche Klinik, I became familiar with the details of the rest cure as carried out by Dettweiler and his followers. I was deeply impressed by Moeller's statement that all his patients found the rest cure extremely beneficial. I remember well my surprise when I read on the train coming home from Saranac this sentence: "I have still to hear of a single patient who found the rest cure irksome. On the other hand, many have said to me that the hours of the 'Liegekur' are to them the pleasantest of the day."

I mused over this a long time, and when the class started, the rest cure on roof, yard, or balcony was our chief reliance in treatment. Every fever-free patient was provided with a reclining chair.

From the outset exercise was regarded as dangerous, and, when taken, the duration of the walks was always exactly prescribed.

We began with one patient, whom Dr. Hawes had discovered in the outpatient department of the Massachusetts General Hospital, where she had been under treatment for more than six months, and in spite of her faithful efforts was slowly but steadily getting worse. She has now been well and working for ten years.

I have preserved the report written by Miss Strong, the class nurse, of the first visit to the first patient in 1905. This patient had received the ordinary treatment as carried out in a tuberculosis dispensary. The letter is as follows:

I visited the first member of the class this morning and everything goes well. I think I showed her how to take her temperature, and taught her her lesson thoroughly, I hope. She is being cared for by an aunt, and therefore has no money. Could we buy a chair for her? She says she cannot. I went to Paine's and they carry the $2.00 chair. I found she could not sit out on the little piazza in the afternoon because of the sun, so I visited a neighbor and made arrangements for her chair to be placed under a tree. I find she is going in to Boston and taking electric car rides, etc. Will you give explicit directions about the amount of exercise? I told her absolute rest for the first week anyway. Her temperature at 12 noon was 98.8 and pulse 80. I also told her to take it every two hours. I find she is taking cold sponge baths every day. I believe you said twice a week. She had a chest protector on, in fact two, which I asked her to remove; also she is taking olive oil, three teaspoonfuls in twenty-four hours. Yesterday she vomited curdled milk, and as I could give no other cause I suggested diminishing the oil to see if that was the trouble. She sleeps very well, and is faithful to the outdoor orders. She asked me when she could come again to the dispensary, and if she could join the Parker Day Camp Hill. I believe they spend the day in tents, and are gathered from the different dispensaries. It seems to me she is quite well situated now. I told her I would bring a record book to her later on when you have them.

I feel rather doubtful about the baths and exercise, not knowing exactly what you would say. Perhaps we could have a rule for all patients for the first week or ten days.

Waban, July 6, 1905.

I quote this in full to show that from the beginning we realized the importance of careful supervision of the individual patient and to let you see that I had a very good supporter in Miss Strong. Much of the success in organizing our work was due to her.

This class was the beginning of the social service work at the Massachusetts General Hospital. Three months later Dr. Richard C. Cabot broadened the work there to cover the investigation and, where possible, the solution of the various social problems of the outpatients by trained and by volunteer workers. At Dr. Cabot's request a second tuberculosis class was organized by Dr. Hawes for the treatment of patients who lived in the suburbs of Boston. Within the next few years many classes were formed in various parts of the country. Most of them, like the seed sown on thin soil, sprang up quickly, but quickly withered away, as adequate financial support was lacking and the vital elements underlying the success in our work were not understood. One class, an off-shoot of ours, organized by one of my assistants, Dr. N. K. Wood, is still in existence after ten years of successful work. The nurse in this class for the entire period has been our first class member.

In New York City in 1906 a tuberculosis class was established by D

Walter L. Niles, called the Christ Church Tuberculosis Class. It had an efficient, friendly visitor, and our methods were carried out by Dr. Niles most successfully. He demonstrated clearly and conclusively that it was possible to treat tuberculosis by substantially the same methods in the heart of New York City. That experiment should be known to all of you. It was very successful, and Dr. Niles deserves great credit. It was abandoned in a few years because money for its support was discontinued.

Shortly after the Christ Church Class was formed, a class was organized at St. George's Church in New York and was carried on successfully by Dr. N. Gilbert Seymour and Dr. Tasker Howard for a period of three years or more. It is important to emphasize the success of these classes, because of the impression that has gone out throughout the country that the class method had been tried but had been given up as unsuccessful. I hope very much that these physicians in New York will publish reports and state the advantages and difficulties of class work. I believe that Dr. Landis who organized and conducted the class at the Phipps Institute in Philadelphia is planning to issue such a report. I know of no class that has carefully followed the same methods we have employed that has not been successful. Dr. Hawes, who was my first assistant, has lost his faith in the class method. Some of you may have been at New Haven and heard his criticism. He considered my success a matter of personality rather than of method. When Dr. Hawes was associated with me in the Emmanuel Church Class, much of the detail work was in his hands. This he did with enthusiasm and success. His own experiment with the Suburban Tuberculosis Class he now regards as a failure. I think I should have failed had I attempted, as he did, to treat 88 patients in one year—to say nothing of the fact that he had no funds at his disposal and that he depended on volunteer visitors to give instructions in the homes, while we had a trained visiting nurse from the start.

In the beginning we sought only far-advanced cases that were refused admission to the only public sanatorium in the state—that of Rutland. Of the 17 patients admitted to the class in the first six months, one was incipient, six advanced, and ten far-advanced. The next year, 1906, 15 of the 31 patients taken into the class were in the far-advanced stage of the disease. That answered the criticism that we selected our cases.

At first we had our weekly meetings in my consulting room. Later we moved to a dispensary on Washington Street, supported by Dr. Haynes, and after that to the Massachusetts General Hospital, where we still have our headquarters. A few years ago we were forced by lack of space in the growing outpatient department to the basement, where we meet in a rather cheerless room. Nevertheless, we are very thankful to the hospital authorities for the aid they have given us.

I wish to emphasize the one point: We are not a church class in the ⌐nse that we meet in a church; the only connection comes through financial support. The St. George's Class was a true church class. They met in the parish house.

Our path even at the start was not wholly smooth. When Miss Strong made the second visit to the first patient two or three days after the one described in her letter, she found that her explicit instructions regarding rest had not been followed, as the patient had been to church on Sunday.

One day that hot first summer the visitor came to me in a discouraged hour and said: "Why insist that these poor consumptives with far advanced disease follow the strict rest treatment out-of-doors, when you know that they cannot recover?" Speaking with the wisdom of hope, if not of experience, I assured her that it was my conviction that some would get well, and they did. We allowed a few patients to go to the day camp that year, but I learned from observations that the exertion of the trips to and from the camp were so injurious as to offset any advantage to be found there. The first member failed to gain for several months, and some who died, I believe, might have been saved if I had kept them in bed for a long period of time.

Within two years my ideas regarding rest were definitely formed, and in a paper read before the National Association for the Study and Prevention of Tuberculosis, in the spring of 1907, I write as follows regarding the rest treatment:

> The chief reason that so many of our moderately advanced cases have recovered seems to lie in the fact that we have insisted on absolute rest in every instance. Even in cases without fever, rest in the recumbent position is continued until symptoms have disappeared. I find less difficulty in keeping a patient quiet all the time than half the time. The rest treatment simplifies wonderfully the management of the case. It saves the patient from many dangers. Each patient is provided with a comfortable canvas reclining chair. The friendly visitor at her first visit selects the exact spot out-of-doors where the cot bed and chair are to be placed. The chair must not be moved without permission. Many of the members spend the greater part of the day on their cot beds. This is encouraged. The patients are never allowed to take any of the prescribed rest in a sitting position or in any form of rocking chair. No sewing or other hand work is allowed, and only a moderate amount of reading. The "cure" consists simply in keeping in the recumbent posture all the time, except that members free from fever are allowed to dress themselves and to take their meals at the table. The members do not find the enforced hours of rest irksome. It is, of course, hard to keep quiet for the first week or two of treatment—much harder for some than for others. But the rest habit is soon acquired. In the past year not a single member has begged me for exercise. It is rare, indeed, that they ask for it after the treatment is fairly begun.

In the years that have passed since this was written I have used more rest rather than less, as a study of the records show. The average time at which exercise in the form of walking was begun in 30 cases admitted from 1905 to 1907 was 7 weeks. In a second group of 30 cases covering the years from 1908 to 1911 it was four months, and in a third series, 1911 to 1913, it was again four months. The average duration of treatment in the first group was 8 months, in the second 8½, and in the third 11 months.

In a paper read in Dublin, Ireland, 1908, I stated my belief "that a case of pulmonary tuberculosis during the active state should be given the same form of rest treatment that is employed in typhoid fever."

My ideal has been immobilization of the patient, and this word gives perhaps a clearer idea of our form of treatment than the word rest. Unfortunately in this work among the poor, with the limited facilities at our disposal, the immobilization has been far from complete. Many of the patients have been obliged to walk to the bathroom and to take their meals at the table. Furthermore, the visits to the class have involved an amount of exercise that has doubtless been distinctly harmful in some cases, but the class meetings have proved so helpful to the members in keeping up their courage and their determination to persevere in the rest treatment that the physical work entailed upon attendance has seemed a necessary evil. Some patients have attended only once in three or four weeks, and none except those who are nearly ready for discharge, and for whom walking and work in considerable amount are prescribed, are allowed to come to the class meetings oftener than once in two weeks. The rest treatment is now carried out in cot beds, and very few of the patients during the past five years have used reclining chairs. The only chair that we can recommend—Dr. Brown's Adirondack model—which is patterned after that of Dettweiler, is too expensive for our patients.

When we discovered that the rest treatment at home was giving better immediate results than those obtained in the sanatorium open to wage earners in Massachusetts, we no longer advised patients in the early stages of the disease who sought admission to the class to go to a sanatorium in preference to taking the treatment at home. The end results of home treatment in the class were better than those obtained at Rutland, although this is a sanatorium limited to favorable cases, while patients in all stages of the disease have been admitted to our class, and no one has been refused because the outlook seemed hopeless. The percentage of Rutland ex-patients able to work after a period of 8 to 10 years was less than 25, while 42 per cent of our class members were working after this length of time.

The class meeting has been described in earlier papers. The patients bring their record books for inspection. Each one is weighed and the temperature and pulse taken and recorded. The gains in weight are posted on a blackboard. After a few words of commendation and cheer, or a brief talk, the members in turn come forward to my desk or to that of my assistant. The record book is carefully inspected, advice given, and an entry made on the clinical history of the patient's condition. If a candidate for membership is present one of the "star" patients is frequently asked to testify what the rest treatment has done for him, and this is done with the enthusiasm that exerts a powerful influence on the newcomer. But the healthy appearance of most of the patients probably makes a deeper impression than anything that is said. At least this was true in the case of James M., who is often requested to tell his experience at the class meeting.

Soon after the death of his wife, James, who was a longshoreman of middle age, and a free user of alcohol, developed a severe cough and rapidly lost weight and strength. At the dispensary at Burrough's Place tubercle bacilli were found in his sputum. His lungs were extensively diseased, and he was advised to go to the city tuberculosis hospital for advanced cases at Mattapan, but he refused. A nurse called several times but he remained obdurate and insisted on staying at home.*

Finally, in despair, his brother having gotten my name somewhere as one who knew something about tuberculosis, brought him to me as a private patient. I explained to James the seriousness of his condition, and the importance of taking the rest treatment, but he remained taciturn and unmoved. On leaving my consulting room he told his brother frankly that he didn't think much of me. I did not make any impression upon him. My personality did not work that time. He said to his brother: "I don't think he is a doctor: he didn't say anything about medicine. He is more like a Christian Scientist, or a professor of physical culture, or something like that." The idea of lying down all day out-of-doors just as though he were a log of wood did not appeal to him at all.

He sought out a doctor who gave him medicine, but he felt that it did him no good. Finally he heeded the persuasions of my class visitor, herself a former member of the class, and came rather reluctantly to one of the meetings. He saw there two or three men who had made good progress, and who had followed the rest treatment faithfully for months. Out of complete discouragement, a hope arose in his mind that he, too, might recover. At the end of the meeting he accepted at once the invitation to join the class, and a more faithful patient in following out the rest treatment we have never had.

To the question often asked by doctors "How do you induce your patients to take the strict rest treatment?" the answer is: the class meeting.

Results obtained 1905-1915. These were briefly reported at the last meeting of the National Association for the Study and Prevention of Tu-

---

* Long afterwards we learned the reason for his refusal. He had known sixteen or seventeen men who had been sent to Mattapan. All but one had died. "They made a quick cure of that patient," James said, "he left in forty-eight hours and is well today." In this experience is a lesson for all who think the segregation of advanced cases in hospitals devoted to this purpose is the essential feature in the tuberculosis campaign Many, like James, will refuse to go to a hospital for advanced cases when they know of many deaths there and no recoveries. The solution of this difficulty is the care of early and advanced cases in the same institution, although not in the same ward.

berculosis. Of all patients discharged from 1906 to 1913, 58.2 per cent were well and working in 1915, two to nine years after their discharge.

Few sanatoriums publish detailed reports of the after-history of their patients. This is most regrettable, and it has often raised the suspicion that the end results are so poor that those in authority do not care to go to the expense of collecting and publishing data that will have a discouraging effect on workers in the tuberculosis campaign. Among the few sanatoriums that have published excellent reports of the after-histories, the Gaylord Farm Sanatorium and the Adirondack Cottage Sanatorium in this State deserve special mention.

One of the most detailed reports of results was published in 1914 by the Brompton Hospital Sanatorium located at Frimley, in England. This institution was opened only a year before our class was formed. There various forms of graduated labor have been employed as the essential element in treatment. At first the patient is given walking exercises, varying from one to six miles daily. After two or three weeks a small basket is carried or light gardening is begun. The after-histories of their cases are given in sufficient detail to permit the construction of tables placing side by side results obtained by two radically different methods of treatment.

In comparing results it should be remembered that we were dealing with unselected cases and that the Brompton Hospital was dealing with selected cases. To quote from the Brompton official report: "The cases sent here have been carefully selected, only those patients being chosen who were free from fever or other serious constitutional symptoms, who possessed considerable vitality and had already begun to show signs of improvement. So far as possible, also, patients with signs of limited disease have been preferred, although it was early found that patients with the disease extensive, but of a quiescent type, often did remarkably well. The presence of pulmonary symptoms, such as cough, expectoration and occasional slight haemoptysis has not excluded the patient from this class, provided the general condition has remained good and the capacity for work has been maintained."

In this report the staff of Brompton admits that the end results are disappointing. "In view of the careful selection of cases for the Frimley Sanitorium, it was hoped that a larger percentage would have retained their health." They point out that their results compare not unfavorably with the German Sanatoria established under the insurance law. But Cornet has clearly shown that the end results in these sanatoria are bad—so bad, in fact, as to bring the sanatorium treatment for wage-earners largely into discredit in Germany. He found that among 19,938 persons who received treatment in the German sanatoria for working men, 13,891, or 70 per cent, were either dead or invalided at the end of four years.

68.4 per cent of those with positive sputum were dead or invalided four years after discharge from Brompton. Our form of home treatment has given better results, as 21 per cent less, 46.7 per cent instead of 68.4 per cent, of the patients with positive sputum treated by the class method were dead or invalided four to ten years after their discharge.

Of 416 patients discharged from the Brompton Hospital Sanatorium 112 were well and able to work five to seven years after their discharge. Deducting the 147 untraced, the percentage is 41.6.

At the end of five to seven years following their discharge from the class 40 of the 59 patients were well and able to work. Deducting the two untraced, the percentage is 70.

Of the 55 patients discharged from Brompton in 1905, only 8 were well seven years later, while of the 21 discharged from the tuberculosis class in 1908, 14 were well seven years later. Patients who were in the sanatorium less than two months are not considered.

The Frimley method found almost instant favor in America. On all sides one heard that work, not rest, was the proper treatment for tuberculosis. Yet Brehmer,* the father of the sanatorium treatment, was convinced after years of clinical observation that labor was injurious in the active stages of the disease; he would not let his patients play croquet or billiards, and he warned them against the danger of breathing exercises. It is strange that all his teaching and that of Dettweiler and Cornet should have been cast aside in favor of the Frimley method, without any evidence except that some carefully selected consumptives, without fever, who had had three months of rest treatment at the Brompton Hospital, could do hard work without any immediate ill effects.

The class method is sometimes criticized as too limited in its scope, because we find it necessary to spend so much time, energy, and money on a single patient. Miss La Motte in her book on the *Tuberculosis Nurse* says that the tuberculosis class "deals with so few people that it makes no real impression on the situation." She adds that the tuberculosis problem is what can be done for a thousand patients, not for twenty. With these statements I cannot agree, and I am convinced that the view widely held that little can be done for the individual patient explains in large part the disappointing results obtained thus far in the tuberculosis campaign. The tuberculosis problem as it presents itself to the practicing physician and the nurse is, or should be, the individual patient. Give him the proper treatment, whether he be the sole consumptive in a small hamlet, a member of a tuberculosis class of twenty, or a patient in a sanatorium for a thousand patients, and the tuberculosis problem will be largely solved.

* It should be made clear that Brehmer did employ exercise in the form of walking. He held the mistaken idea that the disease was due to weakness of the heart, and he maintained that walks of increasing length, by strengthening the heart, brought about the cure of the disease. Great care was taken to avoid fatigue which he recognized as injurious. The following was one of his dictums: "The healthy person sits down when he is tired; the consumptive sits down that he may not get tired."

Not only may one tuberculosis class make a real impression on the tuberculosis situation, but the efforts of one nurse expended on a single patient may exert a widespread influence. The history of Robert D. illustrates the truth of this statement. To many nurses it might have seemed that efforts to make a poor ignorant Negro with far-advanced consumption take the proper treatment were a waste of time, especially as the patient was unwilling to heed her advice. He might readily have been placed in the group of unteachable consumptives. Mrs. Green, the class nurse, was unwilling to admit that this man was unteachable, although she made a dozen visits before he agreed to follow the treatment. After he had yielded, she persuaded the landlord to build a balcony at the cost of $11.50. The picture of this simple porch is familiar to many. It appears in the pamphlet on outdoor sleeping published by the National Association for the Study and Prevention of Tuberculosis and in the widely distributed pamphlet issued by the Metropolitan Life Insurance Company. It is also to be found in Dr. Knopf's "Prize Essay" and Dr. Hawes' two books on tuberculosis. The porch itself is still used as a sleeping place by the patient, although he has been at work for nearly nine years. In the neighborhood in which he lives it serves the purpose of a permanent tuberculosis exhibit. He tells his own story in the following letter:

Cambridge, August 3, 1911.

Dear Doctor:

Please excuse Long Delay. I am all so Sleepy at night after the Days work I culdent keep wake Long enough. this is my after noon of So I have a good chance to write after 5 or 6 years of continuous Sleeping out of dose I am thorley convinced that your way of living in the fresh air is the onley way for me. I have allso convinced my meny Collard Friends who come around after the Nurse had gorn and Beg me not to take that treatment as it would give me more Cold. what I wanted was a warm Room and Some thing that would loosen the Sputum and bring it up all this Seamed just the thing for me expecially the medison which was rum and molasses your Friendly visitor was coming every day telling me of her wonderfull treatment all of her treatment seamed hard Sleep out in the Backyard where the cats was fighting all Night. take cold watter bath that I never did while in the South wher it was warm and this was February. I allmost Beleaved what my Friends had told me that they was trying to kill me so I would not be exspence to the city of Camb or they was experimenting on me So the would know how to cure the nex fellow.

Your friendly visitor Miss Orieon exsplained the treatment to me in Such a way that I Beleaved if I could take the treatment and do every thing just as She wand me to do I would be cured. I desided with my Self I would do everything She want me to do exactly the way She want it don. One month be for the month was up She gave me a Chest Bath in a cold Room before a open window in month of Feb. and Bandaved my Body with wet Bandages. I desided I would not take the treatment enny Longer. When

she came her kind and earnest talk perswaded me to keep on. thank god today I am feeling better than I felt for years Befor I was Sick god bless you
and you Class. Just think where would I been now if you had not taken me
in you class. I remain

R—— D——

R.D. admitted to class Jan. 6, 1906. Far advanced. Positive sputum.
Unable to work since July, 1904. Wt. 145 lbs. Wife and 2 children slept
in room with patient. Porch built by landlord. Photograph appears in
Knopf's Prize Essay, and Carrington's Pamphlet on Open Air Sleeping.
Allowed to work May to Nov., 1907. Resumed treatment Nov., 1907. Dis-
charged March, 1908. Wt. 209. Well and working 8 years. (July, 1915.)

Many of the discharged patients that had learned any sort of trade before their sickness have followed the same occupation since returning to
work. When indoor workers have taken out-of-door jobs they have rarely
held them. It is usually far less fatiguing for ex-patients to do work to
which they are accustomed than to take up some unfamiliar employment.
It is most encouraging to find that those who have recovered their health
at home are able in the majority of cases to work full time month after
month and year after year.

Of 124 patients the occupations when taken ill were as follows:
housewives 38, schoolchildren 14, engaged in various sewing trades 11,
tailors, machinists and laborers, and factory operatives 4 each, clerks, teamsters, printers, and stenographers 3 each, shoe factory operatives, sales girls,
tinsmiths, and designers 2 each, and 1 of each of the following: store
owner, traveling salesman, peddler, barber, deaconess, letter carrier, comedian, confectioner, electrotype molder, scrub woman, lawyer, watchmaker,
jeweler, conductor, detective, note broker, cobbler, Pullman car cleaner,
milliner, waitress, bindery worker, telephone operator, tobacco stripper,
boardinghouse keeper, school teacher. Two had no occupation, and of two
the occupations are not known.

The occupations of the same 124 patients in 1915 were: housewives
46, nine of whom had had children since leaving the class; engaged in sewing trades and store owners 6, schoolchildren and tailors 4 each, machinists, clerks, teamsters, shoe factory operatives, traveling salesmen, peddlers,
foremen, farmers, janitors, attendant nurses, social workers, and bookkeep-
ers 2 each, and 1 of each of the following: printer, designer, barber, deaconess, letter carrier, comedian, confectioner, die forger, scrub woman, col-
lector, forester, writer and photographer, stewardess, hotel checker, music
teacher, ticket seller. Two changed occupations too frequently to be classified. One was a patient in a sanatorium; three were still class members.
Five had no occupation, and of five the occupation was not known.

Space permits only two examples of what has been done in the way of
family rehabilitation. The first patient who returned to work was a tailor.
During the period of class treatment the family resources reached such a

low point that his wife, without our knowledge, pawned her wedding ring. This man was rated on admission as a third stage case with signs of a cavity at the apex of the right lung. He was paid by Dr. Cabot to attend one of his clinical exercises as a subject for demonstration in physical diagnosis. I mention this as an indication that he had definite physical signs. After he was thought ready for work we were loath to send him back to a sweatshop, so an appeal was made to one of the generous friends of the class, who gave him enough money to start in business in a tiny shop of his own. He later moved to a larger place on a busier street and has supported himself and family for more than ten years. At the time of his illness his only child was a little boy of four. The boy now is a first year student in the English High School with a good record in scholarship, and his father is planning to send him to college.

At Christmas 1907 one of the Church workers learned of a family that were without money or food. Investigation brought the fact to light that both husband and wife were sick with pulmonary tuberculosis. There were three children, the oldest of which was only 11. The children were placed in families. After long search, a boarding place for the two patients was found in a colored family. A tent was purchased and the treatment was taken on the flat roof. Both recovered. The family was reunited. The woman has been doing her own housework for years, and the man has been self-supporting for seven years. He is a motorman.

It is often stated that the consumptive should not be treated at home because of the danger that others of his family may become infected. Our experience confirms the opinion expressed many years ago by Cornet that "the consumptive in himself is almost harmless, and only becomes harmful through bad habits." We have statistics on the health of all members of 131 families who had representatives in the Class between 1905 and 1915. Although 83 (41 per cent) of our 200 patients had a family history of pulmonary tuberculosis, since their connection with our class, only 3 new cases of pulmonary tuberculosis (2.3) have developed among the 131 families of which the subsequent report is complete. There have been two cases of tuberculous meningitis and two of tuberculosis of the lymph nodes. In these 131 families there were 220 children.

8

THE USE OF DEJERINE'S METHODS IN THE TREATMENT OF THE COMMON NEUROSES BY GROUP PSYCHOTHERAPY

Joseph H. Pratt

A simple form of psychotherapy that has been successfully employed in the treatment of the common neuroses requires no special training in psychology or psychiatry yet is unfamiliar to most physicians because it is rarely taught in the schools.

Nearly forty years ago, on the street one day I chanced to meet Dr. Isadore Coriat, the late well-known psychiatrist, as he was coming from the Boston Medical Library. He had just been reading Dejerine's new book on the treatment of the psychoneuroses by psychotherapy and recommended it so enthusiastically that I at once obtained a copy. It was a revelation to me.

Sir Arthur Hurst, in his recently published reminiscences, writes of Dejerine as follows: "At a time when in England and America neurotic patients received either no treatment at all or were treated by isolation, rest, overfeeding, and massage according to the routine invented by the poet physician Weir Mitchell, Dejerine had discarded purely physical treatment for a form of psychotherapy which differs little from the best methods practised today. He summarized his methods in these words: 'Expliquer au malade, après lui avoir fait confesser sa vie, comment et pourquoi il est tombé malade, comment et pourquoi il arrivera à se guérir.'"

Joseph Jules Dejerine's book *Les Manifestations Fonctionnelles des Psychonévroses; Leur Traitement par la Psychothérapie** was published in 1911. About the book, Sir Arthur wrote, "It is in my opinion the wisest ever written on the subject, and even today it gives a better introduction to

Reprinted from the *Bulletin of the New England Medical Center*, Vol. XV, March 1953, pp. 1-9.

* E. Gauckler, co-author.

psychotherapy than any more modern book, except perhaps T. A. Ross's *The Common Neuroses*, which, as Ross acknowledged in his preface, was largely based on Dejerine's teaching. Every medical student should read these two books before going into practice, as they will help him to deal with almost any patient who seeks his advice."

Before writing the account of his methods and the results he had obtained, Dejerine had developed methods of emotional reeducation and employed them in hundreds of cases over a period of fifteen years. He was the first to recognize that the neuroses are of emotional origin and that emotional training and reeducation are the essential elements in their treatment. I have followed Dejerine's methods ever since reading his book and can pay no greater tribute to this great master of medicine than to acknowledge the gratifying success that has followed my efforts.

Dejerine's book was translated into English by Dr. Smith Ely Jelliffe and published in 1913. It attracted little attention and has apparently remained almost unknown to American psychiatrists and internists, since it is rarely referred to by American writers. When the book could no longer be obtained from dealers in medical books and I wrote the publishers suggesting that it be reprinted, they replied that the book had had such a poor sale the plates had been destroyed. A number of recent medical school graduates have told me they never heard the works of Dejerine or Ross referred to by their teachers. Ross' *The Common Neuroses* is listed by Dr. Edward A. Strecker in Musser's *Textbook of Medicine* and by Dr. Thomas A. C. Rennie among the references given at the end of his article on the psychoneuroses in the eighth edition of Cecil's *Textbook of Medicine*; Dejerine's book is not mentioned by either author.

The milder neuroses occur chiefly in patients whose emotional maladjustment is slight. They complain only of physical symptoms such as fatigue, headache, and indigestion. Convinced as these patients are that their trouble is wholly physical, they would not think of consulting a psychiatrist—and they should not be treated by a psychiatrist. They should be treated by internists and general practitioners. The general physician usually knows better than the psychiatrist the means of distinguishing between functional and organic disease of the physical organism. He needs, however, to study the effect of injurious emotions on the bodily functions and learn how to correct them. I talked with recent graduates of six medical schools, and all of them told me they had received no instruction on the use of psychotherapy in the treatment of the everyday complaints of emotional origin.

Even in 1953, in our best hospitals, great harm is done to patients by members of the treatment staff who see them as cases instead of as sick human beings. As Dr. Jerome D. Frank of the Phipps Neuropsychiatric Institute, Johns Hopkins Hospital, stated in a paper read at a meeting of the American Group Psychotherapy Association, the result is that the patient thinks "the purpose of a general hospital . . . is to treat patients' bodies exclusively." He added, ". . . it is a fact of the unwritten hospital code that members of the treatment staff are not expected to be concerned with patients' personal problems . . ." and ". . . the duties of the physician are so organized that there is little time for such matters." These are strong statements, but I believe they apply to all hospitals. Dr. Sara Dubo, in a psychiatic study of children with pulmonary tuberculosis, found that it was the disease and not the children that received treatment. In one ward in which she interviewed the children she found they were afraid of the interns, called them "ghosts," and referred to the attending physician as the "head ghost."

There have been voices crying in the wilderness for nearly a century at least, and probably longer, proclaiming that hospital patients are persons and should be treated as such. Let us listen to a few of these. In 1855, in his "Letters to a Young Physician," the leading Boston physician Dr. James Jackson pointed out that the original sense of the word *cure*, which comes from the Latin *cura*, is "to take care." "The priest had the parish for his cure, the physician the sick for his." In the original sense of the word, the duty of the physician to his patients is to cure all of them.

Ernest Wagner, professor of medicine in the University of Leipzig, wrote, "We do not treat diseases, but sick human beings." This statement was made about seventy-five years ago. It is all the more remarkable because Wagner had previously been professor of pathology in Leipzig, in his work therefore dealing with the structural changes in the body wrought by disease, yet uninfluenced by his materialistic background into thinking that treatment dealt exclusively with patients' bodies.

The same criticism on the attitude of hospital physicians that Dr Frank makes today, Dr. Francis W. Peabody made in his famous lecture "The Care of the Patient" nearly a quarter of a century ago. "When a patient enters a hospital," he wrote:

> the first thing that commonly happens to him is that he loses his personal identity. He is generally referred to, not as Henry Jones, but as "that case of mitral stenosis in the second bed on the left." . . . The trouble is that it leads, more or less directly, to the patient's being treated as a case of mitral stenosis and not as a sick man. The disease is treated but Henry Jones, lying awake nights while he worries about his wife and children, represents a problem that is more complex than the pathologic physiology of mitral stenosis. . . . But if teachers and students are inclined to take a limited point of view even toward interesting cases of organic disease, they fall into much more serious error in their attitude toward a large group of patients who do not show objective, organic, pathologic conditions and who are generally spoken of as having "nothing the matter with them." Up to a certain point, as long as they are regarded as diagnostic problems, they command attention; but as soon as the physician has assured himself that they do not have organic disease, he passes them over lightly.

The other day it was reported to me that the chief of a medical outpatient clinic said that all neurotic patients should go to the psychiatric clinic for treatment. He should have known better. The treatment of the simple neuroses belongs in the field of general medicine. As Peabody so well pointed out, "In the first place, the differential diagnosis between organic disease and pure functional disturbance is often extremely difficult, and it needs the broad training in the use of general clinical and laboratory methods which forms the equipment of the internist. Diagnosis is the first step in treatment." I might add that the psychiatrist is often confused as to the significance of bodily symptoms such as severe pain in the chest or abdomen. Not long ago, a woman suffering from anxiety was referred by me to a psychiatrist for confirmation of the diagnosis. A thorough examination had shown that the patient was free from organic disease, although she complained bitterly of severe pain in the region of the gall bladder. It was a simple case of anxiety neurosis, yet the psychiatrist reported to me that he would like to have another X-ray examination of the gall bladder before making a diagnosis. The average internist is no more ignorant of what goes on in his patient's head than the average psychiatrist is of the functional disturbances located below the collar.

Peabody told me he had not read Dejerine's work but had learned and taught the simple method of psychotherapy described by T. A. Ross in *The Common Neuroses*. It was his conviction that the majority of the emotionally maladjusted patients "can be helped by the internist without highly specialized psychologic technique, if he will appreciate the significance of functional disturbances and interest himself in their treatment. The physician who does take these cases seriously—one might say scientifically—has the great satisfaction of seeing some of his patients get well not as a result of drugs or as the result of the disease having run its course, but as the result of his own individual efforts."

Every medical student should have instilled in his heart and mind the truth so well stated by that leading German internist and teacher Rudolf Krehl when he wrote that the physician "is only a true physician when he seeks to know and to influence the inner life of the patient." Lord Horder defines successful medicine as "understanding touched with sympathy."

Dr. Merrill Moore, visiting neurologist at the Boston City Hospital, states in a recently published paper that "there are already hundreds of psychiatric problems on the wards of the Boston City Hospital that are not being adequately cared for."

The word *psychiatry* comes from words meaning "mind" and "healing." Since a physician is "one skilled in healing," it is the duty of the physician to practice psychiatry—his skill in healing—to treat the mind as well as the body, for to do otherwise is to neglect the whole man. To establish close, friendly, personal relations with a patient is an elementary form of psychiatric therapy.

When the Medical Clinic of the Boston Dispensary was reorganized in 1927, the staff took a special interest in the symptoms and diagnosis of the psychoneuroses. Kaplan and Davis found by actual count that such cases constituted 36 per cent of 2,000 consecutive admissions to the clinic. Several studies were made. In one of these, Ayman showed that the early symptoms in hypertension were identical with those in the psychoneuroses. Later, an experimental study of pain of psychic origin was conducted by Golden, Rosenthal, and Pratt.

Even if the young physicians had been trained in the use of psychotherapy, effectual individual treatment would have been impossible, the number of cases was so great. To cope with the situation, group therapy was begun. This was in April, 1930. Within a few weeks it was apparent that this form of treatment was worth while. It has been continued to the present time, a period of 23 years. I determined at the outset that I would use the methods I had learned from the writings of Dejerine and which I had employed successfully with private patients for many years. Dejerine held that:

> reasoning by itself is indifferent. It does not become a factor of energy or creator of effort; but the moment an emotional element appears, the personality of the subject whose mentality one is seeking to modify is moved and affected by it. . . . Psychotherapy depends wholly and exclusively upon the beneficial influence of one person on another. One does not cure an hysteric or a neurasthenic, nor change their mental condition, by reasoning or by syllogisms. They are only cured when they come to believe in you.

At the outset, I had no plan for conducting the meetings except to address the group as if talking to a single patient. I decided that I would make no preparation for the meetings in the form of a formal lecture or address of any kind. If that had to be necessary for success, no busy internist could give the time required week after week. The plan would therefore not be practicable unless psychiatrists or psychologists were available; and in the majority of medical outpatient clinics, they would not be available.

I spoke to the group informally on the nature of their emotional maladjustments and how to rectify them. It was a short talk, lasting about ten or fifteen minutes. I was appealing primarily to the emotions of the members; I did not reason by argument, which, as Dejerine has pointed out, is not sufficient in itself to change the state of mind.

We soon adopted a plan of procedure which has been followed ever since. The meeting begins with a roll call. Each member gives his name and states the number of sessions attended. A slip of paper is given him by a "floor secretary," and on it he writes a signed statement of his present condition. These reports are collected, and the leader reads them to the group without indicating the name of the writer. The slips are then arranged by him in three piles. If the member is feeling well, the slip is placed in the pile to the right; if the condition is stationary or "a little better," in the center pile; and if symptoms are still present, in the one to the left. The number in each lot is then announced. The great majority of the reports are usually favorable. The leader knows how many of the twenty or more present need individual help and how many are doing well. Appointments for personal interviews are made for those whose symptoms persist. This procedure thus serves as a screening process.

A relaxation exercise with eyes closed follows the reading of the reports of the present condition of the members. The short talk given by the leader is followed by testimonies of improvement or by a question period.

We were amazed at the speed with which a change in the emotional state was often effected. This was apparent soon after the group was organized. One of the three women who were the first members of the class got a job within three weeks although she had not worked for the previous five years owing to her ill health.

I have looked over the reports handed in at the last meeting. Twelve members are doing well, five are somewhat improved, and eight are still complaining. This is an unusually large number with symptoms still persisting. The previous week there were thirteen doing well, five stationary, and only three who needed individual help. Typical reports handed in that week were: "Good morning, I am feeling fine and I look forward to coming to this wonderful class." From the middle pile: "Feel good this morning, but have not learned yet to cope with my anger and to control my mind." And from the left-hand column: "Could it be possible, subconsciously, I do not want to get well?"

In the twenty-two years from 1930 to 1952, 3,434 patients have been admitted to the class. There were 566 who attended only one session, indicating by their failure to return that they did not wish to follow this form of treatment. Most of them insisting that their symptoms were due to organic disease, they were referred back to the Medical Clinic. In these cases, the symptoms persisted.

Persons returning for a second meeting are entered as members of the class. These now total 2,868 (84 per cent). New members are urged to come five times before concluding that group therapy is not improving their condition. Those who have attended five times or more number 1,469, 51 per cent of all those enrolled as members.

A large percentage of the members report that they are much improved. Many state that their symptoms have entirely disappeared. To our astonishment, a large number continue to attend the meetings after their recovery. Our records show that 185 members have attended 25 meetings or more, and 62 have attended more than 100 times. The presence and testimony of those who have regained their health in the class is great encouragement to new members. There is a remarkable spirit of comrade-ship among the members in spite of differences in race and religion. They say that they like to come to a place where they are understood and ap-preciated and that they continue to profit from the meetings.

One member who entered the class in the summer of 1930 has at-tended 619 times. She had suffered from severe manifestations of hysteria. Her condition had been mistaken for chronic arthritis, as she had severe pain in the joints on even slight movement. She recovered within a few weeks after entering the class. During World War II her four sons were in the military service, but in spite of natural anxiety for their safety she re-mained well.

Giles W. Thomas, in a historical review of the development of group psychotherapy, published a chart in which our method was placed midway between the pure analytical and the pure repressive inspirational proce-dures. A better designation of our method would be emotional reeduca-tion and persuasion, terms used by Dejerine in describing his method of individual therapy.

During the past 17 years our work in group psychotherapy has been carried on by men of outstanding ability. Winfred Rhoades, consulting psychologist, was a full-time worker for ten years. He organized an eve-ning group for day workers and conducted the morning class after my re-tirement. Out of his experience he wrote *The Self You Have to Live With*, which was reprinted fifteen times, and other helpful books. Outpatients of the Medical Clinic of the Boston Dispensary were referred to him in all cases diagnosed as a psychoneurosis. He would take a detailed history of their emotional life and invite them to enter the class for group therapy. When he retired, this part of the work was taken over by Dr. Rose Hilferd-ing, whose help has been acknowledged by hundreds of the patients that have been referred to her. The classes were conducted by Dr. Paul E. Johnson, professor of the psychology of religion in the Graduate School of Theology, Boston University, who for over five years worked with strik-ing success.

The present director of the group is the psychiatrist, Dr. David Lan-dau, a member of the Dispensary staff. He is assisted by Dr. Joseph H. Kaplan, an internist with large experience in the treatment of the neuro-ses. In recent years the Monday evening class has been under the consecu-tive direction of two clergymen with advanced training in therapeutic counseling and group therapy: Rev. Robert E. Leslie and Rev. James H. Burns. The former is now chaplain of the Boston State Hospital for men-tal patients, and the latter is chaplain of the Massachusetts General Hos-pital. The present director of our evening group is the Rev. Donald L. Col-burn. I believe that clergymen who have done graduate work in psychol-ogy can carry on group psychotherapy successfully if associated with a physician trained in psychotherapy.

In addition to the weekly morning and evening classes, there was for a short time an afternoon class, successfully conducted by Dr. Herbert L. Harris of our staff, which was terminated only when he entered the military service. Dr. Harris has published an excellent study of group psychotherapy.

The distinguished psychiatrist, Dr. Alfred Hauptmann, formerly director of the neuropsychiatric clinic at the University of Halle, Germany, served us as consulting psychiatrist from his arrival in America until his untimely death. After a thorough study of the method and the patients at the Boston Dispensary, he wrote "there is convincing proof that at least 90 per cent of the neurotic patients who fill the offices of physicians of all specialties and who throng outpatient departments of our hospitals . . . can be successfully treated by the Pratt method."

9

GROUP THERAPY AND
THE PSYCHIATRIC CLINIC

L. Cody Marsh

Two previous communications[1] described certain projects in an attempt to treat frankly psychotic individuals by the use of group therapy. In the latter communication on this subject, brief reference was made to group therapy projects with psychoneurotics in the open community.

I now wish to give a more detailed description of these experiments and those which have been performed since the writing of that report.

Private psychiatry is available to very few persons, principally on account of its necessarily high cost. Whereas physicians in other specialties see four or five and even more persons in an hour, a psychiatrist ordinarily requires an hour for each patient. We are constantly being asked, "When are you going to develop a type of psychiatric therapy which is financially within the reach of the average patient with the average sized purse?"

Those who cannot afford to pay the fees of a private psychiatrist have ordinarily but one alternative, and that is the psychiatric clinic. These clinics leave much to be desired. In the first place, they have a morbid taste to them, a taste which has been built up in the mind of the community and for which we psychiatrists are not entirely responsible. Then it is not always possible to have psychiatrists for these clinics who can give regular attention throughout the treatment history of all cases.

To be sure there is the psychopathic ward of a growing number of general hospitals, but these suffer from unsavory reputations built up principally by the fact that the psychopathic ward is too often the place where the community's inebriates are sobered. What is far worse, it is the place where the criminals and near criminals and other notorious characters are housed for "observation." Thanks to the energy of the press for morbid stories, the psychopathic ward of the general hospital is about as inviting

Reprinted from the *Journal of Nervous and Mental Diseases*, Vol. 82, 1935, pp. 381-392.

to the twentieth-century public as the Bridge of Sighs was to the medieval populace. Another objection to the psychopathic ward is that it has the setup and general coloring of a typical hospital ward, and so called "nervous people" and others who require psychiatric care do not feel that they are *sick* and do not wish to be treated as such.

The private sanatorium for nervous diseases is also beyond the reach of the average purse, and very few of them have an Outpatient Department.

Lastly there is the State Hospital, and many of our large cities have these. To be sure, an all too few of them are becoming interested in maintaining an Outpatient Department, but the average citizen, no matter how pressing his emotional conflicts may be, certainly does not wish to admit to himself, much less to his friends, that he is going to the Outpatient Department of "Such and Such an *Insane Asylum*."

In psychiatry, we are dealing with a group of people who, consciously or unconsciously, cling to their maladies because they are serving a very definite purpose, whether they are aware of this or not. The result is that it is only with the greatest difficulty that they can be induced to take any form of treatment. Persons suffering from other maladies than those grouped under psychiatry generally seek treatment energetically and are more or less glad to cooperate. For this reason it is all the more important that we, in psychiatry, offer not only a form of treatment which is financially accessible to patients but which is so adroitly and cleverly presented that this therapy becomes attractive and disarms the sufferer of his forebodings.

THE GROUP APPROACH

Group therapy is not a new thing. The students who clustered about such ancients as Pythagoras, Socrates, Zoroaster, and probably most of the classic philosophers were partly seekers for knowledge, but they were also seekers for emotional help. Many of those early teachers conducted the so-called peripatetic schools, wherein the students walked about with the teacher as he taught. The physical effort involved in these walks, together with the interesting sights encountered, probably combined with the instructor's teachings, to make a form of group therapy as well as a form of education.

Religion has utilized the forces bound up in crowd psychology to produce cures, both alleged and real.

At the Boston Dispensary, Dr. Pratt has successfully treated psychoneurotics in whom organic lesions could not be demonstrated, by the class method.

I have reported certain values of this type of approach for those who are frankly psychotic. It is freely granted that there are types of psychoneurotics whose sufferings are said to be made worse by being placed in a group. However, I have found that where the class work is supplemented with individual attention that this objection is overcome.

There is a compulsion at work in the group which is rarely at work with equal force when the physician meets the patient privately. Another advantage of the group treatment is that the transference is a group transference and a less impersonal one than is made in private treatment. The patient not only makes the transference to the physician but to the group. The transference is more readily broken.

The patient comes to regard the proceeding as an educational one and takes a more sunny attitude toward it. Since he sees that others in the group whom he can respect do not differ greatly from himself, he concludes that he is not in a morbid situation.

The class also takes on a certain enthusiasm which one rarely gets in a private contact. Because of this enthusiasm and the compulsion at work in the group, the case seems to move on more rapidly toward betterment, if not recovery. It is my experience that patients seem more willing to accept a new point of view in the group than they do when approached singly.

In going over some five hundred private cases, I believe that most psychiatrists will agree with me that something like seventy-five per cent of the material which is offered to the patient is material which could be embodied into a course of lectures. That being so, it occurred to me to devise a course of lectures which included this material and supplement this with individual work for the more intimate and specific matters which persons naturally dislike to discuss in an open class.

It has seemed to me that patients also liked the *impersonality* of the class situation. In spite of one's success in developing the so-called objective or psychiatric attitude in the task of psychiatric therapy, private consultation necessarily constitutes a very intimate and personal situation. This very situation seems to act as a fearsome thing, against which the patients build up a whole congerie of defenses.

The descriptive matter following is drawn from the writer's experience with:

(1) *Mental Hygiene Classes Conducted at Worcester State Hospital.* These classes were primarily for the relatives of patients, but in time they came to include many others from the community, clergymen, school teachers, nurses, parents, and a various assortment of persons who could be classed as psychoneurotics and prepsychotics. Of this last group, most of them sought the help of the Group Clinic of their own accord, although there were several who were referred to the Clinic by physicians in the city of Worcester, social service agencies, Y.M.C.A., Y.W.C.A., district nurses, clergymen, and others. Of course no charge was made, although I believe that one should have been made.

In spite of the fact that most of these people had at some time taken a firm but silent vow that they would never enter the doors of what they called "the insane asylum," they seemed to enjoy coming to the classes because of their educational accent and certain other features which they considered attractive. For one thing, the psychoneurotic and psychotic recognized at a glance many persons who occupied substantial places in the community and instantly he identified himself with them, so that membership in the class gave him a tone feeling of comfort and a certain degree of pride. In short it did not strike him as a *clinic* for *queer* people or "crazy" people. Furthermore it was never called a clinic. Many of the class members were given private attention and in most instances, they sought this private attention.

(2) *A Group Class for Normal and Psychoneurotic Persons in the City of Worcester.* This class had a membership of sixteen. All were school teachers, females, and of one religious faith. The religious and sex homogeneity seemed to have certain advantages. This was also an intelligent group and they were taken into the writer's confidence as to what he was trying to do. Because of their splendid cooperation, much was learned about what to do and what not to do in the group approach.

(3) *The Reeducational Institute in Boston.* This was founded by the author in June 1932. A large, high-ceiled studio with two small entrance rooms was engaged for the purpose. The studio was furnished with chairs, blackboard, grand piano, and attractively decorated, and gave the atmosphere of a classroom rather than of a cold treatment room. Twelve series of classes were held in this studio in the course of a year. Classes contained normal persons, physicians, clergymen, educators, teachers, nurses, college students, and so on, and also others who were frankly psychoneurotic, prepsychotic, and others definitely psychotic. This particular experiment, which I have called the Reeducational Institute, gave very gratifying results. Certain social agencies referred cases, but only five physicians in Boston referred cases, although announcements were sent to some two thousand. In this connection I have often wondered what the average physician does with those cases which should be referred to a psychiatrist. In a previous paper I once mentioned that of a long series of patients I had admitted to a State Hospital, and all of whom had family physicians, only in a scant half dozen had these physicians referred the case to a psychiatrist. Certainly the psychiatric clinics are few, and they also are not overcrowded, so I wonder again what the medical profession does about cases which are referable to a psychiatrist.

PROCEDURE

(1) *Enrollment.* Patients were enrolled as *students*. In the case of some of the classes, these students signed a pledge to give their fullest co operation in the course, to do the assigned homework, and to be regular

and prompt in attendance. The pledge went into some detail as to what was to be accomplished in the course and was, in fact, called the "Psychiatric Pledge." Ordinarily tuition was payable in advance, the understanding being that time taken privately with the instructor was to be an additional cost.

(2) *The Lecture Course.* The course consisted of four lectures. The following is a brief outline of the lecture material:

> *Family Situation.* A constructive sociological study of one's own family to obtain a sunny and sympathetic understanding of family relationships and the role of each member in the family drama. The meaning of "good family" and "good birth."
> *Foundations of Personality in Childhood.* Formation of habits of feeling and thinking which condition us throughout life. Beginnings of play life and dissipation trends. School life. Significance of the Intelligence Quotient. The orderly use of the mind.
> *Economic Equipment.* Job integration, aptitudes, and ambitions. Job behavior. Production drive.
> *Emotional Life.* Understanding one's emotional pattern. The conflict between love and fear. Emotional Agility, the measure of one's modifiability. "Monkey Wrenches" in the emotional machinery. Emotional outlets.
> *Social Life.* Social assets and liabilities. The development of charm and "personality." Sex attraction. Small talk. Free association.
> *Religious Life.* The conflict between religion and modern needs. The new ethics. A psychiatric interpretation of sin, conscience, faith, and so on.
> *Sex Life.* A short history of the philosophies of sex. Influence of sex glands on behavior. Dangers of adolescent period. Values and dangers of sex repression and sex indulgence. Love life and marriage at the juvenile, adolescent, and adult levels.
> *Abnormal People.* Beginnings of "mental trouble" in the rigid, shut-in, and selfish personalities. Common types of nervousness, their meaning and management.
> *Normal Adult Personality.* Health without fads, control over environment, healthy emotional mechanisms, thrift, happiness, the open mind, integrated reaction to life, free association, fact-facing, self-understanding, ability to play, articulacy, social ease, success in small things, security feeling, sense of freedom, satisfactory family and love life, independence without pugnacity, lovableness, push.

In several instances students repeated the lecture course, a few of them three and four times. In the deeply seated neuroses, patients even in classwork put up formidable resistances to instruction. However, this is not so marked in the class approach as in the individual approach. The group compulsion tends to overcome these resistances. It may be said, parenthetically, that neurotics tend to put up resistances to any type of instruction. This accounts in part for the difficult time that most neurotics have in all educational institutions.

(3) *Questions and Answers.* When the lecture was concluded, opportunities were given for asking questions. At first students had to be encouraged by writing out questions and leaving them on the instructor's desk. After the first session, however, few questions were written and, in general, students tended to become amazingly frank in asking the most intimate and personal questions which were clearly descriptive of their own difficulties. Oftentimes the instructor asked for answers from class members, and occasionally a consensus of opinion would be taken. It was not long before each class developed a sound mental hygiene point of view. The class thus became a democratic, educational project wherein the instructor was rather a moderator than a lord.

(4) *Class Atmosphere.* The instructor was always careful to maintain an atmosphere of academic dignity. The language used was rarely scientific, that is, the writer rarely indulged in the "slang," "lingo," or "neologisms" of psychiatry. On the other hand, popular slang was not used, except rarely with apologies. On the other hand, the atmosphere was kept sunny, and the subject matter was handled with a certain lightness of touch. The writer believes that there are great dangers in presenting mental hygiene or the subject matter of psychiatry, unless an air of sunniness and lightness of touch is maintained. Students in this type of a setup must be impressed from the outset that they are not queer, that the subject is not queer, but that, on the other hand, they are people like any other group of persons and that the subject matter is just as normal, sunny, informative, and valuable as any other subject.

The emphasis in the class atmosphere is on *teaching* rather than on *treating*. During the actual lecture period, the atmosphere was distinctly dignified, moderately formal, and academic. But before and after class, the students were encouraged to be sociable, and if they showed a tendency here and there to be rowdyish, this was ignored. Flowers were always placed in the classroom, and the writer generally saw to it that there was someone who could play the grand piano or sing before and after class, but always in a spontaneous fashion. If the group or any part of it wanted to sing, they did so, but the initiative came from the students and not from the instructor, who stood apart from all of these activities. It was remarkable, at times, how these spontaneous social activities socialized the whole group, including two incipient, paranoid praecox young men who looked quite hopeless on admission. This latter situation suggested that there may be great therapeutic values in hazing, for oftentimes students seem to have the ability, by means of hazing, of correcting situations which the "prof" would rarely reach. At least some mild hazing did great things for these two paranoid young men. It is suggested that in attempting to do or improve upon this experiment that this particular feature be encouraged, perhaps with some backstage instruction. Neither the psychiatrist nor the teacher can haze. But students may haze their fellows.

(5) *Organization*. Students were assigned to various tasks, so that by the time the lecture course was completed, each one had done something which gave him or her a sense of ownership in the project. They were assigned to such special tasks as being monitors, "greeters," "introducers," to arrange chairs, care for the flowers, clean the blackboard or write thereon the lecture outline, and in keeping the roll. These activities tended also to dispel the atmosphere of morbidity which is apt to cling to things psychiatric, especially the clinic.

(6) *Notes*. Students were always asked to take notes, and whether they took them or not, they were always given pencils and paper if they did not bring notebooks. The art of taking notes, like the art of studying, is something that very few people learn. It was observed that even college people would, oftentimes, prefer to listen without note-taking. There should be some place in our education plan to teach students how to listen to a lecture, how to take notes, and how to study. After all, these are tokens of our powers of attention and concentration. Neuroses often develop from failures, and failure may be due to an inability to listen, or to observe, or to take notes, or to study. Some attention was given to this with some of the groups, and with profit. However, the notes are not an end in themselves, and it is granted that most of the notes should be taken in the head.

(7) *Grading*. In certain of the courses, each student was given a grade on the following points:

(a) Attendance
(b) Punctuality
(c) Attentiveness
(d) General cooperation
(e) Standing with class members
(f) Evident improvement
(g) Avowed improvement
(h) Insight and judgment

These grades were discussed with the student when he came for the private interview after the lecture course was completed. In one class the students were asked to grade each other on most of these points. In this one instance, it was valuable.

(8) *Outside Reading*. At one time I was rather enthusiastic about giving outside reading to those who have so-called mental difficulties. I am beginning to feel now, however, that it is like certain drugs which we use in medicine, that is, they are very valuable if given under the direction of a physician but never ought to be self-administered. It may be that we have not yet developed the right kind of mental hygiene literature. At least my

feelings are mingled about the advisability of giving outside reading in psychiatry or related subjects. Anyone familiar with the general type of person who registers for "Abnormal Psych" in our colleges must agree that study of these things is only an intellectual achievement and not an emotional one. Some of the best authorities I know on the subjects of mental hygiene and psychiatry are also the unhappiest people I know.

I found it more valuable to send students to the library to work up a little outline on some cultural but unrelated subject as a test of their powers of attention and concentration.

(9) *Treating Each Other.* In most of the classes some of the students were asked to assist the instructor in "teaching" some classmate. In most of these cases the assistant so deputized was one of the outstanding class problems. But in helping a confrere, he was inspired to make an effort which he would not otherwise make. This also gave the instructor an opportunity to give experience to certain ones who were interested in the project. Of these, two were clergymen, a physician in general practice, a young psychiatrist, two social service workers, two mothers with problem children, and a Salvation Army official.

Oftentimes when the instructor noted a flagging interest in a student, an assignment to assist "teaching" another student restored his interest.

(10) *Class Exercises.* First of all there were the exercises which bore directly upon the subject matter. The first one was the preparation of the family case history. The class members were asked to make a family case study of their own families, but with the objective point of view rather than the usual, carpingly critical point of view, which ordinarily characterizes the family member. A form for these studies was put on the blackboard, discussed, and questions answered. Other and similar group tasks were:

(a) My Earliest Memory
(b) Ingredients of My Inferiority Complex
(c) Things I Am Afraid Of
(d) Emotional Monkey Wrenches
(e) Disarmament Conference of the Human Heart
(f) Social Assets and Liabilities
(g) Sources of Inspiration and Happiness
(h) Night and Day Dreams

These classroom tasks, if one made contribution to them, gave an opportunity for a good deal of laughter and also for each one to see that most of the material in the secret recesses of his heart was not sinful, or morbid, or abnormal and that he was quite like anybody else. These tasks also assisted the class members in making out their own private tabulations under the above headings.

In addition to this purely academic work and apart from the spontaneous stunts in which students indulged before and after class, they were required to do certain socializing things under the direction of the instructor:

(a) Class was required to organize within five minutes at the third lecture.

(b) Occasionally the class was given tap dancing instruction en masse. This was found most valuable and would have been used more had the finances of the Institute permitted it. The writer knows of nothing that is better calculated to limber up an individual or a group. It served as an emotional stramonium.

(c) In a few instances the class was conducted as an informal dramatic group. This is also very helpful. The shyest person, for example, is willing "to play" the part of the gayest social lion, and this eventually gives him the courage to *live* something approaching that.

(11) *Homework.* Each student was asked to write out and hand in his own personal tabulations under the headings listed in paragraph (10) above. In addition he wrote a "mood history," so that I could ascertain what his favored emotional mechanisms were and thus help him make a better selection of these mechanisms, if necessary, planning and developing new and better ones. He was also asked to make a list of his problems, first of all to find out what they were. They are ordinarily profound secrets to most people. In some instances, class members were asked to make a brief outline of their love life history, their job history, and a simple description of their physical development and illnesses.

(12) *"Private Consultation."* The writer believes it is highly important in psychiatric work to rid ourselves of this expression for reasons which have been given. The expression was not used at the Institute, and this particular task was always referred to as "tutoring" or "coaching." As a rule, the students sought this, and this was a valuable bit of psychology. If the instructor suggested to the student that he had better have some private tutoring, he was quite apt to put up defenses which had to be overcome. If he asked the instructor for it, he brought to the task a genuine interest and at least some enthusiasm. However, he was not given the tutoring until he had completed the lecture course. In most cases, he came to this private hour with a definite list of questions and problems written out. He knew most of his needs and was ready to receive suggestions about them. Most of this did not require more than two or three hours of private consultation. They were charged a reduced coaching fee, where they had limited finances. Cases referred by welfare organizations were charged five dollars an hour. In several instances my assistants took over this task, and with credit to themselves. Certain agencies advised me that, whereas they had been lugging along for months, at considerable expense, problem people referred to the Institute, the work we had done at very slight expense had relieved the welfare agency of any further responsibility and cost.

Doubtless the great majority of people who are ordinarily being carried on the backs of our welfare agencies are people who need a constructive job in mental hygiene, rather than food, clothing, and money allowances.

(13) *Physical Examination.* In most cases, the physical examination was included "among the privileges for which tuition was paid." The examination given was rather thorough and disclosed many things which needed correction, mostly mistaken ideas. The outstanding need here was to reassure the student that he did *not* have a bad heart, that he was *not* about to die of tuberculosis, that she did *not* have cancer of the breast, or that the snapping feeling felt in the head was not disintegrating nerves in the brain. Thus the value of the physical examination was more for reassurance than as an excuse for some medical treatment.

(14) *The Progress Card.* Students were asked to keep a record of their progress or lack of progress and show this frequently to the instructor. It was a single card, ruled into three columns. The first one named briefly a life situation which was a source of discomfort or unhappiness. The second column listed, quite as briefly, the usual response of the individual to this situation. In the third column the student indicated a newly planned but improved response to the situation described in the first column.

Unfortunately the finances of the Institute did not permit of a staff of social service workers, occupational therapists, and many others the writer could name who would be most helpful in the project. In a few instances, volunteer workers helped with some of these special activities, but only enough to demonstrate the great need of well-trained workers.

We indulged in one type of follow-up which was pleasurable and helpful, and that was the student reunion. These were held occasionally, and all past students were invited. They were allowed to indulge their own spontaneous activities, compare notes about progress, show each other their cards, to tell proudly of achievements of which they had previously despaired, and otherwise renew auld acquaintance. The instructor gave a brief lecture on some mental hygiene topic, suggested by what was being reported in the press, for example, "The Psychiatric Slant of the New Deal." Sometimes we had simple refreshments.

CASES TREATED

(1) Psychoneuroses
(2) Prepsychotic conditions
(3) Psychoses
     (a) Epilepsy with schizoid behavior
     (b) Postencephalitic psychoses
     (c) Involutional melancholia
     (d) Hypomanic state
     (e) Dementia praecox, simple type

(f) Dementia praecox, hebephrenic type
(g) Dementia praecox, paranoid type
(h) Traumatic psychoses
(4) Organic states with neuroses
    (a) Cardiac states
    (b) Gastric ulcer
    (c) Hay fever
    (d) Asthma
    (e) Orthopedic conditions
(5) Stammerers

Occasionally there were persons in the class who spoke little English, Italians, Russians, e.g., but they seemed to derive as much benefit as the others. The classes generally represented varying social strata and varying intellectual levels. However the lecture material was presented in the simplest language, and even those not well favored intellectually seemed to grasp nearly all of the material. The psychology of the group levels off human distinctions, and very shortly the group takes on a uniformity of interests as well as of progress.

The writer is especially enthusiastic however about "teaching" special and homogeneous groups. It is suggested that physicians dealing with such groups as cardiac, orthopedic, asthmatic, and hay fever, gastric ulcer, and diabetic cases have them taught by a consulting psychiatrist or mental hygienist in groups. This will make more certain the purely medical task of the respective specialist.

A group of stammerers, consisting of fourteen men and two women, was a special case in point. One of the secrets of the group psychology is that the group share some one great and common need. This was certainly true of the stammerers, and they were helped a great deal by the group work. Already specialists dealing with diabetes and tuberculosis, to mention but two examples, have found the value of teaching their patients in groups. Here, however, they have, for the most part, dealt with purely medical aspects of the situation. The class has been found to be not only a timesaver but a progress maker.

RESULTS

It is most difficult to appraise results in the field of psychiatry. We do not have the palpable evidences of improvement or failure of improvement which other branches of medicine enjoy. However, both the writer and those students who attended the classes feel that psychiatric patients may be treated successfully by the class method, followed by individual consultation.

It is certain that this method cuts down the expense to the patient considerably, and the method is offered as a contribution toward the solution of the problem: How shall we offer an acceptable plan for psychiatric treatment which is within reach of the average purse?

SUMMARY

1. Attention is called to the fact that facilities for private treatment of psychiatric cases, at the present time, are quite limited.

2. Attention is called to some of the shortcomings of our present facilities for psychiatric treatment.

3. Very few persons can afford the services of a private psychiatrist.

4. The group treatment of psychiatric patients has certain special advantages over individual treatment, particularly in providing a therapeutic compulsion, a helpful transference which is easily broken, an educational and attractive setup; resistances of patients are more easily overcome; enthusiasms are engendered which are not so prominent in private treatment; and the impersonality of the situation makes the patient more amenable to treatment.

5. It has been found, by experience, that at least seventy-five per cent of the material covered in private treatment of patients could be embodied in a course of lectures.

6. The author's experience with the group treatment of psychiatric patients is described.

7. It is believed that the plan, as described, is superior to the psychiatric or mental hygiene clinic, and would enable us, with present facilities, to handle a great many more patients.

8. Emphasis is placed on the belief that patients should be regarded rather as *students* than *patients*, and the process should be an *educational* one rather than a *medical* procedure.

REFERENCE

1. L. Cody Marsh, "The Group Treatment of the Psychoses," *Ment. Hyg.,* April 1931; "An Experiment in Group Therapy," *Ment. Hyg.,* July 1933.

10

THE GROUP METHOD OF ANALYSIS

Trigant Burrow

A paper that sets out with a paradoxical title can hardly be expected to invite one's confidence unless we can somehow get square with this initial misnomer. An analysis presupposes, of course, the isolation and examination of a part or element representing the structure of a system, combination, or group of elements. But biologically, a group represents a synthesis, and only its parts are susceptible of analysis. So that a group method of analysis is of its nature self-contradictory. One could as consistently speak of a synthetic method of analysis as of a group method of analysis. And yet there is in fact the group material to be confronted, and there is, as I see it, only the analytic method of confronting it. And so, in attempting to reconcile processes that are so obviously opposed—the one group or synthetic, the other individual or analytic—there is clearly some consistent explanation called for. It is this explanation for which it is difficult for me to find words. If, however, as far as may be, you will participate with me in this endeavor, I think that we may together arrive at some common interpretation that will reconcile this seeming contradiction—a contradiction that has for a long time, I confess, been too little clear in my own mind.

I think we do not realize to what extent we have come to employ the term *group* or combination in an entirely artificial and conventional sense. The landscape gardener arranges a group of trees, the historian a group of chronological events. The educator will form a group of students, the sociologist a group of welfare workers. There may be a group of scientists or ironworkers or artists. But such grouping is entirely external and arbitrary. There is no organic inherency uniting the several elements composing such groups. Where elements are assembled in such manner, what is really represented is but a collection or placing together of elements. On the

Reprinted from *The Psychoanalytic Review*, Vol. XIV, No. 3, July 1927, pp. 268-280.

contrary, when we come to speak of such a group as is represented in a colony of ants, let us say, or a herd of deer or a tribe of primitive men, we are at once connoting an assemblage of elements that is grouped into one integral whole by reason of an inner organic bond common to the several elements of which it is composed. It is this type of group that unites the elements of the species. In such organic groups the connecting link among them is an essential and instinctive one. It is not one that is separable by any arbitrary or external process of arrangement.[1]

The life of man today in the midst of his complex civilization embodies still the organic bonds of this instinctive racial unity. The essential biology of the race is not in the least altered from that of the days of man's early primitive societies. Organic principles do not vary under the variations of external circumstance. Racial instincts do not wear out with time. But something has interposed itself unconsciously within the group life of man. Unlike the groups or colonies occurring within the lower orders, man's societal life has been arbitrarily affected by this unconscious factor, and he has not been allowed to group or colonize in response to the natural behest of primary instinctive bonds. On the contrary, man has gathered or disposed himself in various forms of groupings and affiliations—social, political, economic, national, religious—that have been wholly superficial and utterly alien to him from the point of view of his instinctive group life. And so it is necessary that the synthetic and instinctive group life of primitive tribal man be very clearly distinguished from the collective or pseudogroup formations into which man has entered at the dictates of social and conventional tradition or authority.

Naturally in a group that embodies but an arbitrary collection of individuals the part or element within such an assemblage may, without jeopardy to organic instinct, be readily drawn aside and subjected to a process of isolation and examination—the process we know as analysis. Isolating the individual or part of such a conventional association of elements entails no organic breach—not any more than would the disturbance of the landscapist's arrangement of trees or the school principal's distribution of pupils. But tearing the leaves or petals from their stalk in order to analyze them is a process that necessarily severs the part under examination from functional continuity with the organic whole of which it is a part. The continuity of the organism as a whole is instantly destroyed. So with the ants removed from their colony or the deer withdrawn from their herd. But, after all, the operation of this organic group law within the life of gregarious animals is not an observation restricted by any means to the biological expert. It is a circumstance of practical utility among all intelligent keepers of wild animals. Hagenbeck was not less familiar than Darwin or Kropotkin[2] with the significance of this organic principle uniting the individuals of a species. But while we all tacitly admit that there is this tribal or racial instinct extending throughout and binding together the elements or individuals of a species, we have yet to recognize it within ourselves as *an organic principle of consciousness*. We have yet to see that this societal principle, observable in the spontaneous clusters of primitive man, exerts its instinctive and biological sway equally today within the life of civilized communities.

From these considerations I have come to an altered outlook in my analytic work. I have come to the position that, with respect to the organism of man, an analysis, which presupposes the isolation and private examination of the individual elements apart from their instinctive racial congeners, leaves out of account the larger societal organism of which the individuals are a part and without which it is not possible for them to survive in their coherent unitary life. Such an isolated process of analysis, when applied to the individual of the species man, destroys the organic integrity of the organism as a group or race as truly as we destroy the integrity of the organism composing the flower when we isolate its petal or leaf in order to examine it apart from its structural continuity with the whole. The organic principle uniting the group or societal aggregate represents functional solidarity; the isolated element represents its disruption. So that the analysis of the individual element is contradictory to the preservation of the whole. In other words, the continuity of the group and the isolation of the individual are processes which are of their nature exclusive of one another.

In order to offset this inexorable breach as it operates within the system represented by our own psychoanalytic method, with its inevitable isolation of the single individual, the group of students with whom I have in the last years been working in association have undertaken, through a long and exacting experimental method, a process of analysis that takes account of reactions as they pertain to the species as a whole. This comprehensive scheme of analysis has the merit of leaving intact the material of our societal and instinctive group life, while at the same time it proceeds from this group background to examine analytically the social as well as the personal substitutions and repressions embodied in the arbitrary collective sum or pseudo group represented in this selfsame societal organism.

In order to accept with scientific sympathy the analytic basis of this group technique, it is necessary that as analysts we forego, at least tentatively, certain personal and pseudogroup convictions—convictions that rest rather upon the artificial covenants of single individuals in their merely collective expressions than upon the organic bonds of their essential group biology. We need to rid ourselves of the idea that the neurotic individual is sick and that we psychopathologists are well. We need to accept a more liberal societal viewpoint that permits us to recognize without protest that the individual neurotic is in many respects not more sick than we ourselves. For we quite lose count of the circumstance that the neurotic in his private substitutions and distortions has merely failed to ingratiate himself in the collective confederacy of substitutions and distortions which you and I, with no less an eye to our self-protection, have had the cunning to sub-scribe to under the cover of our arbitrary, pseudogroup symptomatology. It begins to be clearer to me that only in this inclusive outlook shall we be prepared to take account of factors which otherwise are quite closed to us as social individuals thinking only of our social self-protection.

If we will make a disinterested survey of our psychoanalytic work upon its present personalistic and confidential basis of technique—a tech-nique that concerns itself solely with the isolated element or individual—I think it must become evident that, from the point of view of science, our attitude is quite sadly in arrears. The esoteric practice of closeting a patient in our private consultation room in order to hear a story of ineptitudes and maladjustments that are due to social interpositions and substitutions common to the race and therefore identical with one's own, has, I think, nowhere its counterpart in any sphere of scientific procedure. We make no secret of the various physical anomalies to which man is subject. Cardiac and digestive disorders are willingly submitted to medical investigation. Likewise diseases due to the abuse of our organisms, such as overeating, excess of alcohol, or even venereal disease, we accept quite openly in the clinic or laboratory. The reason is not far to seek. The individual no longer holds himself morally responsible for such conditions. Today he no longer regards them as providential visitations. He does not think of them as in any sense reflecting upon his personal integrity. And yet the no less or-ganic distortions represented in our emotional and sexual inadvertences and pathologies we treat in a wholly moral and semireligious manner, and in compliance with the attitude of mind we now hold toward these conditions we invite patients to meet us in secret conferences that are out of all relation to their medical and scientific significance.

Were we observing data presented in the chemical or biological labo-ratory, surely none of us would think of attempting to observe such proc-esses in any other than in a consensual scientific attitude of approach.[3] Consensual observation is synonymous with scientific precision of tech-nique. The noting of immediate data under conditions of observation that establish a correspondence of sense perceptions among the several ob-servers is the acknowledged prerequisite of the laboratory criterion. And so I think we must come to see that it is only our unconscious social resist-ances that have all this while kept us psychoanalysts from adhering to the same basis of scientific procedure that has been the acknowledged criterion in every other sphere of scientific investigation. I think we must bring a social analysis to our own social resistances and gradually recognize that in the sphere of our mental observations we have adhered to an esoteric and imprecise basis of determination which we would not for a moment have employed regarding data pertaining to any other field of observation.[4]

In the laboratory or group work of my associates and myself, such factors as sexual fantasies, the unseemliness of family conflicts, the incongruities and deceptions that mark many of our social or pseudogroup contacts become the materials of our laboratory observation. These ineptitudes, to which not only the moralist or preacher but also the layman generally holds himself, at least by implication, superior and which the psychoanalyst concedes mention of only behind closed doors, are openly presented and observed by us in sessions composed at times of as many as twenty people. After all, the point that we psychoanalysts have missed, because unconsciously we like to miss it, is not at all that an individual is a victim of sexual conflicts but that *all individuals under our present social system of repression are equally the victims of equal sexual conflicts.* The reason that the nervous patient wishes to make so deep a secret of the inadvertences of his sex life is not at all because these matters are really private to him but because society says to him "do not dare to presume that these matters are *not* private to you." And we psychoanalysts have unconsciously fallen in with the prevalent attitude of the social system that blindly bullies the so-called neurotic into inviolable self-concealment and isolation. And so we invite in him this absurdly timorous and isolated attitude toward the social system because our own social attitude is equally timorous and isolated.

I have stated what seems to me the inadequate basis of the private method of analysis. In various writings I have made as clear as I can the altered position to which I have been brought through the researches of my students and myself during recent years. It may seem to some that I have not placed sufficient emphasis upon the results of our work in the usual sense of an objective tabulation. But results in the subjective field cannot possibly have more than a theoretical meaning to those who through circumstances have felt obliged to leave entirely to others the task of securing these results. It is experimentally demonstrable that people who show most theoretical interest in the social processes which others have taken the pains to collaborate in understanding are precisely those who stand in greatest need of participating in the same group study of their own social processes. So that I would remind the reader that the spirit of the mere onlooker at processes common to all of us as social beings is very far removed from that of the direct investigator of those processes as they may be witnessed within oneself, and that "results" must of necessity have a very different connotation according as they are perceived from within or without. There have been results—very definite results—but the results people have in mind, who merely want to look at them, are results which imply something objectively pat and conclusive, like an experiment in chemistry, for instance, with its postulate and conclusion expressed in set terms of mathematical exactness. But the course and development of man's life is a process. It is a condition of continuous flow, of uninterrupted movement. It is not a static, fixed condition. So that in the sense of a neat pharmaceutical remedy, obtainable upon application, one cannot speak of results as they pertain to the instinctive and evolutionary processes of man's growth.

The reader will readily understand, though, how much more thorough and effective is the result of an analysis that stirs to the bottom not only a patient's individual situation but also whatever pseudogroup situation a patient finds himself a social participant in. This new process of analysis has the merit of uncovering complexes which are socially sustained under the covenant of the secret family-cluster as well as those occurring in the individual neurosis. Under these conditions we have experienced again and again how much more readily the schizoid, for example, resting in his intrauterine lethargy, is roused from his dreaming inactions and learns to enter into the objective immediacy of the surrounding actualities; how much more radically the hysteric is ousted from his egocentric reveries and at length lends himself to the day's constructive demands; and, finally, with what greater dispatch the cyclothymic surrenders his bidimensional mood-alternatives in favor of an adaptation to life that represents a symmetrical, unitary effort. The result of this more encompassing program, therefore, has assisted toward a rapid technique of restoration in our neurotic subjects and furthered the freeing not alone of individual but also of mass reactions as a whole, whether represented in families or in other unconscious community clusters.

In summary, certain of the outstanding results among those of us who have been dealing at first hand with our own immediate reactions are as follows:

1. The disclosure socially of a universally unconscious social suggestion (the condition first recognized scientifically by Freud in its individual expression under the term "transference").

2. The phyletic dissolution of the bipolar fixation comprising the mother-child relationship such as underlies this social hypnosis or transference as represented in each individual.

3. The determination of the completely vicarious and socially unconscious reaction represented in the factor of "sublimation."

In addition the following mechanisms have been observed and studied by us in their social setting:

1. The "vicious" alternative of the image-fixation underlying the composite mother-child relationship as it exists within the personality of each individual and the bipolar impasse of this image basis.

2. The social extension of this private image basis leading to the substitution unconsciously of social images for reality—"God," "love," "virtue," together with "marriage" and "family" regarded as "institutions." [5]

3. The social mechanism of projection as a universal manifestation and its gradual resolution into its ontogenetic source.[6]

4. The ambivalent irreconcilability of personal mood reactions within the "normal" as well as in the neurotic individual and their compulsively

alternating phases of good and bad, love and hate, praise and blame, as shown in the interreaction of these moods within the social milieu.[7]

5. The psychological identity of the pseudosexual images now commonly divided as "homo-" and "heterosexual" and the complete dissociation socially of both these components from man's societal or organic sex instinct.

6. The presence of distorted states existing in social clusters, such as paranoia, homosexuality, hysteria, and the like, but heretofore commonly regarded in clinical isolation as disease entities peculiar to the "neurotic" individual.[8]

7. The experimental evidence for *the principle of primary identification*[9] of the individual with the mother and the demonstration of a preconscious mode in its phylogenetic or societal significance that is comparable to this primary subjective phase of the infant psyche hitherto posited in regard to its ontogenetic basis.

The foregoing categories, I fully realize, cannot possibly be wholly clear to the reader in the absence of a laboratory background of experience in the study of subjective social reactions. Students of conditions which are the result of objective laboratory findings would not think of attempting to reckon with the processes leading to those findings in the absence of familiarity with the objective laboratory technique requisite to their understanding. But because of the factor of social resistances involved in the study of subjective processes those who have not as yet participated in the group study of these processes, notwithstanding their lack of training and experience, too commonly hold the subjective laboratory answerable for making a clear presentation of its findings. While the inadequacy of the preceding statements may be attributable in part to my own ineptness in formulating them, certainly the responsibility for the understanding of our methods and aims cannot rest wholly with me as long as the reader lacks familiarity with the processes and technique of the laboratory from which these results have sprung.

What the scientific inquirer is really interested to learn primarily, after all, are the advantages, if any, of the group method of analysis as compared with the restricted method that limits the analysis to conferences between the physician and his individual patient. First it should be pointed out that the group method of analysis by no means excludes individual conferences between physician and patient. In point of fact every patient's analysis begins with such personal interviews, and he is at liberty to return to them as his need demands. But it is of significance that such interviews do not rest upon the arbitrary and pseudogroup basis that presupposes only the neurosis of the patient while the physician stands as a mere onlooker in respect to it. The patient is at once expected to look at his own disorder as part of a neurosis shared very generally by a social community in which his physician is, along with him, also an integral part. From this organic group basis composed thus of two persons the patient later comes into conference with three or four individuals and gradually into the larger group conferences which may be composed of as many as eight to twelve. A significant aspect of these group sessions lies in the circumstance that the patient is from the outset observer as well as observed. He becomes at once a responsible student of our common human problems, personal and social. Besides, there is this further advantage in a patient's entering upon the group analysis. In his association with a group whether as individuals or as a whole, quite apart from the analytic sessions, he becomes part of a societal plexus, as it were, along with people pursuing an interest common with his own. Still preserving these biological amalgamations inherent to his organism he has the opportunity to form social relationships with maturer, more experienced students upon a basis that preserves throughout the day their mutually analytic aims. This means that the hysteric and paranoidal types have opportunities for social contact without being forced up against the vicarious accommodation of our socially galvanized pseudo-group adaptations. It means that the psychasthenic or precoid type of personality comes into group relationships which, while in no sense critical of his ingrowing habits of self-accommodation, do not permit him to regress into the privacy of his own introversion.

In the personal analysis the consummation upon which the analysis depends from the outset is the transference. This must be brought about and preserved at all costs. *Keine Uebertragung, keine Psychoanalyse.* In our group procedure this condition of a patient's dependence upon his physician is from the outset precluded. We know very well that the essence of the neurosis is the mother-child relationship, that this is the neurotic patient's unconscious impasse, that fixation is his unremitting quest. But, in the group, the mother-child relationship is from the very beginning submitted to consensual observation and study, and no surrogate for this relationship such as obtains in the usual technique of analysis is permitted to creep in unconsciously and defeat the real purpose of a psychoanalysis. I do not mean for a moment that there is not in each patient the tendency toward such a fixation or transference in the group situation. It is constantly present. But under conditions of group association naturally there is not the opportunity favorable to its secret lodgment and entertainment as is the case in the private work involving months of solitary confinement with the individual analyst. What would be the individual transference in a private analysis becomes neutralized in the social participation of many individuals in their common analysis.

There is further inherent in the group method the opportunity for each student to see disinterestedly the elements composing his own neurosis as they are directly reflected to him in the neurosis of another. For in a group analysis the manifestations in another are repeatedly shown to be identical with one's own. This factor of our group method is of the great est significance in its influence upon the central factor of resistance. I recall so well Freud's words at the Second International Psychoanalytic Congress in Nuremberg in the year 1911. It was in reference to a statement of Jung's. And I remember Freud's saying that the task of psychoanalysis lay not at all in the discovering of complexes but in the dissolving of resistances. It is precisely here, it seems to me, that the group technique offers its most distinctive advantage. For the essence of resistance is undoubtedly one's sense of isolation in one's own conflicts. Where conditions allow the individual to recognize the common nature of his conflicts, naturally a sense of isolation is gradually resolved and with it the resistances which are the backbone of his neurosis.

It must be remembered that our group work is still in its very beginning. There have been in all but four years of actual group analysis. The two years prior to that consisted simply of experimental variations upon the original analytic theme and in mere tentative adaptations of it. Naturally with a method that is as young as ours and still in the process of its growth other aspects are from time to time coming to light which yet remain to be tested in their fuller implication. But the outstanding interest of our work has been the realization of what is man's commonly neglected societal or essential group basis and its challenge of our commonly accepted or pseudogroup amalgamations. From this essential group basis the careful analytic study of the manifest content of our so-called social consciousness has revealed, and is daily revealing, latent elements in which there is not less contrast with our manifest social adaptations than that which Freud first discovered to be the contrast between the dream life of the individual patient and his actual or manifest adaptation as expressed in his daily life.

I do not wish to be understood as repudiating our conventional social forms of association. They undoubtedly have their place in the process of man's conscious evolution, precisely as our primitive societies had their place in the structural or organic sphere of our evolutionary scheme. I have in mind only to repudiate the substitutive factors whereby such external social groupings are made to replace the organic feelings and instincts which unite man as an integral colony, species, or race.

Persons who have become acquainted with our group method of analysis tend to think of it as an innovation in the psychoanalytic method. They seem to think that my thesis offers a departure from the original aims of Freud. I do not share their view. For this is to judge Freud upon wholly external and accidental grounds. It is to miss the internal significance of Freud's original direction of inquiry. In my interpretation the group method of analysis is but the application in the phylogenetic sphere of the individual analysis as first applied by Freud within the ontogenetic sphere.[10] In a just appraisement of the work of Freud one must not fail to recognize the essentially laboratory spirit of procedure that was Freud's approach to the study of consciousness. From the very beginning Freud attempted to replace personal prejudice with scientific observation. He observed what he saw in human consciousness not only as it exists in his patients but in himself, and he reported faithfully what he saw. This was the application to the field of consciousness of the same precision of laboratory technique that had hitherto characterized our scientific attitude of observation in respect to the biological sciences. In brief, Freud raised the study of consciousness to the sphere of the biological sciences. The result was an outrage to social sensibilities and the social mind with all the weight of its traditional social unconscious has opposed itself so compellingly to Freud's laboratory method that its extension to include the social organism was promptly intercepted.

Instead of receiving the support of a consensual group of co-workers Freud was met by an unconscious resistance that was social and pertained to the collective, pseudogroup reaction. He was alone in his position, and alone he was powerless to meet this reaction in its uncoordinated social form. This was inevitable. In the absence of a consensual societal group of co-workers it was not possible for Freud's work to proceed to the inclusion of the generic social unconscious. Though it was inherent in the very nature of Freud's discovery that a consensual laboratory spirit of observation is alone competent to envisage the problems of consciousness, the social resistance with which Freud was confronted from the very beginning is still unrecognized and unresolved within our psychoanalytic ranks. It is the position of my associates and myself, working as a group, that the pseudogroup prejudices that are the unconscious basis of our social resistance will not be resolved until we have recognized that they are as definitely unconscious a manifestation on the part of the social mind as the individual resistances that are met in the individual analysis. The condition which our group investigations have led us to emphasize is that this resistance within the social mind can no more be resolved in the absence of a social analysis than in the absence of an analysis it is possible to resolve the private resistances of the individual patient.[11] In any other recourse we become Freud's followers merely in the sense of collective, arbitrary, pseudogroup participants, and the spirit of the discoverer and of the laboratory becomes submerged under the mass weight of an imitative or competitive social unconscious. Far from being a departure from the essential significance of Freud's basic discoveries the results that are now issuing from our group analysis are simply the results which with Freud were temporarily intercepted through an absence of a consensual collaboration on the part of his social congeners.

The sum of our findings resolves itself into this. The prevailing view that man is an individual is one which the psychopathologist needs bring into serious question. Man is not an individual. He is a societal organism. Our individual analyses based upon differentiations, which along with others of our kind we have assumed to rest upon legitimate scientific ground, rest in fact upon very transient social artifices and lack the support of a true biological basis. Man's analysis as an element is his isolation as an element. And his isolation is an essential affront to an organic group principle of consciousness.

REFERENCES

1. T. Burrow, *An Ethnic Aspect of Consciousness*. Paper read at the mid-year meeting of The American Psychoanalytic Association, New York City, December 28, 1924.
2. P. Kropotkin, *Mutual Aid* (New York: Alfred A. Knopf, 1921).
3. T. Burrow, "Psychiatry as an Objective Science," *Psychoanal. Rev.*, Vol. XIII, No. 2, 1926.
4. T. Burrow, *The Need of an Analytic Psychiatry*. Paper read before the joint session of The American Psychiatric and The American Psychoanalytic Associations, New York, June 10, 1926.
5. T. Burrow, "Social Images versus Reality," *J. Abnorm. Psychol. Soc. Psychol.*, Vol. XIX, No. 3, 1924.
6. T. Burrow, *The Reabsorbed Affect and Its Elimination*. Paper read at the Sixteenth Annual Meeting of The American Psychopathological Association, New York City, June 11, 1926.
7. T. Burrow, "Our Mass Neurosis," *Psychol. Bull.*, Vol. 23, No. 6, 1926.
8. T. Burrow, "Insanity a Social Problem," *Am. J. Sociol.*, Vol. XXXII, No. 1, Part I, 1926.
9. T. Burrow, "The Genesis and Meaning of Homosexuality," *Psychoanal. Rev.*, Vol. IV, No. 3, 1917.
10. T. Burrow, "The Laboratory Method in Psychoanalysis," *Am. J. Psychiat.*, Vol. V, No. 3, 1926.
11. Just as no one has ever yet really understood the significance of the individual analysis except as he himself entered upon the individual anaylsis, so no one will by any process understand the group analysis except as he himself enters upon it. From the first Freud emphasized the futility of knowledge *about* or *in regard to* psychoanalysis. Knowledge of psychoanalysis is not an intellectual process. Resistances which are the barrier to an understanding of psychoanalysis do not reside in the intellect. Only as one submits one's own feeling, personal or social, to the process of analysis does one truly come into an understanding of psychoanalysis in the only true sense of understanding—namely, into an internal acceptance of the significance of man's unconscious processes.

11

A SUMMARY NOTE ON THE WORK
OF TRIGANT BURROW

Hans Syz

The concepts and procedures introduced by Trigant Burrow represent a pioneer undertaking in the field of social psychiatry.[1] He early took the unorthodox position that "an individual discord is but the symptom of a social discord,"[7] and that "it is futile to attempt to remedy mental disease occurring within the individual mind as long as psychiatry remains blind to the existence of mental disease within the social mind."[8] He suggested that "the psycho-pathologist must awaken to his wider function of clinical sociologist and recognize his obligation to challenge the neurosis in its social as well as in its individual intrenchments."[5]

Kurt Goldstein wrote Burrow in 1948: "You are one of the few scientists who make one feel that for him life and work are closely related."[20] This comment gives a clue to Burrow's endeavors. Applying theory to life, he questioned accustomed self-identity and its elaborate security devices which impede basic capacities for freedom and creativity. Acting upon this altered insight, Burrow included in his observation his own behavior as enacted in family, social, and professional situations.

We may distinguish four periods in Burrow's life and activities: (1) 1875-1909: youth, medical and psychological studies; (2) 1909-1920: training with Jung, charter member of the American Psychoanalytic Association, psychoanalytic practice, activity in psychoanalytic and psychological societies, beginning emphasis on social as well as physiological aspects of behavior disorders; (3) 1920-1932: development of group- or phylo-analysis, focusing investigation on socially sanctioned forms of destructive trends (*the social neurosis*),[9, 25] organizing The Lifwynn Foundation for Laboratory Research in Analytic and Social Psychiatry; (4) 1932-1950: inten-

Reprinted by permission of the *International Journal of Social Psychiatry*, 1960, Vol. 7, No. 4, pp. 283–291.

sive group work with increasing emphasis on proprioceptive aspects of man's behavioral health and illness, differentiation of contrasting attentional patterns, and instrumental recording of associated physiological changes.

With regard to Burrow's psychoanalytic background, although he had studied with Jung, he did not side with him when it came to Jung's break with Freud. Rather he considered the positions of Freud, Jung, and Adler[3] as complementary and not mutually exclusive. Burrow thus anticipated the trend to recognize converging principles in various behavior theories—a trend that has come to the fore in recent years. Throughout, he showed the highest regard for Freud's work, and wrote him in 1925 that he had tried to extend and apply "the principles first enunciated by you to the social as well as to individual repressions." [20]

Even in his early psychoanalytic papers Burrow drew attention, not only to harmful environmental influences occurring in a patient's early family situation, but also to the close interrelation of the individual's neurosis with noxious processes embodied in the customary norm of behavior. In the years before he entered upon his group-analytic studies, Burrow referred repeatedly to "the hideous distortion of human values embodied in the repressive subterfuge and untruth of our so-called moral codes and conventions"; "normality" was in his view "nothing else than an expression of the neurosis of the race." [4]

Along with his emphasis upon "the social neurosis," Burrow early proposed concepts which for him were basic in understanding the human organism as an inherent element in the social and phylic setting, and in interpreting behavior pathology. That is, he drew attention to the "preconscious" * phase of development and to the infant's "primary identification" with the mother. For Burrow, the recognition of the "preconscious" and preconative phase of prenatal and postnatal existence with its psychophysiological continuity with the mother, entailed "no dissent whatsoever from Freud and the unconscious as envisaged by him"; in fact, it was "not only not incompatible with Freud, but . . . a requisite correlate of his teaching." [3]

The evaluation of this early stage of development was essential to Burrow's interpretation of neurotic reactions. While still engaged in psychoanalysis, he suggested that the neurosis is an accentuation and fixation of the original subjective mode of continuity which has not been brought to

---

* Burrow's "preconscious" is to be distinguished from the concept of the preconscious as generally used in present-day psychoanalysis for those phases of psychological function which are not conscious but not repressed and to a large extent capable of becoming conscious.

Clarence P. Oberndorf wrote that one of the four "most noteworthy and original among American contributions before 1920" in the field of psychoanalysis was "Trigant Burrow's emphasis of a 'primary subjective phase' in the infant chronologically preceding the Oedipus situation." [21]

mature social expression. Thus homosexuality was not interpreted as resulting from the repression of love for the mother on the objectifying level of
the Oedipus situation, but rather as a direct outgrowth or extension into
adult life of the pre-objective feeling identification with the mother. That
is, mother fixation, narcissism, and latent homosexuality were seen as different aspects of a single basic principle.[2]

A second, but interrelated, phase of interpretation was the concept
that the organism's basic physiological harmony and feeling-continuity
with the mother-organism and with the world has been interfered with by
the processes of objectivation and cognition, leading to oppositeness, ob-
sessive desire, and neurotic self-defense on an individual and social scale.
Burrow considered incest-awe as an expression of this inherent protest
against the encroachment of the cognitive, objective process upon the
spontaneous, subjective process of the "preconscious," prelibidinal phase
—as a reaction against the affront to the basic psychobiological principle
of unity. "Incest in not forbidden, it forbids itself." [4]

During his psychoanalytic period Burrow assembled much evidence
from everyday life, from dreams and pathological conditions, from the
phenomena of creative, aesthetic, and religious experience, to show the
significance of this powerfully unifying and integrative urge which is commonly expressed in incomplete, distorted, or symbolically substitutive
forms.*

In these early formulations we find also an emphasis upon physiology
which characterized Burrow's work throughout. The principle of the infant's "preconscious" identification with the mother lays stress, of course,
on physiological foundations. From these conceptions Burrow advanced
consistently toward his later neurophysiological interpretations, and toward
the practical procedure in which proprioceptive awareness of motor activations plays an important role.

These interpretations embody a far-going change in perspective. As
mentioned above, Burrow considered neurotic disorders not primarily as
individual events but rather as symptoms of a general social or phylic disturbance. Conflict was not traced primarily to society's interdiction of
instinctive and aggressive trends, to an antagonism between primitive impulses and supposedly mature and socially coordinated forces. The essential conflict was seen to consist rather in the internal imposition of the
objectivating, symbolizing function upon the early unitary mode of existence. This basic interference, as Burrow increasingly emphasized, constitutes a pathogenic complication which, aggravated by social conditioning,
is a source of antagonism, detachment, and image-preoccupation, thus
causing repression, neurotic developments, and social conflict. That is, together with his challenge of "the social neurosis," there was with Burrow

---

* Burrow's unpublished material on the "Preconscious" has been collected and
edited by the late W. E. Galt; it is now being prepared for publication.

a consistent recognition of an integrative matrix for individual growth and phylic cohesion. The individual was always considered as an interreactive part of the larger sociobiological structure, an entity whose growth and freedom springs from its integration within the phyloörganism. This positive emphasis represents a significant departure from Freud's concept that antisocial forces are basic in human organization. Burrow's discrimination between an organismically-rooted feeling continuity and image-dependent, egocentric complications which characterize "transference" relations throughout[11] is important for the understanding of behavioral pathology as well as for the therapeutic or reconstructive process.

Burrow's group-analytic studies had their start in 1918 when he accepted the challenge of his student-assistant, Clarence Shields, that they reverse the roles of analyst and student.[10] This mutual analysis later included other participants, both normal and neurotic. The *group analysis*[13, 22] which thus developed took place in everyday activities as well as in formal laboratory meetings. The approach was a phenomenological one and at the same time revaluative, uncovering affects and motives existing in group interactions at the moment of exploration. It meant dealing directly with a social situation in which the psychiatrist's, the observer's, own perceptions, attitudes, and concepts were inquired into as part of the social reaction tissue. The attempt was made to relinquish the restrictions of outlook and feeling due to established roles and status, and to get in closer touch with dependencies, moralistic pretenses, self-justifications, and defenses, as they are commonly enacted. The purpose was to determine the latent content of these manifestations which could be observed in the individual's self-structure, in the interactions of the participants, and in the mood pervading the group as a whole. After consistent and long-continued observation, these interrelated phenomena appeared increasingly as variations of a common theme, as interreactive components of a total constellation in which the defensive emphasis upon the symbolically isolated self plays a major role (Burrow's *social images*[5] and *"I"-persona*).[12] The investigative group effort centered upon clarification of this socio-individual problem[23] of autistic image-bondage[31] and its relation to clinically neurotic as well as overtly antisocial behavior.

A development of this social analysis was the incorporation of The Lifwynn Foundation (1927), which was established by Burrow and a few of his co-workers to give a community setting to their group- or phylo-analytic studies. A distinguishing mark of the foundation's function was that its own administrative activities were material for the study which it was organized to sponsor. Thus a modest beginning was made in investigating, by specific procedures, distortions of community organization.

In the course of this investigation, it gradually became evident that behavior analysis had definite limitations in dealing with the socially patterned autistic trend. The frustration of accustomed self-identity and its socially sanctioned value systems led to an unforeseen development: with consistent challenging of habitual affect-reactions, attention shifted to the perception of tensions related to specific neuromuscular activations.[14, 17, 26] Local strain in the forepart of the head (Burrow's *affecto-symbolic segment*) came to awareness which seemed to be directly related to self-referent affect-imagery. With continued experimentation, this oculo-facial stress was increasingly sensed against the tensional pattern perceptible throughout the organism as a whole. This proprioceptive reconstellation was found to go along with a dissipation of self-reflective and affect-laden images of others and oneself, and with the affirmation of an inclusive feeling attitude, with more objective observation, and with more direct application to immediate tasks. While the shift of attention from behavioral imagery to the "feeling sensation" of endorganismic patterns was at first only momentary, it gradually became possible to maintain the integrative orientation for longer periods and to carry it into everyday activities.

These observations led Burrow to distinguish between two modes of attention, between *ditention,* the usual self-reflexive attitude, and *cotention,* in which a more direct and organismically-oriented contact is established with the world. Instrumental recordings indicated that changes in respiration, eye-movements, and electrical brain-wave patterns accompany the shift from ditention to cotention, further supporting the conclusion that we are dealing with a deep-seated organismic reorientation.[16]

The sweeping discrimination between two major attentional modes cuts across academic and conventional classifications, and implies a unifying interpretation of behavior disorder. Viewing the social neurosis always from the background of the organism's inherent capacity for coordination and species solidarity, Burrow introduced the terms *phylobiology, phylopathology,* and *phyloanalysis.*[15, 18, 27] These concepts take full account of the pervasive character of the defective biosocial dynamics which in Burrow's view could not be relegated to any specific type or phase of personality or culture. Biology and the behavior sciences provide increasing evidence for this phyloörganismic basis.[19, 24, 29] Burrow proposed that the integrated mode of attention (cotention) be investigated further with regard to its potential significance as a criterion of behavioral health. The altered perspective thus developed by practical measures seemed to substantiate the common denominator to which Burrow, in his group-analytic studies, had related important dynamics of behavior disorder. While in his later formulations Burrow continued to emphasize the noxious implications linked to man's use, or rather misuse, of image-symbol and language, the recourse in this dilemma was not seen as a return to a primordial state of unity. The aim was rather to submit the problem to "consensual observation"[6] and to apply measures which would reinstate basic, "phylic" integration on a mature and culturally advancing level.[28]

It is evident that Burrow's early studies in group analysis had considerable influence upon the later developing group psychotherapies, though this influence often remained unacknowledged. In fact, his investigation of the individual's neurotic deviation as part of the deflection within the interrelational structure of groups, was the only forerunner in the United States of dynamic group psychotherapy. However, there are distinguishing marks, in that Burrow's group- or phylo-analysis was (1) essentially an investigative procedure; (2) it included in its scope the behavior defect in community life, as well as in the observer himself; and (3) it made use of specific proprioceptive measures for bringing about constructive behavioral modifications on the socio-individual level.

I should like to mention that these behavior studies, especially in their later phases, were not without reintegrative influence upon individual participants, and in my own therapeutic work with neurotic patients I find this background most valuable.[24, 29, 30] However, the essential goal of the phylobiological studies continues throughout to be concerned with the release of healthy function within the community.

It may be in order to add a few remarks regarding the reaction to the concepts and procedures introduced by Burrow. The breaking down of established formulations, which is a prerequisite to scientific advance, is especially difficult where these formulations are tied in with our socially validated self-structure. Although there has been a thorough revision of concepts during the last fifty years in other fields of science, notably in physics, we are confronted in the field of human behavior with an especially intricate situation. I know from my own experience as a participant in group analysis how intensely the socially patterned self tends to cling to its prejudices and emotional defenses. On a social scale these resistances are indeed formidable—in the writer, the reader, and in the community generally. With regard to Burrow's formulations, several scholars have commented on what have been called "conspiracies of silence"—an almost neurotic hesitation to acknowledge one's involvement in man's behavioral predicament, and a failure to recognize the urgent need to approach it by scientific methods. Freud himself acknowledged in a letter to Burrow[20] that his irritation with some of the latter's statements had led him to misinterpretation. Perhaps the complexity of Burrow's style was an expression of this same resistance—at least he himself thought so. In any case there was lack of response on the part of Burrow's colleagues to the specific issues to which he drew attention when he presented his observations and concepts at psychiatric and psychoanalytic meetings. However, certain of Burrow's ideas reappeared later in the writings of others, and many of his formulations seem to be particularly applicable to the community problems with which we are confronted today.

It is true, we are faced with a seemingly insoluble dilemma. But while the individual investigator may feel that he can make hardly a dent in the vast problem of human discord, he can perhaps realize that he is a part of a sociobiological process to which he may make a positive contribution. A generic conception of behavior disorder does not necessarily imply that we are dealing with unalterably set dynamic formations. Rather we may have reached a stage of development in which man, as individual and group, can take an active and constructive hand in guiding his own evolution.

REFERENCES

1. Trigant Burrow, "The Psychoanalyst and the Community," *J.A.M.A.* 62:1876-1878, 1914.
2. Trigant Burrow, "The Genesis and Meaning of 'Homosexuality' and its Relation to the Problem of Introverted Mental States," *Psychoanal. Rev.* 4:272-284, 1917.
3. Trigant Burrow, "Notes with Reference to Freud, Jung and Adler," *J. Abnorm. Psychol.* 12:161-167, 1917.
4. Trigant Burrow, "The Origin of the Incest-Awe," *Psychoanal. Rev.* 5: 243-254, 1918.
5. Trigant Burrow, "Social Images versus Reality," *J. Abnorm. Psychol. & Soc. Psychol.* 19:230-235, 1924.
6. Trigant Burrow, "Psychiatry as an Objective Science," *Brit. J. Med. Psychol.* 5:298-309, 1925.
7. Trigant Burrow, "Insanity a Social Problem," *Amer. J. Sociol.* 32:80-87, 1926.
8. Trigant Burrow, "Our Mass Neurosis," *Psychol. Bul.* 23:305-312, 1926.
9. Trigant Burrow, "Psychoanalytic Improvisations and the Personal Equation," *Psychoanal. Rev.* 13:173-186, 1926.
10. Trigant Burrow, *The Social Basis of Consciousness—A Study in Organic Psychology* (New York: Harcourt, Brace; London: Kegan Paul, Trench, Trubner, 1927).
11. Trigant Burrow, "The Problem of the Transference," *Brit. J. Med. Psychol.* 7:193-202, 1927.
12. Trigant Burrow, "The Autonomy of the 'I' from the Standpoint of Group Analysis," *Psyche* (London) 8:35-50, 1958.
13. Trigant Burrow, "The Basis of Group-Analysis, or the Analysis of the Reactions of Normal and Neurotic Individuals." *Brit. J. Med. Psychol.* 198-206, 1928.
14. Trigant Burrow, "Physiological Behavior-Reactions in the Individual and the Community—A Study in Phyloanalysis." *Psyche* (London) 11:67-81, 1930.
15. Trigant Burrow, *The Biology of Human Conflict—An Anatomy of Behavior, Individual and Social* (New York: Macmillan, 1937).
16. Trigant Burrow, *The Neurosis of Man—An Introduction to a Science of Human Behavior* (London: Routledge & Kegan Paul; New York: Harcourt, Brace, 1949). Full text is included in *Science and Man's Behavior—The Contribution of Phylobiology*, by William E. Galt, ed. (New York: Philosophical Library, 1953).
17. Trigant Burrow, "Prescription for Peace—The Biological Basis of Man's

Ideological Conflicts," in *Explorations in Altruistic Love and Behavior*, by Pitirim A. Sorokin, ed. (Boston: Beacon Press, 1950).

18. William E. Galt, "Phyloanalysis—A Brief Study in Trigant Burrow's Group or Phyletic Method of Behavior Analysis," *J. Abnorm. & Soc. Psychol.* 27:411-429, 1933.

19. William E. Galt, "The Principle of Cooperation in Behavior." *Quar. Rev. Biol.* 15:401-410, 1940.

20. William E. Galt, *et al.*, eds., *A Search for Man's Sanity—The Selected Letters of Trigant Burrow, with Biographical Notes* (New York: Oxford University Press, 1958).

21. Clarence P. Oberndorf, *A History of Psychoanalysis in America* (New York: Grune & Stratton, 1953).

22. Hans Syz, "Remarks on Group Analysis," *Amer. J. Psychiat.* 8:141-148, 1928.

23. Hans Syz, "Socio-individual Principles in Psychopathology," *Brit. J. Med. Psychol.* 10:329-343, 1930.

24. Hans Syz, "The Concept of the Organism-as-a-Whole and its Application to Clinical Situations," *Human Biol.* 8:489-507, 1936.

25. Hans Syz, "The Social Neurosis," *Amer. J. Sociol.* 42:895-897, 1937.

26. Hans Syz, "Burrow's Differentiation of Tensional Patterns in Relation to Behavior Disorders," *J. Psychol.* 9:153-163, 1940.

27. Hans Syz, "Phylopathology," in *Encyclopedia of Psychology*, Philip L. Harriman, ed. (New York: Philosophical Library, 1946).

28. Hans Syz, "New Perspectives in Behavior Study—A Phylobiological Re orientation," *J. Psychol.* 31:21-27, 1951.

29. Hans Syz, "An Experiment in Inclusive Psychotherapy" in *Experimental Psychopathology*, by Paul H. Hoch and Joseph Zubin, eds. (New York: Grune & Stratton, 1957).

30. Hans Syz, "Trigant Burrow's Thesis in Relation to Psychotherapy," in *Progress in Psychotherapy*, II, Jules H. Masserman and J. L. Moreno, eds. (New York: Grune & Stratton, 1957).

31. Hans Syz, "Problems of Perspective from the Background of Trigant Bur-row's Group-Analytic Researches," *Int. J. Group Psychother.* 11:143-165, 1961.

12

A NEW THEORY OF NEUROSES

D. H. Lawrence

(A review of
THE SOCIAL BASIS OF CONSCIOUSNESS
by Trigant Burrow)

Dr. Trigant Burrow is well known as an independent psychoanalyst through the essays and addresses he has published in pamphlet form from time to time. These have invariably shown the spark of original thought and discovery. The gist of all these essays now fuses into this important book, the latest addition to the International Library of Psychology, Philosophy and Scientific Method.

Dr. Burrow is that rare thing among psychiatrists, a humanly honest man. Not that practitioners are usually dishonest. They are intellectually honest, professionally honest, all that. But that other simple thing, human honesty, does not enter in, because it is primarily subjective; and subjective honesty, which means that a man is honest about his own inward experience, is perhaps the rarest thing, especially among professionals. Chiefly, of course, because men, and especially men with a theory, don't know anything about their own inward experiences.

Here Dr. Burrow is a rare and shining example. He set out, years ago as an enthusiastic psychoanalyst and follower of Freud, working according to the Freudian method, in America. And gradually, the sense that something was wrong, vitally wrong, both in the theory and in the practice of psychoanalysis, invaded him. Like any truly honest man, he turned and asked himself what it was that was wrong, with himself, with his methods and with the theory according to which he was working?

This book is the answer, a book for every man interested in the human consciousness to read carefully. Because Dr. Burrow's conclusions,

Reprinted from *The Bookman*, November 1927, by permission of Laurence Pollinger, Ltd., and the estate of the late Mrs. Frieda Lawrence.

sincere, almost naïve in their startled emotion, are far-reaching, and vital.

First, in his criticism of the Freudian method, Dr. Burrow found, in his clinical experience, that he was always applying a *theory*. Patients came to be analysed, and the analyst was there to examine with open mind. But the mind could not be open, because the patient's neurosis, all the patient's experience, *had* to be fitted to the Freudian theory of the inevitable incest-motive.

And gradually Dr. Burrow realised that to fit life every time to a theory is in itself a mechanistic process, a process of unconscious repression, a process of image-substitution. All theory that has to be applied to life proves at last just another of these unconscious images which the repressed psyche uses as a substitute for life, and against which the psychoanalyst is fighting. The analyst wants to break all this image business so that life can flow freely. But it is useless to try to do so by replacing in the unconscious another image—this time, the image, the fixed motive, of the incest complex.

Theory as theory is all right. But the moment you apply it to *life*, especially to the subjective life, the theory becomes mechanistic, a substitute for life, a factor in the vicious unconscious. So that while the Freudian theory of the unconscious and of the incest-motive is valuable as a *description* of our psychological condition, the moment you begin to *apply* it, and make it master of the living situation, you have begun to substitute one mechanistic or unconscious illusion for another.

In short, the analyst is just as much fixed in his vicious unconscious as is his neurotic patient, and the will to apply a mechanical incest-theory to every neurotic experience is just as sure an evidence of neurosis, in Freud or in the practitioner, as any psychologist could ask.

So much for the criticism of the psychoanalytic method.

If then, Dr. Burrow asks himself, it is not sex-repression which is at the root of the neurosis of modern life, what is it? For certainly, according to his finding, sex-repression is not the root of the evil.

The question is a big one and can have no single answer. A single answer would only be another "theory." But Dr. Burrow has struggled through years of mortified experience to come to some conclusion nearer the mark. And his finding is surely much deeper and more vital, and also, much less spectacular than Freud's.

The real trouble lies in the inward sense of "separateness" which dominates every man. At a certain point in his evolution, man became cognitively conscious: he bit the apple: he began to know. Up till that time his consciousness flowed unaware, as in the animals. Suddenly his consciousness split.

It would appear that in his separativeness man has inadvertently fallen a victim to the developmental exigencies of his own consciousness. Captivated by the phylogenetically new and unwonted spectacle of his own image, it would seem he has been irresistibly arrested before the mirror of his own likeness and that in the present self-conscious phase of his mental evolution he is still standing spell-bound before it. That such is the case with man is not remarkable. For the appearance of the phenomenon of consciousness marked a complete severance from all that was his past. Here was broken the chain of evolutionary events whose links extended back through the nebulous aeons of our remotest ancestry, and in the first moment of his consciousness man stood, for the first time, *alone*. It was in this moment that he was "created," as the legend runs, "in the image and likeness of God." For breaking with the teleological traditions of his age-long biology, man now became suddenly *aware*.

Consciousness is self-consciousness. "That is, consciousness in its inception entails the fallacy of *a self as over against other selves*."

Suddenly aware of himself, and of other selves over against him, man is a prey to the division inside himself. Helplessly he must strive for more consciousness, which means, also, a more intensified aloneness or individuality: and at the same time he has a horror of his own aloneness, and a blind, dim yearning for the old togetherness of the far past, what Dr. Burrow calls the preconscious state.

What man really wants, according to Dr. Burrow, is a sense of togetherness with his fellow men, which shall balance the secret but overmastering sense of separateness and aloneness which now dominates him. And therefore, instead of the Freudian method of personal analysis, in which the personality of the patient is pitted against the personality of the analyst in the old struggle for dominancy, Dr. Burrow would substitute a method of group analysis, wherein the reactions were distributed over a group of people, and the intensely personal element eliminated as far as possible. For it is only in the intangible reaction of several people, or many people together, on one another that you can really get the loosening and breaking of the me-and-you tension and contest, the inevitable contest of two individualities brought into connection. What must be broken is the egocentric absolute of the individual. We are all such hopeless little absolutes to ourselves. And if we are sensitive, it hurts us, and we complain, we are called neurotic. If we are complacent, we enjoy our own petty absolutism, though we hide it and pretend to be quite meek and humble. But in secret, we are absolute and perfect to ourselves, and nobody could be better than we are. And this is called being normal.

Perhaps the most interesting part of Dr. Burrow's book is his examination of normality. As soon as man became aware of himself, he made a picture of himself. Then he began to live according to the picture. Mankind at large made a picture of itself, and every man had to conform to the picture, the ideal.

This is the great image or idol which dominates our civilization, and which we worship with mad blindness. The idolatry of self. Consciousness should be a flow from within outwards. The organic necessity of the human being should flow into spontaneous action and spontaneous awareness, consciousness.

But the moment man became aware of himself he made a picture of himself, and began to live from the picture: that is, from without inwards. This is truly the reversal of life. And this is how we live. We spend all our time over the picture. All our education is but the elaborating of the picture. "A good little girl"—"a brave boy"—"a noble woman"—"a strong man"—"a productive society"—"a progressive humanity"—it is all the picture. It is all living from the outside to the inside. It is all the death of sponaneity. It is all, strictly, automatic. It is all the vicious unconscious which Freud postulated.

If we could once get into our heads—or if we once dare admit to one another—that we are *not* the picture, and the picture is not what we are, then we might lay a new hold on life. For the picture is really the death, and certainly the neurosis of us all. We have to live from the outside in, idolatrously. And the picture of ourselves, the picture of humanity which has been elaborated through some thousands of years, and which we are still adding to, is just a huge idol. It is not real. It is a horrible compulsion over all of us.

Individuals rebel: and these are the neurotics, who show some sign of health. The mass, the great mass, goes on worshipping the idol, and behaving according to the picture: and this is the normal. Freud tried to force his patients back to the normal, and almost succeeded in shocking them into submission, with the incest-bogey. But the bogey is nothing compared to the actual idol.

As a matter of fact, the mass is more neurotic than the individual patient. This is Dr. Burrow's finding. The mass, the normals, never live a life of their own. They cannot. They live entirely according to the picture. And according to the picture, each one is a little absolute unto himself, there is none better than he. Each lives for his own self-interest. The "normal" activity is to push your own interest with every atom of energy you can command. It is "normal" to get on, to get ahead, at whatever cost. The man who does disinterested work is abnormal. Every Johnny must look out for himself: that is normal. Luckily for the world, there still is a minority of individuals who do disinterested work, and are made use of by the "normals." But the number is rapidly decreasing.

And then the normals betray their utter abnormality in a crisis like the late war. There, there indeed the uneasy individual can look into the abysmal insanity of the normal masses. The same holds good of the bolshevist hysteria of today: it is hysteria, incipient social insanity. And the last great insanity of all, which is going to tear our civilization to pieces, the insanity of class hatred, is almost entirely a "normal" thing, and a "social" thing. It is a state of fear, of ghastly collective fear. And it is absolutely a mark of the normal. To say that class hatred *need not exist* is to show abnormality. And yet it is true. Between man and man, class hatred hardly exists. It is an insanity of the mass, rather than of the individual.

But it is part of the picture. The picture says it is horrible to be poor, and splendid to be rich, and in spite of all individual experience to the contrary we accept the terms of the picture, and thereby accept class war as inevitable.

Humanity, society, has a picture of itself, and lives accordingly. The individual likewise has a private picture of himself, which fits into the big picture. In this picture he is a little absolute and nobody could be better than he is. He must look after his own self-interest. And if he is a man, he must be very male. If she is a woman, she must be very female.

Even sex, today, is only part of the picture. Men and women alike, when they are being sexual, are only acting up. They are living according to the picture. If there is any dynamic, it is that of self-interest. The man "seeketh his own" in sex, and the woman seeketh her own: in the bad, egoistic sense in which St. Paul used the words. That is, the man seeks himself, the woman seeks herself, always and inevitably. It is inevitable, when you live according to the picture, that you seek only yourself in sex. Because the picture is your own image of yourself: your *idea* of yourself. If you are quite normal, you don't have any true self, which "seeketh not her own, is not puffed up." The true self, in sex, would seek a *meeting*, would seek to meet the other. This would be the true flow; what Dr. Burrow calls the "Societal consciousness" and what I would call the human consciousness, in contrast to the social, or "image-consciousness."

But, today, all is image-consciousness. Sex does not exist, there is only sexuality. And sexuality is merely a greedy, blind self-seeking. Self-seeking is the real motive of sexuality. And therefore, since the thing sought is the same, the self, the mode of seeking is not very important. Heterosexual, homosexual, narcissistic, normal or incest, it is all the same thing. It is just sexuality, not sex. It is one of the universal forms of self-seeking. Every man, every woman just seeks his own self, her own self, in the sexual experience. It is the picture over again, whether in sexuality or self-sacrifice, greed or charity, the same thing, the self, the image, the idol: the image of me, and norm!

The true self is not aware that it is a self. A bird, as it sings, sings itself. But not according to a picture. It has no idea of itself.

And this is what the analyst must try to do: to liberate his patient from his own image, from his horror of his own isolation, and the horror of the "stoppage" of his real vital flow. To do it, it is no use rousing sex bogeys. A man is not neurasthenic or neurotic because he loves his mother. If he desires his mother, it is because he is neurotic, and the desire is merely a symptom. The cause of the neurosis is further to seek.

And the cure? For myself, I believe Dr. Burrow is right: the cure would consist in bringing about a state of honesty and a certain trust among a *group* of people, or many people—if possible all the people in the world. For it is only when we can get a man to fall back into his true relation to other men and to women, that we can give him an opportunity to be himself. So long as men are inwardly dominated by their own isolation, their own absoluteness, which after all is but a picture or an idea, nothing is possible but insanity more or less pronounced. Men must get back into *touch*. And to do so they must forfeit the vanity, and the *noli me tangere* of their own absoluteness: also they must utterly break the present great picture of a normal humanity: shatter that mirror in which we all live grimacing: and fall again into true relatedness.

I have tried more or less to give a *résumé* of Dr. Burrow's book. I feel that there is a certain impertinence in giving these *résumés*. But not more than in the affectation of "criticizing" and being superior. And it is a book one should read and assimilate, for it helps a man in his own inward life.

13

GROUP PSYCHOTHERAPY
FROM THE POINT OF VIEW
OF ADLERIAN PSYCHOLOGY

Rudolf Dreikurs

It can be assumed that the practice of group psychotherapy is to a large extent the same, regardless of the psychological orientation of the therapist. There are certain procedural differences which emanate from the theoretical orientation and varying technical approaches characteristic for each school of thought. However, the greatest and most significant difference between the various practitioners of group psychotherapy is probably their different interpretation of the observed phenomena. The clearest example is the assumption by analytically oriented therapists that transference is the basis for all therapeutic results. Therapists who are not psychoanalytically indoctrinated would not consider this factor at all but would attribute the effects of the therapy to entirely different mechanisms.

The formulation of the theoretical premises can then explain both the technique used in group psychotherapy and the therapeutically effective factors seen from each point of view. I will try to present the Adlerian position, being fully aware of the difficulty to clarify in a short presentation the complexity of Adlerian psychology.

THE PRINCIPLES OF ADLERIAN PSYCHOLOGY

The "individual psychology" of Alfred Adler can be characterized as a *socioteleological* approach to an understanding of human motivation. It is in contrast to the physiologic-mechanistic concept of Watson's behaviorism, which considers all human qualities as the result of stimulus-response reflexes, or to Freud's biological-instinctual concept of man, ac-

Reprinted from the *International Journal of Group Psychotherapy*, Vol. VII, No. 4, October 1957, pp. 363-375.

cording to which the individual is primarily driven by instincts which then are repressed or transformed by superimposed cultural demands. Adler perceived man as a social being, primarily and exclusively. He was the first to emphasize that human behavior is *goal-directed,* purposive. These two basic principles in Adlerian psychology distinguished it from any other school of thought until recently when the various psychoanalysts abandoned the original biologic-instinctual premise for a more social orientation.

These two basic principles deserve some further clarification, since neither of them is easily understood in our present cultural and scientific setting. It is rather paradoxical that the social nature of man should require clarifying comments 2,400 years after man has been called by Aristotle a *zoon politicon,* a social animal. It must be admitted, however, that the assumption of the truly social nature of man is difficult to defend at a time when his obviously antisocial behavior offers convincing proof to the contrary. Conflict, tension, and the threat of all-engulfing war characterize our contemporary cultural scene; they do not testify to man's fundamentally social nature. Yet all human conflicts are essentially social, although the structure of our society does not facilitate the solution of interpersonal conflicts and antagonisms.

Adler described an "ironclad logic of social living" as a basis for prevention and solution of conflicts. This inner logic of social living presupposes the recognition of a fundamental human *equality,* which has first been described by the Greek Stoics, then made into law by the Roman legislators, and put into practice by the early Christians. However, human equality, greatly increased in the democratic evolution of the last few centuries, has not been recognized yet in its significance. While the individual in certain countries, especially in the United States, has gained an unequaled degree of social equality, people have not yet learned to live with each other as equals and solve their problems on the basis of mutual respect. The obvious antisocial behavior of most individuals and groups does not, therefore, require the assumption of fundamentally antisocial elements within human nature.

Opponents of the social orientation may say that man could live without society but not without air, water, and food. Does this not prove that biological concepts are more accurate? True enough, man could live without society, but he would also stop being human. It is not always easy to evaluate properly the relationship of several coexisting factors. Let us take as an example the role of sex in the total human personality. No one can deny that sex exists; but we say "man has sex," rather than "sex has man." From our point of view, all human faculties, needs, and desires are subordinated to the *social* needs and outlook of the individual. All human qualities are expressions of social interaction, all human problems are of social nature. The *desire to belong* is the prime human motivation. The individual may develop devious means to find a place, and he may have a distorted concept of his possibilities to do so; but he never loses his desire to belong. According to Adler, social interest—the ability to participate and the willingness to contribute—is an innate human potentiality. The development of sufficient social interest is a prerequisite for adequate social functioning; its lack is the cause of deficiency and social maladjustment.

The second fundamental principle of Adlerian psychology, the teleo-analytical approach to human behavior, was even more difficult to comprehend in Adler's contemporaries, steeped as they were in the mechanistic tradition of nineteenth-century science. True enough, the teleological mechanisms were described before him by the neovitalists in medicine who recognized the purpose of physiological processes and by philosophers like Bergson and others who recognized basic finalistic perspectives. However, it was still considered unscientific in Adler's time to assume self-determination. Limitations of mechanistic determinism, of the causal principle on which the great scientific progress of the last few centuries has been based, were hardly recognized. Adler was fifty years ahead of his time. Only in the last few years has science discovered the teleological mechanism as a universal principle, applicable not only to an understanding of an individual human being but of physical processes as well. Not until physicists realized the limitations of strict determinism and replaced it with the law of "statistical probability" did Adler's concept of man have a chance to become accepted scientifically.

The struggle between a causal-deterministic orientation and a teleological point of view which perceives the possibility of self-determination will not be waged primarily in the fields of psychiatry and psychology. It seems probable that the necessary changes in epistemology will be brought about by research in the basic and not in the applied sciences. However, these changes are already taking place; they favor Adler's concepts of man, and not the heretofore accepted mechanistic-deterministic ones characteristic of constitutional-hereditary, behavioristic, or psychoanalytic postulates.

According to Adler, all human actions have a purpose, and purpose is primarily of social nature. All human qualities express movement, movement in relationship to others. The individual sets his own goals, both the immediate goals in his present field of action and the over-all goals for his whole life, which form the basis for his personality, his *life style*. Even within the once established general frame of reference of his life style, the individual is free to choose his immediate objectives. He acts at any given moment according to his dominant goals which he sets himself. It does not make any difference whether he is aware of his goals or not; he always acts accordingly. Most often the individual is not aware of his goals and intentions. Consciousness is also self-determined. The individual knows only what he wants or needs to know. And the need for conscious awareness is highly overrated. Most emotional, mental, psychological, and physiological processes take place without any awareness, which has only too often an inhibitive effect. The same principle explains the function of memory. While all experiences are retained cerebrally, the recall depends on the needs of the individual. He takes from the vast filing system of his engrams only what he needs for the moment. His conscious intention may not coincide with his actual goal, and therefore he may find himself forgetting what he seemingly wants to know, or be unable to push out of his mind what he would "like to forget." In either case, a close analysis reveals that he is doing only what he really intends to do, although he does not admit his true intentions to himself and operates on pretense.

Our contemporary picture of man is not inducive to self-understanding. Prevalent psychological constructs prevent us from knowing what we could know about ourselves, although nobody ever will be able to know himself fully. Subjectivity, spontaneity, and creativity are not yet recognized in their full social significance at a time when objectivity and rationality are overrated. The crucial factor which deserves attention and reconsideration is the functions of *emotions*. Adler recognized their purposiveness. We create our own emotions for our own purposes while we subjectively feel driven by them. They seem to be our master while they are actually only our tools. Naturally, we cannot admit to ourselves the purpose for which we create our emotions, otherwise they could no longer serve us. We need emotions to act forcefully, to support our self-determined goals, to fortify them against obstacles. Without emotions, we could not act forcibly. They are the steam which we generate to increase and maintain our movement. They come and go as we need them. Emotions are not irrational; they express our *private logic*, what we really think and believe. Reason and emotions only seem opposed to each other, like the left hand "opposes" the right one when both try to hold an object. Reason and emotions are tools which we use alternately as they best fit our purpose. When they seem to oppose each other, this seeming opposition serves merely as an excuse for our actions, "explained" by our emotions. Any conscious opposition to our emotional impulses is a false pretense—but this is difficult to comprehend. Guilt feelings too are only pretenses, pretenses of good intentions which we do not have. They emerge only when we do not want to amend or change, but to demonstrate our good intentions. We feel guilty only if we are not willing to do what we know we should do. In this sense, guilt feelings too have an obvious social purpose.

Similarly, *dreams* are purposive. Adler called them "the factory of emotions." In our dreams we create situations which stimulate those emotions which we may need for the coming day. Through dream analysis we can recognize a patient's plans, his attitudes, and preparation for his coming problem. Neurotic symptoms too have a purpose. They safeguard the individual against failure, they permit him to withdraw or to gain special privileges and services. Freud also recognized such mechanisms. In his *Psychopathology of Everyday Life*, written while under the influence of Alfred Adler, he describes more than anywhere else the social purpose of actions and deficiencies. However, he relegated them later to be merely "secondary gains" since the primary dynamics were considered within the unconscious. It seems to us that no human action can be understood unless we recognize its purpose. It does not make any difference whether this action is socially acceptable or not, productive or destructive, on the "useless side" or helpful—it always has a purpose.

The third basic principle in Adlerian psychology, which is responsible for its name, is the *unity of the personality*. For Adler, the individual is indivisible, a whole. The holistic concept of man, which in theory is generally approved, is far from being understood today, and was less so in Adler's time. At that time his only support came from Gestalt psychologists who also realized that the whole is more than the sum total of its parts. In the meantime, Smuts developed his theory of holism, which is gaining acceptance. Despite this scientific trend, most references to the totality or unity of the personality give merely lip service to this concept. All mechanistic approaches in psychology, be they experimental, behavioristic, or psychoanalytic, try to understand the individual through an exploration of isolated psychological mechanisms and processes under the assumption that their analysis may lead to an understanding of the whole person. True enough, many helpful insights have been gained in such scientific research; but the individual himself cannot be explained nor understood in this way.

Adler indicated the only way in which the totality of personality can be perceived, not merely theoretically, but in practice, be it in psychotherapy, in education, or in any other field where an objective understanding of the total individual is attempted. It is the *movement* of the individual, the goals which he has set for himself, which indicate his total personality and permit a recognition of it. The direction in which the person moves encompass his whole past, all his shortcomings and assets, abilities and deficiencies, and at the same time his perception of the future. He uses all his faculties, his mind and his body, his thinking, feeling, and physiological functions to pursue his goals. Only in his goals can he be recognized in his uniqueness. Without looking at the individual phenomenologically, one cannot see him as a whole. What makes him move are not any parts operating in him, be they emotions, drives, complexes, or other phenomena within him. The force that makes him move is *he* himself, his own determination, his pursuit in line with his goals.

Adler developed a technique which permits a clear recognition of the goals of the individual. It is not difficult to detect them if the individual is *observed in action*; the result of his actions are usually in line with his immediate goals. The individual may be convinced that he does not want what he brings about, but then he is merely not aware of the objectives he set for himself. It is more difficult to recognize his *basic* goals which are the foundation of his life style, the fictitious goals, as Adler calls them. They represent a scheme of action by which the individual hopes to find his place in society, a set of convictions about himself and life which underlie his social movements. The exploration of the *family constellation*, the interaction of the patient with all the members of the family during the formative years of early childhood, permits a clear picture of the pattern according to which he moves. The *early recollections* indicate the concept of life which he has developed and maintained since childhood. We remember from our early childhood only those incidents which fit into our concept of life. Once we have developed such a concept, we perceive only what fits into the scheme. Our "biased apperception" fortifies our "private logic" and permits us to maintain our basic convictions regardless of how wrong they may be. The "guiding lines" which we have set up in our childhood separate the desirable from the undersirable, the possible from the impossible, the superior from the inferior. Masculine superiority may be such a guiding principle, although the individual, man and woman alike, may rebel against the assumption that a man has to be superior. Adler called this rebellion "masculine protest." Moral or intellectual superiority may be other sets of guiding principles. They indicate the safeguards which the individual may set up for himself when his idea of superiority cannot be realized, when he is confronted with failure.

The question has often been posed why Adler considered the inferiority feeling as the main source of deficiencies, of social and emotional maladjustment. How could one psychological mechanism be at the root of all the manifold disturbances? To understand this assumption one must keep in mind that the individual, as a social being, is primarily concerned with finding his place in the group. A feeling of belonging is essential for social and emotional well-being. It permits the endurance of all hardships and adversities. Not belonging is the worst contingency man can experience; it is worse than death. This explains the supreme significance of status. Feeling deficient and inferior deprives the individual of the realization that he has a place. His "social interest" is restricted by the development of inferiority feelings. The extent of his social interest can be clearly measured by the areas where he feels belonging. The smaller his area is, the more vulnerable becomes the individual. As long as he can move in a field where he feels belonging, where his adequacy is not questioned—at least in his own mind—no safeguards, which are the real defense mechanisms, are necessary. But as soon as he is impressed with his inadequacy and inferiority, be they real or assumed, he seeks detours and compensations, either through socially useful means, or—if he is too discouraged—on the useless side of life.

ADLERIAN GROUP PSYCHOTHERAPY

This orientation of Adlerian psychology explains why Adler and his co-workers were among the first to conduct group psychotherapy. Since man's problems and conflicts are recognized in their social nature, the group is ideally suited, not only to highlight and reveal the nature of a person's conflicts and maladjustments, but to offer corrective influences. Inferiority feelings cannot be more effectively counteracted than in a group setting. Furthermore, at the root of social deficiencies and emotional maladjustments are mistaken concepts and values. The group is a value-forming agent; it influences the convictions and beliefs of its members. For this reason, Adler and his co-workers used a group approach in their child guidance centers in Vienna since 1921. My first experience with group psychotherapy—at that time called "collective therapy"—was, besides in child guidance, in the treatment of alcoholics. In 1929 I began to use group psychotherapy in my private psychiatric practice, and I have continued to do so ever since. Our particular orientation permits specific approaches in group psychotherapy and leads to an interpretation of the observed phenomena which may offer some insight to other group psychotherapists in their own dealings with their patients.

Describing the characteristic dynamics of group psychotherapy in the light of Adlerian psychology, we may use the scheme of the four phases of psychotherapy which seem to be present in any form of uncovering therapy. I have described these four phases, which overlap, as consisting of (1) the establishment and maintenance of the proper therapeutic relationship; (2) the exploration of the dynamics operating in the patient (analysis in the wider sense); (3) communicating to the patient an understanding of himself (insight); and finally, (4) a reorientation.

The establishment and maintenance of a proper therapeutic relationship implies more than a good relationship in general. More important and more difficult is the alignment of goals of patient and therapist so that both work toward the same end, which unfortunately is neither self-evident nor implicit in every case. It is obvious that the therapist wishes the patient to get well, and through a process which he, the therapist, deems necessary. The patient who comes for help, may either not want to get well and merely demonstrate his good intention; he may be determined to prove that he is hopeless. Or he may wish to get well but without doing anything about it, expecting the therapist to do the job, or without acceding to the need for a change in personality.

The therapy group can contribute greatly to fortify the patient's *relationship* to the therapist and to overcome disturbances as they are inevitable in any therapeutic procedure. Confidence in the therapist and his ability may be easily impaired by a hostile group, but is equally enhanced in a well-functioning group. Whatever distrust the patient may have, either due to his general personal inclination or due to his disbelief in psychiatry and the effectiveness of therapy, it may vanish under the impact of the faith exhibited by other patients. The group can undermine as well as build up the morale of the therapeutic setting. An individual patient may feel not understood, or he may be in rebellion against any authority figure and regard the therapist as such. Consequently, he might find it easier to participate fully in the therapeutic process as a member of a group than being alone with the therapist. Many patients who can hardly be reached in individual therapy respond in the group; many who oppose psychological investigation, often because they refuse to consider their condition as anything but organically determined, begin to realize the need for a psychotherapeutic approach which they had resented previously.

The group does not only influence each member in his attitude to psychotherapy and to the therapist, but also to the possible outcome of the procedure. We experimented recently with a group which was almost entirely composed of depressed patients, each of whom felt utterly hopeless. It was interesting to note how each one was equally convinced how wrong the others were in their pessimism and how right he was in his. Each one was sure that *he* did not belong in the group, that *he* did not need it and could not benefit from it, but all the others could. The effect of this recognition was dramatic on all participants. Several patients who for a long period of time maintained a distant, reserved, and defeatist attitude to therapy responded within a short period of time after this group experience.

The *analysis* of the psychodynamic forces operating in the patient, the methods which we use to determine the life style of each patient, can be applied in an individual session as well as in the group setting. However, the patient's goals and movements become much more obvious in the interaction with his fellow group members than in the limited interaction between him and the therapist. Furthermore, the therapist no longer depends entirely on the verbal reports by the patient about his interaction with others outside of the therapeutic session; he sees him in action during the session. Not infrequently, the patient appears in a quite different light when confronted by other members of the group than when he is alone with the therapist. Certain façades of his personality may become more pronounced, or visible.

The greatest benefit of the group is in phases three and four. In individual therapy it is relatively difficult to provide *insight* for the patient, particularly in regard to his goals. We are so used to rationalize that we all find it difficult to recognize our own goals and true intentions. This is the more so when the patient is ambitious and overconscientious, as many neurotics are. The group facilitates the process of gaining insight; for many, it is almost a prerequisite without which they never are able to learn about themselves what they need to know. How is this greater ability to understand oneself achieved in the group?

Interestingly enough, the individual patient may show the same blocking to interpretations in the group as in private consultation. What helps him to overcome his resistance is the similar resistance observed in his fellow patients. There he can clearly see the validity of the psychological interpretation and the difficulties of the patient to recognize the obvious. Most psychological disclosures and interpretations in the group are not for the benefit of the patient to whom they are directed, but for the benefit of the others who learn from it. There is sufficient fundamental similarity in faulty motivations and mistaken approaches among all participants so that each one can, time and again, recognize himself in others. This is particularly true if the members of the group are selected because of their similar problems, a group of mothers, of teenagers, of obese women, of executives, of patients with depression, and so on. We try to arrange our groups in such a way that some common element of either personalities, psychopathology, interests, age, or education is evident. After all, patients learn from each other. This seems to be a fundamental principle, explaining the therapeutic efficiency of group psychotherapy.

In this sense, it is characteristic for all group psychotherapy that the patients help each other. What they tell each other is often much more significant to them than what the therapist has to say. They accept each other more in their corrective endeavors, because they feel equal to each other. This is the reason why some patients can only benefit from group psychotherapy and less so from individual therapy, like juvenile delinquents, alcoholics, drug addicts, the crippled and the blind, and other groups which perceive themselves as a minority. The therapist, regardless of how acceptable he may be to them, is still a member of the hostile or at least different majority. His influence depends on his ability to win the active support of some group members.

Insight is not necessarily a strictly personal matter. Certain psychological dynamics, which operate in all of us alike, are hardly known. While man probably never will be able to understand himself, he will, before long, learn a great deal more about human nature. The significance of inferiority feelings, of guilt feelings, the fallacy of prestige and of the desire for self-elevation, they all are still unknown to most. The patients in the group learn not only about themselves, but about people. As they begin to understand people, they begin to understand themselves. Psychotherapy, as we understand it, is primarily an educational process, the intellectual stimulation being supported by strong and impressive emotional experiences. It seems that the group as such facilitates all learning. A seasoned teacher often prefers a small group to individual instruction. Similarly, the learning process called psychotherapy is greatly facilitated by the group.

Insight is not the basis for cure, improvement, or adjustment; it is merely a step toward it, and not even a necessary prerequisite. Many forms of therapy do not use any analysis and insight and still can be highly effective, like hypnosis, suggestive therapy, and many other nonanalytic forms of therapy. They proceed directly from phase 1, the establishing of the proper relationship, to phase 4, the reorientation. The experience in the therapy group provides stimulations which arc highly conducive to *reorientation*.

The most decisive change necessary for a lasting therapeutic effect is relinquishing the faulty premises on which each patient had operated heretofore; this implies a change in the life style, in the fundamental attitude to life. These changes are not only expressed in improvement of functions, amelioration of symptoms, and general well-being; they can be tested by characteristic changes in the early recollections of the patient, since these recollections always represent the basic outlook on life. The group facilitates these changes due to the general improvement of the therapeutic relationship, the greater opportunity to recognize oneself, and above all, through the increased awareness of the patient in the group that his concept of himself and the premises which he had found for himself in his childhood are incorrect and unjustified.

Even greater is the stimulation by the group to recognize faulty value systems on which most of its members have operated and which were induced by our culture. Psychotherapy, to a large extent, offsets certain social stimulations within the community. They induce the patient to consider self-evaluation as most important. This concern with personal prestige limited the patient's ability to cooperate, to take life in his stride, and made him vulnerable to incidents which spelled for him defeat and personal worthlessness. Counseling and psychotherapy lead the patient to a sounder approach to social living, enable him to cooperate, and provide him with healthier and more practical sources of satisfaction and security than those which he previously had considered necessary. Individual psychotherapy may not always be recognized as a means for social reorientation and acceptance of new and better social values; in group psychotherapy this aspect of every psychotherapy cannot be overlooked and becomes obvious. Every group develops its own conventions, its own rules. And the therapy group, dealing with human relationships and with the task to offset or remedy disturbed relationships, cannot escape concerning itself with morals and values conducive to better social functioning.

The most important therapeutic factor in our concept of psychotherapy is the removal of inferiority feelings, or to say it in a positive way, the increase in self-respect. This process can justifiably be called *encouragement*. It is our contention that the effectiveness of *any* corrective procedure, be it called analytic, therapeutic, or educational, rests with the degree of encouragement which it entailed. Without increased self-confidence, without restored faith in his own worth and ability, the patient cannot improve and grow. This aspect of therapy may not be recognized by the therapist, or be minimized by him as constituting mere "supportive" assistance; however, it seems to be the essential factor in all cures and improvement.

In which way does the group contribute to the encouragement of each of its members? To understand this all-important aspect of group psychotherapy, one must take into consideration the peculiar social structure of the therapy group. It is quite unique and different from any other group found in our society. It is characterized by a status of social equality which each member enjoys. Unlike any other group, here, individual differences and particularly deficiencies do not lower the patient's status. Conversely, leadership qualities and personal assets do not necessarily give the patient a status of superiority or envy, since this very envy can be openly expressed by less fortunate members of the group who then see to it that the patient's attempts to achieve elevation is thwarted.

It is this social atmosphere of equality which characterizes a therapy group and which exerts one of the most effective therapeutic influences on each one of its members. First of all, it removes the need for distance. The highly competitive atmosphere of our civilization produces a state of emotional isolation for everybody; revealing oneself as one is entails the danger of ridicule and contempt. In the therapy group this danger is eliminated. For the first time the individual can be himself without fear and danger. This is an utterly new experience and counteracts the basic fears and anxiety which are usually concerned with possible personal failure and defeat.

In this sense, the group provides subtle but all-persuasive encouragement for each member. It permits an unrestricted feeling of belonging without necessary personal bonds or attachments. Unlike personal and close relationships based on friendship or love, the feeling of solidarity is not based here on a union of personal aspirations. It is truly a feeling of human fellowship without any ulterior motives of personal benefits or advantages, which characterize the relationship of friends and lovers. Accordingly, the desire to help each other in the group springs from the deepest source of human empathy and fellowship, from a feeling of solidarity, of genuine humaneness. We have seen patients who never concerned themselves with anyone's interests or needs and who were moved in the group to give assistance and support without any one of the attributes which those acts usually have in our society, namely the demonstration of personal superiority.

It seems necessary to state clearly that all these strong therapeutic factors operating in the therapy group do not make it a cure-all, by any means. No therapeutic procedure guarantees success. Unfortunately, it is a tacit assumption in many quarters that any form of psychiatric treatment is inadequate if it does not bring full success in all cases. In no other branch of medical practice are such demands made. Methods of medication, surgery, and treatment are acceptable and esteemed even if they provide cure only in a small percentage of cases. The advent of group psychotherapy has certainly improved psychiatric effectiveness. It permitted reaching patients who previously were not accessible; it brought often dramatic progress in heretofore refractory cases. It promises new avenues for providing help actually to millions who are in need of emotional adjustment. Particularly its aspect of mutual help of the patients themselves may lead to new experimentations in line with the model which Alcoholics Anonymous has provided and with the pattern of Self-Help which Dr. A. A. Low has established.

14

C. G. JUNG ON THE PRESENT TRENDS IN GROUP PSYCHOTHERAPY

Hans A. Illing

For the purpose of research in connection with an article concerning a new perspective in group psychotherapy[1] the writer communicated with Professor Jung in order to clarify certain points that, in the writer's mind, were ambiguous. The correspondence ensuing from the initial communication was made in German, and the letters have been translated into English essentially, although not completely.

Los Angeles, California
January 14, 1955

Dear Dr. Jung,

For some time I have been engaged with a psychologist in preparing a historical survey of group psychotherapy at the request of a German medical journal.

While my collaborator and I belong to different schools of thought and while each of us is taking different parts of the subject, both of us agree on one point fully: our admiration of the school founded and headed by you, your creation of the theory of the Unconscious, and the vast potentialities of your theories relative to group psychotherapy, which you don't seem to have appreciated so far as we could ascertain from the literature.

As I understand your conception of the *Wandlungserlebnis*, it centers around the identification of the individual with several individuals, who, as a *group*, undergo a collective *Wandlungserlebnis*. In such an experience it can happen that a deeper level of consciousness is excited than in the ordinary experience of the individual. If I understand you correctly, a species of common *Tierseele* (animal soul) is born when the group is

Reprinted from *Human Relations*, Vol. X, No. 1, 1957, pp. 77-83.

large enough. It seems that you draw the conclusion from this that the "morale" of large organizations is always low. In my opinion, however, some therapies can be much more effective in the group because the togetherness of many produces virtually a mass suggestibility. Certainly I will admit that inevitably psychological regressions may take place in a group; however, these regressions are partially checked by ritual, i.e. cultic action. Cultic action seizes the attention of the individual and, simultaneously, makes it possible for him to experience his own catharsis in the group and to become conscious of his catharsis. If, on the other hand, a connection with the center is missing, a connection which symbolizes the unconscious, then the *Massenseele* (group-soul) will inevitably become the center and will absorb individual instinct or initiative.

Having studied your writings much and long, I note that you repeatedly emphasize that there are positive experiences which inspire the individual to good deeds or, as you call it, *ein positives Gefühl der menschlichen Solidarität*, a positive feeling of human solidarity, to me, perhaps, the finest piece of expression I have ever come across in the literature, especially if applicable to group psychotherapy. On the other hand, my collaborator and I believe that, conceivably, you are in error to equate the group with the loss of the ego. To us, this is a generalization, since the belonging to a group per se does not constitute regression but rather a greater understanding of the ego! As we shall point out in our paper, "as the therapist applies clinically both factors, heightened suggestibility and group pressure, the methods of group psychotherapy will become particularly effective in the exploration of the unconscious of *every* member of the group."

Our paper is not yet completed. I am turning to you with the request to submit some personal comments on the question whether your antipathy to group psychotherapy derives from the general logic of your theory of the maturing of the individual or from other causes. We have attempted to be as objective as possible in the description of the various schools of thought in our paper; yet it seems to me that nothing could be more "objective," more scientifically accurate, than an explanation, however brief, from the inaugurator of a school himself.

May I add that I have just received a copy of the first English translation of your *Answer to Job*,[2] which I was asked to review. I also received the German edition of your contribution to *Der Göttliche Schelm*.[3] After a hasty examination of both books I feel that these are superb works, worthy of their author and a fitting present for your forthcoming (80th) birthday on 26 July.

Thanking you in advance for your courtesy,

Very respectfully,
Hans A. Illing.

Dr. Jung's answer to the above letter was as follows:

Kuesnacht bei Zürich
January 26, 1955

Dear Dr. Illing,

As a physician, I consider any psychic disturbance, whether neurosis or psychosis, to be an individual illness; the patient has to be treated accordingly. The individual can be treated in the group only if he is a member of it. If he is, this should be a great help, since, being submerged in the group, he apparently escapes his self to some degree. The feeling of security is increased and the feeling of responsibility is decreased when one is part of a group. Once I ran into a thick fog, while crossing over a treacherous glacier with a company of soldiers. The situation was so dangerous that everybody had to stop wherever he happened to be. Yet there was no trace of panic, but rather the spirit of a private party! If only one or two persons had been there, the danger of the situation would probably not have been recognized. Now, however, the brave and the experienced in the company found the opportunity to show off. The timid ones were able to lean on the strength of their brave comrades, and nobody said a word about the possibility of having to camp unprepared on the glacier, which could hardly have been done without some limbs being frozen, let alone the chances of death in attempts to climb from the glacier. This is typical of the mind of the group.

Younger people, in larger groups, often do mischief, which they would never undertake alone. So, in war as a result of group pressure, neuroses disappeared in our soldiers overnight. The group experiences of sects, e.g. the so-called Oxford Movement, are well known; likewise the cures of Lourdes, which were unthinkable without an admiring audience. Groups cause not only astonishing cures but just as astonishing psychic "changes" and conversions, *because the suggestibility is increased.* This was recognized a long time ago by the totalitarian dictators; hence the mass parades, noise, etc. Hitler inspired the greatest group experience of change which Germany has undergone since the Reformation; it cost Europe millions of dead.

Increased suggestibility means the individual's bondage, because he has been delivered to the influences of his environment, be these good or bad. The capacity to differentiate is diminished, also the feeling of individual responsibility, which, as in the Oxford Movement, is left to the "Lord Jesus." People have wondered about the psychology of the German Army. It was no wonder: Every single soldier and officer was just a mass product of suggestion, stripped of moral responsibility.

A small group, too, may be controlled by a suggestive *mind of the whole group* (Gruppengeist), which, if it is a good one, may have socially favorable influences, though at the expense of the mental and moral independence of the individual. The group *increases the ego*; i.e. the individual becomes more courageous, more impertinent and assertive, more secure, fresher, and less cautious; the *self*, however, is reduced and is pushed into the background in favor of the average. For this reason all weak and insecure persons wish to belong to clubs and organizations, even to a nation of 80 million! In this relationship the individual feels important, because he identifies himself with everybody else; on the other hand, he loses his self (which is the soul the devil is after and wins!) and his individual judgment. But the ego will only be pushed into the background by the group if it is not in accord with the opinion of the group. For this reason there is always the tendency of the individual in the group to give his assent to the majority opinion to the largest possible degree or, if this be possible, to attempt to impose his opinion on the group.

The annihilating influence of the group on the individual will be compensated for by one member, who identifies himself with the *Gruppengeist* and thus becomes the *leader*. For this reason there are always conflicts over prestige and power in the group, springing from the increase of the ego and the egotism of the mass. The ego's social self, so to speak, is multiplied by the number of members in the group.

I do not have any practical objections to group therapy, as I do not have any to Christian Science, the Oxford Movement, and other therapeutically effective sects. I myself founded a group almost forty years ago; however, that group was composed of "analyzed" persons, whose purpose was to define the social position of the individual. This group is still active today. For social position does not function in the dialectic relationship between the patient and the physician and, therefore, is unadjusted, which was the case with the majority of my patients. This misfortune became only apparent when the group was formed and therefore called for a mutual adjustment.

In my opinion, group therapy is only capable of educating the *social* human being. Attempts in this regard are being made in England, particularly with "unanalyzed" persons, on the basis of psychological theories inaugurated by me. Mr. P. W. Martin, Talboys, Hall Hill, Oxted, Surrey, England, could give you detailed information. I welcome these attempts positively. However, what I have said above about group therapy should not be taken to mean that it can replace individual analysis, i.e. the dialectic process between two individuals and the subsequent intrapsychic catharsis, the dialogue with the unconscious. Since the only bearer of life and the absolutely essential element of any kind of community is the individual, it follows that he and his quality are of consummate importance. The individual must be complete and must endure; otherwise, nothing can exist, since any number of zeros still do not amount to more than zero. A group of inferior people is never better than any one of them, i.e. the group is also inferior; and the state which is composed of sheep only is never anything else but a herd of sheep, even though the herd is led by a shepherd with a biting dog.

In our time, a time which puts so much weight on the socialization of the individual because a special capacity for adjustment is needed, the psychologically oriented group formation is of even greater importance. In view of the notorious inclination of people, however, to lean on others and on isms rather than on inner security and independence, which should have first place, there is the danger that the individual will equate the group with father and mother and will, thereby, remain as dependent, insecure, and infantile as before. He may become adjusted socially. But what of his individuality, which alone gives meaning to the social fabric? Surely, if society consisted of superior individuals only, such an adjustment would be profitable; but, in reality, society is composed mainly of unintelligent and morally weak human beings, so that their *niveau* lies beneath that of one of its superior representatives, let alone the fact that the mass naturally suppresses the values of individuality. When a hundred clever heads join in a group, one big nincompoop is the result, because every individual is trammeled by the otherness of the others. There used to be a funny question: Which are the three largest organizations, the morale of which is the lowest? Answer: Standard Oil, the Catholic Church, and the German Army. Especially in a Christian organization one should expect the highest morality, but the necessity to bring into harmony various factions requires compromises of the most questionable kind. (Jesuitic casuistry and distortion of the truth in the interest of the institution!) The worst examples of recent date are National Socialism and Communism, in which the *lie* became the *raison d'être*.

Real virtues are relatively rare and constitute usually the achievements of individuals. Mental and moral laziness, cowardice, prejudice, and unconsciousness are dominant. I have behind me fifty years of pioneer work and, therefore, could tell a few things about these: there is, perhaps, scientific and technical progress. However, one has not heard yet that people in general have become more intelligent or morally better.

Individuals can be improved because they let themselves be treated. Societies, however, let themselves be seduced and deceived, temporarily even for the good. This refers only to temporary and morally weakening effects of suggestion (*Suggestiveffekte*). (It is for this reason that, with few exceptions, medical psychotherapists a long time ago abandoned any real therapy of suggestion.) One can never achieve the good easily; the more it costs, the better it is. Thus the socially good effects have to be paid for, usually later; but then with interest (e.g. the era of Mussolini in Italy and its catastrophic end). Summing up these reflections I arrive at the following conclusions:

1. Group therapy is necessary for the education of the social human being.

2. Group therapy does not replace individual analysis.

3. Both types of therapy complement each other.

4. The danger of group therapy lies in a standstill on a collective basis.

5. The danger of individual analysis lies in the neglect of social adjustment (*Anpassung*).

With kindest regards,
C. G. Jung.

Most of Professor Jung's points seemed to be well taken. However, the writer still did not feel that some of the points were clarified, points over which he had communicated with Dr. Jung initially. His answer to Jung's detailed letter is as follows:

Los Angeles, California
February 3, 1955

Dear Dr. Jung,

Your prompt and detailed reply to my recent inquiry relative to your attitude toward group psychotherapy was greatly appreciated and I shall treat it accordingly. My associate and I believe that your statements were of such importance that we intend to quote your letter in our article to be published soon, provided that you won't object.

Much of your letter's contents was already familiar to me through your books and, therefore, did not come as a surprise; yet you have admirably achieved your purpose to expose the quintessence of today's *societäre Gesellschaft*.

It seems to me immodest to engage in a dispute with a man who can look back "at 50 years of pioneer labor," as I am considerably younger in years and experience as a therapist than you. However, if I, nevertheless, undertake such a correspondence, I do so only because I was encouraged by your expressions of contempt for *unseren lieben Pöbel*, the great mass; you seem to esteem only nobility of soul and the solitude of the creative mind. I sympathize with you the more because I, too, have often had similar notions about *die Minderwertigen*, the inferior, as you choose to call them. However, in my case I could only say: "*Quod licet Iovi non licet bovi*," for the *Pöbel* did not think, rightly, that I was another "Jung." You seem to be an outspoken protagonist of individuality, which, according to Goethe, is *das höchste Gut der Erdenkinder*. Yet although I share your zeal to uphold the dignity and freedom of the individual, I would also venture to cross swords with you on behalf of the "discriminated" group, of which the individual is an integral part.

Firstly, I wish to emphasize my complete agreement on the Five Points with which you sum up the applicability of group psychotherapy. I even agree where I have some reservations, which are probably due to the fact that some words have different meanings to both of us.

One of these words is your term *Individualanalyse*, probably intended as a contrast to *Gruppenanalyse*. Although there is a faction of psychoanalysts who adhere to the school of thought that the psychoanalysis of groups is possible, I never considered it possible, finding myself, I might say, on the side of the majority of group therapists everywhere. No! I meant to say group *therapy* or psychotherapy, terms which are used synonymously in America, being applied to the patient as an adjunct or substitute for individual psychotherapy. Analysis may often be therapy—though not necessarily so—but, in my opinion, psychotherapy can never be equated with psychoanalysis. To the best of my knowledge, based on the analytical literature of Freud and his pupils, Fenichel, Abraham, Reik, Jones, *et al.*, the *principles* of psychotherapy are alike whether they are applied in individual or in group psychotherapy. You speak of suggestibility as a heightened risk in the group, since "one is delivered to the influences of the environment." If I have understood you *and* Freud correctly, it is the suggestibility of the individual therapist (in contrast to the free association in analysis) which is much greater, more dangerous, and more dependent on the temperament and personality of the therapist than on that of the group, the therapist's "influence" on which is virtually modified or even cancelled! Is not the person of the therapist in individual psychotherapy the symbol of the *Umweltseinfluss* for the patient?

If I remember correctly, you once said—I believe in *Spirit and Nature*[4]—that, the more unconscious the human being is, the more he integrates into the circle of the general psychic behavior. But the more conscious he becomes of his self, the stronger is his feeling of the differentiation from others. . . . And the more the single consciousness is emancipated from the rules of society, the stronger becomes the empirical freedom of the will in comparison to the growth of a larger consciousness. In this connection I would like to make a point: Those who are not familiar with the methods of group psychotherapy (according to which groups are being used *de facto* to further individuation, to stimulate and to complete it) can easily be mistaken about it. For instance, you state that, by equating the group, a loss of the self will result. This appears to me a generalization. Belonging to a group *per se* does not constitute a regression, i.e. does not require of the individual an involuntary expression of his self, an expression which may derive from archetypal and unconscious rites. On the contrary! Participation in well-prepared groups will lead to a greater understanding of the ego and to a greater toleration of individual differentiations. In the fact that the therapist applies clinically both factors, namely the heightened suggestibility and the group pressure, the group psychotherapeutic methods will become particularly effective, as, above all, *in the exploration of the unconscious of every member of the group.*

Perhaps you are right when you speak of the instinct of the herd (I think you used the analogy of sheep). Perhaps, too, you made a point in stating that the "reality consists mostly of nincompoops and moral weaklings" (Schiller said: "Majority is nonsense; sense is but with a few"). However, it seems to me that we have to live together with these "nincompoops and moral weaklings" unless those of us who do not qualify as nincompoops can manage to live aside as hermits, in "splendid isolation."

With best wishes,
Hans A. Illing.

Replying to the above, Jung wrote:

February 10, 1955

Dear Dr. Illing,

I fully approve of the integration of the individual into society. However, I want to defend the inalienable rights of the individual; for the individual alone is the bearer of life and is, in these times, gravely threatened by degradation. Even in the smallest group, the individual is acceptable only if he appears to be acceptable to the majority. He has to be content with toleration. But mere toleration does not improve the individual; on the contrary, toleration causes a sense of insecurity, by which the lonely individual who has something to champion may be seriously hindered. I am no advocate of solitude; I have to make the greatest effort to shield myself from the demands of people. Without intrinsic value social relations have no importance.

Sincerely,
C. G. Jung.

REFERENCES

1. G. R. Bach and H. A. Illing, "Historische Perspektive zur Gruppenpsychotherapie," Z. Psychosom. Med., I:131-147, 1956.
2. C. G. Jung, Answer to Job (London: Routledge and Kegan Paul, 1954).
3. C. G. Jung, K. Kerényi, and P. Radin, The Trickster (London: Routledge and Kegan Paul, 1956).
4. C. G. Jung, Spirit and Nature (London: Routledge and Kegan Paul, 1955).

15

SOME APPLICATIONS OF HARRY STACK SULLIVAN'S THEORIES TO GROUP PSYCHOTHERAPY

George D. Goldman

A brief summary of how I view psychoanalytic theory and Sullivan's place in it[1] seems to be in order before I proceed to his specific formulations. Psychoanalysis originated in a nineteenth-century Vienna to help the people of that day and place with their specific problems in living. In these earliest days it dealt primarily with problems of sexual and love frustrations that were experienced in growing up in this particular, rather restricting, setting. These conflicts seemed to be handled by the patients in fairly specific common ways—mainly through the development of hysterical symptoms. The therapy was therefore geared to peel back the layers protecting the patient's disrupting sexual memory and allow for a more effective solution to this experience. After Freud discovered that these "memories" were oft more fancied than real, a different theory to account for the patient's problems in living had to be formed. The advent of libido theory and renunciation of the recall method necessitated interpreting the patient's experiences in terms of this new theory. Soon one was not said to be doing psychoanalysis unless one was making the patient's unconscious conscious and accomplishing it through "analysis of the transference." It appears to me as though the patient's memory of events had been replaced by his being educated to use a new and exclusive system of words and ideas to explain himself to himself.

This brief, not too complete, characterization of Freudian theory is not meant to minimize Freud's monumental contributions to the field but to point out factors that underlie the limitations of using any one frame of reference. This theory is in many ways outmoded, specifically, to name a

Reprinted from the *International Journal of Group Psychotherapy*, Vol. VII, No. 4 October 1957, pp. 385-391.

few of these ways, in the areas of infantile sexuality, libido theory, and structure of the personality.

In the years since Freud formulated his theories of personality our economic, political, and social worlds have changed greatly, and with these changes have come concomitant changes in the people in it. Vienna of the nineteenth century is not New York of 1956. Perhaps this can in some way help us to understand that our present-day patients are different and have different ways of handling their problems. This theme is amplified in a previous paper[2] so I will not discuss it further at this time.

Sullivan was a product of our present-day American culture, he was exposed to and influenced by the scientists and social scientists of our time. Meyer's influence was most strongly felt in his early ideas of psychiatry.[3] Cooley's work was seen in Sullivan's formulations of the self-system.[4] Lewin's field theory and Moreno's situational approach parallel his work.[5] I have tried to apply these theories of group dynamics to group psychotherapy in an approach utilizing Sullivanian principles in a study previously reported.[6]

As a man, he appears to have used "the obsessional dynamism" more than most, and his theories with their intricacies of language and thought reflect this as well. The various major theoreticians had to, by the very nature of their being human beings, focus on specific core problems in a specific way which not only characterized the patients they met in their practice but characterized their own individuality and personal view of life and the major problems human beings face. This paper presents an approach that I have found consistent with my view of life and one which I can use effectively with the patients in my practice.

I see Sullivan as having been quite concerned with what are psychiatric problems and what are not.[7] While it surely is one's task to help people and, more specifically, to help people understand their behavior, there are many ways in which this can be done. One could give direct advice or even be the warm, loving, giving parental substitute who would make up for all the deprivation the patient had suffered. Sullivan, however, felt that the most respectful role, as well as the most scientifically and empirically correct role, was that of an expert at understanding those events which would clarify for patients the processes that involve or go on between people. The patient, of course, was the expert on his specific history of significant interrelationships. Sullivan felt that the analyst could function most effectively by *sampling* those events that are characteristic of the patient's interactions with other people. What better laboratory to observe and document these dynamic events than in the therapy group, where the analyst is, in the fullest sense of Sullivan's usage, participant observer of human interaction?

Interaction, characteristic of the patient's interpersonal operations, is thus constantly under observation for its anxiety-laden overtones and for awareness of what else might have been going on other than what the patient assumed was happening.

Having mentioned the patient and his anxiety I feel I cannot go any further without briefly outlining both how the patient got to be first a person and then a patient, and how and why his anxiety appears. Sullivan did not see patients as being different in kind from other human beings; it was rather a matter of degree.[8] The human animal with its biologically determined substratum becomes a distinct person through an infinitely complex series of interactions throughout its developing years with a multitude of significant persons ranging from parents to chums. To be a bit more specific: The "self-system" comes into being very early in the child's education and socialization as the developing human copes with the complex demands, expectations, limitations, appraisals, and security operations of the parents. The self-system controls the patient's awarenesses to his environmental pressures, to the specific demands and attitudes of significant others that are intolerable, by specific dynamisms. The overuse of a specific dynamism, whether it be selective inattention or obsessionalism, differentiates *the patient* from other persons. The self-system develops through the various eras from infancy through late adolescence, learning from the social heritage passed on by the developing human's parents, teachers, and friends. This learning has to take place since humans in their humanness have characteristically certain tendencies to interact and integrate interpersonally. These interactions are governed by the nature of the "need systems," the goals, or integrating tendencies of human beings. These can be classified under two main headings: those having to do with the individual in his culture, his comfort, belongingness, apartness, his security or insecurity with others are called the "pursuit of security"; those that have to do with his more biologically derived needs are grouped under the "pursuit of satisfactions." The person, in his living with other people, is thus constantly striving to avoid anxiety in the pursuit of these two universal needs.

Sullivan saw the vast majority of the work we do in therapy as having to do with acquainting the patient with the various processes and techniques which are his maneuvers for minimizing or avoiding anxiety. Anxiety responses are derived from antecedent historical events involving earlier human situations. These earlier human situations occurred as interaction with *all* significant persons as the developing person with his biologically given substrata progressed (through the stages of development) from infancy to adulthood. Mental illness can be defined as interference with this progression and in the attainment of satisfactions and security.

As an example of what I have been saying, let me illustrate by telling an event that recently took place in one of my groups, showing how it was handled and relating it to the above theoretical framework.

About twenty minutes after one of my group sessions had started,

Ann timidly poked her head in the doorway of my office, looked around, and scurried to a seat. Within the next five minutes she had verbally lashed out at three different group members, especially the analyst. Joe, who had been in the group with Ann for some time, observed that this was a fairly typical way of behaving for Ann when she felt she had done something wrong. Focusing on Ann in this event, let us examine her behavior as the group interaction highlighted it. As the group members confronted Ann with their reactions to her conduct, she became vividly aware of her anxiety. Our initial task was to understand what her behavior was geared to do for her in relation to minimizing anxiety and later to understand the historical perspective of her behavior in the safety of the analytic relationship. This, parenthetically, is my therapeutic method in individual treatment as well. The interpersonal operation involved was delineated as follows: When Ann felt she had done something that would be thought of as bad, wrong, or incorrect by those around her she anticipated a rebuke of such severe intensity that it would destroy her self-esteem. To block the expected attack Ann attacked first at what she felt were the weak spots in those around her. In her framework she was neutralizing those in the group who might hurt her. If they were shown to be weak they were not to be feared. In reality she was acting in direct opposition to her wish to be accepted and was provoking the very behavior she feared most.

Our next task was to explore the historical perspective of this interpersonal operation in order to understand the parataxes involved and advance toward a more mature integration. By parataxes I mean the carry-overs into the present of her personalized childhood fantasies about a situation. Thus, as a child, to be yelled at disapprovingly was seen by her as being destroyed, and to err ever so slightly was the invitation to be yelled at. The developing self-system could not tolerate the destructive criticism of Ann's mother (in this case). The dynamism used in adjusting could keep the disruptive appraisal of her mother out of her awareness and thus avoid the anxiety. This approach is both Sullivanian and a distinct contribution in its awareness of personality being studied only in an interaction with another human being; in its realization that it is the adult Ann that gets into difficulty as an adult from using an adaptation of a childhood pattern (rather than exact repetition); in its understanding of dynamisms to keep unfavorable appraisals by others out of our awareness; and finally that these appraisals historically could have come from any significant person. I am going to omit the specific details of Ann's history since my emphasis is only on presenting an example of Sullivan's method.

To apply this method specifically to further our understanding of group therapy theory, I want to mention that this same behavior had been previously brought to Ann's attention in our individual session with little apparent effect. I feel it was the *immediacy* and *vividness* of her being confronted with behavior that had been acted out in a life situation, analogous to the original childhood situation, helped her accept the present interpretation. For this lonely and isolated girl, the security that came from belonging to a group and the knowledge some part of her had that she was really accepted by the group gave her the strength to "look at herself" in the group. Also operating for Ann as a support to go on to explore her problem was the experience she had had in the group of how similar exploration had helped others. The group in this case was a valuable adjunct to Ann's individual treatment.

More generally speaking, the group is an ideal place vividly to act out patterns of interaction that are characteristic of the patient's particular relatedness; in turn, the relatedness of specific group members often stirs up unique reactions in fellow patients. Consensual validation can indicate the parataxic elements in the various reactions. To clarify this, let me illustrate more of the various forces and pulls going on interpersonally during "an event" and how this is characteristically handled in my groups. The patients in the group all have concomitant individual treatment. The group interaction therefore can center around the various group members interrelating with each other. These interactions are seen as representative of their relations in general and are used to spark further exploration of patterns of operation. A specific event, then, could potentially affect each of the ten patients in the group and enable them to learn something about their feelings, reactions, attitudes, and so on. Turning once more to the event previously used as an illustration, we could have focused on Joe and tried to understand what was behind his sensitivity to Ann. What was there in him that was awakened by this angry woman? Was he defending the analyst? If so, what did this mean? Why did he remember that Ann attacked when she felt she was wrong? To clarify Ann's behavior, four members of the group gave identical reactions to her being destructively belittling. It is this consensual validation by a group of significant peers that made her realize her behavior. The importance of the people and strength of their reactions was too great to have been kept out of awareness by the dynamism of selective inattention. Once vividly aware of what she was doing, Ann could and did analyze her behavior. As Ann talked of her feelings in anticipation of being criticized, a strong reaction was stirred up in Art, another group member, who spoke of his perfectionistic music teacher and his demands. In this way the group members' characteristic interpersonal operations are highlighted, thus giving each the opportunity to feel the anxiety concomitant with the reaction and to become aware of acts and feelings that he has been perhaps totally unaware of.

In the group situation the patient can become aware of unsatisfied strivings that are typical of some early developmental stage. He can reexperience the pain of the frustration of his desires in as close to the original situation as his chronological age allows with a minimum loss of self-esteem, for the group is a place where his imaginary or fantasied people come to life and are most vividly felt. This re-experiencing with its concomitant bringing to awareness the feelings that have been dissociated makes for growth. The patient in his group treatment can relive, in a symbolic way, all his life experience, and can experience the unique opportunity to live his psychic life over again.

Let me amplify this point. The groups that I have are heterogeneous in composition, with all age ranges represented. It is possible in the group situation to relive and work through feelings and attitudes that are typical of infancy, childhood, the juvenile era, preadolescence, early or late adolescence. At one time for one or more patients the group is a peer group, and we would find cooperation, banding together of peers against authority, competition, and conformity. Another patient may see the group as the family, and he may be experiencing some of the somatic feelings of anxiety that had their origins at a preverbal level in infancy. If the patient had never had the experience of finding one person who was particularly important to him, a chum, he might start this type of relationship in the group. It is through the development of this relationship that Sullivan felt that one's capacity to love matures. From the above it is clear that I believe the group is not necessarily either a family or a peer group, but will become for the patient what his and his therapist's parataxes demand and allow respectively.

In terms of directly handling a patient's needs for satisfactions and security, group membership gives one the feeling of being part of something and belonging that is often so hard to find in our present-day urban society. His emptiness and loneliness are more directly alleviated in his contact with other people, who are, after all his fears and expectations, human and therefore more similar to than different from himself.

I do not feel that I can conclude this paper without a brief word on this last point—humanness and the respect of it that characterized Sullivan, the man, and his technique. For it is not only the expertness of the analyst that helps the patient to grow and change. Rather it is his personality and the respect for other human beings and feelings for their suffering that he communicates. In the group situation by his gestures, facial expression, or nonverbal acceptance, as well as his verbalizations, the therapist communicates his respect for others. This is sensed by all and helps in the formulation of the group atmosphere, an atmosphere where each can without humiliation and with dignity expose his specific patterns of interpersonal relations. It is in such an atmosphere that parataxes can be pointed out without overwhelming anxiety and their resolution can take place.

In summary, we have attempted to show the relevance of Sullivanian principles to meet the challenge of working with patients in our present-day practice. These principles were shown to be based on the concept of an ever-interacting, constantly changing human being evolving from the human animal through absorbing the social and cultural perspective of those around him. The developing self-system was shown to have used certain dynamisms to protect itself. Through the example of an event in the group used to make the patients vividly and dramatically aware of their interpersonal operations, Sullivan's theory was applied to group practice. Group treatment was thus seen as an effective laboratory to explore and vividly verify one's patterns of interpersonal reaction as a prelude to learning their historical perspective and eventually changing one's behavior.

REFERENCES

1. For their invaluable teachings in this area, I thank Drs. Mary White Hinckley, Meyer Maskin, and Clara Thompson.
2. G. D. Goldman, "Group Psychotherapy and the Lonely Person in Our Changing Times," *Group Psychother.*, 8:247-253, 1955.
3. *The Common Sense Psychiatry of Adolf Meyer*, edited and with biographical narrative by Alfred Lief (New York: McGraw-Hill Book Co., 1948).
4. C. H. Cooley, *Human Nature and the Social Order* (1902), in one volume with *Social Organization* (Glencoe, Ill.: The Free Press, 1955).
5. K. Lewin, A *Dynamic Theory of Personality* (New York: McGraw-Hill Book Co., 1935); J. L. Moreno, *Who Shall Survive?* (Washington, D.C.: Nervous and Mental Disease Publishing Co., 1934).
6. J. L. Singer and G. D. Goldman, "An Experimental Investigation of Contrasting Social Atmospheres in Group Psychotherapy with Chronic Schizophrenics," *J. Soc. Psycho.* 40:23-37, 1954.
7. H. S. Sullivan, *The Psychiatric Interview* (New York: W. W. Norton & Co., 1954).
8. H. S. Sullivan, *The Interpersonal Theory of Psychiatry* (New York: W. W. Norton & Co., 1953).

16

KAREN HORNEY'S THEORY APPLIED TO PSYCHOANALYSIS IN GROUPS

Louis DeRosis

What makes us what we are? Freudian theory of motivation sees man as caught up in ingrained and inherent instincts, as described in the libido theory. But Karen Horney's view of human motivation questioned the Freudian viewpoint of the dominance of libido. For Horney, cultural patterns underpin the formation of character structure; character, as dealt with by Horney's theories of psychoanalysis, is molded by the impact of psychological factors in the environment upon the individual.

Examination of Horney's concepts can cast light on our understanding of, and our attempt to reorder, the character structures of people in group therapy. I believe that examining the application of her theory of human motivation to group psychoanalysis also permits us to study some aspects of the human scene.

For Horney, the influence underlying character development was not a matter of the impact or sum total of instincts, but, rather, the impact of the character of one human being upon that of another. Environmental influences of people upon the individual were for her the emotional greenhouse that encouraged individual growth and character development. Unfortunately, that greenhouse contains a variety of distortions that hamper growth and lead to man's loss of his essential being. Essential traits become distorted; these distortions pass from parent to child, child to child, adult to adult, and are responsible for the continual loss of time and energy to anxiety and hostility.

For Horney, the pressures of physical survival alone do not account for the horror man visits upon man. Rather, the motivation underlying that horror springs from the distortions imbued in the psychological environment in which we grow up.

Freud committed the common human error of confusing his own personal biases with those of his milieu. We are all prone to this error. It is a dominant trait from our earliest days, inducing emotional and intellectual blindspots. Through bias we are prone to make hasty conclusions and prejudgments. Our minds close when they should remain open to the possibilities and the wonder of taking in stimuli. Because of our tendency toward bias, with its unconscious roots, neurosis exists and is transmissible.

Horney's approach to group therapy comes to grips with the fundamental bias of our experience by concerning itself with the influence of human beings upon each other. Since Horney considered human existence to be the result of such interaction, logically, the group therapy situation is an ideal one since it permits a human being suffering from the effects of outwardly imposed conflict to change and grow by examining and understanding the roots of that conflict.

For Freud, "inner conflict" involved a struggle between the person and *impersonal* forces such as instincts, moral institutions, other social structures, and so on. For Horney, "inner conflict" arises as a result of contradictory influences imposed on the child.

In Horney's view, the child attempts to walk a razor's edge to selfhood. Few of us make that journey successfully. The child, whose development underlies the adult we become, loses his way. In his effort to cope, to present at least a seemingly solid, whole front to the world and to himself, the child generates a precariously balanced, stress-filled, easily disturbed order. In this delicate state he is blocked from understanding or expressing his true spontaneity. This separation is the beginning of neurosis, and neurosis is the cause of our suffering. We suffer not because we are involved in contradictions, for the ability to be so involved is crucial to our development. Rather, we suffer because we become *caught* in contradictions. In this maze of contradictions, the child loses access to his spontaneity. That loss hurts and injures us the most, for in the freedom to respond to our deepest being there is a quality of life we crave, however dimly we may be aware of it. We all seek to satisfy this hunger, though we may deny it or have it denied by some insistent influence around us.

Either that craving for spontaneity is awakened in therapy, or there is no true therapy. Strictly speaking, the past cannot be changed, but the appetite for spontaneity can be renewed or touched, depending on the circumstances of the individual's past. This is no mean achievement; it is the difference between being entangled in misery and having a vitality with which to pursue contentment.

Horney saw that the struggle toward healthy development involves conflict between two kinds of forces: (1) those that foster spontaneity, continuity, and self-evolution; and (2) those that are antithetical to this development toward self-liberation.

A child or an adult is like a pregnant woman who is living to bring forth her child. Forces within her and beyond her control produce the child; she must respond to those forces or endanger her own being. So it is with all of us all of the time. If we were not damaged by the encroach-ments of other human beings, we would always be wanting to deliver our-selves of the numerous "babies" we would constantly be generating. This is our nature; it is the process of unfolding life and of our development as human beings. Just as a baby cannot be conceived without two people, we must have contact with other human beings if we are to conceive and fulfill the healthy elements within ourselves.

To be inclined toward such "maternity" is to be involved with other people. This is the essence of Horney's emphasis on the matter of character development.

THE GROUP: SEEDBED OF BEING

In 1950 Horney encouraged a group of young people—Elinor Crissey, Benjamin Becker, Louis Landman, Benjamin Wassell, and myself, along with others—to set up groups for therapeutic work, in order to try out her then innovative concepts. She pointed out new problems that had to be faced, such as the possibility of the therapist's unwitting exacerbation of neurotic conflict in the group and the possibility of falling in with neurotic needs involving the danger of behavioristic reinforcement. She pointed out the danger of intensifying anxiety and depression with the attendant sequelae, the increased demand on the therapist for his attentiveness, the desirability of intrepidness, and the urgency of sizing up the possibility for multiple reactions and responses which dwarf the one-to-one of the ordinary analytic relationship. Although Horney realized that there were certain inherent drawbacks within the group situation, it was also apparent to her that the same factors, when employed judiciously and at the appropriate time, became the determinants of disengagement from the compulsive patterns of behavior that comprised the body of neurosis.

At the heart of being human is the urge for self-realization. Left on his own in the human situation (if not impaired by surrounding impedi-ments), according to Horney, a human being would pursue intermin-ably the process of realization until death; since the process, in terms of its inner momentum, is boundless.

This does not mean that a person must be isolated in the midst of the human situation. Quite the contrary. He is a participant in the human situation, weaving it into a new form through the workings of his own particular individuality and uniqueness. His individuality is in turn con-stantly renewed and refreshed by its contact with other people, from whom it receives opportunities for self-realization and continuity.

Those who suffer from the emotional blockages and distortions which comprise neurosis do not enjoy a free, creative, restorative exchange with the world around them. They give too much; they struggle to get, at best, a meager portion of nourishment; they weary; they despair.

A creative exchange is the central focus of group therapy. What happens among the members contributes directly to the emergence of the spontaneity in its members. This freeing of the individual to give and take, to ebb and flow with the group, marks "the cure"; it is at once the goal of therapy and the signal that a release from neurosis is taking place.

In the struggle against neurosis, the issue is not, as Freud contended, the return to regressions, as if in some magical or mechanical way a person has to restart his life's journey from the point at which his real self was blocked. Freud's therapeutic process involved that sort of genetic methodology, overlooking the fact that human existence occurs at the interface, the meeting place between two persons. That meeting does not occur in some hidden recess of the mind, nor does it matter whether or not we are trying to be correct in our relationship to the other.

Even though one may be unaware of an attitude that is being communicated, one is not responsible for it until one *can* be. Here is the heart of human discord. We tend to be more reactive in our response to that which the other is *in no way intending* to present. In so reacting, we tend to increase the other's hurt, for it is from that which hurts him most (in his scarcely tenable life position) that he is seeking to protect himself. And we merrily or viciously or unwittingly expose him to it!

We act from *our* unawareness of the impact we have on others, because we are seeking relief from the toils of what hurts *us*. We relieve ourselves by mindlessly ascribing our inner injury to the other, while never intending to hurt him. This happens in the group, as it does elsewhere, and it is upon faulty perceptions that the therapist must exert his influence, *at once furthering a free interchange while stopping the regrowth of that which injures.*

Horney, like Freud, saw that the engine of neurosis takes its power from conflict, but they did not agree as to the nature of the conflicting design. Freud saw man as a creature inevitably squeezed on all sides by the forces of the instincts within him and by those forces of an institutionalized morality as rigid in its demands as to make it nearly as compelling as those Freud held to be biologically ordained. Freud contended that through this inescapable miasma, the self struggles until it is overwhelmed.

Freud did not believe in immortality and he resented death, ascribing to it a malevolence so great as to be accounted for only in terms of an intricate battle fought against biology, an unbeatable foe, and an almost equally formidable historicized and mythologized morality. In this tortured and pathetic vision, Freud himself struggled to gain an upper hand, if only a rhetorical one, on death. His pessimism was consistent with this dilemma.

It is not surprising, then, that for Freud human development was fragmented into stages. Pessimism is not induced by knowledge of one's finiteness, but develops through an insistence on immortality that robs life of even the possibility of hope.

Freud turned simple human concerns into rigid, desperate absolutes, thus carrying over into psychiatry the same distressing traditional concerns that organized religion had evolved and inadequately dealt with in terms of man's emotional development. There is no way out of an impossible insistence except through relinquishing it; to insist on the impossible, the inhuman, is to become fixed on that which cannot grant human freedom.

The neurotic's "cure" lies in this process, in his becoming free enough to relinquish the various insistences on which he has wrongly staked his survival. He must be led to the discovery of aspects of existence that may free him from depending on the neurotic devices that have seemed to him, at the cost of so much pain, to be necessary to living. Those devices stem from emotionally fraught developments in man that displace real development, and they cancel out the possibility of a continuous relationship to the world and to himself. Freud saw this discontinuity as inevitable: to be lived with and somehow temporized. Horney did not view this discontinuity as inevitable, unless the patient's inner requirements made it unavoidable. She saw man's evolution of personality, given the freedom to develop, as a potentially life-long process.

For Horney, wholeheartedness of being was the foundation of the therapeutic relationship. It was, I think, also the foundation of her personality. She approached the human predicament in a wholehearted and positive manner, and though she experienced fatigue like any of us, she did not tire in spirit. Horney's sense of unrelenting continuity is the very stuff for which one yearns, even if there are no words to express the feeling, or even if one cannot admit that one believes such a state of being is possible.

The patient who seeks out an analyst has the beginnings of such awareness. He has begun to sense that he has lost touch with his true desires, with some force that could sustain him from day to day, despite the buffetings of the world. Instead he finds himself repeatedly going astray, losing touch, and experiencing discontinuity without knowing why. He also begins to feel a new sort of distress, something deeper; out of that new discomfort and pain, therapy may commence.

Because he is riddled with misconceptions and self-deceptions about the nature of being, the neurosis-plagued person can rarely come to such a realization without first leading himself into a long-term slough of misery or personal tragedy. That which he *must* see as true is fraught with falsehoods made seemingly workable because it feeds the false self which he believes he must evidence or he will perish.

Even Freud's efforts to demythologize what religions were purveying only served further to entrench the root of the problems of man's misconceptions and self-deceptions about the nature of being. Freud created enemies for his cause and then mistook this enmity for proof of the validity of his system. It is true that it *was* evidence of the effectiveness of his attack, but not of the effectiveness of his grasp of the human condition, which required not merely an attack but the simultaneous pointing to a way out of the status quo—another realm, a somewhere else, that the culture and the patient had yet to dream about.

To insist that something be torn down and discarded as unworthy is of little value if, once having destroyed the entity, one has nothing with which to replace it. We talk here not of Camelot or Shangri-La; we talk, rather, of a better way to be in a world which will not change to accommodate us. The question is: What is the best life we can have if we can make the most of our attributes? Freud held out little hope of any real improvement, except in coping with the fixed nature of ourselves and those around us.

Horney, on the other hand, worked to show how individuals might regain touch with their original selves and find a richer, more human existence even as they continued to live in an indifferent, confusing, and hostile world. To the extent that the truly vital person could move with the force of himself, he could, Horney believed, persist in the face of such environmental conflict and progress to the realization of selfhood. Is the world our oyster? No, Horney saw the world too realistically for that. But she surely believed the world could be, short of personal calamity, oyster enough.

BASIC ANXIETY: CHILDHOOD MENTAL DEVIL

What goes wrong? What destroys or gets in the way of the basic continuity which could sustain us? What shatters our original sense of being? What horror is induced in children that requires them to give up their connection to the source of their humanity? How long can any child hold out before relinquishing his hold on the simple impulses which would carry him wherever his sense of delight and interest might take him?

The extreme tragedy resides, of course, with those who lose all sense of continuity and cast themselves adrift on the shoreless sea of psychosis, losing touch not only with themselves but with the world. Hope for these must be limited; it is far greater for those who, however wounded, still seek to interact with the world around them.

The question persists: What destroys our capacity for serenity in our relationship to the world? A beginning toward the answer lies in an understanding of the anxiety that possesses our hearts and drives out peace when wholeness is shattered.

If we concur with Horney that at the heart of neurosis is conflict induced by the already conflict-ridden and conflicting character structures of parents and society, then it follows that life first inflicts upon a child this nameless sense of disarray, fragmentation, and unwholeness. The child's early sense of the environment is one of fearsome kaleidoscopic fragmentation. Everything splits; nothing holds together. Anxiety is triggered within an atmosphere fraught with conflict. Conflict and anxiety go hand and hand in our mental chemistry.

Even in utero, the infant may not have that sense of physiological harmony which an anxiety-free, vital mother would send coursing through her child's circulatory system. With demonic consistency, children come into a parental world where existence may be an almost constant sensing of jeopardy and living tension. Personal and interpersonal parental conflicts are silently visited upon the child. Long before he has the capacity to name these oppressive and subverting feelings he suffers their effects. It will be a long time, if ever, before he will be able even to name them, far less understand them.

By then, if that day ever comes, he can collect his feelings into symbols; but the transformations they have undergone are so numerous, so complex in the coverings of the real with the false-but-seeming-real, that he may be almost overwhelmed by the difficulty of the task that lies before him. This is generally apparent in the school situation, in which the child is unable to grasp the simplest of human connections. He responds as if he were mute, or his answers are completely inappropriate. Finally he ceases to be an active agent in his existence. Such a child might be labeled "retarded."

At that point the ultimate crisis ensues. With the disappearance of a relationship to oneself, there occurs a sense of impending disaster, of insufferable disordering. When one's sense of continuity is being constantly impaired, it is imperceptibly supplanted by a sense of anxiety. Horney called this "basic anxiety." The term is misleading if one ascribes inevitability to it. I am referring at this point to the term as it is used in formal existential thought, that is, "existential anxiety."

Existential psychotherapists believe that this kind of anxiety is a usual accompaniment of being alive. Horney would hold, I think, that it is not inevitable that we all suffer basic anxiety, but she would admit that very few of us escape it.

HUMAN RELATIONSHIPS: THREE MOVES

We have referred to the contradictory approaches to which the child, and then the adult, is subject. Horney posited that most of these contradictory impulses consist of three irreducible components, or "moves." They pertain to relational modes between persons. We can address ourselves to each other, against each other, or we can isolate ourselves from each other. As long as these moves, *toward, against,* or *away* from each other remain choiceful and relevant, they are consistent with growth-producing development. It is only when they become rigidly compulsive—that is, *choiceless* —that they may be regarded as neurotic.

Furthermore, one must remain acutely aware that at the center of a civilizing process is the essential continuity of human relationships. It is interrupted only by sleep. The child has little sense of the interruption; he feels he wakes immediately after having fallen asleep. Horney believed that the three primary moves of *toward, away,* and *against* were only diverse ways of sustaining this continuity. They are the basic triad that sustains human encounter. They *may* be divisive, implosive, or explosive, but they are not necessarily so; they *may* have the effect of carrying us to the gratifications of self-realization. Indeed, when the possibilities for variation among these three moves are abundant and unfettered, we have optimal conditions for human growth. But when the child is hindered in moving freely, eccentric and ultimately brutalizing varieties of development will occur. Human beings need to move *toward, away,* and *against,* but if the individual is to enjoy his existence that need can be fulfilled only along paths of development of the genuine, original self.

Blockage of such freedom results, generally, in these effects upon the child: (1) the child will appear to be overly dependent if the *toward* mode predominates; (2) he will seem overly inclined to isolation and solitude if he is intent upon *awayness;* and (3) if his vitality is such that he is inclined to be oppositional—negativistic, a fighter—this comprises the *against* mode. Such a person strives to manipulate others. A child may develop all three of these now *insistent* modes consecutively or intermittently. In fact, all neurotically afflicted persons enact some combination of all three modes, as I shall explain later.

SENSE OF CONTINUITY

We all have an inclination, however subdued it may be, to relate wholeheartedly to each other. We all yearn to "identify" with our fellow human beings, to be the same as others. We yearn to find a sameness within the identity of others, though we know that this identity is not wholly ours, for to identify totally with another human being is rank emulation and results in a loss of self, a submerging of one's own identity. On the other hand, the inclination to discover elements of sameness between oneself and others is substantially the means of deriving our sense of self-identity.

If a child is made to feel that he is totally outside the pale of human sameness, he will not perceive elements of sameness with others. He will therefore have no sense of being and no sense of his being will be part of the civilizing process which may lead to self-discovery.

I believe that our exaggerated emphasis on individualism, our over-emphasis on various forms of apartness and the value of "standing on your own two feet," have been major factors in the many-faceted "identity crises" in which our children are caught. They feel they are not merely different from their parents, but in an indescribable sense alienated from them, a world apart. They want no part of the "establishment" that is the world of their parents as they experience it, or rather as they fail to get a chance to experience it.

Here is the rub. One cannot feel *that* different, *that* alien, and sustain a sense of identity. Thus the movements of toward, away, and against occur in the free sense only when they exist in a matrix of unimpeded parental acceptability. The source of this matrix can exist only if the parents themselves are free to move among these three modalities. Their child simply presents them with a new opportunity to impart whatever patterns of being, whatever sense of existence, they themselves are free to live or are caught up in. And since so many of us are so caught, "hung up" as the current idiom so well expresses it, it is no wonder that basic anxiety is diffused from generation to generation. When this transmission of anxiety exists, there can be little or no continuity between parent and child. We cannot develop a wholesome relationship with that which we fear or which conveys fearful things to us.

Parents confuse their desire to have things a certain way with having to hurt their child. The parent, who is clearly the greater force, has only to be firm in his position to help the child grow. The child may try "to have his own way," but he will discover that opposing and resulting from his effort is neither hurt nor fear, but indifference. The parent is not inclined to alter the mode of relationship at that time. In this fashion he stands and thus "opposes" the child. There is no way for the child to proceed; he has no recourse but to let it go. Neither hurt nor frightened himself, he suffers no sense of rejection. On this occasion, nothing has gone on. The parent is still firmly there, as is the child. Here are the makings of equality.

Parents in a shop with a child who wants a toy demonstrate diverse modes of relating in action. One child will get all he wants and be satiated, as it were, automatically. Because there is no "opposition," what happens in the store is simply the transporting of whatever toys he wants to his bedroom. Often that same child will also be impelled to gorge himself with food, so our picture now becomes one of an obese child getting all the toys his urges fix upon.

But if, as in other cases, the parent is confused and arbitrarily passes from "yes" to "no," then we will observe a child who seems to employ various strategies as cleverly as he can. The nature of these strategies will depend on his intelligence, his ingenuity, and his past experience. We will observe some very intricate steps associated with the parent's relationship to his own main modes of relating. If the mother is in a "good mood," the child will sense that by pushing just a bit harder he will have his way. The child will adapt his strategy to meet the conditions of the moment.

What evolves, outwardly expressed and occurring along with the obtaining of the toy, is *the inner experience of playing effectively on his mother's (or father's) feelings.* It is unspoken, not acknowledged in any way, because it is not part of the child's awareness. This is the prototype for "the making of the unconscious." Contrary to Freud's views, I believe that the unconscious is not only preceded by the conscious, but that it would be totally superfluous if children could grow openly and directly in relation to the parental world. The unconscious would not occupy so forceful a role, for it would not be *occupied* by various warring forces.

The only unconscious worth the name would be the gestating baby. This unconscious is not the dark and murderous id, but a positive force that marks the onset of new possibility, whether one is moving *toward*, *away*, or *against*. As one moves, so does one's life move, if one remains free to relate creatively to others.

By contrast, when we are "at war," literally or verbally, how are we engaged? Is there an alteration of the unconscious? Is its ability to allow the mind to move freely along creative paths incapacitated? I believe so. Let us consider this analogy.

The military "psyches" you to kill. Even though the killing may be in self-defense, it still means that one must give up some creative propensity; one must transform oneself into a life destroyer. In the past, a knight in battle chose a specific opponent and, as the combat raged, heard the grunts of his chosen victim, saw the blood gush out of the man's wounds, and finally killed him, experiencing a sense of relief at remaining among the living.

Somehow this is supposed to be less alienating than the anonymous death dealt out with bombs and rockets. In my view, this is not so, nor do I believe that in the days of knighthood killing one's enemy served to heighten one's own loyalty to life. Today and yesterday, killing serves only to inflame the urge to destroy. To the extent that we are in any way "heightened" by the adversity we visit or see visited upon others, we are lessened as human beings sickened by this dehumanization.

The child who "got his way" by manipulating his "good-mood-today" mother is unaware that he has thereby "destroyed" her. It is no longer *what* he does that matters. What becomes important to him is that he must get his way, and eventually he will need to do so no matter what the cost, because he will lose all sense of defining the cost in any way that could be authentic to him. Getting his way becomes a stand-in for his sense of being with the other. He has, in the deepest sense, gotten rid of the other. He has his own way, but the result is that he is alone. When we are "having our way" we are alone, no matter how successful we are or what sort of accolade we receive.

Accolades can have the effect of confirming us in our "splendid" manipulation of the other. Who manipulates, he who praises or he who receives the praise? The one, the other, or both? Vicariously, the praise provider wants to be on the stage as well. This is the game of the unaware manipulator, no matter what its form, whether ultimate as in war or temporary as in a performance that sends the audience into wild applause.

Praise, compliments, accolades in any form, do not admit to participation or to genuine openness with one another. "You were great" is a hollow statement, no matter how well meant. If dialogue is to mean something to us, it must have substance or lead us to a statement of our own which opens our minds. The game of the accolade cannot do that; it is not true dialogue of the sort that makes us take part in a meeting of minds. As with the accolade, so with the verbal brickbat; it is all one-way. I kill you or you me, I praise you or I deride you.

Does this rigidity come from the id? I believe it comes from encounters with a world that does not respond and does not heed our assertions. What could be a conferring becomes, instead, a stage on which we are not granted a chance to do our thing, on our own terms. In other words, one is not allowed to enter into dialogue with others; a one-way communication becomes fixed.

IDEALIZED IMAGE OR INVENTED SELF

In order to understand the implications of the condition of being caught up in, preoccupied with, and even possessed by issues of victory and defeat, Horney's concept of the idealized image must be examined. Long before the current spate of allusions to "self-image" developed, Horney had discovered the psychic formation which she saw as a substitute growth for one's sense of being. She called it the *idealized image*. I like to think of it as the *invented self*.

According to Horney, this idealized image takes diverse forms. At heart, it represents the idealization of any of three major moves: (1) "I can become a giant of a fighter, fighting, like Don Quixote, the impossible dream"; (2) "I can become the most gloriously abject, saintly provider, worthy only of your contempt for not being able to be even more abject and generous"; or (3) "I can become the most exalted of lonely travelers thinking the greatest of thoughts in the solitude of my paneled study."

The first form comprises the *against* mode, the second is *toward*, and the last is *away*. By the time the child forms such images of himself, he is too repressed to allow himself the freedom to sense his own spontaneity. His parental world failed to provide him with that human matrix of which we have spoken. Instead, he has been used by his parents to further their own needs and ends. The child had no recourse but to react in kind.

The child whose existence is determined by a mother's fickle moods must pursue his existence as if it were a predetermined matter, and so it is, for this is how he has been conditioned to *feel* his existence to be. His continuity now depends on how well he manipulates these predeterminations, and not on the certainty of creative dialogue.

He has substituted the predictability of his tried and true manipulations *for* spontaneity. It is a deadly transformation and one that, as time passes, is deepened, complicated, and embellished. It is bedecked with attributes which are caricatures of the life that might have been. To a small boy, hungry for closeness, a chance home run in a schoolyard ball game becomes the stuff out of which he, now the recipient of seemingly universal applause, weaves a picture of himself as loved by all. Whether he is shy or arrogant about it, he sees himself rigidly as existing through that single act. He has moved himself into the center of that stage, surrounded on all sides by people who *look up* to him. Until this moment, he was lost in a subservient position in which he was required to despise himself. Now he has turned the tables. He controls all during that applause. This is probably the single greatest falsification in his long series of would-be self-fortifications. Although in turning the tables he achieves a sense of static certainty which he mistakes as life, the event cannot provide him with real continuity. Quickly he feels empty; he needs more of the same. He is now required to pursue the certitude of this concoction he mistakenly perceives as his self. With each "success" he puts another chain around the bondage of himself, all the while believing he is coming into a "splendid" state of life.

Can he realize that this course of action really means a kind of death, the death of his capacity to sense life freely, on his own? Unfortunately, he cannot, for he is now on a search without the original compass of self; he has a substitute compass deflected by the ways of being foisted on him by others. Because it is unconscious, his deflected quest now seems real to him. It is automatic, and he is an automaton.

The neurotic deflection, or distortion, always contains the makings of its own undoing. Even though the child forms an idealization to stand in for himself, his original self is still looking for its own expression. Conflict between these two forms asserts itself constantly.

In the child, the forms of this conflict are rather simple and easily discerned. A child is almost always busy, occupied, self-revealing; his actions and usually his motives are clear-cut. For example, if he is moving *toward* people in order to be pleasing, he is seeking the approval of the others. If he is of the *against* variety, his tendency is to oppose others. If he is employing the *away* mode, he is distant. All the while he keeps his eye on the adults around him, giving clues concerning the nature of his quest for identification.

Since it is clear that the child involved in these actions is not free to pursue his own particular inclinations, why the "weather eye" on what the adults might appear to be feeling toward him? He needs to know how he must continue to relate to them. In imagining he knows what is behind their gaze and/or the set of their faces, he loses his capacity to be at one with himself. What we mean by his self is his acceptability to the world as he is involving himself with the spontaneous impulses that arise in him. Instead of relating to his own spontaneous impulses, he is diverted; he must relate to the world in ways that he believes are required of him. Thus he buys his way into being a wanted member of the group.

By contrast, how rare is the child whose parents are simply pleased at the fact of his existence and are capable of accepting him exactly as he reveals himself to them. Rare indeed is the child who has the good fortune to be born to a father and mother who impose no conditions on his remaining in the midst of their company. Such a child has internalized a sense of the unchangeable fact of his being a member of a group. This, too, is automatic, but not in a compulsive or rigid sense. Rather, he is suffused with a sense of self-perpetuated knowledge that he belongs without question, doubt, or hesitation. That child lives with the continuity experienced by the other members of his group. This group feeling explains, at least in part, the raison d'être of ghetto structures, religious groups, and so on, that attempt to generate "belonging."

Only in the matrix of such feeling can the child "forget" his basic survival needs, because they will have been taken care of as part of his belonging to the group. When these needs are filled automatically he is also automatically free to engage his spontaneous impulses as he meets the world. Optimally, this freedom is sustained as his capacity to engage the world evolves in greater and greater complexity. Such a child will experience no conflicts of the kinds we have described. He is free and at peace —a happy contrast with the child who must be constantly on the alert against those upon whom he depends for at best a semblance of a communal, nourishing life.

The "on guard" child must continually qualify the modes that are available to him; instead of growing freely, he develops in ways he regards as self-protective. He conducts himself as if he were literally being threatened in his attempt to survive as a member of the group.

In such a self-protective context, food may become inordinately important, a prime example of the distorted perceptions of such a child. He mistakes the parents' overfeeding of him as a sign of his being a part of and acceptable to the group. Overeating becomes a continual reentry rite into the group, his revalidated membership card. He eats excessively as a means of exciting safety-inducing feelings. If the child cannot pursue his spontaneous impulses, this block constitutes a threat to his human existence, or the guise of humanity which he sees as the only way to be.

We love to please each other, but *toward* persons transform pleasing into appeasing. We love to oppose each other, as when we are engaged in games. But the child engaged in protecting himself doesn't love his need to oppose the other; he opposes others out of fear. We also sometimes love to be alone. But when the troubled child resorts to solitude out of fear, he clearly cannot love that solitude. Rather, it constitutes an attempt to get away from people who are out to hurt him. Far from being a pleasant retreat for the purpose of recreation, his is a desolate withdrawal into loneliness from a field of combat where wounds were inflicted on him. To escape from loneliness, he must face the prospect of returning to that battlefield.

A patient once said that the feelings derived from watching her parents epitomized her childhood. "All I ever did was look at them," she said. She looked at them to determine how best to appease them in the next instant. Gradually she came to realize that the underlying disposition of her parents was to hate her. Later, she experienced whatever criticism or differences that were leveled at her as hate; any conflict between her and her parents was, she felt, a sign of their ill feeling toward her.

By contrast, the child who feels the true acceptance of his parents experiences criticism as simply an occasion on which a parent helps him make new distinctions about the nature of the world and his relation to it. Patients in group therapy feel, in various ways, as unacceptable as the patient just mentioned.

THE GROUP

Such patients, although they long to do so, cannot verbalize their feelings at first. They struggle for an expression of feelings which have remained denied, and they begin to want to belong to the therapeutic group. The struggle to belong becomes apparent when an alignment of their respective idealized images for *confronting* each other, rather than *presenting* themselves to each other, occurs.

After the initial phase of the struggle for recognition (of their images) a phase of stand-offs and standstills begins, and group members resort to silence. No one wants to talk and no one is inclined to give an inch. Some become bitter, some quietly disappointed. Some look for redress. The question is: What are they wanting? Are they looking for redress for the unfairness of a childhood that deprived them of their chance for a spontaneously and humanely cherished existence? That is what we would like to believe. But, as already indicated, because of the development of the idealized self, such is not possible at this time; the person thus blocked is not aware of the terms and conditions of that blockage.

The "child in us" has no way of knowing that it desires to be wanted on that basis. What the patient seeks at that time is redress of his self-image, a self-image that has not been properly admired or properly accepted. The patient cannot know that his being is safe from outside influences; only he can violate his being. No one "out there" can "put it down" or inflate it. Outside influences can, however, induce him to take refuge in a false image of self.

The patient cannot know that his true self is inviolate because parental assaults induce in him a shift away from *being* toward the idealized self, a shift which cannot be altered without therapeutic help. For most, the very devices that are invented in childhood to deal with assaultive influences only serve to extend further the distance from the true self. The external assaults split us; then we split ourselves even more in trying to live with the disturbances caused by external factors.

Thus, the therapist must face the fact that group patients experience their invented selves as if they were their true selves. It is safe to assume that most people unwittingly come to group therapy in order to have their self-images repaired or somehow "debugged." The intensity of this demand is illustrated by the quality of rage that is evinced when these reparations are not forthcoming.

Group members are not aware that they live lives of despair out of a failure to attain their respective images, or out of a failure to gain confirmation of that image from others. A sense of futility is not the outcome of "underachievement," "excessive ambition," loneliness, or lovelessness. It is the pursuit of the creation and support of an idealized (inhuman) image that results in hopelessness and despair. Even when the patient is led to believe that he is meeting with success, there is always the underlying, haunting feeling that "it will not last," or "it isn't really for me," or "why do I feel hollow when I should feel good?" That day may arrive when the patient recognizes despair and hopelessness not as signs of an authentic self, but as the hopelessness of a way of life that he had evolved in a struggle to deal with the assaultive and inhibiting effects of relationships experienced within a parental or cultural context.

Once the idealized self has been mobilized, it becomes the stand-in for the real self. In evolving an idealized, invented self one sets into motion a process which is probably the most deleterious of any which has ever beset man. What is worse, the person comes to hate that fabricated self when it fails, as it inevitably must. Thus, his original self becomes the enemy of an idealized self. He regards the former as infirm, unpredictable, and fickle. He explains that his failure is not his responsibility. He regards the very events that would verify and underscore his humanness as the causes that signify and compel his ignominious failure and defeat.

Humanness is marked by attentiveness to spontaneous impulses and to efforts to relate those impulses to the world. Humanness feeds on the individual's joyful awareness of what he has the capacity to do, free of any requirement about what others must do or be. Spontaneity flows from such attributes, but it is also drawn forth by what are perceived as the attributes of the world around one. One takes in order to give of his being, and that trade-off can never lead to anything but enrichment of self, for we all draw inspiration from our worlds.

To the *invented self*, however, spontaneity is an enemy because of its unpredictability. This point is illustrated in the story of Aladdin. The magician, who is trying to regain the lamp Aladdin took from him, goes through the streets of Baghdad crying out, "New lamps for old, new lamps for old!" By this means—trading the new for the old—he does get hold of the magic lamp again. But in repossessing the lamp he simply assures the inviolability of his glorified self. The magic of the lamp is not of himself, though he cannot imagine life without it; he must have the lamp he regards as the essential prop of his existence.

The invented self does not *exist* (exist, to come out). Its chief raison d'être is to insure itself against the encroachments of spontaneity. This is the principle impediment to creativity with which the neurotic person must deal. Creative output in the neurotic person occurs in spite of the attempts of an invented self to insure a changeless state of nonbeing. The struggle for and against creativity is probably one of the most profound sources of conflict arising in us. Conflict occurs between the healthy urge to engage one's spontaneous impulse—from which all creativity takes its origins—and the neurotic struggle against these impulses. The block to one's nascent impulses, the spontaneity of self, derives from a static, invented self. Nothing must happen that is unexpected or unforeseen, for it could contain the seeds of change, and change portends disaster. Anything that threatens to modify the invented self must be avoided.

The human concoction I label the *invented self* is powered by every inner resource available to an individual. These resources include one's physical vitality, intelligence, sensitivity, creativity, talents, and experience. In addition, the source-experience, the dynamo giving rise to the invented self, derives from experiencing physical pain. Infants experience pain when they are wet or hungry. We all wish to avoid pain, a wish seminal to our need to move toward self-realization, to give of our being to the world, and to gain a sense of well-being; the persistent blocking of that seminal wish gives rise to malaise and eventual neurosis. Automatic interest in avoiding pain insures the use of pain as the means for parents to enforce demands. The parent may literally beat the child if he does not comply, and often without the child's understanding the reason for the chastisement.

Authority demands obedience and visits punishment upon those who do not comply. Adam and Eve were thrown out of paradise for their act of disobedience. The pain they experienced due to this act was willed upon them by their parent. It is not an accident that this story, told and retold by mankind from the early days of civilization, represents the ultimate authority as inscrutable and answerable to no other entity. An authority that imposes rules and punishes rule breakers implacably, and sets up standards too demanding for mankind, while denying and deriding that essential spark of man's uniqueness—his curiosity. The wonder is that so many people, generation after generation, have taken the "authoritarian" charge of disobedience to heart, feeling both the guilt of being human and the need to treat their offspring as likewise tainted with humanness.

God as parent neither took the time nor had the inclination to discover what his errant children were about as they exercised their curiosities. Far be it from him to explain what underlay the punishment he was meting out. The monopoly he wanted to exercise was a secret. In such terms, we can infer from the millennia-old tale which is the source for the earliest chapter of Genesis that God, the original parent, could not tolerate equality—a fair psychological process between people—any more than the great majority of parents who have succeeded him throughout the ages of man. We are all unwitting exploiters; we cannot strike a balance between give and take with those who are in any way less powerful than we. Those of us who are, for whatever happy reason, clearly aware of being exploiters rarely know the originating impulses which drive us. In any event, the sense of clear evidence of our being both free of and involved with each other is piteously lacking in the vast networks of exploitation and counter-exploitation which are all about us. Although exploitation exists everywhere in our lives, the process whereby it occurs and keeps on occurring is, I believe, largely unconscious.

Specifically designed to deal with overt instances of exploitation, even the law, at best, is inadequate, for it must be limited to the conscious realm of human behavior. Its methods are the same as the biblical ones of revenge and punishment. Much as we like to think that our laws are fair, justice, it turns out, is on the side of God, interested in preserving a monopolistic state of affairs. So-called impartiality of the law is really non-partiality to the human condition. The law believes itself to be better equipped to manage the affairs of humanity itself, even though there is something to be abstracted from humanity. Because of abstractions, the law must move to the side of interests vested in the status quo. I do not mean, in this connection, the establishment or the so-called rich. They suffer no less than the poor, though they do it with more gadgetry, pomp, and airs.

The status quo to which I am referring is that imposed by a shift from the evolution of the original self to the insuring of the maintenance and influence of an invented self. This variety of self depends on strategies for its survival. It has given up the freedom to pursue those original impulses by means of which newness, a sense of continuous discovery, open wonderment, and enlivening curiosity, would have come to exist as the foundation of the personality. Instead of an original self, we are given the concept of original sin and its accompanying punishment. And just as God took his vengeance on Adam and Eve, so does the law avenge itself for any infringement of its codes.

Similarly, when the invented self is unable to compel the residual original self to live by its codes, it too will take its revenge. This is a step that the invented self takes in turning upon the original self—whatever vestiges of it remain—as a means of forcing it to do its bidding. In this manner, all sense of concern for that first self, the real self, is gradually lost. That self becomes utterly expendable to the means and ends of the invented self. In short, the invented self employs the machinery of pain, hate, torture, and even the threat of death in order to enforce itself, in order to become and remain dominant.

SUICIDE

Suicide is largely understandable in terms of the ultimate rage of an invented self which has been beaten on all sides and takes its revenge by destroying the self, the real self, which it holds responsible for failure.

Whether or not the individual comes to such a critical pass, the tug-of-war between the "hollow man," or the invented self, and the man-who-might-have-been, the real self, produces our patients' eternal inner hell. Contradictions and inconsistencies abound. Seemingly wise and protective counsels of the invented self collide with the longings of the real self, creating the tensions and conflict of a constant inner splitting, or dividedness. It is a struggle that goes on within most of us, a struggle between the "rigged" self and the self that was choked off but not entirely destroyed in childhood. Thus we are split, and the extreme form, a so-called "split personality," is not uncommon.

Those who have reached a stage of "image-failure" so stressful that they are on the brink of destroying themselves are not good candidates for group therapy. This applies especially to those who have a drive to take out their need for self-punishment (the need to kill themselves) on others. This process *can* have a self-relieving effect, but the group members would then be mere targets, scapegoats, a role which would scarcely be healthy for them.

Such punishing drives against the group are unavoidable to some extent, however; they act as safety valves for such people. The therapist must watch closely for the appearance of such behavior; indeed, monitoring it is one of his main occupations, especially early in the group's existence. If such attacks on the group by self-punishing persons become too strong they will cause the group to fragment, and may even drive some members away. In any event, they cause needless suffering. To minimize such eventualities, the therapist must exercise all possible judgment in the selection of the group.

CHOOSING GROUP MEMBERS

Clearly one ought not to compose a group in which all the members are the type of person driven to experience himself only in opposition to and dominating toward others. Equally ill-advised would be a group in which all members were isolates. Likewise, a group in which all members spent their time outdoing each other in being compassionate and comply-ing would also be unbalanced. In such groups there can be no mobilizing of the essential conflicts that the individuals experience in everyday life, for no movement or service to the group members could occur.

On the other hand, when a group has been properly composed and yet fails to "take," we can either look to the therapist or to the struggles among the group members in order to determine which conflicting forces are meeting other conflicting forces and resulting in a stalemate. The search for such root-causes comprises the therapeutic process. The goal of that search and that process is the freeing of the patient to experience not the conflict between himself and the other group members, but *the conflict which is the outcome of strategical compulsions in service of a way of being that denies life itself, both to himself and others.*

WORKING WITH THE GROUP

One of the larger problems in group therapy is: How are we to grasp the crosscurrents of conflict which are at work from moment to moment? It becomes apparent that group members can move in two major ways. They can move toward greater coherence—"in-groupness"—or they can move toward more and more fragmentation and, finally, toward dissolu-tion of the group itself. Further observation reveals that these modes of group behavior occur in behalf of neurosis as well as in behalf of whole-ness, or cohesion.

Fragmentation may involve the breakup of the group into subgroup discussions or into a silent state—the "silent treatment." Cohesiveness may show itself in a variety of forms, such as intense focusing on a single member's material, or focusing on a subject of general interest, which can itself take diverse forms. In cohesion there is a coming to a centralizing point.

In fragmentation there occurs a fracturing of a point, or effective insur-ance against any possibility of a point being established. The group will splinter into subgroups; there is listless inattentiveness; members read maga-zines or newspapers, knit, or eat with total concentration on what they are eating; they leave to go to the bathroom more often than biological func-tions require.

Such fragmented patterns can vanish suddenly if there is an injection of material which commands involvement. Such material may sometimes present itself after the session ends and the group has gone out to a coffee shop and group members share in lively conversation; suddenly they are together, cohesive. Similarly, an in-session cohesiveness can be dispersed just as soon as the members leave the consulting room.

These modes of cohesion and fragmentation of the group's attention move toward the spontaneous as well as the compulsive. In other words, at certain junctures the group may fragment—that is, divide itself into subgroups or no group (silence, eating, "hiding" by whatever device)—for the sake of facilitating the coming into being of a new perspective; *or* the group may enter into the same behavior in order to *insure* the operation of an old (neurotic) way. The same pattern is evidence in behalf of the cohesive dimension.

This multidimensionality of modes of behavior is in keeping with the goal of group therapy. That is because the group comes together for destructive involvement as well as for constructive involvement. At the beginning of a group's life, the preponderance of these processes exists for neurotic needs. We can be fooled into believing that a group's cohesiveness at the outset is constructive. On the surface everything is oh, so jolly, and the members appear to be "all for each other." But some months later it is clear that a jolly togethernesses was the means whereby each member staked out his "gold mine"—"I have been good to you and you must now pay me back."

Many of these dynamics are visible in the life of the usual groupings that occur in a given culture. No doubt the "character" of a group will take many of its forms from those to which we have been conditioned in our "subcultures": religious, scientific, political, and so on. These are, of course, groupings to which many patients have been exposed. Such experiences tend to lend a sense of "ready-madeness" to the group's character which we can bring into play in the course of composing a group, or this sense of "ready-madeness" may turn up on its own during the group's life. This condition we may describe as the "we're all in the same boat" feeling.

The American culture mix contains, among other things, the tendency toward "togetherness" and another, though less prevalent, tendency toward "individualism." Today, involvement in individualism is occurring more by default than did the insistent individualism of the past. Today the preponderant bias works against fragmenting in behalf of a tenuous cohesiveness bought by way of Woodstocks, communes, and the like. The old "rugged individualism" is being replaced by the enforced individualism of the rebel, the dropout, the drug user. From these ranks are coming our newest heroes, whose heroics are employed in gathering worshipers about them. The old-time individualist had no such end in view. He walked alone on the beach or on the mesa, and in this way "resolved" his life course. John Wayne types are not troubled by conflict. Such a he-man typifies "the man of decision," the man who meets his problems squarely and "makes it all come out right."

Fifty years ago the weight of sympathy would have inclined us more toward isolation or fragmentation. In today's groups, the inclination is toward "togetherness." This trend alerts us to a variety of influences and biases that operate within the group, exerting an impact softly or harshly, suddenly or gradually, covertly or overtly. These forces bear on the issue of selection of material. They also bear on timing: when to raise questions on matters of relevance, appropriateness, and so on.

It comes as no small relief when the group realizes that much of its tendency toward togetherness is the result of culture-push, rather than a self-produced interest. Similarly, group members feel liberated when they realize that some measure of their aloofness is the outcome of another "cultural *should*" that requires them to perform as Amy Vanderbilt and similar authorities so rule.

Fig. 16–1.   Framework for working with a group.

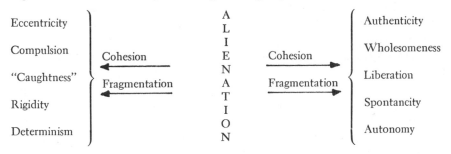

The framework of theory for working with a group can be laid out on the axis shown in Figure 16–1. As the therapist composes the group, he must be able to "manage" the left side of these equations from the beginning. If he cannot do this, the group will disintegrate. If he keeps it together by various "tricks"—such as authoritarianism, holding out "magic" help, giving olympian assurances, or using scare tactics such as expressing the dangers implied by various symptoms—he will have to face the wrath of the group when his threats and/or promises are not fulfilled.

Such tricks, or tactics, may work if the analyst profitably uses the time gained by those tactics to help the group members begin to grapple with the attitudes and feelings which have inhibited their growth. The key to real progress in group therapy involves the therapist's ability to take whatever steps are necessary to reduce the patients' feelings of rage, hostility, helplessness, and inner aloneness, the tortured emotions that have kept them from experiencing their own beings as a foundation for coming into touch with the *being of the other.*

Whatever the therapist does to assist the patient in touching his own possibilities of life and those of the world around him is "money in the therapeutic bank." It is the stuff which, little by little, will further the patient's sense that his life is in his hands as well as in the hands of the group.

It is a great day when the patient sees that the group is essential to his "discovering" himself, meaning the connections with those aspects of himself which he has repudiated because of his need to compel his old strategies to work. Now, through the group's offices (sometimes constructive and sometimes destructive), he begins the arduous task of accepting the dreadful fact that his *dis-ease* is in him, a fact which he has been disavowing since it did not jibe with his arduously achieved invented self. Only *he* knows how hard he worked to make a go of it.

A WORKING THEORY

A theory, if it is to be relevant, must account for the workings of its various parts. In a group, the "parts" in one sense are the members, even though we must consider as well each member as part of the whole.

The therapist is in the unbalancing position of having to consider both elements concurrently—the part (member) and the part as a member of the whole. But there can be only analysis of the member and his relationship to the others; there is no "analysis of a group." What we call group therapy is, at most, an experimental expedient generated by us for the sake of the *persons* who comprise the group. A theory of group therapy is here proposed in order to facilitate the knowing of the *holding patterns*, so that the therapist becomes freer to attend to the inner movements through which the individuals are passing. As his sensing attention moves back and forth on these axes, the therapist can tell just how much, and in what ways, the group is furthering its potentials for neurotic, or constructively liberating, moves; he can tell whether it is moving toward freedom or toward restriction.

Left to itself, a synthetically instituted group would most likely move toward fragmentation and dissolution. But the theory admits of the possibility that the group could be so constituted that it coheres out of destructive tendencies—that is, to prove to the therapist that he is not indispensable, to relieve anxiety by "togetherness" strategies which include everything from sex to pot parties. (Everything, I realize, indicates a broad range, but in my experience the group has proved extremely inventive in filling up time and expending energy in a very wide range of "togetherness" activities.) There are also the more intransigent strategies which deploy sadomasochistic needs, or members using each other as escape valves for the release of their anxiety by whatever other symptoms are generated. Such strategies can be quite vicious, for once the binds are made the group may cohere on this basis for a long time.

A group once set itself up as a do-good, "big brother" undertaking, a self-styled social agency which was to serve less fortunate souls than themselves from the problems of drug abuse. Each week I was bombarded by demands that I permit their new-found drug-afflicted strays to join the group. It could be said that their work was worthy, for undoubtedly it helped to get many of the people they "worked on" into drug therapy clinics. But it hid the underlying anxiety that would have fragmented their tenuous holds on each other if it had been permitted to operate, to come to the surface of their group dialogues.

At any given moment, simultaneous cohesion and fragmentation may be observed in a group, forces moving in the direction of health and of neurosis, as Figure 16–1 indicates. As can also be seen in the figure, there are four movements. These can alter from moment to moment, depending on the thrust of the neurotic movements and their attempts to "resolve" these new discomfitures with their old solutions.

The members who "move against" will take on the task of shaping up the others in accordance with their accustomed modes. Depending on how well they appeal to the "towarders" they will be effective in inducing a "cohesion." The *away* position will lend itself to joining in if it tends to strengthen their cherished solution, that of feeling at bottom more self-sufficient in the very act of seemingly joining the group. Such persons use the others in order to move more deeply and assuredly away. They will toy with the feeling of closeness for a moment so that their apartness will feel all the sweeter later. But these are the ones who are most prone to splinter the group by implicit means. They usually remain on the sidelines, where they look upon the rest of us with refined contempt, superiority, and self-satisfying independence. As Horney says, these individuals have a lien on freedom. They want freedom in the "from" form, and they want it for everybody. In that way they want the most for all of us. Thus is joined the struggle between these loners and the "againsters," who have plans of their own for herding the compliant ones into their camp.

"Love" has great appeal. The opposers need it to ameliorate their hardness. The independents need it to lend themselves an aura of social goodness within their otherwise all-too-rigid demands for unswerving fidelity to their ideal of splendid aloneness. A dose of compliant "love" is innocuous enough when it gets cold on those olympian heights they inhabit above all other mortals.

Such contention holds a dangerous fascination for the therapist. Indeed, there is danger for the therapist in a variety of fascinations that can overtake him as he observes the myriad pushes, pulls, maneuverings, openings, and closing, as each subgroup jockeys for the assertion of the power of their respective "solutions" to work upon the others. It is heady stuff because it is suffused with narrative threads of man's history.

The threads are those in which man has time and again become entangled, to his loss: the endless neurotically oriented chronicles of mankind believing all the while that somehow underpinning existence is the very struggle in which people are engaged. Victory in this struggle means the actualization of some truth which is the essence of their lives; something very precious will be made real by the triumph which shall be theirs at the happy end of the struggle.

Under the press of such feverish motives people struggle with marvelous ardor and dedication. We must not interfere with their momentum, for it comes out of their primordial selves—the selves which are still seeking their assertion in the world, despite the debris of years piled upon them. No, the therapist must only interfere with the content of the struggle, not the passion of the zealot.

We can have no quarrel with freedom, for example. Freedom in itself is the goal of all man's struggling. We do, however, move to combat so-called struggles for freedom when they are being deployed against the self or the other. Moves to counter damaging ploys contain an element of love, for love is a mark of our capacity to want not only our own well-being but that of others.

But when love is made a condition to an end, is it really love? How much have we destroyed in the name of Love, of God, of Country, of Lady Fair? Recently, American culture has tended to blind us to the hidden conditions of modern love. The women's liberation movement is trying to expose this in cultural terms, but its actions contain a new danger in that they provide the liberationists with an opportunity to exercise their repressed malice as if it had a new-found legitimacy.

On the other hand, the dominator-opposers stand out as "the buddies" for, by contrast, the "aggressives" in American culture are now on the wane, John Wayne notwithstanding. Their type reached its zenith with John F. Kennedy and sank to its low with the Vietnam debacle. The hidden effects of these cultural peakings-out of neurotic drives surface in the various subtypes, for each enjoys a variety of reinforcements as various phases are passed through.

This is meaningful to the therapist for it emphasizes the factors with which he must deal in the group, factors which militate to increase or decrease the entrenchment of the various "solutions" for anxiety and conflict. Such ersatz remedies or "solutions" are often influenced by some new fad or credo espoused by some important figure, such as a politician or movie star. There are fads in neurotic forms just as there are in fashions.

We are all too painfully aware of the lobbyists who tout their wares brashly with the innocence of a worker who has an honest day's work to do. Behind all such special interest groups is some need to be served at the expense of the rest of the people. The gun lobbyists espouse a cause; why and for whose benefit is it intended? For self-effacing "love" people? For solitary tower-dwelling people? Or are the gunmongers for the militants, the opposers?

It is comforting to realize that these axes of relationship in the group reflect an over-all wholeness. Witness to this is the fact that we have endured and increased in number to a total of three billion people the world over, now struggling to survive and gain what we perceive as the life course that will provide for our greater welfare. The pattern and the prospect of that struggle are, in most cases, fraught with the pain and blindspots of neurosis, one's own and that of others. Hence, the stress experienced by most men. But entwined thoughout the complex fabric of life is the overarching fact that the civilizing process appears to have an indwelling capacity to endure. From this we take heart as we see ourselves through some very bleak moments, moments when the neurotic entanglements feel oppressive and, at the extreme, suicide seems the only escape route.

For some, the pain may subside as they participate in group therapy. The most reassuring moment—one we may liken to the moment when medicine begins to make us feel better—is when a certain event marks the onset of the cure. The therapist knows that such an event may occur in many forms. One of the most poignant, and one for which group therapy was designed, is the massive shift of consciousness that can occur when the dwelling of the surface dialogue of the self-effacing "love" member and his would-be protectors, the dominators, is exposed for what it is, a self-obliterating ruse which the love member has been using to choke off real selfhood.

A woman came to this realization when she recalled a dream in which she offered her child to a rabbi for sacrifice. (The dream occurred shortly after Yom Kippur.) She awoke from the dream in disconsolate terror. At first she was filled with feelings of guilt and a strange disquieting remorse; then the shift occurred. She realized that the dream was precisely what she had been presenting to the world. The dream portrayed her approach to life: she had been relinquishing her autonomy in order to placate not the men in the group but her own exploitative tendency, which had been concealed behind her "face" of compliance and so-called love—a polarized substitute self symbolized by the rabbi. The ultimate prick of insight occurred with the help of the group. They told her something to the effect that they had seen her at times act like a baby, alternating with saccharine sweetness and struggling rage when her demands were unfulfilled. Swiftly, she connected with feelings of unacceptability she had felt early in life because of her father's criticisms of her.

She had disappointed him by the mere fact of being a girl. Twenty years of her life were spent trying to make up this loss to him, and a pattern of behavior was established through which she sought to achieve all her wants, authentic or otherwise.

In the group, however, one of her "protectors" could not abide her coming into herself, for he knew in his grandiose heart that she was slipping out of his grasp. He tried some diversionary tactics in order to siphon off attention from her, but to no avail.

The others sensed the scope of her transformation in progress and wanted to observe and take part in the liberation of this young woman. This infuriated the protector. How could they, he wanted to know, fall for her usual sympathy mongering? No one took his bait. At this point he picked himself up to leave. He paused, willing to be held back. It was a moment of truth; no one stirred an inch. The others kept looking at the woman whose dramatic change had triggered this development. He sat down, at which point I said that he had made an important decision, a decision constructive both from his standpoint and the group's.

The *against* types are the most fragile, for once they "shoot their loads" they have little else to fall back on, especially if their compliant and self-effacing acolytes are beginning to feel stirrings against their entrapments. The detached, *away* types are the longest-lived in the group. Their solitariness makes them best equipped to withstand the encroachments of the other two varieties. For these reasons they are also the most difficult to involve in the group's relationships. They explain it all on the basis of "tolerance" and "understanding." In this way they *appear* to be tolerant while effectively putting off the risk of living in the world with others.

In sum, the early hours of the group's life are spent in jockeying for the position which will tend to confirm all of the old, favored "solutions" for their distressed ways of being in the world. They are all busy repairing their invented selves, believing that only there lies their salvation. As we all too sadly know, this can be a ruthless process, holding for each of us our very survival. It is a precarious survival; a word, a glance can be felt as the beginning of a schism in that already too fragile cohesion.

The therapist tries to minimize this outcome in composing the group. The degree and varieties of sensitivity must be carefully gauged. The member who is "too far out" will quickly be pushed out of the group. A degree of difference will be tolerated, but if the difference is too great the "strange one" will be shunned, abandoned, and ridiculed, until his endurance is exceeded, at which point he will quit. Clearly, we wish to avoid such outcomes. There is enough distress involved in the group therapeutic process without adding to it by insufficient sizing up of the essential factors in group selection.

In addition to group selection, the therapist must conduct the group in ways which will facilitate two main outcomes at all times. First, he must work to prevent reinforcement of the members' usual neurotic solutions. Second, he must assume the task of developing a position of central trust, of openness, of the tacit promise that he, the therapist, is the new factor in their lives. Without the effective possibility of the *new*, there is no hope. Without this implicit hope, there is no "therapy" worthy of the name.

THE THERAPIST

There is a widespread belief that patients in group therapy will "take care of themselves" using their well-developed defenses. Therefore, the belief goes, the therapist is free to "be himself" with these patients, while they come up against each other and, in the process, discover the infeasibility of those defenses and work out new, more vital approaches to one another. So, under this and other rubrics, a new sort of license has been emerging for the therapist. Let us examine some of the implications of this "be yourself" approach.

The therapist, it is said, should be free to express his feelings to the group, free, that is, of all the circumspection in which he engages in a one-to-one therapeutic relationship. Somehow the fact of the group's being will suffice to smooth out the therapist's unwarranted intrusions and irrelevancies, no matter how much he sounds off, for he is one of the group.

The "we're all in the same boat" feeling is supposed to work in many ways, some of them mysterious, to ameliorate the rough spots and the triggerings which may set into motion all manner of defensive maneuverings. It is argued that it is good to activate these maneuverings, for then we can analyze that which was set free by the accidental occurrence. No one will deny the desirability of using what happens to emerge by accident, but this should be kept to a minimum, especially at the beginning of the group's life. The group members will trigger much more than can be handled, so there is a constant need for direction. Since the group members are triggering an overabundance of neuroticisms, what is the value of the therapist doing the same and adding to the burden which he must handle? Is he not the guide of, rather than contributor to, the maze of data and stimuli the group members are putting out?

It is one of the special features of group therapy that the therapist can render himself more effective *precisely* because he can sidestep involvement in the "output" dialogue while using the information elicited by members acting upon each other. And he can do so in more pertinent, timely, and appropriate ways if he does not attempt to contribute to and get caught up in the exchange of group dialogue. He is able to build the crucial sense of trust more rapidly and more pointedly by far than he could if he "sat in the boat" with the group.

Defenses are the unfortunate concoctions the patients have invented at a terrible cost to their primordial sense of being. We do not want those defenses to be reinforced at the therapist's instigation, for he would only ally himself with the hostile world which induced the bizarre, tortuous developments of these patients. Nevertheless, the therapist must engage himself wherever and whenever it is possible. And he must do so with all his feeling, knowledge, and experience, toward the goal of helping the members of the group.

That is why group treatment is so much more demanding than the relatively moderated, single-track quality and content of one-to-one. In both settings the therapist conducts the patient or patients through whatever is the current order of business coming into consciousness.

"Consciousness," as stated above, is employed by the patients early in the group's life as a means of sustaining, reinforcing, and, if necessary, extending and elaborating the neurotic solutions for their conflicts. The therapist, in turn, must be careful not to reinforce their solutions, and must simultaneously employ himself in ways which permit constructive feelings to emerge from the group members. That is, the therapist must not induce feelings of anxiety or panic in group members. (This element of theory opposes Freud, who maintained that one must keep the patient anxious in order for therapy to proceed.) Anxiety in the patient is the enemy with which the therapist must not be identified; if he is so tainted in the patient's mind, he becomes, along with other adverse forces in the patient's life, a generator of anxiety.

At best, anxiety arising in the patient from his dialogue with the therapist is a sign that a crossroad has been reached. The patient dreads being caught in conflict at a time when he is helpless, alone, weak, and devoid of resources. The therapist does not want him to be in this weakened condition, and so aims to help him gain strength. To move beyond that crossroads is the aim of therapy, the index of whether or not the patient is being helped. Therefore the therapist must do all he can to avoid being a party to anxiety, the great depleter of human strength.

SUMMARY

Horney's theory of neurosis consists in showing how the child gradually passes from being at the center of his true existence to living at its periphery. This happens, according to Horney, in well-defined phases.

First the child molds himself by distortedly conforming to the parents' requirements. These distortions take their forms from the three major modes by means of which we relate to each other: *toward*, *away*, and *against*. The *toward* child is the compliant, dependent, good child. The *away* child is the self-sufficient and solitary one. The *against* child is aggressive, using force to gain his ends.

With experience, the child will embellish these strategies and, as he grows older, make them into a substitute for himself. Thus he invents an image, relying on the above attitudes and ploys for its formation. When he cannot make the image work *at all times* he resorts to blaming others for his failure. In meting out that blame, he is externalizing his alleged imperfections (the allegations he is inferring from the stated and unstated criticisms of early authority figures) so that he always emerges untouched, unscathed, by them. But should he fail continuously at keeping his image "intact and perfect" as defined by him, he will be compelled to experience himself as "no good." Should this happen, he will form a despised image of himself.

Horney also found that a person may form other ways of keeping the self-image intact. Among these are: blindspots, compartmentalizing, rationalizing, rigid self-control, arbitrary rightness, elusiveness, and cynicism.

In taking any or all of these steps, the person moves farther away from his "alive" center. From this center, the site of original being, come elemental impulses which make possible new and creative relationships to the world of people and things. That world is the world which may sustain a vital existence, a world where one may find more constructive activities and interests than one has time for, a world with which the neurotic person has lost touch and the possibility of which he cannot even fathom.

For the person so troubled there are no new, creative openings into life; there are only renewed constrictions of the old mechanisms of defense. Life is a bore, a weary pattern of repetition; or a realm of oppression; or a series of triggers of anxiety and depression. The mix may differ but the constant in the mix is this: a sense of being hounded, enslaved, rather than being where we all once sought to be—free to let our minds and bodies, our beings, play.

When the therapist composes the group, Horney maintained, he should try to involve persons in a balance of the three major responses, or solutions, in order that all may experience the impact of the full range of those responses. Any weighting toward one or two of the three responses will distort the experience of the group and obstruct the course of the dialogue and, ultimately, the therapy.

Horney also set forth the theory of cohesion/fragmentation—the group's movement in two directions, holistically and neurotically. On this theoretical framework the positions of the group members with respect to each other can be represented and tracked. By this means we have a general sense of the group's impact on each person, how the resultant forces may be affecting the members. And such perceptions afford the therapist tip-offs as to the effectiveness of his interpretations and their follow-through outcomes.

Part 3

THEORY
AND TECHNIQUE

ALTHOUGH THIS SECTION is labeled "Theory and Technique," close inspection of its contents would indicate that we have presented essentially a collection of papers on a variety of techniques used to treat individuals in group therapy. The theory behind these techniques leaves a great deal to be desired. This is the weakness in group therapy even after the experience of many years. The original papers by Wender, Schilder, Lowrey and Slavson, Moreno, and Ackerman communicate some of the history of the development of group psychotherapy. A study of the papers makes it increasingly obvious that technique came first and theory later. Many techniques used by the earlier practitioners of group psychotherapy were based on psychoanalytic concepts. For the most part emphasis, in working with groups, was on the individual, and at times there was a denial of certain concepts advanced by social psychologists. We have included papers to illustrate the varied evolving approaches to group psychotherapy and technique.

The paper by Moreno has been included because he feels "it should be of value to the readers because it contains the first comprehensive table of the basic categories of group psychotherapy, a tabulation which has hardly been surpassed in the course of years."*

We have included a nonanalytically oriented paper by Drs. Truax and Altmann which stems from a Rogerian phenomenological approach to psychotherapy. The paper is a pithy survey of relevant psychotherapy research. Wolf's paper on the psychoanalysis of groups is a current summary. His extensive, earlier article in the original edition of this volume was deemed too lengthy for this edition. His paper may be considered representative of much of the thinking of group psychotherapists who stem from a psychoanalytic tradition. In another setting, he has expressed his

---

* Personal communication from Moreno. The editors believe a more basic article is the paper by Moreno entitled "Psychodrama and Group Psychotherapy," which appeared in *Sociometry*, 10:249-253, 1946. We were unable to secure the right to reprint it here.

concern that social theory will not give the answer to resolving individual psychopathology. For example, Wolf has expressed the belief that "the group qua group cannot become the means by which its members resolve intrapsychic difficulty. The need for such differentiation led us to change our concept of the psychoanalysis of groups (Wolf, 1949–1950) to that of psychoanalysis in groups (Wolf, 1959). We do not treat a group. We must still analyze the individual in interaction with other individuals."*

Wolf and some of the people associated with him recognized the early pessimism which Freud expressed toward the psychotherapy of individuals in a group setting. This point has previously been noted by the editors in relationship to LeBon's concept of the mob and LeBon's influence on Freud. Wolf also recognizes Freud's unwillingness to see the healing potential within the group of individuals. Yet he expresses a very strong point of view when he states: "There is as yet no clinical evidence demonstrating that attention to these phenomena (group dynamics) is useful to the understanding and treatment of the patient in a group setting. How do group dynamics help achieve a healing objective?"* The opinion that Wolf expresses indicates the confusion of many analysts regarding group dynamics. It is very much related to the desire to root all psychotherapy in the group setting to a psychoanalytic base. It does not recognize the possibility that psychotherapy in a group setting goes beyond analytic concepts and thinking. The fact that patients are brought together and treated psychoanalytically within a group setting does not deny the current relevant findings of the students of group dynamics.

Too much attention has been given in the literature to Americans, with the pioneer contributions of British group therapists ignored for the most part. The senior group therapist on the British scene has been S. H. Foulkes. Originally the most highly trained psychiatrist who began to work with group techniques in Great Britain, his descriptions of the work he carried out have been the most refined and thoughtful. While others in Great Britain carried out different approaches, they did not express the degree of therapeutic sophistication that Foulkes' work conveys. The article that we have included represents an early and yet very comprehensive statement of his ideas and therapy approach. It communicates the degree of his analytic sophistication.

Sherif, White, and Harvey† found in working with a group of boys that even on a task of supreme importance to them, in this case handball

---

* E. Schwartz and A. Wolf, "Psychoanalysis in Groups: The Mystique of Group Dynamics," in *Topical Problems of Psychotherapy*, Vol. II, *Sources of Conflict in Contemporary Group Psychotherapy* (Basel: S. Karger, 1960), pp. 119-154. Quote is from p. 137.

* Ibid., p. 126.

† M. Sherif, B. J. White, and O. J. Harvey, "Status in Experimentally Produced Groups," *American Journal of Sociology*, 60:370-379, 1955.

throwing, boys base their predictions and judgments of another boy's performance mainly on his status in the group. This kind of observation is extremely valuable when we work with a *group* of patients. If we deny the influence of status in the group setting, we deny the possibility of ascertaining a perceptual base for another patient's functioning. Many firmly psychoanalytically oriented practitioners of group therapy deny the social variable and discount the group influence on personality function. Wolf, for example, is strongly oriented toward the family concept in his perception of the psychotherapy group. The group becomes the historic recreation of the original family milieu. Yet if this concept is too rigidly held, there is a denial of the evolutionary aspects of group psychotherapy and its roots in sociology, psychology, education, and philosophy.

There is denial, too, that group psychotherapy may be essentially different from individual psychotherapy; that the individual in a group is considered unique as well as ill; that there is an immediacy and spontaneity in the face-to-face relationship of patient to patient and patient to therapist within the group experience which is entirely different from the somewhat intellectual and impersonal therapeutic relationship which often occurs when the patient is alone with the therapist. The group experience encourages a sense of equality and commonality. Overemphasis on the individual denies an important facet of human behavior, that the group is both a conforming and an impelling force. (See Maurice Friedman's article and his discussion of Martin Buber in Chapter 55 of this volume.) It is unnecessary to deny the closeness of familial or parafamilial ties, but we also depend on the group to which we are closest, whether it be the family, the squad, or the team. It is conceivable that in the emphasis on the *individual*, the therapist may deny the growth of the *person*—of the "mensch." The potential to become a real person is only fulfilled in relationships with other persons.

Klapman's article summarizes a "state mental hospital approach." It is direct and to the point and yet based on theoretical awareness. Corsini and Rosenberg's paper on the mechanisms of group psychotherapy indicates that many of the terms used in attempting to find basic mechanisms derive from the literature of social psychology and group dynamics.

The excerpt from Rosenbaum's article, "The Challenge of Group Psychotherapy," emphasizes the resistance mechanisms of analysts working with groups. While the focus in this paper is upon the individual analyst, the resistance mechanisms may certainly be applicable in all group settings in which leaders have difficulty relating to a group because of what the group represents for them.

The remaining articles deal with the techniques of treating individuals within the group setting as well as the selection and classification of patients. Particularly pertinent today is Rosenbaum's paper on co-therapy and styles of leadership.

Berger's article on nonverbal communications in group psychotherapy recognizes the different sets of symbol systems that may be used as individuals communicate with one another. For example, some students of semantics differentiate between the linguistic (phonemes) and the paralinguistic (sighs, drawls, slurs, inhalations, loudness and softness, breathiness, speech coughs), and note that these communicate something about the behavior of each speaker, as well as what the total impact of a message is to another individual.

The paper by Kadis stresses the importance for patients' growth of encouraging them to meet, interact, and assess themselves, so that they may clarify their difficulties in living without the professionally trained therapist. We note that Kadis' paper and her position stem originally from the work of Wolf, who, while he is opposed to group dynamics in group psychotherapy, would still encourage patients to meet with one another outside of regularly scheduled psychotherapy settings. Such meetings are called alternate meetings. This concept of peer relationship would appear to accept the validity of group functioning, of the importance of group membership for the individual, and the importance of allegiance to a group. It stresses the fact that the stronger and more cohesive the group, the more impact and influence it has upon each individual member. Interestingly, it also communicates something about the importance of a leaderless group.

Before his death, Eric Berne, the founder of transactional analysis, reviewed four books on group therapy. The review is actually a statement of Berne's point of view toward psychotherapy in general and group therapy in particular. We have included this review and invited Robert L. Goulding, who worked with Berne, to comment on it.

The papers in this section indicate that many leading group psychotherapists scarcely acknowledge that students of group dynamics can contribute to the effective practice of group psychotherapy. While the situation is changing, it has not yet done so dramatically.

17

THE DYNAMICS OF
GROUP PSYCHOTHERAPY
AND ITS APPLICATION

Louis Wender

Group psychotherapy has been practiced at the Hastings Hillside Hospital for nearly six years. Initial experimentation with this method was prompted by the need for devising forms of therapy adapted to meeting the peculiar problems created by the segregation of mild mental patients and psychoneurotics under one roof. Carefully tested experience with this method has convinced the writer that this form of therapy is efficacious in selected situations and that it merits much wider application in hospitals where patients amenable to psychotherapy receive care.

In distinction to the method of extramural group analysis described by Trigant Burrow, which is psychoanalytic in technique and carries large sociological and philosophic implications, group psychotherapy is a method confined to the intramural treatment of certain types of mild mental disease.

In the ensuing material the writer will attempt to review some of the conditions that prompted the adoption of this approach, to define this method of therapy, to show its ideologic basis, to describe its application and scope, and to evaluate its results.

In considering the treatment of patients within a hospital, one has to bear in mind that the choice between extramural and intramural care is not arbitrary. Hospitalization is the last resort, after efforts at extramural care have failed, and it is usually the severity of the patient's condition that precludes continued treatment on the outside. To the patient himself hospitalization is a crisis. His sporadic efforts in the direction of adjustment need no longer be maintained, since not only has his illness been

Reprinted from the *Journal of Nervous and Mental Diseases*, Vol. 84, No. 1, July 1936, pp. 54-60.

acknowledged to himself, but there has been a corresponding certification to society and a meting out of "punishment." Hospitalization also deprives the patient of the attention he received from his family group and of the power he exercised over them because of his illness. He compensates for this loss by identifying the hospital with his family group (home) and proceeds to seek recognition in the new milieu. Since he no longer competes for supremacy with normal people, who accede to his demands because of the illness which distinguishes him from the rest, he resorts to an intensification of his complaints in order to focus attention on himself in the new setting, where he has to endure the competition of other sick people.

Another condition prevailing in hospitals, as in other assemblies, which requires recognition in considering approaches to therapy is the formation of friendships and cliques and the choice of "buddies." Problems are frequently analyzed and discussed among patients with greater candor than with the physician, and it is a common occurrence to learn the problems and conflicts of a patient through his confidant.

McDougall's theory "that the gregarious impulse receives the highest degree of satisfaction from the presence of human beings who most closely resemble the individual, who behave in like manner and respond to the same situations with similar emotions" is amply demonstrated in hospital life. One encounters daily a group interaction, with its resultant infectiousness of symptoms and suggestibility of moods, that demands the diverting of these impulses and the utilization of group interaction into positive therapeutic channels, if we are not to promote "symptoms orgies."

In viewing intramural methods of therapy, one is impressed by the gap between the profound influence psychoanalytic thinking has exerted on our understanding of the individual patient and the barriers to the wide application of individual analysis to hospital patients. In this connection one must remember that as a therapeutic method psychoanalysis has a limited field of application. Hospitalization still further restricts the use of this method for the following reasons: (a) the difficulty of establishing transference where separation of patients cannot be maintained as in private practice and where patients have opportunities to compare physicians and to develop jealousies of one another while sharing a therapist; (b) the prohibitive financial cost; (c) the dearth of patients with a suitable intellectual and cultural equipment; (d) the practical barrier of extending the length of hospitalization to make possible the completion of an analysis.

The conditions enumerated, as well as many minor ones into a discussion of which we have not the time to enter, make clear the need for seeking and crystallizing methods of approach that are applicable to wider groups of patients, that are shorter in duration, and that are realistically adapted to prevailing hospital conditions. To meet these requirements a proposed method of therapy would have to take cognizance not only of the individual through a psychoanalytic approach but also of the psychology of the group with its common reactions, its individual-to-individual identifications, and its responses to the therapist.

Group psychotherapy is based on the assumption that the application of some of the hypotheses and methods of psychoanalysis, in combination with intellectualization, when applied to a group for the purposes of treatment under conditions of active therapeutic control, will lead to the release of certain emotional conflicts and a partial reorganization of the personality and ultimately to an increased capacity for social amalgamation. In distinction to individual psychoanalysis this method places greater emphasis on sociological factors (group interaction) and on intellectual comprehension of behavior. The material for this form of therapy is elicited through theoretical discussions with a group of patients, affording a natural tie-up with the individual participants' experiences and problems. The base, or meeting ground, for these patients is established through what Giddings calls "consciousness of kind." He says "that this consciousness is the basis of alliance, of rules of intercourse, of peculiarities of policy and that our conduct toward those whom we feel to be most like ourselves is instinctively and rationally different from our conduct toward others who are different from ourselves." These patients are in the same predicament; they have diminished need for concealment; in a sense, they are temporarily in a different state of society, with different mores, and their resistance to a relatively intimate sharing of problems is reduced by prevailing attitudes in the new setup. These comments are not hypothetical. They are deductions from extended observation of patients and the progressive changes in their perspective and attitudes during hospitalization. These changes are inevitable; the only question that arises is whether one is to permit them to lie fallow or whether they are to be utilized and released through some method such as this form of therapy.

Experience has shown that group psychotherapy is applicable only to disorders in which intellectual impairment is absent and in which some degree of affect is retained. It is believed that the following groups lend themselves to this type of treatment: (a) early schizophrenics where the delusional trends are not fully systematized and in which hallucinatory phenomena are completely absent; where the splitting of the personality is not marked and there is no blocking; (b) depressions without marked retardation and those who libidinize their ideation—depression *sine* depression; (c) psychoneuroses, with the exception of severe compulsion neuroses of long duration.

The application of this method does not preclude the continuance of individual treatment. As a matter of fact, individual interviews are undertaken in conjunction with the patient's participating in a group, and in many instances it has been found that the group stimulated the patient's desire for individual treatment and that during these interviews such patients spoke readily of experiences the discussion of which they had avoided previously.

A group consists of six to eight patients of the same sex. Attendance is entirely voluntary. The procedure is elastic. No patient is introduced into a group immediately upon his arrival in the hospital, as some degree of adaptation to the hospital is considered essential. A new patient learns soon after his arrival that this form of therapy is an established procedure and that some of his fellow patients participate in a group. Frequently requests for this form of treatment come from the patients and great tact and patience have to be exercised in explaining the exclusions. A group has two or three one-hour sessions each week and continues for a period which varies according to the needs of its members and the objectives of the therapist (usually four to five months). New patients are not admitted to a group already in session. At early meetings the group is instructed not to discuss the content of sessions with patients outside the group, but they are encouraged to discuss the material freely with one another.

Sessions are begun with what is almost lecture material: a simple exposition of why we behave as we do, a description of primitive instinctual drives, conscious and unconscious elements, significance of dreams, early infantile traumata, reaction formations, repressions, rationalizations, and so on. The material is presented in elementary form, with simple, everyday illustrations, the intellectual content and method of presentation being adapted to the general cultural and emotional tenor of the group, and varying accordingly. Presentations are planned with a view to arousing sincere interest in the background of everyday life without inculcating a "psychology hobby." This pitfall can be avoided by the therapist, and the response obtained from groups has always been on the level desired. The use of theoretical material in the beginning stimulates intellectual interest and serves to divert patients from their immediate problems. It also serves as an instrument of facilitating a kind of intimacy and social good will that is analogous to the reaction which we experience after spending an evening with a group in stimulating and vital conversation that gives us a feeling of closeness to people toward whom we have never felt this previously.

Even in the early period of the group's existence, there are individual members who have established a transference to the therapist and there are others who have identified themselves with patients who have this transference. What occurs progressively is a common rapport, patient-to-patient transference and patient-to-therapist transference. A sense of intimacy within the group develops, greater freedom from inhibitions is observed in theoretical discussions and is followed by a spontaneous readiness on the part of some patients to discuss their own problems in relation to the theoretical material. Beginning with illustrations of individual incidents in their own lives which they regard as traumatic or significant, the patients go on to a discussion of their own and one another's symptoms and adjustments. They discuss dreams, which are interpreted on a superficial level with some of the patients participating in the interpretation. The therapist exercises no pressure, and when the term "active control" is used, it is in the sense of active awareness, in distinction to any form of manipulation. Whenever resistances are observed in any particular patient, skillful guidance can divert the discussion into safe and still theoretical waters until such a time as the patients wish to resume the subject. Moreover, the use of this more generic approach minimizes resistance and trauma, since the patient is left free to accept as much as he is ready to accept as applying to him, and to the degree necessary for him is also able to project explanations painful to him on to other patients. Nevertheless, the most carefully gauged awareness as to the individual and collective reactions of the group is essential. Both the theoretical material and the guidance of the patients' own discussions have to be adapted to the changing attitudes and receptivity of the group so that even the tempo of discussion and the duration of a group will be determined accordingly.

It is the writer's intention to make available at a later date the complete material of one group throughout its entire duration so that the techniques may be more intensively scrutinized and evaluated. At the present time it seems expedient to summarize briefly some of the dynamics operating in group psychotherapy.

1. *Intellectualization.* In our awareness of how prominent and destructive a role the conscious can play, we may have neglected it too completely as a factor in the healing process. While there may be no pure intellectual acceptance and everything that may seem like logical acceptance is accompanied by emotional tone, the fact remains that a synthesis of intellect and emotion dominates every phase of our lives and is the basis of all social adjustment. Nor can we overlook entirely the fact that there are intellectual disciplines like the yogi philosophy, the application of which results in the regulation of emotional responses through a self-determined intellectual discipline. What we term "insight" or emotional acceptance may have similar components of self-discipline. While group therapy in no way professes or strives to be an intellectual discipline, it does tend to a comprehension of emotional reactions that enables the patient to meet new situations with greater awareness and skill. The writer is convinced that intellectual awareness is a therapeutic aid as indisputable as the fact that while we may be panic-stricken at an unexpected noise coming from behind, we accept such a noise calmly when we know its origin.

2. *Patient-to-Patient Transference.* The influence exerted by one individual on another may contain elements corresponding to the psychoanalytic transference. In group psychotherapy this patient-to-patient transference is made use of in several ways. It is used to facilitate transference to the therapist through the identification of one patient with another who

has established such transference. This type of transference is encouraged, since it serves to meet the needs of the patients more permanently than the transference to the therapist which has to be abrogated for practical reasons as well as for the purpose of sustaining the patient's independence. It is also believed that the relationship which is established between patients in time takes an outward course, embracing a wider area of interests and activities (socialization).

3. *Catharsis-in-the-Family.* In the group there is undoubtedly a transference of tendencies originally directed toward the parents and siblings. There is a possibility that the entire group setup provides a kind of "Catharsis-in-the-Family," with an accompanying resolvement of conflicts and the displacement of parent love on to new objects. The patient finds himself sitting on terms of equality with the therapist (symbolic of the parent) and the other patients (who represent the siblings). He experiences (it may be for the first time in his life) the receiving of understanding from the just parent whom he shares with siblings who are equal in the eyes of that parent. He is not only receiving understanding but is also free to rebel openly, thus averting repression with its concomitant sense of guilt. In the writer's opinion this experience serves as a means of effecting a degree of emotional release, particularly in situations where the early traumata in child-parent relationships have remained unresolved. The fact that the actual setup is on an adult level and that the patient is conscious of it only as a treatment process makes it acceptable to him.

4. *Group Interaction.* Group interaction is a phenomenon to which every patient was exposed prior to his hospitalization. His development, his ego ideal, and his sense of values had their roots in his societal experience. In this method the patient's association with other patients, his new group experience, is made use of. Inevitably this association will influence his mode of thinking and his reactions, as manifested by the patients' competing with their respective complaints during their early sojourn. Under guidance this interaction results in the development of a changed perspective on behavior, which in turn gives rise to new ego ideals and strivings. In the group the patient develops criteria for evaluating his own problem against the problems of others in a way that is not feasible in individual treatment. An individual who prior to his hospitalization regarded his problems as unique and peculiar to himself learns through exchange with the group that many of his fellows have similarly predicated ego conflicts and begins to view his own problems with greater detachment. The individual experiences a resultant lessening of personal tensions, his attitudes undergo modification, and his whole outlook on behavior changes. In this entire experience he is reinforced by the experience of his group.

The patient's drive to get well derives greater impetus through this method than when only individual treatment is undertaken. This drive is motivated in part by the new ego ideal which the individual has adopted and is strengthened by the apparent feasibility of attaining health, since the recovery of other members of the group presents convincing evidence.

It may be argued that suggestion is a major factor in the results gained through group interaction. If by suggestion we mean the concepts as defined by MacDougall or Freud, these types of suggestion play no greater role in this method than in any other technique. In no sense is there acceptance without logical basis or a continued infantile emotional dependence, implicit in suggestion. In the use of group psychotherapy, the patient derives an understanding of the nature and direction of his unconscious trends, experiencing simultaneously an emotional release. This is accompanied by his being exposed to observation and experience which involve himself and others, ultimately leading to a partial reorganization of his personality. In this unified process it is not an outside agent like suggestion which accomplishes the change but the saturation of the individual with the forces of his own experience.

The results yielded by this method, which has been used in the treatment of about seventy-five patients over a period of six years, cannot be computed statistically. Interpretation on the basis of follow-up (in some cases for four to five years), since that is the only form of evaluation open to us in analyzing material of this nature, shows fairly conclusively that this form of therapy carries positive values for social adjustment. It has been observed repeatedly that friendships formed while groups were in session persist on the outside; that these patients retain a common bond of mutual interest, helpfulness, and understanding which is a source of strength to them; and that their drive to remain well is more dynamic and characterized by a competitive quality. While the recovered patients' opinions cannot be interpreted as having scientific validity, it is significant that they attach importance to this form of therapy and attribute to the group experience their continued capacity to discuss their problems freely and their enhanced ability to deal successfully with new and difficult emotional material and experience.

18

RESULTS AND PROBLEMS OF GROUP PSYCHOTHERAPY IN SEVERE NEUROSES

Paul Schilder

The problem of adequate psychotherapeutic care for neurotic patients who frequent the outpatient departments of public hospitals is an urgent one. Psychoanalysis is undoubtedly an efficient therapeutic weapon, but it makes great demands on the time both of the physician and of the patient. Thus it has become in our economic structure a method employed only for the wealthy. In addition, the general trend in psychoanalytic technique is to prolong the treatment; indeed, daily treatments for two or three years are not considered unusual. If psychoanalysis is the best treatment available at the present time, the community should utilize it; but if this be impracticable, experiments should be conducted in an attempt to find an alternative. In public hospitals surgical cases receive care that is in no way inferior to that given the private case. It is our social duty to set up the same standards in the care of the neurotic patient.

Psychoanalysis is based upon a definite and well-studied relationship between two human beings—the analyst and the patient. Other human beings appear in a way suggestive of ghosts during the analysis. The patient confides in an analyst whom he trusts not to divulge his secrets. To be sure, the analyzed person, reëxperiencing his past life with the analyst, finally finds his way back to the social continuum in which he lives. There is no doubt but that the transference situation, carefully as it has been studied, is still full of pitfalls. When one considers that isolation and secrecy are basic factors in the psychology of the neurotic, one is tempted to discard both of them in the therapeutic situation. In group psychotherapy, a number of patients are seen simultaneously by the physician, and each patient is

Reprinted from *Mental Hygiene*, Vol. XXIII, No. 1, 1939, pp. 87-98.

aware of the problems of the others. A second physician may join the group and add his interpretations.

A year and a half ago, I began an experiment in group psychotherapy in the Outpatient Department of the Psychiatric Division of Bellevue Hospital. Up to the present time about fifty cases of severe neuroses and mild psychoses have been treated. Only severe cases have been taken into this group. Most of the neuroses were of long standing and had been previously treated by other methods. A definite therapeutic plan was followed.

Human beings live not only in a group—they live also as comparatively independent entities. A therapy dealing only with the group would be as one-sided as a purely individualistic treatment. Every patient was seen individually before he joined the group, and these personal interviews were continued throughout the treatment. The groups meet once or twice a week, from two to seven patients participating. This type of therapy emphasizes the leadership of the physician, through the mere fact that he directs the group. Patients should have insight into this relationship. They should not be blind believers. The physician should be not an authority, but a leader, and it should be clear that his leadership is based not upon any intrinsic superiority, but upon the particular task to be solved by the group. Basically, he is a fellow human being confronted with the same problems as any other member of the group.

The various forms of psychotherapy emphasize specific sides of interhuman relations. If a physician gives orders to patients without giving them any insight into the nature of these orders, his therapy is based upon the necessity for authority in human life. In hypnosis, therapy is based upon the human relationship of erotic submission. In cathartic hypnosis, the patient is forced into insight. Again, one may treat a patient as a sensible fellow human being with whom problems can be discussed. An attitude of friendly helpfulness may be added.

In psychoanalysis the semblance of an impersonal relationship may be insisted upon, but the patient is in reality in a state of submission which is more or less one of complete surrender. In the further course of analysis, insight accrues with the revival of significant childhood attitudes. The therapeutic situation, if in any way valuable, is based upon a human relationship of fundamental importance. Hypnosis, for instance, which stresses submission and surrender to a magic power of love, reveals at least one important side of human relations. The technique immediately reaches a higher level if the patient has insight into this. The part truth of the hypnotic attitude and of any psychotherapeutic attitude should be seen at its real value. The final aim of psychotherapy can only be insight. Psychoanalysis comes nearest to this goal. Insight means more than verbalization. It means the ability to see the structures of the real world and to act accordingly.

Psychoanalytic insight was utilized in this group treatment. In every case the life history of the patient was discussed and elucidated in detail and early infantile material was particularly studied. A written report was asked of the patient after he had gained partial insight. Not only had he to write his life history, but he also had to discuss his relationship with father, mother, siblings, and nurses. In addition, a report of his sexual development was required. Further reports were called for according to the needs of the therapeutic situation. Dream interpretation and so-called free associations were used both in the individual treatments and in the group treatments. Sexual development was studied as completely as possible. Besides an historical approach to the personality, the ideologies of the patients and their general orientation to life were investigated. No individual can be understood unless his objective is known—his goal and his life plan. One must know his expectations for the future. The individual, too, must gain deeper insight into his own needs and wishes. He must learn to understand the social setting and his social and sexual ambitions.

These basic problems may be formulated briefly as follows: (1) body and beauty; (2) health, strength, efficiency, superiority, and inferiority in a physical sense; (3) aggressiveness and submission; (4) masculinity and femininity; (5) the relationship between sex and love; (6) the expectation for the future; and (7) the meaning of death. Particular attention must be given to the language in which the patient expresses his attitudes toward these basic problems. Certain phrases are very often used in order to enable the patient to hide his real attitudes from himself. Phrases not fully understood in their true meaning are very often found at the turning point of an individual's life. It is necessary that the individual's conscious and unconscious goals come into full light with insight. Modern psychology has all too often forgotten the social nature of human experiences. I have been able to show that even the experience of one's own body, the body image, acquires its final expression only in a continuous interplay with the body images of other human beings.

Hartshorne has justly emphasized the social character of every sensation. Any problem of money, occupation, and sex that may be met has its true meaning only in a social setting of which it is a part, and cannot even be thought of apart from this social setting. Obviously, then, the significance of any detail of an individual life history will be clearer if it is brought forward in a group and appraised by a group. In one discussion, for example, a patient remembered an attempted sexual assault against his sister. It was astonishing how many members of the group recalled similar experiences in their own lives, so that a correct appreciation of such an event became possible. On Mother's Day one of the patients brought forth bitter complaints against his mother, who had curtailed his freedom, had not given him enough love, and had had a sex life of her own. This outcry provoked a whole series of similar associations from the other patients. The deeper social meaning of the Oedipus situation revealed itself, and the patients experienced their specific attitudes merely as variations of a general attitude. The relief patients experience when they no longer feel excluded from the community because of urges and desires that society does not openly tolerate is remarkable. To be sure, in the strictly analytic situation, the analyst offers a like relief, but there he is merely the representative of a group, whereas in the group treatment the patient actually experiences the breaking through of similar or identical impulses in others. Group treatment is in this respect a step nearer to reality.

Feelings of guilt result from sexual drives and actions and from aggressiveness. Both seem to excommunicate the individual from a society that sets up for him a system of ideals that cannot be fulfilled. Mothers are supposed always to love their children and children are expected always to love their parents. There should be no destructive impulses against any one; good deeds from the individual are not enough—the demand is also that he think only good thoughts. Morally we live in a state that punishes not only actions, but thoughts as well. In a general way we feel that the authorities of a country should permit liberty of thought. But the unwritten ideologies and prejudices, the demands of misunderstood morality are much more tyrannical than written laws, since the former punish for thoughts. Thoughts must come out into the open quite in the same way as ideologies if individuals are to be liberated from their feelings of guilt.

In a group, the patients realize with astonishment that the thoughts which have seemed to isolate them are common to all of them. This enables them clearly to see their aggressive instincts and helps them to understand that aggressive instincts and social conduct are compatible.

The thoughts and ideologies of one patient become the common medium for the group in their continuous emotional interplay. Most of the threads are united in the person of the analyst, who enters into the discussions, the language analysis, and even into the free associations of the patients. The definite interpretation of a symptom or of an action of a patient is the work not merely of the analyst, but of the whole group.

The phenomena of positive and negative transference to the analyst are not less outspoken in the group than in the usual psychoanalytic treatment. They express themselves in generally known terms. The reaction of one patient to the transference situation of another patient is very often remarkable. The patient in a state of positive transference feels a need to defend the analyst against the negative transference of another patient. In the negative transference, the group particularly stress that the physician is not sufficiently interested in their fate, that as a public employee he must spend his hours with them regardless, and that he is less interested in the fate of the patients than in the scientific problems they offer. Very often discussions of problems of this type have a very important effect upon the fate of a group. They can be shown that nobody has the right to expect the complete emotional surrender of another person—that the other person has to live his own life even if he does happen to be one's father or one's relative or one's physician.

The patients brought together in one group are not particularly selected, but men and women have been treated separately. It has been my general plan to bring every patient who is at a given time under treatment into contact with the other patients of the same sex. I hope that it will be possible to have persons of both sexes in the same group when we have gained a deeper understanding of this method.

The method I have described will not escape the reproach of being too intellectual and putting too much emphasis upon the factor of insight. Skepticism may be increased when I confess that I do not refrain from using an elaborate system of questionnaires. These contain such questions as what the patient remembers about his father, what he thinks about him, and what fantasies he has had about him. These questions are concerned not only with the sexual problems relating to the father, but with every phase of the father's life, as whether he was considered strong, healthy, gifted, clever, successful, and so on. Similar questions are elaborated about the mother, siblings, nurses, and teachers. A further series relates to ideas about one's own body. Others probe the castration complex, masturbation, intercourse, breasts, urination, defecation, the attitude of the family and of the patient toward disease, food habits, and so forth. A different set sought to discuss aggressiveness and attitudes toward death, the opinions the individual has about himself, his goals in life, and, finally, the general attitude of human beings toward one another. At least one should try to discover the basic attitude of an individual in the following spheres of experience: (1) the need to love and be loved (according to Watson, love means stroking); (2) the tendency to maintain one's own support (in childhood, against gravitation); (3) the tendency to maintain the integrity of the body (sudden noise, sudden impressions are a threat in this respect); (4) the tendency to eat and drink and to get as much property as possible, to acquire and to retain; (5) the tendency to expel what the organism can no longer use and to push away that which is threatening; (6) the tendency to handle and to destroy objects and human beings and to get an insight into their structure; (7) the tendency to help others in the pursuit of the same aims.

This is a reformulation of the problems that we considered as most important in an individual's life.

One of the discussions arising out of the individual problems of the patients is here reproduced in a slightly altered form.*

B., twenty-one years old, had a severe social neurosis which caused him to withdraw from contact with others and to suffer from severe feelings of

* I have added the brief remarks on the history of each patient. Every one in the group knew the histories of the others.

inadequacy; his speech was actually hesitant. He stammered when he checked impulses of rage directed against those who he believed were ridiculing him. Excessive ambitions had developed to overcompensate for his sense of being threatened. In school games he did not want to be on the losing team. He was interested in auto races and in all speed races involving motor-driven vehicles, seeming to feel that their force was added to his. He did not like sports in which he was dependent only upon his own ability.

E., twenty-one years old, with a basal metabolism of minus 23, had felt that he had no energy and no drive. Accordingly he would exert himself too much, feel bewildered, and then give up almost completely, until he really had become inefficient. His sexual energy seemed to have little vitality. There were no sex fantasies or sex impulses when he came for treatment. In spite of a rise in the basal metabolic rate to minus 8 under the influence of thyroid medication, he did not change until psychotherapy had given him insight into his problems. Sexuality then awakened. The question is, Where did he get the energy with which to drive himself forward? One may draw the conclusion that human beings should gaily acknowledge their shortcomings. They should be taught neither to overcompensate for them nor to brush them out of consciousness. Every one should be aware of the necessity of having shortcomings. The ideal of general efficiency and of striving to be blameless is a wrong one. If one is a minus variant as a personality, one should accept the fact. Minus qualities in ourselves and in others make us human, and the attempt to be perfect only makes us into caricatures.

F., twenty-one years old, an anxiety neurotic with the fear of sudden death, had no problems of this kind. He lived in an emotional attachment to his mother and brother and expected protection from them against the dangers connected with his own lack of strength. It did not matter whether this attachment to the mother was sexual or not, but it was important that he have no inferiority feelings in the ordinary sense. There is no reason to believe that there is only one fundamental problem lying at the base of neuroses. One should evaluate life situations as human problems in their varieties of expression.

C., twenty-four years old, suffered from inferiority and guilt feelings because of obsessional sex drives against children and men, and obsessional aggressions, such as kicking and pushing. He had been forced into this situation by his mother, who overpowered him. If there were feelings of inferiority, they were the result of a complicated sexual development. He was very much frightened by his impulses, whose strength he overestimated. Perhaps too much is expected of us in a moral way, and it should be acknowledged that there are impulses which go against the standards of society. One should be lenient to one's own morality, especially if it harms no one. It is probable that tolerance of one's own impulses does not strengthen them, but reveals them as inefficient and weak—that is, if they do not fit into the structure of the personality and into society.

In the case of W., nineteen years old, the fight against the father and the protection of the mother against the father (also sexually) were prominent. In W.'s attempt to substitute for the father he cultivated intellectuality. He denied himself sexuality because he condemned it in his father and mother. Since he wanted to convince himself and others that he was superior to his father, he was concerned only in having others acknowledge his superiority. He was shy and self-conscious with people who he believed gave him exaggerated attention.

Modern men suffer from the idea that they should be perfect. They expect perfect health and are unduly perturbed and excited by minor symptoms. W., for example, has palpitations when in bed. One should have patience with one's own body and not be afraid of being weak and tired. People want to be highly efficient, to show speed and energy, when they should have the courage to be slow and adynamic. It is easier to be tolerant toward one's self if no comparison is made with others. Humanity should be considered as consisting of varied types, and those who are not highly gifted are still an important part of society as a whole. The imperfect human being is needed as well as the one approaching perfection, and one should be tolerant toward one's own stupidities. The stupid person is more than a mere background for the intelligent.

If humans ask of themselves speed of movement and of speech and strength, why should they not ask to be beautiful in all the parts of their bodies? The perfection sought for oneself is demanded of others, and intolerance ensues. This intolerance is greater toward the members of one's own family, and they are expected to be ideal figures without blemish. Of course, they can't live up to these images. Parents have to pay dearly for every perfectionistic ideal they put into their children's minds. The child will soon measure his parents against the ideals implanted in him and find them wanting. When parents teach children suppression of sex, children retaliate by fighting against the sexuality of their parents. Asexuality belongs to the perfectionistic ideal. Sometimes it is expected that sexuality shall awaken only at the conventional signal. Perfectionistic ideals exist not only for physical functions, but also for one's strivings, and can be positive as well as negative. They demand, for instance, from one's self and from others (1) absence of hate, (2) a continuous flow of love toward one's love object, (3) continuous sexual impulses toward a socially acknowledged love object, and (4) absence of promiscuous impulses or sexual impulses.

The foregoing paragraphs summarize the record of one group treatment. The objection of intellectuality may again be raised. The account given here does not indicate how closely these general remarks were related to definite experiences of the patients. The discussion shows in detail how the patient developed his attitude. It should not be forgotten either that this is only one of the phases in the treatment. The truth of the formulation is considered only as partial truth which must be completed by the other aspects of the situation. In connection with this specific record, for instance, a discussion would be necessary to show how the individual fits his impulses into society.

In modern psychopathology, the difference between intellectual and emotional processes is too greatly emphasized. To be sure, though it has never been formulated, there is an underlying assumption that intellectual processes are pale and without strength, and this at a time when everybody speaks of the personality as a whole. Attitudes express themselves in thinking as well as in emotions, and emotions also have goals and aims. A separation of intellect and emotion is artificial and is justified only if one considers them as two sides of the unified attitude of an individual, one or the other facet scintillating more strongly according to circumstances.

One might further object to the procedure as recorded because it involved a more or less definite stand on the part of the physician, while psychoanalysis has attempted an attitude of neutrality on questions of morals and values. But as I have stated, Freud is deceiving himself in holding that he is purely scientific and has no "*Weltanschauung.*" Psychoanalysis has in fact a definite attitude toward certain moral problems. A body of definite knowledge contains in itself a definitely moral point of view and invites definite actions. One should know this. If one is practicing psychotherapy, and especially group psychotherapy, one should know what to expect from life.

As one would suppose, group psychotherapy is especially effective in cases of what I should characterize as social neuroses. These are cases that do not feel comfortable in the presence of others. They feel that they cannot concentrate, they cannot think, or they are merely embarrassed and uncomfortable. Physical symptoms, such as palpitation or discomfort in the gastrointestinal tract, may be present. Sweating, blushing, awkwardness in movement, may become obvious signals of this discomfort. The individual feels that he is the center of attention, that not only is something wrong with him, but that others realize it. Every object becomes, in this respect, an important object on a sado-masochistic level. To be seen and to be observed means to be hurt and to be pushed into an inferior position.

Twelve cases of social neurosis have been treated by our group method. Three can be considered as cured. In the case of E., mentioned above, sexuality, which had been dormant, appeared in spite of the organic background in the situation. Only two cases showed no improvement. The remaining seven were decidedly improved, and some of them are still under treatment.

In one case of stammering, the stammering was not overcome, but there was an improvement in social attitude.

Nine cases of obsession neurosis have been treated. There has been no complete failure in this series. Two severe cases were cured. In a third an involuntary bromide intoxication led to a complete disappearance of the symptoms. Two cases with slight encephalitic signs showed a very decided improvement. Two other cases, both severe and of long standing, were mildly improved; both were still under treatment at the time this paper was written. The two remaining cases improved to the point where they are adapting well to society and enjoying themselves.

Of three cases of anxiety neurosis, two were cured and one was improved.

Of four hysterias, two were cured, one was unchanged, and one ceased treatment too early.

Three cases of hypochondriasis were not influenced by the treatment.

Two cases with organic vegetative symptoms adapted better, but the organic symptoms did not disappear.

Of three cases of character problems, one was discharged and was well adjusted at the time of writing; the other two were considerably improved and are still under treatment.

Of six depersonalization cases, one was cured and one decidedly improved; one who did not come back for treatment was slightly improved at the time the treatment was broken off. Three were unimproved. One of these three was a schizophrenia and another a depression.

Two cases of depression (in addition to the depersonalization case) were unimproved. One of them committed suicide. The family had been warned.

Among four cases of schizophrenia in which treatment was attempted (besides the depersonalization case) two cases were not influenced. One case, in which the diagnosis was dementia simplex, adjusted much better. The fourth case completely recovered, and was socially and sexually adapted at the time of writing. Fear of homosexuality and homosexual ideas of reference had been in the foreground. I was in no doubt about the diagnosis of schizophrenia when I started the treatment, which lasted several months. The possibility of an atypical depression might have been considered, but I adhered to my original diagnosis.

Many of the cases treated in this group could not have been treated individually even with the classical analysis. They reacted only in the group. This is especially true of social neuroses.

This is only a very brief report of the experiment. It is difficult to judge therapeutic results after so comparatively short a time, and perhaps I have been too optimistic. If this should be so, it lies in the nature of the psychotherapeutic approach. It is probable that not all of the results are permanent and there may be relapses sooner or later. But I believe, as do the patients, that they have been helped to get a better orientation to life. I have had an opportunity to compare the results of this method with those of others. In some cases the approach is preferable to the strictly analytic technique, and again there are cases in which the psychoanalytic approach is doubtlessly superior. However, one will have to learn. A definite technique has been utilized. I hope that this technique can be taught and can be learned.

SUMMARY

A method of group psychotherapy has been developed which attempts to give the patient a deeper insight into his individual life history, his ideologics, his problems, and his expectations for the future. The basis of this treatment is a written report of the patient concerning the various phases and aspects of his life and of his relationships to the persons in his world. Sexual development is elucidated. Dream interpretation and free association are utilized. The patient must understand how much he has been under the influence of merely verbal formulations in his life plan. In individual interviews and in group discussions various aspects of the personality come into the foreground. The analyst as a member of the group is compelled to greater activity. The patients gain a new direction and new orientation in life.

The therapeutic results so far are promising, especially in the social neuroses and obsession neuroses. This truly social method, though it, too, requires much time, enables the physician to treat a relatively large number of cases and to help them in the development of their personalities.

19

GROUP THERAPY
SPECIAL SECTION MEETING

Lawson G. Lowrey, Chairman
S. R. Slavson*

CHAIRMAN: My interest in the utilization of procedures involving a group has been developing over the past twenty years. Our first efforts in this direction—recreational groups for our "problem" cases, family councils, mothers' and parents' discussion groups—were certainly not specifically planned to be directly therapeutic in the sense in which we would use that term today. But, although primarily thought of as recreation, education, and socializing experiences, there were important therapeutic effects as well—as indeed there may be and frequently are in all sorts of interpersonal relationships.

My first experience with a sort of group therapy—again not precisely viewed that way—was with a special camp setup for "problem" boys in Cleveland during the summer of 1926. That first summer, when I spent weekends at the camp, was really one of groping experimentation. The work was later carried on from the psychiatric side much more effectively by Doctors E. S. Rademacher and A. T. Childers. Mr. Newstetter, in his report on this work,[1] stated three major practical considerations which led to the initiation of the project. These were: the lack of generalized knowledge of the primary group; the problem of adjusting individuals referred by caseworkers for group adjustment; and the problem of practical utilization of mental hygiene contributions.

At our 1939 meeting, in reviewing *Trends in Therapy*,[2] mention was

Reprinted from the *American Journal of Orthopsychiatry*, Vol. XIII, No. 4, October 1943, pp. 648-690. © 1943, American Orthopsychiatric Association, Inc. Reproduced by permission.

* *Editors' note:* Because of space limitations, we have not included here all of the papers presented at this meeting. The other contributors were Dorothy Spiker, H. B. Peck, Helen Glauber, and N. Ackerman.

made of several *group therapy* approaches, and there was a brief discussion of the "open approach" as I had seen it in operation abroad and as used in this country, notably by Ira Wile in the Mental Health Class at Mt. Sinai Hospital in New York. It is clear to me now that I then had only an imperfect realization of the potential group psychotherapeutic values of the open approach. From recent correspondence with Dr. Wile (who is unable, I regret to say, to be present at this meeting), it is clear that he regards the methodology in his clinic as *group psychotherapy*. In one letter he states regarding this program:

> We have always had papers [in the programs] on music, puppets, play and all sorts of group activities. . . . It is interesting to note . . . that the common factor in almost all of these therapies *inheres in the group* [italics mine]. This group reflects the factors of interplay, intercommunication, interfeeling, interstimulation, interdependence, with heightened suggestibility, both from active and passive participation. . . . The moment a child meets a medical attendant, a psychologist, or a social worker, particularly if they form a group, active therapy is under way, even though little is said. The theory of work with Scouts, Big Brothers, and Big Sisters, has always involved group therapy. The development of associations and the concept of socialized education involve principles entering into group therapy.

These concepts refer to therapy only in a very broad sense. In another letter, Wile narrows the field somewhat. "Inasmuch as therapy has been based upon conscious and unconscious and even hypnagogic reactions, one must distinguish the effects sought for, the effects secured and known, the effects registered but not expressed. Whether we give a child a toy that can be torn apart or one that cannot, helps to determine a play therapy." He then makes some comments on technique and "reducing terminology to what one wishes to have it mean and appropriating it," and raises interesting questions regarding objective measurements of group therapy and play therapy.

We propose today to discuss not the open approach but group work specifically and consciously planned as therapy, with a background of theory and a body of practice, which has been studied objectively, at least to a degree, and where the dynamic role of the group as such is the important therapeutic tool. This is a much more definitely oriented and circumscribed use of technique than is true in the more general situations mentioned above.

A leading characteristic of modern life is the large number of groups in which an individual lives and functions. Each of these affects the individual, as the latter also affects the group. In this reciprocal relationship, the group is quick to take steps to conserve its own interests, protect itself from hostile aggression, develop its prosperity, maintain its inertia, and so on, at the expense of the individual, who, in turn, exploits the group.[3]

Why, then, should not the specific impact of the group upon the indi-vidual's attitudes and behavior be utilized in consciously planned therapy, as it is used more vaguely in education and "socialization"? Speaking broadly, the treatment of mental disorders and delinquency by the use of specially organized and controlled environments is an example of a basic general principle of therapy from which use of the group as a therapeutic tool may be said roughly to stem. Many variations and refinements and considerable differences in theory and practice usually operate under differ-ent names.

Turning now to the topic of the day, my first contact with this therapy program of the Jewish Board of Guardians was during the first half of 1941, in the course of a survey of the clinical facilities of that organization and those of the New York Association for Jewish Children. Then, this past year, by special invitation and arrangement, I made a study of the pro-cedures, techniques, and results of group therapy as practiced at JBG, un-der Mr. Slavson's direction, since 1934. It is not my purpose to review that study at this time, but certain conclusions reached explain my interest in this meeting, which was suggested and arranged by Mr. Slavson.

In my study, a total of 176 children (of 500-550 who had been in groups) were identified in reading 19 of 72 available group records, 55 case records of the child guidance department . . . , and 34 group therapy "in-dividual" records. In a total of 101 cases there were data enough in the rec-ords read to permit a *personal* judgment of the results of the group therapy. There were 74 cases with good results, and 27 with poor or no results. These results were in cases taken from all the seven years studied, in groups con-ducted by 14 different workers, included both sexes, and covered all age ranges. The material therefore represents an adequate random sample, the analyses were rigorous, and the findings must be regarded as significant.

Accordingly, it is obvious that here is a technique which is as effective as is individual therapy. Questions promptly arise concerning the nature of the technique and the types of situations and cases to which it is applica-ble. For, if the technique can be defined, described, and transmitted and the limitations of its applicability determined, we shall have added a most important instrumentality to our therapeutic armamentarium.

With the final comment that this type of treatment is therapy *by* the group, rather than therapy *in* the group, we pass to descriptions and anal-yses by the speakers of the day.

The first speaker, Mr. S. R. Slavson, is the Director of the Department of Group Therapy at the Jewish Board of Guardians and the one who de-veloped the technique and analyses of procedures there. He is a Lecturer in Education at New York University. His concepts of group therapy stem from group work, progressive education, and psychoanalysis. Many in this audience will be familiar with his books, *Creative Group Education* (1937) and *Character Education in a Democracy* (1939). Mr. Slavson will present the *Principles and Dynamics of Group Therapy,* which is the general subject of his book.[4]

S. R. SLAVSON: This paper is based on the experience of about nine years in group therapy with approximately 800 children, 63 distinct groups, and 96 group years. It deals with a type of interpersonal therapy for young children developed at the Jewish Board of Guardians and has since been tried in many centers in the United States.

The idea of treatment of adults in groups is not altogether new. It has for some years been employed by Doctors Trigant Burrow, Paul Schilder, Louis Wender, James Sennett Greene, and others. Treatment is carried on through interviews in groups in which the patients' problems are ventilated, inner pressures and anxieties released, and guidance given by the therapist as well as the patient participants.

We, on the other hand, deal with children of the ages from 8 to 15, through activity (rather than interview), and with the resultant interpersonal interactions and their therapeutic effect. It must be made clear that activity therapy which is emphasized here is not the only type of group therapy being employed either at our agency or in similar efforts at other agencies. Because of different treatment needs of clients, we introduced "group interview treatment" or *collective psychotherapy* for adolescents, a combination of activity and interview for younger children, group treatment with mothers, and *transitional* groups for children.

Activity group therapy here described is a type of noninterpretive therapy in which no interview is held during the treatment period. If interview therapy is required, it is given by a caseworker or psychiatrist at another time. Thus, among our clients are children who receive individual treatment concurrently with group treatment (cooperative cases), and children who are treated in groups only (exclusive cases).

The general setting for activity group therapy is work in simple arts and crafts for an hour or an hour and a half. This is followed by a period during which the clients and the group therapist cook, serve, and eat together. They then clean up the room. The meetings are varied by occasional trips, picnics, and excursions, in accordance with the needs and readiness of the members and the seasonal opportunities offered. It will be readily seen that the group is a substitute family with the positive elements a family should have and that the worker is a substitute parent. In fact, many of our children refer to the workers as mama, pop, and "unk."

The clients accepted for treatment have all experienced destructive or undesirable relations with people. We therefore aim to correct attitudes and perceptions through a new type of experience so that the children can enter into constructive personal relations. In addition to the total friendly and permissive atmosphere of the group, the materials and tools serve to prevent mutual invasion on the part of the members before they are ready to accept one another. They work on materials rather than on each other. This is a rather important phase in the treatment, for it serves to redirect aggression and, in some instances, is also a means of sublimating it.

Group therapy is *situational therapy* as differentiated from interview and treatment by interpretation. We have evidence, however, that insight is acquired by our young clients as a result of their own thinking and comparing their abilities and attitudes with each other and their own in the past. "I used to fight all the time," says a boy. "Now I work and am too busy to fight." Another addresses one of his fellow members thus: "You remember when we were enemies? Now we are friends." And still another: "I used to think my little sister was a pest. Now I think she is kind of cute." With security and self-acceptance comes also acceptance of others and a more friendly and relaxed attitude toward the world.

To young children, experience as understood in terms of subjective response and adjustment to an external occurrence, is often more telling than verbal formulations. In fact, in individual treatment, skill is most manifest where the interview is made an emotional experience. This inevitably proceeds from a well-adjusted relation between therapist and client.

The *situational configuration* of a therapy group can be said to consist of (1) the client, (2) the therapist, (3) the situation, and (4) the activities. We shall discuss these elements at different points, but it will be necessary to keep in mind that they are functionally one and inseparable.

What type of problem child can best be served by group therapy? What is it that a child with personality difficulties and social maladjustments needs to get from such a group? By and large, we can say that in order to gain from any group experience, it is necessary that the individual have some initial capacity to relate himself to others; he must have a desire to be with other people, to belong, to be a part of. This we designate as *social hunger*. Whatever the psychologic syndrome or personality problem, clients assigned to groups have some measure of social hunger, latent or overt, for without it no contact with them is possible.

Since eventually satisfactions must come from constructive activity rather than from destruction, and people must become sources of gratification rather than of pain and threat, the child must give up his need to resent or fight the world. Instead, he needs to develop a desire to be a part of it. Psychotherapy can help in this, but it can be successful only when there is a foundation for it within the personality of the client. We found that only children who have this initial capacity and some degree of social hunger respond to treatment. Thus, intensely psychopathic clients and those with some forms of behavior disorders are not suitable for group therapy. Social hunger in group therapy corresponds to the transference relation in individual therapy. Just as a patient who is unable to establish a transference with the therapist is not accessible in individual treatment, so is a client with no social hunger inaccessible in group treatment.

We have found that even narcissistic children gain from a nonrepressive group. They take, however, a very long time and improvement is first observable in other relations—the home, the school, the play group—even though their behavior is not affected in the group itself.

We are dealing with the child whose ego structure is defective. Our clients are those who were directly infantilized by anxious or overprotective mothers or whose infancy was prolonged by rejecting, rigid, hard, unloving parents. They are also children whose identifications had been established with wrong models or images in the persons of the parents or parent surrogates. It is therefore necessary to supply them with opportunities for corrective identifications. This is done through the group therapist and the other children in the group. It becomes clear even from this brief statement how important is the personality of the therapist as well as the choice and grouping of clients.

In many of our clients the superego is either overintense and tyrannical, as in the neurotic child, or it exerts inadequate control over impulses and primary narcissism, as in the child with a behavior disorder and in the child with prolonged infancy. In the one case, the child must find release from the emotional pressure under which he lives; in the other, he must internalize restraints and controls. The authority, restraint, and controls that arise spontaneously and naturally from the group relationships and working conditions are, in most instances, acceptable to the client. He submits because he derives basic satisfactions from the situation. Here we rely on the child's social hunger and the *supportive ego*. This supportive person may be the therapist or a comember whom the client naturally likes or who meets his emotional needs at a given period in his growth.

In the initial stages of our treatment, and as a result of the permissive atmosphere of the group, group therapy temporarily suspends the child's superego. He can act out his problems and difficulties; he can reveal his true nature and his hidden impulses without fear of retaliation, criticism, or punishment. This may create considerable confusion, aggression, and turmoil at the meetings, but *activity catharsis* is essential to equilibrate the personality of each of the participants. The withdrawn child remains quietly at his task; the assertive and aggressive gains release through action, until balance is attained.

We see how important is the choice and grouping of patients. If grouping is incorrect, the anxious and neurotic child grows too frightened to come to the meetings, or when he comes, his anxieties are further increased. He is thus traumatized. The overaggressive provokes and instigates aggression to a point where no group equilibrium is possible and therefore no therapy can occur.

Because the child is plastic, and because he absorbs from experience at a greater rate than do adults, his total personality is affected through the release, control, and relationships in the group. One of the results (and we consider this a major outcome of group treatment) is that his superego is extended and, to a varying degree, also transformed. The early superego is derived from the fear and anxiety of being abandoned, punished, or maltreated. As he matures, the average person learns restraint, not because of fear of punishment, but because of identification with the desires and needs of other people. This growing awareness of others engenders a superego which can be designated the *group superego*, as differentiated from the *infantile superego*. It proceeds from satisfying group experience, growing identifications and associations with individuals, and finally leads to integration into groups. Thus, the child no longer perceives other people as a danger and a threat, and can therefore establish relationships without fear.

In the disturbed and maladjusted child, identifications and strivings toward the group have not supplanted, as it were, the fear-laden, infantile superego. A therapy group, such as we have described, helps in the process of extending the early fears of mature self-restraint. Hyperactive children have gained greatly through the free, unimpeded release in our groups. Some attach themselves to a satisfying interest such as carpentry and canalize their energies in sublimitory, *libido-binding activity*. Children who are too inhibited to communicate their problems to a caseworker are freed from their inhibitions, and as a result, there is greater movement in individual therapy as well.

Then there is the child who is nonverbal—with language limitations, either constitutional or cultural. He may be inhibited, distrustful, frightened, of low intelligence. These conditions would impede communication and understanding in individual treatment. Group therapy is evidently indicated in these cases.

Through the work in arts and crafts, eating together, trips and excursions, and the accepting and permissive atmosphere in the group, the schizoid child is activated. He need not use his self-protective withdrawal in an environment that is friendly and nonthreatening. The mildly schizophrenic child, too, has here a conditioned and attenuated situation of things, occupations, an adult, and the other children to lead him back to reality. Children whose compensatory fantasies interfere with their social adjustment and with the development of an adequate sense of reality, have actualized some of these flights into unreality through their free, undirected work with art and other materials. The recognition they receive from the group therapist, fellow members, at home and at school reduces their need for self-maximation and grandeur. Many children in this category have entirely given up this mechanism. As they gained status, they substituted achievement for fantasy. Children with prolonged infancy and the over-protected child gain much from the experience provided by a free group life with the emergent restraints and graded group pressures. The most perfect attendance is found in this group of clients. The neurotic child can act out his anxieties without fear of retaliation or threat. With security gained through this, he is able to talk out his problems with his caseworker or psychiatrist.

Perhaps the group of clients with whom we were most successful are the emasculated boys who had overdominating mothers, who grew up in an exclusively or predominantly feminine environment, or have been in competition with sisters. Such boys acquire feminine characteristics, become submissive or ingratiating, and are commonly known as sissies. They build up fantasies about the danger and destructiveness of masculinity and some express a wish to be girls and actually imagine themselves as girls. The improvement in these children as a result of a nonthreatening masculine group environment and relations is really quite remarkable.

The primary and most essential element in a therapy group is that it must be a carefully planned and a consciously organized body. A therapy group stands or falls on the insight and skill in grouping. Essentially, the group must consist of children who potentially have therapeutic value to one another. Obviously, a beaten down and rejected child would only be more traumatized if he were to be assigned to a group where he would be beaten and persecuted. A frightened, withdrawn, and sensitive child becomes only more frightened and withdrawn in a tumultuous and aggressive environment. If these children are each to be helped to make better social adaptations and overcome their personality problems, they must have an environment in which their particular difficulties are counteracted and their needs are met. This is accomplished through a planned group in which the interpersonal relations have, in the long run, positive values for every participant.

The difficulties that arise in fitting together seven or eight children who would be useful to each other in treatment are apparent. Luckily, there is no need to fit in all of the children in this manner. In a group of eight, there emerge a number of subgroups of two and three who are suited to each other. A weak and dependent child will attach himself to another member who gives him security, or he may lean upon the group therapist for such support. In either case, this supportive ego functions only for a brief period. The friendly and comforting environment and relations soon make the child secure enough to go on his own and to interact freely with others in the group.

The aggressive child whose aggressiveness does not proceed from serious pathology, and whose social hunger is adequately strong, soon curbs himself because of group pressure. Children gang up on him, demand that he conform and not interfere with their comfort and activities. If this restraint does not arise from the group spontaneously, which is usually the case, we place in the group an equally aggressive or an older child. The conflict for power is then confined to these two and is usually resolved as they become fast friends. The danger here lies in that these two together may tyrannize over the group. If this occurs, a third aggressive child is added. Three children do not act in unison because rivalry is set up among them. Sometimes nothing can be done to check such hostility, and in our experience so far, thirteen children have had to be removed from groups as inoperable despite all our strategies. Restraint may come from the group therapist as well as from the group.

We are able to identify, so far, four types of clients as related to their function in the group: *instigators, neutralizers, social neuters,* and *isolates.* Children of various clinical syndromes and diagnostic categories are found in each of these classifications. Hyperactivity and withdrawal may be neurotic symptoms; they may also be character manifestations more or less normal to the particular individual temperament, or they may be behavior disorders. In assigning clients for interpersonal therapy, the child's function picture rather than the clinical diagnosis is important. However, one must be aware of the latter in order to anticipate future developments. Free expression of hostility may be in some cases not only bad for the group, but destructive to the client as well. One must at all times know the meaning of each child's behavior, as well as understand the effect of that behavior upon the child himself, other children, and the total group atmosphere.

Another major element of the group setting is that it is a *permissive environment.* In the early stages, the child can use the environment in whatever way he wishes. He can make friends or withdraw, work or idle, construct or break, quarrel, fight or fraternize. This free use of the environment by the client in accordance with his own particular needs is of utmost importance. The child is convinced that he is loved, since he is allowed to do whatever he wishes. He discovers that the world is not necessarily frustrating, denying, and punitive. The client gains in his feeling of autonomy, and because of the friendly and accepting attitude of the adult, he relates himself to people. Inability to relate is the predominant cause of our clients' maladjustments, and when they can find their own way into a group at their own pace in their own particular manner, we have a truly therapeutic medium.

The neurotic patient finds in this permissiveness relief from his feelings of guilt concerning his behavior and impulses. He discovers that hilarity, aggressiveness, and destructiveness do not destroy one. He feels reassured. For a long time he watches from a distance the play and aggressiveness of his fellow members, but cannot bring himself to take part. Gradually he begins to participate vicariously by looking, laughing, turning lights on and off, or tripping another child. After some months, he takes part furtively at first, and quite freely later, in all the activities of the other children. Display of hostility makes these children very anxious, and some may not return for a number of weeks. In some cases release through individual treatment must precede group treatment. Almost all of the neurotic clients have overcome the fear of their impulses, with constructive effects upon their total adjustment. In fact, one study of our work indicates that neurosis is one of the four characteristics of our successful cases. The others are: aggressiveness at home, having no friends, and the child must be under thirteen years of age.

The opportunity we offer to each child to use environment in accordance with his particular needs is of immense importance. We believe that psychotherapy consists of removing the patient's resistance to the world, his self-encapsulation, as it were. Once this is done, living in a social environment is itself a therapeutic situation. As long as the patient isolates himself either through resistance, active aggression, or withdrawal, the world cannot get at him. He remains in a state of isolation and develops or continues with antisocial attitudes. When we make it possible for our clients to go out into their environment to a degree to which they are ready and in a manner suitable to them, we not only give them release and comfort, but their perception of the world as a hostile, destructive force to be feared or attacked changes. It is in this changed attitude that our therapy largely lies.

The therapeutic processes in individual treatment and group therapy parallel each other in many respects. Transference, catharsis, insight, relationship, attitude formation, authority, and limitations that are present in individual treatment have their counterparts in a therapy group. Group therapy, in fact, can be effective only when this similarity exists. The therapeutic process is the same whether it is in individual treatment or in the group. The difference is that the elements are derived largely from different sources and in different ways.

In some respects the group situation is more realistic to the young child. He is with other children, is active—which is a basic need of the young organism. He interacts with numerous facets of a realistic situation; he gains status, evolves interests, and relates to his contemporaries. Throughout, he tests this reality. He seeks to discover its nature and response. Will it hurt or reject him? Is it in any degree dangerous? Is it friendly and accepting? As he acts out his impulses and problems, the group reacts to him, and if he desires to be a part of the group, he curbs or modifies his behavior. As the withdrawn child gains strength and assurance, he tests himself against the group situation and the activities to gain further reassurance. He does this time and again, each time growing in strength, self-reliance, and self-acceptance.

The reality which we set for our clients extends beyond the group and its permissiveness. Eating in restaurants, trips, and excursions serve to take the children beyond the comforting confines and relations in the meeting room. Some children cannot face this challenge and stay away, but they gradually gain in power and take part in these extramural activities. Reality is further extended and each client is tested against it through the addition of new members, being assigned to a new group, changing of the therapist, and similar devices and strategies. Nurturing and feeding are also gradually reduced, materials become unavailable and their use restricted, food is no longer supplied, the therapist exerts mild pressure and constraint, and other methods are employed to dissolve dependence and aid the maturing process.

Such a group as described is one in which there is considerable *social mobility*. Our clients cannot fit into organized and stratified groups. They either cannot or are only too willing, as an escape, to submit to rules, regulations, group purposes and aims. Such groups of *social fixity* threaten some; others find their regimen and rules a comfort and escape through submission and ingratiation. To belong to a group of social fixity requires a certain amount of depersonalization, and many of our children are not capable of it. Others are depersonalized and need to build up confidence, self-assertiveness, and aggression. The value of a neutral environment from which each can draw according to his needs is obvious. Personal balance is achieved in a therapy group, however, not through habit formation or "learning," but rather by correcting intrapsychic disturbances, acquiring substitute mechanisms and sublimations.

We have stated that the first condition in our work is proper grouping. The second major factor is the personality of the group therapist. From what we have already said, it would seem that he is required to be all things to all children. Some may project upon him their hostilities toward parents and teachers; some become dependent upon him, some monopolize him, and others may seem indifferent. It would appear that the adult must meet the needs of all the children, which is, as can be readily seen, not a very simple matter. Should he attempt to do this actively, he would set up much confusion, emotional chaos, and hostility of the members toward one another. He can meet the requirements of the children by being a neutral person and as passive as one can be in a group. It is rather important that he does not activate a strong transference relation. Transference upon the adult is established to varying degrees by the clients themselves. This is almost inevitable, but what is important is that transferences be established toward fellow members, for it is because of their inability to do this that we accept children for group treatment. In this particular type of therapy, the focus of treatment is the relations among the members, and the adult should play a recessive role. This he can achieve by not obtruding himself, by not becoming the center of activity or the sole source of information, by abstaining from actions that stimulate and feed dependence.

Such neutrality on the part of an adult means to children that he is a kind, accepting, and approving person. Coupled with the facts that the therapist supplies and gives food, furnishes tools and materials, is helpful in case of need, and is kind and responsive, the adult emerges in the role of the all-sanctioning and comforting principle in life. In the child's mind this role is translated in terms of *unconditional love*. The child tests the genuineness of this love by exaggerated, aggressive, and irrational acts to see whether the therapist is really what he appears to be, and he must pass this test. He cannot become anxious, express disapproval, or display irritability by facial expression, muscular tension, or verbally. This requires a personality structure in the therapist capable of withstanding, without a feeling of discomfort, the turmoil, cruelty, and aggressiveness of the members toward each other. The fact that aggressiveness is accepted by an adult in the presence of others convinces the child he is being accepted and loved. Whether he intends it or not, the adult is a restraining agent by the very fact of his being an adult. When the child comes to us, he has already built up attitudes toward adults. To him, they have a definite prestige. He expects prohibition. Try as we may, we cannot entirely divest ourselves of the symbolic authoritarian role the child projects upon us. However, by accepting the child, and by not frustrating him actively, the therapist does not arouse resentment, aggression, or defiance toward himself. Restraint continues the child in his state of dependence, and the fact that he is thrown upon his own resources helps the maturing process, even though it may temporarily increase anxiety.

A child of prolonged infancy, if it is not charged with too intense emotions, needs restraint. The child who is loved but overindulged tends to persist in his infantile pattern. This may be manifested by annoying and interfering with others, by wheedling and whining, and dependence. The group therapist restrains and guides such a child even in the early period of treatment. However, even in these cases, restraint cannot take the form of disapproval or rejection. It must be given with a kindly mien, though firmly, with no emotion, and on a realistic basis. It should never take on the form of repression or nagging. Usually, infantile behavior continues in a group when there is more than one such immature child present, for they tend to reinforce each other, and reassignment of these clients into groups according to individual therapeutic needs have proved effective.

Control and setting of limitations by the worker is not confined to such children alone. At appropriate times in treatment, some limitations and denials are imposed upon all clients, but they are never arbitrary nor unkind. The timing of limitation and denial and their discriminative use with specific clients are of utmost importance. Bad use of these may undo many months and even years of treatment. When denial occurs before *frustration tolerance* is established in the members of the group, the consequent feeling of rejection only reinforces the child's conviction of the cruelty and unfairness of the adult world. It intensifies his hostility and defiance, activates retribution on his part, which may take subtle and indirect forms.

Rebuke and restraint if applied prematurely often bring on the defeat of the adult. Children have numerous ways in which they can defeat us. They can challenge or disobey, they build up patterns of passive resistance, they steal materials and tools, they incite the hostility of other children. Authority, therefore, must be used with caution and adapted to the total group and the individuals in it. It should be employed at stages of treatment when it can be effective. When this is not done, it may destroy the treatment situation. It must be kept in mind that attendance in groups is entirely voluntary, and when we fail to satisfy the children's cravings or hurt them, they drop out. This is another way in which they defeat us.

Since our project in group therapy was set up in 1934, there have been a large number of similar experiments in group treatment in different parts of the country. There is some disagreement on the part of other workers in this field as to the function of the therapist. We feel that there is unanimity in the basic concepts. The differences proceed from the fact that work was carried on in different settings, with different age groups, different types of workers, and probably different groups of children in regard to problems, age, and cultural backgrounds. Variation in any of these and other factors require adaptations of techniques. Since group therapy is situational therapy, any changes in the elements of the situation must of necessity require appropriate readjustments. We, too, have found it necessary to adapt our basic techniques to the treatment needs of different groups of clients.

An important fact must be recognized in group therapy which does not exist to the same degree in individual treatment. A number of sources of restraining authority besides the adult are present here. These arise from the group situation. Interest in a project, for example, restrains the child's impulses for immediate and easy results. Eating together makes it necessary to evolve some order at the table. Among the other restraining relations and situations are those which arise from the need to share and take turns with tools and materials from other children and the building superintendent.

In conclusion, a word of caution is perhaps necessary. Group therapy, in any of its forms, is no substitute for other types of psychotherapy. It is effective only with clients whose treatment needs are specifically met by it. It must be related to age, the nature of the difficulty, the readiness of the client to enter into a group relation, and numerous other factors. Under no circumstances must it be viewed as anything approaching universal application.

In our experience we have found that group therapy is entirely adequate in the treatment of some children, for some it is only of partial value, it is of no value to others, and may be injurious to clients whose problems and personalities are such that they are traumatized by permissiveness. It can be employed only in agencies where there is psychiatrically trained personnel and where psychiatric consultative service is available.

REFERENCES

1. W. I. Newstetter, M. L. Feldstein, and I. M. Newcomb, *Group Adjustment* (Cleveland, Ohio: School of Applied Science, Western Reserve University, 1938).
2. L. G. Lowrey, "Trends in Therapy," *Am. J. Orthopsychiat.*, IX, 4:697-699, 1939.
3. L. G. Lowrey, "Program for Meeting Psychiatric Need in the City," *Ment. Hyg.*, X:464-479, 1926.
4. S. R. Slavson, *An Introduction to Group Therapy* (New York: The Commonwealth Fund, 1943), p. 352.

20

SCIENTIFIC FOUNDATIONS
OF GROUP PSYCHOTHERAPY

J. L. Moreno

The late arrival of group psychiatry and group psychotherapy has a plausible explanation when we consider the development of modern psychiatry out of somatic medicine.[1] The premise of scientific medicine has been since its origin that the *locus of physical ailment is an individual organism*. Therefore treatment is applied to the locus of the ailment as designated by diagnosis. The physical disease with which an individual A is afflicted does not require the collateral treatment of A's wife, his children, and friends. If A suffers from an appendicitis and an appendectomy is indicated, the appendix only of A is removed; no one thinks of the removal of the appendix of A's wife and children too. When in budding psychiatry scientific methods began to be used, axioms gained from physical diagnosis and treatment were *automatically* applied to mental disorders as well. Extra-individual influence as animal magnetism and hypnotism was pushed aside as mythical superstition and folklore. In psychoanalysis—at the beginning of this century the most advanced development of psychological psychiatry—the idea of a specific individual organism as the locus of psychic ailment attained its most triumphant confirmation. The "group" was implicitly considered by Freud as an epiphenomenon of individual psychodynamics.[2] The implication was that if one hundred individuals of both sexes were psychoanalyzed, each by a different analyst with satisfactory results, and were to be put together into a group, a smooth social organization would result; the sexual, social, economic, political, and cultural relations evolving would offer no unsurmountable obstacle to them. The premise prevailed that there is no locus of ailment beyond the individual,

Reprinted from *Group Psychotherapy*, edited by J. L. Moreno, Beacon House, 1945, by permission.

that there is, for instance, no group situation which requires special diagnosis and treatment. The alternative, however, is that one hundred cured psychoanalysands *might* produce a societal bedlam together.

Although, during the first quarter of our century, there was occasional disapproval of this exclusive, individualistic point of view, it was more silent than vocal, coming from anthropologists and sociologists particularly. But they had nothing to offer in contrast with the specific and tangible demonstrations of psychoanalysis, except large generalities like culture, class, and societal hierarchy. The decisive turn came with the development of sociometric and psychodramatic methodology.* [3]

The change in locus of therapy which the latter initiated means literally a revolution in what was always considered appropriate medical practice. Husband and wife, mother and child, are treated as a combine, often facing one another and not separate (because separate from one another they may not have any tangible mental ailment). But that facing one another deprives them of that elusive thing which is commonly called "privacy." What remains "private" between husband and wife, mother and daughter, is the abode where some of the trouble between them may blossom, secrets, deceit, suspicion, and delusion. Therefore the loss of personal privacy means loss of face, and that is why people intimately bound up in a situation fear to see one another in the light of face to face analysis. (They prefer individual treatment.) It is obvious that once privacy is lifted (as a postulate of individual psyche) for one person involved in the situation, it is a matter of degree for how many persons the curtain should go up. In a psychodramatic session therefore, Mr. A, the husband, may permit that besides his wife, his partner in the sickness, the other man (her lover) is present, later his daughter and son, and some day perhaps, they would not object (in fact they would invite it) that other husbands and wives who have a similar problem sit in the audience and look on as their predicaments are enacted and learn from the latter how to treat or prevent their own. It is clear that the Hippocratic oath will have to be reformulated to protect a group of subjects involved in the same therapeutic situation. The stigma coming from unpleasant ailment and treatment is far harder to control if a group of persons is treated than if only one person is under treatment.

But the change of locus of therapy has other unpleasant consequences. It revolutionizes also *the agent of therapy*. The agent of therapy has usually been a single person, a doctor, a healer. Faith in him, rapport (Mesmer), transference (Freud) toward him, is usually considered as indispensable to the patient-physician relation. But sociometric methods have radically changed this situation. In a particular group a subject may be used

---

* Sociatry is applied sociometry. The group psychotherapies and the psychodramatic methods are subfields of sociatry, as the latter comprises also the application of sociometric knowledge to groups "at a distance," to intergroup relations, and to mankind as a total unit.

as an instrument to diagnose and as a therapeutic agent to treat the other subjects. The doctor and healer as the final source of mental therapeusis has fallen. Sociometric methods have demonstrated that therapeutic values (tele) are scattered throughout the membership of the group; one patient can treat the other. The role of the healer has changed from the owner and actor of therapy to its assigner and trustee.

But as long as the agent of psychotherapy was a particular, special individual, a doctor or a priest, besides being considered the source or the catalyzer of healing power—because of his personal magnetism, his skill as a hypnotist or as a psychoanalyst—the consequence was that he himself was also the *medium* of therapy, the stimulus from which all psychotherapeutic effect emanated, or at least, by which they were stimulated. It was always his actions, the elegance of his logic, the brilliancy of his lecture, the depth of his emotions, the power of his hypnosis, the lucidity of his analytic interpretation, in other words, he, the psychiatrist, was always the medium to which the subject responded and who in the last analysis determined the mental status which the patient had attained. It was, therefore, quite a revolutionary change, after disrobing the therapist of his uniqueness, showing for instance that in a group of one hundred individuals every individual participant *can* be made a therapeutic agent of one or the other in the group and even to the therapist himself, to go one step further and to disrobe all the group therapeutic agents themselves of being the media through which the therapeutic effects are attained. By means of a production on the stage a *third* element is introduced *besides* the healer and the patient-members of the group; it becomes the medium through which therapeutic measures are channelized. (This is the point where I went with psychodramatic methods beyond the methods I had used previously in group psychotherapy, even in its most systematic form— the group psychotherapies based on sociometric procedures and socioanalysis.) In psychodramatic methods the medium is to a degree separated from the agent. The medium may be as simple and amorphous as a still or moving light, a single sound repeated, or more complex, a puppet or a doll, a still or a motion picture, a dance or music production, finally reaching out to the most elaborated forms of psychodrama by means of a staff consisting of a director and auxiliary egos, calling to their command all the arts and all the means of production. The staff of egos on the stage are usually not patients themselves, but only the medium through which the treatment is directed. The psychiatrist as well as the audience of patients are often left outside of the medium. When the locus of therapy changed from the individual to the group, the group became the new subject (first step). When the group was broken up into its individual little therapists and they became the agents of therapy, the chief therapist became a part of the group (second step) and finally, the medium of therapy was separated from the healer as well as the group therapeutic agents (third step). Due to the transition from individual psychotherapy to group psychotherapy, group psychotherapy includes individual psychotherapy; due to the transition from group psychotherapy to psychodrama, psychodrama includes and envelops group psychotherapy as well as individual psychotherapy.

The three principles, subject, agent, and medium of therapy can be used as points of reference for constructing a table of polar categories of group psychotherapies. I have differentiated here eight pairs of categories: amorphous vs. structured, loco nascendi vs. secondary situations, causal vs. symptomatic, therapist vs. group centered, spontaneous vs. rehearsed, lectural vs. dramatic, conserved vs. creative, and face to face vs. from a distance. With these eight sets of pairs, a classification of every type of group psychotherapy can be made.

Table 20–1   Basic Categories of Group Psychotherapy

SUBJECT OF THERAPY

1. As to the *Constitution* of the Group

Amorphous	vs.	*Structured (organized) Group*
Without considering the organization of the group in the prescription of therapy.		Determining the dynamic organization of the group and prescribing therapy upon diagnosis.

2. As to *Locus* of Treatment

Treatment of Group in Loco Nascendi, In Situ	vs.	*Treatment Deferred to Secondary Situations*
Situational, for instance within the home itself, the workshop itself, etc.		Derivative, for instance in especially arranged situations, in clinics, etc.

3. As to *Aim* of Treatment

Causal	vs.	*Symptomatic*
Going back to the situations and individuals associated with the syndrome and including them *in vivo* in the treatment situation.		Treating each individual as a separate unit. Treatment may be deep, in the psychoanalytic sense, individually, but it may not be deep groupally.

AGENT OF THERAPY

1. As to *Source* or *Transfer* of Influence

Therapist-Centered	vs.	*Group-Centered Methods*
Either chief therapist alone or chief therapist aided by a few auxiliary therapists. Therapist treating every member of the group individually or together, but the patients themselves are not used systematically to help one another.		Every member of the group is a therapeutic agent to one or another member, one patient helping the other. The group is treated as an interactional whole.

2. As to *Form* of Influence

Spontaneous and Free	vs.	*Rehearsed and Prepared Form*
Freedom of experience and expression. Therapist or speaker (from inside the group) is extemporaneous, the audience unrestrained.		Suppressed experience and expression. Therapist memorizes lecture or rehearses production. The audience is prepared and governed by fixed rules.

MEDIUM OF THERAPY

1. As to *Mode* of Influence

Lecture or Verbal	vs.	*Dramatic or Action Methods*
Lectures, interviews, discussion, reading, reciting.		Dance, music, drama, motion pictures.

2. As to *Type* of Medium

Conserved, Mechanical, or Unspontaneous	vs.	*Creative Media*
Motion pictures, rehearsed doll drama, rehearsed dance step, conserved music, rehearsed drama.		Therapeutic motion pictures as preparatory steps for an actual group session, extemporaneous doll drama with the aid of auxiliary egos behind each doll, psychomusic, psychodrama, and sociodrama.

3. As to *Origin* of Medium

Face-to-Face	vs.	*From-a-Distance Presentations*
Any drama, lecture, discussion, etc.		Radio and television.

VALIDITY OF GROUP METHODS

All group methods have in common the need for a frame of reference which would declare their findings and applications either valid or invalid. One of my first efforts was therefore to construct instruments by means of which the structural constitution of groups could be determined. An instrument of this type was the sociometric test, and it was so constructed that it could easily become a model and a guide for the development of similar instruments. My idea was also that if an instrument is good, its findings and discoveries would be corroborated by any other instrument which has the same aim, that is, to study the structure resulting from the interaction of individuals in groups. After social groups of all types had been studied, formal and informal groups, home groups and work groups, and so forth, the question of the validity of group structure was tested by using first deviations from chance as a reference base, second by control studies of grouping and regrouping of individuals.

Deviation from Chance Experiments.[4] A population of 26 was taken as a convenient unit to use in comparison with a chance distribution of a group of 26 fictitious individuals, and three choices were made by each member. For our analysis any size of population, large or small, would have been satisfactory, but use of 26 persons happened to permit an unselected sampling of groups already tested. Without including the same group more than once, seven groups of 26 individuals were selected from among those which happened to have this size population. The test choices had been taken on the criterion of table-partners, and none of the choices could go outside the group, thus making comparison possible. Study of the findings of group configurations (resulting from the interacting individuals) in order to be compared with one another, were in need of some common reference base from which to measure the deviations. It appeared that the most logical ground for establishing such reference could be secured by ascertaining the characteristics of typical configurations produced by chance balloting for a similar size population with a like number of choices. It became possible to chart the respective sociograms (graphs of interactional relations) of each experiment, so that each fictitious person was seen in respect to all other fictitious persons in the same group; it was also possible to show the range in types of structures within each chance configuration of a group. The first questions to be answered read: What is the probable number of individuals who by mere chance selection would be picked out by their fellows, not at all, once, twice, three times, and so on. How many pairs are likely to occur, a pair being two individuals who choose one another. How many unreciprocated choices can be expected on a mere chance basis? The experimental chance findings followed closely the theoretical chance probabilities. The average number of pairs in the chance experiment was 4.3, in the theoretical analysis 4.68 (under the same condition of 3 choices within a population of 26 persons). The number of unreciprocated choices was in the chance experiments 69.4; the theoretical results showed 68.64 under the same conditions.

Among the many important findings the most instructive to the group psychotherapists were: (a) A comparison of the chance sociograms to the actual sociograms shows that the probability of mutual structures is 213 per cent greater in the actual configurations than in chance, and the number of unreciprocated structures is 35.8 per cent rarer actually than by chance; the more complex structures such as triangles, squares, and other closed patterns of which there were seven in the actual sociograms were lacking in the chance sociograms; (b) a greater concentration of many choices upon few individuals, and a weak concentration of few choices upon the majority of individuals, skewed the distribution of the sampling of actual individuals still further than took place in the chance experiments, and in a direction it need not necessarily take by chance. This feature of the distribution is called the *sociodynamic effect*. The actual frequency distribution compared with the chance distribution showed the quantity of isolates to be 250 per cent greater in the former. The quantity of overchosen individuals was 39 per cent greater while the volume of their choices was 73 per cent greater. Such statistical findings suggest that if the size of the population increases and the number of choice relations remain constant, the gap between the chance frequency distribution and the actual distribution would increase progressively. The sociodynamic effect has general validity. It is found in all social groupings whatever their kind, whether the criterion is search for mates, search for employment, or in sociocultural relations. The frequency distribution of choices shown by sociometric data is comparable to the frequency distribution of wealth in a capitalistic society. In this case also the extremes of distribution are accentuated. The exceedingly wealthy are few, the exceedingly poor are many. Economic and sociometric curves are both expressions of the same law, a law of sociodynamics.

Control Studies.[5] Two groups of individuals were compared. In the one, Group A, the placement to the cottage was made hit or miss, in the second, Group B, the placements were made on the basis of the feelings which the incoming individuals had for the cottage parent and for the other inhabitants of the cottage, and vice versa. Sociometric tests were then applied at intervals of eight weeks so that we could compare the structure of the control group A with the tested group B. Among other things it was found that the tested individuals undergo a quicker social evolution and integration into the group than the individuals who have been placed in a cottage hit or miss. At the end of a thirty-two-week period the control group showed four times as many isolated individuals as the tested group. The tested group B showed twice as many individuals forming pairs than the control group.

Indications and Contraindications of Group Psychotherapy. The indication of group psychotherapy or of one particular method in preference to another must be based on the sociodynamic changes of structure which can be determined by means of group tests of which two illustrations have been given above. Group psychotherapy has come of age and promises a vigorous development largely because group theory and group diagnosis have paved the way and have kept pace with the rapidly expanding needs for application.[6]

REFERENCES

1. G. Zilboorg and G. W. Henry, *A History of Medical Psychology* (New York: W. W. Norton & Co., 1941).
2. S. Freud, *Massenpsychologie and Ich-Analyse* (Leipzig: Internationaler Psychoanalytischer Verlag, 1921).
3. J. L. Moreno, *Das Stegreiftheater* (Berlin: Kiepenheuer, 1923); J. L. Moreno and E. Stagg Whitin, *Application of the Group Method to Classification* (New York: Beacon House, 1932); J. L. Moreno, *Who Shall Survive? A*

New Approach to the Problem of Human Interrelations (Washington, D.C.: Nervous and Mental Disease Publishing Co., 1934); "Interpersonal Therapy and the Psychopathology of Interpersonal Relations," *Sociometry*, I:9-76, 1937.

4. J. L. Moreno and Helen H. Jennings, "Sociometric Measurement of Social Configurations," *Sociometry*, Vol. I, Part II, 1938; U. Bronfenbrenner, *The Measurement of Sociometric Status, Structure and Development* (Sociometry Monographs No. 1; New York: Beacon House, 1945).

5. Helen H. Jennings, "Control Study of Sociometric Assignment," in *Sociometric Review* (New York: Beacon House, 1936).

6. J. L. Moreno (ed.), with a foreword by Winfred Overholser, *Group Psychotherapy* (New York: Beacon House, 1945).

21

PSYCHOANALYSIS AND GROUP PSYCHOTHERAPY

Nathan W. Ackerman

At the present time, the effort to shed light on the dynamics of group psychotherapy, through the application of psychoanalytic concepts, is fraught with complications. It is a task indispensable to progress, nevertheless, and in the end promises a substantial reward. The serious interest of psychoanalysts in group psychotherapy is distinctly on the increase. A number of them, myself included, have been groping toward a better understanding of the relevance of psychoanalytic principles for the dynamics of group treatment.

With the wide gaps of knowledge which prevail in this field, there is great room for prejudice in the approach of individual analysts to the issues of group therapy. My present views, highly tentative as they are, may reflect some amount of personal prejudice. For this reason, it may be useful to offer the background on which I have developed these views:

1. A primary orientation as a psychoanalytically trained psychiatrist.
2. Experience in the application of group psychotherapy to school-age children, adolescents, and adults.
3. Acquaintance with the literature on group psychotherapy.
4. A personal incentive toward the study of processes of social interaction, expressed in membership in two committees: The Committee on Social Issues of the American Psychoanalytic Association and the GAP Committee on Social Issues.

One episode out of the past will illustrate the particular slant with which I approached the problem of group psychotherapy. At a luncheon meeting of the American Orthopsychiatric Association, at which the plan for the American Group Therapy Association was launched, I timidly sug-

Reprinted from *Group Psychotherapy*, Vol. III, Nos. 2-3, edited by J. L. Moreno, Beacon House, 1949, pp. 204-215.

gested that a study of the processes of group therapy might provide a natural setting for the acquisition of sorely needed knowledge in a new science, social psychopathology. My remark was not then received with favor, but I still cling to that same prejudice. I believe careful study of the processes of group psychotherapy may yet give real substance to the new emerging science of social psychopathology.

I should like, first, to point concretely to some of the difficulties involved in applying psychoanalytic thinking to the problems of group treatment. Immediately, three types of phenomena and three kinds of knowledge are involved:

    1. The psychodynamics of group behavior, including both the processes of group formation and the processes of group change.
    2. The dynamic processes of emotional integration of an individual into a group.
    3. The internal organization of individual personality.

In all three areas, we are handicapped by an insufficiency of knowledge, but the lack of knowledge is conspicuously great in categories 1 and 2; i.e. in the processes of integration of an individual into a group and in the dynamics of group formation and group change. In addition, there is the difficulty of correlating the intrapsychic functions of personality with those adaptive operations of personality which are involved in the integration of an individual into a group. Partly because of these handicaps, we are not yet able to set up an adequate conceptual frame for applying psychoanalytic principles to the processes of group treatment.

At the very outset, we are confronted by a thorny semantic problem. Conventional psychoanalytic terms and definitions have not yet achieved a satisfactory level of scientific clarity and precision. The term "psychoanalysis" itself has come to mean many different things. The more important usages of this term offer at least four distinct meanings:

    1. A theory of personality.
    2. A therapeutic technique.
    3. A method of investigating the unconscious life of man.
    4. A special point of view toward human nature and toward the problems of living.

In addition, each of these connotations of psychoanalysis has been continuously changing through a process of evolution, especially the psychoanalytic theory of personality and the psychoanalytic concepts of therapy.

It is now almost axiomatic that psychoanalysis, as a device for systematic exploration of unconscious mental life, does not by itself guarantee therapeutic change. In exceptional circumstances, it may even constitute a crucial danger to the therapeutic objective. Mental health is not achieved in a simple way: It is not achieved merely by increased awareness or release of unconscious urges. It means not only the elimination of specific disabilities of personality, but also the positive fulfillment of the potentialities of the individual in the context of prevailing patterns of social relations. It is reached through the establishment of an optimal balance between the individual's orientation to his deeper strivings and his orientation to the real requirements of his relations to other persons and to the group as a whole.

This immediately sets up a distinction between psychoanalysis as a means of study of the unconscious and as a therapy. This consideration has direct relevance for both the goals and processes of group psychotherapy.

Psychoanalysis, as a theory of personality, has added a wealth of insight into the nature of man's inner conflicts, but has not yet reached the status of a scientifically unified theory. As a biological psychology, psychoanalysis has done much to correct the deficiencies of the older academic theories of personality. Yet, this very advantage has introduced certain complications. Psychoanalysis stresses the individual's deeper relationship to himself and those operations of personality which are oriented to the task of gratifying basic biological needs. It emphasizes unconscious motivation, the individuality and the egocentricity of man, and the primary importance of the individual's relation to body function. It gives rise, however, to a definite complication; namely, the difficulty of integrating the concept of man as an individual and man as a social being.

From the first, Freud admitted the importance of the social determinants of behavior, with special reference to the conditioning influences of family life, but a measure of ambiguity has always characterized Freud's formulations of the interrelationship of the biological and social determinants of behavior. This is rather clearly reflected in Freud's own statement concerning individual and social psychology:

> A contrast between individual psychology and social or group psychology, which at first glance might seem to be full of significance, loses a great deal of its sharpness when it is examined more closely. It is true that individual psychology is concerned with the individual man, and explores the paths by which he seeks to find satisfaction for his instincts, but only rarely and under exceptional circumstances is individual psychology in a position to disregard the relations of this individual to others. In the individual mental life, someone else is invariably involved, as a model, as an object, as an opponent, and so from the very first, individual psychology is at the same time social psychology as well.[1]

Here we have an illustration of Freud's brilliantly penetrating wisdom and yet, at the same time, a fair sample of his tendency to somewhat beg the question as regards the precise relationship between the biological and the social determinants of behavior. While making his bow to the "social man," he tends to show a preferential interest in the "individual man." He sought to explain the social role of man and woman in terms of biologically determined instincts and the related unconscious drives; the social function of man was represented as a projection onto the social scene of his unconscious strivings and fantasies. The broader patterns of culture were similarly interpreted.

While sharply illuminating the role of family life in shaping the child's personality, he tended, nevertheless, to stereotype the roles of mother and father, failed adequately to take into account the cultural patterning of these roles, isolated the dynamics of family life from surrounding social institutions, and subordinated the feminine half of humanity. He failed to see the way in which child-rearing concepts were influenced by cultural as well as the developmental factors of neurosis.

But what has all this to do with group psychotherapy? Mainly this: In order to illuminate effectively the dynamics of group therapy, the conceptual frame for a theory of personality must be expanded in a way that satisfies two necessary conditions:

1. The operations of personality must be conceived in terms of a biosocial unit. The biological and social determinants of behavior cannot be dissociated. Out of the interaction between the organism and environment, a new unit of behavior emerges which is biosocial. The adaptive functions of personality must be so viewed as to take into account the continuous interplay between those processes that reflect the individual's relation to his inner (biological) being and those which reflect his orientation to social participation. It is necessary, furthermore, to find criteria for the dynamic relations between the adaptive expressions of personality in group action and the relatively more fixed internal structure of personality, as conditioned by developmental influences. In other words, man has an identity that is, at once, both individual and social.

2. The functions of personality must be defined within the context of a broader theory of social organization and social relations. The adaptive behavior of the individual must be viewed in relation to the characteristics of the group to which he belongs. Differences between individual and group behavior must be understood. The behavior of a group has certain unique characteristics of its own, and the adaptive processes of personality, both normal and pathological, need to be viewed within this wider frame.

Until we satisfy these requirements in the basic concepts of personality structure and function, it will be difficult to usefully transpose psychoanalytic principles to a group treatment setting.

In a group setting, the therapist cannot directly observe, nor does he have access to, the total potentialities of individual personality; instead, the therapist establishes emotional contact with the shifting adaptive phases of the personality in action, which are expressed through the role of the person in that social situation. The role of the individual in the group represents a particular form of integration of his emotional tendencies in a specific situation. The adaptive expressions of the person are limited and shaped in two ways: by the relatively fixed organization of the individual personality and by the requirements of a given situation, as this individual interprets them.

It must be emphasized, therefore, that the immediate therapeutic influence in a group is exercised not through what is called "total personality," but rather through those particular forms of emotional expression through which the patient displays his personality in the group—namely, through his role in the group. The continuity of group therapeutic experience is such, however, as to induce in the person a series of changes in adaptive role, and through these changes, the therapist may gradually achieve access to a variety of layers of the personality.

Thus, social interaction can be understood only if we broaden our conception of personality so as to consider the continuous interplay between the individual's relation to his biological make-up and the individual's orientation to social participation. Each individual has layers of emotional reactivity which are relatively fixed and others which are more pliable. Each individual is capable, within the limits set by his fixed intrapsychic structure, of modifying his adaptive form in diverse social situations; he can change his "social role." The identity of each individual holds both individual and social components. In a shift from one social situation to another, the dynamic equilibrium between the individual and social components of personal identity undergoes change.

In a recent paper, "Social Role and Total Personality," I endeavored to illuminate the relationship between the social functions of personality and individual personality. I suggested that the adaptive forms or roles of personality in different groups might be appraised by the application of the following criteria: the group-conditioned aim of the individual, his quality of apperception of surrounding interpersonal realities, the concept of self projected into the role (including personal values, ideals, standards, and so on), his techniques for control of the group environment, his pattern of conflict, the quality of anxiety engendered by this role, and the defenses mobilized against it.

It seems to me that some attempt to define the adaptive functions of the personality can be made in these terms, and this adaptive role can then be correlated with our knowledge of the fixed intrapsychic structure of this individual. In order to establish such correlation, more exact knowledge of ego functions is needed.

When we turn to a consideration of the relation of psychoanalytic therapeutic technique to the techniques of group treatment, it becomes imperative to contrast the different psychosocial potentialities of the two therapeutic situations. The two-person psychoanalytic relationship provides a unique experience in which the earlier patterns of child-parent relations are relived and their destructive elements removed. Group psychotherapy, involving three or more persons, however, has its dynamic base in the fact that the child's character is influenced not only by the mother, but all the interacting relationships within the family group, especially the relationship between the parents. These multiple interpersonal patterns, each affecting the other, also contribute to the distortion of personality.

The psychoanalytic method applies to a pair of persons, but the techniques are pointed almost exclusively to the experience of only one of these persons—the patient. In considerable part, the analytic relationship does not constitute a true social experience; it provides no model for society. It is a process of working-through of the patient's internal conflict with self, with the analyst acting as catalyzer of this process. External conflict with the analyst becomes translated back into terms of the patient's internal conflict with self. A further aspect of analytic therapy involves a degree of temporary shedding of the patient's inhibiting ego, of his rational control, a denuding of the social layers of the patient's identity, so as to accentuate the patient's awareness of inner conflicted emotion and biologically conditioned urges. Thus, the importance of outer reality, and reality as personified by the analyst, is temporarily diminished. Such an experience heightens the patient's deeper communication with his private self and his unconscious, but at some cost in terms of temporary subordination of social communication. As access to the deeper self is achieved, the reality elements of the patient's ego and the reality of the analyst are reasserted and play their part in reintegration of the patient's emotional life. In this sense, analysis is predominantly a therapy which moves from "inside outward."

The group situation is different. Interpersonal processes emerge in a group which either are not present in a two-person relationship, or at least not in an identical form. Contact between two persons provides the potentiality for a social relationship, but does not provide the foundations of a society. Only a group of three or more persons makes possible an organized social unit, with a set of dominant aims, ideas, emotions, values, and patterns of social relations. Here we have multiple interpersonal patterns, interacting continuously with each other. Some of these relationship patterns may be in harmony; others in conflict. They vie with each other for a position of dominant influence. The way in which the group forms, integrates, changes, and is affected by leadership, determines the channels along which emotion is released or restrained. Thus, in a group, a tangible social reality is always present. The patient's contact with this reality is immediate and inescapable. The therapeutic process moves back and forth between this social reality and the patient's inner emotional life. Here we have a basis for continuous impact between the patient's image of interpersonal relations and their actual nature, as perceived and interpreted in the group interaction.

In order to try to see the extent to which therapeutic mechanisms operate similarly or differently in the group and individual settings, it is useful to outline the partial processes of psychotherapy, in general:

1. The development of an emotional relationship with a dynamic "give-and-take" between patient and therapist.

2. Through this relationship, provision of emotional support for the patient.

3. Reality testing; modification of concept of self, and patterns of relation to others in the direction of more realistic perception.

4. Release of pent-up emotion.

5. Expression of conflict, both conscious and unconscious.

6. Change in patterns of resistance and defense against anxiety.

7. Diminution of guilt and anxiety.

8. Growth of new insight, and emergence of new and healthier patterns of adaptation.

All of these processes overlap, influence each other, and together they provide the dynamic basis for therapeutic change. A number of questions arise.

Is therapeutic change in the group and individual settings dependent on the same or a different set of processes? Are there some processes which are specific and unique for one or the other form of psychotherapy? Do some particular processes play a more important role in one form of treatment than in the other? Or, if the basic processes are in essence similar, are the separate elements of therapy integrated and balanced differently in the two situations? On these questions, I offer my present views humbly, tentatively, with keen awareness of the handicap of limited knowledge.

First, I would tend to doubt that the group therapy situation involves any unique processes. I do believe, however, that the different psychosocial potentialities of the group necessarily modify the pattern of the balance between the partial processes of therapy, intensifying some, lessening or inhibiting others. The therapeutic processes in a group tend to operate on an interpersonal level, rather different from that which prevails in psychoanalysis. The nature of group experience is such as seems to place a first emphasis on conflict with the environment, rather than with the self. In the group, conflict tends to be externalized, projected into the social scene. Through such projections are reflected the patterns of inner conflict with self. Externalization of conflict encourages some measure of "acting out" in the group relations. Expression of feeling in a group, therefore, is more than verbal, it extends to the sphere of social action and fosters a higher degree of motor discharge of tension. In individual psychoanalysis, the primary emphasis is in the opposite direction; namely, on conflict with self, and in harmony with this, the tendency to "act out" is discouraged. Through the conflict with self, one gets, in turn, the mirror reflections of conflict with the environment.

But there are other differences as well. The pattern of intensive exclusive dependence on one person is not so readily possible in a group as in psychoanalysis. Relationships in a group tend to be more influenced by reality. The irrationalities of transference are held in check. The multiple interpersonal relationships provide opportunity for displacement, division, and dilution of transference emotion. Magic expectations and omnipotence strivings are restricted.

In the group, the function of providing emotional support for the patient is divided. The therapist is not the sole source of security and gratification of emotional needs. The group, as a whole, shares this responsibility.

In the group, discharge of pent-up emotion takes place on a selective basis. Emotion which can be experienced in common with others is reinforced. Other types of emotion may be inhibited.

Free association, in the analytic sense, occurs on a more limited scale, if at all. In its stead, we have the spontaneous emotional interactions between members and with the therapist.

In the interaction between the person and the group environment, there is a two-way selective process. The individual takes out of the group what he needs. The group takes from each individual what its processes require. The individual combines his force with those tendencies in the group which will strengthen the effectiveness of his chosen role. Also, he may submit to being used by others in the interest of their self-assertion. This two-way selective process plays a part in the assertion of certain types of control, in releasing basic drives, and in dealing with conflict, guilt, and anxiety.

In the group setting, the therapist does not have immediate or direct access to the unconscious of the patient. In this respect, the analytic situation enjoys greater favor; here the access to unconscious conflict is more direct, and more systematic. In the group, conscious conflict is the first to appear. The working-through of such conflict and its reduction to concrete terms will often bring to light significant clues as to the nature of deeper conflict. Frequently, the manner in which conflict is externalized and "acted out" in group interaction, offers hints as to the content of unconscious conflict.

Some further comment may be in order here in relation to the therapeutic connotations of a patient's tendency to "act out" his impulses. In the analytic situation, "acting out" is conceived as harmful and is systematically discouraged. In a group setting, the urge to express conflict through "acting out" is, to some degree, natural. Group psychotherapy is intrinsically an "acting out," rather than a "thinking out," type of experience. Here, a patient deals with conflict by projecting it into a relationship; he lives it out with the other person. In this manner, inner conflict is translated into outer conflict with another person. It is this "acting out" in relationships which enhances the motor discharge of emotional tension. In this setting, the therapist can work with the irrational elements of conflict not in the form of fantasy but rather in those forms which are projected onto the social scene. The group therapist may then translate this back into the context of the patient's inner conflicts. Because of the selective nature of the group process, however, some kinds of unconscious conflict may remain totally inaccessible.

Patterns of resistance and defense against anxiety are dramatically transparent in the proceedings of a group. Resistance should not be regarded as pathological behavior; it can be defined as the natural mechanism of self-protection when a patient fears harm through exposure of himself in a close relationship. Anxiety, the defenses against anxiety, and patterns of resistance are a functional unit. By tracing out the resistance paths, and the types of defenses employed, one sees the way in which a patient attempts to escape his anxiety and conflict. By pursuing closely these paths of escape, one is led, step by step, to the actual content of the conflict.

Individual patterns of guilt can be modified to a variable extent by group treatment . . . some forms temporarily, others more permanently. The more superficial types of guilt are easily reached and relieved, especially if they represent a shared form of guilt. The technique of universalization is a device for mitigation of guilt through reassurance, but may not alleviate it at its source. A lasting relief of guilt in the more rigid, automatized types of reaction is more difficult in a group. In general, however, the impact between the impulse tendencies of the individual and the fluid standards and moral reactions of the group does offer a substantial basis for diminishing guilt feeling. Here, the standards of individual conscience, immature and inappropriate as they often are, are checked against the more balanced and realistic standards of the group.

The group situation provides a wide range of possibilities for the testing of reality. In this setting, social reality is not a fixed entity. Each member of the group, and each pattern of relationship, personifies a given form of interpretation of social reality. In this sense, social reality is fluid, relative, and is represented by multiple interacting concepts, rather than by a single fixed interpretation. As the group evolves, however, there is increasing unity and stability in these interpretations of reality. On this background, the patient tests out his fear of dangers from the real world, and his fear of his own impulses. In this setting, the clash between his impulses and the standards of this fluid form of social reality offers a chance to expand his emotional orientation to his own nature and the nature of society. Such increased understanding may develop with or without therapeutic interpretation. Patients often spontaneously offer their own interpretations. Sometimes these are uncanny in their accuracy, sometimes utterly inappropriate because of the patient's egocentricity and projections. It is the therapist's task to guide these emotional crosscurrents toward correct understanding. He may use the technique of interpretation sparingly and only when the emotional trends have become sufficiently ripened. Here we have a broad opportunity for growth of insight, modification of social standards and values, and the development of healthier patterns of social adaptation. Of particular importance in a group is a growth of confidence in dealing with people and a basic increase in self-esteem.

Some Differences between the Psychoanalytic Two-person Situation and the Group Therapeutic Situation

Psychoanalysis	*Group Therapy*
1. Two persons.	Three or more persons.
2. Couch technique.	Face-to-face contact.
3. Temporary subordination of reality.	Reality continuously asserted by group though reality takes fluid form.
Analyst reasserts reality according to patient's need.	Patient's impact with reality is immediate.
Analyst is observer; suppresses his own personality.	Group therapist is more real person, participant as well as observer.
Relationship is not social, except in later stages.	Group provides genuine social experience.
Social standards not imposed.	Group standards emerge, but remain flexible.
4. Exclusive dependence on therapist.	Dependent need is divided, not exclusively pointed to therapist.
Emergence of irrational attitudes and expectations.	Irrational attitudes and expectations appear, but checked by group pressures.
Magic omnipotent fantasy prominent. Irrational motivation may rise to dominant position.	Magic omnipotent fantasy is controlled. Irrational motivation not permitted dominant position.
5. Direct gratification of emotional need not given.	Group offers some direct gratification of emotional need.
6. Communication largely verbal; communication less real.	Communication less verbal; greater expression in social action and reaction.
Patient communicates deeply with self; also with therapist.	Higher degree of social communication.
Patient feels alone.	Patient belongs to group, shares emotional experience, feels less alone.
7. "Acting out" suppressed; little motor discharge of tension.	Higher degree of "acting out," and motor discharge of tension.
8. Access to unconscious conflict more systematic; greater continuity in "working through."	Access to unconscious conflict less systematic; lesser degree of continuity in "working through."
Emphasis on inner conflict with self; conflict with self mirrors conflict with environment.	Conflict is projected, externalized. Conflict with environment mirrors inner conflict.

Psychoanalysis	*Group Therapy*
Modification of specific internal disorders of personality more effective.	Modification of specific internal disorder of personality less effective.
9. Patterns of resistance and defense more uniform and specific.	Patterns of resistance and defense more variable.
10. Relief of guilt and anxiety more specific.	Relief of guilt and anxiety less specific.
11. Dynamic movement to large extent from "inside outwards."	Dynamic movement to large extent from "outside inwards."
12. Emotional change and insight more immediately related to intrapsychic conflict.	Emotional change and insight more immediately related to extrapsychic conflict.
Method more suitable for specific psychiatric symptoms; predominantly a therapy for disturbance in basic drives.	Method more suitable for change in character traits; predominantly an ego therapy.

REFERENCE

1. S. Freud, *Group Psychology and the Analysis of the Ego* (London: International Psychoanalytic Press, 1922).

22

RESEARCH IN COUNSELING AND PSYCHOTHERAPY

C. B. Truax
H. Altmann

Man is a many splendored thing. Infinitely plastic, he can be molded into almost any psychosocial shape—for better or for worse. He can be either productive, happy, and a joy to those about him, or he can be incompetent, unhappy, and a pain in the neck to those about him. Counseling, psychotherapy, and related professions are in the business of promoting or facilitating the former and extinguishing or changing for the better the latter state.

There is a fad now to say that everyone ought to "actualize" oneself. Nonsense! We each have many potentialities. It is the work of counseling and psychotherapy to help make the client or patient productive and happy—not to put him on a guilt trip by implying or saying "actualize all of your potentialities." You contribute and actualize as *you* choose. There is no "moral" or "psychological" compulsion to run madly to "actualize *all* of your potentialities." Instead, clients, patients, people, and we ourselves should decide what we enjoy, and maximize productively just that. Life is endless growth and change, so our task is easy—we facilitate positive growth and change and inhibit negative growth and change.

Counseling or psychotherapy, whether conducted in an individual or group setting, is aimed at producing constructive behavioral and personality change in the clients it seeks to serve. It has become a principal part of the rehabilitation process: it is a common tool of psychology, psychiatry, social work, school counseling, marriage counseling, rehabilitation counseling, and vocational counseling, and plays a major role in the work of parole officers, group workers, recreation and playground workers, physical therapists, antipoverty workers, welfare workers, clergymen, educators, nurses, family physicians, and teachers.

In spite of its widespread adoption, there exists a considerable amount of evidence which seems to suggest that counseling or psychotherapy is not superior to "no treatment." Since Eysenck's (1960) assessment of the evidence and his conclusion that on the *average* the therapeutic enterprise was ineffective, a number of further studies have been conducted which, over-all, lead to a similar conclusion. Truax and Carkhuff (1967) found that the overwhelming evidence does indeed demonstrate that the *average* effects of counseling and psychotherapy do not *substantially* contribute to the rehabilitation process. This conclusion is based on studies of thousands of clients. That review, however, also indicates just as clearly that while counseling and psychotherapy have no over-all average positive effect, there are valid specific instances in which individual therapists, counselors, or clinics are indeed positively effective. While these studies showing positive effects are in the minority and based on smaller samples of clients, they were obtained in well-controlled studies utilizing adequate control procedures. Putting together these two bodies of evidence, it logically follows that if therapy has only minimal over-all average effect but does under some circumstances and with some therapists produce positive effects, then there must also be specific instances in which it is decidedly harmful. That is, to have an average minimal effect, if some clients have been helped, then other clients must have been harmed. When one examines the available evidence that appears to be the case. Thus while some clinics, hospitals, counselors, or therapists do seem consistently to produce results beyond that observed in similar clients receiving no treatment, other agencies or individuals seem consistently to produce effects considerably *worse* than that obtained without treatment.

Examples in a recent book by Calia and Corseni (1973) of unbelievably bad counseling and good counseling with critiques by a variety of highly experienced counselors and therapists give vivid reality to the "for better or for worse" effects of counseling or psychotherapy suggested earlier by Truax (1961, 1963, 1966), Truax and Carkhuff (1967), and Bergin (1966).

Indeed, a close examination of Eysenck's original table also shows this in his combined report on nineteen evaluations covering over 7,000 cases treated by eclectic, relationship-centered, or psychoanalytic approaches to treatment. Although the over-all improvement rate is 64 per cent (which tends to be somewhat poorer than the estimates of "spontaneous improvement" rates in nontreated comparable populations), one study (Ross, 1936) reported an improvement rate of 77 per cent for 1,089 patients, while another (Matz, 1929) gave an improvement rate of only 41 per cent in 775 cases. In terms of their relationship to the over-all average, the first study shows slight benefit and the other notable harm. Even more striking variability occurs in the findings presented by Levitt (1957), who obtained an average of 67 per cent improvement on 3,999 cases. In that survey, improvement rates as high as 91 per cent (Irgens, 1936) were combined with improvement rates as low as 42 per cent (Maas, 1955) to obtain the over-all averages. Clearly, the 91 per cent improvement rates from some studies differ significantly from the 42 per cent improvement rate of others, but in terms of the improvement seen in nontreated clients, one would be considered helpful and the other harmful. The line of evidence obtained from control studies shows a similar pattern, with some individual therapists or agencies being more helpful than "no treatment" and others being harmful in comparison to "no treatment": over-all, however, counseling and psychotherapy have not been shown to be greatly superior to "no treatment." In describing Paul Bjerre's famous case example (1922), Paul H. Hoch humorously observed:*

> The patient had a very elaborate paranoid content, and the psycho-analyst who treated him claimed the patient was cured by his analytic efforts. Later on there was a follow-up on this case in which the patient claimed that someone had pushed him from a horse; that this caused him to suffer a concussion and that following the concussion he was well—he no longer had the paranoid ideas. Now, I do not know who is right—the patient, the horse, or the analyst. But from this you must be aware of one thing, even though it appears a little far afield: It would be most interesting to some day determine just how far the influence of therapies in general, and psychotherapies in particular, can be assessed. In other words what functions are being performed and what is actually being accomplished by the various therapies.

The continual aim of the helping profession must, as Hoch suggested, involve the study of antecedents and processes which facilitate or retard constructive personality change during counseling or psychotherapy, and thus to contribute to a better utilization of therapy in the helping process. It would seem sensible for clinics, hospitals, schools, and agencies to attempt to identify effective and ineffective or harmful individual practitioners. That is, inasmuch as the available evidence indicates that psychotherapy and counseling as currently practiced have minimal average over-all beneficial effect (due to the presence of large numbers of practitioners who have negative effects offsetting the large number of those who have positive effects), it would seem that only by keeping records on individual practitioners can the clients' welfare and the public good be best served. Unfortunately this sort of individual record keeping is almost never practiced. Almost never do individuals or agencies keep even crude outcome measures of a given practitioner's effectiveness. This is equally true for professional organizations, universities, licensing boards, and other agencies or bodies. Both our public and moral responsibilities require that we exert our efforts toward evaluating average client response to specific

---

* M. Strohl and N. D. C. Lewis, eds., *Differential Diagnosis in Clinical Psychiatry: The Lectures of Paul H. Hoch, M.D.* (New York: Science House, 1972), p. 703.

individual practitioners; in spite of growing research knowledge, there seems no surer way of improving the effectiveness of a hospital, a clinic, a school, or an agency.

Indeed, it seems that one of the main reasons that professional, government, and agency bodies have not pursued such a policy in the past is simply that it is often difficult for the helping professions to accept the notion that counseling or psychotherapy can be and is harmful as well as helpful. We have too often implicitly assumed that although we could help, we would rarely prove harmful. The available evidence unfortunately indicates that on the average our therapeutic enterprise may be harmful almost as often as helpful, with an average effect only minimally better than no professional help.

The evidence does suggest that certain relatively unspecified kinds of therapists or counselors are effective. Further, it is clear that what is grossly labeled as counseling or psychotherapy is in fact a heterogeneous collection of ingredients or psychological conditions that produce varying degrees of both positive and negative change in the all-too-human client. This latter point is the critical one. It suggests that research can make significant and meaningful impact on the effectiveness of the rehabilitation process by concerning itself with identifying, isolating, measuring, *and relating to client outcome, specific ingredients or dimensions of the therapeutic process.*

THE COUNSELOR'S INTERPERSONAL SKILL IN PROVIDING BASIC THERAPEUTIC CONDITIONS

Despite the growing and bewildering array of theories about effective interpersonal relationships, and despite the difficulty in translating concepts from the jargon of one theory to that of another, several common threads weave their way through almost every major theory of human relationships, whether the theory is behavioristic, psychoanalytic, existential, eclectic, or humanistic. In one way or another, all have emphasized the importance of one's ability to be integrated, genuine, authentic, or congruent in interpersonal relationships. All have stressed the importance of the ability to provide a nonthreatening, trusting, safe, or secure atmosphere by one's acceptance, positive regard, caring, valuing, or nonpossessive warmth for the other person. Finally, virtually all theories dealing with effective or facilitative interpersonal relationships emphasize the central importance of one's ability to understand, be with, or be accurately empathic toward the other person.

In recent years there has been a dramatic breakthrough in measurement and training of certain central facilitative interpersonal skills. The measurement and research grew initially out of the psychotherapeutic relationship between therapist and patient. Gradually they were extended across different patient and therapist groups, different counselor and client groups, then to normal friendship relationships, parent-child relationships, and finally in educational settings from preschool to adult education. In all cases, high levels of these communicated interpersonal skills brought improvement on a wide range of behavior change, low levels of these facilitative relationships were decidedly harmful. This balance seems to apply equally to the relationship between a therapist and severely disturbed schizophrenic patient as to the relationship between the normal classroom teacher and a fourth-grade student studying reading or arithmetic.

From a massive and growing body of research evidence it is now clear that at least three *communicated* interpersonal skills have central positive effects on others: (1) an effective person communicates that he is nondefensive, nonphony, authentic, or *genuine* in his relationships with others; (2) an effective person is able to provide a nonthreatening, safe, trusting, or secure relationship through his own communication of acceptance, valuing, positive regard, or *nonpossessive warmth* for the other person; and (3) an effective person is able to understand, be with, grasp the meaning of, or communicate a high degree of *accurate empathic understanding* of the other person on a moment-by-moment basis. These three ingredients of communicated empathy, warmth, and genuineness are aspects of human encounters which cut across virtually all theories of interpersonal relationships.

THE EFFECTS OF COMMUNICATED ACCURATE EMPATHY, NONPOSSESSIVE WARMTH, AND GENUINENESS IN PSYCHOTHERAPY AND COUNSELING RELATIONSHIPS

For many years, particularly since the early writings of Freud, a great deal of the emphasis in psychotherapy, and as a consequence in counseling, focused upon psychopathology in the patient or client and specific strategies and techniques applied by psychotherapists or counselors. Relatively little attention was focused upon the *interpersonal skills* of the therapist or counselor. Indeed in the early 1950's psychoanalytic, eclectic, learning theory approaches, and even client-centered psychotherapy, were almost exclusively *technique* oriented. A series of retrospective studies by Whitehorn and Betz at Johns Hopkins University Medical School provided evidence that the way the therapist related to a patient dramatically affected the patient outcomes (Betz, 1963a; Whitehorn, 1964; Whitehorn and Betz, 1954).

Whitehorn and Betz's now classic contribution was a retrospective study of seven psychiatrists who had an improvement rate of 75 per cent in their schizophrenic patients, as contrasted with seven other psychiatrists of similar training and background who had an improvement rate of only 27 per cent. That is, if you were seen by any one of the seven psychiatrists with a high improvement rate you had three times as much chance of improvement as if you were seen by the seven other psychiatrists who had only a 27 per cent improvement rate. Their evidence indicated that the successful therapists were warm and attempted to understand the patient in a personal, immediate, and idiosyncratic way, whereas the less successful therapists (actually harmful therapists) tended to relate to the patient in a more impersonal manner, focusing upon psychopathology and the more external kind of understanding. In Betz's further delineation of successful and unsuccessful therapists (1963b), the descriptions were consistent, although not identical, with communicated empathy, warmth, and genuineness. It should be emphasized that the two groups of psychiatrists were equally well trained in the classic sense and were involved in one of the most prestigious psychiatric facilities of the day. Still, if we look at the normal 60 per cent improvement rate at that facility, we would have to conclude that one group of therapists were skilled at increasing the normal recovery rate (15 per cent better) while the other group were even more skilled at preventing normal improvement (33 per cent less improvement than no treatment). Clearly the relationship dramatically outweighted professional-technical skills in its impact on psychotherapeutic treatment.

The four-year study of psychotherapy with sixteen hospitalized schizophrenics, conducted at the University of Wisconsin under the leadership of Rogers, Truax, Gendlin, and Kiesler, has yielded a number of studies (Rogers, 1963; Truax, 1963; Truax and Carkhuff, 1963; Truax & Carkhuff, 1967; Rogers, Gendlin, Kiesler, and Truax, 1967; Truax, 1970). Findings from these reports indicate that: a) patients receiving psychotherapy and those under control conditions showed little difference in average constructive personality change, and particularly no difference in subsequent hospitalization; b) patients whose therapists communicated high levels of nonpossessive warmth, genuineness, and accurate empathic understanding showed significant positive personality and behavior change on a wide variety of indices; and c) patients whose therapists communicated relatively low levels of these interpersonal skills during therapy exhibited deterioration in personality and behavioral functioning. Their ability for "spontaneous improvement" had been destroyed. The evidence thus indicated that the three central therapeutic ingredients were predictive of outcome, and that, since in the sample studies the number of therapists communicating high levels of these interpersonal skills approximated the number offering low levels, the average therapy patient outcome was not markedly different from that of the average patient in the control group.

Truax, Carkhuff, and Kodman (1965) extended research into group psychotherapy or counseling with forty hospitalized mental patients, all relatively chronic, who were given group therapy sessions twice weekly over a three-month, time-limited period. Those patients receiving high levels of accurate empathy showed improvement equal to, or greater than, that of the patients receiving relatively low levels of accurate empathy on all subscales of the Minnesota Multiphasic Personality Inventory (MMPI), which was administered pre- and posttherapy. Statistically significant differences occurred on the Pt scale, the Sc scale, and the Welsch Anxiety Index obtained from the MMPI. Surprisingly, the data on the therapist's genuineness were in direct opposition to the prediction, although the data on nonpossessive warmth came out much like the data on communicated accurate empathy. In this study and in the Johns Hopkins study (to be discussed later), the three interpersonal skills were not all positively correlated. In the Hopkins study, warmth was negatively correlated with empathy and genuineness, and therefore negatively related to outcome. In the group therapy study of schizophrenia genuineness was negatively correlated with warmth and empathy, and therefore negatively related to outcome. When there are negative correlations among these three interpersonal skills it is statistically necessary that all three cannot show positive relationships with outcome. The data thus suggest that when two conditions of the therapeutic triad are highly related but the third is negatively related, then the prediction of outcome should be based on the two that are most highly related.

Studying 160 mixed hospitalized patients who met for only twenty-four sessions over a three-month period, Truax and Wargo (1967a) secured data indicating that significant differences in improvement favoring patients receiving relatively high levels of empathy, warmth, and genuineness were obtained on Q-sort measures of self-concept, the Welsch Anxiety Index, the MMPI Subscales of Mf and Sc, and particularly on time spent out of the hospital during a one-year follow-up. The patients receiving high levels of communicated interpersonal skills showed twice as many days out of the hospital than those receiving low levels of interpersonal skills.

Extending the prior findings to eighty institutionalized juvenile delinquents receiving three months of group counseling, Truax and Wargo (1967b) reported similar but much stronger findings, again indicating a significant association between the level of accurate empathy, nonpossessive warmth, and therapist genuineness offered by the group counselor and the degree and direction of behavioral and personality change occurring in the juvenile delinquents. Replicating the same basic design and study on a population of eighty outpatients receiving group psychotherapy, Truax and Wargo (1969) obtained essentially similar significant findings for all interpersonal skills combined. When accurate empathy, nonpossessive warmth, and genuineness were analyzed separately, the data suggested that nonpossessive warmth in particular and genuineness to a slightly lesser extent were more critical than accurate empathy for outpatients in group therapy. In contrast to the earlier reported findings concerning deteriorative effects of low levels of interpersonal skills with inpatient populations, the findings from the group therapy study with outpatients suggested very little evidence of absolute deterioration from pre- to posttherapy. However, since spontaneous improvement is relatively frequent with outpatients, the effects of low levels of interpersonal skills were to reduce and often eliminate spontaneous improvement rather than to result in absolute deterioration.

A cross-validation study of forty outpatients treated in individual psychotherapy by resident psychiatrists at the Phipps Psychiatric Clinic at Johns Hopkins (Truax, Wargo, Frank, Imber, Battle, Hoehn-Saric, Nash, and Stone, 1966) indicated greater improvement on two over-all measures for patients seen by therapists communicating high levels of combined accurate empathy, nonpossessive warmth, and genuineness, in comparison with patients receiving relatively lower levels of these combined interpersonal skills. When the interpersonal skills of accurate empathy, nonpossessive warmth, and genuineness were analyzed separately, the data indicated identical findings for empathy and genuineness, but a reversed tendency for nonpossessive warmth, again suggesting that when one of the interpersonal skills is negatively related to the other two, predictions of outcome should be based on the two that are most highly related. Of particular importance was that those patients receiving high communicated interpersonal skills showed a 90 per cent improvement versus a 50 per cent improvement for low levels of communicated interpersonal skills.

The above studies, taken together, support the theoretical view that the level of therapist accurate empathy, nonpossessive warmth, and genuineness are related to constructive change in patients. Still, the research reported above deals with relatively successful and relatively unsuccessful cases, rather than comparisons with control groups receiving no psychotherapy. Eysenck (1952), for one, has insisted on the value of comparisons with control groups by suggesting that even under the best conditions psychotherapy might not be significantly superior to no treatment. A number of studies have now been completed utilizing control groups.

The Wisconsin study, involving sixteen schizophrenics receiving individual psychotherapy and sixteen carefully matched control patients (Truax and Carkhuff, 1963; Truax, 1963), found an over-all significant difference in psychological functioning among patients receiving high levels of communicated interpersonal skills, patients receiving low levels of interpersonal skills, and control patients. In terms of the number of patients at or above the median change in psychological functioning, the control group had a rough 50-50 split; *all* patients in the group receiving low levels of interpersonal skills were below the median; and six of the eight patients receiving high levels of interpersonal skills showed positive change. The findings indicated that patients receiving high levels of communicated interpersonal skills in psychotherapy spent significantly more time out of the hospital than either the control group or patients receiving low levels of interpersonal skills, in psychotherapy, while patients who received low levels of interpersonal skills in psychotherapy did not differ from the control populations.

Working with a group of college underachievers, Dickenson and Truax (1966) found that those students receiving group counseling showed significant improvement in grade-point average over those students who did not receive counseling. One of the more striking findings from that study was that after therapy the total group of students receiving counseling functioned at the level predicted by their college entrance exam scores, and were thus no longer underachievers, while the control population continued to achieve college grades at a level significantly below their predicted level. Moreover, those receiving high levels of interpersonal skills showed a 90 per cent improvement versus a 50 per cent improvement for both the low level and control groups.

A further study (Truax, Wargo, and Silber, 1966) involving juvenile delinquents in group counseling indicated that on all twelve measures obtained pre- and posttherapy, the delinquents receiving high levels of interpersonal skills in group psychotherapy showed improvement significantly beyond that seen in the control group. Of particular importance is the fact that not only did the over-all differences in amount of time spent out of the institution significantly favor the delinquents who had received high levels of communicated interpersonal skills, but the superiority over the controls extended throughout a follow-up of one year.

That the effects of high and low levels of empathy, warmth, and genuineness can be extremely long lasting in their effects is shown by the recent follow-up study on a population of schizophrenics (Truax, 1970). The follow-up was made nine years after patients entered psychotherapy and focused on hospitalization. The findings across nine years indicated that patients seen by therapists high in these interpersonal skills tended to get out and stay out quicker than the control group as well as patients seen by therapists low in empathy, warmth, and genuineness. What was more striking was the negative effects exerted over a nine-year period by therapists low in empathy, warmth, and genuineness. There was no tendency for those patients to get out with the passage of time. Thus the poor interpersonal relationship had such profound influence that it disrupted and prevented the normal recovery process throughout a nine-year period.

These same findings have been confirmed at the University of Hamburg in a series of studies using the research scale translated into German. Thus several studies (Tausch, Eppel, Fittkau, and Minsel, 1969; Sander, Tausch, Bastine, and Nagel, 1968) studied a total of over 250 clients receiving therapy. Their findings showed significant high relationships between therapist level of accurate empathy and client level of self-exploration ($r = .72$). Moreover, they found that both the therapist's level of accurate empathy and the client's level of self-exploration were significantly related to measures of therapeutic outcome. Another recent study (Truax, Wargo, and Volksdorf, 1970) showed very strong relationships between the levels of communicated interpersonal skills provided by group counselors and improvement in delinquency behavior, including follow-up measures. On a study of psychoanalytic therapy, Vanden Bos (1970) showed that these interpersonal skills were significantly related to a variety of outcome measures in what was designed as a purely psychoanalytic study of therapy. In a study investigating largely nonverbal play therapy with children (Truax, Altmann, Wright, and Mitchell, 1973), ratings of empathy, warmth, and genuineness from videotape recordings were compared to improvement measures. Significant relationships were found between the level of the therapist's interpersonal skill and improvement or deterioration in the child as evaluated by both the parents and the participating therapist. Interestingly, children seen by the play therapist who communicated low interpersonal skills were evaluated by their parents as showing average deterioration, while those children seen by play therapists relatively high in empathy, warmth, and genuineness showed marked improvement.

Research seems consistently to find that counselors and therapists who are able to *communicate* a high level of accurate empathic understanding, nonpossessive warmth, and personal genuineness produce constructive behavioral and personality change in their clients, while those who are unable to communicate these qualities by reason of their training or personality tend to have damaging or harmful effects on their clients. The growing body of converging evidence on the importance of these conditions has serious implications for our personal conduct toward clients.

To be facilitative toward another human being requires us to be deeply sensitive to the moment-to-moment being of the other person, and to grasp both the content and the meaning and significance of his experiences and feelings. To do this requires that, at least to a certain great degree, we value, nonpossessively prize, and accept this other person. Moreover, none of these interpersonal skills can be constructively meaningful in a human encounter unless it is "real." Unless the helping person is genuine in relating to the client, his warmth, caring, and understanding have no meaning. Indeed, they may even have a potentially threatening meaning when they are artificial, contrived, or unauthentic. We should aim at being what we are in our human encounters—we should openly express the feelings and attitudes that we are experiencing. Basically, this might mean coming into a direct personal encounter with the client without the professional facade or screen—a meeting on a person-to-person basis, which is unfortunately rare.

These findings suggest that, to be therapeutic, we should personally aim toward communicating warmth in relation to the client without attempting to dominate him. To be maximally therapeutic we should move toward becoming listeners as well as talkers. We must develop abilities to perceive sensitively and accurately the client's feelings and experiences and their meanings to him, and to communicate a greater degree of this understanding in a language consistent with his language.

Procedures developed to teach prospective counselors, therapists, and laymen the art and skill of being able to communicate high levels of accurate empathy, nonpossessive warmth, and personal genuineness have shown significant positive effects. These procedures, now involving less than fifty hours of training time, made heavy use of the research scales used to measure these qualities in an integrated didactic and experiential program. One experienced trainer and an assistant can teach up to eighty trainees at one time by rating between small groups (Truax, 1973a).

Beyond the ability of the counselor or therapist to communicate generally high levels of these therapeutic interpersonal skills, the research has produced findings which add a totally new dimension to our understanding of the therapeutic role of empathy, warmth, and genuineness: their role as effective reinforcers in counseling and psychotherapy. The therapist who uses moment-to-moment variations in these therapeutic interpersonal skills to reward or reinforce the client's own self-exploration is significantly helpful, while the therapist who fails to do this or, even worse, actually rewards "nonself-exploration," has harmful effects. This means that we may be helpful or harmful depending not only upon our average level of therapeutic interpersonal skills, but upon how we use them on a moment-to-moment basis to reward and shape the client's behavior. While we may individually wish to abjure the role of a "reinforcer," shunning any attempts to control the client, the evidence is clear that, wittingly or unwittingly, therapists and counselors respond selectively. The remaining question is whether they shall respond selectively on a rational basis that will enhance their helpfulness to the client, or whether they allow themselves to respond selectively on the basis of personal preference to the detriment of their client.

SELF-EXPLORATION

While there are many areas of client functioning that could be rewarded or reinforced with benefit, the research indicates that self-exploration is an important client behavior within the process of counseling and psychotherapy, except in the case of juvenile delinquents. Studies with all other populations indicate that client self-exploration is an important antecedent to constructive behavioral and personality change: the more a client engages in deep self-exploration, the more successful the therapeutic outcome.

Much of the research in this area has been stimulated by the work of Rogers (1951). One of the early studies by Peres (1947) investigated differences between benefited and unbenefited patients in client-centered group counseling. Using tape recordings of the actual sessions, she developed a classification of patient statements based upon whether or not the statements referred to personal problems. Her findings indicated that, early in group counseling, both the benefited and unbenefited patients made equal numbers of references to personal problems. However, during the last half of group counseling, the successful clients made significantly more references to personal problems than did unsuccessful clients. This finding is perhaps related to Cartwright's finding concerning the critical significance of the therapist's final rather than initial level of understanding. Even considering all sessions combined, the successful clients in group counseling made almost twice as many references to personal problems as the unsuccessful ones.

Focusing on the degree of exploration of problems in individual counseling using a client-centered approach, Steele (1948) did a comparative study of more and less successful cases. The findings indicated that more successful clients increasingly explored their problems as therapy proceeded, while the less successful ones tended to explore their problems less. Similar results were reported by Wolfson (1949), while corroborating evidence dealing with client-centered counseling is available in the reports of research by Seeman (1949) and Blau (1953).

Using data from individual psychotherapy carried out from a client-centered orientation, Braaten (1958) attempted to determine the amount of *change* in self-references for successful and unsuccessful cases. Findings for the more emotionally disturbed part of his sample indicated a greater increase in the amount of self-references for the more successful than for the less successful cases, particularly those self-references involving expressions of the private self (awareness of being and functioning, internal communication).

Tomlinson and Hart (1962) used the Process Scale developed by Rogers, Walker, and Rablen (1960) in comparing successful and unsuccessful counseling cases. Their data indicated that the successful cases tended to score higher on the Process Scale, which essentially measures degree of self-exploration, rigidity of concepts, and degree of immediate experiencing. Similarly, Wagstaff, Rice, and Butler (1960) reported data from a study of client-centered counseling indicating that patients with successful outcomes tended to explore themselves more in the course of psychotherapy, whereas patients who could be classified as therapeutic failures showed little self-exploration and emotional involvement.

The research on individual psychotherapy with schizophrenics (Truax and Carkhuff, 1964) involved use of the Depth of Intrapersonal Exploration Scale applied to tape recordings of psychotherapy. The over-all findings indicated that patients who were high in self-exploration showed significantly greater personality change than patients who were relatively low in degree of self-exploration. This finding held both with the final outcome criterion, based on a number of psychological tests including a blind analysis of the Rorschach and percentage of time hospitalized, and with a number of specific measures. The over-all analysis indicated that the patients engaging in a high level of self-exploration showed an average improvement one standard deviation beyond that of patients low in self-exploration. In specific subanalysis, the data suggested that the basal level of self-exploration (the average of the three lowest samples of self-exploration per patient) was most highly related to outcome, but that the altitude (highest levels) of self-exploration was not significantly related.

Of particular interest, serial analyses of the first thirty interviews, covering a period of up to three and one-half years, indicated that for the most part this positive relationship between level of self-exploration and outcome held whether measurement was taken early or late in the process of therapy. There was one significant exception to this, a clear reversal of the pattern at approximately the fifth interview of therapy: Successful cases who started off significantly higher in self-exploration appeared to show a sharp drop in level of self-exploration at about the fifth interview and then returned to a high level by the tenth interview and thereafter; cases who were later to show deterioration or no change showed a relatively constant lower level of self-exploration. Analyses using the Problem Expression Scale developed by van der Veen and the Experiencing Scale developed by Gendlin yielded similar findings. The relationships to outcome were somewhat less and in some cases not at all significant, and there was an even sharper reversal at around the fifth interview.

Although the available data could not yield conclusive findings, an analysis by Rogers and Truax (1962) obtained findings suggesting that the Depth of Intrapersonal Exploration Scale, the Experiencing Scale, and the Problem Expression Scale measured something akin to readiness for help. That is, the data, while not totally conclusive, favor the hypothesis that low levels on the scales describe clients who are relatively rigid and unready for help, and high levels describe clients with a readiness to change, who are already exhibiting some "changingness" by their self-exploratory behavior.

One intriguing finding from those studies was the indication that successful cases, as a group, showed significantly more self-exploration as early as the second interview. The correlation between level of self-exploration in the second interview and the final case outcome was .70, even though some cases were continued for more than three and one-half years. When comparisons were made using a control group, the data indicated that patients who engaged in a relatively high level of self-exploration showed improvement significantly greater than the control patients, but those showing low levels of self-exploration showed less improvement (even deterioration) than the controls. Significant differences, favoring greater improvement for those high in self-exploration, also showed in the time patients spent hospitalized during a three and one-half year period. Here improvement was measured by psychological tests: the sum of the clinical scales of the MMPI as well as the Pd, Mf, Pt, and Ma subscales.

Analyses were also made relating the levels of accurate empathy, non-possessive warmth, and genuineness offered by the therapist throughout the course of therapy to the levels of patient self-exploration. Although it was not strong, there was a significant relationship between the levels of accurate empathy and nonpossessive warmth offered by the therapist and the average level of self-exploration engaged in by the patient. The level of congruence tended to show a similar pattern. Using the same data that had been used for analysis of the therapeutic conditions, an attempt was made to determine the relative contribution of therapist and patient to the patient's level of self-exploration. With data from the study in which hospitalized patients had each seen a different therapist, the findings indicated that both patient and therapist significantly affected the level of patient self-exploration. That is, different therapists, when seeing the same set of patients, tended to *evoke* different levels of patient self-exploration; different patients, when seeing the same set of therapists, tended to engage in different levels of self-exploration.

That the patient plays the major role in determining his own level of self-exploration is further indicated by an analysis making use of the sampling interviews in the schizophrenic research study. For each case, the level of self-exploration occurring in the periodic sampling interviews with a constant standard interviewer was computed. Then the average level of self-exploration occurring for each case in actual therapy was computed separately. With such data, the degree to which self-exploration was solely a product of the patient (and not the therapist) could be examined more closely. The obtained correlation of .67 between the level of self-exploration occurring in therapy per case and the corresponding level in the sampling interviews strongly suggests that although the therapist may indeed *influence* the patient's self-exploration by offering certain levels of therapeutic conditions, the patient himself is the one who primarily *determines* his level of self-exploration.

In more recent attempts to extend the findings on self-exploration to group therapy, Truax and Wargo (1966) studied the relationship between level of patient self-exploration and outcome on an initial population of eighty juvenile delinquents. The findings were quite equivocal. On a few specific measures the differences favoring those in groups where high levels of self-exploration occurred reached statistical significance; however, on some of the other submeasures the exact reverse was found. Self-exploration, then, did not seem critical for delinquents.

In a study of eighty outpatients receiving time-limited group therapy (Truax, Wargo, and Carkhuff, 1966), the findings suggested that successful outpatients in group therapy engage in greater self-exploration than outpatients who show poorer outcome in group therapy ($p < .05$).

In the related study by Truax and Wargo (1966) of 160 hospitalized patients, evidence for the importance of patient self-exploration in group therapy was stronger. On twenty-one of the twenty-eight specific measures of outcome available for analysis, patients in groups with high levels of self-exploration showed greater improvement than patients in groups low in self-exploration ($p < .001$). The findings indicate that the patient's level of self-exploration is significantly affected both by the average level of the counselor's accurate empathy, nonpossessive warmth, and genuineness, and by the degree to which the counselor systematically uses empathy, warmth, and genuineness to reward greater self-exploration.

OTHER IMPLICATIONS

Another important implication of the research findings deals with the therapeutic impact on high and low prognosis clients during psychotherapy or counseling. It is widely argued that until psychotherapy, counseling, and the total rehabilitation services are widely and uniformly available, it might make more sense to concentrate efforts on the high prognosis clients. It has already been pointed out that we know little, if anything, about prognosis. What have been considered prognostic indicators in the past have been taken from studies attempting to predict therapeutic outcome without consideration of the effectiveness and differential effectiveness of the treatments applied to the client population. The evidence therefore deals with the prediction of degree of expected change with or without treatment, and does not indicate degree of client *benefit*. The present findings in general indicate that empathy, warmth, and genuineness tend to have similar effects in high and low prognosis clients. The evidence suggests that the absolute degree of client change is determined both by the treatment and by the client's current status, but that the degree of *benefit* (how much he changes with treatment as opposed to without treatment) is not markedly different for the high and low prognosis client.

The findings on the use of alternate sessions in group psychotherapy would indicate that alternate sessions are of significant value to the rehabilitation process with neurotic and mildly disturbed outpatients, but harmful or damaging for institutionalized juvenile delinquents and hospitalized mental patients. The evidence is fairly clear in indicating that the use of alternate sessions in group psychotherapy detracts from effective treatment of institutionalized juvenile delinquents and hospitalized mental patients. On the other hand, its effectiveness with groups of outpatients spread geographically from the Midwest to the South and Northeast United States would mean that counselors and therapists could provide more clients with group therapy services without increased cost by the use of alternate sessions with outpatient populations.

The research findings on the impact of vicarious therapy pretraining indicate that the cognitive and experiential structuring for the client provided by a single tape recording of examples of good therapeutic interaction has modest therapeutic benefit in a wide variety of patient populations. The use of vicarious therapy pretraining which can be applied throughout the field of rehabilitation quite economically (requiring only the duplication of half-hour tapes to be played to prospective group counseling or group therapy clients) would have significant therapeutic benefit. The findings suggest that vicarious therapy pretraining has the most beneficial effect for outpatients, and modest benefit for hospitalized mental patients. At the same time, there appears to be no therapeutic benefit (but also no harmful effects) when vicarious therapy pretraining tapes are used with institutionalized juvenile delinquents. This latter fact, combined with the indication that degree of self-exploration is irrelevant to outcome with juvenile delinquents, suggests that the usual psychotherapeutic models of process, appropriate to emotionally and mentally disturbed clients, may be inappropriate for juvenile delinquent populations. That is, juvenile delinquents may make use of such therapeutic factors as empathy, warmth, and genuineness to deal with problems concerned with external relating rather than internal relating.

From the number of research studies conducted, there is much evidence to confirm, and none to disconfirm, the line of reasoning that overall, counseling and psychotherapy, *on the average*, do not greatly enhance the rehabilitation process. Further, the evidence clearly confirms the expectation that this over-all lack of therapeutic impact of counseling and psychotherapy is due to the presence of much counseling and psychotherapy that is psychonoxious or harmful. The widespread impact of harmful counselors and therapists, and harmful therapeutic practices, obscures the equally widespread presence of beneficial counselors, psychotherapists, and therapeutic practices.

While it is clear that agencies, clinics, hospitals, schools, and indeed all responsible institutions should attempt to identify the effective and ineffective or harmful individual practitioners by keeping careful records which would enable them to judge future effectiveness by past performance, a number of the present findings point to antecedents and processes which facilitate or retard constructive personality change in the client. To have impact on the effectiveness of the total rehabilitation process, it is necessary to apply the understanding gained from the research.

In a recent address to the Ontario Psychological Association, Truax

(1973a) presented comparative outcome effects of interpersonal skills training (one trainer for eighteen clients) versus traditional counseling and psychotherapy (one therapist per client: N = 14) versus behavior therapy (one therapist per patient: N = 15). The findings indicated little difference between traditional counseling and psychotherapy and behavior therapy, but revealed significant differences suggesting the superiority of interpersonal skills training. Significant differences were obtained on the neurotic and anxiety scales of the MMPI and an over-all change in adjustment and functioning, change in work or school adjustment, relationships with friends and relations, and other specific areas of adjustment as judged by pre- and posttesting of the patient or client and by his or her closest friend.

This finding is striking. Most clients or patients have difficulty in relating to other people, not to objects. If they learn to relate well to others, then through the principle of reciprocal affect others will at least minimally reciprocate by returning warmth, genuineness, and empathy.

A further line of evidence reviewed by Truax and Mitchell (1971) together with the above data suggests that clients, patients, and people in general (including counselors and therapists) will have a more satisfying, productive, and fruitful life if they surround themselves in their personal environment with others who communicate high levels of empathy, warmth, and genuineness—and *avoid like the plague* (which psychologically they are) others who are nonempathic, cold, indifferent, dominating, phony, or defensive.

The essence of training in ability to communicate the interpersonal skills of empathy, warmth, and genuineness is *feedback*.

While training programs can be elaborate and rely on the research scales (Truax, 1961; revised for teachers, 1970), self-rating is also significantly effective in improving interpersonal skills. Simply tape-recording oneself and rating on a scale of one to five by self or self and friends or colleagues produces significant improvement in these interpersonal skills.

These studies taken together suggest that therapists or counselors who are accurately empathic, nonpossessively warm in attitude, and genuine, are indeed effective, and this relates to the degree of self-exploration by the client. These findings seem to hold with a wide variety of therapists and counselors (regardless of their training or theoretic orientation), lay helping persons, peers, and friends or relations. They also hold in educational settings and with a wide variety of clients or patients, including juvenile delinquents, hospitalized schizophrenics, mild to severe outpatient neurotics, the mixed variety of hospitalized patients, and disturbed children. Further, the evidence suggests that these findings hold in variety of therapeutic contexts and in both individual and group psychotherapy and counseling.

BIBLIOGRAPHY

Bergin, A. E., and Jasper, L. G., "Correlates of Empathy in Psychotherapy: A Replication," *J. Abnorm. Psychol.*, 74:447-481, 1969.

Betz, B. J., "Bases of Therapeutic Leadership in Psychotherapy with the Schizophrenic Patient," *Am. J. Psychother.*, 17:196-212, 1963a.

———, "Differential Success Rates of Psychotherapists with 'Process' and 'Non-process' Schizophrenic Patients," *Am. J. Psychother.*, 11:1090-1091, 1963b.

Bjerre, P., "Delusions and Obsessions and Their Treatment," *Hggiea*, 84:1009, 1922.

Braaten, L. J., "The Movement from Non-self to Self in Client-centered Psychotherapy," Ph.D. dissertation, University of Chicago, 1958.

Calia, V. F., and Corseni, R. J., *Critical Incidents in School Counseling* (Englewood Cliffs, N.J.: Prentice Hall, 1973).

Dickenson, W. A., and Truax, C. B., "Group Counseling with College Underachievers: Comparisons with a Control Group and Relationship to Empathy, Warmth and Genuineness," *Personnel Guidance Journal*, 45:245-248, 1966.

Eysenck, H. J., "The Effects of Psychotherapy: An Evaluation," *J. Consult. Psychol.*, 16:319-324, 1952.

———, ed., *Behavior Therapy and the Neuroses* (New York: Pergamon Press, 1960).

Irgens, E. M., "Must Parents' Attitudes Become Modified in Order to Bring About Adjustment in Problem Children?," *Smith College Student Social Work*, 7:17-45, 1936.

Levitt, B. E., "The Results of Psychotherapy with Children: An Evaluation," *J. Consult. Psychol.*, 21:189-196, 1957.

Maas, H. S., et al., "Socio-cultural Factors in Psychiatric Clinic Services for Children," *Smith College Student Social Work*, 25:1-90, 1955.

Matz, P. B., "Outcome of Hospital Treatment of Ex-service Patients with Nervous and Mental Disease in the U.S. Veterans Bureau," *U.S. Veterans Med. Bull.*, 5:829-842, 1929.

Peres, H., "An Investigation of Non-directive Group Therapy," *J. Consult. Psychol.*, 11:159-172, 1947.

Rogers, C. R., *Client-centered Therapy* (Cambridge, Mass.: Riverside Press, 1951), pp. 73-74.

———, "The Interpersonal Relationship: The Core of Guidance," *Harvard Ed. Rev.*, 32:416-429, 1962.

———, Gendlin, E. T., Kiesler, D., and Truax, C. B., *The Therapeutic Relationship and Its Impact: A Study of Psychotherapy with Schizophrenics* (Madison: University of Wisconsin Press, 1967).

Rogers, C. R., and Truax, C. B., "The Relationship Between Patient Intrapersonal Exploration in the First Sampling Interview and the Final Outcome Criterion," *Brief Research Reports*, Wisconsin Psychiatric Institute, University of Wisconsin, 73, 1962.

Rogers, C. R., Walker, A., and Rablen, R., "Development of a Scale to Measure Process Changes in Psychotherapy," *J. Clin. Psychol.*, 16:79-85, 1960.

Ross, T. A., *An Enquiry into Prognosis in the Neurosis* (London: Cambridge University Press, 1936).

Sander, K., Tausch, R., Bastine, R., and Nagel, K., "Die auswirkung experimenteller anderungen des psychotherapeutenverhaltens auf klienten in psychotherapeutischen gesprachen," im manuskript 1968.

Seeman, J. A., "A Study of the Process of Non directive Therapy," *J. Consult. Psychol.*, 40:157-168, 1949.

Steele, B. L., "The Amount of Exploration into Causes, Means, Goals, and Agent: A Comparison of Successful and Unsuccessful Cases in Client-centered Therapy," Master's thesis, University of Chicago, 1948.

Strohl, M., and Lewis, N. D. C., eds., *Differential Diagnosis in Clinical Psychiatry: The Lectures of Paul H. Hoch, M.D.* (New York: Science House, 1972).

Tausch, R., Eppel, H., Firrkau, B., and Minsel, R., "Variablen und Zusammenhange in der Gesprachspsychotherapie," *Zeitschrift Fur Psychologie, 176:* 93-102, 1969.

Tomlinson, T. M., and Hart, J. T., "A Validation Study of the Process Scale," *J. Consult. Psychol.*, 26:74-78, 1962.

Truax, C. B., "A Scale for the Measurement of Accurate Empathy," *Psychiatric Institute Bulletin*, Wisconsin Psychiatric Institute, University of Wisconsin, 10, 1961, rev. 1970.

————, "Effective Ingredients in Psychotherapy: An Approach to Unraveling the Patient-Therapist Interaction," *J. Clin. Psychol.*, 10:256-263, 1963.

————, "Counseling and Psychotherapy: Process and Outcome," VRA *Final Report*, Arkansas Rehabilitation Research and Training Center, University of Arkansas, 1966.

————, "Effects of Client-centered Psychotherapy with Schizophrenic Patients: Nine Years Pretherapy and Nine Years Posttherapy Hospitalization," *J. Consult. and Clin. Psychol.*, 35:417-422, 1970.

————, "Training in Interpersonal Skills: A Viable Alternative to Traditional Counseling and Psychotherapy or Behavior Therapy," Address to the Ontario Psychological Association, Toronto, February 1973a.

————, "Effects of Short Term Training on Teacher Interpersonal Skills," in press, 1973b.

————, Altmann, H., Wright, L., and Mitchell, K. M., "Effects of Therapeutic Conditions in Child Therapy," *J. Comm. Psychol.*, 1:(3) 313-318, July 1973.

Truax, C. B., and Carkhuff, R. R., "For Better or For Worse: The Process of Psychotherapeutic Personality Change," Paper read at Academic Assembly on Clinical Psychology, McGill University, Montreal, Canada, 1963.

————, "Concreteness: A Neglected Variable in the Psychotherapeutic Process," *J. Clin. Psychol.*, 20:264-267, 1964.

————, and Kodman, F., Jr., "Relationships Between Therapist-offered Conditions and Patient Change in Group Psychotherapy," *J. Clin. Psychol.*, 21:327-329, 1965.

Truax, C. B., and Mitchell, K., "Research on Therapists' Qualities in Relationship to Process and Outcome," in Allen E. Bergin and Sol L. Garfield, eds., *Handbook of Psychotherapy and Behavior Change* (New York: Wiley, 1971).

Truax, C. B., and Wargo, D. G., "Antecedents to Outcome in Group Psychotherapy with Hospitalized Mental Patients: Effects of Therapeutic Conditions, Alternate Sessions, Vicarious Therapy Pretraining, and Patient Self-exploration," Unpublished manuscript, University of Arkansas, 1966.

―――, "Antecedents to Outcome in Group Psychotherapy with Hospitalized Mental Patients: Effects of Therapeutic Conditions, Alternate Sessions, Vicarious Therapy Pretraining and Patient Self-exploration," Unpublished manuscript, Arkansas Rehabilitation Research and Training Center, University of Arkansas, 1967a.

―――, "Antecedents to Outcome in Group Psychotherapy with Juvenile Delinquents: Effects of Therapeutic Conditions, Alternate Sessions, Vicarious Therapy Pre-training and Patient Self-exploration," Unpublished manuscript, Arkansas Rehabilitation Research and Training Center, University of Arkansas, 1966.

―――, "Antecedents to Outcome in Group Psychotherapy with Outpatients: Effects of Therapeutic Conditions, Alternate Sessions, Vicarious Therapy Pre-training and Patient Self-exploration," *J. Consult. and Clin. Psychol.*, 33, 1969.

―――, and Carkhuff, R. R., "Antecedents to Outcome in Group Psychotherapy with Outpatients: Effects of Therapeutic Conditions, Alternate Sessions, Vicarious Therapy Pre-training and Patient Self-exploration," Unpublished manuscript, University of Arkansas, 1966.

Truax, C. B., Wargo, D. G., Frank, J. D., Imber, S. D., Battle, C. C., Hoehn-Saric, R., Nash, E. H., and Stone, A. R., "Therapist Empathy, Genuineness, and Warmth and Patient Therapeutic Outcome," *J. Consult. Psychol.*, 1966.

Truax, C. B., Wargo, D. G., and Silber, L., "Effects of High Accurate Empathy and Non-possessive Warmth During Group Psychotherapy upon Female Institutionalized Delinquents," *J. Abnorm. Psychol.*, 71:267-274, 1966.

Truax, C. B., Wargo, D. G., and Volksdorf, N. R., "Antecedents to Outcome in Group Counseling with Institutionalized Delinquents," *J. Abnorm. Psychol.*, 76:235-242, 1970.

Vanden Bos, G. R., "Therapist Conditions in Psychoanalytic Psychotherapy," *Michigan State Psychotherapy Research Project Bulletin*, 11, 1970.

Wagstaff, A. K., Rice, L. N., and Butler, J. M., "Factors of Client Verbal Participation in Therapy," *Counseling Center Discussion Papers*, University of Chicago, 6:1-14, 1960.

Whitehorn, J. C., "Human Factors in Psychiatry," *Bull. N. Y. Academy of Medicine*, 40:451-466, 1964.

―――, and Betz, B. J., "A Study of Psychotherapeutic Relationships Between Physicians and Schizophrenic Patients," *Amer. J. Psychiat.*, 3:321-331, 1954.

Wolfson, K. S., "Clients' Exploration of Their Problems During Client-centered Therapy," Master's thesis, University of Chicago, 1949.

23

PSYCHOANALYSIS IN GROUPS

Alexander Wolf

Claims are occasionally made that the beginnings of psychoanalytic group therapy were undertaken by one therapist or another. Perhaps one could demonstrate that group therapy began at meetings of young philosophers around Socrates and Plato or among the Apostles and Jesus. Ernest Jones suggests that psychoanalysis in groups began aboard ship in 1909 when Freud, Jung, and Ferenczi analyzed one another's dreams on the way to the United States. If any priority needs to be respected, it should perhaps be rendered to Freud and his shipboard companions.

Group psychotherapy began in the first decade of this century. Psychoanalytically oriented group psychotherapy began in the 1930's, years that were especially conducive to the development of all sorts of collective activity for a variety of ends. The leadership of Roosevelt and the concerted social need helped to lay the groundwork for the flowering of group therapy. It was a time of protest against failures in the establishment, a protest that took various social forms. Today this rebelliousness takes the form of withdrawal, isolation, and retreats into fantasy. This is done even in groups where experiencing one's feelings in acting out inappropriate affect is being promoted as therapeutic when it is, in fact, regressive.

It is of some interest to speculate why there was in the 1930's such readiness to seek therapy in a group, when generally there is reticence about exposing subjective disorder. This was the time of the great economic depression. It was a time of restlessness, when people sought one another out in collective endeavor. Most people were short of money and tried to find solutions in common struggle, whether in attempts to deal with their impoverishment or their anxiety. Most patients could not pay the cost of an individual analysis. There were needs that were met by the opportunity to undertake analysis in a group: the availability of reconstructive therapy; treatment at a very reasonable fee; a sustaining and col-

Reprinted from *Major Contributors to Modern Psychotherapy*, published by Roche Laboratories, division of Hoffman-La Roche Inc.

laborative membership under the leadership of a clinician in a joint effort against an outer threat, an impoverishing social structure, and an inner threat, neurosis.

In the middle 1930's I became interested in the possibility of doing psychoanalytic therapy in a group setting. I read the papers of Trigant Burrow, Paul Schilder, and Louis Wender, visited J. L. Moreno, and participated as an actor in one of his psychodramas.

Moved by the success of these clinicians, I suggested to several of my patients that they forego their individual analytic work and continue their further treatment with me in a group setting. With little obvious resistance they evidenced an eagerness to pursue my proposal. In 1938 my first group had its initial meeting. The patients were stimulated and moved by the experience. Our enthusiasm spread, so that by 1940 five groups of patients were in treatment with me, one of them made up of five married couples.

It is not possible in this space to provide a history of the development of psychoanalysis in groups. What follows is a brief statement of my present concepts of its underlying theory and clinical practice.

Psychoanalysis in groups is the use of analytic means—free association, the analysis of dreams and fantasies, and the working through of resistance and transference—in the treatment of eight to ten patients in a group setting. Psychoanalysis in groups entails an understanding of unconscious processes and motivation. It seeks out the historical basis for current behavior in order to resolve its persistence in the present. It requires the working out and working through of repetitive and compulsive psychopathologic maneuvers. Psychoanalysis in groups pursues the latent as well as the manifest in patient interaction and function. The search for unconscious processes is achieved by the promotion of the freedom to express any thought, fantasy, or feeling. The pursuit of unconscious motives moves patients away from attending only to the present and toward an understanding of intrapsychic processes, historical determinants, and the working through of transference distortions.

INDIVIDUAL ANALYSIS

The traditional psychoanalyst tends to reject the group as a therapeutic milieu. He is more anonymous and less interactive with the patient than are group members or the group analyst. The individual analysand is thereby rendered more passive, regressed, introspective, isolated, and concentrated on the intrapsychic rather than on the interpersonal. He pursues his early history, and the focus of attention is largely upon himself, on his associations and reactions. The individual analyst is inclined to reject the idea that his values, individual characteristics, and predilections provoke particular responses in the patient. The group analyst, however, becomes increasingly aware from his observation of group interaction that his commitments, his personal qualities, choices, and preferences elicit special reactions in his analysands.

The individual analyst is denied in the dyadic relationship a multi-faceted view of his patient. He does not see the analysand in the multiplicity of reactions stimulated by other group members. He is not witness to the patient's responses to his projected nuclear or current family, his boss, his friends, authorities, and peers. He does not actually observe the multiple transferences that a group evokes. He is also less aware of the patient's positive resources in the healthy ways he deals with people. The individual analyst is inclined to regard the patient as more helpless than he is, because the therapist is in the vertical position of helping a dependent person. In the group, however, every member occasionally offers support and insight to a co-patient. This is a new role for an analysand, one that exposes a previously unseen side of his character, the strength and perceptivity to encourage and offer insight to another patient, which is mutually ego-building. The presence of other patients provides new kinds of activity and responsive feelings induced less readily in individual analysis. The group analysand experiences peer interaction that is not available in dyadic therapy.

In individual analysis the patient has more difficulty in asserting himself. Co-patients in a group support each other in dealing with the authority-invested group analyst. The individual analyst is more easily able to govern one patient than he is several of them assembled. They encourage one another to express attitudes toward the leader less readily ventilated in isolation with the therapist.

GROUP THERAPY AND PSYCHOANALYSIS IN GROUPS

There are differences between nonanalytic group psychotherapy and psychoanalysis in groups. These differences are relative, not absolute, so that in the following list of distinctions between them there is some overlapping. The group therapist tends to treat the group as a whole and to use group dynamic interpretations. The group analyst is more attentive to individuals in the group and their particular unconscious motivation. The group therapist is more interested in the here-and-now, while the group analyst is more attentive to the there-and-then, its persistence in the present, and working through. The group therapist is inclined to organize his membership more homogeneously and to treat the homogenized group as one with a bipersonal psychology. The group analyst tends to organize groups more heterogeneously and to treat the patients with a multipersonal psychology. The group therapist looks for similarities in the membership, so that adjustment and conformity are therapeutic outcomes. The group analyst values differences among his patients, so that insight, individual uniqueness, and freedom are therapeutic derivatives. The group therapist focuses on the manifest behavior made evident by interaction and interpersonal processes. The group analyst scrutinizes the latent content, the intrapsychic processes, the unconscious material, and promotes self-examination to this end. As a result there is less anxiety in nonanalytic group therapy and more anxiety in psychoanalysis in groups.

In group therapy which is not analytic, the patient may repeat his submission to the original familial expectation that he yield to parental dictates. This resistance to differentiation repeats the earlier ego-repressive experience. In group analysis the examination of unconscious processes helps the patient to grasp in detail the character of his yielding up his own ego to his parents in the past and to group members in the present. He is emboldened to search for a way out, to repossess his own ego. The analytic group supports his distinguishing attributes, his difference, the emergence of his repressed ego.

SIX PRIMARY PARAMETERS

The analyst in groups has in mind the existence of six primary parameters, which in part differentiate group from individual analysis.

The first of these is the presence of *hierarchical and peer vectors* in the group. They become apparent in the interplay of vertical and horizontal reactions that characterize parental and sibling transferences. Co-patients in a group provide a peer vector and peer relatedness. The analyst provides a hierarchical vector, a responsible authority and projected parental figure. The presence of leadership in the person of the analyst and of peers in the patient members makes for a setting in which vertical and horizontal interaction can take place that promotes parental and sibling transferences.

Second, there are *multiple reactivities* in the group in which each patient utilizes other members and the leader in healthy and neurotic ways. Some of the distortions are in terms of multiple transferences, identifications, abuse of another patient seen as oneself, and so on. This multiple interaction engages group members with one another and the therapist in their feelings, thoughts, and behavior. Multiple interaction tends to impel the more uncommunicative patient to participate. Reserved or silent members find it difficult to maintain their detachment. They are reacted to for their nonverbal attitudes until they are able to speak. In the course of multiple interaction, group members are sometimes inclined to gratify each other's transference expectations, so that the therapist is obliged to analyze the patients' inappropriate fulfillment of one another's archaic demands, until the members themselves are able to undertake this mutual analysis. Some masochistic patients manage to provoke the members into scapegoating them. This, too, requires analytic intervention.

Third is the dimension of *interpersonal and intrapsychic communica-*

tion. The intrapsychic process stresses self-knowledge leading to personal integration. The interpersonal process emphasizes knowledge of the self and others leading to personal and social integration. Individual analysis often tends to be more of an intrapsychic experience. Group analysis tends to be more of an interpersonal experience, but properly conducted can be equally intrapsychic. In dyadic analysis the analytic process usually proceeds from the intrapsychic to the interpersonal; in group analysis, from the interpersonal to the intrapsychic.

Fourth is the principle of *forced interaction.* Some patients are reluctant to reveal themselves in the group setting. There is, however, pressure on the less participant to become engaged. It is difficult to hold oneself apart in the face of the general push for collaborative interaction.

Fifth is the principle of *shifting attention* which helps to resolve the expectation of the patient who was an only child that he receive all the attention. Group analysis confronts the monopolistic only child with the reality that there are others beside the self who need to be heard and attended. Sometimes it is the originally favored or unfavored child who tries in the group to exclude his siblings. Such a maneuver is less apparent in dyadic analysis, where there is little if any necessity to compete for the therapist's attention.

In a group the focus of attention shifts from one patient to another. No one has exclusive possession of therapeutic scrutiny. The analyst and the patients do not give any one member their exclusive regard. This shifting attention gives each member an opportunity to digest the insight that has been offered him. Others use the relaxation from examination as a breathing spell from what may be experienced as a somewhat threatening exploration. Still others may resistively seek avoidance of such attention in order to maintain their psychopathology.

Sixth is the principle of *alternating roles.* The group structure necessarily gives rise to the phenomenon of alternating roles. Every member is obliged or at least inclined to listen, to try to understand the other. Novel kinds of feelings, reactions, and activity are evoked. Each patient talks, gives advice, tries to comprehend, responds, feels sympathetic, irritated, and bored, and evokes appropriate and inappropriate reactions. He wants to help and extends help. He is giver and taker, helper and helped. His roles are enlarged by new kinds of activity. He feels frustrated, angry, flattered, pleased. Now he is trying to understand the others. Later, they are trying to understand him. At one moment he is interacting spontaneously. The next he is thoughtfully contemplating what has just been said to him about himself.

GROUP ORGANIZATION AND GOALS

The group analyst tries to organize a diversified membership. Although he recognizes similarities among his patients, he tries to be awake to each member's novelty and originality. He is alert to every patient's right to be distinctive. There is unhealth in the cohesion of a homogeneous group that too often excludes the new member as an alien foreigner. The group analyst sees health in the reciprocity and interdependence of unlikeness, in men and women working creatively together just because of their complementarity, in parents and children acknowledging their reciprocal need of one another. He views homogeneity as separating and isolating.

It is not possible to form a group heterogeneous in every respect. Patients are alike in many ways and their similarities make for some homogeneity. The leader does not assemble children, adolescents, and adults in groups. He treats these different patients in groups homogeneously organized with respect to their age. He does not mix the intelligent with the mentally retarded or the sociopath with the responsible citizen. While he is obliged to make some concessions to the need for homogeneity, as analytic treatment progresses, the members become more diversified.

If the leader promotes homogeneity, he limits the intensity of analytic investigation. Patients who made advances in treatment begin to ask for differentiated and complementary others in the group. This kind of request is some indication that the group leader is practicing analytic therapy. The more the analyst and analysands search for the latent beneath the manifest, uncover repressed past history, and seek out psychic determinants, the more individual differences, heterogeneity, and diversity emerge among the members. The analytic approach to group members sponsors their individuality and makes the group heterogeneous. Each patient emerges as a distinct person with a singular past, evolution, and current psychodynamics. The members become more responsive to one another in their differentiation in pathology and in health. A struggle develops to understand and accept the stranger in the other.

CONFIDENTIALITY

Occasional patients claim they cannot join a group because there is too much anxiety or danger in exposure to strangers whose commitment to confidentiality cannot be trusted. Such patients can usually be induced to join a group in time as their anxiety and resistance are analyzed. Confidentiality among members needs to be maintained. If a patient reveals to an outsider what goes on in his group, he arouses a good deal of fear and anger among the members. The therapist needs to analyze the resistive gossip. Such a breach of mutual trust is a resistive leak that threatens the secure existence of a group unless the problem can be quickly resolved. If not, the tattler may have to return to individual analysis until this difficulty is overcome.

THE ALTERNATE MEETING

The alternate session is a scheduled meeting of patients without the presence of the analyst. It alternates with regular meetings at which the analyst is present. Regular sessions take place once a week for about one and one-half hours. Alternate meetings take place once or twice a week and last two or three hours.

There are a number of reasons for organizing alternate sessions. For one thing, such a regimen says to the patient in effect: "One of our objectives in treatment is to resolve your need of me. I believe you can function effectively with your peers. I will be available to you at regular sessions or in individual consultations should they prove to be necessary. But I believe it is in your interest to try to use and develop your own resources. You can do this, I am certain, at the alternate meeting." These sessions, then, are an attempt even at the very beginning of analysis to work through pathologically dependent transferential ties to the parental surrogate in the analyst, to move the patient toward autonomy. It is a movement toward ending at the beginning. It is a trial for the child-self in the patient—a trial without the parental figure. The good analyst, like the good parent, believes in paying judicious attention and judicious inattention.

The alternate session provides the opportunity to compare thought, feeling, and behavior in the two climates, the regular and the alternate, for patients to a certain extent think, feel, and act differently in the presence and absence of the authority figure. And these differences become the basis for defining, elucidating, and working through parental transferences to the group leader. Many patients interact more freely in the absence of the analyst when authority transferences are experienced as less oppressive. As a result, often a good deal of material is expressed that is withheld in the analyst's presence. This material frequently is concerned with feelings about the therapist. With the support, encouragement, and sometimes "betrayal" by other members, the attitudes and feelings expressed at alternate meetings are brought into regular sessions.

The parental transferences patients make to one another at the alternate session tend to be somewhat attenuated by an awareness that they are, in fact, among their peers. The absence of the helping analyst at alternate sessions forces the peers to help one another and promote their sharing and their equality at the same time that it reduces their childlike dependency on the analyst.

A by-product of psychoanalysis in groups, more particularly when alternate sessions are provided, is socialization. Socialization is usually looked upon as resistance, and in some instances this may be so. However, this is not necessarily true, if socialization is explored analytically for its resistive elements. Socialization has a reparative and humanizing function. Socializing may, however, limit the pursuit of unconscious processes. As a result, the group leader needs to examine the way patients use or misuse the alternate session, their participation in extragroup cliques or subgroups.

The therapeutic use of the alternate session provides further advantages. One of these is the clinical experience of spontaneous mutual support. There may be concern that patients left to their own inexperienced devices may do wild analysis and psychically, if not physically, damage each other. But patients do not become decorticate and barbaric at alternate meetings. If some of the insight they extend is premature, poorly timed, too penetrating, or widely off the mark, the member who is the target for analysis usually discounts or resists it on the ground that the proffered help is coming from an inexpert peer. However, as patients become more experienced, sophisticated, and familiar with one another's psychological and pathological maneuvers, they often make very astute clinical observations which tend also to be carefully considered. If these insights fit, they are gradually accepted and worked with. For certain patients who have extreme difficulty in accepting insight when offered by the authority figure of the analyst, these same observations coming from peers appear to be more readily acceptable.

RESISTANCE

Resistance is dealt with quickly in group analysis. Patients question the appropriateness of each other's resistive operations. They will not let a member sleep. They urge the silent patient to speak. They energetically press for an end to resistive maneuvers. They incite one another to change. They ask for new activity, demand interaction, protest against withdrawal or monopoly, and object to compulsive intrapsychic self-absorption or to inappropriate ways of relating. They induce participation until there is freely expressed and examined interaction.

DREAMS, FANTASIES, AND FREE ASSOCIATION

Analysts are often skeptical about whether group members can associate freely in the group, where there are so many interruptions of spontaneous expression. But even in individual analysis free association must to an extent be limited, restrained, and bounded. It needs, in any case, to be used selectively. The leader's concern with interruptions of free association may be looked upon as his wish to do individual analysis in the group. The discontinuity in free association may clarify the fantasy or dream of a given patient, but may also be used to analyze the interruptive associations of other members in multilateral interpretations. The leader's view of co-members' communications as discordant prevents the group from engaging in multilateral analysis. It demands individual analysis in the group and supports a competition to interrupt each other, a rivalry to win the attention of the therapist.

Supporting the right of the members to join in with their associations gives all the patients the right to be in treatment rather than just one person at a time. The therapist must, therefore, deal with presentations as reciprocal and interdependent, so that patient mutuality is improved. By this means all patient free associations are increased rather than limited. In a group a patient in his free associations is obliged to function with some awareness of others. This expectation of consciousness of the other is health-facilitating. Unlimited free association without such awareness may lead to more serious pathology.

Free association may be interrupted or facilitated by co-members. If a patient in a group is searching in his associations for previously unexamined unconscious material, he generally excites and holds the attention of his peers and is, as a result, encouraged to continue. If he reproduces the same pathology, the members become bored with the repetition and usually try to stop him and plead for a more mutually gratifying alternative —like a fresh dream or fantasy. If his free association discloses more realistic or less compulsive imaginings, the other patients become more receptive in the hope that he will continue to make freer choices. If his associations take the course of an isolating autism, the members object to his masochistic and detached free association.

The presentation of a dream is followed by the dreamer's associations. Then the other members associate in relation to the dream. Following this, the patients try to interpret the dream as well as the latent meaning of each member's subjective associations. In this way the dreamer is prevented from monopolizing a group session, for every patient's unconscious contribution to the original dream is made conscious and insightful.

ACTIVITY AND ACTING OUT

Acting out is more readily discovered and revealed in the group than in the therapeutic dyad and can, therefore, he more easily examined for resolution. Patients who reveal "secrets" to one another in private dyads outside of group meetings engage in a form of cliquing, a resistive leakage that subverts the analytic process. It is an acting out, a resistance to treatment. Members are, therefore, encouraged to expose one another in the group setting. They are urged to "betray" one another's secrets to the whole group.

In any therapeutic group there is a good deal more activity than in the therapeutic dyad. The activity may be appropriate or an acting out. Much of the activity is not acting out but a wholesome consequence of vigorous group interaction. There is lively expression of good will, friendliness, and support as well as anger and aggression. When acting out occurs, it is partly a consequence of the strong emotional multilateral excitement. If the analyst pursues an interpretive role with respect to acting out, it can commonly be checked. When analytic confrontation fails to limit acting out, the therapist may, all else failing, be obliged to forbid it. Such imposition of restraint generally provides so much relief from anxiety that patients usually appreciate the superimposed control.

Even when the analyst does not limit acting out, the patients themselves put an end to it before long. If they seem unable to do so, they plead with the therapist to help them exercise control. There is finally such frustration among acting-out patients that they turn to the group and the leader for restraint and insight.

Clinical experience has demonstrated that there need be little concern about acting out. If patients can function twenty-three hours a day without the analyst, they can be relied upon as a rule to exercise reasonable restraint. Factors supporting control over acting out are the wholesome realistic goals patients set for themselves and the preservative influences in various healthy ego functions. Other sources of restraint are the projection of reasonable authority, regard for the analyst as an appropriately controlling influence, and the wish to be guided by conventionality and tradition, by what is fit and unfit, by rules of conscience. A deterrent to acting out is that it will in time be exposed. All acting out ends in such frustration that self-corrective needs and leadership in the group move the members to set their own curbs on the pathological activity.

WORKING THROUGH

It becomes apparent in any therapeutic group that the analyst's advocacy of freedom to express associations, fantasies, dreams, thoughts, and feelings leads to a good many highly charged responses. These interactions are both appropriate and inappropriate. Group members become increasingly aware of the typical distortions that characterize each one of them. As time goes on, these transference reactions are traced to specific familial antecedents. The process of working through entails a conscious struggle to choose more reasonable and realistic alternatives to the persistent transference maneuvers.

There is more reality-boundness in group than in individual analysis. In the group, even while the patient reveals what he thinks and feels, he is obliged to be regardful of the thoughts and feelings of his peers. This consideration for others prevents pathological retreats into loss of realistic bounds. It enables each member to become aware of his own provocative behavior. Not only is self-understanding meaningful, but consciousness of one's effect on others is equally relevant.

Patients and therapist offer different kinds of help. Patient help is offered more spontaneously, more impulsively, and more compulsively. The therapist's helpfulness has more purpose, more usefulness, and is suggested with more discrimination.

A concern of some therapists is that a patient may inappropriately offer another an insight with which he is not yet ready to cope. The impression is that a poorly timed proffer of insight may be damaging to a member as yet unable to deal with the anxiety evoked by the penetration of his defenses. Patients, however, seem able to deal with insights from their peers either by rejecting them or by gradually assimilating them. When the analyst times his interpretation poorly, the patient becomes more upset, because the insight comes in the authority vector.

A patient does not have the knowledge and skill that the therapist has in timing interpretations. Patients nevertheless often make useful comments about one another with good intuition and considerable acuteness. They are not by nature experts in psychoanalytic theory and technique. It is rather their common sense, straightforwardness, unpremeditation, plain matter-of-factness, liveliness, and naïveté, free of the technical language of psychoanalysis and the manifest wish to be helpful, that enable them to be constructive with one another. The emotional intensity associated with their observations is also an element in their influence on each other.

Understanding and confrontation among co-patients are both more easily resisted and invited because they emanate from peers. The group analyst can more often than not simply permit the patients to interact, for they generate less anxiety than he does. He may then selectively interpose his own impressions when they are most useful. Interaction and interpretation among patients generally invigorates, supports, and intensifies the improvement of the members.

ROLE OF THE GROUP ANALYST

The primary ingredient of psychoanalysis in groups is attention to unconscious material, the study of intrapsychic processes. The therapist sets the tone of group meetings by his lead in the pursuit of unconscious material, free association and the analysis of dreams, resistance and transference. The search for unconscious processes and motivations leads the patients to their suppressed history, awareness of its compulsive repetition in the present, and speculation about the conscious choice of more realistic alternatives.

As multiple interaction develops in the group, the therapist leads the patients into the exploration of unconscious motivations and their genetic determinants. If the leader permits the group simply to interact without analysis, he supports resistive and defensive behavior.

Analytic intervention needs to be made in such a way that the interactive participants are given insight multibilaterally. One member should not for long be the exclusive focus of analytic attention. If he is so scrutinized by the whole group, the therapist should examine the contribution of the observing co-patients and confront them with their resistance. In so doing, the analyst does not permit any one member to stand alone under critical analysis. A single patient subjected to group scrutiny often has the support of certain other members. If he does not have such allies and needs one, it is the function of the therapist to afford him whatever support is needed.

TERMINATION

The end of treatment for any given patient stirs the remaining members. Their being witness to one patient's recovery is encouraging to them. The departing member impels the others to try harder to attain a similar state of well-being. He may animate them in a time of relative despondency. He may make them more introspective in order to learn how he attained his goals. He may induce in them a competition to succeed as well. Occasionally, the success of a "graduate" may induce a contentious resistance in which another member may insist on his readiness for discharge when he is hardly, in fact, ready to do so.

CONCLUSION

Psychoanalysis in groups can be effective because patients become aware of one another's appropriate needs and develop increasing ability to understand and cope with their transferential distortions. Patients achieve in groups a remarkable ability for mutual exploration and understanding and for multilaterally reparative behavior. In the group, interaction is examined as it occurs, not just between patient and analyst but among co-patients as well.

The psychoanalyst in groups has been up to now the student, the pupil of the individual analyst. Developments in group analysis over the last thirty-five years may now improve and intensify individual analytic treatment. If individual analysts would acquaint themselves with the value of group interaction, of socialization, of engagement with personalities other than the analyst, of resolving hierarchical and horizontal vector difficulties, of working through compulsive preoccupations with rank and status, of multiple interaction in attaining intrapsychic gains, these phenomena would receive the attention they deserve—even in the course of individual analysis.

It is of some interest to set down some of the integral characteristics that determine the content and process of group as compared with individual analysis. The numbers of patients in the group provide for the simultaneous presence of vertical and horizontal dimensions. The analyst is experienced as more distant and co-patients as more accessible. Transference reactions are aimed at both the leader and at fellow patients. Transferences in the group are less uniform and less entrenched than the dyad. The number of provocative members in a group makes it more difficult at the outset to detect what is a reasonable response from what is irrational in the course of the manifold interactions. Despite this, the excitation of feeling, whether positive or negative, healthy or sick, provides each patient many opportunities for experiencing assurance and insight. In the group, there are both more securities in reality and hazards in unreality than in the analytic dyad. Still, the leader's distortions are more acutely examined by his assembled patients. And the possibility of the therapist's acting out is generally excluded in a group setting.

The multilateral character of transference becomes more obvious in a group. The affective intensity of transferences among patients is more easily tolerated than is one-to-one transference because its power is lessened when aimed at a fellow patient. Occasionally, lateral transferences bind patients together and become a force that keeps patients in treatment. Such intense feeling for an individual analyst might induce an analysand to flee therapy or to feel helpless or terrified. In the group, interaction is engaged in by the patients, and the therapist can maintain a somewhat detached but active observing role. It is not easy for a patient to isolate himself in a group, because others push for activity, reactivity, and mutual responses. As a result, relationships become transferentially intensified. The occasion for more provocation of pathology as well as analytic therapy coexist because of the interactive intensity in the group. Following such interpersonal interaction, analytic examination of unconscious processes provides insight.

No one patient monopolizes analytic attention. Examination of intrapsychic material follows the interaction of dyads, triads, and so on. No member is expected to play only one kind of role, to subscribe to a group dynamic, or to be homogeneous with his group. The patient is so encouraged to engage in noncompulsive and liberating activities that he is finally free to leave the group.

BIBLIOGRAPHY

Durkin, H., Glatzer, H. T., Kadis, A. L., Wolf, A., and Hulse, W. C., "Acting Out in Group Psychotherapy; A Panel Discussion," *Am. J. Psychother.*, 12:87-105, 1958.

Schwartz, E. K., and Wolf, A., "Psychoanalysis in Groups: Three Primary Parameters," *Am. Imago*, 14:281-297, 1957.

———, "Psychoanalysis in Groups: Combined Therapy," Paper read at the Postgraduate Center for Psychotherapy, New York, November 1957.

———, "Irrational Trends in Contemporary Psychotherapy: Cultural Correlates," *Psychoanal. and Psychoanalyt. Rev.*, 45(1-2):65-74, 1958.

————, "Psychoanalysis in Groups: The Mystique of Group Dynamics," in B. Stokvis, ed., *Topical Problems in Psychotherapy*, II (Basel: S. Karger, 1960), pp. 119-154.

————, "Psychoanalysis in Groups: Some Comparisons with Individual Analysis," *J. Gen. Psychol.*, 64:153-191, 1961.

————, "Psychoanalysis in Groups: Resistance to Its Use," *Am. J. Psychother.*, 17:457-464, 1963.

————, "On Countertransference in Group Psychotherapy," *J. Psychol.*, 57:131-142, 1964.

————, "The Interpreter in Group Therapy: Conflict Resolution Through Negotiation," *Arch. Gen. Psychiat.*, 18:186-193, 1968.

Wolf, A., "The Psychoanalysis of Groups," *Am. J. Psychother.*, 3:525-558, 1949; 4:16-50, 1950.

————, "On the Irrelevance of Group Psychotherapy in Mass Conflict," *Group Psychother.*, 5:78-79, 1952.

————, "Code of Ethics of Group Psychotherapists: Comments," *Group Psychother.*, 10:221-223, 1957.

————, "The Advanced and Terminal Phases in Group Psychotherapy," New York, *Proc. Second Annual Inst. Am. Group Psychother. Assoc.*, 1958, pp. 66-79.

————, "Potentialities of Group Therapy for Obesity," *Int. Rec. Med.*, 171:9-11, 1958.

————, "Discussion of S. H. Foulkes: The Application of Group Concepts to the Treatment of the Individual in the Group," in B. Stokvis, ed., *Topical Problems of Psychotherapy*, II (Basel: S. Karger, 1960), pp. 16-23.

————, "Psychoanalytic Group Therapy," in J. Masserman, ed., *Current Psychiatric Therapies*, IV (New York: Grune & Stratton, 1964).

————, "Short-Term Group Psychotherapy," in L. R. Wolberg, ed., *Short-Term Psychotherapy* (New York: Grune & Stratton, 1965), pp. 219-255.

————, "Group Psychotherapy," in A. M. Freedman, and H. I. Kaplan, eds., *Comprehensive Textbook of Psychiatry* (Baltimore: Williams & Wilkins, 1967), pp. 1234-1241.

————, "Psychoanalysis in Groups," in G. M. Gazda, ed., *Basic Approaches to Group Psychotherapy and Group Counseling* (Springfield, Ill.: Charles C Thomas, 1968), pp. 80-108.

————, "The Discriminating Use of Feeling in Group Psychotherapy," in B. F. Riess, ed., *New Directions in Mental Health* (New York: Grune & Stratton, 1968), pp. 173-186.

————, and Schwartz, E. K., "The Psychoanalysis of Groups: Implications for Education," *Int. J. Soc. Psychiat.*, 1:9-17, 1955.

————, "El Psicoanalisis de Grupos: Consecuencias para la Educacion," *Criminalia* (Mexico, D.F.), 22(2):70-75, 1956.

————, "Psychoanalysis in Groups: Clinical and Theoretic Implications of the Alternate Meeting," *Acta Psychother.*, 7 (Suppl.):540-573, 1959.

————, "Psychoanalysis in Groups: The Role of Values," *Am. J. Psychoanal.*, 19:37-52, 1959.

————, "Psychoanalysis in Groups: The Alternate Session," *Am. Imago,* 17: 101-108, 1960.

————, "Psychoanalysis in Groups: As Creative Process," *Am. J. Psychoanal.,* 24(1):46-59, 1964.

————, "Psicoanalisis en Grupos," *14th Colección Ciencias del Hombre,* editorial, Pax-Mexico, Libreria Carlos Cesarman, S.A., Rep. Argentina 9, Mexico 1, D.F., 1967, pp. 1-383.

Wolf, A., *et al.,* "The Psychoanalysis of Groups: The Analyst's Objections," *Int. J. Group Psychother.,* 2:221-231, 1952.

Wolf, A., *et al.,* "Sexual Acting Out in the Psychoanalysis of Groups," *Int. J. Group Psychother.,* 4:369-380, 1954.

Wolf, A., *et al.,* "Training in Psychoanalysis in Groups without Face to Face Contact," *Am. J. Psychother.,* 23:488-494, 1969.

Wolf, A., *et al., Beyond the Couch: Dialogues in Teaching and Learning Psychoanalysis in Groups* (New York: Science House, 1970).

24

ON GROUP-ANALYTIC PSYCHOTHERAPY

S. H. Foulkes

Group-analytic psychotherapy, or group analysis, as it is called for short, is a special form of psychological treatment in small groups. Many forms of group therapy have come into being during the last twenty years, and increasingly during the last ten. They have been developed more or less independently by various psychotherapists in the United States and Great Britain. I do not know whether group therapy has had any independent source of origin on the European continent or elsewhere but it is now beginning to be practiced everywhere. The common feature of all forms of group therapy is that more than one patient is taking part at one and the same time, usually a small number between five and ten. Of course, there are as many forms of group therapy as there are of individual psychotherapy, but they do not strictly correspond to them. The reason for this is that the group situation introduces quite new features of its own, which are not present in the individual situation between one therapist and one patient. This is true even though the majority of group therapists are not aware of this at the present time. The special features of group analysis, as I am trying to set it out in this paper, have been developed and are being developed by myself. It was first practiced in civil life, in private practice and outpatient clinic, about ten years ago, later on being applied in a modified form on a large scale and by a number of different psychotherapists in a Military Neurosis Centre in the British Army during World War II. At the present time about half a dozen group therapists (group analysts) apply it in various teaching and other hospitals, particularly in London.

By way of an introduction, I can best explain the nature of group analysis by commenting upon its name, which name is meant to pay tribute to two facts: first, that it has common ground with psychoanalysis in its general clinical and theoretical orientation, and, secondly, that it has

Based on a paper read in New York City, on January 25, 1949, before the New York Psychoanalytic Society.

a place inside group therapy similar to that which psychoanalysis has inside psychotherapy, from its intensity and its intentions. There is a risk, however, that this name may mislead some people into thinking that they have to do with psychoanalysis in groups, a sort of substitute or cheap edition, embarked upon maybe for reasons of economy of time or expense. Being a psychoanalyst myself, I want particularly to emphasize that nothing of this sort is in my mind. The psychoanalytical situation, which is the essence of psychoanalysis as a method, can only be established between one therapist, the psychoanalyst, and one patient, the analysand, alone. The quintessence of psychoanalytic therapy, the analysis of the unconscious, infantile Oedipus conflict in a transference situation, would not permit of anything else. Group analysis, on the contrary, focuses on the dynamics of the group. Its more elaborate designation of "Group-Analytic Psychotherapy" does justice to both points just mentioned: it is a form of psychotherapy, not of psychoanalysis, and its frame of reference is the group as a whole.

Group analysis in the strict sense as a form of psychotherapy takes the group as a whole as its instrument of operation but is concerned with the social integration of the individual. In this sense it puts the individual patient into the center of its attention.

The following is a short account of the elementary features, both in practice and in principle, of group analysis. It leaves largely out of account the technique of the conductor's part. For this, as well as for any more detailed information, I must refer to my introductory book, which gives a concise account in more detail.*

HOW DOES GROUP ANALYSIS TAKE PLACE?

A small number of patients, who are suitable for a common approach, preferably seven or eight in number, assemble regularly, as a rule once a week, at an appointed time and place. The room should be comfortable and of adequate size, seating arrangements are best left flexible, with movable chairs so that all participants can see each other and talk to each other. As a rule members sit in a circle or semicircle, maybe round a fireplace or table, for instance. The atmosphere is informal and details are allowed to be flexible according to the prevailing circumstances and surroundings. The duration of each session is approximately one and one-half hours. The group can be composed of men, women, or a mixture of both sexes.

In the extreme case, there is no other contact apart from *this group* treatment, either between patients among themselves or between any of them and the therapist. One may keep rigidly to this, but experience has

---

* S. J. Foulkes, *Introduction to Group-Analytic Psychotherapy* (London: W. M. Heinemann, Medical Books Ltd., 1948).

taught me that the possibility of a personal talk with the therapist alone is better not denied. This can be done either in that the therapist makes himself available immediately before or after the group session, or sets a special time aside, maybe on a different day, for such a purpose. This facility must be used with discretion, but if so used, its advantages outweigh possible disadvantages. To avoid contact between patients themselves outside the group meeting entirely is almost impossible; in addition, an attempt to enforce such a rule would introduce an unwarranted note of rigidity and artificiality into the situation. It is, however, important to avoid these contacts of patients outside becoming a cause of leakage or a nucleus of subgroup formation. This can be done by appealing to the understanding of the participants and by pointing out the adverse effects of such occurrences in time. As a rule members become cooperative in abstaining from discussing topics or individuals connected with the group, or if they ever do, to bring the matters discussed back to the group in the presence of all.

On the other hand, the group can be combined with individual treatment. This can take the form of a regular appointment once or more a week, or of occasional appointments if and when there is a special request for such. Such combined groups seem to be the optimum arrangement under the conditions of private psychiatric practice.

Two forms of group have emerged and become more clearly defined: the open and the closed group. In the open group individuals join and leave on their own merits. Numbers can be slightly larger, selection more loose, and there is not too much emphasis on regular attendance. The group tends to be more individual-centered and more leader-centered, the discussion on a more everyday level, less likely to reach deeper psychopathological levels. This is a typical outpatient's group, not differing necessarily much from the usual group psychotherapeutic sessions, unless the conductor's orientation is group-analytic.

The closed group is formed in order to go through the therapeutic process together as a group. Regularity of attendance is essential here. It lends itself well to more deliberate selection according to problems or syndromes. The group can become more truly group-centered, reach deeper levels. This type of group can be run over a predetermined course of time, maybe three months, six months, a year, or more. It is more likely to take place under inpatient conditions or in a group center where a variety of different types of group meetings can take place. The essence of this closed group is that its participants begin and end their treatment together as a group.

Midway on between these two forms of group is what I have called a "slow-open" group. Whereas it is principally open and its course indeterminate, it does in fact approximate a closed group over longish periods, both in composition and intensity of therapeutic orientation. There is emphasis on regular attendance and the number of participants at any one time is fixed and limited to seven or eight patients; only very occasionally one or two patients might terminate treatment and vacancies so arising can be filled by new admissions. This is, as it were, a standard form.

The keynote in group-analytic sessions is informality and spontaneity of contributions which leads to what I have described as a "free-floating discussion." The conductor gives a minimum of instructions and there are no set topics as to the content of discussions, no planning. While he is in the position of a leader, he is sparing with leading the group actively. He also keeps himself in the background as a person. He thus weans the group from wanting to be led—a desire which is all too strong—from looking upon him as an authority for guidance, for instance, as a doctor who will cure them. The group does not like this, especially in a group of psychoneurotics, because he thus undermines one of the strongest neurotic defense positions. The more the conductor succeeds in this weaning, however, the more he provokes active participation on the part of the patients. Their personalities become more actively engaged and can be observed in action in their dynamic interplay.

What is latent in one person is manifestly stressed in the other. Both symptoms and defenses are mobilized. Moreover, they can be observed in action, their meaning and significance are revealed in a living situation. Different attitudes, character and symptom formations are represented by concrete, living present persons. These cannot be denied and the members of the group have to cope with these experiences. Changes are observable directly, and one is not dependent on the self-reflective report of the patient. The consensus of the group forms an important check on all this. The group proves a fine and reliable indicator in the last resort, because it agrees with the social community of which it forms a part.

Need for understanding and acceptance forms an ever present stimulus for communication. As to mechanisms involved, we find all our old friends which we know from individual analysis: becoming conscious of the unconscious, catharsis, insight, the analysis of defense mechanisms, and—above all—working through. But there are many group specific factors, of which I will mention activation, exchange, mirror reaction, active participation, social interaction, and communication. The group is also a potent source of support and a powerful forum.

One of the significant experiences a patient can have is that morbid ideas, e.g., obsessions, impulses, which appeared to be confined to himself, sometimes literally confined to himself alone in the whole world, are present often to the most minute detail in that haphazard selection of people he finds in the group. The other experience, by contrast, happens to him when peculiarities, which appear to have no echo in him, are voiced by other participants. This is very important because he now changes roles. He is himself a witness and observer of strange manifestations, toward which he at first impulse would be inclined to take up an attitude similar to the one which he had so often experienced, namely to pooh-pooh matters, pointing out how ridiculous or unreasonable they are, that one must pull oneself together, and so on. More important, however, than this is what he always imagines other people would think if they knew. That is what he dreaded most, and most of all, unconsciously. Now he is himself one of these "other people"! In other words, the patient in a group sits on both sides of the fence of a neurotic conflict, a conflict for which his symptomatic disturbances are an uneasy compromise. Moreover, he experiences either side both actively and passively. In this he also experiences how one's attitude changes, one's toleration increases as soon as things can be understood and their meaning becomes intelligible.

The patient also learns, as disguise becomes unmasked, distortion removed, and entanglement unraveled, that his troubles, as well as those of the others, arise from conflict over basic human needs which all have in common, not only in the group at hand but in the community at large. In this process he is greatly helped where other people's disguises make use of the same mechanisms, in particular defense mechanisms, as his own, and equally, on the other hand, where they use quite different ones. In the latter case he has less immediate understanding but is emotionally more detached. He gains a better appreciation of the dynamics of such a display from his more detached position, which in turn helps him where he is more entangled. It is obvious that therapy can proceed and progress in the processes here described, can be directed toward increasing transformation from autistic neurotic symptom formation to articulate formulation of problems which are basic for human beings, and can be shared and faced by all in common. This is a very different proposition from what it was at first: a host of complaints for which one looked to a doctor for a "cure." While this whole therapeutic process takes place, other dynamisms of no less fundamental importance are implied. Isolation is replaced by social contact, even on deep levels, and in such affairs as previously were considered particularly intimate, private, and secret, and charged with anxiety, apprehension, and guilt; rivalry and competition are replaced by cooperation, superstitious imagination about other people's minds by genuine information based on testing in frank and mutual exploration. One's individuality emerges as not in contrast to that of others but as complementary to the group. Superstition and prejudice give way to insight and enlightenment, insight, most important, gained by one's own living experience made by one's own effort with one's own means. Thus it can never be static again, since one has had to change while making these experiences.

Now for a few words on the conductor's function, without being able to enter into his technique. He is a participant, observes, has his eye on the group as a whole, as well as on the individual members whom he perceives against this background.

While he allows the group to make him into what they like, typically into an omnipotent father, leader figure, he does not actively assume such a role, but uses it in the best interests of the group, as the group's most devoted servant. While the immature group needs the sanction and support of such a leader-image, with growing maturity and integration that need diminishes. The group analyst makes a significant move by encouraging the independence of the group (and its members) so that they can eventually accept him as a leader on a mature level. This process has great significance in the modification of the superego of each individual. The conductor has to observe and watch the balance between analytic, disturbing, processes and integrative, supporting processes. In the same way, he must see to it that this coming down to earth is a gradual process, in accurate relationship to the group's growing independence, and does not come as a sudden disappointing disenchantment which would produce bewilderment and shock.

These effects of group-analytic treatment, of which some indication has been given above, might appear somewhat idealized. It could indeed be said that if a group can behave like that, they should not be in need of treatment. It must, however, be kept in mind that what has been outlined is the ultimate aim of the therapeutic group's "climate" or culture. It can only be reached in approximation, but while the tendency is in that direction, one of the therapist's tasks is continuously to point out, bring to light, and interpret everything in the group as a whole, or in any of its individuals, which counteracts this tendency. In this way he analyzes resistances and defenses which impede the therapeutic process, and this forms an integral part of his contribution.

Leaving out of account those therapeutic factors which take their place in any individual treatment and therefore also in the group setting, enough has been said to show that there are factors quite apart which can only happen in a group: group specific factors. The group-analytic situation in particular is characterized by the basic attitude of the conductor, as indicated, with its stress on active participation, unreserved discussion of interpersonal relationships, insight based on the articulation of all contributions as they arise spontaneously without direction or selection. It thus does full justice to the unconscious dynamics.

As an over-all assessment, all sets of therapeutic factors seem to fall into two categories: (1) analytic; (2) supportive. The first are, on the whole, of a more long-range nature and more responsible for lasting change. In their immediate effect they are rather more upsetting and disturbing to the patient. The second are more of immediate help, relieving, stabilizing, and encouraging. As has been pointed out, both these sets of factors work hand in hand, their favorable blending being one of the important things the conductor has to watch and direct. Like anything else in group therapy, they must be seen as they affect: a) any one individual, and b) the group as a whole. They can be set in motion in any one of the following ways, separately or in combination:

(1) By the conductor on the group as a whole
(2) By the conductor on any one individual
(3) By any one individual on the group as a whole
(4) By any one individual on any other individual or individuals
(5) By the group as a whole on the whole group
(6) By the group as a whole on any one individual

The above scheme should be kept in mind for everything happening in group therapy. It refers to effects upon the patients and leaves out of account the effects upon the conductor, who is after all an individual member of the group and subject to the same influences. He is the only member of the group who has to observe this process, including how it affects himself and his own position. For this reason he cannot be fully submerged into the group but has to stay outside it and retain a certain detachment.

In group therapy, including group analysis, it may be said that the supportive factors on the whole outweigh the analytic ones. This is certainly the case in comparison with the psychoanalytic situation. It is not to be overlooked, however, that in group analysis a good deal of modification produced by the process of social communication itself is of a lasting kind, although not strictly analytic.

It is evident that such experience can be of value to anyone. Taking it more strictly as a therapy, the indications for group therapy are still very wide. They certainly include all forms of psychoneuroses, such psychoses as are amenable to treatment, psychosomatic disorders, psychopathies, and delinquencies. In a sense its indications are as wide as those of psychotherapy altogether, and group therapy may be said to make a category of patients amenable to treatment who would not respond to individual psychotherapy. As an example of this, one might think, for instance, of the favorable effects of group approach to psychotics, even in deteriorated conditions. Indications should not be seen as competitive to individual treatment but rather as supplementary and complementary to it. Practical considerations inevitably play their part also.

In saying a few words on indication and selection, I shall confine myself to group analysis itself and to the type of patient for whom it would appear the optimum form of treatment, the treatment of choice. By inevitable overlap this will include such patients as might equally well respond to other intensive forms of psychotherapy or to psychoanalysis. It must be kept in mind that group analysis is an intensive, deepgoing form of psychotherapy. It makes high claims as to the qualities and training of the group analyst and also on his current resources. I, for one, would not undertake to conduct more than four different groups of patients at the same period of time, and prefer not more than one on any one day. If one conceives in the future of specialists who concentrate almost entirely on this work, this program might be doubled, but I do not think they could do more without losing a desirable standard of their work, their freshness, interest, and spontaneity. I mention this because indication and selection of patients should be looked upon rather in the light of whether they qualify for and merit such treatment than merely whether they might benefit by it. Having this in mind, one might give the following conditions special consideration.

General

(1) Degree of cooperation, genuine preparedness to take stock and to change, not superficial keenness

(2) Relative, at least potential, stability in character and potential social integrity

(3) Capacity to learn, and to gain insight, intelligence not below average, preferably high

(4) Potential social value of individual

More specific

(1) More favorable: character disturbances, social difficulties, lack of success in life, inhibitions of all sorts, recurrent neurotic conflict situations ("fate neurosis"), anxiety states, phobias, certain psychotic or psychosis-near states with well-preserved personality (like depersonalizations and some forms of schizophrenia), psychosomatic conditions

(2) Less favorable: obsessionals, predominantly conversational hysterics, epileptics, perversions, manifest sex disturbances, for instance, vaginism, frigidity, impotence, addictions, deep hypochondriacal syndromes (all of these can, however, benefit considerably, and some of these types can be expected to do very well in specially selected groups)

(3) Unfavorable: paranoia or pronounced paranoid states; depressions

Such a list is, of course, wholesale and too static. The best test for any individual is often the group itself. Much depends on the particular group and the conductor. This list also envisages outpatient conditions. Inside a suitable setting, corresponding to inpatient conditions, selected groups of psychopaths, delinquents, addicts, can do very well, as experiences in the U.S. and those of Dr. J. C. Mackwood with groups inside prisons seem to show.

In conclusion of this short survey of group analysis as a therapy, I want to stress that its aims and effects are not those of a symptomatic treatment, relying on relief, reassurance, encouragement, and so on, but a laying open and dealing with the very basis of neurotic conflicts and suffering. It mobilizes the "character basis" (W. Reich, *Charakteranalyse*, Berlin: Soppol Verlag, 1933, 288 pp.) itself and can lead to radical changes or a considerable modification of personality. In this respect it can only be compared to psychoanalysis itself or similar deepgoing psychotherapeutic procedures. For practical purposes, however, and for a fair assessment of its results, it must be kept in mind that it is very much more economical in time and expense than these long methods. This can be made clear easily if we compare the following: Suppose we take two years of psychoanalysis, comprising, say, 400 sessions, as a standard figure, which is certainly not too high, and we assume that the same patient would have two years of combined group-analytic psychotherapy at the rate of one weekly group session and one weekly individual session. This would consume 200 hours during the same time, taking the group session as one and one-half hours. As regards the therapist's time, however, 120 of these hours would be shared among eight patients. Thus to treat eight patients at that rate by daily psychoanalytic treatment over two years would take 3,200 hours; by combined group analytic treatment, which is a very intensive form of treatment, it would take 760 hours. In my experience, by and large, the therapeutic achievement—and I mean genuine and lasting results—in relation to the time spent is incomparably greater in group-analytic treatment. Important as this economy in time undoubtedly is, in view of the vast problem of neurotic and other mental suffering, I want to emphasize once more that this is not, in my opinion, the essential merit of group analysis. The really essential contribution which group therapy, in particular group analysis, makes to psychotherapy is that it adds another dimension to it, thus bringing for the first time the basic social context of human psychology and psychopathology into full view and living perspective. On this rests also its value as a method of investigation and research, which I rate even higher than its value as a therapeutic instrument, and of which we will now have to say a few words.

GROUP ANALYSIS AS A DIAGNOSTIC AND PROGNOSTIC TEST

Every experienced psychotherapist will agree that a patient's diagnosis, prehistory, and present state, important as they are, give only a rough guide as to the degree by which he may or may not benefit from treatment. What may really be achieved depends far more on the degree of contact, emotional rapport, resulting cooperation, strength and rigidity of defensive mechanisms, in particular character defenses, capacity for understanding and for expression, reaction to life circumstances, and a great number of imponderabilities, all of which reveal themselves only in the course of treatment, that are in the living relationship between patient and therapist. Even in long analyses we often cannot tell what we may have achieved until it is all over and settled and has passed through the test and impact of life itself. Now all these factors mentioned are openly displayed and activated in a group situation. Such a situation indeed activates all the patient has got in him and it is astonishing how much reveals itself, and how soon. Thus the group situation is a testing ground of the first order and presents a living diagnosis and living prognosis.

Moreover, it throws light not only upon the kind of relationship the patient is able to form with the therapist alone, but at the same time with quite a number of people of all sorts, so that there is a good chance that they can serve as prototypes of all the different figures in life with whom the patient can or cannot deal satisfactorily. The group-analytic situation, in addition, confronts the patient with an everlasting flow of unexpected material with which he has to cope and forces the task upon him of participating actively in the creation, organization, and manipulation of a situation which is deliberately only vaguely defined for him. He has to take his fate into his own hands in that situation. In this way it not only develops and extends his spontaneity and his capacity for handling life social situations, but at the same time it reveals his latent resources, or deficiencies, for doing so. It shows the meaning of his symptomatology in the light of action.

GROUP ANALYSIS AS AN INSTRUMENT FOR TEACHING AND RESEARCH

The group situation has another important advantage over the individual situation in that it can be watched and observed by the student. It is scarcely necessary to elaborate on the importance of this feature for teaching purposes. This does not refer merely to the student of psychiatry and psychotherapy but to doctors in general, teachers, psychologists, sociologists, anthropologists, administrators, magistrates, and men of affairs, in short, to everybody who has to deal with human beings in a responsible position.

As to the scientific value, the group situation not only displays what we know from individual psychology and psychopathology in operation, and thus allows us to study it, but it throws new light on these concepts and may eventually lead to a considerable modification and revision of them. It is my conviction that many of the problems which psychoanalysis finds difficult or impossible to solve on its own ground, and just those problems, will eventually find a satisfactory answer from the study in the group.

Apart from this contribution to the science of the individual's psychology, the group situation, of course, is the medium of choice for the study of the group itself. Problems such as human interaction, tensions and their solution, leadership, and so on, can only be studied in the group itself. This is where the investigations in therapeutic groups merge with the wider field of sociological study. The group-analytic situation, through its peculiar features, will, however, have its particular contribution to make.

WIDER APPLICATIONS OF GROUP-ANALYTIC PRINCIPLES

From what has been said, it should be clear that the principles involved in the group-analytic therapeutic situation can be applied in wider fields, such as education, industry, or special problems of any community. Of particular interest in this connection are experiments in the interaction of groups upon each other. An interesting quasi-laboratory experiment, of which some details have been published in my book mentioned above, has been the so-called Northfield Experiment, which gives an example of the application of these principles within the framework of the Armed Forces.

25

THE CASE FOR
DIDACTIC GROUP PSYCHOTHERAPY

J. W. Klapman

It is not to be expected that any new discipline or art, any new mode of therapy, should receive unqualified and universal approval and acceptance at the very outset. As a matter of fact, the method of group psychotherapy has gained quite wide acceptance and numerous adherents with rather astonishing rapidity. There is no cause for disappointment on that score. Nevertheless, a consideration of the resistance to its adoption here and there necessitates a recapitulation of its basic assumptions.

With some presumption it is here suggested that even the art of mental healing itself would appear to need some analysts and psychotherapy, for it is not wholly free of its own species of rationalizations. In a recent work on treatment in psychiatry the authors remind us that there is a body of scientifically well-founded therapies, such as hyperpyrexia, anticonvulsant chemotherapy, hydrotherapy, chemical sedation, and so on and on, more or less in contradistinction to the more nebulous and, by implication, less scientific psychotherapies. Among the scientific procedures are listed such methods as electroshock and insulin therapy. Now, any cursory perusal of the history and course of development of the shock therapies will easily reveal the chance character of their origins. But they are mediated through physical agencies; insulin in the one case and an electric current in the other, and the tendency to aquate the physical and tangible with the scientific dies very hard indeed.

But as psychotherapy it is to be noted that group treatment, being juxtaposed with the individual therapies, cannot avoid the implication of rivalry and competitiveness. Psychotherapy having long been considered as a certain relationship between two individuals with certain subtle interactions, has established itself as the framework and model of psychother-

Reprinted from *Diseases of the Nervous System*, Vol. XI, No. 2, February 1950, pp. 35-41.

apy more or less exclusively. When compared with actual prevalent conditions and needs it will be found deficient in a number of respects.

Even excluding the frankly psychotic individuals it is well known that many patients are not amenable to individual psychotherapy. When it comes to that *ne plus ultra* of psychotherapy, psychoanalysis, it is well known that the patients presenting themselves for its ministrations are already self-selected. Usually the subject has some smattering of knowledge of what the treatment will consist. He has no doubt deliberated some time over his decision. But even then the psychoanalyst may further exercise considerable selection, excluding major psychoses, those beyond an optimal age level, and those with more severe psychoneuroses, the so-called character neuroses. In other words, the candidate for psychoanalytic treatment must be of good intelligence, with psychopathology not too severe and still in *status nascendi,* and with deeper insights more or less ready to erupt into consciousness. And even in spite of all these favorable conditions failures with psychoanalysis are not infrequent.

Yet the total stratum of patients who would qualify for psychoanalytic treatment and similar therapies forms a very thin veneer over the vast numbers of individuals who are in dire need of psychotherapy. It would therefore seem like a bit of presumptuous nonsense and a plain breach of psychiatric obligation to insist that since these vast numbers cannot be reached by psychoanalysis or any similar individual therapy there is actually no treatment for them. The difficulty does not lie primarily with psychoanalysis per se, but rather in the failure to recognize that there are different levels of psychopathology and the failure to recognize the importance of calibrating techniques to conform with such varying levels. If, as Gardner Murphy[1] sees it, personality constitutes the individual plus his immediate environment, it must even appear reasonable that psychotherapy in some instances need not at all concern itself with what is inside the skin.

Now, because group psychotherapy assays to treat patients in groups the assumption is that the original impetus for its development was the scarcity of therapists and an attempt to economize on their time and thus reach larger numbers of patients; in other words, that it was originally devised as a kind of desperate expedient and makeshift. That is not entirely borne out by its brief history, because, as so often happens, its birth was as much a matter of chance as design. Its earlier pioneers such as Emerson[2] and Pratt[3] were not psychiatrists or psychotherapists and chanced upon this mode of therapy in the treatment of tubercular patients. Even Marsh[4] and Lazell[5] did not approach group therapy purely from the point of view of expedience; in the case of Lazell he was seeking a means of reaching regressed patients. That, incidentally and subsequently, especially during the recent war, its advantages in reaching numbers of patients was recognized, in nowise establishes its origin as a pure makeshift.

Misconceptions which arise from a poor perspective must inevitably lead to rivalries between schools of psychotherapy. This is especially true in the failure to realize that psychotherapy in itself is a kind of spectrum and that particular segments of the spectrum apply optimally to particular levels of psychopathology. Naturally, there is considerable overlapping, too. Such a statement looks to a time when specific indications and contraindications for psychotherapy based on a knowledge of psychopathology are so well worked out that a fairly exact prescription for the patient's therapy can be made. Such a point of view is not sufficiently appreciated even in certain authoritative circles, as witness the following quotation:[6]

> "Because so little is known about group therapy and because so many forms are employed, it is obvious that it is very difficult to assess and compare successes and failures. We have group therapies where the group is regulated by itself and the therapist acts as a catalyst. Other group therapies depend on leadership. Again others are actually nothing more than instructive lectures given to a group of people. It is interesting that all the group therapies which I am acquainted with even the most successful ones, can not compete with faith healing. . . . Group therapy should be the answer to many of the present day psychiatric difficulties, because a fairly large number of patients could be treated simultaneously. Therefore it is interesting that even though a good deal of experimentation has been done with it, it is still not very popular, most likely because no method has yet been found to compete successfully with the individual treatment procedures."

"Actually nothing more than instructive lectures," echoes a bias that has gained wide currency. As frequently happens, the pendulum swings back to a presumably outmoded method of treatment with a new conception and some new "twist." This has happened with hypnotherapy. This must happen, too, with the role of education. The question of education will have to be revaluated with regard to its place in mental health and mental ill health.

Time was when we naïvely assumed: "Only make the means of learning accessible to people; only multiply the printed word and education will become universal." We had not properly taken into account the factor of motivation. For, despite the present-day suffocating profusion of the printed word, despite the radio and other present-day means trumpeting their information and misinformation to the world, if the Gallup poll is any kind of reliable index there is surprisingly little education prevalent— often in unexpected quarters.

But education, in the sense of biological conditioning, is not the mere summation of facts and figures, although as part of the amalgam it constitutes, factual data can be extracted from it in considerable quantity. Neither is education a time interval spent in designated halls of learning, which interval is formally certified to by designated persons and institutions.

Education in its true and biological significance means the acquisition of a broad perspective of the surrounding world leading to adequate attitudes and beliefs. It imparts a sense of relationship of man to man and to the universe he inhabits. It encompasses mature judgment in the light of abiding values. It is one means by which that currently much bandied about desideratum, "emotional maturity," is acquired; also emotional stability, a stability which is not founded on insensitivity, but which, rather, is the fruit of a profound appreciation of the human scene, its significances, and connotations.

Have we swung so far in psychotherapy in our preoccupation with the manipulation of instinctual drives and affects as to lose sight of and generate a contempt for the role of conditioning and "education" in the maintenance of psychic homeostasis? Freud did not entirely lose sight of it when he voiced his hopes for the "future primacy of the intellect" in man's motives and behavior.

The contempt for pedagogy as an instrument of therapy is unwarranted on still other grounds. It is not difficult to demonstrate that what transpires in the class or the group of the skillful pedagogue is something more than mere exposition, and it should be recalled that it is often said of a professor or instructor, "He certainly knows his stuff, but he just can't teach." For it cannot be denied that what transpires in the class of the skillful pedagogue is a process akin to the transference of psychotherapy. The process of learning is not merely one of passive absorption, for its most powerful implement is motivation, and the most successful teacher consciously or unconsciously comes to employ it through the transference relationship.

The pedagogue is more concerned with the quantity and quality of the knowledge acquired by his students than the transference process per se; the group therapist quite deliberately attempts to enhance and manipulate the transference process though not entirely ignoring the therapeutic value which inheres in intellectual growth and perspective. That there is considerable overlapping of both disciplines cannot be considered discreditable to group psychotherapy.

It must be emphasized that group therapy is not merely an adjunct to individual psychotherapy. It does not appear sufficiently evident to many that it is the therapy of choice at certain levels of pathology. Mental and emotional disorders do not invariably arise at the deeper levels of psychopathology, nor do they always proceed primarily from maldisposition of instinctual energies. "A. Paranoiac" [7] has cited a number of interesting and amusing examples of personality disturbances originating from misapprehensions on the cognitive levels of psychic functioning. In the following case example it may be seen that that order of psychopathology can lead to dire consequences quite as much as the deeper instinctual disturbances.

Mr. A. was a little man in his sixties who had developed gastric symptoms, having suffered a sudden rupture of a peptic ulcer, and an emergency operation had barely saved his life. He was found to be the epitome of the henpecked husband. A more subdued and browbeaten male could hardly be imagined, and overshadowing the entire picture was the domineering, disciplinary Mrs. A. She was the second oldest in a sibship of seven sisters. Her father, a widower, arrived in this country with his bevy of daughters when Mrs. A. was in her early teens. She had practically no schooling, having adroitly outsmarted the truant officers. However, in the recurrent economic depressions of the last part of the nineteenth and the early part of the twentieth centuries there was considerable need for her scanty earnings. The father was a docile, ineffectual person, who, faced with the task of raising seven obstreperous daughters without the assistance of a wife, apparently threw up his hands in complete surrender and resignation. It is certain the girls quarrelled and bickered among themselves *ad nauseam*. In this setting and probably also by a variety of incidental and accidental circumstances, Mrs. A. may be seen to have adopted a life philosophy which may be paraphrased somewhat as follows: "If I have nothing to do with the 'other guy' he cannot harm me. I must look out for myself, and what the 'other guy' does and how he fares is no concern of mine. I want nothing to do or know of matters that do not touch me, and if I concern myself not with anything outside myself and know not what transpires about me no evil can assail me." Mrs. A. thus demonstrates that the state of pristine ignorance is sometimes an active process which has to be labored for to maintain pure and unsullied by alien information and "stuff." In fact, Mrs. A. sometimes boasted she did not think and cogitate or make plans as some misguided people are wont to do. Any question which implied the fulfillment of a personal obligation by her was apt to be countered with the staccato reminder to tend to one's own business. This philosophy, in any case, served Mrs. A. as an effective insulation, and her personality thus remained maximally insulated.

A personality cannot remain absolutely insulated in society, for other strong instinctual drives urge in a different direction. For example, marriage and a family, because of which "the other guy" comes to occupy a more preferential position than originally calculated. However, the insulated personality never concerns itself with such inconsistency, for the intellectual exercise necessary to its solution is alien to its nature; and thus, the insulated personality cannot realize that in having acted so contrary to the original intent the wall of personal insulation has been made slightly porous.

After their marriage Mr. and Mrs. A. established a small retail business in which they were quite successful. But Mr. A. soon found himself submerged under a barrage of orders, reprimands, browbeatings, belittlings, and every manner of conceivable insult from which he has never emerged. Even when his two daughters reached maturity he found no champion for his cause, for the three formed an iron-bound matriarchy and gynecocracy, and Mr. A. was more deeply submerged than ever.

Having been successful in the business by methods and management, which, though honorable enough, would not have earned any commendation from Better Business Bureaus, Mrs. A. arrogated all the credit to herself. Consciously or unconsciously, in her mind her close adherence to her philosophy, epitomized in that shining motto, "It pays to be ignorant," had been amply vindicated. It was not long before one arrived at the realization that Mr. A. was not the bearer of the original or most important psychopathology. The disease and pathological entity was constituted by the family as a unit, and the nidus of the disease process and source of infection was none other than Mrs. A.

When a slump came in the business Mrs. A. always had a convenient scapegoat. In no way could the lesser income be attributed to deficiencies in her management or poor economic conditions. Such a conception would have violated her self-image. The adversity was invariably ascribed to Mr. A.'s bungling and ineptitude. Be that as it may, the true reasons for any business *contretemps* were apparent to Mrs. A. Obviously Mr. A. as the "other guy" was helping himself to the contents of the cash register. For what purpose? To support a certain lady. Certainly! Some of the customers had informed her of seeing Mr. A. in that lady's hotel. From what was known of Mr. A. such an escapade was inconceivable, violating every tenet of sound psychological reasoning. And, furthermore, it was highly doubtful that the business in its palmiest days could have supported such a lady in the style to which she was accustomed. One could demur at this allegation only at the risk of indicting Mrs. A. as an outright liar.

Serving as a commentary on the dynamics of *folie a deux*, or *trois*, or *quatre* was the concurrence of opinion of Mrs. A. and her older daughter about Mr. A.'s playing the horses, another of his alleged depredations. Well, if the man found some pleasure and compensation in betting small sums why deny that to him? Small sums, nothing! Five and ten dollars a day and even twenty-five, and by way of proof the daughter and her mother deposed they had seen him at some distance sidling up to a newspaper stand and making a hurried transaction with the man. Seeing his wife and daughter approaching, Mr. A. had made a speedy getaway. They, wife and daughter, then went up to the newspaper man and told him that if he did not immediately return the money to them they would call the police. The man silently refunded two dollars. This certainly sounded like incontrovertible truth, but it was altogether inconsistent with the behavior of the self-effacing little Mr. A. The daughter, privately, was asked: "Were you there yourself at the time?" She hedged. After some further persistent questioning she finally admitted she was not present at the time, but that her mother had informed her of the incident of the two-dollar refund.

There were many other characteristics demonstrating Mrs. A.'s insularity, consequent immaturity, and paranoid reactions toward the "other guy." If, for example, Mrs. A. momentarily misplaced her diamond ring or other valuables, even her daughters, despite their well-nigh organic attachment to their mother, were not above suspicion (again, both the daughters' marital adjustment is another story). Many asocial characteristics and mannerisms in speech and deportment also resulted. When some acquaintance related some incident or event Mrs. A. frequently interrupted saying,

"No," then proceeded to relate the same occurrence giving precisely the same data, much as a child insists on holding the center of attention and at the same time, making light of the "other guy's" capacities and abilities.

In Mrs. A.'s case one may postulate theories about masculine protest, Oedipal situations, penis envy, and castration complexes. But it would not appear to the impartial observer that the psychopathology resides primarily within the skin. It lies primarily outside of the organism in the faulty interpersonal relationships, in the defective orientations, and in poor social conditioning. It lies predominently in the plan which Mrs. A. adopted early in life, which for her became a fixed set by which she has lived and which she has lived up to with singular devotion. In the goal of remaining as unaware as possible of the "other guy," of having no truck with him, and remaining as ignorant as possible she has achieved amazing if not praiseworthy success. This situation conforms far more closely to the Adlerian concept of the "life plan" or "life style" than to the concept of deeper instinctual or emotional disturbance. We are not yet fully accustomed to thinking in terms of suiting psychotherapeutic approach to the level of psychopathology predominantly involved, and in all situations we insist on the grand technique of individual psychotherapy exclusively. Even if Mrs. A. were treatable by psychoanalysis one wonders what would be the fate of the supernatant intellectual hiatus.

The educational role of group psychotherapy, then, may be one of the most important therapeutic functions, and from our point of view not lightly to be dismissed. It is possible to cite numerous examples in which a process of preparation must precede individual psychotherapy. What does observation of the usual psychiatric patient reveal? In one way or another, despite much initial resistance, he has finally mobilized enough courage to consult a psychiatrist. He sneaks into the doctor's office, if possible, by the byways and alleyways as if en route to a sorcerer's den. Finally, he finds himself closeted with a strange man who makes quite unusual requests of him. The patient has no idea what to expect. If he could concretize and verbalize his vague expectations they probably would be that the doctor will feel the bumps on his head, would administer a simple "twist of the wrist" to his spine or head; would try out some strange electrical gadget on his head, look deeply into his eyes and read his thoughts, or, at any rate, give him some strange nostrum or potion. When, instead of such procedures, the doctor tells him to go ahead and state what is in his thoughts and so much of the burden of treatment is thrown right back on his own shoulders, many of the patients are actually insulted, at least rendered highly uncomfortable. It is, at any rate, all very weird to the patient.

However, in group therapy, in the protection that the presence of his fellow patients provide he finds a much more natural setting. While he preserves a kind of anonymity he can at the same time hear and see that his own case is not so unique and that he has a great deal in common with the problems and difficulties of his fellow patients and classmates, and he is thus gradually brought out of his isolation and gradually induced to ventilate his own emotional problems. The class atmosphere is much more of a natural setting than the one in which he finds himself when closeted with a strange inquisitor. It has, indeed, far greater verisimilitude, for personality is to a very large extent the product of the social scene about us. Murphy[8] has put it this way:

> "But for the most vital purposes a cell must be understood as an aspect of the life of an organ and the organ as an aspect of the life of man. In the same way personality must be understood as an aspect of the social process; it cannot in most cases, be considered as a self-contained unit. Individually we balk at this fact, for it is very deflating; nevertheless we are reflections of a broad social process."

Obviously disorders which have their origin, at least in part, in social interrelationships are best treated in the setting from which they arose. As one of the direct benefits of group therapy we may see that at the very least it is a good preparation for intensive individual psychotherapy. This can be illustrated by the following case history example:

> B.C. was a young matron who had suffered a schizophrenic breakdown and had had one period of state hospital commitment. She was now out on conditional release. Required to return to the clinic for periodic checkup she is found exceedingly tense and uncomfortable. Asked about herself she gives a halting, very laconic summary of symptoms, and from there on any attempt to elicit biographical or psychological data meets with absolutely no success. Asked to talk about herself she is rendered extremely uncomfortable. "But what shall I say? I've told you everything." The best she can manage is to scrape up additional data about her symptoms, as if, as is usual in such cases, the individual believed the very accretion of such signs and symptoms, this continual piling of Ossa on Pelion, will of itself miraculously effect a cure. However, it was suggested that she attend group psychotherapy class. Two days later she attends such a session wherein the nature of mental illness, the injustice and groundlessness of the stigma are dealt with. The following day she is seen in individual interview. She now brings along notes she has made of her interim thoughts as she has been directed to do before but which she has not carried out until this interview. She now also relates many traumatizing incidents of her childhood. Another thing which greatly bothered her, she relates, was her resentment toward her husband and mother for having had her committed to a state hospital. "But," she hastens to add, "I wrote this down before I had been to the class. Now I don't feel that way any more."
>
> It is noteworthy that now she not only produces material more abundantly and freely, but her voice is louder and more steady, and her manner indicates greater self-assurance.

From the foregoing example it may be seen that not only may group therapy serve as a preparation for individual treatment but that it also acts as catalyst, speeding up and intensifying positive transference, helping to resolve negative attitudes and negative transference. That this should be so is not surprising in the light of what is already known of group behavior. Contrary to the critic of group therapy quoted earlier in this paper there is some scientific basis for this form of treatment, and to mention only a few such references we might cite Freud's *Group Psychology and the Analysis of the Ego*,[9] McDougall's *The Group Mind*,[10] Le Bon's *The Crowd*,[11] Redl's work [12] and so forth. One will find in these works some of the fundamental reasons why group dynamics are effective in treatment. While it is true the field is in great need of further experimental investigation, it would be a gross understatement that little or no psychological or scientific rationale is known for its employment at the present time.

As to the character of approach it is to be noted that there is a wide range of intensity of group therapy. The polarity of this range is marked by the repressive-inspirational at one end and the more or less analytical method at the other end. Marsh [13], who worked with groups as large as two hundred, apparently achieved a mild form of inspirational therapy, while Schilder[14] with groups of four to eight selected patients conducted intensive psychoanalytic group psychotherapy. As to method of implementation a division has already been made into analytic forms and didactic forms of group therapy. The distinction cannot be hard and fast, for much depends on content. The use which the therapist makes of his materials determines in large part how didactic or how analytical the treatment turns out to be.

Teaching or pedagogical methods are administered in a variety of ways. In many instances the therapist will depend on the patients bringing problems to the class for general discussion, therapist acting as leader and moderator and, where indicated, making appropriate interpretations. It may be remarked that such a regimen is successful when dealing with an unusually articulate group of patients who harbor strong resentments. In most other cases it devolves on the therapist to produce stimulus material to set the class into action. Such stimulus material is usually furnished by therapist's delivering a series of talks or lectures with subsidiary procedures combined in a variety of ways. Now, it would seem obvious that if the therapist delivers a series of lectures these should be reasonably well organized and planned. If the therapist has carefully planned this material and has designed it to be maximally stimulating to and provocative of patients' emotional responses and abreactions, it is patent he may as well commit them to writing. The fact is that many a treatise and textbook has had such an origin. An instructor gives a series of lectures which is well received and is for that reason induced to collect and edit them for publication. This is the case in group therapy employing the medium of a textbook.

The writer has used such a textbook and feels there are a number of advantages from its use. These advantages are:

(a) The textbook provides a systematic, planned, and logical sequence of material which serves to stimulate patients' associations, as well as serving the purposes of education and reeducation in the broadest sense.

(b) Instead of patients being passive auditors as they would be at lectures they become active participants when they read aloud from the book, recite, comment, and associate to the material.

(c) The textbook furnishes material which does not depend on therapist's forensic skill for effectiveness; which is always available and is especially useful in retaining continuity of purpose and method when a new therapist is required to take over.

(d) Although it would not seem possible to standardize the practice of group psychotherapy in all its phases, use of a textbook supplies the nearest approach to a standard and basis of comparison as between one class and another.

(e) The printed word carries some additional authority. Of course, the printed word is capable of great abuse. But in this case, employed in the interest of therapy, the stratagem is justifiable.

(f) Silences during class sessions have been noted by several group therapists. It is believed by Foulkes[15] that silence is not always an evidence of resistance. But whatever the silence of the group may connote it appears to be disconcerting. With the textbook always at hand to turn to, the therapist need have no concern about these arid interludes in the class sessions.

No grades are given and no constraint is exercised. While it is very desirable to absorb knowledge that is not the main desideratum. Nor is the quantity of material dealt with in any given session a great concern. If in the entire session only one little phrase of the book has been dealt with, which has led to copious comment or abundant associations; in which patients' attitudes and beliefs have been objectified and commented on liberally by the whole class, it is deemed a very worth-while session, indeed. At the end of each chapter is a list of review questions by which the preceding section is more or less recapitulated and summarized.

But the group therapy need not be confined to the textbook. As already indicated, the text performs the function of stimulus, calling forth patients' responses and reactions, often stimulating the production of deeper material and associated abreaction. But in addition to this central thread, this nucleus of the classwork, there are outside assignments for book reviews, and this in itself would constitute a form of bibliotherapy. Symposia and debates may be arranged and conducted. Written autobiographies may be called for. Even a well worked up case history of one of the class members may be discussed and commented upon by the whole class. This has been found very effective.

Results of group psychotherapy are not easy to assess. However, the clinical impression is not a totally unreliable guide. The factors which make for improvement in any given patient seem to be multiple and of some complexity. Many patients, invited to the class, appear once or twice and then drop out of sight; but, clinically, of those who attend regularly for any extended period of time, with only few exceptions, practically all show definite improvement. This observation is corroborated by psychological testing[16] which shows gains in personality organization in all patients with few exceptions. In one patient in the writer's group the improvement has been spectacular and dramatic.

To the skeptical inquisitor we can do no better by way of conclusion than again to quote from Murphy.[17]

> "It is quite likely (as in a dialectical moment) selfhood will be better understood when reference is made to the primordial non-self matrix from which it arises, and the synthesis, the capacity of human nature to function at self and non-self levels at the same time, to alternate when it so desires, may prove to be an enrichment of personality far greater than that which the cult of self-contained, self-defined individuality can grant."

REFERENCES

1. G. Murphy, *Personality* (New York: Harper & Bros., 1947).
2. W. R. P. Emerson, "The Hygienic and Dietetic Treatment of Delicate Children by the Class Method," *Boston M. and S. J.*, 164:326-328, 1910.
3. J. H. Pratt, "The Principles of Class Treatment and their Application to Various Chronic Diseases," *Hosp. Social Service*, 6:401, 1922.
4. L. C. Marsh, "Group Treatment of the Psychoses by the Psychological Equivalent of Revival," *Ment. Hyg.*, 15:328-349, 1931.
5. E. W. Lazell, "The Group Treatment of Dementia Praecox," *Psychoanalyt. Rev.*, 8:166-179, 1921.
6. P. H. Hoch, "Summary of Symposium Findings," in *Failures in Psychiatric Treatment* (New York: Grune and Stratton, 1948).
7. A. Paranoiac, "Paranoia from the Subjective Point of View," *Psychoanalyt. Rev.*, 13:200-209, 1926.
8. Murphy, *op. cit.*
9. S. Freud, *Group Psychology and the Analysis of the Ego* (London: International Psychoanalyt. Press, 1922).
10. W. McDougall, *The Group Mind* (New York: G. P. Putnam's Sons, 1920).
11. G. Le Bon, *The Crowd* (New York: Unwin, 1922).
12. F. Redl, "Group Emotion and Leadership," *Psychiat.* (White Foundation), 5:573-596, 1942.
13. Marsh, *op. cit.*
14. P. Schilder, "Results and Problems of Group Psychotherapy in Severe Neuroses," *Ment. Hyg.*, 23:87-98, 1939.
15. S. H. Foulkes, *Group Analytic Psychotherapy* (New York: Grune and Stratton, 1948).

16. J. W. Klapman and W. H. Lundin, "Objective Appraisal of Textbook-Mediated Group Psychotherapy with Psychotics," *Int. J. Group Psych.,* II:116-126, 1952.

17. Murphy, *op. cit.*

26

MECHANISMS OF GROUP PSYCHOTHERAPY: PROCESSES AND DYNAMICS

Raymond J. Corsini
Bina Rosenberg

Scientific progress in psychotherapy is dependent to a large extent on the ability of psychotherapists of different schools of thought to communicate. Lacking the universal language of mathematics which has enabled the rapid and orderly development of the natural sciences, social scientists may find that the medium of verbal communication sometimes actually forms a barrier to understanding and progress. The question of semantics and syntactics in psychotherapy is an important one and needs to be explored.

Group psychotherapy has expanded greatly in the past two decades and has already developed a considerable literature. But as may be expected, no differently from individual therapy, it has generated a number of special concepts couched sometimes in esoteric language. While diversity of language per se is not to be deplored, it does seem necessary to find means of effecting maximal communication between people exposed to different frames of reference. The question arises as to whether it is possible to come to semantic generalizations. This paper is devoted to an attempt along these lines.

THE PROBLEM

A central issue of psychotherapy is the nature of the dynamics that lead to successful therapy. What within the group therapeutic situation is of the essence?

A simple way to find the answer is to examine the literature. This is

Reprinted from the *Journal of Abnormal and Social Psychology*, Vol. 15, No. 3, November 1955, pp. 406-411.

perhaps the best way since it must be expected that those who have written on this subject, having gained their knowledge from clinical experience, should have at least partially valid opinions. However, the inquirer finds so much, stated so variously, often so convincingly, and mostly without reference to anyone else, that it is not to be wondered at that one often retires from the literature sadder but not wiser. This can be illustrated in miniature. Three articles are searched for the answer to the question of the dynamics of group therapy.

The first writer lists five dynamics: relationships, catharsis, insight, reality testing, and sublimation.[1] This list seems to make sense and the author's contention that these *are* the dynamics may assure the reader that the answer has been found. In the second article the reader finds five dynamics. This time they are transference, catharsis, abreaction, loss of isolation, and ego support.[2] The comparison is interesting. Only one dynamic, catharsis, is mentioned by both authorities, and between them they have listed nine mechanisms. Going to the third article, once again five mechanisms are listed: reassurance, reeducation, desensitization, catharsis, and transference.[3] The three writers each have contributed five mechanisms, of which only one, catharsis, is mentioned by all three; transference being mentioned by two. Each of the other ten mechanisms is mentioned by only one of the three experts.

How can this be explained? Have the authorities had different experiences and so found different mechanisms? Are there really 12 different mechanisms, and has each expert recognized only some of them? Or is it possible they are saying the same things in different ways? This problem, here illustrated in miniature, extends throughout the literature on psychotherapy. Had samples been taken from ten or from one hundred writers the list would have been longer and still more puzzling. What is needed is to find some way of arranging, classifying, and synthesizing these separate elements into an orderly and meaningful system. It is this that we have attempted to do.

THE METHOD

The procedures used were based on two assumptions. The first was that all writers on the question of the dynamic mechanisms of group psychotherapy are correct in their opinions, no matter how unusual or how unique their observations. The second assumption is that it is possible for the authors to make certain unifying classificatory judgments about concepts.

The procedures involved four steps:

Step 1. The literature on group psychotherapy was searched for expressions of dynamics. Data were sought in approximately 300 articles, amounting to about one-quarter of the entire literature on group therapy.

Step 2. More than 300 statements were abstracted from the literature and then examined critically to determine whether they could be considered dynamics rather than results, or something else. Eliminating doubtful items left 220 statements to be analyzed.

Step 3. All identical statements were combined. This resulted in 166 different mechanisms.

Step 4. The 166 statements were put on cards and examined to find combinatory hypotheses. For example, it was noted that some of the statements indicated that an often-occurring concept was one that involved a person doing something for another, being philanthropic or altruistic. All cards were then examined to locate statements such as "patient is a therapist to other patients," [4] "advice by patient," [5] "patients help each other." [6] All cards involving "altruism" were isolated to form a cluster. In this manner hypotheses were suggested and the remaining items searched and combined until a number of cards remained that could not be placed in any established category but yet did not seem to form other categories.

RESULTS

Ten classes of mechanisms were finally isolated by this procedure, nine of which could be assigned specific labels. A tenth group, consisting of items not otherwise assignable, was also formed. The nine chief mechanisms will now be defined. The actual statements will also be listed to show the diversity of opinions in this field and to permit further independent research on this problem.

Mechanisms

Acceptance. This statistically most frequent concept was taken to mean respect for and sympathy with the individual. Acceptance implies belongingness, a warm, friendly, comfortable feeling in the group.

Altruism. Closely related to acceptance, but in addition involving wanting to do something for others, is the mechanism of altruism. The essence of this mechanism is the desire to help others.

Universalization. This concept refers to the realization that one is not unique, that there are others like oneself with problems either identical with or very similar to one's own.

Intellectualization. This is a process of learning or acquiring knowledge in the group. Intellectualization leads to insight, which itself we considered not a mechanism, but a result of intellectualization.

Reality testing. This concept means that the group situation is one where real and important things happen; it is not only a temporary artificial environment. It assumes reality and in it the patient can test himself in a safe and unthreatening atmosphere.

Transference. This concept implies the existence of a strong emotional attachment either to the therapist, to separate members of the group, or to the group as a whole.

Interaction. Perhaps the most difficult of the mechanisms to understand and classify is the one which relates to relationships of unspecified nature within the group. What this process seems to amount to is that any interaction engaged in by a therapeutic group manages to have beneficial results.

Spectator therapy. Through this mechanism people gain from listening to and observing themselves and others.

Ventilation. As in individual therapy, one of the important mechanisms in the group is the release of feelings and the expression of ideas usually repressed in other nontherapeutic situations.

Miscellaneous. A number of statements remaining after classification are listed separately. It must be understood that the concepts in this set of statements need not be considered any less important or any less universal than others that have been either more frequent or easier to combine. Classification is not intended to be value-forming.

The Statements

Below are listed the original data from which the classifications were made. In many cases statements were compressed or reworded to get the essence of the authors' ideas. They are listed according to their classifications in order of statistical frequency, with bibliographic notations to the original articles.

Acceptance

> Group identification (23), (40), (58)
> Group status (25), (55)
> *Esprit de corps* (5), (33)
> Friendly environment (54)
> Communal feeling (7)
> Unification of the group (31)
> Group socialization (33)
> Loss of isolation (27)
> Emotional acceptance (63)
> Feeling of belonging (25), (31)
> Acceptance by the group (64)
> Cohesiveness (61)
> Identification with others (32), (62)
> Togetherness (16)
> Strength through belonging (6)
> Group is tolerant of the patient (52)
> Protection of the group (52)
> Ego support (27)
> Security of the group (52)
> Conviction of social approval (17)

Friendly relations between patients (28)
Permissivism (12)
"No longer feel alone" (33)
Security in a nonthreatening environment (6)
Supportive relations (54)
Therapist tolerant of patient (37)
Therapist is accepting of patient (37)
Loss of feeling of isolation (27)
Permissive environment (53)
Feeling of reassurance (25)
Group support (6)
Group cohesion (15)
Emotional support (4)

Universalization

Universalization (47), (5)
Patient recognizes his behavior has been duplicated by many of his mates (48)
Realization others have the same problems (28)
"People fighting what I am fighting" (26)
Realization others similarly affected (26)
Demonstrative universality of problems (51)
Recognize similar problems in others (13)
Illness not individualized (13)
Recognize other patients have same difficulty (60)
Resonance (36)
Realize others are in the same boat (41)
Realization of similar problems (34)
Knowledge of others with same problems (57)
Discovers he is not unique (55)

Reality testing

Testing reality (4), (35), (40), (45), (55), (56)
Working through (31), (33), (35)
Relive old family conflicts (60)
Put patient where he cannot fail (14)
Experience for personal interaction (53)
Recapitulation of family relationships (32)
Practice field for social relations (23)
Provides a testing forum (9)
Living out of ego frustrations (64)
Outlet for aggression (18)
Patient finds a setting where he can re-evaluate his concepts (8)
Test social reality (4)
Recreate family setting (49)
Surrogate family (64)
Reality of hostilities (33)
Revival of conflicts (51)

Defenses can be tested (25)
Field where one can relate self to others (54)
Catharsis-in-the-family (63)
Substitute family (55)
Appropriate targets for hostility (55)

Altruism

Encouragement (10), (66), (34)
Advice by patient (44)
Direction by patient (44)
Sense of being important in the lives of others (26)
Interpretation by patient (23)
Suggestion by patient (44)
Altruism (24)
Patient a therapist to other patients (21)
Patient sacrifices personal interest to group (39)
Patients help each other (44)
Reassurance by compassion (33)
Giving love (3)

Transference

Transference (5), (15), (16), (27), (31), (46), (49)
Transference to therapist (19), (20), (38), (40)
Transference to group (15), (20), (22), (32), (63)
Continued flow of emotional support (4)
Patient-to-patient transference (63)
Countertransference (31)
Attachment to therapist (58)
Identification to therapist (28)

Spectator Therapy

People patient can imitate (54)
Testimony of members (28)
Patient listens to himself objectively (19)
Passive participation (19)
Spectator therapy (42)
Example of others (44)

Interaction

Interaction (38), (49), (56)
Contagion (39), (61)
Relationship (55), (56)
Group interaction (34), (63)
Relationship to leader (46)
Relationship pattern (2)
Interaction atmosphere (67)
Contact with others (26)
Relationship of patient and therapist (34)

Experience for personal interaction (53)
Interstimulation (51)

Intellectualization

Interpretation (4), (19), (31), (55)
Intellectualization (19), (29)
Awareness of interpersonal relations (1)
Learning common thoughts of others (50)
Explanation (57)
Understanding defenses of others (1)
Understanding (18)
Intellectual comprehension (63)
Learning (61)
Reeducation (15)
Analysis of dreams (31)
Analysis of resistance (31)
Proper evaluation of symptoms (30)
Relearning (21)
Subject evaluates symptoms in others (48)

Ventilation

Catharsis (15), (21), (25), (27), (33), (35), (40), (43), (55), (56), (59), (63)
Abreaction (27), (62)
Ventilation of hostilities (9), (63)
Ventilation (33), (35)
Animosities abreact (20)
Verbalization of fantasy (40)
Emotional release (2)
Release of hostilities in a socially acceptable way (66)
Relief of guilt through confession (33)
Ventilation of guilt (11)
Release of hostilities (66)
Activity catharsis (56)
Ventilation of anxiety (21)
Attitude of verbal expressions (52)
Release of unconscious material (63)
Expression of unconscious tendencies (2)
Activate emotional release (4)
Release of repressed drives (4)
Releases emotional tension (55)

Miscellaneous

Sublimation (65), (66)
Spontaneity (43), (61)
Rivalry for improvement (28)
Suggestion (10)
Authority of the therapist (31)

Suggestibility of the group (28)
Heightening action (61)
Closure of tension systems (21)
Therapist's confidence in the patient (37)
Substitution (5)
Facing the traumatic past (6)
Inspired by others to greater effort (26)
Social coercion to think rationally (33)
Sharing mutual experiences (17)
Sharing (62)
Relief of isolation through sharing (51)
Reinforcement (61)
Integration of contradictory tendencies (6)
Shock (42)
Relaxation (61)
Desensitization (15)
Sharing difficulties (41)
Reassurance (15)
Rivalry (39)
Intensification (56)
Emotional infection (56)

DISCUSSION

The process of combining separate elements into general classes is known as taxonomy. Whether the reductions here effected are the most efficient possible, and whether others operating on other premises or even using the same procedures would have come to the same conclusions, is open to question and to further research. In any case, a rational beginning has been made in the combining of elements into general classes and in the providing of a series of relatively independent factors. This process can be utilized for more effective communication through the reduction of terms.

The nine classes found appear to reduce to three still more general factors. An *intellectual* factor consisting of universalization, intellectualization, and spectator therapy appears. Also, an *emotional* factor including acceptance, altruism, and transference evolves. And, there is an *actional* factor of reality testing, interaction, and ventilation.

From this arises the possibility of evaluating any method of group psychotherapy in terms of these three factors. For example, it seems that Klapman's textbook-mediated therapy and Dreikurs' group counseling have a high component of the intellectual factor; that Rogers' nondirective group counseling and Schilder's analytic group therapy have a relatively high degree of the emotional factor; and that Moreno's psychodrama and Slavson's activity group therapy have a large amount of the actional factor.

SUMMARY

Some 300 articles in the literature of group psychotherapy were examined to locate expressions referring to effecting dynamic processes of therapy. Some 200 items were obtained and reduced by inspection to nine general classes and a miscellaneous class. The nine general classes appear to reduce to three factors: an *intellectual* one, consisting of universalization, intellectualization, and spectator therapy; an *emotional* one, consisting of acceptance, altruism, and transference; and an *actional* factor, consisting of reality testing, interaction, and ventilation.

It is believed this reductionism can be useful in providing better communication between group therapists and can be the basis for further research in the basic components of group therapy.

REFERENCES

1. S. R. Slavson, "Advances in Group Psychotherapy," *Int. Congr. Ment. Health*, 24-26, 1948.
2. S. B. Hadden, "Dynamics of Group Psychotherapy," *Arch. Neurol. Psychiat.*, 65:125, 1944.
3. J. M. Cotton, "Group Psychotherapy: An Appraisal," in P. H. Hoch (ed.), *Failures in Psychiatric Treatment* (New York: Grune and Stratton, 1948), pp. 121-128.
4. J. M. Enneis, "The Dynamics of Group and Action Procedures in Therapy," *Group Psychother.*, 4:17-22, 1951.
5. H. Mullan, "Some Essentials of Group Psychotherapy," *Group Psychother.*, 5:68-69, 1952.
6. *Ibid.*

BIBLIOGRAPHY

1. Abrahams, J., "Preliminary Report of an Experience in the Group Therapy of Schizophrenics," *Am. J. Psychiat.*, 104:613-617, 1948.
2. Ackerman, N. W., "Group Therapy from the Viewpoint of a Psychiatrist," *Am. J. Orthopsychiat.*, 31:667-681, 1943.
3. ———, "Psychotherapy and Giving Love," *Psychiat.*, 7:129-137, 1944.
4. ———, "Some General Principles in the Use of Group Psychotherapy," in B. Glueck, ed., *Current Therapies of Personality Disorders* (New York: Grune & Stratton, 1946), pp. 275-280.
5. Altschuler, I. M., "One Year's Experience with Group Psychotherapy," *Ment. Hyg.*, 24:190-196, 1940.
6. Bettelheim, B., and Sylvester, Emmy, "Therapeutic Influence of the Group and the Individual," *Am. J. Orthopsychiat.*, 17:684-692, 1947.

7. Betz, K., "Gruppentraining und Bilderlefen," Z. *Psychother. Med. Psychol.*. 1:71-76, 1951.
8. Blackman, N., "Ward Therapy—A New Method of Group Psychotherapy," *Psychiat. Quart.*, 16:660-667, 1942.
9. ———, "Group Psychotherapy with Aphasics," *J. Nerv. Ment. Dis.*, 111: 154-163, 1950.
10. Buck, R. W., "The Class Method in the Treatment of Essential Hypertension," *Ann. Int. Med.*, 11:514-518, 1937.
11. Caplan, G., "Mental Hygiene Work with Expectant Mothers," *Ment. Hyg.*, 35:41, 50, 1951.
12. Coffey, H., Friedman, M., Leary, T., and Ossorio, A., "Social Implications of the Group Therapeutic Situation," *J. Soc. Issues*, 6:44-61, 1950.
13. Colthorp, R. W., "Group Psychotherapy in Patients Recovering from Psychoses," *Am. J. Psychiat.*, 104:414-417, 1947.
14. Cotton, J. M., "The Psychiatric Treatment Program at Welch Convalescent Hospital," *Res. Pub. Ass. Nerv. Ment. Dis.*, 25:316-321, 1946.
15. ———, "Group Psychotherapy: An Appraisal," in P. H. Hoch, ed., *Failures in Psychiatric Treatment* (New York: Grune & Stratton, 1948), pp. 121-128.
16. ———, "Group Structure and Group Psychotherapy," *Group Psychother.*, 3:216-217, 1951.
17. Curran, F. J., and Schilder, P., "A Constructive Approach to the Problems of Childhood and Adolescence," *J. Crim. Psychopath.*, 2:125-142, 305-320, 1940-1941.
18. Curran, F. J., "Group Therapy: Introductory Remarks," *Neuropsychiat.*, 2:43-47, 1952.
19. Dreikurs, R., "Technique and Dynamics of Multiple Psychotherapy," *Psychiat. Quart.*, 24:788-799, 1950.
20. Dreyfus-Moreau, J., "A Propos du Transfert en Psychotherapie Collective," *Rev. Franç. Psychoanal.*, 14:244-257, 1950.
21. Enneis, J. M., "The Dynamics of Group and Action Procedures in Therapy," *Group Psychother.*, 4:17-22, 1951.
22. Glatzer, H., "Transference in Group Therapy," *Am. J. Orthopsychiat.*, 22: 499-509, 1952.
23. Golden, M. M., "Some Mechanisms of Analytic Group Therapy," *Int. J. Group Psychother.*, 3:280-284, 1952.
24. Greenblatt, M., "Altruism in the Psychotherapeutic Relation," in P. A. Sorokin, ed., *Explorations in Altruistic Love and Behavior* (Boston: Beacon Press, 1950), pp. 188-193.
25. Grotjahn, M., "Experiences with Group Psychotherapy as a Method for the Treatment of Veterans," *Am. J. Psychiat.*, 103:637-643, 1947.
26. Hadden, S. B., "Group Psychotherapy: A Superior Method of Treating Larger Numbers of Neurotics," *Am. J. Psychiat.*, 101:68-72, 1944.
27. ———, "Dynamics of Group Psychotherapy," *Arch. Neurol. Psychiat.*, 65:125, 1951.
28. Harris, H. I., "Efficient Psychotherapy for the Large Outpatient Clinic," *New England J. Med.*, 221:1-15, 1939.

29. Johnston, M., "Experiment with Narcotic Addicts," *Am. J. Psychother.*, 5:24-31, 1951.
30. Jones, M., "Group Treatment with Particular Reference to Group Projective Methods," *Am. J. Psychiat.*, 101:293-299, 1944.
31. Kew, C. E., and Kew, C. J., "Group Psychotherapy in a Church Setting," *Pastoral Psychol.*, 1:36-39, 1950.
32. Klapman, J. W., "Group Treatment of the Mentally Ill," *Survey Mid-Monthly*, 82:80-81, 1946.
33. Kline, N. S., and Dreyfus, A., "Group Psychotherapy in a Veterans Administration Hospital," *Am. J. Psychiat.*, 104:618-622, 1948.
34. Konopka, G., "Group Work and Therapy," in C. E. Hendy, ed., *A Decade of Group Work* (New York: Association Press, 1948), pp. 39-44.
35. Krise, M., "Creative Dramatics and Group Psychotherapy," *J. Child Psychiat.*, 2:337-342, 1952.
36. Lebovici, S., Diatkine, R., and Kestenberg, E., "Applications of Psychoanalysis to Group Psychotherapy and Psychodramatic Therapy in France," *Group Psychother.*, 5:38-50, 1952.
37. Lipkin, S., "Notes on Group Psychotherapy," *J. Nerv. Ment. Dis.*, 107:459-479, 1948.
38. Lowrey, L. G., "Group Treatment for Mothers," *Am. J. Orthopsychiat.*, 14:589-592, 1944.
39. Marsh, L. C., "Group Therapy of the Psychoses by the Psychological Equivalent of the Revival," *Ment. Hyg.*, 15:328-349, 1931.
40. Mayers, A. N., "A Psychiatric Evaluation of Discussion Groups," *J. Nerv. Ment. Dis.*, 111:499-509, 1950.
41. Miller, H., and Baruch, D., "Psychological Dynamics in Allergic Patients as Shown in Group and Individual Psychotherapy," *J. Consult. Psychol.*, 12:111-115, 1948.
42. Moreno, J. L., "Psychodramatic Shock Therapy," *Sociometry*, 2:1-30, 1939.
43. Moreno, J. L., and Toeman, Z., "The Group Approach in Psychodrama," *Sociometry*, 5:191-194, 1942.
44. Mullan, H., "Some Essentials of Group Psychotherapy," *Group Psychother.*, 5:68-69, 1952.
45. Parrish, M., and Mitchell, J., "Psychodrama in Pontiac State Hospital," *Group Psychother.*, 4:80-84, 1951.
46. Pederson-Krag, G., "Unconscious Factors in Group Therapy," *Psychoanal. Quart.*, 15:180-189, 1946.
47. Pfeffer, A. Z., Friedland, P., and Wortis, S. B., "Group Psychotherapy with Alcoholics," *Quart. J. Stud. Alchol.*, 10:198-216, 1949.
48. Rome, H. P., "Group Psychotherapy," *Dis. Nerv. Syst.*, 6:237-241, 1945.
49. Scheidlinger, S., "Group Therapy: Its Place in Psychotherapy," *J. Soc. Casewk.*, 29:299-304, 1948.
50. Schilder, P., "Introductory Remarks on Groups," *J. Soc. Psychol.*, 12:83-100, 1940.
51. Shaskan, D. A., and Jolesch, M., "War and Group Psychotherapy," *Am. J. Orthopsychiat.*, 14:571-577, 1944.
52. Shaskan, D. A., "Development of Group Psychotherapy in a Military Setting," *Proc. Assoc. Research Nerv. Ment. Dis.*, 25:311-315, 1946.

53. Slavson, S. R., *An Introduction to Group Therapy* (New York: Commonwealth, Fund, 1943).
54. ———, "Differential Methods of Group Therapy in Relation to Age Levels," *Nerv. Child*, 4:196-210, 1945.
55. ———, "The Field and Objectives of Group Therapy," in B. Glueck, ed., *Current Therapies of Personality Disorders* (New York: Grune & Stratton, 1946), pp. 166-193.
56. ———, "Advances in Group Psychotherapy," *Int. Congr. Ment. Health*, 24-26, 1948.
57. Snowden, E. N., "Mass Psychotherapy," *Lancet*, 11:769-770, 1940.
58. Sternbach, O., "The Dynamics of Psychological Treatment in the Group," *J. Child Psychiat.*, 1:91-112, 1947.
59. Swenson, W. M., "Round Table Group Psychotherapy at St. Peters State Hospital," *Group Psychother.*, 4:63-65, 1953.
60. Teirich, H. R., "Was Ist Gruppenpsychotherapie?" *Psychother. Med. Psychol.*, 1:26-30, 1951.
61. Twitchell-Allen, D., and Stephens, F. M., "Some Theoretical and Practical Aspects of Group Psychotherapy," *Group Psychother.*, 4:9-16, 1951.
62. Wender, L., "The Dynamics of Group Psychotherapy and Its Applications," *J. Nerv. Ment. Dis.*, 84:54-60, 1936.
63. ———, "Group Psychotherapy Within the Psychiatric Hospital," in B. Glueck, ed., *Current Therapies of Personality Disorders* (New York: Grune & Stratton, 1946), pp. 46-58.
64. ———, "Current Trends in Group Psychotherapy," *Am. J. Psychother.*, 5:381-404, 1951.
65. Willner, G. P., "Preliminary Report of the Introduction of Group Psychotherapy on a Chronic Ward in a Mental Hospital," *Psychiat. Quart. Suppl.*, 26:86-92, 1952.
66. Wittenberg, R., "Psychiatric Concepts in Group Work," *Am. J. Orthopsychiat.*, 14:76-83, 1944.
67. Wolf, A., Locke, N., Rosenbaum, M., Hillpern, E. P., Goldfarb, W., Kadis, A. L., Obers, S. J., Milberg, I. L., and Abell, R. G., "The Psychoanalysis of Groups: The Analysts' Objections," *Int. J. Group Psychother.*, 2:221-231, 1952.

27

THE CHALLENGE OF
GROUP PSYCHOANALYSIS

Max Rosenbaum

(The first part of this article, relating to the resistances of patients, has been deleted.)

Up to now we have tried to describe the common types of reaction and resistance of patients who are asked to join a group. At this point it would be illuminating to discuss the reactions and resistances of psychoanalysts themselves. Many of the analyst's reactions are what we would recognize as resistance on the part of a patient.

During the fall and winter of 1951 this writer surveyed, via questionnaire, a group of thirty-nine practicing psychoanalysts as to their reactions to group analysis. Of the twenty-one analysts who replied to the questionnaire, all showed an awareness of the field. Six of the twenty-one had some experience with group therapy. The reactions of these six varied from enthusiastic acceptance, in the case of one analyst who had prolonged experience in private practice, to rejection of the method by another who had been in charge of some psychiatric services in the army. This "rejecting" analyst felt that group therapy was an unfeasible technique since it requires "an integrated and skilled therapist" who is able to "stand the manifest transferences or see them all. Since it is not possible to be such a therapist, it seems that those who do group therapy do not see all the problems involved." Between these two extreme reactions there was mild acceptance of the method as an adjunct process which was effective, but not as effective as individual analysis; and acceptance as an "interesting technique that is not a substitute for individual analysis. These are two completely different techniques."

The fifteen analysts who had never worked in the area of group ther-

Reprinted from *Psychoanalysis, Journal of Psychoanalytic Psychology*, Vol. I, No. 2, Fall 1952, pp. 50-58

apy or group analysis were in the main favorable. Three were planning to acquire training in the method. This "no experience" group contained analysts who were strongly convinced that "the method is feasible," as well as analysts who felt that the "method is in the experimental stage but this should serve as a stimulant." There was a good deal of skepticism as to the depth of the method. There was question as to whether transferences could be explored and resolved in the group analytic situation. By some the group was accepted as a "more real situation" but suitable only for "carefully selected cases." One analyst commented that "since anything works in therapy . . . since life is therapeutic . . . group analysis may help in shot gun fashion. . . ."

It is worth noting at this point that the responses of the entire group of analysts surveyed are in the main favorable to the idea of group therapy. Yet there is a great discrepancy between the answers to the questionnaire and the actual clinical practice of even those analysts who are favorable to the concept of group psychoanalysis. These same analysts indicate considerable resistance to referring patients for group psychoanalysis. Is it possible that these analysts, in writing an answer to a questionnaire, must fulfill a self-concept of the permissive, accepting therapist? Do they actually fear the resolution of their own resistances toward the psychoanalysis of the individual in a group? This question will be discussed at length in a future paper.

It seems then that analysts object to group psychoanalysis because:

(1) They don't feel there is any "depth" to the method.

(2) They have questions regarding the technique and procedure of the method and consequent dangers to the patient who is exposed to the method.

(3) They don't feel there is a real substitute or equivalent for the individual analysis and the relationship which exists between analyst and analysand in such a method.

With regard to the objection as to the depth of group analysis there is the fear expressed that, in the group, transference relationships are diluted. It seems to be assumed that transference reactions can occur only toward the therapist and that patients therefore will have only short periods of time in a group framework where they can develop and work through transferences. But what of the multiple and shifting transferences that patients project upon one another? Are these transference reactions inaccessible to analysis? Experience has indicated that patients who are introduced into the group react in a manner never met in the individual analysis. The analyst is often seen as quite different—even in the first group session. With the support of the other group members the patient can feel much less anxiety about expressing hostile as well as loving fears. In the group the patient finally permits himself the expression of affective reactions, so long repressed for fear of the analyst.

A stimulating study by Drs. Powdermaker and Frank has indicated neglect of analytic methodology among psychiatrists conducting the groups studied. They state ". . . the doctor's uncertainty may cause him to confuse the group by being unpredictable in his attitudes and methods." It should be emphasized that the method of group analysis is the method of individual analysis. Group therapists who do not proceed analytically because of their anxieties cannot then conclude that the method lacks depth. Such criticism reminds us of the "mirror" concept of the analyst in early psychoanalytic history, which served as a convenient theory to absolve analysts of their shortcomings, since they could always blame the shortcomings on the patient. This same attitude is manifested when analytic methodology such as dreams, free association, transference, and countertransference are not used in group analysis and where, as a result, the therapist concludes "lack of depth."

The analyst who is reluctant to use analytic methodology in the group setting may have anxieties about his own individual responses and capacities, or he may have real anxieties about the ability of people to get together and to act in their own interest. There are group therapists who circumvent their anxieties by organizing groups with a common psycho-visceral complaint, or nearly uniform character structure. This desire for homogeneity may be in reality a resistance of the analyst, who does not want to take advantage of the special opportunities the heterogeneous group offers. Or a therapist may reject group procedure because of his own unresolved overprotectiveness of his patients. Not unlike overprotective parents we find overprotective analysts who encourage dependency, out of a need to dominate patients. In a group, however, when the members combine both their neurotic and healthy rebellion, such an overdominating analyst will find very rough going indeed. Such analysts often conduct a group in a rigid lecture pattern and forbid any contact among patients outside of the regularly scheduled meetings.

It would seem that overconcern for patients can often mask the analyst's fear of patient insight regarding the analyst. One individual with whom this writer worked described a relationship with a psychiatrist whom he saw individually and then in a group. He saw this man for five years altogether and was assured that he was receiving analysis. While it is true that the method of analysis was used in some part, it is also true that the therapist sat behind a desk with the group seated in front of him, refused to permit the group to meet outside of regular sessions, and held a ruler in his hand "to emphasize my points." The reader can judge whether a helpful therapeutic relationship could exist in such a setting, although the therapist continues to be unaware of any shortcomings. The patient, after five years, finally recognized that, since his problem was fear of authority, he wasn't really going very far.

It is important to recognize that depth can often evoke countertransference on the part of the analyst, since he cannot escape careful scrutiny in the group: Depth works both ways. The analyst's own reactions are analyzed by group members who leave little or no time to think over or work through challenging situations. There is constant evaluation of the analyst's unconscious as the group makes him examine his reactions. Often the therapist rejects the group method because there is unconscious anxiety about exposing himself in the countertransference. His concern about depth often relates to self-concern.

Let us now survey some questions regarding the technique, procedures, and dangers of the group method. There are those who criticize the training of the group analyst as not being as thorough as that of the individual analyst. The answer is simple; the training must be even more thorough. The group analyst must have the training of the individual analyst plus knowledge and experience in the area of group functioning. Since group analysis is a relatively new method, the group analyst has, until the postwar period, been forced to search for adequate training. At present, however, there are constantly developing opportunities for study and training.

Some analysts feel the privacy of the individual analytic relationship is basic to analysis. But psychoanalysis is a two-way street. Discussions of method touch upon the therapist as well as the patient. Both analyst and analysand can hide in the "small get-together," where the perceptive patient can always be accused of projecting, since there are no checks on the analyst's judgment. Privacy in the individual relationship can be overemphasized and may be questioned. The transference cure under such conditions is often an authoritarian cure, based on the patient's inference that the analyst is all-powerful. The patient may experience deep guilt and anxiety about questioning this all-powerfulness. In the group, on the contrary, the analyst may have a healthier relationship with the patient, strengthened and expressed in many ways. In a group the dependent personality soon expresses aggression when the longed-for parent-figure has relationships with other siblings and family figures, whereas aggression is rarely expressed by the dependent person in individual analysis until considerable time has passed, for fear of estranging the analyst-parent.

One of the analysts who answered our questionnaire, describing his work with group therapy in an army setting, was concerned about the ability of the analyst to recognize and withstand the many transference reactions that are directed at him in the group. He seems to have assumed that all transferences on the therapist are expressed at the same time. While such reactions are present and latent, it is only in the process of working through that they come to the surface. They rarely come to the surface at the same time. Even if a group of patients should all attack the analyst at once, it is possible to handle this temporary revolt, which is historically representative of rebellion against authority in the family. The therapist always finds several individuals in the group who will help explore the dynamics of the revolt. More usually, however, the patients express their hostility individually and the group forces them to compare their views of the therapist with the divergent feelings of the other members.

As in individual analysis, there are times when the analyst will fail to pick up a transference reaction in the group. But the pattern of reactions, as in individual analysis, comes through again and again. If the analyst is not perceptive enough, there are the patients who, as increasingly skillful adjunct analysts, will pick up the transference reactions. The group is active and moving. There is little opportunity for patient or analyst to escape into personal fantasies.

One often sees graphic illustrations of how the patient's transferences change constantly in the group. The patient who is constantly involved in a sexual contact and *loves* the analyst can see how *love* for the analyst is used by another or several other group members. The patient then works it through not only with the analyst but with all of the group members. The microcosm of life exists in the group. The transferences exist as they do in life—constantly shifting and variable. The analysis broadens from the first "unique" relationship with the analyst to a group relationship which is more helpful.

Many analysts show anxiety about the group structure because they feel that patients may move too quickly. They fear "acting out." Experience *has* indicated that most patients move more quickly in the group than in individual analysis. The presence of the stimulating group is vital for the patient. The analyst's authority and presence are diluted by the presence of other neurotics "in the same boat." Patients may minimize the reaction of another patient with the comment that "you're a neurotic and you're too sick to know what's going on . . ." but this does not minimize the effect when a fellow patient makes an analytic observation. Many problems do develop much more quickly within the group framework than in individual sessions. One analyst commented that such development was dangerous because the analysand ". . . might have a psychotic breakdown."

Yet in the combined clinical experience of the ten analysts who are members of the Workshop in Group Psychoanalysis there have been only three psychotic episodes reported by one analyst although a wide variety of personality problems have been handled. This analyst's patients had had psychotic episodes prior to his contact with them or their entrance into the group. The psychotic episodes which occurred while they were in group analysis were successfully handled in the group.

The reason why patients in the group are not endangered by "acting out" seems to lie in the fact that the group "goes with" the patient. The group leaves a session with the patient, who is thus still able to communicate with siblings in his "family"—siblings who often help him get through difficult periods—where the individual analyst would find it impossible to follow up. Group members have often noted that in individual sessions the patient leaves after the scheduled hour and "that's that. . . ." One of the limitations of the individual session is, indeed, that time schedules must be followed. While we can defend such a procedure on the basis of "reality"—a reality which the patient is asked to accept—it is undeniable that patients do sometimes leave analysts' offices under considerable stress and that many analytic hours terminate with the analysand depressed or overanxious.

Analysts who express concern over "acting out" in a group setting might well explore their own anxieties about patient behavior. "Acting out" takes place frequently enough. When it does, it is analyzed as part of the neurosis and resistance mechanisms. Patients also "act out" in individual analysis, but often do not discuss this with the analyst. Even experienced group therapists who do not want to use analytic methodology speak with anxiety about the combination of men and women in a group and the possibilities of sexual promiscuity. Are they not losing sight of the fact that the promiscuous patient has a problem which must be analyzed? Promiscuity does not result from group analysis. Patients who have been promiscuous will continue their pattern. But within the group framework these patients come to realize that such behavior should be analyzed and worked through. Let us not overlook the experiences of some patients who have met in group analysis, gone through neurotic love experiences, and analyzed these experiences. Nor those patients who have met within the group framework and developed healthy relationships.

Since patients get so much that is positive from the group and are sustained in moments of anxiety, some analysts object that the group reinforces the overdependent patient and encourages dependency generally. Experience indicates, however, that the group extends aid to those in need, but does not permit itself to be used by dependent patients. Patients recognize the distinction between a cooperative relationship which leads to growth and a relationship which is neurotically draining in nature. True, there are always some patients who permit themselves to be used, but this neurotic "missionary" type is exposed and analyzed. In one of my groups, one patient felt constantly driven to be a father figure. In every relationship he strove for this role, although he unconsciously rejected it. This compulsion was repeatedly analyzed as it occurred in the group, until ultimate clarification ensued.

Theodore Reik has aptly described psychoanalysis as a place where "dere's no hiding place." This apt observation certainly describes a group. Neither patients nor therapists can hide in the group setting. Therapist as well as patient shortcomings appear in the group, and the therapist is under constant scrutiny in the group. The therapist may overwork the phrase "it's your distortion" in the individual relationship. But can he really continue such comments when a group—albeit neurotic—with varying personality problems sees the problem that the analyst fails to see in himself? The analyst in the group often finds himself indebted to patients for sound insights. But there are analysts who can't accept such a relationship.

Martin Grotjahn, in a beautifully written exposition on analysis, has spoken of the competition that exists between the training analyst and the student analyst. Dr. Grotjahn notes the necessity of a secure training analyst. We may further note the extension of the same problem in a group where the analyst feels competitive with patients. Dr. Grotjahn in another article describes the group as a "gallery of mirrors"; certainly the insecure analyst has good reason to fear mirrors! The group always forces the analyst to evaluate his countertransferences. No one escapes scrutiny in the group, not even the analyst. The possibility that the analyst may escape into nonparticipation simply does not exist. A nonparticipating analyst, experience indicates, will only lead to group dissolution.

Analysts who fear the overactive group with consequent chaotic conditions may reflect upon their own analytic practice, which in many ways consists of an "all day" group. Patients often express anxiety in individual analysis as to whether the analyst can handle all the information that patients bring forth. The average individual analyst does manage, simply because he is not compelled to handle all his patients at the same time. But the situation is similar in a group. Group patients do not permit chaos to exist unless the analyst is unable or unwilling to interpret and handle this disorder. The group is bound by the common desire to get well. The autistic patient is brought out of his autism or is not accepted by the group. The psychopath is rejected. Nevertheless, even the patient who hallucinates in a group may be helped through his experience by the warmth and understanding of his "family."

One of my patients has said that "saying goodbye to a neurosis is like saying goodbye to an old friend. You don't know the new friend in advance. You are frightened by the effort needed to make new friends and are therefore reluctant to give up the old friend—neurosis. So very often you're afraid to cross the river and find out what's on the other side." The group offers the warmth and support to cross the river.

Basic to those who practice group psychoanalysis is the belief that the group process tends to maximize all healthy constructive elements in the individual. The individual may often seem so sick, and his resources so limited, that we forget that he does have some resources. In the group his healthy resources are reinforced manyfold through interaction. Group members do not confuse one another. Rather they see one another clear of all the psychological vocabulary that critics of psychoanalysis often rightly attack us for using. The group is the beginning area for communication. Analysts should take advantage of it.

Historically, new ideas are always met with doubt, and frequently with hostility and opposition. Group analysis faces skepticism and justly so. But analysts who have taken upon themselves the role of the questioner must also question their opposition to the practice of psychoanalysis in the group setting. If we as analysts do not question, who will?

BIBLIOGRAPHY

Alcoholics Anonymous (New York: World Publishing Co., 1939).

Freud, S., *Group Psychology and the Analysis of the Ego* (London: Hogarth Press, 1927).

Grotjahn, M., "The Process of Maturation in Group Psychotherapy and in Group Therapists." *Psychiat.*, Vol. 13, No. 1, February 1950.

———, "The Role of Identification in the Training of Psychiatrists." *Monthly Review of Psychiatry and Neurology*, Vol. 117, 1949.

Hobbs, N., "Group-Centered Psychotherapy," in C. R. Rogers, ed., *Client-Centered Psychotherapy* (Boston: Houghton Mifflin Co., 1951).

Klapman, J. W., "The Case for Didactic Group Psychotherapy." *Dis. Nerv. Sys.*, Vol. XI, No. 2, February 1950.

Powdermaker, Florence, and Frank, J. D., "Group Psychotherapy with Neurotics." *Am. J. Psychiat.*, December 1948.

Schilder, P., *Psychotherapy* (New York: W. W. Norton & Co., 1938).

Slavson, S., *Analytic Group Psychotherapy with Children, Adolescents, and Adults* (New York: Columbia University Press, 1950).

Wender, L., "The Dynamics of Group Psychotherapy and its Application." *J. Nerv. Ment. Dis.*, Vol. 84, No. 1, July 1936.

Wolf, A., "The Psychoanalysis of Groups." *Am. J. Psychother.*, Parts I and II, October 1949; January 1950.

Wolf, A., Locke, N., Rosenbaum, M., Hillpern, E., Goldfarb, W., Kadis, A., Obers, S., Willberg, I., and Abell, R., "The Psychoanalysis of Groups: The Analyst's Objections." *Int. J. Group Psychother.*, Vol. II, No. 3, July 1952.

The works cited here accompanied the original, longer, article.

28

GROUP COUNSELING WITH PARENTS

Hanna Grunwald
Bernard Casella

It has often been our experience, in casework treatment of mothers who request help for their children's behavior problems, that although a change in attitude brings about improvement in the child, friction with their husbands comes to the surface. The friction appears to be intolerable for the mothers and jeopardizes the treatment gain. The mothers voiced their feelings about the problem by stressing their inability to explain to their husbands what had really brought about their change in attitude toward the child. When they were enabled through treatment to be more clearly directive with the child, the husbands accused them of being cruel. When they were more lenient, the husbands accused them of coddling the child. Mothers with better ego integration than those of the group with which we were concerned can be helped to overcome this problem. However, the mothers with whom we were working felt overwhelmed by the threat to the equilibrium of their marital relationship and longed desperately for a return to the former marital situation. We believe that the mother's gain in self-esteem resulting from casework treatment led to lessening of dependency on her husband, to which he had reacted with fear and anger.

The problem was aggravated when the child's rebellious behavior had been a source of unconscious satisfaction to the father. At times the father retaliated for being deprived of this satisfaction by pressuring another child whose behavior was a source of unconscious satisfaction to the mother. This in turn made the mother more anxious and led to a return of the children's problems.

This recurrent problem stimulated us to look for a new treatment method. We looked for a way out of it by trying to draw the father into a

Reprinted from *Child Welfare*, Vol. XXXVII, No. 1, January 1958, pp. 1-6.

meaningful contact. We were always aware of the importance of the father's role in the child's development and felt it unfortunate that, primarily due to technical reasons, we have to work more with the mother than with him. It is usually considered an achievement when we are able to see the father once or twice during the course of a one-year treatment of mother and child, since he may have long working hours which overlap with our office hours. We are also aware that the father's unavailability for treatment is due not only to technical reasons but also to the husband's strong feeling that any need for outside help with family problems reflects his own inadequacies. He may also feel that the responsibility for the children's rearing is mainly the mother's because he is so tied down realistically and emotionally with the obligation of wage earner. Basically, however, their defense against the deep-seated longing for dependency makes a help-seeking process too threatening to these fathers and therefore they avoid it.

We have been working in our agency for the last seven years with case-work-oriented counseling groups. Often this is the treatment method of choice. Many clients who would have been lost in an individual contact were helped in group treatment. In individual treatment the client often is overwhelmed by the fear of overdependency and uses various defenses to ward off this danger. In a group contact he feels protected against this danger. Energies that would have been needed for defensive purposes in individual contact are thus freed in the group and can be utilized for constructive purposes.[1]

We formed a parents' group in the belief that the benefits of group counseling would aid us in our attempt to help both mother and father. In three of these families the mothers had been seen for treatment either individually or in a group. They all had reported the problems in family living described earlier. We chose a fourth couple who had only recently come to our attention; however, we had sufficient evidence to assume that they had similar problems. The parents ranged in age from thirty-four to forty-one; the children's ages ranged from five to fourteen years. All of the couples had two children. The couples came from similar cultural and economic backgrounds. They were intelligent; some had superior intelligence. There was a conspicuous lack of spontaneity in their thinking. All members of the group had suffered from extreme emotional deprivations in early childhood. Severe rejection by their own inadequate parents led them to a constant search for ideal accepting parents, which they hoped to get by "behaving perfectly." This unrealistic goal, coupled with limited ability to form relationships reflected vividly that the behavior of these clients was determined largely by pre-Oedipal needs. Such clients require a more active and assertive role with regard to guidance and counseling.[2]

Because of this need for more active roles we felt that the presence in the group of a male and a female counselor would be an advantage, facilitating the application of major techniques (i.e. displacement) needed for the treatment of these clients. The presence of a father and a mother figure further enhanced the possibility of recreating a family situation. The fathers seemed to be especially encouraged by this arrangement. Since their wives had initiated the contact, they often were apprehensive that the treatment process would be "woman-dominated."

CHARACTERISTICS OF GROUP MEMBERS

The couples managed rather well on a surface level. The husbands were hard-working men. They had various white collar and semiprofessional positions. Because of their wish for security, they avoided competition, preferring instead sheltered work below their capacities. Their social life was restricted because of their concern to be "polite and friendly." The women were well groomed and meticulously dressed. They assumed the major responsibility for cohesiveness of the family and determined its cultural standards. They had a distinct quality of "going through the motions of living" caused by their wish to avoid conflict. Under great stress such a defense system cannot hold: Most members of the group had suffered from "nervous breakdown" for brief periods when under great stress. Some had previously benefited from brief psychiatric care. Two psychiatrists who had earlier treated two members of the group encouraged us to choose the counseling method rather than psychotherapy for their former patients.

The marriage of each couple was "an armed truce"; the partners had an unspoken agreement to be tolerant of each other's weaknesses. Occasional flare-ups reflected the unrest of the truce. The suspension of hostilities was especially threatened by the parents' differences about rearing the children. Some pressure was eased by leaving this responsibility to the mother. Both parents were terribly frightened whenever it seemed that the child's behavior would thwart their efforts to remain inconspicuous to the outside world. However, in many instances a child's behavior may have caused panic in one partner while satisfying unconscious needs of the other partner, which led to a complication of the marital conflict.

This need to conceal what was going on inside their homes was strong, and the mothers had come to the agency only because of great outer or inner pressure. The fathers fought longer against this involvement. Not having had the benefit of earlier treatment in the agency, they were at a disadvantage at first. Prior to the meetings, the male and female counselors each took the opportunity to see every father and mother individually. When they came to the first meeting the male counselor introduced the members to each other. Then he repeated what they had been told in the individual interviews: that we had invited them to participate in the group in the hope that they might be assisted through this to help their children in constructive ways. The members understood that they could discuss whatever they liked in the group. They were not obliged to talk when they preferred to remain silent. The requirement for keeping the names of the members confidential outside the group was especially stressed by the counselor.

He had barely ended this introduction when Mrs. Clare burst into an almost hysterical complaint: "Jack is still wetting the bed—it's terrible! What can I do?" This plea for help brought out from the members run-of-the-mill advice about controlling bed-wetting. This quickly resulted in a back-and-forth questioning about the ages of their children. They started telling one another about the problems of the children which had brought them to the agency: bed-wetting, restlessness at night, failure in school, shyness, inability to make friends. After several weeks group members frequently voiced their feelings of satisfaction when "right in the beginning" they came to see that the other members were "such likable people." They were pleased to find that the moral standards of the members were up to their own strict expectations. They quickly sensed that the other couples suffered from similar problems because "they are as sensitive as we." Of major benefit in group counseling is the help members derive from identification with each other. The members selected for the parents' group were quickly enabled to identify with each other because they were able to "like each other."

ISOLATION OF THESE PARENTS

The process of identification was enhanced by the fact that the members were victims of "social hunger." [3] They suffered from their isolation, which resulted from their fear that rejection by the outside world would constitute too much outrage to their sense of self. However, they were not isolated because of pronounced narcissistic make-up. Once the presence of protecting parental figures made them feel safe enough to communicate with other persons, they were quickly enabled to establish good rapport.

The members of the group were sensitive to each other's needs and it was gratifying for them that they were able to help each other.

> When Mr. and Mrs. Alden complained about the "circus" at night in their home, the children running back and forth into the parent's bedroom, the Bateses and Clares helped them with support and understanding. Mr. Alden was angry that his wife was "too soft with the girls" when they did not stay in bed at night. The members in the group helped him to understand gradually that at least part of the difficulty stems from the fact that many children are afraid at night. They suggested that parents should help their children to cope with these fears. After more meetings, Mr. Alden was proud to report that he had read a story to the youngsters at

their bedside. He also told them, "anyone can get afraid when it gets dark." He boasted, "They were like angels."

At times there were setbacks which were worked through by the members. A warm, positive climate developed in the meetings, in which there was a constant back-and-forth evaluation of daily problems. No topics were planned, the group process was unstructured, and associative material led to a nonsystematic flow of discussion.

A husband, feeling that his wife was under attack, might come to her rescue by holding her hand for a short time, or a wife may have looked at her husband with amazement and pride because he advised another member in a sure, patient, and intelligent manner.

> Mr. Clare said to Mr. Alden: "You get so mad at your wife's daily calls to her mother as if this takes something away from you, as if she spites you. Don't you see that she needs these calls to mother, that she is not yet quite grown up. . . ." Mr. Alden reported, after a number of meetings, that since he stopped nagging his wife about the calls by showing some "paternal concern" for her, she has let go of the daily calls. After the end of the group sessions Mrs. Alden told the counselors: "We had been married eight years when we came to the group. After some time in the group we had our honeymoon."

It was interesting that Mrs. Clare had started the discussion in the first meeting by complaining about Jack. In prior contact she had focused upon her strained relationship with her daughter whom she pushed forward, wanting her to be self-sufficient. In her husband's presence she immediately turned to discussion of the other child who was rejected by him.

WORKING THROUGH PROBLEMS

Gradually some focal theme became crystallized out of the group discussion. The members came to understand that they had equated human inadequacies with sin. They acted as if weaknesses might lead to a disastrous point of no return. They came gradually to see this concept as wrong when applied to the problems of other couples, but they took a longer time to understand that it was wrong as it applied to themselves. It was impressive to see how skilled each member became in unraveling the many rationales developed by the others in their attempt to ward off this new insight. In the beginning many members felt that they would prefer to be faced with the problem of another couple instead of types of problems they had to cope with in their own home. Gradually, however, they began to accept problem situations in their own homes. Towards the end of the group sessions they even came to feel that they preferred their own problems to those of the others.

The process of mutual help was intricately interwoven with assistance from the counselors. At times the members asked one or the other counselor a direct question which was always answered briefly. Questions on problems of feeding or weaning were usually addressed to the female counselor; those on educational problems and problems of contact with the community, to the male counselor. When a female member of the group was attacked by the male members—specifically by her husband, with resulting overwhelming anxiety—the male counselor came to her rescue. This technique was also used by the female counselor when one of the men was attacked. The rescue was usually given with the help of the method of universalization.

> Mr. Clare complained about Jack's "black hands" when coming to the table. "I won't tolerate it. My wife is too soft with him." "Oh you———," Mrs. Clare retorted. "No wonder he doesn't wash his hands! I have to remind you each week to take a bath." Mr. C. became white with rage, pounded his fists on the table, and stammered that he would not take this. He got up retreating to the door. The female worker in a quiet way stated that anyone would feel like running away when his weaknesses are suddenly and openly discussed—"we all would prefer to keep some habits to ourselves." Mr. Clare returned to his chair, the other members helping to reassure him. Mrs. Clare was still angry. She attacked him further and when he again threatened to leave, she insisted that "this is a place where to bring the dirty laundry—if not here, then where?"

In the next meeting the Clares reported that "After the storm last time we had a wonderful time." They also reported, with pride, some improvement in the boy. Treatment was enhanced because husband and wife cooperated in working throughout the week on newly gained understanding. Working together was a constructive experience as was the opportunity to report this to the group.

The couples found that since attending the meetings they were able to talk more readily with each other. Channels of communication which had been blocked for a long time were opened when they experienced that in the group such discussions were safe. The Bateses began to talk things over at home, even though Mr. Bates did not talk in the group sessions. However, he listened intently and even imitated some of the male counselor's mannerisms in greeting people, and later came to smoke the same kind of pipe. Mrs. Bates reported in a few of the meetings that during the last week her husband had spent some time reading to his son or playing ball with him. This revealed that Mr. Bates derived benefits from the group without verbal participation. The members of the group seemed to sense his need to remain silent. In individual counseling such a tendency might have blocked or even led to an interruption of treatment.

TRANSFERENCE IN THE GROUP

Group counseling differs from group therapy in that we do not inter-pret the transference that takes place both to the therapist and to the members of the group. However, just as in individual casework treatment, the counselors must understand the transference phenomena. In this parent group the transferences were subjected to a variety of modifications, different from that in groups of members of the same sex or of members of both sexes not belonging to the same family. The presence of a person important in the client's life, with whom he is in daily contact, reduces the intensity of some of the transference phenomena. The presence of the marital partner brings more reality of the living situation to treatment, which prevents the development of some aspects of the transference. Our group manifested fewer aspects of sibling rivalry and fewer attempts to gain special attention of the counselors. We believe that this was due to the fact that the partners' sympathies remained with each other rather than with individuals outside of their marriage.

At the same time other aspects of transference are more pronounced. The presence of a male and female counselor enhances the reproduction of the family scene which partially may account for this intensification. The presence of the partner and the other group members reduces the clients' fear of overdependency, thus allowing him to refrain from building up defenses against the transference. This may account for the fact that the members of the group faced the two counselors with less defensiveness than usually experienced either in individual counseling or in groups conducted by a male or female counselor alone. The fact that there was so much reality in the treatment situation lessened the chance of the establishment of a dependency relationship. This allowed the counselors to feel freer to nurture the members than is done in most other treatment processes. In turn, the clients' need for accepting parental figures was somewhat satisfied, which released energies for constructive purposes that heretofore had gone into the endless search for ideal parents. Their destructive hold on the children was therefore considerably lessened. We feel that we are not yet prepared to analyze completely this question of transference, after experience with only one group. However, these two trends of transference development were quite pronounced.

Another trend observed in this child-centered parents' group is similar to one often found in joint interviews with married couples. In interviews of this type, as in our group, we find that conflicts pertaining to the early childhood are less often recalled and that there is a lesser degree of hostil-ity released against the partner and the child. However, the less the amount of hostility released, the greater is the impact upon reality testing. Hostility released against the partner or child in the presence of the partner is not accompanied by an ensuing overwhelming guilt when later seeing the partner, as might happen after an individual interview. Although this problem can be worked through with many clients it appears too difficult for the type of persons selected for our group. The availability of reality in this group also enhanced the utilization of the client's healthy ego strengths. Since regression occurred seldom, there was less manifestation of illness. This is desirable in counseling, in contrast to psychotherapy.

THE COUNSELORS' CONTRIBUTIONS

It was especially helpful that the parents could witness discussions of differences between the two counselors. Although both counselors have the same training, their responses often differed. The male counselor may have supported a parent who felt it was important to help a child to be weaned away from the parents, whereas the female counselor at this point may have stated that although it certainly is important to help the child to be independent, this can be very difficult. She remembered that she too had felt qualms, for instance, when it had become necessary to allow a child to cross the street alone for the first time. Such differences did not lead the counselors to change their attitudes toward each other. The members would witness that differences of opinion do not have to lead to conflicts.

Some therapy groups have a male and a female therapist, one of whom is a helper to the other. In our group the contributions of each counselor were equally valid. Differences stemmed from the distinction in sex and the individuality of human temperament. However, in basic professional social work training their understanding was similar. It was a new experience for both counselors to work together in the same interviewing situation and both approached this new task with the excitement of the untried. We had questioned, for instance, how we would discern which one should react to certain occurrences within the group. However, throughout the group sessions this did not prove a problem. The counselors took turns recording the interviews and found that discussing the material together was more stimulating in many ways than discussing it in consultation with someone who was not present during the meeting. The staff psychiatrist was available to the counselors on the same basis as in our individual casework.

The group started to meet in the fall once a week for an hour and a half. In addition to the group meeting, some members were seen individually when necessary. As in our work with individuals, children were seen when it seemed important for diagnostic clarification or for help with acute problems. We terminated the group at the time of the summer vacation period. The members of the group felt that they were helped through their group participation. Life at home became more enjoyable for them. They were especially pleased to report improvements of their children's behavior. Jack still has dirty hands at times but they no longer lead to stormy scenes at the dinner table. However he stopped wetting the bed and for the first time he even got interested in his school work. He no longer felt that his parents thought of him as a nuisance. They were enabled through treatment to communicate to him that they liked him and that they were proud of him—which in turn helped Jack to gain a better self-image. This enabled him to make better use of his potentials. The teacher was amazed that Jack no longer was a reading problem, although he had not received remedial reading help. The Clares' daughters learned to trust their parents more. The parents being less panicky about the children's fears helped the girls to lessen their fears. The Aldens and the Danes came to understand that although their children had improved they needed professional help for internalized problems and accepted referral for psychotherapy. They would have become panicky if we had referred them to a child guidance clinic prior to the group experience.

CONCLUSION

We felt that a child-centered parents group can be an important device in the treatment of specially selected clients. These parents, as mentioned above, were primarily motivated by pre-Oedipal needs. It seemed to us that they would not have had the strength to be amenable to psychotherapy, where they would have been helped to understand their own involvement in the child's symptom and the meaning a child's behavior has for them. Their good intellectual equipment would have enabled them to be active participants in a group educational project; however, their emotional limitations would have prevented them from applying the newly gained knowledge about child-rearing. We felt that these parents were best helped in changing their attitudes towards their children when they could become less panicky about the child's behavior. This kind of help is the proper domain of casework.

Individual casework often does not reach this type of client. We feel that group treatment filled this gap. In the group described the parents were able to raise their self-esteem through a positive identification with the counselors and the other group members. This, coupled with release of hostility, freed energies for bringing about change of attitudes towards the child, and in turn the child's behavior improved.

The emotional experience provided by the group was shared by both parents. This prevented a dangerous shift in the precarious family balance, which was essential to the parents and children for their emotional survival.

We are planning to work with more groups of this structure in the hope of widening our experience with this important new casework method.

REFERENCES

1. For an analysis of the modification of casework-oriented group techniques from methods used in individual contact see *Group Methods in Casework Agencies*, Welfare and Health Council of New York City, May 1955, Part I, p. 2; S. Sherman, "Group Counseling," *Casework Papers from 1955 NCSW* (New York: Family Service Assn. of America, 1955); Hanna Grunwald, "Group Counseling in a Casework Agency," *Int. J. Group Psychother.*, 4:183, 1954; 7:318-326, 1957.
2. S. L. Green, "Casework Diagnosis of Marital Problems," in V. Eisenstein (ed.), *Neurotic Interaction in Marriage* (New York: Basic Books, 1956), p. 241.
3. S. R. Slavson, *An Introduction to Group Therapy* (New York: The Commonwealth Fund, 1943), pp. 5, 85, 187, 200, 272.

29

CO-THERAPY

Max Rosenbaum

Today, a sense of excitement pervades the field of psychotherapy, especially group psychotherapy. But enthusiasm often becomes a substitute for a rigorous and thoughtful approach, especially when psychotherapists become defensive about their capacity to help troubled people. Because of the difficulty that therapists face as they approach work with groups of patients, they tend to seek techniques that will ease the practice of psychotherapy. As therapists try to ease the emotional burden they face and to function more efficiently as therapists, they are more and more drawn to the idea of co-therapy, a technique that, although apparently recent, has actually been practiced in many forms since the outset of dynamic psychotherapy. Ever since Freud decided to treat Little Hans by conferring with Hans's father and ever since supervisors started guiding trainees in the practice of psychotherapy, therapists have used co-therapy. In the larger view, co-therapy practice has been in existence for some time, even if it was not labeled as such.

Group psychotherapy, because of its very structure, has encouraged the use of co-therapists. Since the relationship is no longer one-to-one but is, rather, one-to-a-group, the group members are more responsive to the idea of another therapist coming to the therapy group. In many training institutions, beginning therapists are often encouraged to visit groups. This writer feels that a visitor is disruptive to the group. It is more advisable for the therapist to enter the group as a trainee, recorder, or observer. Finally, he should be encouraged to take over as a co-therapist.

For the most part, clinical practice validates the use of a co-therapist as an aid to therapy. The co-therapist appears to enhance group process and increase interaction. Also, the co-therapist often increases the validity and intensity of the interpretation. Patients are more prone to accept two inter-

Reprinted from H. Kaplan and B. Sadock, eds., *Comprehensive Group Psychotherapy* (Baltimore: The Williams & Wilkins Co., 1971), pp. 501-514.

pretations that are consonant than one solitary interpretation. One of the side benefits is that the group therapist becomes accustomed to co-therapy and may be responsive to the idea of having a co-therapist for an individual session. Sometimes the presence of another therapist helps break through a therapeutic impasse. This use of another therapist in individual therapy is called multiple therapy and is an aspect of co-therapy. In both the individual and the group situations, the human qualities of the therapist are accepted and worked with. In addition, the therapist's neurotic problems are acknowledged and may be neutralized or clarified by the presence of another therapist.

The use of co-therapists aids group therapy in the following ways: First, the patient has another figure to whom he may transfer. This added person causes an imbalance in the traditional transference response of patient-therapist. But the presence of other group members has already modified the traditional transference response. The co-therapist simply modifies it further. Second, more movement is promoted in the therapy group. Third, the group members appear to move toward greater depths. Fourth, co-therapy offers an effective method to break through blockages. Fifth, one therapist may undercut while another supports the patient's defenses. Sixth, one therapist is able to take more risks in depth interpretation, since another therapist is present as a kind of ballast, especially in work with psychotic patients, where a therapist may fear the loss of his own psychic balance as he enters the world of the acutely disturbed.

The use of more than one therapist at a time in individual or group psychotherapy has been given many names. Besides co-therapy, they include dual leadership, role-divided therapy, three-cornered therapy, multiple therapy, three-cornered interviews, cooperative psychotherapy, conjoint therapy, and joint interview. Additional names are probably being formulated as this is being written. Anywhere from two to ten therapists may work with a single patient, and groups of therapists may join groups of patients.

HISTORY

As noted, Freud used a kind of multiple therapy in the case of Little Hans. Adler and his co-workers at the Vienna Child Guidance Clinic consistently used forms of co-therapy. Moreno has for many years used a trained auxiliary ego to play the part of the patient and has used other people as aids in his psychodramatic approach. Dreikurs (1950), one of Adler's leading students in this country, has used co-workers to side with the patient and expound his logic. At the same time, another therapist argues with the therapist who is playing the role of the patient. Meanwhile, the actual patient observes what is happening. This technique is particularly effective with psychotic patients, as it communicates the intensity of the therapist's desire to be of aid.

Until the 1960's, co-therapy was used to help resolve specific problems in therapy or to teach certain goals. But many of the people who used multiple therapy or co-therapy stumbled on the technique without any planning and with no awareness of the work that others were doing with the technique. The present confusions concerning the concept of co-therapy go back to the early days of group psychotherapy. For example, the early literature contains many cursory references to visitors or observers who participated in some manner in group psychotherapy. Often the group therapist paid little attention to the impact of the visitor or observer.

Samuel Hadden, one of the early pioneers in group psychotherapy in the Philadelphia area, encouraged interns and psychiatric residents in the 1940's to observe sessions of didactic group therapy with neurotic patients. The residents and interns became involved in group discussions and were encouraged to take part as group leaders. From this start, a more structured approach was developed. In 1949 Whitaker reported that for the previous six years he had used techniques of multiple therapy to encourage general practitioners of medicine in their work with patients who had emotional difficulties. He is not clear as to how he arrived at this practice.

Lundin and Aronov, whose work was carried out at Chicago State Hospital with psychotics, stated in 1952 that the use of two therapists in a group psychotherapy setting was a relatively unexplored field. What they really meant was that there was no clear statement of the method. They noted that the original purpose of co-therapy was to help train psychotherapists, as Hadden had reported in 1947. Until Lundin and Aronov's 1952 article, only vague references to multiple therapists or participant observers had appeared in the literature, and there was no clearly defined position or theoretical presentation.

Gradually, with clinicians more or less fumbling along, the ideas of multiple therapy and, finally, co-therapy were formalized and a few clinicians began to theorize about the implications of their work.

REASONS FOR CO-THERAPY

MacLennan (1965) has pointed out that in some places co-therapy is used routinely without any awareness of its dynamic implications and consequences. But therapists must have a theoretical rationale to justify the use of co-therapists.

Training Therapists

As group therapy becomes more and more popular in private practice, clinics, and hospitals, administrators display a certain urgency to train future group therapists quickly. And co-therapy seems to be excellent on-the-job training. But administrators must clearly delineate the co-therapists' roles in such a training situation. If they do not, tremendous rivalry comes to the surface. Often the more experienced therapist runs the group while the trainee just sits at the feet of the master. Worse yet, the trainee finally becomes the experienced co-therapist and begins training juniors. He may never, alone, lead a group of his own or withstand the pressures he is exposed to.

Gans (1957) notes that the training of psychotherapists is built around a core of transference and countertransference reactions. He stresses the valuable opportunities for such reactions that co-therapy opens up. Granted, the student benefits from co-therapy. But is it fair to use patients in order to train students?

Contrary to the popular assumption, co-therapy is not an easy technique. It requires considerable maturity on the part of both leaders, and it should be used cautiously and with experienced therapists. It seems unfair to patients to use co-therapy for training therapists. And the practice of using co-therapy to train group therapists ignores the complex issues of group therapy—the many relationships and the complex transference problems.

Simulating a Family

Many advocates of co-therapy feel that the patient can use the group as a second family, often a more helpful and healthy family than the original one. With the helpful reassurance of the second therapist, the patient can try to cope with unresolved problems toward the dreaded parent or, in some cases, an overwhelming sibling. For example, a patient can confront a feared parent in the person of one therapist only because he feels that he has another therapist to turn to. The second therapist is somewhat like the parent who supports the child while the other parent is angry. Of course, in some situations both parents turn on the child, but there are no reports in the literature of both co-therapists being destructive.

Groups led jointly by a man and a woman therapist seem logical in view of the wide agreement that a basic value of group therapy is that the patient can experience and work through multiple transferences. Many therapists believe opposite-sex co-therapists activate sexual transferences. The rationale is that co-therapy permits the patients to identify with a therapist of the same sex and to clarify problems with a therapist of the opposite sex. Actually, in this situation the use of co-therapy is generally restricted to a specific goal or problem.

Dreikurs (1950), an Adlerian, found co-therapists effective for creating a familial setting. Lundin and Aronov (1952), who worked with psychotics, also felt that co-therapists simulated the family structure, which is created

> by the presence of two authority figures. The child must learn to adjust to a reality determined by the presence of two adult figures. . . . Our experi-

ences to date indicate that the two therapists need not be of the opposite sexes. As might be expected, the physical characteristics of the therapists become less important than the subtle psychological differences which schizophrenic patients can easily detect and respond to. One therapist will be seen as more aggressive and masculine, the other as more protective and feminine; one will be reacted to with more or less fear and guilt; one will be closer to the idealized image of the patient.

Hulse (1956) hypothesized that co-therapists of different sexes would "stimulate the creation of a milieu that repeats family and society." But he did not explore the transference phenomenon that might arise in such a milieu.

Certain patients may profit from the use of therapists of different sexes. For instance, juvenile delinquents who have not been exposed to a man and a woman living together in marriage, to a couple with healthy differences as to how they perceive the world, may be able to work out their oedipal problems and their distorted perceptions of the man-woman relationship if they have a man and a woman as co-therapists. Some therapists find that teenagers profit from observing the substitute parent figures in the persons of the man and the woman co-therapists as they disagree with one another and yet present themselves as adults who are able to communicate with each other. The larger question here is whether group psychotherapy is the appropriate setting for corrective experiences in living. This question is particularly pertinent in community health programs and in work with socially deprived patients from broken or unhappy homes.

Economy

Many of the economic reasons advanced for co-therapy, some of which sound rather mercantile, are not supported by full consideration of the theoretical implications. For example, some of those who advocate co-therapy feel that co-therapists can treat larger groups. This argument denies the importance of intimacy. Many patients suffer from intimacy problems and would prefer to obscure these problems. Large groups meet this preference. Also, advocates of larger groups assume that the therapists possess an enormous capacity to comprehend the dynamics of an expanded group, thus endowing them with extraordinary strengths. Actually, patients may so maneuver co-therapists that they engage in rivalry, thereby masking the patients' own conflicts.

Convenience

Some therapists advocate co-therapy because it gives them more freedom. One therapist can lead the group while the other is absent because of illness or an emergency or because he goes on vacation. This argument ignores the patient, who may not express but almost invariably feels a sense of rejection when the therapist is casual about his own presence and doesn't appear to be very committed. When a patient is absent from scheduled group meetings, many therapists are outraged and wonder about the patient's commitment. Yet they themselves find all sorts of rationalizations for their own absence and lack of commitment.

Mutual Support

Some therapists welcome the idea of co-therapy as a means of coping with their own anxiety about their adequacy as therapists. A mutual support mechanism is at work here, and patients often spot the mechanism and wonder about the unresolved anxieties of the group leaders. Actually, some therapists are not prepared for the groups they undertake to lead, so they invite another therapist to help them cope with the task. One therapist who works with schizophrenic patients both in groups and in individual sessions routinely invites a co-therapist to work with him when he enters the patients' intense fantasy life. He is fearful that he may become psychotic, and so he wants the control of another therapist.

Self-Therapy

The therapist who contemplates co-therapy must be on guard, since some therapists have a neurotic need to pair off with one another. They use co-therapy as therapy for themselves. For psychotherapists to work out their countertransference problems at the patients' expense is exploitation of patients. Some therapists who are fervent supporters of co-therapy completely ignore their own marital distress and loneliness, which are quite obvious to observers, as they recruit male or female therapists to work with them in groups. And lonely therapists often become intrigued with marathon therapy.

Other Reasons

At any given time in a deeply involved group, much is happening. The extra observations and support that a therapist may gain from a co-therapist are bound to be of aid in group psychotherapy. And co-therapy serves as a good learning situation for even experienced psychotherapists. One therapist may hold the other therapist in some kind of check.

Current research in learning theory and its relationship to intensive psychotherapy also become more relevant as one therapist checks on another. And co-therapy is helpful in evaluating psychotherapy, a research task that seems at times almost insurmountable because of the complexity of the issues and the many variables involved. Research may also answer a major question concerning co-therapy: Is the amount of time spent by two therapists warranted? Does co-therapy shorten treatment time? Does it produce successful results?

Some therapists feel that transference reactions become more intense in co-therapy groups. In this writer's opinion, the intensity of the transference cannot be related to co-therapy, but oedipal material may possibly come to the surface more quickly if the patient is confronted with both a male and a female therapist.

SELECTION OF CO-THERAPISTS

At this time, no firm rules for the selection of co-therapists can be set down. Co-therapy is still very much an art, and many variables are involved. But clinical experience indicates that certain therapists are more at ease in co-therapy relationships than when they lead a group alone. Some workers speak of the value of mutual and spontaneous choice as sometimes more valuable than pairing based on objective criteria. This writer does not agree. Experience has indicated that spontaneous pairing may not survive the rigors of hostility between co-therapists.

In institutional settings, co-therapists are rarely selected with care. Too much attention is paid to the training needs of the institution, and very little attention is paid to the specific anxieties and problems of the proposed co-therapists. Those who are new to co-therapy have to prepare by reading the literature and working with a supervisor even before co-therapy begins.

Equal clinical experience seems to be important in a co-therapist team. There is a tacit acknowledgment that therapists of equal skill are working with each other rather than *for* each other.

Compatibility of Therapists

Careful attention should be paid to the personality characteristics of therapists who plan to join one another as co-therapists. Most important is compatibility of temperament. Both therapists must be comfortable with intimacy and able to accept their differences. Over the years, experienced therapists establish a style, and co-therapists respect each other's style. Ideally, their styles blend together, so that a smoothly working team of co-therapists has its own style. A degree of trust must be present because on occasion a therapist may interpret or react in a manner that makes no sense at all to his co-therapist. Sometimes, when they lack regard for each other, co-therapists engage in rivalry for the patients' affections. Or they may engage in games or ploys that, exciting at the outset, later prove to be obstructive. In these situations therapists end up performing for patients, not treating them.

The issue of compatible pairing of therapists becomes critical if therapists attempt to work with acutely disturbed patients. Kraus (1970) points out that, in his work with chronic schizophrenics, "each member, including the therapists, was considered to be a participant of equal value." The co-therapists joined in group fantasy, an extension in some measure of the earlier work of Whitaker and Malone (1953).

In private practice, co-therapists often pair on the basis of personal friendship. Such pairing does not appear to be wise. The ostensible convenience may prove to be an obstacle when fantasy material comes to the surface and intense transferences develop. Because of their friendship, one therapist may avoid significant material. Openness and honesty must be present in the co-therapy relationship. Personality differences can be resolved as they occur, and the therapists can serve as healthy models for patients. Lack of authenticity often results in a floundering group that comes to a rapid end.

None of what has been stated precludes co-therapists from developing friendships. Similarity of background, geographic isolation, and a variety of situational circumstances may, in fact, promote close friendships. But a friendship between therapists has an impact on the group, and the therapists should be aware of this fact.

Compatibility of Patients and Therapists

The limited psychotherapeutic research data available suggest that Negro clients prefer and work better with Negro counselors than with white counselors. Some research studies suggest that more positive relationships result when the therapist and the patient are of the same race. But in co-therapy, is it advisable to pair therapists of different races, religions, cultural levels? One major metropolitan psychiatric center makes an effort to use therapists of different races to dissolve ethnic isolation. The ethical problem is one for the reader to evaluate.

Recently, active members of the Women's Liberation Movement have claimed that many psychotherapists are guilty of male chauvinism. These women search for sympathetic therapists. Their comments have the familiar echo of comments made during the 1930's and 1940's by members of the political left, who claimed that psychotherapists were out to convert them to an acceptance of the capitalist system. Their psychotherapists had to pass political tests of acceptability.

Class differences have as much validity as ethnic and religious differences in the selection of therapists. Yet too much attention to the manifest material obscures the psychological reality that the patient responds to in terms of his own unconscious.

Male-Female Co-Therapists

A man-woman pairing is often effective. Here one must not be thrown by surface appearances. Sometimes the man is quite feminine, and the woman is quite masculine, with the patients becoming quite confused.

The co-therapists serve as models for the group. If co-therapists of opposite sexes have unresolved problems concerning male and female roles in the culture, chaos will rapidly ensue. One extremely dominating woman therapist consistently espouses co-therapy and invariably chooses a passive male as her co-therapist. In another instance, an experienced but rather grandiose male therapist consistently chooses very attractive and rather seductive women as co-therapists, almost as if he were showing off a mistress. Because of his prominence and the teaching position he enjoys, his patients and the psychiatric residents he trains rarely challenge him as to his behavior. A follow-up study by this writer indicates that many of his patients have deep fantasy problems and confuse marriage with harem-type living.

In some instances, a husband and wife do co-therapy as a matter of convenience. They may, in fact, be creating the ideal family, with themselves as idealized parent models. One couple, both of whom had been previously married, were unconsciously drawn to the practice of co-therapy. They acted out a model for patients who had had unsuccessful marriages, as though they were telling patients that they—the co-therapists—could relate together in a second marriage and, therefore, so could the patients. There is no objection to this technique if it is conscious. Unfortunately, the therapists were not aware of what they were doing.

Sometimes a nurse is chosen as the female co-therapist. Since she generally ranks low in the hierarchy of a hospital setting, she may be supportive only and may pass on feelings of inadequacy to the women patients in a group. Selection of co-therapists should be intelligent, not a hit-or-miss grabbing of whatever staff is available.

Some groups of aged patients receive tremendous stimulation from exposure to male and female co-therapists, who apparently renew their interest in heterosexuality. In many cases, paraprofessionals can supply a similar corrective emotional experience in group work with this patient population.

A therapist was serving as psychiatric consultant to a home for the aged. He decided to use group therapy to help the aged with their anxieties. He found the group members very wearing in their demands, so he finally started using co-therapy. With a man and a woman as co-therapists, the aged members of the group found a renewed interest in heterosexuality and began to make plans to remarry and leave the home for the aged. There was an immediate storm of protests from the old people's children. They were agitated by the new life of their parents and had no intention of encouraging their parents to remarry or stimulate a more fulfilling sexual life. They had placed their parents in a home for the aged essentially to relieve their own sense of guilt, and the setting was intended to provide for the declining years of these aged people.

The whole affair proved to be a kind of castration experience, with the children overwhelming the parents. The children became angry, the parents became depressed, and the co-therapists ended up enormously discouraged. The administration of the home for the aged complained bitterly that endowments they had counted on were being withdrawn by the children of the aged patients. The situation turned out to be negative for all concerned. Sadly, but amusingly, the aged members of the group were sympathetic and consoling toward the co-therapists. Apparently the old people's life experiences had fortified them to live with disappointment.

RELATIONS BETWEEN CO-THERAPISTS

The idea of a co-therapy relationship promotes anxiety in the majority of psychotherapists who have been practicing individual or group psychotherapy. Co-therapy demands maturity and sensitivity in both therapists. Besides having to define interaction in the group, therapists are confronted with many of their own unresolved problems in a co-therapist relationship. A quality of strain exists at the outset and possibly throughout the co-therapy relationship, as unresolved transference phenomena come to the surface. But in the same way that anxiety serves as a stimulus for change, the acknowledged tension between co-therapists may further therapeutic change.

Most therapists find it difficult to visualize their impact on a group. Videotape can capture some of what is going on. But when another therapist observes a working therapist within the group setting, all kinds of unresolved feelings become apparent. The group therapist who has successfully masked omnipotent behavior, a need to be seductive, a need to avoid anger, or a need to stimulate hostility will almost certainly have his behavior and needs exposed when another therapist joins the group. Of course, the therapist with problems of omniscience may select as a co-therapist someone who will not rock the boat.

For the most part, group therapists resist the exploration of their own countertransference problems as they come to the fore in the group. The co-therapist may quickly perceive the problem, and this perception may threaten one or both of the therapists. A therapist in training may be reluctant to confront his co-therapist mentor. Or the trainee may have the neurotic need to confront the senior therapist. Some therapists experience difficulty leading groups and they turn to the co-therapist as a lifesaver. Although reluctant to acknowledge their need, these inept therapists want another therapist to help with the pressures and anxieties that develop in the group.

Both complementary and symmetrical behavior, as Haley (1963) describes them, are at work in co-therapy. In complementary behavior, each person's behavior complements or fits the other's behavior, as when one person teaches and the other serves as the student, or when one leads and the other follows. In symmetrical behavior, two people engage in the same type of behavior. In this situation, their behavior is both competitive and equalitarian, and the interaction is on a level of parity; in short, it is the behavior of two people who are equals. An effective co-therapy team works on a symmetrical pattern. Some teams may work effectively in a complementary fashion, but their goals appear to be more limited, since one therapist dominates the other. Pairing an experienced and an inexperienced group therapist produces a complementary pattern at the outset. As the team matures and grows in its work together, the move is toward a symmetrical pattern. But some teams never outgrow the complementary pattern.

In clinical practice one therapist can supplement and complement the skills of the other therapist. Co-therapists should be able to accept each other emotionally, understand each other's methods of working in a group setting, and share common aims and goals of treatment. Emotional acceptance and mutual respect are prime requisites. Neither therapist should feel a necessity to mold the behavior of the other, to be defensive with the other, or to use the group and its members to resolve competitive strivings.

Lundin and Aronov (1952) note an important point: "The co-therapist method by its very nature is a potentially powerful stimulus." According to them, if the purpose of co-therapy is to help patients identify with healthy models as contrasted with the original parental figures, who helped traumatize them, the co-therapists must have a healthy regard for each other. If the patient senses in any way the type of disharmony and bickering that characterized his early years, the basic thrust of the method is dissipated. Furthermore, the patient's neurotic defense mechanisms may be reinforced rather than changed for healthier defenses. Of course, Lundin and Aronov's work was with schizophrenics. Disharmony between co-therapists may not be devastating to neurotics.

If the co-therapists do not have a peer relationship, the patients may sense this inequality and play one therapist off against the other, which may be quite traumatic to the patient. But if co-therapists express healthy disagreements, the patients will learn to accept the reality of authentic differences.

On occasion, co-therapists maintain a social contact outside of the group, which invariably affects their behavior in the group. The administrative hierarchy of the institution also effects the group and the co-therapists. Some psychiatric residents in training use co-therapy as an opportunity to attack their mentors—verbally and nonverbally—while both are with the group. Some staff members are fearful of reacting genuinely in the group because of some unresolved reaction to a co-therapist who is perceived as a superior—either intellectually or administratively more powerful. And a senior therapist with power problems of his own may have great difficulty in accepting the contributions of a junior member serving as a peer co-therapist. The patients observe all this interaction whether they comment on it or not.

All the differences that co-therapists feel about the administration of the group and the group process should be clarified before the first group meeting. Obviously, not all the issues will be resolved before the first group session, but a quality of authenticity must be present between the two therapists. The optimally functioning co-therapy group reflects the comfort and openness that exist between the leaders.

RELATIONS WITH PATIENTS

In his leadership of a group, the therapist assumes certain responsibilities. He enters into a therapeutic contract with the patients. The contract is modified when co-therapists work with the group. The patients may become quite confused, unless the therapists clearly define their areas of responsibility and what the patients can reasonably expect from each group leader. Ideally, the co-therapists should work out their relationship and responsibilities before they decide to lead a group, but theory is often complicated by fact. Thomas Huxley, the biologist, refers to the finest theory defeated by the ugly fact. This is very much the case with co-therapy. All too often, the resistances of patients to the group experience are founded in the resistances of co-therapists to the exploration of their own problems in interaction. Even before they organize a group, *both* therapists should, ideally, interview and screen potential members of the group. From the outset, then, the patient is prepared for the experience of co-therapy. The patient may also be able to establish transference reactions from the first contact with the therapeutic situation. Actually, in a dynamic sense, an element of co-therapy is at work even before a patient enters the therapeutic situation. The patient who contacts a clinic establishes some type of relationship with a significant figure at the clinic, whether it be a receptionist or intake worker. This contact plays a part in the intrapsychic reaction of the patient. And the patient who calls a private practitioner for an appointment almost certainly reacts to the answering service, nurse, or secretary. Therapy is an ongoing process and includes many people who are not professional therapists.

Often therapists overlook the fact that they are being carefully observed by patients in the group setting. These same patients compare reactions while out of earshot of the therapists. Co-therapists should take note of their behavior, particularly if patients meet on their own before or after the regularly scheduled group meeting or if they arrive at or leave the group meeting together.

In private practice the question of fees should be clarified before a patient enters a group led by co-therapists. There are no definite rules concerning payment. Some therapists are paid directly by the patient; others divide the fee equally.

If a patient wishes to have an individual session with one of the therapists, both therapists should know about it. Otherwise, the patient may trap one therapist into his patterns of resistance.

A therapist's personal preference for a patient is quickly noted by the group. In the same way that a therapist may unconsciously keep patients in individual therapy because of his unresolved problems in sharing them with a group, he may unconsciously resent sharing patients with a co-thera-pist. Many patients are still working through their unresolved need to separate their parents. And some of these patients may try to separate the co-therapists—by creating emergency situations, for example. In such a situation, both therapists should meet with the patient in an individual session.

In the course of a group experience, changes occur in the lives of therapists. A team of therapists—Sadoff, Resnik, and Peters (1968)— described a long-term, continuous therapy group of convicted pedophiles on probation; they were being treated as part of a project to study the effectiveness of analytic group psychotherapy for sex offenders. One ther-apist, who had been conducting the group for three years, accepted a position in another city. At the time his co-therapist was a third year resident in psychiatry who had been a group member for one year. The transference phenomena became very intense among the group members and the therapists because of the change in leadership of the group.

The death of a leader also has a strong impact on a group. In 1947 Rosenthal described her experience with a group led by Paul Schilder, one of the pioneers in group psychotherapy. She participated for many con-secutive months in the group psychotherapy sessions conducted by Dr. Schilder before his death. It thus devolved upon her to help adjust these abandoned patients to the death of the father figure, a task beyond the psychological means at her disposal.

Even the most vociferous exponents of co-therapy have begun to recognize the problems that may occur. The patient may displace all his hostility onto one therapist rather than risk the censure of the other therapist, whom he prefers. Furthermore, the patient may be locked into feelings for one therapist and deny his ambivalent feelings. The danger is that the co-therapy technique may become meaningful to the therapists rather than to the patient.

If the decision is made to use co-therapists as ego models, the co-ther-apists should be quite clear as to their goals—both individually and in unison—so that they do not engage in a power struggle and vie for the attention and affection of members of the group. For example, co-therapists are useful in coping with the intense negative transference reactions that patients develop. These reactions are often intolerable for a patient to experience and may lead to strong attacks on the therapist, who is accused of being hostile. Indeed, the therapist may become hostile after prolonged attacks. Co-therapists often provide a splitting situation: One therapist is perceived as the good parent, while the other is perceived as the bad parent. In addition, other group members help the patient perceive the distortions or the reality in his complaints about the therapist.

Some group therapists who do not use a co-therapist approach may introduce a therapist into the group for a short time when a patient's anger is so overwhelming that it blocks group movement. Or they may refer the patient to another therapist until the aggression is worked through. MacLennan (1965) writes that poorly formed groups of disturbed children seem to need co-therapists, but in this situation one therapist seems to treat the children while the other merely watches them and acts like a policeman. This situation may arise when there are no limits set on the group.

> At a mental health clinic in the inner city of a metropolitan area, a group was made up of adolescent girls from emotionally and economically impoverished environments. The therapist was a childless psychiatrist, a woman who had an enormous need to be an earth mother. She proved to be very effective, was able to face the orality, and was completely feeding in her relationship with the girls. However, because of her inability to set limits for fear of arousing the teenagers and losing their love, a co-therapist was introduced to set up a structure of discipline. The original group therapist would not respond to another woman as co-therapist, since she feared the other woman would take away the affection of her children. A male co-therapist was effective as a disciplinarian, but he reinforced for several of the adolescents a picture of the male as punitive and nonloving, which did not help them in their heterosexual development.

TECHNIQUES

Probably the most sophisticated description of co-therapy was written by Demarest and Teicher in 1954. Their description is still valid. It was based on an experience with a group of five hospitalized schizophrenic patients who were in intensive psychotherapy for a period of a year and a half. Demarest and Teicher stated that their hypotheses should be viewed within the framework of the

> widely accepted ideas that the goal of therapy is to enable people to effect changes in life patterns and that transference is the enabling instrument, the working tool, which allows therapy to accomplish this goal.

Demarest and Teicher observed that, in group therapy, transference occurs on many levels of relationship:

> patient-patient, patient-therapist, patient-group, and therapist-group. Where there are co-therapists, it also occurs on the therapist-therapist level.

They defined transference as

the process in which a person projects a pattern of adaptation which was learned, developed, and adopted in a previous significant life situation from that previous situation to a current life situation; he then displaces the affect of the previous situation from that situation to the present situation.

The presence of co-therapists in the group described in the Demarest and Teicher paper impressed on them the intensity and variety of the transferences occurring in the group. They felt that the quality and availability of the transference phenomenon in this group was a product of the use of co-therapists of opposite sexes. As early as 1927, Trigant Burrow, one of the pioneer American psychoanalysts, described all underlying behavior in the group setting as transference. But the old arguments continue: Is transference in group therapy the same as transference in individual psychotherapy? Does it have the same qualities? Is transference diluted in a group?

Demarest and Teicher's group of five patients met twice a week for one-and-three-quarter-hour sessions. Although the therapists attempted to establish a careful balance—matching patients on the basis of verbal ability, type of illness, educational background, and motivation for psychotherapy —the balance did not work. There were too many external variables. Even so, say the investigators, the presence of male and female therapists made it possible for each patient to structure a family group, which allowed him to act out family conflicts and set up familial constellations in which problems of sibling rivalry and of mother-son and father-son struggles could be perceived and worked through. Furthermore, having therapists of both sexes allowed a patient to act out his problems with each sex in relation to the opposite sex.

When the woman therapist went on vacation, the group members expressed transference reactions toward the mother deserting them, and displaced their aggression to the male therapist, who remained as group leader. Thus Demarest and Teicher note:

> The absence of one therapist became a valuable device with which to precipitate feelings and fantasies on the therapist-group transference level that could not be experienced or expressed in the presence of both therapists.

The important feature here is that the therapists worked within a consistent theoretical framework. The mere fact that transference is present in a group is meaningless. Transference is a tool that must be consciously used to bring about change. One of the values of co-therapy is that it offers the possibility of more valid and objective observation and evaluation of different levels of the transference phenomenon. In the therapist-patient relationship, there is a process of working through, and generally only one therapist is centrally involved. The co-therapist is able to observe the relationship and the manner in which it expresses itself. Thus, one therapist can continuously check on the other.

Bardon (1966) notes that male and female co-therapists are usually reacted to as father and mother figures, respectively, and feels that patients work through their transference feelings toward the mother and father figures more rapidly in co-therapy than in one-to-one therapy. His groups of six to eight patients were composed of university students, with a generally equal sex distribution in the groups. His orientation was psychodynamic, and the goal was reconstruction of the patients' personalities. He found that the patients developed transference reactions to the actual relationship between the co-therapists and expected the co-therapists to show the same problems in their relationship that the patients' parents did. Consequently, the transferences developed not to the therapists as individuals but to their joint presence and interaction with each other.

This finding seems to validate the viewpoint of Gans (1962), who stated that the added transference possibilities offered by using co-therapists of opposite sexes are not necessarily of value. His experience was that the interplay between the therapists had many disadvantages for the group. He found a definite undercurrent of competition and rivalry between the co-therapists with a division along aggressive versus gentle or active versus passive lines.

Mintz (1965), one of the most enthusiastic supporters of co-therapy, goes beyond the co-therapy situation in which male and female therapists represent mother and father figures to a consideration of them as masculine and feminine authority. The patients see them then as models. In the author's opinion, this type of learning experience is, perhaps, not properly the function of trained psychotherapists.

Exponents of conjoint therapy, in which a patient works individually with one therapist and in group treatment with another, say that this type of therapy helps the patient work through his unresolved intrapsychic conflicts related to his relationship with one or both parents. Here, again, the suggestion is made to use therapists of different sexes. The hope and purpose is to bring oedipal and preoedipal problems to the surface much more quickly than in either individual psychotherapy or group therapy led by one therapist. The belief is that no transference deadlock will develop.

Mathis and Collins (1970a, b) report that, in a mandatory group therapy experience for exhibitionists, male and female co-leaders were used to simulate a family setting that would be nearly the reverse of the earlier pattern most of the patients had known. The group members knew that the male therapist was the organizer of the program, and he adopted an obviously leading role, without being overbearing or harsh. The female therapist remained relatively passive but never obsequious; she was understanding and kind but not seductive or susceptible to seduction. She allowed the patients to practice being masculine without the threat of reprisal or rejection. It was theorized that the patients' past relationships with women had kept them constantly anxious to prove their masculinity yet equally afraid of doing so. The female therapist needed considerable maturity and security in her own feminine identification to carry off her role in the group.

The therapists easily fell into fairly constant roles. The male therapist tended to confront the patients with their overt behavior and its effect on their lives. The female therapist interpreted the more subtle psychological factors. The patients rarely accepted these interpretations of dynamic factors during the first few months of therapy, since the mechanism of denial allowed them to hear exactly what they wished. The denial system became more and more difficult to maintain as the other group members began to make interpretations. The use of male and female co-therapists was felt to be highly valuable, but the authors of the study commented: "There is no reason to assume that it is essential."

Successful group therapy of exhibitionists without this combination of co-therapists has been reported by Witzig (1968). Most of the men in the group apparently viewed women as powerful and dangerous and might have been less likely to talk about their sexual conflicts and vulnerabilities if a woman had been present. With such a patient population, however, the presence of a woman may eventually facilitate the working through of problems with women when a male therapist is present to protect the patients.

In a community mental health clinic described by Teicher (1966), groups of disturbed adolescents from economically and emotionally deprived walks of life met once a week with two co-therapists of different sexes. The author is very specific in his statement about the therapists' roles:

> The therapist has many roles thrust upon him. He represents reality, authority, educator . . . the male therapist should be dominant in the group. Most of the girls in the groups here discussed had no father at home or in some Negro families the mother was very strongly dominant.

When co-therapists work with married couples, one therapist often serves as a balance wheel for his co-therapist, especially when unresolved problems of the therapist come to the surface. The expectation is that the co-therapists will not join in the neurotic behavior and attack either the group members or one another. In family therapy the co-therapists can help pick up faulty patterns of communication in the family, but the primary emphasis is on interaction phenomena. Unconscious conflicts or transference phenomena are largely ignored.

There is a difference between an active co-therapist who takes responsibility and an observer who does not take responsibility for the patients in a group. However, the observer is a person to whom patients do react and transfer. In the overemphasis on the interactional, the intrapsychic is often ignored. But the patient is always reacting, even if he does not care to share his reactions with the observer therapist or active co-therapists.

The more structured situational approach to co-therapy does not seem to this writer to be as relevant as the intrapsychic approach. To say that a male and a female therapist will serve as father and mother figures ignores clinical experience, especially with acutely disturbed patients, who often perceive the therapist of the *same sex* as father and mother. In essence, situational arrangements overlook the patients, particularly in clinical work with sex offenders. Also, transferences are not diluted in the experience of this writer. Therefore, the situational approach cannot be used exclusively.

SUPERVISION

Supervision of co-therapists presents formidable problems. The supervisor must be on guard against favoring one therapist at the expense of the other. He must stress the process of mutualism and not play one therapist against the other or ridicule one at the expense of the other. Both therapists should be present for the supervisory session. In the same way that therapists may discover many unresolved feelings toward patients in the group, supervisors may note for the first time patterns of preference toward one of the co-therapists.

CONCLUSION

If one practices co-therapy, he rapidly comes to grips with his unreal and overidealized expectations. The most experienced therapists have difficulty as they embark on this new collaborative venture. One therapist plus one therapist do not necessarily add up to better treatment. The new team of co-therapists may become quickly disillusioned. Whether they are able to stick it out and ask for help from one another is a test of their maturity. Unresolved problems of sibling rivalry and status needs rapidly come to the fore and can be handled with adequate supervision. However, therapists are not there to treat one another. Doing so is an abuse of the patient's trust. The therapists' primary responsibility is to the patient; on occasion, co-therapists have to be reminded of this responsibility.

The rewards of co-therapy are enormous. The challenges are great. If the two therapists agree to engage in authentic mutualism, the benefits to patients and therapists are endless.

BIBLIOGRAPHY

Adler, A., *Guiding the Child* (New York: Greenberg, 1930).

Adler, J., and Berman, I. R., "Multiple Leadership in Group Treatment of Delinquent Adolescents," *Int. J. Group Psychother.*, 10:213-225, 1960.

Bardon, E. J., "Transference Relations to the Relationship Between Male and Female Co-therapists in Group Psychotherapy," *J. Amer. Coll. Health Assoc.*, 14:287-289, No. 4, 1966.

Barrow, T., "The Problem of Transference," *Brit. J. Med. Psychol.*, 7:193-203, 1927.

Cameron, J. L., and Stewart, R. A. Y., "Observations on Group Psychotherapy with Chronic Psychoneurotic Patients in a Mental Hospital," *Int. J. Group Psychother.*, 5:346-360, 1955.

Demarest, E., and Teicher, A., "Transference in Group Therapy: Its Use by Co-therapists of Opposite Sexes," *Psychiatry*, 17:187-202, 1954.

Dreikurs, R., "Techniques and Dynamics of Multiple Psychotherapy," *Psychiat. Quart.*, 24:788-799, 1950.

Elmore, J. L., and Fowler, D. R., "Brief Group Psychotherapy with Unwed Mothers," *J. Med. Soc. New Jersey*, 67:19-23, 1970.

Fenichel, O., *The Psychoanalytic Theory of Neurosis* (New York: W. W. Norton, 1945).

Fink, H. K., "Adaptation of the Family Constellation in Group Psychotherapy," *Am. J. Psychother.*, 6:189-192, 1958.

Gans, R. W., "The Use of Group Co-Therapists in the Teaching of Psychotherapy," *Am. J. Psychother.*, 9:618-625, 1957.

———, "Group Co-therapists and the Therapeutic Situations: A Critical Evaluation," *Int. J. Group Psychother.*, 12:82-88, 1962.

Grunwald, H., and Casella, B., "Group Counseling with Parents," *Child Welfare*, 37:11-17, 1958.

Hadden, S. B., "The Utilization of a Therapy Group in Teaching Psychotherapy," *Am. J. Psychiat.*, 103:644-649, 1947.

Haley, J., *Strategies of Psychotherapy* (New York: Grune & Stratton, 1963).

Hulse, W. C., "The Social Meaning of Current Methods of Group Psychotherapy," *Group Psychother.*, 3:56-57, 1950.

———, Lulow, W. V., Rindsberg, B. K., and Epstein, N. B., "Transference Reactions in a Group of Female Patients to Male and Female Co-leaders," *Int. J. Group Psychother.*, 6:430-435, 1956.

Kasoff, A., "Advantages of Multiple Therapy with Adolescents," *Int. J. Group Psychother.*, 8:70-77, 1958.

Klapman, J. W., and Meyer, R. E., "The Team Approach in Group Psychotherapy," *Dis. Nerv. Syst.*, 18:95-97, 1957.

Kraus, R. F., "The Use of Symbolic Technique in the Group Psychotherapy of Chronic Schizophrenia," *Psychiat. Quart.*, 44:143-157, 1970.

Leoffler, F., and Weinstein, H. M., "The Co-therapist Method: Special Problems and Advantages," *Group Psychother.*, 6:189-192, 1954.

Lundin, W. H., and Aronov, B. M., "Use of Co-therapists in Group Psychotherapy," *J. Consult. Psychol.*, 16:77-80, 1952.

MacLennan, B., "Co-therapy," *Int. J. Group Psychother.*, 15:154-165, 1965.

Maldonado-Sierra, E. D., Trend, R. D., Fernandez-Marina, R., Flores-Gallardo, A., Vigoreauo-Rivera, J., and De Colon, L. S., "Cultural Factors in the Group Psychotherapeutic Process for Puerto Rican Schizophrenics," *Int. J. Group Psychother.*, 10:373-382, 1960.

Mathis, J. L., and Collins, M., "Mandatory Group Therapy for Exhibitionists," *Am. J. Psychiat.*, 126:1162-1167, 1970a.

———, "Progressive Phases in the Group Therapy of Exhibitionists," *Int. J. Group Psychother.*, 20:163-169, 1970b.

Mintz, E. E., "Transference in Co-therapy Groups," *J. Consult. Psychol.*, 1: 34-39, 1963.

———, "Male-female Co-therapists," *Am. J. Psychother.*, 19:293-301, 1965.

Moreno, J. L., ed., *Group Psychotherapy: A Symposium* (New York: Beacon House, 1954).

Mullan, H., and Rosenbaum, M., *Group Psychotherapy* (New York: Free Press, 1962).

Mullan, H., and Sangiuliano, I., "Multiple Psychotherapeutic Practice: Preliminary Report," *Am. J. Psychol.*, 14:560-565, 1960.

Rosenbaum, M., "Group Psychotherapy and Psycho-drama," in B. Wolman, ed., *Handbook of Clinical Psychology* (New York: McGraw-Hill, 1965), p. 1254.

Rosenthal, P., "The Death of the Leader in Group Psychotherapy," *Am. J. Orthopsychiat.*, 17:266-277, 1947.

Sadoff, R. L., Resnik, H. L. P., and Peters, J. J., "On Changing Group Therapists," *Psychiat. Quart.*, 43 (Suppl.): 156-166, 1968.

Slavson, S. R., "Discussion," *Int. J. Group Psychother.*, 10:225-226, 1960.

Teicher, J. D., "Group Psychotherapy with Adolescents," *Calif. Med.*, 105: 18-21, 1966.

Whitaker, C., "Teaching the Practicing Physician to do Psychotherapy," *Southern Med. J.*, 42:899-903, 1949.

———, and Malone, T., *The Roots of Psychotherapy* (New York: Blakiston, 1953).

Witzig, J. S., "The Group Treatment of Male Exhibitionists," *Am. J. Psychiat.*, 125:179-185, 1968.

30

HOMOGENEOUS VERSUS
HETEROGENEOUS GROUPS

William Furst

This presentation represents the opinions of my former associates, Dr. Lewis H. Loeser, Mrs. Thea Bry, and myself, and is derived from the experimental work and experience we have gained in group therapy during military service and in private practice.

The problem of the homogeneous versus heterogeneous group has interested us from the onset of our work. In using these terms we are referring to diagnostic and psychodynamic criteria. Although the terms may equally well be applied to homogeneity of sex, age, color, religion, and so on, we have used and are now using this terminology only in reference to diagnosis and underlying psychopathology. A homogeneous group then, is one in which a reasonable similarity in psychodynamics and pathology is known to exist among the members of the group. All other similarities or differences, in this discussion, are set aside.

Our accent has been placed on research techniques and we have employed the method of parallel and control group to throw further light on certain basic questions. We have, for example, material based on intensive study of two homogeneous and two heterogeneous groups, otherwise similar in make-up and nature. Each group has been carefully selected; detailed observations of each session were recorded by an observer, and cases were reasonably well followed after treatment. We use an interview type of therapy, analytically oriented, and our patients are all private patients on a free basis who have voluntarily applied for treatment.

Only conclusions will be given here.

Observations on homogeneous groups of anxiety neurotics lead to the following conclusions:

Reprinted from *Topical Problems of Psychotherapy*, Vol. II, 1960, pp. 170-173.

(1) Group identification takes place quickly and transferences are rapidly formed.

(2) Insight develops rapidly.

(3) Psychodynamics are more rapidly laid bare.

(4) Duration of treatment is lessened.

(5) Attendance is more regular.

(6) Resistances and interactions of a destructive nature are lessened.

(7) Intramural groups or cliques are uncommon.

(8) Recovery from symptoms is more rapid.

On the negative side, in dealing with homogeneous groups, we note:

(1) Homogeneous groups are difficult to put together. Careful screening, and a large number of patients from which to select, are necessary.

(2) Because of the absence of interaction factors the level of therapy is relatively superficial.

(3) Despite removal of symptoms, character structure is relatively untouched.

(4) The opportunity for reality testing is lessened by the absence of interaction with heterogeneous personalities.

(5) The opportunity to develop multiple and shifting transferences in accordance to needs is lacking.

Our experience with heterogeneous groups would lead to the following observations. On the negative side we would conclude that:

(1) Recovery takes place more slowly. Anxiety neurotics, for example, in a homogeneous group become symptom-free faster than in a heterogeneous group.

(2) Problems of interaction and resulting tensions within the group become magnified. The problems of the therapist are multiplied.

(3) Group identification takes place slowly.

(4) Transference to the therapist is delayed.

(5) Insight is slow in developing. Common denominators are difficult to work out in the field of psychodynamics.

(6) Attendance is likely to be more irregular.

On the positive side there is evidence that:

(1) Heterogeneous groups by their very nature tend to take the therapist, whether or not he so desires, into deeper levels of therapy.

(2) Character structure as well as symptom formation are influenced by the process of therapy.

(3) Reality testing is more adequate and thorough.

(4) Intragroup transferences of a diverse and shifting nature can be formed readily in the heterogeneous group in accordance with individual needs.

(5) Heterogeneous groups are easy to assemble and screening need not be as thorough.

As a result of our observations, derived from actual comparison of homogeneous and heterogeneous groups, certain broad generalizations are justified. We are firmly convinced that both types of groups can be utilized in group therapy. However, the make-up of the group has an important bearing on the type and nature of therapy, and we submit the following conclusions for consideration:

(1) Heterogeneous groups are necessary for activity therapy, for interaction therapy, and for group psychoanalysis. Homogeneous groups are not as suitable for these types of group therapy.

(2) Interview therapy, analytically oriented, can be carried out successfully with both homogeneous and heterogeneous groups.

The question of "level of therapy" is closely linked to the make-up of the group. It is difficult to do deep therapy with a homogeneous group. It is difficult not to do deep therapy with a heterogeneous group. Homogeneous groups do not put as much strain on the therapist and do not require the skill and experience on his part that heterogeneous groups require.

Homogeneous groups should then be chosen:

(a) When the interview type of therapy is utilized.

(b) When less profound and nonintensive therapy is indicated.

(c) When the therapist is not prepared or trained to handle deep levels of therapy.

(d) When the factor of time and expense are important.

Heterogeneous groups, on the other hand, are to be chosen:

(a) When deep levels of therapy are desired.

(b) When modification of character structure is necessary.

(c) When the training and experience of the therapist is adequate.

(d) When the time and expense are less important.

Glatzer has shown experimentally, by the creation of a heterogeneous group from two dissimilar homogeneous groups, that optimum treatment conditions and facilitation of the flow and handling of conflicting productions in the group were expedited.

Schwartz and Wolf have recently reported highly pertinent observations on heterogeneous and homogeneous groups as follows:

In Homogeneous Groups:

(1) There is created a limited and limiting form of therapy.

(2) There is bound to be more hostility in seeing oneself in others.

(3) There is a limit to any kind of intercommunication because the group analyzand starts with the assumption "I am like everybody else here," thus limiting comparisons and need to change.

(4) Interpretive interventions of the therapist always focus the group

analyzand on intrapsychic rather than interpsychic examination because of the sameness of all the members.

(5) There is a greater tendency in the homogeneous group to act out, to be more isolated from reality, from differences, and from the rest of the culture.

(6) A teaching or a form of social group may be more efficient if homogeneous.

In Heterogeneous Groups:

(1) There is opportunity to work through the problems of difference both with peers and authorities.

(2) Isolation is reduced by experiencing multiple reactivity possibilities.

(3) There is less mirror imaging and less identification.

(4) There are more transference and countertransference reactions, also more reality testing and working through.

(5) Superficially, at least, more interpersonal communication than intrapsychic preoccupation is encouraged.

(6) Eventually, intrapsychic communication is stimulated by virtue of comparison of individual with individual, because of differences.

(7) In the beginning, patients may act out more, but ultimately they will solve their problems.

(8) Differences do not have to come only from the authority figure, as in homogeneous groups, but many come from the peers.

In conclusion, one can make the following generalization:

Level of therapy and make-up of the group are factors which are closely correlated. Any discussion of one must involve the other factor. Neither homogeneous nor heterogeneous groups are best. They are to be used in accordance with the goals of the therapist.

31

CONCERNING THE SIZE
OF THERAPY GROUPS

Joseph J. Geller

The size of therapy groups is related to various techniques and depends upon their aims and goals. In general, the purpose of any psychotherapy is to bring about in the psychiatrically sick person more satisfactory and more effective relatedness to others. Group-psychotherapy techniques serve this purpose by adapting many of the principles of individual psychotherapy, as well as bringing into play two important aspects of group psychotherapy; namely, the effective utilization of group interaction for therapeutic ends and the employment of facilities to reach greater numbers of patients. Experience has shown that there are different sizes of groups that can be related to the different levels of therapeutic aims.

These levels of psychotherapy can be listed as: (1) those approaching the depth, breadth, and totality of psychoanalytic therapy; (2) the analysis and alleviation of the major presenting problems of a patient with these limited goals in view; (3) the use of repressive-inspirational techniques to strengthen the control exercised over symptoms; and (4) the use of group-orientation techniques. The various sizes of groups will be discussed in relation to these levels of therapy. As a general rule, it has been found that there is a correlation between the size of the group and the depth of therapy achieved: The depth of therapy decreases as the size of the group increases.

(1) In the first level of therapy mentioned, the psychoanalytic level requires the smallest size of groups. As few as three or four patients are included by some, while others have from six to ten patients in a group. The intensity of therapy, the need thoroughly to explore data presented by each of the patients, and the close attention given to an understanding of the many aspects of the interpersonal relations within the group, all require a fairly small group.

Reprinted from *The International Journal of Group Psychotherapy*, Vol. I, No. 2, June 1951, pp. 1-2.

(2) The next level is that in which efforts are directed toward handling one or more specific problem areas for a given patient. While psychodynamic concepts similar to those used in the foregoing level are here similarly employed, a more general approach to the treatment problem is used. As a consequence, slightly larger groups are permissible. From eight to fifteen patients is the size commonly allowed for a group of this nature. The essential difference between this level and the deeper one mentioned above is a quantitative, rather than qualitative one.

(3) Still larger groups are permissible in the repressive-inspirational approach to therapy. From thirty to fifty patients are brought together here. It is even possible, although not quite so effective for the individual patient, for such a group to work with one hundred or more people. For this type of therapy, the group is the vehicle par excellence for the development of mass-emotional phenomena which support and strengthen the individual's repressive abilities.

(4) The largest groups are found possible with the most superficial approach to psychotherapy: the guidance and orientation method. Here, theoretical and practical aspects of psychological functioning are presented to interested groups. Fifty or more patients in a group can conveniently be helped with this approach. The larger the size of the group, however, the less opportunity there is for individual discussion of points raised by the material presented.

We see, then, that therapy groups are roughly of four sizes: those under ten patients, eight to fifteen patients, thirty to fifty patients, and over fifty patients. These particular sizes are related to the nature and depth of the psychotherapy contemplated. It has been found that the more intensive and individually directed the therapy, the smaller the size of the group.

A subject related to sizes of groups that, for completeness, may briefly be considered here is that of the make-up of the professional component of the therapy group. As in individual psychotherapy, the usual arrangement consists of one professional person in the group as the therapist. Several modifications of this are made possible by the nature of the group structure. It is quite feasible to have a second professional person present to act as an "observer." This enables the therapist more effectively to validate his procedures and permits more adequate record keeping where this is desired. It is possible also to have the second professional person in the group act as an observer at times and at others change places with the therapist. Thus there is an "alternate therapist," both to maintain continuity of therapy in the absence of the original therapist, as well as to permit of more extensive transference phenomena than occur with a single therapist. Experiments have also been carried out with multiple therapists working simultaneously, from two to five persons being the usual number.

32

THE SUITABILITY FOR THE GROUP EXPERIENCE

Hugh Mullan
Max Rosenbaum

Careful screening of patients is a necessary responsibility when psychoanalytic psychotherapy is undertaken. However, there is no guarantee for psychotherapeutic effectiveness even when the "best" selection technique is employed, because a therapy group is more than just a group of individual patients. There are constantly changing configurations in the group, and different patterns of interpersonal relationships occur in each group and, indeed, at each group meeting. If the beginning group therapist carefully researches the literature on selection of patients for group therapy, he is apt to become confused by the contradictory statements concerning criteria for group suitability. Some group therapists stress only personality dynamics, while others use diagnostic classifications.

A good deal of confusion about suitability is related to the different philosophical systems that motivate group psychotherapists. Those therapists who value an intellectual approach to group psychotherapy will be governed accordingly in their selection of patients. The fact that their goals are generally carefully determined influences their patient selection. Therapists who value the affective and human experience in group psychotherapy will not be doctrinaire or specific, and they will take more risks. Since we believe the group therapy experience to be an experience of creative change for the individual who is hamstrung by his inner emotional conflicts and by his outer perceptual distortions, and since we believe that beyond man's destructiveness or egocentrism, or whatever else it has been called, there are also qualities which compel growth—that is, a desire to change and a desire to relate to other human beings in the great

Reprinted from Hugh Mullan and Max Rosenbaum, *Group Psychotherapy: Theory and Practice* (New York: Free Press of Glencoe; Macmillan Publishing Co., 1962), pp. 93–105. © 1962 Macmillan Publishing Company. Reprinted with permission.

enterprise of creativity—we express an essential optimism regarding the patient's capacities. We are skeptical of overemphasis on pathology in the selection of patients for group therapy. Does not the psychotherapist who is overly concerned about pathological functioning deny the many growth possibilities in the patient-person who comes to his office or who sees him in the clinic, agency, or hospital?

It may be helpful to survey suitability from two points of view, the patient's and the therapist's.

In a report by a patient of our acquaintance on the suitability of the group, beyond the overidealization of the therapist which colors this protocol, there is communicated the intensity of feeling and movement that is to be found in the therapy group. In contrast, it is of interest to survey the varying opinions of therapists on the selection of patients for the group experience.

One writer[1] complains that others ignore the fact that one cannot transpose to group selection the same criteria that one uses in individual therapy. He notes that little attention has been paid to the personality of the group therapist. For example, a strong and directive therapist who leads a group of patients in a basically repressive-inspirational fashion will attract to himself and select relatively dependent patients.

The early group psychotherapists, Pratt, Lazell, and Marsh, in working with specific groups of patients, apparently were concerned about the possibilities of treating groups of patients and spent little time in questioning suitability. When Lazell worked with chronic schizophrenics in a mental hospital, he was so enthusiastic about the use of a group that he simply organized those patients in a group. This practice may still occur. In an institutional framework patients can be ordered to a psychotherapy group.

In 1935 Wender, an early worker in group psychotherapy, stated that his experience indicated:[2]

> that group psychotherapy is applicable only to disorders in which intellectual impairment is absent and in which some degree of affect is retained. It is believed that the following groups lend themselves to this type of treatment: (a) early schizophrenics where the delusional trends are not fully systematized and in which hallucinatory phenomena are completely absent; where the splitting of the personality is not marked and there is no blocking; (b) depressions without marked retardation and those who libidinize their ideation—depression *sine* depression; (c) psychoneuroses, with the exception of severe compulsion neuroses of long duration.

Slavson, who has been specific in his therapy goals, wrote in 1943:[3]

> Group therapy is not a blanket, universally applicable treatment method. Nor can it substitute for individual treatment where such treatment is indicated. Deep-rooted neurotic anxieties or compulsive manifestations cannot be treated in groups alone, just as many character malformations and habit disorders cannot be affected by individual treatment. The area

in which the greatest clarification will be needed is the delineation of problems in personality that are most accessible to one type of treatment as against the other. Some effort in this direction has already been made,* but much more remains to be done in this direction.

But apparently some group psychotherapists, as they gained more and more experience, began to question the earlier exclusivity in determining which patients were suitable for groups. Loeser in 1956 wrote:[4]

What are the criteria for selection of group patients? At one time we had an elaborate and rather complex set of criteria, based on psycho-dynamics, character structure and symptom production. In recent years my personal viewpoint has swung over toward a simple and uncomplicated type of reasoning. In general, today, based on considerable experience, I do not think the criteria for selection of patients for group therapy differ at all from selection of patients for individual therapy. Those patients who are good candidates for psychotherapy, who possess reasonable ego strength, are well motivated, etc. will do well in either form of treatment. On the contrary, the refractory patient, the untreatable patient, the difficult patient will remain just that, whatever the mode of therapy. I no longer have any sharp criteria by which one patient is selected for the group, another for individual treatment. The exceptions are those obvious categories referred to above—the psychotic patient, the addict, the retarded, the homosexual, the psychopath and certain severely ill and demoralized patients who would require adjunct therapy such as drugs, shock therapy or sanitarium care. My conclusion, then, is to the effect that there does not seem to be any sharp criteria by which patients can or must be selected for the group. If they are reasonably good candidates for psychotherapy in general, they will do well in any properly structured group.

The central question that Loeser passes over is what makes a reasonably good candidate for psychotherapy. This is still a dilemma confronting all psychotherapists. All of the kinds of patients that Loeser would *not* treat in a group have been treated in a group setting by other therapists. Barnett[5] combined group psychotherapy and insulin subcoma with patients who did not respond to other methods. He found that 20 per cent of such patients improved markedly and another 50 per cent improved moderately. Rosow[6] introduced group therapy at a state prison in California and organized eighty-five groups totaling 700 men, about 65 to 70 per cent of the prison population. His groups were organized along psychoanalytic lines, and he was quite enthusiastic about the efficacy of the method in a prison facility. He points out that the administration must be supportive of the therapeutic program, a point that we have also stressed. He differentiated

* S. R. Slavson, *An Introduction to Group Therapy* (New York: Commonwealth Fund, 1943), chap. 4.; "The Treatment of Aggression through Group Therapy," *Am. J. Orthopsychiat.* 13 (1943):419-427.

between groups that are supportive—for patients bordering on psychosis who are unable to tolerate an uncovering type of therapy—and groups in which prisoners were similar in their psychodynamics, their capacity for ego integration was adequate, and there was receptivity for therapy. He also felt that members of these groups should be in the same age category.

The continuing differences between therapists as to which patients are suitable for group psychotherapy appear to be rooted in the therapist's conception of the nature of psychotherapy. Joel and Shapiro noted in 1950:[7]

> Diagnostic label per se does not appear to be a very useful index of capacity for social interaction. Group psychotherapy has been conducted with patients of all nosological categories . . . it is safe to state that some patients will respond more quickly or profoundly to group therapy than others, and that these differences are less due to differences in diagnosis than to individual differential capacity for establishing relationships with people. Group therapists, therefore, are beginning to lose interest in diagnostic labels.

Yet in 1955 Slavson[8] still claimed that therapists should be careful not to impose a treatment of their preference rather than a treatment to suit the needs of the patient. He presented an extremely detailed classification for selecting therapy groups composed of children, adolescents, and adults. Since he stated that "the ideal criterion for grouping of patients is their similarity of psychological syndrome and pathology," this basic view toward homogeneity of central problem for all patients influenced all of his criteria for selection. With the passage of time there seems to be some minor modification of his views, for in 1961 he wrote:[9]

> With patients in a state of remission, who are in good contact and have tolerably good ego strengths and defenses, quasi-analytic and even analytic group therapy can be tried. This, however, has to be done with great caution since psychotherapy in which unconscious drives and affect-laden memories and experiences are uncovered is most often not suitable for borderline, latent, or active schizophrenic patients. This rule applies variously according to the defensive resources of a particular patient, however.

He also cautioned:

> It is important that not more than one or two borderline patients be included in an analytic group . . . .

With reference to the treatment of the borderline schizophrenic, Spotnitz, who has had considerable experience with this patient group, noted in 1957 that ". . . the attitude to group psychotherapy for the severely disturbed patient which is reflected in the current literature is becoming more favorable."[10] He favored a homogeneous group of these patients.

In 1956 Pinney was optimistic about including such patients in a group but complained that "perhaps the most difficult problem we have encountered in this group stemmed from the poor choice of a patient."[11]

Graham, the Australian group psychotherapist, noted in 1959:[12]

> It has been my practice to treat mainly psychoneurotics in groups. Patients with strong paranoid tendencies, who have little insight into their condition, tend to be too disturbing an element. Some early schizophrenics seem to do well, but I have seen others deteriorate.

Wolman, based on his work with schizophrenics, stated in 1960:[13]

> Not all latent schizophrenics can be admitted to psychotherapeutic groups. Two categories should be excluded, namely those who cannot stand the group and those whom the group cannot stand. To the first category belong all those who have been much too hurt in their social relationships and therefore should not be exposed to additional and unpredictable social experiences. . . . The other category consists of patients who tend to act out. The group might not be able to tolerate them or some members of the group might be hurt and drop out. . . .

From the broad category of schizophrenics and their suitability for group psychotherapy, there has been recently increasing definition of the dynamics involved. Since Wolman writes from the viewpoint of a therapist who stresses the interpersonal relationship, he is concerned with this phenomenon in a group.

Some group therapists who use a more Freudian approach to work with groups stress a different concept of suitability. Glatzer[14] places basically compulsive personality types in one group and basically hysterical personality types in another group.

An interesting experience is that of Cameron and Freeman,[15] who found that when they chose for group treatment patients suffering from depressive psychoses who had not responded to convulsive therapy, the selection resulted in the presence of patients of different diagnostic categories.

Klapman, in a straightforward clinical presentation in 1957, related his experiences in treatment of patients in a mental hospital:[16]

> Because of prevalent conditions in many mental hospitals . . . it is very difficult to select patients for group psychotherapy and to maintain the selection once the group has started. In the hurdy gurdy of the large institution practices there is usually a shortage of personnel and often no one available to bring patients to the sessions nor to escort them back to their wards. The list of group therapy patients the therapist may send to the attendants may not be adhered to, and attendants may send chance selections, chosen by criteria known only to themselves. Group therapy membership becoming thus scrambled a therapist in sheer resignation may decide to do what he can with what he actually receives and to see what happens when the chips are allowed to fall where they will.

He asked, "Can any therapeutic results flow from such chaotic circumstances?" Klapman concluded that if the therapist employs a structured, leader-led, textbook-mediated approach, with a strong emphasis on lectures by the group therapist and on patients' reading selected material with the group, "from an initially unpromising group of deteriorated appearing patients the group therapy revealed some individuals with residual capacity. Over 25 per cent of these patients improved sufficiently to be discharged."

In 1954 Freedman and Sweet[17] presented a detailed statement concerning selection procedures. In view of Klapman's findings it is interesting to note theirs. Freedman and Sweet researched therapeutic groups, composed of five or six patients, in which intensive therapy was carried out. An effort was made to avoid homogeneity with respect to diagnosis. They found that "members of groups uniform with respect to personality structure tend to reinforce each other's defenses" and concluded that the group is not the best therapeutic medium for neurotics with well-organized ego structures and for character disorders with strong defenses and good reality-orientation. For these patients, individual therapy is the choice of treatment.

They found that the "chaotic and inchoate egos"—patients with strong schizophrenic trends who have experienced emotional deprivation and the lack of good identification figures and who live in a chronic state of agitation, suffering from strong feelings of isolation—are to be placed in a group. For them the group will serve as the steppingstone to an intensive psychotherapeutic experience to be carried out individually. Freedman and Sweet would also include in a group "emotional illiterates" who have "little or no familiarity with the language of feeling," rigid personalities who have an inflexible social role and cannot bear any form of dependency, and "belligerently demanding and exceptionally coercive patients." Thus, group therapy is recommended for the "sickest" types of outpatients. Their recommendation runs counter to the general decisions we have cited.

It may have been the general confusion in the area of patient selection that led Jerome Frank and his co-workers to attempt a different approach and describe this in a series of papers.[18] They suggested that the patterns exhibited by patients in early meetings of therapeutic groups may be used to diagnose and classify patients rather than the clinical symptoms most therapists use. They identified several behavioral patterns: first, a "help-rejecting complainer," a patient who continually asked the group for help, often without actually requesting such help verbally while at the same time either explicitly or implicitly rejecting it. This same patient would constantly attempt to prove that he needed more help than any other patient.

Second, they found a "doctor's assistant," a patient who would attempt to impress all other patients in the group, defend authority, please the group therapist, offer advice to other patients, and hide his own difficulties. The third type of patient is the "self-righteous moralist," who has a constant need to convince others that he is right and has suffered nobly and has sacrificed himself because of ethical beliefs, which account for his failures to achieve status in life. He is a "noble character."

Frank and his colleagues concluded that the therapist who identifies his patient's behavioral patterns according to these three categories will have a much easier time organizing the group and predicting its movement. This type of guide will then lead to a clearer diagnostic framework for neurotic behavior. In their program of research, Frank and his colleagues excluded patients with a diagnosis of organic brain disease, antisocial character disorder, alcoholism, overt psychosis, or mental deficiency. Apparently even more important than diagnosis is the finding that patients who have high expectancies for the helpfulness of treatment are most suitable for all forms of psychotherapy.[19]

Neighbor and his co-workers,[20] after work in an outpatient mental hygiene clinic, became convinced that group psychotherapy is the "treatment of choice for a substantial percentage of patients whose problems are susceptible to clinic therapy of any type." The patients they describe were primarily seen in groups, and only rarely for individual therapy. The diagnostic groups they treated included a mixture of patients with psychoneurotic, psychophysiologic, and personality disorders, and occasional ambulatory schizophrenics. They excluded from groups patients who displayed tendencies toward overt suicidal, homicidal, or infanticidal acts. Also excluded were patients who experienced extreme frustration in sharing a therapist with the group, those who experienced extreme anxiety as a result of group participation, and those with an imminent or active psychosis who might deteriorate further because of the material discussed in the group.

Sometimes the therapist may be overprotective of the group or fail to recognize the flexibility of group members. Thus, one therapist writes:[21]

> There is, however, an advantage to the borderline patients in being part of a "healthy" (nonpsychotic) group environment and identifying with healthier patients. . . . But it is essential that the pre-psychotic patient should not be bizarre or so markedly different from the other patients as to make them uncomfortable . . . .

This has not been our experience. When patients have experienced a break with reality within the group setting, other patients in the group have been extremely helpful and warm and, apparently, nonrejecting. This has resulted in patients' experiencing and working through a psychotic episode in the group.

Since we are risk taking and experiential in our group therapy endeavor and essentially optimistic about the patient's capacity for growth, we are not concerned with a particular diagnosis. The concept of the diagnosis moves toward the direction of selection—a more static concept. "Selection" has been defined in biology as any process that results, or tends to result, in preventing individuals or groups of organisms from surviving and propagating, and in allowing others to do so. "Suitability" is defined as that which is suited to one's needs, wishes, or condition. A synonym for select would be choice; a synonym for suitable would be compatible—which is more in accord with our concept of group therapy.

We are concerned with the patient's capacity for relatedness. We look in his background for some evidence of an experience in mutuality in relationships with family figures or parent surrogates. Rather than classify the patient in any diagnostic category, we attempt to determine his compatibility with others. Therefore we see diagnosis as much broader than its usual meaning—as scientific scrutiny rather than symptom assessment. The patient's desire for a mutuality of experience, in which the other individual is seen as essentially human rather than as an object, is a major factor in determining group suitability. A patient who has experienced minimal gratification in early childhood relationships will require extensive individual therapy before he is ready to trust himself to the group experience. The patient's suitability for the group experience is determined by his belief in mutualism. If his life has been composed of a series of power operations, he will attempt to "wheel and deal" in the group. This behavior may evoke such anger or rejection on the part of other group members that group interaction will cease.

If it is at all possible to set up specific standards for group suitability, we would agree with Leopold[22] and say that any patient is a potential candidate for group psychotherapy in private practice or in an outpatient clinic who fulfills the following requirements:

(1) He has reality contact.
(2) He can be related to interpersonally.
(3) He has sufficient flexibility so that he may reduce or heighten intragroup tensions.
(4) He can serve at times as a catalyst for the group.

To set up standards in a restrictive fashion, we would say that a patient should *not* be placed in a group when:

(1) He paralyzes group interaction over an extended period of time.
(2) He cannot be reached by other group members because of his constant chaotic behavior, stimulated by his own unconscious feelings.
(3) He is constantly in a state of acute anxiety, and his behavior makes him a burden and responsibility to the group.
(4) He shows destructive, antisocial behavior, impulse-motivated, which evokes reality-based fears in other group members.

A patient who still maintains some reality contact would be the patient who has been described as borderline schizophrenic. This patient has not become completely autistic. The group setting permits him to move at his own speed; he can relate to the group and withdraw without pressure. He observes other group members, who often present healthy identifications.

A severely disturbed psychotic patient, who is unable to follow the verbal pace of a group, or who is unwilling to face the world of reality from which he does not obtain gratification, would usually be unsuitable for the group. The anxiety level in the active group exposes more and more psychotic material for such a patient, and the group participation becomes unbearable for him. In an institutional setting, where the therapy is more directive and leader led, these patients obtain relief from the social relatedness of the group experience and gradually become willing to relate to other group members.

The same anxiety-provoking material that makes it inadvisable for the acute psychotic to be placed in a group outside of an institutional setting will keep the patient who is initially suffering from acute anxiety at fever pitch in a group. The acutely anxious patient contributes little or nothing to the group experience since he does not move toward any mutualism. He simply looks for relief of anxiety.

Similarly, the acutely depressed patient may be unable to profit from the group. The tremendous anger, which so often is at the core of the depression, is not released by the group movement; rather it is more blocked. The group members often sense the aggression beneath the depression, and the depressed patient is unable to face this awareness on the part of other group members. He then becomes more depressed or withdraws from the group. Such a patient needs intensive individual therapy before a group experience is contemplated.

Patients who have the capacity to heighten group tension and aid group movement have been labeled *provocateurs*. While they are generally helpful and perceptive about other group members and stimulate group movement, their function is usually limited to their capacity to antagonize. Often these patients are unwilling to explore beyond antagonizing other patients. On occasion, when the patterns of these patients are attacked by other group members, they are unable to participate any further in a group, and must be withdrawn and offered individual therapy.

Patients who have never experienced primary gratifying relationships in infancy—described by some as oral or dependent or narcissistic or a combination of all three—must first experience a gratifying experience with the parent figure, the therapist. Only after this prolonged period of individual treatment, possibly six months to one year, can these patients be considered suitable for the group and willing to experience mutualism. Some group therapists continue to see such patients in combined therapy—that is, both individual and group treatment. The intensity of the group experience is too overwhelming for these patients if they are placed in a group after limited individual therapy. (Such patients include narcotic addicts and alcoholics who are best seen in a homogeneous group where the therapy is less intense. The alcoholic, with his focus on his own desires and the gratification of them, burdens the group.) If these oral patients have never experienced a gratifying relationship with the therapist, they drop out of the group and leave therapy altogether. As these patients feel more secure with the therapist and finally enter a group, the presence of other group members becomes educational, and they learn something about social relationships.

The individual who is overtly destructive—actively homicidal, for example—is unsuitable for the group. One therapist has described in a workshop how he dealt with such a patient, who occasionally would carry hand grenades with him to a group meeting. The therapist would sit next to this patient and serve as an ego control. While this is an ambitious maneuver, it would appear to place an unfair burden upon the other group members. Another therapist has described her experience with an extremely antisocial patient, in which the group accepted this patient while she was inclined to reject him. In this particular group most of the members were not only warm to the patient but also unafraid of him physically. The fact that a majority of the group members were theological students may have played some part in the process. Overt psychopaths who after a long period of treatment finally develop a relationship with the therapist may become "socialized" enough to enter a group. If they have a long history of anti-social behavior, there is a question of group suitability.

Some therapists suggest that the habitual monopolist who feels compelled to dominate the group by any and every measure be excluded from the group. These patients defend themselves against acute anxiety by compulsive talking. The group members become extremely frustrated, and there is no interaction. A skilled therapist who has a strong relationship with such a patient may be able to place the patient in the group and point out to him that silence would finally expose the intense insecurity and anxiety that the patient is unwilling to face and must mask by talking.

Similar to the monopolist but actually quite different dynamically is the patient who paralyzes group interaction because he conceives of psychotherapy as relief from pressing environmental problems. This patient has no desire to explore or gain insight but merely looks for a speedy solution. The group members cannot offer speedy solutions to immediate environmental problems, and a feeling of frustration develops which blocks the group movement; members fall into the trap of giving advice and there is no interaction.

Because there is little to be done for patients who are terminal and dying of an apparently incurable disease, psychotherapy in a group is not indicated for them. The group becomes discouraged and frustrated because of inability to help such a patient. A general attitude of pessimism develops in the group, and therapy becomes a much more difficult task for patients who are already feeling discouraged about living. There are exceptions, however. In a situation in which a group member was found to be suffering from an incurable disease after she had been in group therapy, she was permitted to reenter the group after hospitalization.

We would include in a group patients who are discouraged about living and have ventilated suicidal feelings. The aggression that is often found behind such feelings comes to the surface more quickly within the group framework. Further, patients who experience intensive reconstructive therapy in a group experience deep feelings of despair.

It has been our experience that the sadomasochistic patient is difficult to work with in a group. His constant pattern of suffering first traps the group because it is quite sympathetic. Then, as the group members become aware of the pattern at work, they become enraged by what they consider a ruse and proceed to attack this patient. Because this feeds the patient's need to suffer, no therapy results, and there is a standstill for the entire group.

It is important for the therapist to differentiate between the mentally retarded and the emotionally blocked. A patient who is of true borderline intelligence will have great difficulty in accommodating to a group. A patient who is blocked emotionally and therefore functioning on a minimal intellectual level will generally improve within the group setting.

As the group therapist gains experience, he will become less selective and more concerned with suitability. He will question the appropriateness of the group experience and constantly work with the patient's uniqueness and individuality. He will not be bound by rigid criteria.

To summarize, the group therapist should look for suitability in the patient, based upon the patient's early life experiences and desire to engage in the mutualism of a psychotherapeutic group. This is more important than any effort on the part of the therapist to classify the patient in a diagnostic category and then decide on the wisdom of treating this category in a group.

REFERENCES

1. D. Shaskan, "Selection of Patients for Group Psychotherapy," *Postgrad. Med.*, 23:174-177, 1958.
2. L. Wender, "The Dynamics of Group Psychotherapy and Its Application," *J. Nerv. Ment. Dis.*, 84:54-60, 1936.
3. S. R. Slavson, "Values of the Group in Therapy," *Newsletter* of the Am. Assn. of Psychiatric Social Workers, 13, no. 3, Winter 1943-1944.
4. L. Loeser, "The Role of Group Therapy in Private Practice," *J. Hillside Hosp.*, 5:460-467, 1956.

5. G. J. Barnett, "Group Psychotherapy as an Adjunct to Insulin Subcoma Treatment," *Int. J. Group Psychother.*, 9:62-70, 1959.

6. H. M. Rosow, "Some Observations on Group Therapy with Prison Inmates," *Arch. Criminal Psychodynam.*, 1:866-897, 1955.

7. W. Joel, and D. Shapiro, "Some Principles and Procedures for Group Psychotherapy," *J. Psychol.*, 29:77-88, 1950.

8. S. R. Slavson, "Criteria for Selection and Rejection of Patients for Various Types of Group Psychotherapy," *Int. J. Group Psychother.*, 5:3-30, 1955.

9. S. R. Slavson, "Group Psychotherapy and the Nature of Schizophrenia," *Int. J. Group Psychother.*, 11:3-32, 1961.

10. H. Spotnitz, "The Borderline Schizophrenic in Group Psychotherapy," *Int. J. Group Psychother.*, 7:155-274, 1957.

11. E. L. Pinney, "Reactions of Outpatient Schizophrenics to Group Psychotherapy," *Int. J. Group Psychother.*, 6:147-151, 1956.

12. F. W. Graham, "Observations on Analytic Group Psychotherapy," *Int. J. Group Psychother.*, 9:150-157, 1959.

13. B. B. Wolman, "Psychotherapy with Schizophrenics," *Int. J. Group Psychother.*, 10:301-312, 1960.

14. H. T. Glatzer, "Selection of Members for Group Therapy," *Am. J. Orthopsychiat.*, 17:477-483, 1947.

15. J. L. Cameron, and T. Freeman, "Group Psychotherapy in Affective Disorders," *Int. J. Group Psychother.*, 6:235-257, 1956.

16. J. W. Klapman, "The Unselected Group in Mental Hospitals and Group Treatment of the Chronic Schizophrenics," *Dis. Nerv. System*, 20:17-23, January, 1959.

17. M. B. Freedman and B. S. Sweet, "Some Specific Features of Group Psychotherapy and Their Implications for Selection of Patients," *Int. J. Group Psychother.*, 4:355-368, 1954.

18. D. Rosenthal, J. D. Frank, and E. H. Nash, "The Self-Righteous Moralist in Early Meetings of Therapeutic Groups," *Psychiat.*, 17:215-223, 1954; J. D. Frank, J. B. Margolin, E. H. Nash, A. R. Stone, F. Varon, and E. Ascher, "Two Behavior Patterns in Therapeutic Groups and Their Apparent Motivation," *Hum. Relat.*, 5:289-317, 1952; J. D. Frank, E. Ascher, J. B. Margolin, H. Nash, A. R. Stone, and E. Varon, "Behavioral Patterns in Early Meetings of Therapeutic Groups," *Am. J. Psychiat.*, 108:771-778, 1952.

19. E. H. Nash, J. Frank, L. H. Gleidman, S. Imber, and A. R. Stone, "Some Factors Related to Patients Remaining in Group Psychotherapy," *Int. J. Group Psychother.*, 7:264-274, 1957; J. Frank, L. Gleidman, S. Imber, A. Stone, and E. Nash, "Patients' Expectancies and Relearning as Factors Determining Improvement in Psychotherapy," *Am. J. Psychiat.*, 115: 961-968, 1959.

20. J. Neighbor, M. Beach, D. T. Brown, D. Kevin, and J. S. Visher, "An Approach to the Selection of Patients for Group Psychotherapy," *Ment. Hyg.*, 42:243-254, 1958.

21. Slavson, "Group Psychotherapy," *op. cit.*

22. H. Leopold, "Selection of Patients for Group Psychotherapy," *Am. J. Psychother.*, 11:634-637, July 1957.

33

NONVERBAL COMMUNICATIONS IN GROUP PSYCHOTHERAPY

Milton Miles Berger

INTRODUCTION

Improvement of the processes of communication with and to one-self and others is one of the goals of all psychotherapies, whether the therapist is consciously aware of this or not. To bring man closer to the whole reality of himself and others involves expanding his awareness of and capacity to utilize channels of communication which are potentially available to all men.

Definition: Nonverbal communications are all those manifest and latent messages, other than verbal, which reach ourselves and others about ourselves and others and the time-space continuum of the world we live in. These messages may be perceived through any of our bodily senses such as seeing, hearing, smelling, tasting, touching and through thinking, feeling, dreaming, intuiting as well as extrasensory and other ways still unknown but in process. Expression, transmission, perception, and evaluation are aspects of the communication process. That which is communicated by its absence is often at least as significant if not more significant than that communicated by its presence.

In this paper my use of the term "group psychotherapy" refers to group-psychoanalytic psychotherapy which utilizes free associations, dreams, fantasies, transference-countertransference reactions, verbal and nonverbal communications, and focuses upon bringing that which is unconscious into awareness wherever this is considered therapeutic. Experiencing without awareness may also be in the direction of health. There is an analysis of individual and group processes involved in the interactions and transactions which occur, and our goal is growth and increased use of

Reprinted in slightly condensed form from *The International Journal of Group Psychotherapy*, Vol. VIII, No. 2, April 1958, pp. 161-178.

available constructive forces as well as development of creative potentials in each individual in the group in his strivings toward self-fulfillment. Believing we cannot survive in a completely individualistic society, there is an experiential emphasis on relatedness, on moving toward and being with others as well as self. In the spirit of Rabbi Hillel, we attempt to learn through adventuring in experiencing the implications of "If I am not for myself who will be? If I am only for myself what am I?" while we are being and becoming.

My purpose in this introductory paper is to spell out in greater detail than I have found in the literature pertaining to group psychotherapeutic processes the values for patients and therapist in greater interest in and utilization of NVC.*

Intriguing patients into greater interest in their multiple simultaneously experienced and expressed NVC, intrapsychically and interpersonally, is a process which parallels the interest of the therapist in NVC. Increase of therapeutic interest in and utilization of NVC can help reduce the number of failures in therapy and of interminable analyses. Emphasis upon NVC decreases overfocus on words, intellectual insights, and understanding of psychodynamics which do not sufficiently stimulate and motivate patients toward being, toward self-realization, toward that dynamically knowing self which inherently implies accepting self with and without understanding.

The group-psychoanalytic setting affords an unparalleled opportunity to group members to become familiar with NVC in themselves and to learn that some NVC are primarily expressive and others are primarily communicative. A single nonverbal communication may serve for expression and communication, e.g., squirming in one's chair may serve to discharge and thus relieve heightened neuromuscular tension and at the same time communicate to the patient or others that he is involved in a tension-increasing experience. The therapist and the group may feel it is in this person's interest for him to experience involvement in anxiety, conflict, or discomfort as he is a person always driven to seek escape from tension-increasing, painful aspects of life. They may therefore continue to focus on the content of the moment; or if they feel he has had about all he can tolerate at this specific time, they may "turn the heat off," change the subject, or move away from directly focusing on this person to someone else in the group.

Group members learn through experiencing in the group situation that how a person is really being rather than what he is saying or doing is of prime significance in their attitudes toward him and themselves when they are with that person or persons. They learn that NVC play the most significant communications role in all their relationships.

* NVC is used in this paper to mean *nonverbal communications*.

NVC are processes which may be expressions of pure fact and/or may be symbolic expressions. A man who scratches his arm where he feels his arm itching tells us the pure fact that he is scratching and also informs us symbolically that he is itchy, which may be a reflection of inner itchiness, irritability, turmoil, anger, or unrest, and that he is scratching to seek relief.

SYMBOLS IN DREAMS AND IN NVC

Knowledge of the attributes and values of dream symbols helps us to understand and to utilize more fully the expressive and symbolic aspects of nonverbal communications in our therapeutic work. Familiarity with the dynamics of coming to what is manifest and what is latent in dreams helps us effectively to experience, integrate, and interpret what is manifest and what is latent in NVC.

CHARACTER STRUCTURE IN NVC

NVC, being an aspect of one's total self functioning, are used in the service of healthy and unhealthy character-structure trends and express the compulsive neurotic trends overtly and covertly. The resigned, detached individual [1] with marked alienation from self and people, described by H. Leopold [2] as "emotional illiterates," that is, those who do not adequately know the language of feelings, attempt consistently to deny or hide from verbal or nonverbal awareness and expression of feelings. The moment the group or therapist comments on nonverbal signs that such persons have been reached or touched emotionally by some interaction process, they reflexly activate all their defenses aimed at controlling and squelching and manipulating feelings. Faced with incontrovertible evidence that they have been "caught," experienced by such patients as if in a criminal act, feeling feelings, especially tender sentiments, which to them means weakness, such a patient may react with face-flushing embarrassment of reddening suffusion of his eyes. He may attempt to divert attention from what is going on by provoking laughter at his own expense or by expressing hostility toward the therapist.

The expansive group patient may indicate his drive for power, recognition, and prestige in his aggressive, lordly, [3] or spirited gait, a chip-on-the-shoulder attitude, and an air of inconsideration and callous disdain for the rights, weaknesses, and communications of others. His character pattern may be indicated by his frequent looks of disapproval and disagreement; by an air of excessive independency and self-sufficiency, and not too well concealed facial attitudes of arrogance and snobbery evidenced in whom he attends to and addresses, forms a clique with, and how he functions particularly during, before, and after group coffee klatches and alternate sessions when he attempts to control and master others in numerous ways.

The self-effacing patient reveals himself as a "schnook" in multiple ways. His or her colorlessness in attire, indrawn, constricted body without backbone indicating a body image of weakness and inadequacy; his dependency mannerisms as if constantly seeking a handout of help and approval and affection; the telltale, sickening, repeated, covering-up smile which marks him as "a nice guy" who is compliant, sweet, and everybody's friend—these are some of the clues to this appeasing person who is driven to seek peace and love at any cost.

I shall now describe in greater detail some of the major areas of NVC interest, namely, resistance, silence, body language, transference-countertransference, group atmosphere, the therapist's NVC, acting out, prejudice, art, growth and constructiveness, and some miscellaneous observations. The focus is on multiple simultaneous processes occurring in unison in which the various cues and codes for understanding the communications are perceived in the light of the whole context of each individual in the group and of the group itself.

RESISTANCE

NVC of resistance in the group[4] are expressed to us in the occurrence of the following:

(a) silences; absences from regular or alternate sessions; physically absenting oneself from a session during a session ostensibly to go to the toilet, to leave early because of a previously arranged appointment, to go out for a glass of water, for cigarettes, or to cry in privacy; spiritually absenting oneself during a session by daydreaming or "listening without listening"; lateness;

(b) body language, expressed with the body as object or in motion, or gestures, as with a tight, defiant face, a clenched fist and held-in body or sitting with one's chair back from the group circle;

(c) acting out, e.g., the patient who comes into the group and stretches out on the floor to provoke the therapist and group;

(d) the sudden appearance of signs of fatigue, sleepiness, yawning, or looking blank; or restlessness and looking at one's watch;

(e) a return to former modes of gait, dress, and manners to indicate superior status[5] and to decrease relatedness with peers and therapist.

SILENCE

Therapies and therapists who overemphasize the importance of the intellect and verbalizing tend to regard silences as evidence primarily of resistance to the analytic process. Silence does not invariably mean resistance. Patients in a group who have rarely said a word for many months and sometimes even a year or two have made measurable progress. A patient who verbalized nothing for fifty group sessions spoke up one day, stating, "I'm getting married tomorrow. I want to thank all of you. You've helped me a great deal.*

Contrary to the notion held by some beginning therapists, silence in a group does not mean that "nothing is going on." There is silence which communicates togetherness and cooperation, silence which is questioning, silence which is appraising and asks, "Are you aware of me? Are you with me?"

We must differentiate between silence as a definite expression of or way of communicating something and silent expressions and communications which may concomitantly be occurring in or not in harmony with the verbal expressions of an individual patient or of the group.

The attitude of the therapist in regard to silences and what is nonverbally communicated during silences and/or silently through gestures and bodily expressions will determine through imitation or contagion the attitude of the group members about these processes.

Silence of a group patient or of the therapist may indicate decreasing tension, an increasing sense of belonging, an increasing capacity to sit in and with feelings and fantasies and thoughts of all types with less judgmentalism, increasing awareness of self-limits and the rights, pressures, and tensions of others, and may promote integrative processes.

Some silences are purposive in the direction of resistance. They are in the service of blocking or retarding the growth of the individual and the group. Such general or selective silences may be vindictive, and a patient functioning this way may sit with a smug, arrogant demeanor of face and body. Fear of judgment, criticism, condemnation, or retribution with their accompanying increase of anxiety, pain, and discomfort may also provoke silence.

BODY LANGUAGE

Body language encompasses the body as object and in motion. Nonverbal communications are expressed through total appearance, clothes, body mass, height, and configuration; smells, skin reactions, specific features, and deformities; movements and gestures in gait; walking, standing and sitting postures; head, facial, trunk, arm, hand, finger, leg, foot, and other movements; facial and eye expressions with major emphasis on looks and looking, smiles, laughs, yawns, and tears; respiratory movements, rhythm, depth, and sighs, intestinal gurglings, muscle fibrillations, tics, and

* Personal Communication from A. E. Moll, Montreal, Canada.

attitude toward own sex and body image. Vocal intonations are included by some as NVC and are most revealing of the inner truth.

These and other internal body reactions which may be intuitive and unconscious in their connecting linkages occur in one moment to communicate to us and influence us in our relations to self and others. Particularly significant are the eyes, referred to popularly as the "windows of the soul." The eyes, face and hands perform a major portion of our NVC through the various nonverbal pictures they create.

Probably visual perception and expression through looks make the eyes the most significant nonverbal communications agency. They express unintentionally as well as intentionally what is going on intrapsychically and interpersonally and communicate nonverbally what a person may be unable to state verbally or may not want to or may be unaware of wanting to verbalize. The eye and face expressions can inform us of the following feelings* going on in another person in relationship to himself: confusion, guilt, frustration, anxiety, fear, terror, anger, hate, jealousy, envy, self-satisfaction, self-esteem, self-love, inner peace, agreement, pensiveness, wholeness or self-possession, self-sufficiency, depression, anguish, grief, sadness, enjoying, light-heartedness, rigidity, brittleness, tenuousness, shadowiness, featherlikeness, or emptiness.

And in relationship to others, the eyes can inform us of the following states of being: questioning, provoking, surprised, confused, frustrating, demanding, seducing, piercing, killing, terrorizing, crushing, accusing, grasping, pleading, helplessness, burdened, vulnerable, dependent, independent, tortured, anguished, panicky, fearful, anxious, desperate, absent-withdrawn, blank-vacant, distant-far away, close-togetherness, understanding, communion, loving, appreciating, grateful, abeyance, waiting, watching, innocence, sophistication, knowing, affirming, agreeing, seeking affirmation, differing, denying, suspicious, interested, disinterested, embarrassed, or guilty.

The lids and eyes[6] may be open in the usual interested conversational manner indicating interest and togetherness or closed in the usual manner as in sleeping, resting, free associating, relaxing, or simulating sleep. A patient may appear open-eyed as in surprise, astonishment, amazement, disbelief, a startle reaction, being terror-stricken, angry, or enraged. Droopy lids occur in states of fatigue, tiredness, low blood sugar, not listening, simulating disinterest, active withdrawal, boredom, feeling guilty and therefore finding it difficult to look fully or directly at others, or may indicate a former or present nerve injury or illness such as Bell's palsy. Squinting may serve to reduce peripheral vision and concentrate actual visual perception on a specific person, position, or process. A patient may screw his eyes tight to look more clearly into his own present feelings or past rec-

---

* It is impossible to create a complete list.

ollections and feelings. Eyes squeezed tightly occur in states of forcibly wanting to blind self, to not see, to shut out, to resist perception of something or someone. Unmoving fixed lids occur as with a stare as in a condition of spiritually absenting oneself while physically present, in states of catatonia, seeing without seeing, and in autohypnosis.

Smiles may attest to such states of being as enjoying, feeling good, nostalgia, reminiscence, experiencing pleasure, or humor; irony, as with a sardonic smile; sadness, as with tears and sorrow in one's eyes; contempt, arrogance, or smugness; a covering up of shame, embarrassment, guilt, feeling silly, stupid, or caught; an expression of unexpressed rage especially when accompanied by gritted teeth; smirking, mocking, and ridiculing; expressing resigned, sadistic, vindictive, or masochistic satisfaction. A smile may represent "an arrangement of the face rather than an expression of the heart," according to Jean Stafford, the short-story writer.

Some other miscellaneous body language communications are: (a) chin stroking, which is commonly associated with a reflective state but may also have a sensuous value with the firmness of one's chin serving as a symbolic substitute for one's erect penis or it may stimulate peripheral awareness of one's own solidity; (b) the thumb clasped in the clenched fist which is more common in girl children making a fist than in boy children. In adult patients this may be a security mechanism occurring as it does involuntarily when certain patients are in an increased anxiety-tension state though unaware of this. To some who do this the sensations aroused may give one a feeling of holding onto self as in (a) above, or it may simulate the oral sensations of sucking on a nipple. This thumb-clasp may occur more often in those who do not light up a cigarette to relieve increasing anxiety in the group-interpersonal situation; (c) finger tapping may serve not only as a common sign of nervousness but may, as with one of my patients, be a way of Morse-tapping to oneself certain unedited messages which thus move from unawareness to awareness. The context of their occurrence became a clue to their meaning and associating to the tapped word or phrases became a fertile source for repressed material; (d) doodling with finger or foot in repeated patterns such as a circle, triangle, X, Y, !, or other figures can be a direct clue to "the heart of the matter" if attention is brought to it by the therapist; (e) the patient who repeatedly takes off one shoe and not the other may be expressing his conflict about openly plunging into a significant aspect of his personality.

TRANSFERENCE AND COUNTERTRANSFERENCE

Transference and countertransference reactions are frequently activated and manifested by NVC in the group. This has an evolutionary genetic background in infancy and childhood where many of the child's learning and growth experiences have been for the most part in response to nonverbal pictorial communications from the parents and siblings, especially during the prolonged period when the processes of imitation and modification of undisciplined biological and reactive behavior in response to parental facial expressions are in the foreground.

The marked frequency of looking at the therapist or other authoritative transference figures for facial evidences of approval or disapproval in the group is seen to diminish as such patients feel strengthened by group support and learn through the corrective educational and reeducational experience of the group with its working through and reduction of transference distortions and projections the feeling of acceptance and belonging more or less unconditionally, which is so important in the development of inner security.

The therapist's silence is sometimes considered as evidence of his support of one patient in the group who is attacking or belittling another patient. Either the victim of the attack or other group members may feel hostility toward the therapist for not openly coming to the defense of the target person. This is usually a transference reaction with the demand for a protective verbal response from the therapist as none came from the patient's father. Such patients may be unable to recognize or experience the nonverbal expression of compassion, empathy, or support by the therapist unless it is also verbalized.

The therapist's countertransference reactions may be involved in a situation such as the aforementioned where his silence is in fact related to his countertransference. His nonverbal expressions of favoritism and approval may also be on a countertransference basis.

GROUP ATMOSPHERE

Group atmosphere is a changing process and according to Flowerman[7] "you may notice group atmosphere less by its presence than its change." Group atmosphere is influenced markedly by contagion and there may be one or more atmospheric currents present simultaneously. R. Bross[8] refers to one of her groups as "a congenial group of disturbed people."

Nonverbally, group atmosphere is governed and communicated by such matters as the manner and presence of the current peer group leaders in the pregroup waiting room; the manner of the therapist as he calls the group in; the degree of aliveness and eagerness of the group to be with the therapist or conversely the sluggishness, deadness, reticence of the group to come in; the degree of current competitiveness and sibling rivalry manifested in the movement toward seats, toward the most comfortable seat, the seat nearest the door, the seat nearest or furthest from or opposite to the therapist; the presence or absence of specific group members or an "observer."

THE THERAPIST'S NONVERBAL COMMUNICATIONS

The therapist is the single most influential person in the therapeutic group structure. How and what he is being as well as saying and doing profoundly affect the group as a whole and the individual members of the group.

Through numerous nonverbal means he communicates his attitude toward himself, toward his patients, toward his family, professional associates, and the community at large. The notion of anonymity maintained by some therapists is a myth and the need to attempt to remain unknown to the patient, to remain uninvolved with him may impede and retard the therapeutic progress of the patient. This does not refute the concept that the therapist should not place the burden of his problems on the patient, but implies that the sooner the patient does get to know and feel the therapist as a human being, as an authority who can be loving, giving, rejecting, and accepting, the sooner will he give up magical expectations of the therapist as an omnipotent figure and accept the reality limitations of the therapeutic relationship.

The selection of patients for the group informs the patients as to the therapist's preferences. Is it a group of all women? All men? Younger people? Older people? Mixed ages? Does the fact of the group being homogeneous reflect that that is how the therapist prefers life and people to be? Does it say he is afraid of contrasts and differences and that the price of nonconforming to the values or attitudes of the group majority will bring on disapproval from the therapist? Will there be room to develop and express one's own unique potentials even though they differ from others?

How the therapist furnishes his room for group psychotherapy, whether the chairs are of different types, or all the chairs are exactly alike including the therapist's chair may indicate to patients a feeling for a democratic attitude if this is borne out in other ways. Patients will sense that their therapist is being driven to prove to his patients how democratic he is when his other actions and functioning belie this. Is the office clinical and sterile? Or does it impart a lived-in "let's feel at home here" attitude?

Does the therapist indicate favoritism by the attention and approval he pays verbally as well as nonverbally to one or more group members? Which one is so rewarded? The most intelligent? The prettiest female? The most sexually free group member? The one who pays the most? The one who affirms the therapist most frequently? The one who has the best command of psychoanalytic jargon? Is the therapist aware of his nonverbal cues which indicate interest, support, or approval? Is the group predominantly leader-centered or peer-centered? This development is attributable to the therapist and is evidenced by whether the members more frequently address their communications directly to the therapist or to peers.

Is the therapist really able to trust the constructive potentials of the group? This may be manifested by whether he forbids the group to meet without him for fear of deleterious acting out or whether he encourages pre-, post-, or alternate group meetings, which allow for growth and cohesiveness without his presence, which allow for socialization interaction including some acting out, and allow for release of tension and for airing of repressed experiences which a patient is not yet ready to reveal to the therapist for fear of criticism or censure.

The kind of person the therapist is may be communicated by his attitudes concerning smoking, eating, and sharing of candy, gum, coffee, and so on, by group members and the extent of his own participation in these kinds of shared experiences. Does he ever provide coffee for group members? Food-sharing experiences reach patients and therapists on deep primitive nonintellectual levels and may have profound and long-reaching therapeutic impact. They may be evidence of acting out, of transference and countertransference reactions by the therapist. They may be a form of interaction which implicitly expresses togetherness, trust, and deep communion between the mutually accepting patients and therapists who no longer fear one another. "Breaking bread together" has most significant implications.

The therapist's head-nodding, bodily positions, state of health and physical being, whether he is fresh, clean-shaven, and relaxed or tired, irritable, and unshaven influence the group markedly. They may be afraid to express hostility and have to pussyfoot for fear of guilt or retribution when the therapist seems overtired or irritable.

ACTING OUT

I do not believe that acting out is always a form of resistance. Acting out always implies a transference phenomenon is taking place. It is important to not glibly or too quickly label all acting or behavior other than nonverbal functioning as acting out. If the behavior or action is not based on an unresolved transference, then it is acting or reacting to be experienced and examined in the light of its constructiveness and destructiveness for self and others.

PREJUDICE

Group psychotherapy diminishes irrational prejudices of all types.[9] In the therapeutic group there are revealed prejudices based not only on the more usual differences of race, nationality, color, and religion, but also on sex, intelligence, education, body cleanliness and odors, body build, physiognomy, deformities, manner of dress, age, values, attitudes, cultural background, degree of aggressivity or passivity, dependence or independence, hostility of friendliness, and constructiveness or destructiveness predominant during group meetings with and without the therapist.

The prejudices are revealed nonverbally by looks of superiority, smugness, arrogance, and looking down on others with contempt as well as looking through and ignoring certain group members; by avoidance of sitting next to certain individuals or chancing any bodily contact with that person, or by inattentiveness; by formation of a clique with other group members having similar prejudices.

ART

The use of art forms and processes in psychotherapeutic groups has been increasing as it has been recognized that this is a valuable nonverbal tool for expression and communication. This is especially so for more disturbed persons and others who have stronger inhibitions against verbal communications of inner experiences. The capacity to express contrast may be an index of ego strength.

The bringing into the group of one's artistic creation whether a painting or a poem may be experienced as a gift to the therapist or group or may indicate increasing trust in others; decrease in fear of criticism or needs to be perfect; a desire to bring out what has been taboo as an expression of increasing feeling of self; or a patient may feel his back against the wall and be driven to force himself at least to open up in this way.

NONVERBAL COMMUNICATIONS OF GROWTH AND MORE CONSTRUCTIVENESS

In the group there is less of the initial need to impress, less sibling rivalry, less resistance in all forms, especially absences and collusive resistive silences or excessive verbosity aimed to confuse rather than to clarify, less turning to the therapist for direction and approval, and more of a capacity to go along with what comes up and out and with what is. There is more spontaneous interaction, greater mutuality and respect for others as well as less distrust and hostility.

In individual patients in the group there is a greater capacity to listen with greater ease, to wait in abeyance, to sit in silence, to empathize and identify nonverbally, not to conform where they were formerly driven to conform, and to conform where such patients were formerly driven to defy. There is less looking to the therapist for approval. A formerly alienated patient who can now get up to go to the toilet without embarrassment during the group session indicates his increasing acceptance of his biological being.

CONCLUSION

The story is told in a cartoon of a boy of 5 reading to his younger brother, age 3, and saying, "What are words for? Why, words are for people who can't read pictures!"

The exact manner and timing for the more active utilization of non-verbal communications in the group-psychotherapeutic process is something which calls for the greatest skill and trust in intuitive feelings which the therapist may possess. It is an aspect of therapeutic technique which cannot be more than implied in this paper. The main goal of this paper has been to focus greater interest in NVC. A secondary goal has been to suggest means of interpreting and using the myriad forms of NVC in the hope that this will reduce some of the pain and time involved in the psychotherapeutic experience as it is currently known and make for better therapy.

REFERENCES

1. K. Horney, *Neurosis and Human Growth* (New York: W. W. Norton & Co., 1950).
2. H. Leopold, Lecture to Association for Group Psychoanalysis, October 1956.
3. W. Reich, "Character Analysis," in *An Aristocratic Character* (London: Vision Press and Peter Nevill, Ltd., 1950).
4. S. R. Slavson, "A Contribution to a Systematic Theory of Group Psychotherapy," *Int. J. Group Psychother.*, 4:3-29, 1954.
5. H. Mullan, "Status Denial in Group Psychoanalysis," *J. Nerv. & Ment. Dis.*, 122:345-352, 1955.
6. M. Riemer, "Abnormalities of the Gaze," *Psychiat. Quart.*, 29:659-672, 1955.
7. S. Flowerman, "Group Atmosphere." Lecture to candidates in training with the Association for Group Psychoanalysis, November 1956.
8. R. Bross, Lecture to Association for Group Psychoanalysis, December 1956.
9. G. W. Allport, *The Nature of Prejudice* (Boston: Beacon Press, 1954).

BIBLIOGRAPHY

D. Barbara, "The Value of Non-Verbal Communication in Personality Understanding," in *Your Speech Reveals Your Personality* (Springfield, Ill.: Charles C Thomas, 1958).
C. Beukenkamp, "Further Developments of the Transference Life Concept in Therapeutic Groups," *J. Hillside Hosp.*, 5:441-448, 1956.
M. Buber, *Between Man and Man* (Boston: Beacon Press, 1955).
C. Darwin, *The Expression of the Emotions in Man and Animals* (New York: Appleton Press, 1872).

S. Freud, *A General Introduction to Psychoanalysis* (New York: Boni and Liveright, 1920).

E. Fromm, *The Forgotten Language* (New York: Rinehart, 1951).

T. Hora, Lecture to Association for Group Psychoanalysis, March 1957.

K. Horney, "On Feeling Abused," *Am. J. Psychoanal.*, 11:5-12, 1951.

A. M. Johnson and S. A. Szurek, "Etiology of Antisocial Behavior in Delinquents and Psychopaths," *J. Am. Med. Assn.*, 154:814-817, 1954.

H. Kelman, "Life History as Therapy; Part III: The Symbolizing Process," *Am. J. Psychoanal.*, 16:145-173, 1956.

M. Proust, "The Guermantes Way," in *Remembrance of Things Past* (New York: Random House, 1934).

J. Ruesch and W. Kees, *Non-Verbal Communication: Notes on the Visual Perception of Human Relations* (Berkeley: University of California Press, 1956).

H. A. Witkin, H. B. Lewis, *et al.*, *Personality Through Perception* (New York: Harper & Brothers, 1954).

R. L. Woods, *The World of Dreams* (New York: Random House, 1947).

34

COORDINATED MEETINGS
IN GROUP PSYCHOTHERAPY

Asya L. Kadis

Wolf's introduction of the alternate meeting[1] and later publications on the theory and practice of this procedure[2] have stirred up a lively controversy in the profession. In this paper are condensed several papers on the subject of alternate and other coordinated meetings.[3]

WHAT ARE COORDINATED MEETINGS?

It has been the practice of a number of group psychotherapists to ask members of each group to hold regularly scheduled meetings on their own. In these coordinated meetings, held one or more times weekly, patients are encouraged to continue the group analytic process as in regular meetings when the therapist is present.

In the protective atmosphere of regular sessions it is difficult if not impossible for many patients to resolve their strong transference resistance toward the authority figure, whereas in coordinated meetings they can transfer their displeasure, aggression, hostility, or feelings of love to a substitute parental figure in the group.

The three principal types of coordinated meetings are identified here as alternate, pre-, and postmeetings. Alternate meetings[4] usually take place in rotation at the homes of group members. Refreshments are sometimes served, or everyone may go out later for coffee or a meal, continuing the discussion meanwhile. Although the therapist's office may be used for convenience, a freer atmosphere is likely to prevail elsewhere. The alternate meeting, which represents the ideal integration of the peer and parental group, is perhaps the most desirable form of coordinated meeting.

From *The American Journal of Psychotherapy*, Vol. X, No. 2, April 1956, pp. 275-291. This article was rewritten and based on two articles including the one cited.

Premeetings, held in the therapist's office immediately before regular group sessions, serve as a warming-up process. Closest within the therapist's orbit, they often pave the way for post- and alternate sessions, particularly in institutional settings. In instances where group ego is unlikely to develop, or where the therapist has to be a constant agent of control, the premeeting may be considered an end in itself. This is especially true of hospitals, clinics, and schools, where the group is confined to an authority setup. Patients who mistrust their ability to handle their own anger or positive feelings toward fellow members, or those who fear the group's hostility, find reassurance in the therapist's proximity. His momentarily expected appearance, as well as the time limitation, imposes greater control over premeetings than is sensed in either of the other coordinated sessions.

Postmeetings,[5] the so-called cradle of alternate meetings, are also of three types: scheduled meetings held in the therapist's office in his absence,[6] scheduled meetings held elsewhere, e.g., at members' homes, and spontaneous meetings[7] at a restaurant or other eating place. Even when the members meet in the therapist's office, they feel less confined and anxious than in premeetings where he will soon appear. The postsession is thus characterized by a release in tension and assumes an intermediate position.

Subgroups, spontaneous social gatherings of two or more members,[8] should be strongly discouraged. Such meetings, which are conducive to acting out transference resistances, are bound to come to the therapist's attention. He may take this opportunity to bring up the subject of coordinated meetings, explaining that the emotions engendered among members must be analyzed by the whole group at regular sessions.[9]

The child reaches out to establish himself with his peer group at the same time that he seeks protection at home. He experiences anxiety and hurt—an inevitable part of growing up—as he shuttles back and forth between these two worlds. The consequences are similar when patients alternate between regular sessions with the parental figure and coordinated meetings where they are on their own. The ensuing struggle makes for greater separateness and more profound personal involvement, a basic aim of mature human development.

INITIATION OF COORDINATED MEETINGS

Any new group requires considerable preparatory experience before post- and alternate meetings can be launched. They should be suggested only when the members have developed inner controls and a group ego, including a sense of group belonging, and are able to handle outbursts with some effectiveness.

When group members who have been together for several weeks or months begin to express a desire to increase the intensity of their analytic work, the therapist may say, "You seem to have many things to discuss and not enough time. Why don't you meet regularly once or twice a week and work without me?" Haphazardly arranged meetings are undoubtedly already taking place, and the therapist's expressed interest serves to include them within the total therapeutic framework.

It goes without saying that some patients are reluctant to participate in coordinated meetings. But like a timid diver who finally decides to plunge into icy waters, they experience a certain exhilaration once they have left the pier. Despite feeling safer with a parental figure, they usually welcome the opportunity to explore feelings they have kept firmly locked in their inner recesses. They may restrain feelings of warmth, anger, or rebellion when the therapist is present, simply because of their distorted views of the parental figure. At coordinated meetings, patients begin to shed some of their restraints and defenses; they find it easier to attack a lesser authority than to attack The Authority.

Frequently patients reluctantly agree to participate in coordinated meetings then fail to attend regularly or act out in various ways. The therapist must understand and analyze the fears and rationalizations underlying this behavior.

The criteria of readiness are both subjective and objective. The therapist senses the development of group cohesion and *esprit de corps*. If he is thoroughly comfortable and at ease in the group he is likely to know when the bonds between group members are sufficiently strong for them to carry on for a few hours a week on their own. The therapist's hunches about readiness appear to have objective counterparts: Members tend toward overt manifestations of hostility and also toward feelings of greater warmth; they react to hostile outbursts with less upset and disturbance. In a cohesive group there emerges a system of checks and balances in which the outburst of one member seems to be handled by the reassurance of another. In short, the group has developed ego strength of its own.

THE THERAPIST AU COURANT

Once coordinated meetings are under way they must be integrated into the therapeutic framework. How does the therapist become aware of what takes place in his absence? Communication between sessions is possible without the members' recounting all events that transpire—a type of behavior reminiscent of tattling to the teacher or parent. The desired attitude is for members to bring up their spontaneous reactions to happenings at the last session, whether a regular or a coordinated one, without feeling obligated to relate all the specific events and disclosures.

Therapists frequently open a regular session by saying, "Have there been any after-reactions to your last meeting without me?" Various responses to the same event enable him to understand the interactions. Of course, he may be kept in the dark for some time, especially when the group is in a phase of resistance to him. If this is the case he may say frankly, "Why leave me out of things?" or "I feel hurt at being left out." Such a remark usually brings forth strong positive or negative feelings toward him which had been concealed by resistances. My impression is that little important material is withheld. One of eight or nine group members will bring up his reactions because of overwhelming personal anxiety or fear that the group will lose its equilibrium.

MATERIAL VIEWED IN TOTAL THERAPEUTIC CONTEXT

The characteristic properties of coordinated meetings must be described in terms of the total therapeutic context, not as isolated happenings. In contrasting and comparing patterns of behavior at regular and coordinated meetings, it is apparent that the latter represent a phase of testing, exploring, and consolidating, wherein the patient learns to separate himself from parental dependency in its various forms. Four aspects of the struggle for separateness may be described as exploration, vacillation, acting out, and incorporation. Although simultaneously observed in the course of therapy, they will be discussed separately for the sake of clarity.

Let us first briefly consider the characteristics most commonly shared by persons seeking psychotherapy and the conditions commonly considered essential to their achievement of a fuller measure of well-being. The core feeling of most patients, regardless of the professed complaint, is one of helplessness, loneliness, and mistrust of their own judgment. It arises from a distorted conception of themselves which, by elaboration, leads to distortion of other human relationships. It is assumed that such difficulties in the patient's interpersonal relationships reflect in some degree certain failures in emotional growth. Most therapeutic endeavors are directed toward correcting the personality deficiencies arising from these failures.

THEORETICAL CONCEPTS

Coordinated meetings provide a climate of testing and exploring in which the patient learns to consolidate discriminations between past and present relationships (working through) and is thereby enabled to function without leaning heavily on parental figures. Such meetings represent a mediating bridge which permits peer-group members to use their affective resources independently.

In the historical family setting there is constant interaction between the peer group, the bridge to the external world, and the family group. The child's way of relating to his peers is determined by his status at home, and the treatment he is accorded by his peers is reflected in his reactions to the home situation. Again we find a similar interaction between coordinated and regular sessions. Without special encouragement from the therapist, patients relay their experiences in and reactions to coordinated meetings; conversely, they wait until they are alone with their peers to vent their strong negative and positive feelings or to "act behind the therapist's back."

The above-mentioned therapeutic properties require a particular type of social organization as well as group cohesion and participatory leadership—salient characteristics of coordinated meetings. French [10] has demonstrated that group cohesion is closely related to the members' tolerance for aggression and frustration.

It has been found that individuals tend to shift perceptions of relatively innocuous stimulus material more readily under group-centered leadership than under an authority figure.[11] Furthermore, the changes are either strongly toward or away from group norms. In coordinated meetings, where the stimulus material is highly personal and very powerful, the likelihood of shifts in perception is even greater. Studies by Preston and Heintz[12] show that an important factor in bringing about such shifts is the constantly changing leadership. Also, participatory leadership is proportional to the meaningfulness, personal stimulation, and enjoyment of the over-all group experience. It seems especially desirable to create a group climate fostering group solidarity, participatory leadership, and facile shifting of roles.

Patients interacting in both coordinated meetings and regular sessions exhibit strikingly different behavior in the two social climates, especially early in therapy, and these discrepancies—present since childhood—become a major objective index of their distorted relationships.

THE ASPECT OF EXPLORATION

During adolescent development and neurotic struggles, the individual invariably wishes to conceal an important part of his world from parental scrutiny but will often "open up" to trusted peers.

In coordinated meetings, patients feel free to explore and experience feelings they have previously kept locked in a chamber of secrecy. Those who feel that a show of affection will be punished by a "parent" also may choose these meetings to express their positive feelings. Because of the emphasis in our culture on asexual relationships in the home, patients think they must maintain a similar attitude during regular sessions. Despite the permissive atmosphere that generally prevails there, they regard the therapist as a forbidding parental figure from whom they must withhold sexual and other strong feelings. It is of course true that apparently warm and sexual gestures at coordinated meetings are frequently motivated by concealed hostility, stemming from the patient's desire to act behind the therapist's back and express himself despite presumed parental disapproval. But even these pseudowarm reactions have a positive element for in this way some patients may for the first time experience positive affect.

Patients who are shy and withdrawn at regular sessions may exhibit aggressive and boisterous behavior at coordinated meetings. This is especially true of those with passive dependent traits, who seize this opportunity to explore the assertive feelings they have previously denied.

Discrepancies in behavior at coordinated and regular sessions are found to be more pronounced early in therapy. If patients do not exhibit these differences, combined treatment—individual and group—for a considerable period of time may be valuable, regardless of the clinical diagnosis.[13] Group members come to respond in the same way at all types of sessions as they learn to share parents freely with their peers—an essential part of ego building.

One factor underlying affective exploration at coordinated meetings is a lessening of restraint and defenses in the absence of a titular figure. At times the explosive potential becomes frightening to certain members who seek out the therapist at a regular session to protect them from their own impending explosion. Others dare to explode only in the presence of the therapist who represents a safety valve at the moment, depending on the specific transference phase.

THE ASPECT OF VACILLATION

Joining a coordinated meeting can be likened to the first loosening of family ties. Both the therapist-parent and the group-member-child may at first resist the change. The patient clings to parental shelter and the therapist wishes to protect his children by keeping them under his wing.

The therapist often minimizes his patients' importance to him, despite his intellectual awareness of countertransference factors. His protective clinging manifests itself in subtle rationalizations.[14] The main argument against coordinated meetings is rooted in fear of the parent's losing his children. The charge that patients meeting on their own will become an unruly mob is partly based on the therapist's feeling that they can function effectively only under his surveillance. Similarly, the debate over whether socialization after group meetings should be permitted or forbidden has the ring of benevolent authority. Socialization is inevitable, for children feel that they must break away from home. One of the functions of therapy is to examine each patient's techniques for escaping so that the break can be made in as wholesome a way as possible.

Various rationalizations are offered by patients who resist entering coordinated meetings. An attitude of contempt may alternate with one of professed self-sufficiency. "I can analyze things as well as any of those people. It'll be just a waste of time" or "What's the use of meeting with a bunch of nuts like that?" An examination of such statements reveals the patient's fear of exposing himself or assuming a burden of responsibility he is as yet unwilling or unable to take on. There is also a fear of being exposed to the "wolf pack" of hostility or of expressing or responding to warm feelings.

Refusal of a member to participate must be understood, analyzed, and coped with by the therapist. A resistance, which can be analyzed, is always involved. Whenever a member consistently stays away from coordinated meetings, the other group members become resentful. Failure to attend is usually analyzed and resolved. However, if the group cannot handle the problem the therapist should schedule an appointment with the defecting member to help resolve his negative transference. If he still refuses to return it may be advisable to switch him to another group, an alternative that is preferable to having him stop therapy completely.

In this phase of vacillation some patients with a little encouragement will leave the safe parental orbit to accept the fearful though exciting challenge of being on their own. The therapist may tend to overprotect them by delaying their participation in coordinated meetings where the fluctuating climate fosters independence.[15]

THE ASPECT OF ACTING OUT

Coordinated meetings are not only relatively free of "parental" restraint but directly stimulate freer behavior. Physical proximity, the informal seating arrangement, the likelihood that four-letter words will be used, the socializing over cokes or coffee—all these factors contribute to a more relaxed atmosphere than is usual in regular sessions. Although lowering of defenses may foster acting out, therapeutic use of such behavior may well result in over-all gains.[16] While sexual and aggressive acting out at coordinated meetings is negligible, shouting, tantrums and cursing, and regressive behavior such as stuttering are fairly common.

Acting out in a therapy group and in an individual therapy setting must be evaluated and analyzed differently. Acting out has two essential components: the motor discharge and awareness of the transference context. When there is a considerable time lapse between the two, acting out is truly blind and repetitive. But when the transference nature of a patient's behavior is pointed out immediately after the motor act, he begins to acquire control over his previously blind behavior. Perception of the transference image takes precedence over the motor act, and the patient can act upon his genuine feelings.

The following factors, briefly outlined, facilitate acting out in response to feelings: (1) immediate therapeutic scrutiny of the affective out burst—the concept of simultaneity. The sooner the association is established, the more readily the patient perceives the meaning of his behavior and the sooner the group can analyze it. Also, the group in coordinated meetings tends to challenge the purely defensive aspect of sexual or aggressive outbursts; (2) sharing of the emotional reaction by the entire group. The patient, faced with multiple and varied responses to his acting out, is more likely to alter his perceptions; (3) motor behavior clues. Evidence seems to support the view that in our culture, where the heavy burden of defenses is carried by verbalization, motor behavior breaks through them very effectively. Important working-through components emerge when a patient is immediately confronted with his motor behavior during an outburst.

While the group may stimulate acting out, it may also inhibit such behavior. For example, members often frown on two patients in the group who are especially affectionate toward each other, feeling that the group's unity is thereby threatened. Impending sexual or aggressive acting out is usually strongly opposed, especially if the involved persons tend to act out compulsively and repetitively. On the other hand, sporadic emotional outbursts by a previously silent and "mousey" member usually have a highly salutory effect.

Acting out in coordinated meetings raises the question of the therapist's responsibility. How, indeed, can he be answerable for his patients' safety and well-being when he is not present? Actually, a therapist is responsible for his patients whether he sees them one hour or five hours a week. He cannot possibly survey all their life activities. The best he can do is to select the best possible group for both regular and coordinated sessions[17] and be available when patients express their need for him. Clearly psychotic patients, psychopathic, epileptic, and cardiac patients are not suitable candidates for coordinated meetings.[18]

Besides controlling and preventing certain kinds of acting out, group members always immediately notify the therapist of impending danger which they feel unable to cope with. When one realizes that a patient in acute distress will not see the therapist for four or five days, this protection is not slight. From the outset, group members must be given a certain degree of trust and responsibility. As they grow in therapy the leader gradually surrenders his responsibility until they can fully assume it. The minimal danger inherent in coordinated meetings seems to be overbalanced by genuine advantages which help loosen defenses, overcome exclusive dependency ties, and bring to the surface hitherto repressed affect.

THE ASPECT OF INCORPORATION

Ego building goes forward when patients have an opportunity to assume authority and autonomy and when they learn how to give and withhold affective experiences. The management of giving and withholding is significantly modified according to whether or not the therapist is present.

The patient, only too willing to lean on the therapist and attribute to him any therapeutic gains, tends to say, "My analyst feels . . ." One of the goals of psychotherapy is to effect a transition to "The group feels . . ." and finally to "I feel . . ." His achievement of this objective may be facilitated by working through problems in the intermittent absence of the therapist, whose psychological presence is undeniably felt. Affective experiences, analysis of transference and resistance, and the development of a sense of authority lead to autonomous action.

Patients who compulsively withhold, require considerable support from the group before they can share personal happenings with the therapist as well as their peers. Patients' experiences in the two milieus help them to acquire the means of giving and withholding. In one case, a young woman allayed her anxiety by confessing, although she was not required to share everything with the therapist. To withhold secrets from a parent and still feel accepted appears to be part of a wholesome and trusting child-parent relationship. If a patient feels obligated to share everything with the thera pist at all times, he may develop guilt feelings about consciously or unconsciously withholding material. In fact, the tendency to tell all in great detail may be a form of resistance. After imparting all his antisocial thoughts and actions the patient may feel no further responsibility for them, thereby removing the anxiety implicit in tolerating his own tension —anxiety which is necessary for working through.

In individual analysis the therapist usually controls the timing of material and decides whether the patient is ready for certain interpretations. In group psychotherapy the timing is largely controlled by the members; it becomes less important simply because it is not instigated by the therapist. There is a common feeling that poor timing, both in introducing subject matter and in interpretation, may precipitate a crisis and thus constitute a hazard particularly in meetings without the therapist. In setting up coordinated meetings the therapist is not telling his patients to sink or swim, but is trusting them to confront the unknown. In effect he is saying, "Your feelings are not as dark and you are not as helpless as you think. The group has enough positive resources to handle most crises that may arise. When you run up against something you can't handle, you can call on me." Although the therapist must always have enough time for individual sessions, it is my observation that the less anxious he is the fewer crises will loom up requiring his help.

Participation in concerted group action enables the patient to assume a responsible role himself at a critical time when some member needs support or threatens the unity of the group. He may also request help, in return for help given. The interchange of help, protection, encouragement, and support is a most important element in ego-building activity.

Patients who in all their relationships tend to shield themselves by nonparticipation or withdrawal usually behave in the same way at peer-group meetings. They try to create authority figures of their own so they can resume their dependency pattern. Prominent members accept the authority role for a while but reject it as they progress in therapy. Thus, the less effectual members are thrown on their own again, and this very fact mobilizes their resources.

SELF-ASSESSMENT REQUIRED

Many *avant-garde* leaders in the specialty are convinced of the value of coordinated meetings, while other psychotherapists are either unwilling to try them or have, for various reasons, given them up after a trial. Surely the therapist's personality, value system, and philosophy of psychotherapy and of society as a whole have influenced his strong stand on this controversy.

It has been charged that group regulatory defenses will not permit patients to maintain group structure and boundaries. However, my experience indicates that the therapist's control is only indirect; in practice the group acts as his agent. As we well know the gang acts either positively or negatively and often endorses much stricter disciplinary measures than does the authority. And each member's earnest wish to identify with the therapist makes the group carry out his wishes. Group control is thus exerted mainly by the members—out of their positive identification and transference—not by the therapist.

Built-in group control provides a theoretical and empirical foundation for the generalization that acting out becomes less frequent once coordinated meetings are under way, and when it occurs its impact is less damaging than in situations outside the therapeutic framework. A system of checks and balances helps to control it. But just as children in a family act out their parents' delinquent or antisocial wishes, patients in the group may respond to the therapist's unconscious wishes.

And what of us therapists? While seemingly priding ourselves on noninterference, may we not unconsciously—like some parents—wish to acquire more and more knowledge of how our children behave? Most of the vital material from coordinated sessions comes to us in time, either directly or indirectly. Do we then probe closely because we unconsciously desire to take a greater part in their experiential worlds? It is an oversimplification to label a therapist permissive or controlling according to whether or not he decides to launch coordinated meetings.

Group therapists may be classified under three familiar parental types: (1) Responding to his patients' quest for an ideal parent, he also provides a favorable therapeutic climate (see all, hear all, know all), ideal siblings, and understanding playmates. He strives to be the wise omniscient parent who is constantly concerned with his children's whereabouts and welfare. (2) He attempts to free himself of his patients' dependency demands by adopting a laisser-faire, *laisser-aller* attitude. He unconsciously desires freedom for himself and also wants to close his ears to the children's constant clamoring for attention and satisfaction. (3) He initiates coordinated meetings to increase his control of the patients' lives by receiving additional information about them from other group members.

Before deciding to start coordinated meetings, each therapist must carefully analyze his conscious and unconscious attitudes. He should be wary of this departure if he believes that: (1) his own authority is all-important; (2) group structure, with himself as focus, is immutable; (3) any acting out is destructive; (4) complete control at all times is desirable.

He should try to decide whether he can tolerate—without undue disturbance—a considerable amount of aggression and regression, a conflict between the group's value system and his own, temporary exclusion, or direct challenge by the group. Once started, coordinated meetings should be carried through. Offering and then taking them away would serve to reinforce the patients' early experiences with interfering and punitive parental figures.

The controversy over coordinated meetings did not spring up overnight, nor will it be resolved quickly. The answers to many puzzling questions await further investigation and research. What are the essential differences in patient behavior at coordinated and regular sessions, and what are the origins and consequences of such variations? Can we define and measure the particular contribution made by the therapist, other members, and the group as a whole to each patient's progress? What is the contribution of coordinated meetings as a special variable? Finally, what are the significant therapeutic experiences in any kind of psychotherapy for individual patients and for the group as a whole? Can patient, group, therapy, and therapist variables be described reliably?

If therapists as well as observers and co-therapists continue to pool their clinical experiences and improve research techniques we may find at least partial answers to such questions. In any event self-searching and keen observation should help each of us assess the value of coordinated meetings in the entire group therapy context.

REFERENCES

1. A. Wolf, "The Psychoanalysis of Groups," *Am. J. Psychother.*, Vol. III, No. 4, October 1949; Vol. IV, No. 1, January 1950. [Also reprinted as Chapter 23 in the present volume.]
2. A. L. Kadis, "The Alternate Meeting in Group Psychotherapy," *Am. J. Psychother.*, Vol. X, No. 2, April 1956.

3. Kadis, *ibid.*; "The Role of Coordinated Group Meetings in Group Psychotherapy," *Acta Psychother.*, Vol. 7, 1959; "Alternate Meetings," *Topic Probl. Psychother.*, Vol. 2, 1960.

4. Wolf, *op. cit.*; Kadis, "The Alternate Meeting in Group Psychotherapy," *loc. cit.*

5. G. R. Bach, *Intensive Group Psychotherapy* (New York: Ronald Press. 1954), pp. 107-108.

6. Wolf, *op. cit.*

7. Kadis, "The Alternate Meeting in Group Psychotherapy," *loc. cit.*

8. Bach, *op. cit.*

9. A. Wolf *et al.*, "Sexual Acting Out in the Psychoanalysis of Groups," *Int. J. Group Psychother.*, Vol. IV, No. 4, October 1954.

10. J. R. French, Jr., "The Disruption and Cohesion of Groups," in D. Cartwright and A. Zander (eds.), *Group Dynamics* (White Plains, N.Y.: Row, Peterson & Co., 1953), pp. 121-134.

11. E. W. Bovard, Jr., "Group Structure and Perception," in D. Cartwright and A. Zander (eds.), *Group Dynamics* (White Plains, N.Y.: Row, Peterson & Co., 1953), pp. 177-189.

12. M. G. Preston and R. K. Heintz, "Effects of Participatory Versus Supervisory Leadership on Group Judgment," in D. Cartwright and A. Zander (eds.), *Group Dynamics* (White Plains, N.Y.: Row, Peterson & Co., 1953), pp. 573-584.

13. E. Fried, "The Effects of Combined Therapy on the Productivity of Patients," *Int. J. Group Psychother.*, Vol. IV, 1954; W. C. Hulse, "Transference, Catharsis, Insight and Reality Testing During Concomitant Individual and Group Psychotherapy," *Int. J. Group Psychother.*, Vol. V, 1955; E. Fried, "Combined Group and Individual Therapy with Passive-Narcissistic Patients," *Int. J. Group Psychother.*, Vol. V, 1955.

14. A. Wolf *et al.*, "The Psychoanalysis of Groups: The Analyst's Objections," *Int. J. Group Psychother.*, Vol. II, July 1952; H. Mullan, "Transference and Countertransference: New Horizons," *Int. J. Group Psychother.*, Vol. V, April 1955.

15. E. Fried, "Ego Functions and Techniques of Ego Strengthening," *Am. J. Psychother.*, Vol. IX, 1955.

16. A. Wolf *et al.*, "Sexual Acting Out in the Psychoanalysis of Groups," *loc. cit.*

17. C. Beukenkamp, "An Indication for Group Psychotherapy," *J. Hillside Hosp.*, Vol. IV, April 1955; S. R. Slavson, "Criteria for Selection and Rejection of Patients for Various Types of Group Psychotherapy," *Int. J. Group Psychother.*, Vol. V, 1955.

18. H. S. Leopold, "Who Should Be Excluded from Group Psychotherapy?" Presented at the Second Meeting of the Eastern Group Psychotherapy Society, May 27, 1955.

35

FOUR BOOKS ON GROUP THERAPY:
A REVIEW

Eric Berne

A *Practicum of Group Psychotherapy*, Asya L. Kadis, Jack D. Krasner, Charles Winick, and S. H. Foulkes (New York, Evanston, and London: Harper & Row, 1963), 195 pp., $6.50

Psychoanalysis in Groups, Alexander Wolf and Emanuel K. Schwartz (New York: Grune & Stratton, 1962), 326 pp., $8.00

Group Therapy: A Practical Approach, James A. Johnson, Jr. (New York: McGraw-Hill Book Company, 1963), 467 pp., $10.95

Group Psychotherapy: Theory and Practice, Hugh Mullan and Max Rosenbaum (New York: The Free Press of Glencoe, 1962), 360 pp., $5.95

In 1943 Giles Thomas published the first systematic survey of the literature of group psychotherapy.[1] The following year (October 10, 1944), the famous TB Med 103 was published by the War Department, giving official sanction to this form of treatment and starting many of us on our careers in this specialty. The almost simultaneous appearance, twenty years later, of four books on the subject signals the emergence in this country of a new generation of group therapists. The present review provides an opportunity to appraise the new position.

From the beginning, there was an undignified schism between two schools of practice. Slavson's "expanded Bibliographies" of 1946 and 1950[2] give not a single specific reference of Moreno's, though the "Historical Survey" in Moreno's 1945 Symposium[3] does give two references to Slavson. This schism has persisted to the present day. In the new generation, there is a similar breach, so far unhealed, between two schools of thought, which may be called the "Western" and the "Eastern." The Western,

Reprinted from the *American Journal of Orthopsychiatry*, Vol. 34, No. 3, April 1964, pp. 584-589.

represented chiefly by the prolific Palo Alto family therapists, the transactional analysts, and the SWING group in Los Angeles, is more actionistic: In general, their motto is "Get better first and we'll analyze afterward." The Eastern, well represented by the authors of these four new books, is centered principally in Manhattan (with Los Angeles, as in many other fields, functioning as a suburb of that island), and tends more to the slogan "Let's analyze first and you'll get better afterward." This more recent split is not merely academic or verbal. An experienced transactional analyst, for example, can tell, after listening to no more than five minutes of a tape recording or verbal report of a group meeting, which school the therapist accepts.

These four books, then, represent the classical analytic Eastern approach, and they will be considered mainly from three points of view: their value as instruction manuals for beginners in the Eastern method, their interest for experienced professionals, and their possibilities as "books" in the literary sense, implying durability and readability.

As for *A Practicum of Group Psychotherapy* (Kadis, Krasner, Winick, and Foulkes), it is likely that each of the authors of this joint effort could singly have written a better book, and one of them in fact, Foulkes, already has. Although they have not come up with the camel that is the proverbial product of committees, they have managed a rather discouraging horse. The book starts off with perhaps the best brief exposition extant of the nature, goals, and problems of group psychotherapy, and this is followed by an excellent historical review. At the end is an interesting statistical survey of the training and professional activities of group therapists in this country, with two useful appendixes giving curricula for two-year and for weekend training of group therapists.

The body of the book, which lies between these two stimulating extremities, gives a distressing impression both of co-authorship and of group therapy. Verbosity ("interpersonal socio-psychological problems"), tautology ("anticipated expectations"), solecisms ("Psychodrama is a procedure whereby one or more persons with problems interacts with others"), and misprints ("indentifications," and so on) are rife. The style has a polysyllabic opaqueness that will challenge the penetration of even the most eager reader who tries to relate the verbal content to clinical experience. To take one example, the fascinating subject of "fractionation of the group" is glossed over with undefined terms and self-evident banalities (p. 96): "The group experiencing itself . . . the members experiencing themselves . . . group climate . . . may manifest this withdrawal behavior. . . . Such manifestations are often very significant."

Equally unfortunate is the picture given of the therapist and the world in which he and the patients live. The selection of patients is determined by a continual stream of threats, cautions, and anxieties besetting the therapist from every side; the patients themselves are dangerous because they might succumb to unorthodox impulses and they are continually on the brink of being overwhelmed with anxiety, so that, as the writers remark (p. 141): "The therapist will do well to work toward the increase of ego strength to enable the patient to cope with his emotional conflicts. In so doing, he will increasingly be able to relinquish his somatic problems as a defense." The words "threat" and "anxiety" occur on almost every page, sometimes more than once. The therapist is pictured as helpless to interfere with the machinations of his patients. In general, if the patients huddle more and more closely together through "communication," even if this is boring enough to put some of the patients to sleep ("resistance"), somehow the threats will not be so scary. For patients who do not "threaten" the therapist with "resistance," there are hearty reassurances.

If this sounds like a parody, it is what emerges from the body of the book. Sometimes, indeed, it is difficult to believe that the writers are not parodying themselves, for example, "His reactions to Sophie and to the therapist were continually redefined and altered as a result of his strong reaction to Sophie's attachment to Martin and to the therapist."

The whole situation is saved by the chapter, "Termination of Treatment," which demonstrates that things are much better than they sound, for the terminating patients talk as though they had received considerable benefit from their therapy. This indicates that the writers are better practitioners than preachers, and that they are presenting themselves poorly. No doubt the book is useful as a manual for their students. For the experienced practitioner, it contains little of interest save Foulkes' introductory remarks, the statistical chapter, and the chapter on termination.

A bad book presents to the reviewer the unpleasant task of choosing between duty and friendship. It is a relief to turn to the freedom, competence, sophistication, and objectivity of Wolf and Schwartz. Their book, *Psychoanalysis in Groups,* takes us far away from the type of "therapy group" that at its dreariest becomes a tedium from which no one must shrink lest he be called "resistive"; or at its toughest becomes a Procrustean bed on which he who squirms at being stretched or amputated is accused of "acting out"; or at its most fanciful becomes a *folie à neuf* where healthy skepticism is only for the squares. Wolf and Schwartz shun such vulgarities in favor of one criterion: "We ask that the evidence be made available." And they have only one question in mind: "What is the best way to cure patients?"

This book is in the main an expansion and modification in the light of experience of Wolf's paper of 15 years ago.[4] The thesis is that, not only is psychoanalysis in groups possible, it can be practiced more effectively there than in individual therapy. The merits of this thesis will have to be judged by another generation; the merits of the book can be evaluated in contemporary perspective. As reading matter, despite some redundance, it is well and imaginatively written, it is readable, it is stimulating, and it is logical. As a thesis it is provocative, because the questions are asked in an answerable form, and it is inviting because the authors are willing to listen to their opponents, and even to consider courteously their opponents' trivialities. As a paradigm, the book is singularly free of jargon; when a technical word is used, it is used correctly and distinguished from its debased form. For example, the authors distinguish "acting" from "acting out," and when they use "transference" the transfer is demonstrable. They reject clichés such as "it is necessary to express hostility."

The flavor is best conveyed by some samples from the first half of the book:

> While it is true that rejection by a group is traumatic, at the same time it is also therapeutic. . . . A collective interpretation tends to obscure specific differences. . . . Spontaneous interaction must be supplemented by conscious methodical sifting and planning. . . . Shallowness of therapy results from the lack of exploring each member in uniqueness. . . . It is important that the group not manipulate the individual to comply with a consensual position. . . . The patient will resist drowning in homogeneity. . . . The objective [is] the health of the individual patient who comes for treatment. . . . There are three aspects of a total therapeutic process. All three are directed toward the same goal, the cure of the patient. . . . Whether the therapist is at ease or not is not a criterion. The primary question is whether or not it is therapeutic for the patients. . . . The formulation and organization of therapy may be a reflection of the unconscious pathology of the therapist. . . . What is not tolerated is often automatically labelled acting out [which] is a technical term . . . it becomes a non-specific meaningless mark of opprobrium to designate all activity as acting out.

Every beginner in group therapy should read this book from aspiration, saying to himself: "Some day, if I use my training and intelligence, I can be like them." Those with more experience should read it as a corrective against the diffuseness of some of the current literature. Senior group therapists should read it to redirect their attention to their prime duty of curing patients and teaching others to do so. Because it is based on sound and enlightened empiricism rather than on pious assumptions, it will help the science and art of group therapy attain the dignity that it could but does not yet deserve.

James Johnson, in *Group Therapy: A Practical Approach*, deals with the subject primarily from the point of view of the general psychiatrist with experience in hospital, clinic, and private practice, and in teaching psychiatric residents. His book is the most "clinical" in the field to date in the sense of viewing group therapy as part of the total therapeutic armamentarium of the psychiatrist, along with shock treatment, drugs, other psychotherapies, and the ancillary hospital and clinic facilities. The first five chapters will probably set the standard for the clinical psychiatric approach to group therapy for some time to come. He reviews the uses and limitations of group therapy, offers a systematic program for teaching the subject to psychiatric residents, and discusses its application to each category of the personality types listed in the *Diagnostic and Statistical Manual of the American Psychiatric Association*. In particular he stresses the differences between group therapy and group activity, and between groups and nongroups. He emphasizes that an aggregation of people is not a group unless it has a leader, and that this leader or authority plays the decisive role in determining what the members will do, even if the leader is not aware of that role or tries to deny it, and that in this sense the dynamics of therapy groups are the same as the dynamics of other groups and organizations.

He goes on to describe his model of a therapy group, and by implication of a group therapist, and states the terms of the group contract and the goals of therapy. The bulk of the book (pp. 174-387) is then devoted to an illustrative analysis of seventy meetings of an outpatient group. At this point the exposition gets into serious difficulties, since the example is unfortunately chosen. Everyone concerned seems to be "acting out": tormented patients, depressed and bemused therapists, harassed recorders, and forgetful secretaries, with discouraging results. The repeated proscriptions against addressing anyone in the group individually (pp. 4, 102, 104, 167, 188, 405, and so on) because that is "group destructive" and because "the therapist is there to do group therapy, not individual therapy," are unsupported and questionable. The truth of the matter is that medically speaking the therapist is *not* there to "do group therapy," he is there to cure patients, but this goal is specifically repudiated in the book for reasons never clarified.

The operational model of the therapist that emerges from the text is different from that formally described. He is frequently late for meetings, changes the time of meetings, and misses meetings. One therapist missed four meetings in two months. It is not stated what could be more important to or for the therapist than attending group therapy meetings. There is an implication that extraneous factors took precedence over the needs of the patients. This may explain the stress on "patient hostility," and the instructions to the therapist to plead and insist that the patients express hostility against him. It also means that the group contract is unilateral, since tremendous pressure is put on the patients to attend every meeting, and punctually, while the therapist does not do so. In summary, then, the model of group therapy here is based on a local situation which few institutions would care to emulate, and which has the earmarks of an institutional "game" sanctioned or enforced from the top. Strictly speaking, it represents, not group therapy (the results are disappointing), but an experiment in group dynamics: What happens in a group if the "therapist" is unreliable, or is not permitted to keep his schedules, and refuses to address any of the patients individually? In my own experience, in several cases where the therapists were originally doing "group therapy," the attendance rose markedly after the therapist began to talk freely to individual patients. The patients also got better faster.

It is suggested that the first five chapters of this book be reprinted, omitting the subsequent material in its present form.

Group Psychotherapy: Theory and Practice, by Mullan and Rosenbaum, is readable, interesting, and instructive, and full of well-tempered and well-documented discussions. The worst that can be said about these authors is that they may seem to some readers to be overly sentimental—"I like you very much and I am glad that you are with us" (p. 85)—but their patients evidently forgive them for it, since their attendance is "consistently 90% or more." There must be some sound reason for this devotion on the part of their patients, and it probably lies at the opposite pole from the sentimentality, namely, in the gentle but firm commitment and the incorruptibility of these therapists: "There can be no consideration by the leave-taking patient that should he desire or need to return that he can in fact return to the group. . . . The therapist is solely responsible for preventing this by excluding this member (the egocentric usurper). . . . The difficulty of the individual therapist in contemplating this kind of group psychoanalytic therapy is basically that of facing the group with his own neurotic, possibly incestuous, ties with his individual patients. . . ." Regarding the banal "father and mother" concept of co-therapy, they ask, What if "the male co-therapist is not particularly masculine or fatherly and the female co-therapist is not particularly feminine or motherly?" There is no meanness in their frankness, but merely an objective offering of possibilities, a regard for the patient's welfare rather than the preservation of false status (when it is false) among therapists.

The chapter, "Emergency, Crisis, and Emergence," can be considered required reading for all group therapists from beginners to the most experienced, since it deals in a most admirable and practical fashion with real emergencies (such as the death of a patient), and not with "emergencies" in the therapist's head. The therapist who reads this chapter *before* crises arrive will find himself well prepared to deal with difficult real situations when he is suddenly confronted with them and may have no time to prepare on the spot. There is nothing else quite like it in the literature.

Mullan and Rosenbaum recognize that transference and countertransference (and they distinguish clearly between the two) on the part of the therapist are not rare and interesting occurrences to be greeted with surprise, but regularly occurring phenomena to which every therapist must be continually alert. This, and other attitudes derived from carefully considered experience, pays off in the only legitimate way, which is not the accrual of comfort for the therapist, but of comfort for the patient: "When we return after vacation, we find that everyone has made progress" is a grateful change from the carefully cultivated horrors of separation anxiety as described by other authors. "There have been very few experiences of overt psychosis in the group" is much pleasanter to read than recondite explanations of why patients insist on becoming psychotic at the most inconvenient times for the therapist.

Some of these books, or parts of them, at least, are more suitable for some specialized audiences than for others. For the inclusive potential audience—interested laymen, students of the social sciences, psychiatric residents, beginners in group therapy, and experienced clinicians—Mullan and Rosenbaum's book can be recommended with the most enthusiasm. Patients, of course, will always read books on group therapy, particularly those written by their own therapists, and here, too, Mullan and Rosenbaum would be the book of choice. For the layman, it is readable. For the student, like Wolf's book, it pictures the therapist as a person who knows what he is doing and is at home with his work. For the psychiatric resident, it is intelligible and instructive. For the beginner, it is reassuring, and, for the experienced clinician, it is relevant, even though he may find both central and peripheral points of disagreement.

These four books, which may be taken as representative of the Eastern school, indicate that the first generation has reached an impasse in obfuscation and rigid provincialism, while the second generation has freed itself to reach out creatively and provocatively. Although the new thinkers are psychologically sophisticated, they seem to the Westerner to be naïve in their approach to social action; their superlative understanding of what goes on inside the patient is matched by a groping approach to what goes on outside the patient. While most literate Westerners are familiar with the names of these nine authors, not one of the nine cites a single reference from either the Palo Alto group or from the literature on transactional analysis. One thing that impresses the transactionally oriented clinician, after reading each of these books meticulously from title page through index (over 1,300 pages in all), is the nervousness of these writers, their continual cautioning, their meticulous attention to peripheral issues such as the selection of patients. Even Wolf has his weak spot in this respect: He is as timorous about discussing finances as Johnson is about discussing sex. There are no cowboys here. (A "cowboy," in transactional parlance, is a relaxed therapist who walks into any room where any group of patients is collected, without regard to selection, and proceeds to cure as many as he possibly can in the shortest possible time.)

Since it appears well established, by this time, that any kind of group activity or group therapy is going to benefit a certain proportion of members to a certain extent, it is no virtue to report a reasonable number of "therapeutic effects" from using a given approach, nor does that make it worthwhile to devote time and energy to studying each approach. The

only worthwhile system is one that will cure an unreasonably high proportion of patients in an unreasonably short time with unreasonably stable
results, that is an "above chance" system, so to speak, and for such a system to be demonstrated effectively it will be essential for Easterners to
read Western literature as assiduously as Westerners read Eastern. It is just
as necessary to listen to Virginia Satir talk about messages as it is to hear
Alexander Wolf talk about transference, and there are well thought out
ways of dealing with both simultaneously as a step toward the phantom
ideal goal of group therapy—the complete cure of every patient in one
session. Whenever a group therapist forgets this ideal, he will easily be led
astray. Whenever he keeps it in mind, he will be sure that at each meeting
of each group he adds to his store of hard-boiled knowledge. If the reader
is amused at this concept, his grandfather would have been equally skeptical about the idea of curing syphilis, gonorrhea, or pneumonia by a single
injection, yet that goal is now almost realized. In a more practical way,
we might aim for a thoroughly effective, relatively short group therapy by
1980.

COMMENTS BY ROBERT L. GOULDING

The review by Eric Berne of the four books brings back many fond
memories of him.

When I reread the review, I remembered fondly many meetings with
Eric over the years—from playing poker in the mid-1950's, to sitting beside
him as President of the Golden Gate Group Psychotherapy Society, when
he gave his last speech at the annual meeting, to being turned away when
I went to see him the Sunday before he died, and feeling that my friend,
with whom I had fought bitterly at times, no longer saw me as his friend,
or so I thought.

Eric's position, overtly, was that we could cure patients; that it was
possible to cure them in one session, and that we should look for ways—as
he clearly states in this review. Covertly, or ulteriorly, to use the transactional analyst term, I don't believe that he did so. In *Games People Play*
he had hope for a few patients, but not for mankind. His own life, during
the last year, was not a happy one, with his divorce not quite final when he
died. When Mary and I asked him to come have a drink with us to celebrate our engagement, he said, "I feel too sad about my own marriage to
celebrate with anyone else."

Whatever the ulterior statement was, however, he established an
environment around him wherein anyone with any moxie turned on to the
possibility that patients really could be cured—although I prefer to say that
patients really can cure themselves. Herein lay the greatest difference
between Eric and me. To quote from his last book:[5]

The electrode is the decisive challenge for the therapist. He, together with the patient's Adult, must neutralize it, so that the Child can get permission to live freely and react spontaneously, in the face of the parents' programming to the contrary, and their threats if he disobeys. This is difficult enough with milder controls, but if the injunction is a demand made by a witch or giant whose features are distorted with rage, whose voice smashes through all the defenses of the child's mind, and whose hand is ever ready to strike humiliation and terror into his face and head, it requires enormous therapeutic power.

I see the power as being in the patient, not in the therapist, and that the therapist's real job is to *allow* the patient to find his own power, and to put that power to use in a service, not a disservice. Eric repeatedly wrote and spoke about the "scripting" of patients, of how parents inserted electrodes into children's heads (the electrode is the Child of the Parent in the Parent ego state of the Child ego state), of how injunctions were "locked in solidly," that the script *determined* a person's life plan, and so on. When I said to him one day, "Damn it, Eric, you totally disregard the autonomy of the individual and that all of us have choices," his response was, "If your parents told you that you can get well when you are 37, after you have seen a psychiatrist, then you can get well."

On this we disagreed. I believed, and still believe, that people make whatever decisions they have to make as children to survive psychologically and physically, and that they can remake a decision or make a new one at any time, and thus change the course of their lives. Eric believed the power to be in the "cowboy," as he called our kind of therapist. I believe the power is in the person, and that the therapist's job is to create an environment in which that person can make new decisions in his life, and get out of his script—to live autonomously, responding to the new environment in a way appropriate for this time and place, not hanging onto old feelings from the past, and looking for receptacles for them.

Nonetheless, he was a great teacher, a great creator of new ideas, and, above all, a great listener. He taught me to listen in a way that nobody else could—not even Fritz Perls. I am still listening.

REFERENCES

1. G. W. Thomas, "Group Therapy, A Review of the Recent Literature," *Psychosom. Med.*, 5:166-180, 1943.
2. S. R. Slavson, *et al.*, *Bibliographies on Group Therapy* (New York: Amer. Group Psychotherapy Assn., 1946, 1950).
3. J. L. Moreno, ed., *Group Psychotherapy, A Symposium* (New York: Beacon House, 1945).
4. A. Wolf, "The Psychoanalysis of Groups," *Am. J. Psychother.*, Vol. 3, No. 4, October 1949, pp. 16-50; Vol. 4, No. 1, January 1950, pp. 525-558.
5. E. Berne, *What Do You Say After You Say Hello; The Psychology of Human Destiny* (New York: Grove Press, 1972), p. 116.

Part 4

APPLICATIONS
TO PARTICULAR
DIAGNOSTIC
ENTITIES

THIS SECTION CONTAINS papers which relate specifically to particular settings in which group psychotherapy has proven to be effective. Each of the settings described is important to the student of group functioning, particularly to the sociologist. Research conducted on the hospital as a community has indicated that group therapy cannot be seen in isolation in an institutional setting. Frank engages this point at the very outset of his paper on group therapy in a mental hospital, since he notes that group therapy in state hospitals may awaken in patients a sense of belonging in a hospital community through increasing their participation in a therapeutic program. He is concerned about the hospital culture in this regard. Among group therapists Frank stands out as one of those who is strongly aware of the importance of group dynamics. This probably is related to his original background in the field of social psychology and his early association with Kurt Lewin, as well as his sympathy to Sullivan's interpersonal theory as a theoretical base for psychotherapy. His point of difference from those psychoanalytically trained group therapists who are more rooted in a Freudian approach to human behavior appears in his recognition of the socializing drives of individuals and his belief in group cohesiveness and the importance of membership in a group. He has added some current comments.

Freudian theory, which emphasizes identification with the leader, appears to deny much of the cohesiveness that can stem from the group members' relationships with one another and their discovery that they have a common ground in their difficulty in living. The importance of the group as an experience is also attested to by Standish and Semrad in their work with psychotics. It is interesting that this paper was part of a symposium organized by a group of social workers. The symposium emphasized the group dynamic aspects of group psychotherapy. Semrad has added to his paper with comments by Max Day.

With the increase of the aged in the population there is an increase in emotional difficulties of this same population. Ross has reviewed in detail group psychotherapy with the geriatric population.

Alcoholism remains a major problem in the American culture, and we believe the articles we have included to be as timely today as when they were first published.

Over the last decade there has been awakening of interest in techniques of group therapy with the mentally retarded. The results appear to be promising. The article by Payne and Williams sets forth a practical approach to such a group.

Particularly since America's involvement in Vietnam, the problem of drug addiction has become a major health problem. Kaufman describes the use of paraprofessionals in a treatment program. The specific use of ex-addicts is noteworthy, as is the rationale behind such an approach. A related article by Berger covers work with the addict's family.

We have included a paper by Bilodeau and Hackett relating to the use of group techniques with convalescent male heart patients. We believe group techniques to be valuable in work with patients who are recovering from a variety of different physical complaints.

Although the early work in group psychotherapy, especially during the 1930's, was with children, there has been a paucity of work with youngsters since that time. The article by Rosenbaum and Kraft is both a survey of the field and a practical guide to group treatment of children.

The paper by Sandison covers the common ground between psychiatrists who are drug oriented and use a pharmacological approach and those concerned with group dynamics. Specifically, the article is very encouraging in its recommendations for treatment of psychotics.

The "nitty-gritty" of group psychotherapy is discussed in the article by Chance. In a society where value systems are constantly being scrutinized and questioned, patients often find themselves frustrated as to their own life goals. The therapist occasionally finds himself at an impasse with patients no matter how strenuously he performs. Berger and Rosenbaum illustrate what happens with such an impasse, following logically from Chance's description of the problems to be encountered.

Many therapists have become disenchanted with a psychoanalytic approach to psychotherapy and have explored other techniques. Liberman's paper offers an approach to group therapy from the perspective of behavioral or learning principles.

As psychotherapists organize community clinics and make efforts to intervene in populations that were rarely exposed to or responsive to psychotherapy, they often became frustrated. Strupp and Bloxom discuss the novel use of a film developed for lower socioeconomic groups in paving the way for a more relaxed meeting with mental health professionals.

36

GROUP THERAPY IN THE MENTAL HOSPITAL

Jerome D. Frank

In recent years the use of group therapy in mental hospitals has grown by leaps and bounds. Groups are conducted by aides, nurses, the clergy, social workers, and occupational and recreational therapists, as well as by psychiatrists. The kinds of groups are as varied as the group leaders. Ranging in size from a handful of patients to the population of an entire building, the forms they take are legion. There are discussion groups, social clubs, roundtable groups, psychodramatic groups, administrative groups, and occupational and recreational groups, to mention some of the most common. This proliferation of group activities parallels a similar trend in the larger community and also reflects a changed conceptualization of the functions of the mental hospital.

Our competitive, urbanized, highly mobile culture has drastically reduced opportunities for intimate, nondefensive relationships with others, such as might have characterized the large family of a previous era engaged in running a family farm or business. Each of us meets many more persons in a day than our grandparents did, but these contacts are apt to be superficial and often tainted by some degree of self-seeking. Despite much superficial gregariousness, many Americans suffer from a sense of isolation and alienation. The burgeoning of small face-to-face groups which seek to cultivate emotional intimacy and honest, open communication can be viewed as a self-healing effort by society to counteract this state of mind.

Since psychiatric patients experience isolation and alienation especially keenly, it is fitting that mental hospitals should also seek through group methods to awaken or restore their feeling of belongingness and increase their sense of participation in the affairs of the hospital community.

Reprinted from *Monograph Series No. 1*, December 1955, pp. 1-17, American Psychiatric Association, Mental Hospital Service. Revised and updated, 1973.

The main impetus for the introduction of group methods into mental hospitals, however, came from a change in the view of the hospital environment related to the ascendance of psychodynamic psychiatry. It had been generally assumed that the mental hospital was a psychologically neutral, protective environment which held patients while the staff tried to cure them through individual psychotherapy. Attention to psychodynamics inevitably led to the awareness that, far from being neutral, the hospital abounded with psychologically destructive group forces.[1] To counteract them and substitute therapeutic group influences, psychiatrists developed and implemented the concept of the therapeutic community, organized around group activities.[2]

It also gradually became apparent that most psychiatric illnesses were chronic or recurrent disorders that neither psychotherapy nor antipsychotic drugs could cure. Rather, as with other chronic illnesses, the appropriate goal was the more modest one of rehabilitation. For mental patients, this meant helping them to acquire or enhance communicative skills and to assume more responsibility for their own lives. Group therapies proved especially appropriate for this purpose.

This paper considers group therapy in the mental hospital from the standpoints of its direct effects on patients and its relation to the therapeutic community.

GROUP THERAPY AS A FORM OF PSYCHOTHERAPY

From the standpoint of psychotherapy the functional psychoses are seen as maladaptive processes resulting from disturbance in normal growth and maturation. These disturbances arise from conditions, especially in the formative years, which do not afford suitable opportunities for growth or create chronically anxiety-producing situations with which the inadequately equipped child must deal. As a result of these unfortunate early occurrences, the patient experiences conflicting urges and feelings which he cannot effectively resolve; for example, feeling utterly dependent on a parent whom he at the same time fears. These conflicts and his futile efforts to deal with them lead to habitually distorted ways of perceiving himself and others, resulting in inappropriate responses to current interpersonal situations. That is, he carries over his childhood conflicts into his adult life.

Psychopathological manifestations are seen in part as direct expressions of the emotions involved in these conflicts (such as fear, anger, shame, guilt, anxiety) and in part as bungling efforts to resolve the conflicts in such a way as to preserve self-esteem and to alleviate the unpleasant emotions.

To avoid possible misunderstanding, it should be made clear that this formulation does not by any means imply that patients' symptoms are wholly or even primarily of psychogenic origin. The inability of a patient to resolve his emotional conflicts or to cope with life's stresses is often undoubtedly related to biologically determined vulnerabilities. Just as interventions at the biological level can improve a person's psychological functioning, however, so beneficial psychological interventions can ameliorate organic disturbances.

The crux of the problem from the standpoint of psychotherapy is that mental patients seem unable to profit by experience. Instead they continually repeat the same maladaptive patterns, and each new experience of failure or frustration, instead of leading them to modify their behavior, seems to reinforce the neurotic or psychotic pattern. Perhaps the major reason why psychiatric patients fail to learn by new experience is that they are too demoralized. Their self-esteem is so damaged by their repeated failures that they lack the courage to try new responses but instead cling to their habitual ones which, however self-defeating, are comfortably familiar and often yield pseudo solutions to their problems.

The object of psychotherapy is to restore the patient's morale by supplying new interpersonal influences which help the patient resolve his conflicts, develop a more accurate picture of himself in relation to others, and so become able to behave more fittingly toward them. As the patient begins to experience some successes in his dealings with others, this reinforces the new ways of behaving; if all goes well, the maladaptive patterns are progressively weakened and the more successful ones strengthened. Thus his potentialities for further emotional growth are progressively mobilized.[3] At first glance the means by which psychotherapy tries to produce these fortunate results seem to be legion, but all varieties of psychotherapy share three aims. The first is to strengthen the patient's self-respect so that he gains the courage to seek better ways of dealing with his conflicts. The second is to help the patient to maintain a level of tension or distress sufficient to keep him working toward better solutions, but not so great as to force him back into his maladaptive patterns. With some patients the problem is to increase tension, to stir up inappropriate responses so that the patient becomes more clearly aware of them and is more strongly motivated to correct them. With others, the task is to keep the patient's tension within manageable bounds. In individual therapy with outpatients the desideratum is usually to raise the level of tension; in group therapy, especially with hospitalized patients, it is to keep tension within bounds. This is primarily because a group, with its potentialities for emotional contagion, multiple transference reactions, clashes of differing viewpoints, and so on, presents more opportunities for emotional stimulation than a two-person relationship.

The third aim of all forms of psychotherapy is to supply some guides or models to the patient as he struggles to modify his attitudes, in an atmosphere which encourages him to experiment, provides him with accurate information as to how well he is doing, and minimizes the penalties for failing. All this may be summed up in the phrase "reality testing." This aspect of therapy is more apparent in group methods than in the individual form because of the multiplicity of models afforded each patient by the other group members, the greater freedom with which advice and guidance are offered, and the greater nearness of the therapy group to "real life" situations.

In furtherance of the aims of increasing the patient's self-respect, maintaining an optimal level of tension, and encouraging reality testing, all forms of psychotherapy offer the patient a certain kind of relationship and present him with some sort of task. The common factor in all psychotherapeutic relationships, whether group or individual, seems to be that the patient feels that he is taken seriously by a person in whom he has confidence, and will continue to be taken seriously no matter what weaknesses and faults he may reveal. This permits him to gain self-confidence by finding himself acceptable to a person he respects—to shine by reflected glory. Group therapy, in addition to offering patients this relationship with the therapist, introduces a new dimension of it which may be termed "group belongingness," to be discussed below.

All therapies involve a task in which patient and therapist engage collaboratively. It is with respect to this that therapies differ most. The task provides the medium by which patient and therapist (or patient and patient in a group) relate to each other. The task is also linked to the patient's self-respect in that the more successfully he carries it out, whether it be to free associate or to beat a drum in a rhythm band, the more he is rewarded by the approval of other participants. The nature of the task also affects the amount of tension felt by the patient. The more poorly a situation is defined, that is, the more ambiguous it is, the greater the anxiety it produces.[4] Hence, if it is desired to increase tension, the definition of the task is ambiguous; if it is desired to diminish tension, a task is chosen which is within the patient's grasp and it is clearly defined. Thus it is that classical psychoanalysis and nondirective therapy, in which the task set the patient is only vaguely defined, seem most useful for patients who are not too sick, while therapeutic social clubs and psychodrama, which structure the task for the patient quite elaborately, have found their chief applicability in the treatment of psychotics.

The usual task set by both individual and group psychotherapy is to help the patient to become aware of and correctly label his present feelings and behavior and to reevaluate his past experiences in the light of his current attitudes and goals. In short, it is to increase the patient's self-understanding or insight. This task is based on a sound rationale. To the extent that a patient understands himself better, he is more able to modify his behavior constructively. Without this clearer vision, his renewed efforts to solve his conflicts under the stimulus of psychotherapy will tend to run along habitual patterns, and he will end up more discouraged than before, having again experienced a failure. Increased self-understanding heightens the patient's self-confidence in various ways. Identifying the motives behind a response carries the implication that it is caused by the patient, rather than by circumstances beyond his control. Therefore he has the power to change it. Conversely, finding the explanation for a present faulty attitude in the patient's past experience shifts responsibility from him to figures in his background, with concomitant reduction of guilt. The mere act of naming an attitude or a feeling reduces the anxiety connected with the unknown.[5] Furthermore, a labeled feeling is automatically a shared one, and the patient gains reassurance by finding that the therapist and other group members, knowing the dreadful secret, are not upset by it.

Finally, to the extent that the therapist and other patients accept the task of aiding the patient's self-understanding, they must continually try to understand him better. This helps them to maintain a consistent interest in the patient which in turn increases the patient's feeling that he is taken seriously, and thereby increases his self-confidence.

The task of fostering insight is so admirably suited to producing beneficial changes in so many patients that it is easy to regard it as the only "real" form of psychotherapy and to view all other approaches as merely palliative. It does have one drawback, however, which is that it is beyond the reach of many patients who need psychotherapy most. Insight therapy is the treatment of choice for many psychotics. But quite a few already have too much insight in the sense that they cannot cope with the urges and feelings of which they are aware. Focusing on the feelings of such patients often increases their anxiety to a degree which impedes therapy. Other psychotics are largely incapable of verbalizing their feelings, and when faced with this task by the therapist become more discouraged, frustrated, and angry. The accumulating experience with therapeutic groups has made clear that there are other possible therapeutic tasks which can produce beneficial change of attitude. Even primitive group activities such as rhythm bands may succeed in mobilizing a spark of self-confidence in very regressed patients and in encouraging them to reach out a little toward others. A more complex task, suited to patients in better contact, is posed by the didactic group of Klapman.[6] Here the therapist takes the major responsibility for how the group functions by presenting material to it and guiding the discussion. He can easily control the level of difficulty of the task so as to keep it within the members' abilities, and the use of neutral material stimulates interaction at the intellectual level and dampens emotional interplays which the patients are not ready to handle.

A similar type of task is offered patients by therapeutic social clubs,[7] whose major aim is to strengthen their social skills as a means of combating their isolation and heightening their self-confidence. These groups are organized on parliamentary lines, elect their own officers, and plan their own activities, the therapist functioning as an advisor only.

Rhythm bands, didactic groups, and social clubs aim to strengthen the ability of patients to function socially and to reduce their emotional tensions by channelizing them into rigorously structured activities. A more flexible approach is afforded by the methods of psychodrama.[8] At one extreme, psychodramatic scenes can be used to train patients to handle the ordinary situations of daily life; at the other, to mobilize intense and regressive emotional responses. All have in common that the director exercises control over what transpires, aiming to foster spontaneity in the actors and to minimize the likelihood of emotional experiences too intense for the patient to deal with constructively.

The task of a therapeutic group is an important means of fostering a sense of belongingness among the members. It does this by giving them a common focus which encourages them to relate to each other and supplying a vehicle for them to do so.

GROUP COHESIVENESS AS A THERAPEUTIC FORCE

Members' sense of belongingness to a group, more simply termed group cohesiveness, plays an analagous role in therapy groups to the relation between therapist and patient in individual treatment. As such it is probably the most important therapeutic feature of groups.[9] It supports the self-esteem of members, enabling them to face rejected aspects of themselves and to risk experimenting with new ways of feeling and behaving on the basis of what they have discovered. Cohesiveness also enables the group to tolerate intense emotional interplays without disruption, and emotions supply the motive power for change of attitudes.[10] As it is particularly hard to achieve with psychotics, it requires extended discussion.

All humans possess disjunctive and socializing drives. A philosopher has made an apt comparison of human beings to the supposed behavior of hedgehogs in winter. The hedgehogs try to cuddle together to keep warm, but run into each others' spines and are forced to draw apart. Finally, they find the proper distance which will afford maximum warmth and minimum discomfort. Just so, each of us seems finally to discover that distance from others at which he can function with the most gratification and least uneasiness. Mental patients have particular difficulty in entering into close, satisfying relations with their fellow-man. This is evident in their group behavior, much of which can be understood as the resultant of a conflict between disjunctive and cohesive forces. The most disjunctive end of the scale may be represented by a patient who spent entire group meetings standing with his back to the group and his fingers in his ears, shouting out the window. Even this man, it may be surmised, felt some pull toward the group or he would not have resorted to such extreme measures to shut the others out. A slightly higher degree of cohesiveness, though still minimal, is shown by what has been termed asyndetic communication.[11] By this is meant that a patient hears only enough of what another says to use it as a take-off point for his own fantasies. This phenomenon is not entirely unknown in other group meetings, including those of professional societies.

Perhaps the first reliable sign of group cohesiveness in hospital groups is common griping. From the standpoint of group dynamics, this may be viewed as an attempt of the members to move closer together by directing disjunctive feelings away from each other to targets outside the group. Many other phenomena, especially in early group meetings, can be profitably viewed as attempts to strike a balance between cohesive and disjunctive forces. An example is the search for superficial similarities, whereby at the same time efforts to become more intimately acquainted are forestalled. The conflict between attraction and repulsion is also expressed in the "peer court" in which patients advise and criticize each other, implying both interest and disapproval,[12] in competition for various roles, such as the doctor's assistant,[13] or the sickest, and even in explosions of open hostility. Antagonisms often are a sign that members of the group have come close enough emotionally to get under each other's skins, to return to the metaphor of the hedgehog.

Some of the disjunctive forces underlying these behaviors are easily identified in schizophrenics, though every human probably experiences similar stirrings to some degree under certain circumstances. At the top of the list may be put their deep distrust of themselves and others, leading them to approach each new potential relationship with the expectancy that it will be painful, if not disastrous. This is often expressed in early group meetings as suspiciousness of the motives of the group leader, who is especially suspect because he is in a position of power and because he says he is trying to be helpful. At the close of the first session of a group, for example, a patient buttonholed the observer and with the air of one who invites a great confidence asked to be told the "real" reason for holding these meetings. In another group, one of the patients asked the doctor why she came to the group. When she replied, "To help you solve your problems," this announcement was met by jeering laughter from a number of patients, one of whom stated it was the funniest joke he had heard in a long, long time. In another group, a patient said, "All doctors are insincere. Doctors are trying to learn things about foreign relationships. What trusts are they trying to break?" When the doctor attempted to reassure this patient of his sincerity, the patient immediately demanded a pass from him. When the doctor explained that he did not have the authority, the speaker shouted angrily that he "didn't like people crossing me up."[14]

Another disjunctive force in early group meetings is the fear of the stranger, probably innate in all gregarious animals including humans. A stranger is an ambiguous figure, an unknown quantity, hence he arouses anxiety. In therapy groups, whose task includes self-revelation, the anxiety caused by the presence of strangers is heightened by the knowledge that one is expected to expose one's weaknesses to them.[15] Yet another disruptive force in therapy groups is the mutual contempt of the mentally ill, a reflection of their self-contempt. To the extent that a patient feels stigmatized by having to undergo psychiatric treatment, this feeling is heightened by having to admit it publicly, as it were, especially to a group of people he feels to be equally unworthy.

Fortunately, in addition to disjunctive forces, there is in every human a force, however twisted in its expression, which leads him to seek satisfaction from intimate contact with his fellows. All forms of therapy must ultimately rely on this. In therapy groups this basic drive is strengthened by certain factors. First among these is the dependence of each patient on the therapist. The expectancy of help from the group leader is probably the only cohesive force that the latter can rely on initially. According to Freudian theory,[16] identification with the leader remains a route toward identification with other members throughout the group's life. Another cohesive factor is the existence of a shared task or goal, already mentioned as essential to the therapeutic process. Focus on the task, besides supplying a common point of reference for everyone, diverts members from concentrating on the differences which keep them apart. The development of group cohesiveness is encouraged by the presence in the members of the group of a shared background of experience, including that of suffering from a mental illness. Patients' discovery that they have symptoms or problems in common draws them together. "Misery loves company" expresses a sound psychological truth. Some patients derive self-respect from finding that others are worse off than they are, and this may motivate them to keep attending.

As a group continues other cohesive forces emerge, such as the development of a body of shared experiences and each member's sense of being taken seriously by the others, growing out of the group interactions. A particularly effective binding force is a spirit of mutual helpfulness,[17] which is of slow and uncertain growth but may occasionally be achieved. With luck, all these influences, and others not mentioned, add up to produce a feeling in each member that he belongs to an ingroup, that he is participating in a special and rewarding kind of experience which is not shared by everyone. The therapeutic impact of any group on its members is at least partly a function of the extent to which this sense of group belongingness is achieved.

It is true that a mere aggregation of patients has some therapeutic potentialities. Each may gain sufficient support from his individual relationship with the therapist to derive some therapeutic benefit despite tensions created by the presence of the others. Moreover, such a situation is useful diagnostically in that it tends to elicit from each patient his characteristic interpersonal ways of dealing with his anxieties, affording valuable clues to an observant therapist. The special values of group therapy, however, are in large part dependent on some feeling of cohesiveness among the group members, and the therapist should consciously work to foster its development. In order to do so successfully he must first of all have a realistic appraisal of the potentialities and limitations of group treatment. A therapist who starts a group reluctantly or lacking faith in its therapeutic possibilities is handicapped in his efforts to create a cohesive atmosphere. The same holds for the overenthusiastic therapist who expects miracles. He is bound to be disillusioned, and the resulting discouragement will infect the members of his group.

With respect to group composition, a basis for cohesiveness is provided by including in the same group patients who are undergoing a common experience in the hospital. Thus patients may be selected from the same administrative unit, since they have the same physical environment and the same treatment personnel. This also facilitates transfer of administrative responsibilities to the group, which will be considered presently.

The experience of being admitted to a mental hospital forms another useful basis for organizing groups. Intake groups are useful in their ability to convey quickly to patients information they should know about the hospital regimen. They also give the patients a chance to express feelings of anger, anxiety, and humiliation or other reactions to being hospitalized. Thus they admit the patient at once into a treatment relationship.

Similarly, groups may be based on the shared experience of being about to leave the hospital. Such "exit groups" have been found useful for patients who, because of prolonged hospitalization, have lost the confidence to face the outer world. This anticipatory anxiety may be effectively combated by opportunities to rehearse their behavior in situations they expect to face. The psychodramatic approach seems especially helpful for this purpose. Therapeutic social clubs are also useful in easing the transition from the hospital to civilian life, as they focus on developing and strengthening social skills. They also supply patients with a continuity of relationship in that they join a club while in the hospital and continue in it after they leave. This continuity is strengthened by the fact that relatives of patients often attend these groups while the patients are still in the hospital.

Though the presence of a shared experience in the hospital is one basis for organizing a group, further selection may have to be exercised to avoid including in the same group patients who are unlikely to be able to interact in any useful way. This is especially important if a type of group therapy is contemplated which fosters direct emotional interactions. Here clinical diagnosis is of some, but limited, aid. The same group should not contain patients who are too far apart with respect to degree or type of illness, for example belligerent paranoids and regressed hebephrenics. On the other hand, a group should not necessarily consist exclusively of patients with the same clinical picture. It depends on the nature of the condition. Alcoholics do well together, but—to take an extreme example—mute catatonics do not.

More important than diagnostic categories in guiding composition are the ways in which characteristics of the patients in a given group can be expected to interact. Thus one excessively aggressive patient in a group of timid ones may create an unworkable situation, but several may foster useful interaction. They hold each other in check, and encourage the timid ones by their example or by seeking allies among them in their battles with each other. Similar considerations apply to the personal characteristics of patients in relation to the therapist. For example, certain therapists seem to enjoy aggressive patients and can do well with them, while others may have to struggle so hard to control urges to counterattack that they cannot be therapeutically effective. A motherly woman therapist may do better with a group of dependent patients than a younger male colleague.[18]

Even before the first group meeting, its cohesiveness will have been influenced by how the therapist offered the group to the participants. Since the patients' reliance on him for help is the chief unifying force in initial meetings, it is important that his approach to the patients inspire confidence in him. This is done by presenting group therapy to the patient in terms that he can understand, discussing his misgivings with him, and then simply prescribing it as one would any other form of treatment, with the understanding that the patient may reopen the question after trying a few meetings, should he wish to do so. Unless the patient is so ill as to be unable to assume any initiative at all, he should probably not be compelled to attend a group, because this damages his self-esteem. On the other hand, it is perhaps worse to leave the decision entirely in the patient's lap. This amounts to abdicating one's therapeutic responsibilities. The patient may interpret it to mean that the therapist does not have much faith in the treatment. Also, seeming to let the patient decide may confuse him because he knows that the staff has the power to compel his attendance if they wish. Thus a therapist's take-it-or-leave-it attitude may diminish the patient's confidence in him and so weaken one of the main cohesive forces in the group.

In conducting the group, the therapist can foster cohesiveness by deliberately making himself the focal point and by keeping the group's task clearly before it. Even in a free discussion group he should be definitely in charge, facilitating communication between patients and encouraging those types of interaction which seem to him to hold most promise. He should define his role clearly to combat the ambiguity with which he is certain to be initially perceived, and thereby lessen the patients' anxiety. The group's task should be one within the members' capacity, and the therapist should try to avoid letting the members experience failure. In this connection it must be kept in mind that psychotic patients often resort to irrelevant activities, and the therapist's disapproval of these may further demoralize them. He should set the task and guide the group by example more than precept, permitting the group to follow him by identifying with him rather than by taking orders from him. In this way he may be able to avoid becoming the target of disruptive resentments as an authority figure, while encouraging the group's sense of responsible participation in what goes on.

THERAPEUTIC GROUPS AND THE
THERAPEUTIC COMMUNITY

The development of a sense of belongingness to a therapy group facilitates patient participation in an over-all hospital program organized along democratic lines; that is, a therapeutic community. Democracy means many things to many people. A British Peer defined it as a society in which every man considers himself to be the equal of his betters. In the first flush of enthusiasm for the democratic ideal, many hospital staffs attempted to hand over to the patients more responsibility for decisions about each other and the management of their ward than they were qualified to make. Since each is primarily interested in his own welfare, and his judgment is frequently impaired by his psychopathological state, his decisions about his fellow-patients are not likely to be fully objective or well-considered. Moreover, as the length of hospital stay progressively decreases, patients are less and less able to accumulate the experience needed for wise decisions about how a ward should run. For these and other reasons, a more realistic concept of the therapeutic community soon prevailed. According to this view, each patient shares actively in arriving at decisions about the welfare of the group and its members, but only to the extent commensurate with his capacities. The staff retains ultimate responsibility for all major decisions, but arrives at them only after taking the patients' views into full consideration.

The most direct way of using patient groups to increase the democratization of a hospital is by giving them limited administrative responsibilities. In accordance with the principle of suiting the difficulty of the task to the capacity of the patient, the degree of responsibility entrusted to these groups depends on how sick the patients in them are. For example, Cruvant [19] describes administrative groups of patients on a maximum-security ward. These groups are run along parliamentary lines and elect their own officers, but follow an agenda prepared in advance. Their activity is limited to discussing administrative problems of the ward, not of individual patients, and communicating these to the leader who is the administrator of the ward. Cruvant comments that in this way he may unearth conditions of which he might otherwise be totally unaware and which he can readily correct. Competent attendants appreciate the group. Less competent ones often improve in response to group-developed social attitudes, and the others can be easily identified in a way not otherwise possible.

Wender and Stein [20] describe groups of less ill patients in a private hospital which assume responsibility for organizing their own activities. In addition, members are encouraged to make suggestions concerning the over-all hospital program, but the final decision about these is made by the director of the hospital. Wender and Stein note that the patients in such groups tend to lose their originally indifferent attitude about the hospital: "They had begun to think of the hospital as something in which they had a share, and they tried to make it something of which they could be proud." A further extension of administrative responsibility is illustrated by the round-table groups of McCann.[21] These groups are self-selected; that is, patients elect new members to the round table as vacancies occur. Their administrative responsibility extends to making recommendations for parole or discharge of patients which are taken seriously by the administrator. Thus the round-table group assumes a high degree of responsibility for the conduct and welfare of its members.

The goal of patient participation, in short, does not mean that all patients should join in making all decisions, but rather that each has an opportunity to participate to the extent that his condition allows. Democracy can be overdone. Those aspects of state-hospital life which have been severely criticized as antitherapeutic, such as conformity, utter simplicity or routine, and relief from all responsibility, may be helpful to certain patients at some stages of their illness. By keeping the ambiguity of the situation at a minimum they help to reduce anxiety. Under such an organization patients are not apt to be set tasks beyond their ability so that they are not faced with the threat of failure, and this may permit restitutive forces to begin to operate. It is not rare for patients to show prompt improvement on transfer from a private hospital to a state institution, suggesting that active therapeutic efforts may have impeded the recovery process of such patients by setting them tasks they could not manage. However, it seems true that for most chronic patients a highly simplified hospital program offers little help. If a patient after a few months has not been able to mobilize his healing processes under this regime, its continuance is self-defeating, since he progressively loses his incentive to get well as he becomes more and more remote from his usual activities and relationships.

The successful functioning of a therapeutic community depends on free, undistorted communication within and among all its levels, coupled with a feeling of shared responsibility. Ideally this atmosphere fosters in each member a feeling of self-respect and inner freedom. Therapy groups heighten patients' sense of freedom by increasing their options through enabling them to enter into previously unavailable interactions and activities. Since these activities require cooperation, controls exerted by a successful group on its members are felt by them as enhancing rather than diminishing their freedom. Members' sense of group identification leads each to experience guides imposed by the group not as external forces but as coming from within themselves. Thus the parliamentary rules of a successful therapeutic social club are experienced by members not as restrictions on their freedom of activity but as means of progressing toward shared goals.

In this connection, since patients identify more easily with each other than with a staff member, controls exerted by other group members are more apt to be internalized than those imposed by the staff.

Just as a successful group both enhances and constructively limits the freedom of its members, so it heightens each member's sense of responsibility but makes the burden easier to bear by sharing it. Group cohesiveness implies a greater awareness in each member of the problems of the others and therefore some assumption of responsibility for their welfare. But since the group shares these responsibilities they do not fall with crushing force on any one patient. Baker and Jones point out, for example, that a patient group which dealt with patients who broke hospital rules was often more lenient to the offender than he was to himself.[22]

The development of a sense of freedom and responsibility in members of a group is concomitant with improvement of communication among them. All groups foster communication among their members. Even at the level of a rhythm band members must learn to respond a little to each other in order to keep in time. Groups with a common task, such as discussing a book or organizing a party, stimulate mutual communication, because the successful carrying out of the task depends on this. In discussion groups the major task is to improve communication, and the extent to which this is achieved is a measure of the group's success.

Parenthetically, increased communication between schizophrenic patients may not be an unmixed blessing. These patients are extraordinarily easily upset by close emotional contact, and their initial reaction to a group experience may be an increase in behavioral disturbance. In a study at Perry Point Veterans Hospital it was found that the introduction of group therapy was accompanied by an increase in combative and destructive behavior on the ward as compared with a control ward not receiving group therapy. These and other signs of disturbance, however, fell off more sharply in the group therapy than in the control ward with the passage of time. More importantly, they were accompanied by evidence of improvement at a deeper level, such as a drop in night-time sedation to about half the previous level and a striking decline in urinary incontinence, which was probably a sign of increased self-respect.[23]

Concomitant with improving communication among patients, group therapy intensifies communication between patients and staff and within the staff. Communication between patient and staff is enhanced by the well-known fact that patients can more easily express their real feelings, especially hostile ones, to an authority figure in a group than when they are closeted with him face to face. The therapist is literally a terrifying figure to many schizophrenics. This was vividly illustrated by two in different groups, both of whom were ambulatory, who were also being seen in individual treatment and who would never sit next to the therapist in a group meeting. They always saw to it that another patient was interposed. Both finally confessed in the group that they were afraid the therapist would strike them. Neither had been able even to hint at this in individual sessions. Thus the group facilitates expression of feelings to the therapist simply by its geographical arrangement. In addition, the public nature of the occasion diminishes the patient's fear of retaliation, such as might occur in private where others would not be aware of it. Patients are further encouraged to speak up when they sense that they are spokesmen for other group members.

Sometimes a group may communicate too successfully with the staff in the sense that the group leader identifies too closely with the patients. Patton[24] reports this experience with residents starting groups. The young doctors tended temporarily to identify with the patients and echo their complaints against the hospital administration. After a difficult period the end result, here as elsewhere, was that the doctors recovered their objectivity while achieving a better understanding of their patients. In another hospital in which the doctors saw in the group the same patients that they were treating individually, it was noted that they began to see them more as whole human beings and less as examples of psychopathology. The doctors became more aware of the patients' integrative powers and ego strengths, and began to speak about them in everyday language instead of psychiatric jargon.[25]

An example of how the group improves communication between patient and staff was shown by a group of adolescents at the Henry Phipps Psychiatric Clinic. This group was started because the adolescents were creating minor disturbances on the ward—teasing the nurses and finding various ways of irritating their doctors. In early group meetings their attitude toward the therapist, a staff physician, was markedly reserved. In the course of a discussion in which the leader participated about how to accumulate some athletic equipment, the group gradually came to see him as one of themselves. This was neatly shown when the group advised him how to best approach "them"—the other staff members—to facilitate getting the equipment. Incidentally, the behavior of these boys on the ward improved remarkably after the group was started.

In the context of the therapeutic community, greater freedom of communication between patients and staff may not be an unmixed blessing. It may also heighten tensions as patients become unwilling to follow the orders of staff members blindly, demand explanations, and, with the support of the group, may talk back.

The concept of treatment as the responsibility of everyone on the ward has also led to increasing participation of lower-echelon personnel, with concomitant changes in the roles of the professional staff. Since emerging roles cannot be clearly defined, the resulting role-blurring can create considerable tension as staff members jockey for position.[26]

Increased communication between patients and staff inevitably stimulates increased communication among staff members—and not only by posing a threat to their authority. Groups arouse emotions in their leaders and present them with challenging new experiences to share with their colleagues. A group therapy program also increases the number of staff members on whom patients impinge. Typically the patient's individual therapist, if he has one, is not the same as his group therapist, so that each patient automatically is involved with at least two staff members. As patient groups participate in administrative responsibilities, problems arise which can only be solved by a meeting of the staff members involved.

In short, the introduction of group activities has repercussions at all levels. Successful transition from the traditional authoritarian structure to the more democratic one of a therapeutic community requires continuing examination by all concerned of what is transpiring, efforts to resolve problems as they arise, and familiarization with the new treatment philosophy and methods for its implementation.

Achievement of these aims requires not only frequent community-wide meetings in which the staff must take the lead in promoting communication and imparting information, but also frequent informal group discussions among staff members. Through these they can experience something of what patients feel in group therapy. More importantly, their misgivings can be met, conscious or unconscious efforts to sabotage the program can be exposed and forestalled, and new roles defined and clarified. Staff groups also afford an opportunity for treatment personnel to familiarize themselves with principles of group dynamics, leadership, and administration—topics not ordinarily included in the training or experience of psychotherapists. For this purpose, didactic sessions can be interspersed with the informal ones.[27]

This discussion may be concluded by reference to a recurrent phenomenon which well illustrates how therapeutic groups foster the growth of freedom, communication, and responsibility. The first activity of almost every therapeutic group is patient griping about aspects of the hospital such as food, passes, and cleanliness of the ward. Griping, as already mentioned, is one means of facilitating group cohesiveness by diverting hostile feelings to targets outside of the group. It also means that patients feel freer in that they can talk about matters which they were unable to bring up in other settings. Griping also implies a willingness to communicate more openly with the staff and perhaps some increase in self-respect in the sense that the complainer must have a trace of hope that his complaint will be received seriously or he would keep silent. In initial group meetings patients imply that the responsibility for doing something about the complaints rests solely with the staff, and inexperienced leaders share this view. In this way the attitudes of both reflect the dominant hospital culture. The patients express it by their demands that the leader do something, the leader by pointing out that he is not the administrator or in other ways trying to evade having to act. A properly oriented leader, however, strives to shift the discussion from the complaints to what the individuals or the group can do about them. This is easiest, of course, with respect to the discharge of a patient since when a patient leaves depends ultimately on himself. A skillful leader can divert a barrage of demands for discharge into a discussion of what one does in order to achieve discharge. Similarly, complaints about aspects of the hospital can be referred back to the group for suggestions as to what is best done. In this way along with freedom and increased communication there is gradually built up in the group a sense of individual and group responsibility which is a powerful therapeutic agent for the members and increases their participation in the functioning of the hospital.

In summary, group therapy programs can benefit hospitalized patients in two ways: through direct influence on the patients themselves and by facilitating beneficial changes in the hospital organization. With respect to their effects on patients, two potential advantages of group over individual therapy have been stressed. First, groups offer a wide range of therapeutic tasks which can be tailored to the needs of different types of patients. Secondly, through fostering a sense of belongingness they strengthen patients' feelings of freedom and of responsibility for themselves and each other. These inevitably lead to improved communication throughout the social structure of the hospital. Thus from the standpoint of the hospital, therapy groups are both expressions of the democratically oriented therapeutic community and necessary means toward this end.

REFERENCES

1. E. Goffman, *Asylums: Essays on the Social Situations of Mental Patients and Other Inmates* (Chicago: Aldine, 1962); A. H. Stanton and M. Schwartz, *The Mental Hospital* (New York: Basic Books, 1954).
2. M. Greenblatt, R. H. York, and E. L. Brown, *From Custodial to Therapeutic Patient Care in Mental Hospitals* (New York: Russell Sage Foundation, 1955); M. Jones, *The Therapeutic Community* (New York: Basic Books, 1953); H. Wilmer, *Social Psychiatry in Action: A Therapeutic Community* (Springfield, Ill.: C. C Thomas, 1958).
3. J. D. Frank, *Persuasion and Healing: A Comparative Study of Psychotherapy* (2nd ed.; Baltimore: Johns Hopkins University Press, 1973).
4. E. S. Bordin, "Ambiguity as a Therapeutic Variable," *J. Consult. Psychol.*, 19:9, 1955.
5. E. F. Torrey, *The Mind Game: Witchdoctors and Psychiatrists* (New York: Emerson Hall, 1972).
6. J. W. Klapman, *Group Psychotherapy: Theory and Practice* (New York: Grune & Stratton, 1959).
7. D. A. S. Blair, "The Therapeutic Social Club," *Ment. Hyg.*, 39:54, 1955.

8. J. L. Moreno, "Psychodrama," in H. I. Kaplan and B. J. Saddock (eds.), *Comprehensive Group Psychotherapy* (Baltimore: Williams & Wilkins, 1971).

9. J. D. Frank, "Some Determinants, Manifestations, and Effects of Cohesiveness in Therapy Groups," *Int. J. Group Psychother.*, 7:53, 1957; R. Liberman, "Behavioural Group Therapy: A Controlled Study," *Brit. J. Psychiat.*, 119:535, 1971; I. D. Yalom, *The Theory and Practice of Group Psychotherapy* (New York: Basic Books, 1970).

10. R. Hoehn-Saric, B. Liberman, S. D. Imber, A. R. Stone, S. K. Pande, and J. D. Frank, "Arousal and Attitude Change in Neurotic Patients," *Arch. Gen. Psychiat.*, 26:51, 1972; J. C. Whitehorn, "Physiological Changes in Emotional States," *Research Publication, Association Nerv. Ment. Dis.*, 19:256, 1939.

11. E. A. Martin, Jr., and W. F. Hill, "Toward a Theory of Group Development," *Int. J. Group Psychother.*, 7:20, 1957.

12. G. R. Bach, *Intensive Group Psychotherapy* (New York: Ronald Press, 1954), p. 245.

13. J. D. Frank et al., "Behavioral Patterns in Early Meetings of Therapeutic Groups," *Am. J. Psychiat.*, 108:771, 1952.

14. Florence Powdermaker and J. D. Frank, *Group Psychotherapy: Studies in Methodology of Research and Therapy* (Cambridge, Mass.: Harvard University Press, 1953).

15. J. Mann, "Some Theoretic Concepts of the Group Process," *Int. J. Group Psychother.*, 5:235, 1955; D. S. Whitaker and M. A. Lieberman, *Psychotherapy through the Group Process* (New York: Atherton Press [Prentice-Hall], 1964).

16. S. Scheidlinger, *Psychoanalysis and Group Behavior: A Study in Freudian Group Psychology* (New York: W. W. Norton, 1952).

17. W. McCann and A. A. Almada, "Round-table Psychotherapy: A Technique in Group Psychotherapy," *J. Consult. Psychol.*, 14:421, 1950.

18. Powdermaker and Frank, *op. cit.*

19. B. A. Cruvant, "The Function of the 'Administrative Group' in a Mental Hospital Group Therapy Program," *Am. J. Psychiat.*, 110:342, 1953.

20. L. Wender and A. Stein, "The Utilization of Group Psychotherapy in the Social Integration of Patients: An Extension of the Method to Self-governing Patient Groups," *Int. J. Group Psychother.*, 3:210, 1953.

21. McCann and Almada, *op. cit.*

22. A. A. Baker, M. Jones, J. Merry, and B. A. Pomyrn, "A Community Method of Psychotherapy," *Brit. J. Med. Psychol.*, 26:222, 1953.

23. J. D. Frank, "Group Therapy with Schizophrenics," in E. B. Brody and F. C. Redlich (eds.), *Psychotherapy with Schizophrenics* (New York: International Universities Press, 1952).

24. J. D. Patton, "The Group as a Training Device and Treatment Method in a Private Psychiatric Hospital," *Int. J. Group Psychother.*, 4:419, 1954.

25. J. Miller, S. Kwalwasser, and A. Stein, "Observations Concerning the Use of Group Psychotherapy in a Voluntary Mental Hospital: Effects of Group

Psychotherapy on the Training of Residents," *Int. J. Group Psychother.*, 4:86, 1954.

26. R. Rubenstein and H. D. Lasswell, *The Sharing of Power in a Psychiatric Hospital* (New Haven: Yale University Press, 1966).

27. K. L. Artiss and S. B. Schiff, "Education for Practice in the Therapeutic Community," in J. H. Masserman (ed.), *Current Psychiatric Therapies* (New York: Grune & Stratton, 1968), 8:233; R. W. Sherman and A. M. Hildreth, "A Resident Group Process Training Seminar," *Am. J. Psychiat.*, 127:372, 1970.

37

GROUP PSYCHOTHERAPY WITH PSYCHOTICS

Christopher T. Standish
Elvin V. Semrad

A general review of group psychotherapy with psychotic patients was done by Drs. James Mann and Elvin Semrad of our staff in 1947 in a paper entitled "Notes on the Use of Group Therapy in Psychoses." This present paper for the greater part is an elaboration of their earlier paper bringing up to date our collective experience in group psychotherapy at the Boston State Hospital.

Group techniques were first used with psychotic patients by Dr. E. W. Lazell at St. Elizabeth Hospital in 1919. Until recently, in contrast to other modes of psychiatric treatment, group psychotherapy in psychoses has remained a relatively unexplored sphere of endeavor. Important contributions in this field have been made however by Moreno, Schilder, Blackman and Klapman, in addition to Lazell. Gifford and Mackenzie have reviewed the literature in 1947.

The principal types of group psychotherapy as applied to the psychoses may be classified according to the method of approach. Opposite extremes are seen in the repressive-inspirational and the analytic or investigative methods. Between these two extremes lies a third approach which may be appropriately designated as didactic.

The repressive-inspirational technique exploits the strong collective transference to the leader and the force of suggestion exerted over the group. Evangelists and political demagogues attest to the effectiveness of this method with normal groups of people. The investigative technique on the other hand in general makes use of productions and interplay in the group while the therapist maintains a neutral role. In the didactic method, emphasis is placed upon some form of lecturing to the patients. The therapist is a teacher and mental mechanisms are interpreted in order to impart conscious intellectual insight.

Reprinted from the *Journal of Psychiatric Social Work*, Vol. 20, 1951, pp. 143-150.

Group therapy was begun at the Boston State   Hospital in June, 1946 in an effort to define the role of group therapy in the treatment of the psychoses. The discussion that follows covers some of the problems of organization and technique with an estimate of our observations and results growing out of our experience in the active use of group therapy with psychotic patients.

The organization of a group of psychotic patients for the purpose of instituting group therapy is accompanied by many misgivings and anxieties. We could not help but notice in our own project a marked reluctance to begin and often to continue group therapy. In seminar discussions before and during our project we found it helpful to acknowledge honestly our own fears, indecision, and ignorance of the situation. The exchange of such feelings among members of the staff served as a source of security and allayed anxieties preventing progress in conducting group therapy. These seminars were expanded to include not only staff psychiatrists, but, in addition, social workers, clinical psychologists, and experienced psychiatric nurses now working with psychotic patients in groups. It is our feeling that one of the chief obstacles to group psychotherapy lies in the therapists themselves, assuming that the patient in his desire for health constantly seeks our assistance, albeit in a manner evoking uneasiness in those who try to help him.

Having overcome our initial reluctance to begin group therapy, further problems arose in the course of treatment. These too were aired in seminar discussion, and as a result further observations and experiences were better understood and formulated.

Diagnosis does not seem to be of great importance in terms of choice of patients for group therapy. In the early stages of our work, it was generally felt that the inclusion of a manic patient would be certain to stimulate conversation in the group. Similarly, articulate paranoids were found to be equally helpful. We no longer regard these as necessary preliminary selective measures, since the need for a flow of conversation in the group, we feel, is in large part an expression of the need of the therapist. As the therapist proceeds, the nature of group dynamics is apparently such that sooner or later most of the members of the group will participate verbally while all participate on a nonverbal level.

The location of the meeting place is of some importance. The meeting place in our experience should be free from distraction and sufficiently attractive so as to afford an atmosphere of importance to this special type of treatment. The therapeutic setting should be one that the patient feels has been selected for a special type of helping situation.

Seating arrangement of the group members is not prescribed so that each patient is free to select his own seat. As members come to know each other, they will sit near those whom they like. Invariably one or more patients will vie for a seat near the therapist. On the other hand a patient will sometimes indicate his hostility and remoteness from the group by sitting far away from it or even turning his back to it. After a number of sessions, seating arrangement tends to become static.

In determining the frequency of meetings, we considered the following points: How many meetings best serve the interests of the group? How much can the group take? And how much can the therapist take? In our experience two or three meetings weekly have worked out to good advantage. Meetings last usually about one hour. Meetings of this duration permit arrival at a subject of common appeal and interest, as well as time for discussion, without undue fatigue on the part of either the therapist or the patients from the emotional tensions that go with the discussions.

Attendance in our groups is not compulsory although we do use social pressure to enforce attendance. All therapists respect the patients' wishes by leaving open invitations to all recalcitrants. Reiterance of this invitation by the therapist between sessions and by nurses and attendants before each session reduces the problem of absenteeism. In some cases pressure is exerted by members of the group on the absentees.

We have found it desirable to limit the group to a maximum of fifteen patients. In a larger group it is very difficult for the therapist to keep track of what is going on in the group. Many of us feel that even smaller groups of about ten or eleven are preferable as the therapy progresses. Addition or subtraction of members seems in the long run to make little difference to the progress of the group. In our Reception Services rotating groups have been successfully conducted.

All of our therapists introduce the first meeting with a brief orientation as to the purpose of the meetings. Patients are asked to express their opinions freely and are assured that they can speak of anything they care to. It is suggested that in this way the patients may be able to help each other. With further experience we introduce a meeting with a contract of sorts in which we more specifically define the objectives of the group meetings and what the therapist expects of the members as well as some definition of his own role in the group. In general, no restrictions are placed on behavior.

Our technique can be described as "Participation in Casual Conversation" with appropriate comments being made at opportune times. The therapist's role we term as that of a catalyst in which he attempts to arouse action and reaction on a feeling level.

The term catalyst was borrowed from the field of chemistry and was chosen by us to emphasize that a catalyst keeps a reaction going. The implication for therapy is that the therapist facilitates interaction between patients but takes care not to use the situation to act out his own personal conflicts or problems.

In this respect we feel it better to avoid a lecturing or all-questioning role, thus not becoming established as forbidding or authoritative figures. Rather we try to insinuate ourselves as members of the group. We feel that the therapist should be discouraged from impressing on the group what an intelligent person he really is or how much he really knows about emotional problems.

It has been our experience that a therapist's sincere interest in the patient as a person and an appreciation of the patient's dilemma is a great asset in therapy. Patients seem to sense very keenly when the therapist, by his attitudes and comments, shows a lack of interest. It also seems helpful if the therapist is honest with patients particularly with regard to his own feelings and actions towards them. It is quite a comfort to patients when the therapist can objectively discuss his own responses in the treatment situation. In this way he can indicate that he also is human and subject to much the same feelings as his patients. Indicating respect through attempting to understand the patients' feelings and difficulties is also of help in the therapeutic situation. We have our own special way of saying this; that is, "the therapist must provide an atmosphere of 'all-rightness'!"

In treatment we make use of ordinary everyday conversation in preparing the patient for investigation of more intimate material regarding personal conflicts and problems; what we have called participation in casual conversation with appropriate comments at opportune times. We are not exclusively preoccupied with the content of what is said by patients, thus focusing attention on feelings which lie behind what is said or done at the moment. We might say that we are more concerned with what the patient means rather than what he says.

We talk with our patients on any topic whatsoever, no matter how trivial or inconsequential the conversation may appear to be. Such apparently trivial conversation is an excellent entree into the emotional life of the patient and may often reveal a good deal about his sentiments and attitudes. We have also noticed that just as much feeling can be linked with superficial conversation as with so-called "deeper productions."

We use the term "appropriate comment" mainly in an attempt to define the role of the therapist with respect to the interpretation of material brought forth by the patients. In general we do little in the way of interpretation in the sense of relating present conflicts and interpersonal issues to those of infancy and childhood. Rather we attempt to understand what the patient is trying to convey to us in terms of what he feels. The appropriate comment may be a query, approbation, mild disagreement, or any sort of remark which helps to stimulate the flow of conversation and the emergence and recognition of these underlying feelings. Ideally the appropriate comment should indicate the "all-rightness" of the feelings expressed by the patient. It should also show that the therapist has some appreciation and understanding of the preoccupations of the patient which are hinted at in the material brought forth. The appropriate comment is more effective in our experience when use is made of the patient's own words.

The therapist has further opportunity to indicate his understanding when questioned about psychotic symptoms such as delusions and hallucinations. Such questions are usually phrased so as to create an issue over the validity or truth of the experiences. We prefer that the group answer questions of this sort. However we may often comment from a premise which runs roughly as follows—that hallucinations, for example, are not only valid but also very vivid personal experiences and that it is of interest to both the therapist and the patients to figure out what possibly could have given rise to them, for they are without doubt unusual and naturally clamor for explanation. This diverts discussion from the validity of the experiences to a more profitable area; namely, what everyday experiences and feelings past and present are associated with these psychotic symptoms.

The therapist has the opportunity to indicate his understanding of questions in which the patients ask about themselves, but in disguise, as it were. It seems helpful to answer such questions as much as possible in terms of the patient's own needs rather than the therapist going into any details of his own personal life. Patients of course do show a personal interest in the therapist. Personal opinions and preferences are frequently asked of him. Such questions seem better answered in a brief and straightforward fashion.

Our patients seem to be much more sensitive to the therapist's inadvertent or unconscious behavior than to his conscious attitudes. A warm smile, the twist of a lip, the tone of one's voice, a quick adjustment of one's clothing, a glance at one's watch, and so forth, are much more accurate indicators of the therapist's actual interest and understanding than anything he might say to his patients. The therapist indicates interest, boredom, anxiety, or frustration mainly through his own inadvertent responses or nonverbal cues. This may easily affect the material which the patients bring forth. In this way the sentiments and prejudices of the therapist have their effect on the therapeutic process.

We usually find it unnecessary to actively restrict or prohibit patients in their overt behavior. It seems to us however that the therapist sets limits to the patient's behavior by his own inadvertent responses and may even in the same way invite patients to go too far. Occasionally it is necessary to interfere actively.

The setting of limits may possibly have a more subtle meaning for the patient than is at first apparent when attention is focused on the mere prohibition of antisocial behavior. A patient may for example feel quite ineffectual in his everyday experience when other people behave aggressively towards him. By being aggressive towards the therapist, he is forcing the therapist to give a practical demonstration of how such situations can be handled more effectively. Instead of seeing "how far he can go" with the therapist, the patient may rather be challenging the therapist to show him how he can learn to handle these disturbing situations in a more grown-up way. The setting of limits may thus have potentialities for emotional growth of the patient.

Our experience indicates that group therapy with psychotic patients goes through recognizable stages. The first stage is one of testing out the situation and is characterized chiefly by hostility in as many forms as the patient has at his command. The conversations deal quite exclusively with the hospital and the representatives of the hospital (rarely direct attacks on the therapist) and the special situation the hospital produces. Agreement in this sphere fosters a good deal of group unity which permits the advent of the second stage.

In the second stage there is fairly free expression of anxiety-laden psychotic material. Hallucinations and delusions are most frequently disclosed and such repeated disclosures are finally met by attempts of the various members to explain such phenomena. It must be said in this regard that some of the most astute observations are made by the patients.

Gradually the material discussed takes on a more personal tinge in relation to feelings about the self and feelings about others. Thus the third stage is entered as the patients begin to introspect, mutually criticize, and work through some of their emotional problems.

A fourth or closing phase of the group is not yet entirely clear. However it is observed that patients who show the most improvement gradually begin to speak about their future plans and become more concerned about their situation outside the hospital, the persons in that external situation, and the problems that the total situation of leaving the hospital and returning to the community presents.

Recently in a paper by Drs. Rosen and Chasen, attention was focused more closely on individual group sessions in an effort to clarify some of the ways in which psychotic patients resist frank discussion and easy interaction in a group setting, as well as the issues lying behind such resistances. Those who published this study felt that it could not be categorically stated that overcoming particular difficulties would bring about good results. Rather the immediate goal is to help what might be called a "poor" group to change in the direction of a "good" group.

A "poor" group we feel is one with much disorganization and chaos and great indirectness of language. Many evidences of regression and persistent lack of change over a period of months fall into the same category. A "good" group on the other hand is a group in which there is a general feeling of cohesion or working together with attentiveness on the part of individual members and participation and interaction of at least a few of the members. Fairly clear language with some direct verbal expression of feeling, some attempts to deal with present and past problems, and absence of a persistent and unrelieved block also indicate a "good" group.

We have observed many manifestations which serve as resistance to straightforward discussion. It is our impression that perhaps they arise out of the current situation between the patients and the therapist. Some of these indicators of anxiety and resistance follow.

First, hostile acts in general may indicate anxiety and resistance. These acts range from the most obvious and overt to the most subtle. References in speech to violence and destruction are frequent. Hostile imitations of the therapist occur as well as hints about evil or authoritative persons. Patients may aggressively take over in the group or become excessively passive or inhibited.

Accentuated defenses are seen, both neurotic and psychotic, including the more typical symptoms of schizophrenia. To these, we would add evidence of specific regression both in speech and behavior.

Finally, we would mention persistent and unrelieved block with freer discussion outside the group, formation of cliques, and more obvious signs of group disintegration. Some of the latter would include patients aimlessly wandering about the room, much hubbub and murmuring, and various expressions of desire to quit or leave. As therapy goes on there may appear direct verbal expression of feelings of emptiness, of worthlessness, and even of being dead. Expression of emotions like fear and hostility usually leads into or accompanies the issues which are currently disturbing the patients. These feelings are frequently expressed to another member of the group before being directed at the leader.

It would seem that nearly everything we see happening in the group or to the patients is meaningful for the immediate situation among the patients, and in particular between the patients and the therapist, since these phenomena are seen arising out of or being accentuated in any given group session.

It should also be mentioned that sometimes a useful clue that something is wrong in the group is the therapist's awareness of his own discomfort. He may sense that the patients are making him feel tense or hostile in some way or are forcing him into unintended activity. As a result he may be didactic, overtalkative, or make premature comments arising from his own associations instead of clarifying from patients' associations.

In a general sort of way the issues lying behind the various resistances shown in therapy seem to concern ideas of physical danger, rejection, and feelings of being attracted to the therapist. Usually the patients have to deal with problems concerning their relationship with the therapist and the hospital before they feel free to discuss the prototypes of these problems in their prehospital and earlier life.

There is no doubt that the therapist is at times actually rejecting to the patients. This may be rather subtle, as when the therapist is excessively interested in some special attribute or talent of the patient, thus frequently through implication rejecting the rest of his personality. Also in the category of rejection is treating the patients like children, as for example, bringing in unannounced guests, acting in a dogmatic or patronizing manner, sleepiness, not consulting the patients about changes in schedule, broken promises, lateness, and missed meetings.

Some problems are inherent in the group situation itself. Jealousy over the many patients sharing the therapist's attention and the reluctance of patients to expose their private problems before a crowd are to be expected. More difficult to detect are resistances growing out of conscious or unconscious preferences by the therapist of patients who are most intelligent or who verbalize better than others. It is difficult for the therapist to remain objective in such circumstances and to discuss the patients reactions as problems of the patient even if they are provoked by real attitudes in the therapist.

The resistances are handled by clarifying their manifestations and investigating the feelings and issues lying behind them. We usually assume that the resistance grows out of some issue that has currently arisen between the patients and the therapist. When the therapist arrives at some appreciation of what is causing the patients' concern, the issue can be discussed honestly and realistically. The therapist need not feel that resistances are caused by his own mistakes; they are inevitable during the course of therapy. An observer is frequently useful in clarifying causes of resistances which may be in the therapist's blind spots, since many of the issues are precipitated through the therapist's unconscious behavior. The more the therapist can tolerate severely irritating attitudes and promote interaction, the more secure, accepted, and understood the patients will feel.

We are aware that in spite of much recent work on psychotherapy of chronic psychotic patients the idea is still rather widely held that psychotics are living in their own world and do not respond to cues in the immediate environment. The great preponderance of our experience contradicts this view.

It might be of interest at this point to comment on some observations made in comparing normal groups with psychotic groups. Resistances in psychotics though more easily recognized as such are exceedingly tenacious. Resistances can be much more subtle in normal groups, but at the same time we see a stronger desire to investigate, a much shorter period of testing, and a more rapid emergence of tender feelings. We have noticed that normal persons work much more effectively as a group in helping and trying to clarify for one another and in trying to apply what they learn. Psychotics on the other hand have a marked tendency to monopolize the therapist. The tendency for normal groups to use a show of excessive positive feeling for the group experience as a resistance is rarely seen in psychotic groups and then only on an individual level.

Although therapeutic results must be reckoned in long-term changes, general benefits to the patients are fairly specific. The group situation provides the patient with a safe permissive tool of relating himself once more to others. It encourages the expression of suppressed hostility, mobilizes unconscious tensions, and permits their release. It further provides a setting in which the patient can learn more about how he operates as a person in his dealings with others and possibly acquire more effective ways of dealing with other people.

The self-imposed isolation of the patient may relent as the opportunity is offered him to compare himself with others who also have severe conflicts over problems of everyday living. He is provided with a setting in which he may acquire a better perspective on his own problems and feelings.

Group therapy facilitates the task of caring for patients. Patients become more cooperative and less resistive with attendants, less abusive and assaultive on the wards. Many of those who are incontinent show better control of excretory functions. Others are less destructive of clothing and property, and the majority show greater neatness in dress and appearance.

In addition to these benefits to the patients, group therapy contributes to the general therapeutic atmosphere of a large state hospital in that it is possible to have more patients under treatment. The feeling that something is being done for the patients permeates the allied personnel, who often show subtle but definite improvement in their attitude toward the patients.

The therapist shares too in the benefits of group therapy. It contributes to his growth by affording the observation of patients in a new light. The group functions as a miniature of society in many ways and reveals much about how patients handle themselves with others. In addition, the therapist becomes aware of the effect he has on the group as a person while he also learns his limitations. Certainly the therapist will become more keenly aware of the nonverbal cues through which human beings so often convey their most intimate feelings to one another.

The effectiveness of group therapy in terms of statistical results is much more difficult to evaluate, though we have attempted such an evaluation of our group therapy program which was begun in June, 1946. This was done with a total of 165 patients who had been or were currently in group therapy in April of 1947 when an initial survey was made by Dr. Gurri and Chasen of our staff. It was decided at the time to keep these patients in group therapy as long as they remained in the hospital and to periodically evaluate benefits to these patients.

A total of 165 patients were treated, originally in 12 separate groups. Of this number 52 per cent were schizophrenic disorders, 28 per cent affective disorders, and the remainder other types including psychopathic personalities, alcoholic psychoses, organic psychoses of different kinds, and so forth. The age range of these patients was from 14 to 84 years. The average age was about 35 years and the average hospital stay about three years. Of the 165, slightly less than one third were acute patients, the remainder chronic. Four-fifths of the patients were females. This disparity was due only to the fact that most of the participating staff members were on female services.

In April, 1947, our survey showed that results with acute patients were, as would be expected, much better than results with chronic patients. Of the acute patients, 51 per cent had been released on trial visit as compared to 27 per cent of the chronic patients. An additional 25 per cent of the acute patients showed noticeable improvement as compared to an additional 37 per cent of the chronic patients.

Three years later in January, 1950, a survey by Dr. Gurri showed that 65 per cent of the acute patients were now on visit as compared to 34 per cent of the chronic patients. In other words, in the intervening three years additional patients, both acute and chronic, were released on visit. The increase in patients on visit in this period was 14 per cent in the acute and 7 per cent in the chronic patients. The proportion of patients showing progressive improvement over the three-year period was slightly lower than the percentage of patients who had showed initial improvement in April, 1947.

BIBLIOGRAPHY

Chasen, M., Finlayson, M., MacKenzie, J. M., "Further Follow-up of Results of Group Therapy in Psychoses." Read at Massachusetts Society for Residents in Psychiatry, May 1948.

Fidler, J., Jr. and Standish, C., "Observations Noted During Course of Group Treatment of Psychoses." Dis. Nerv. Sys., Vol. IX, No. 1, January 1948.

Gifford, S. and MacKenzie, J., "A Review of Literature on Group Treatment of Psychoses." Dis. Nerv. Syst., Vol. IX, No. 1, January 1948.

Gurri, J., Personal communication re follow-up of patients in group therapy, January 1950.

Gurri, J. and Chasen, M., "Preliminary Survey of Results of Group Therapy of Psychotics." Dis. Nerv. Syst., Vol. IX, No. 2, 1948.

Mann, J. and Mann, H., "The Organization and Technique of Group Treatment of Psychoses." Dis. Nerv. Syst., Vol. IX, No. 2, February 1948.

Mann, J. and Semrad, E. V., "Notes on the Use of Group Therapy in Psychoses." J. Soc. Casework, May 1948, pp. 176-181.

Rosen, I. M. and Chasen, M., "Study of Resistance and its Manifestations in Therapeutic Groups of Chronic Psychotic Patients." Psychiat., Vol. 12, No. 3, August 1949.

Semrad, E. V., "An Analytically Oriented Group Therapy Program in Boston State Hospital." Read before the American Psychoanalytic Association, mid-winter meeting, December 16, 1947.

Standish, C. T., Mann, J. and Rosen, I. M., "Further Observations on Organization and Technic of Group Therapy in Psychoses." Dis. Nerv. Syst., Vol. X, No. 12, December 1949.

38

GROUP THERAPY WITH PSYCHOTICS—
TWENTY YEARS LATER*

Max Day
Elvin V. Semrad

There has been a growth of interest in the past twenty years in working with psychotic patients analytically as well as in other ways. Analytic approaches have grown in various parts of the Western world.[1, 2, 3, 4, 5, 6] Many reports have continued to appear about analytic group therapy with psychotics in state hospitals all over this continent. There have also been trends in working with psychotics using pharmacological approaches, social psychiatry, community psychiatry,[7] and manipulative techniques. In the onrush of so many approaches, analytic approaches at times seem to fall behind.

The approaches and problems presented in the preceding paper are still true. The problems seem to be different—yet the same. The anxiety of the therapist in approaching such sick patients poses the same problem it did in the past in doing analytic group therapy. The existence of psychotropic and psychoelevating drugs is a reality, and they are often used to mask the therapist's resistance in facing such infantile patients. The increase in availability of drugs serves the wish to manipulate rather than understand patients. The repressive-inspirational approaches mentioned in the first paper were franker in their intent. The biggest clinical challenge in dealing with psychotics in group or individual therapy is in dealing with the afteraffects of past inadequate therapy.

Therapists have somewhat more courage in approaching psychotics than in the past, in part because of the existence of these same drugs and because of the other approaches mentioned. It seems as if patients are not as regressed as they used to be over twenty years ago, at least not in the big teaching centers. Perhaps some of them are just as regressed at home,

* Dr. Standish died in 1963 after the publication of the preceding paper. The present paper brings developments in the field up-to-date.

but they are not so visible en masse in their sickness; surely patients suffer just as much. One of the biggest problems currently is the difficulty of getting freely at psychological material from patients because so often they are completely blanketed with various drugs that do not allow them to express their needs, tensions, worries, fears, or concerns. In practice, with patience, as the therapist learns to trust his supervisor, he may reduce the drug intake of the patient to the point at which he can more properly get at the patient's feelings. Usually this brings surprising results, since the patient that the therapist has regarded as being at a stalemate in therapy suddenly starts verbalizing his inner feelings and worries. Most residents in psychiatry approach working with groups of psychotics as the necessary running of the gauntlet of their training. It is something that they feel they have to be exposed to only to be forgotten so they can then get onto most sophisticated, comfortable neurotics. A few who remain interested in the field may then try innovative approaches in prolonged therapy.[8]

It is ironic that psychotics, patients for whom loss is one of the chief issues in life, are exposed repeatedly to the loss of a therapist—losses which are not worked through constructively. In training centers there is a changeover of therapists every one, two, or three years, depending upon the nature of the training program. As a result, psychotic patients learn to steel themselves against the loss of their therapists. Some even waste a year of work waiting for the inevitable loss, when this issue is not faced and analyzed directly. Out of their own guilt for wanting to abandon psychotics, therapists play into this fear on the part of the patients by announcing their departure at the beginning of therapy, by providing enforced co-therapists (so that the intercurrent loss of the therapist need not be faced), by never permitting the group to skip a meeting in their absence, and by preparing long in advance of their own leaving another therapist for more therapy. This endless assembly line of group therapy for such patients has the feel of a fantasy of an ever-flowing good breast. Supposedly for the benefit of the patient, this setup is contrived for the relief of the therapist's guilt and to "soften" the blow of separation for the patient. It does neither. It denies reality for both.

Patients often become psychotic after termination as the next group starts. Others with more intense denial nag the next therapist to be like the former therapist of last year, or two or three years ago. It is very discouraging for the new therapist, and the patient is insulated against regarding the current therapist as an individual, since he, too, will be leaving to be replaced by another and need not be taken seriously. Thus the acceptance of group therapy as a mode of treatment for psychotics is a change, but changes and popularity do not necessarily connote progress. The repressed anxiety of the therapists returns to undo this form of therapy as well. It is our impression that it may be wiser to encourage that work not necessarily be completed with psychotics, should the therapist have to terminate prematurely, and to allow the psychotic to go out and face the problems of his loss on his own for half a year or a year before thinking of further therapy. Such patients who work through the issues of loss may do much better than those who are put on the endless assembly line of group therapy.

Groups tend to be smaller than fourteen, which was the figure given in the earlier work. Perhaps fourteen was a response to the scope of the problem posed in the large state hospital setting, namely, the large number of patients and the dearth of therapists. Commonly nowadays we see groups of six or eight patients working together.

Interpersonal issues are stressed now as in the past. The stress on such issues works with psychotics generally in individual therapy as in group therapy. Certainly, interpersonal issues have to be stressed in group therapy or there will be no group therapy. The coincidence of this necessity in both kinds of therapy probably accounts for the general impression that group therapy is so useful with psychotic patients. It is not eaiser in a group; rather, the same factor works best with this population and this mode of therapy. Outpatient work with psychotics increased as group therapy became part of the general approach of working with psychotics and the same patients continued to be followed in the community who had been treated in the hospital.[9]

In private practice, psychotics are more often seen in a group of mixed diagnoses. Including psychotics in private work poses special problems. In general, we limit the number of psychotics to one or two in a group. Beyond that point, the flavor of the group and the kinds of issues that come to the fore would be changed. One is then faced with the usual problems of working with an all-psychotic group, as mentioned earlier. The problem for a mixed group is that neurotics must face their fear of the psychotic. They do this partly out of guilt toward the patient and partly out of fear of and loyalty to the teacher. This goes only so far. There is a problem of difference in aims in life and differences in character structure in mixing these two categories. The aim of the psychotic is survival, since for him living is a matter of life and death. He uses extreme passivity or rage to manipulate a compliant object to sustain him in life. His defenses include denial of painful reality, distortion of reality, blaming a compliant object (projection), daydreaming and hallucinating, and some reaction formation, along with acting out and manipulative techniques.

The aim of the neurotic patient, on the other hand, is to love and be loved with less than full responsibility for these aims at a neurotic price. This neurotic price may include some inhibition, whether frigidity or impotence, some obsessive-compulsive devices, and some phobias, all of which allow less than total responsibility in love, sexuality, and work. The neurotic resorts to denial, reaction formation, some projection, but also a fair amount of sublimation. It is clear that both kinds of people live at different levels of aim in life and use different levels of operative techniques. One can see why it would be hard for them to get along together in a group without the persistent expectation of the therapist to hold them together as a unit. After all, most therapists with character structure like the neurotic avoid treating psychotics. Why, then, should not just plain neurotics want to avoid psychotic patients? They stay with the psychotic patients in group out of love for the leader and his persistent expectation that they can work it out, out of lack of finances (since group therapy is cheaper than individual therapy), or out of a fear of individual therapy (the hope for less involvement in the group than in individual therapy).

The most common reaction of neurotics to the psychotic patient is to humor him and cover him with substitutive goodness as a poor child or a lost soul, thereby isolating him. Approaches to communicate are tentative in both directions. This may precipitate some crisis for the psychotic, including hallucinations, delusions, a suicide threat, or a "reality problem" (such as loss of apartment or loss of job or a change in the home). Since the group is quick to appease and humor the psychotic, this kind of reaction must be analyzed so as to get at the fear that the neurotic feels and wants to avoid, and that the psychotic repeatedly instills in others. Analyzing this approach is difficult and takes a long time, since the neurotic shies away from facing such massive anxiety. If the patient is paranoid or in an agitated depression, the impatience of the members in having to face this stress with him is increased. When the group faces and resolves a crisis with a psychotic and sees their similarities and differences, the team is given a feeling of accomplishment for working it through and comfort that things are not as bad for themselves.

On the other hand, the psychotic patient is usually quite glad to be in the group. He gets a great deal of support just from being with reasonable neurotic people. He may insist on his right to sit quietly for long periods of time, even for months, and still benefit from the group. It takes the group a long time to overcome their dread of the silent psychotic on whom they can project so many fears and worries. One must keep in mind two separate measuring rods in expectations when one mixes neurotics and psychotics in the same group. As long as the therapist is comfortable with both of these and with mixing them, the group will fare well.

What is missing in such an office group, which was easily available in the hospital group, is the social pressure to come to group therapy. This has to be replaced by the strength of the bonds built up between patient and therapist as well as among the patients. The strengthening begins during evaluation interviews before group therapy itself has even started. We ask each psychotic patient to have at least one interested relative who will be prepared to bring him to meetings regularly—from the hospital, if necessary, during any regressions that may take place. So long as such a relative is provided one can ensure continuity of treatment for the patient and for the group, and mere increases of psychotic anxiety will be expected, tolerated, and encouraged, while interruption of treatment is discouraged completely. Nevertheless, despite this aim, if the patient is hospitalized far away, one has to expect short interruptions for a month or two before he can resume treatment in the same group. Bond strengthening also requires the therapist to provide extra moments before or after a group therapy meeting, individual hours, telephone calls, and other matters in order to maintain the bonds with the group.

One of the realities of treating psychotics and people generally nowadays is the general social climate—the availability of all kinds of drugs, mood elevators, tranquilizers, and so on. We discourage their use. This comes as a matter of consternation to the group members. We look on such devices as a necessary evil or crutch that we hope the patient will get rid of as soon as possible. At first the group cannot understand an approach like this, but it gives all the members courage in seeing that one can face anxiety, and massive amounts of it, and grow because of it, rather than immediately snuffing it out chemically. Actually, most psychotic patients resent the use of drugs that deprive them of responsibility for their feelings, and therefore they take heart from such an approach. Where drugs are given by the group therapist or by another physician, a detailed analysis of their meaning should be made. This is because they usually feed on the patient's earliest fantasies of poisoning or good feeding, and their use affects not only the use of the drugs themselves, but the use of comments by the therapist (another type of feeding).

The continuity of therapy is one of the most striking features for the psychotic. He is encouraged to come whether in or out of the hospital, whether suicidal or not, whether sicker or not so sick. This approach sets an example for all the patients in the group, with the neurotic patients benefiting as well as the psychotic. Another approach used as a necessary support for some psychotic patients is combined therapy. While this is not a necessary way of dealing with the psychotic, it is a common one, since psychotic patients in individual therapy elsewhere will often be referred for group therapy. It necessitates extra time to work out issues for the patient for which there is not enough time in the group. Where the patient is referred from individual therapy to the group, the usual hope is that he will be exposed to other kinds of people and learn to see what feelings are aroused in him in dealing with them. Our own impression is that, where possible, the group therapist should see the patient individually in order to accomplish whatever detailed work is necessary, and in this way encourage the patient to keep all the material in the group with the other members. If the group therapist does not have the extra time, he has to share the burden with another therapist. This does not necessarily encourage the tendency to split the therapists that had been a concern in the past. Yet where therapy is split between two therapists there may, in time, be a tendency to split off from one kind of therapy.

In general, the goals with psychotic patients in analytic group therapy are the same as in treating any psychotic patient individually. There is not enough time in a group to work out all the details of the psychotic character structure and all the details of their fantasy life. Instead, one must work out major portions of pathology analytically by interaction in the group. A great deal of the work is done by the patients sitting silently in the group or on their own outside of the group. This is as true for the psychotic patient as for any other member. Some psychotics may stay in a group for three or four years to work out certain issues. Others may work for a year or so to gain enough strength to accomplish a goal in life, go out to work at it, and then come back in the future for further work. For example, one woman in her early twenties, in the midst of a desperate struggle about her feelings of identity and separating from her parents, was referred to group therapy for additional work. During a year of group therapy she found that she could be accepted by other people despite her extreme agitation, depression, self-depreciation, and other strange ideas. She also began to learn more actively that although her father was immersed in his professional career he did not loathe her as much as she had always believed. In fact, he loved her. She further realized that her mother was not the all-loving reliable mother that she had always imagined her to be. She then left the group to take a year of intensive professional work, intending to return for further work in the group when that was accomplished. Such segmented or limited pieces of therapy are as useful with psychotics in group therapy just as they are in working with psychotics generally.

All in all, group therapy offers a reasonable and feasible approach for working with psychotic patients analytically. But this approach must be tied together for the therapist with his work with psychotics individually and intensively in order to provide him with the understanding of psychotics in groups or individually. Analytic group therapy by itself cannot exist for the therapist.

REFERENCES

1. Joseph Abrahams and Edith Varon, *Maternal Dependency and Schizophrenia* (New York: International Universities Press, 1953).
2. W. R. Bion, *Experiences in Groups* (New York: Basic Books, 1959).
3. M. Day and E. V. Semrad, "Group Therapy with Neurotics and Psychotics," in Harold I. Kaplan and Benjamin J. Sadock (eds.), *Comprehensive Group Psychotherapy* (Baltimore: Williams & Wilkins, 1971), pp. 566-580.
4. M. Edleson, *Ego Psychology, Group Dynamics and the Therapeutic Community* (New York: Grune & Stratton, 1964).
5. H. Spotnitz, "The Borderline Schizophrenic in Group Psychotherapy," *Int. J. Group. Psychother.*, 7:158-174, 1957.

6. C. A. Whitaker, *The Psychotherapy of Chronic Schizophrenic Patients* (Boston: Little, Brown, 1958).
7. Maxwell Jones, *The Therapeutic Community* (New York: Basic Books, 1953).
8. David Blau and Joan J. Zilbach, "The Use of Psychotherapy in Post Hospitalization Treatment. A Clinical Report," *Am. J. Psychiat.*, 111:244-247, 1954.
9. *Ibid.*

39

COMMUNITY GERIATRIC GROUP THERAPIES: A COMPREHENSIVE REVIEW

Mathew Ross

It is estimated that by 1985 there will be twenty-five million persons aged sixty-five and over in the United States![1]

If we are to improve the quality of life in old age, we surely agree with Martin Roth[2] that "psychiatric problems of old age present major challenges in their own right and are an inescapable responsibility for modern psychiatry both in a practical and a scientific sense."

Whereas in the past a good deal of therapeutic nihilism characterized the relationship between the geriatric patient and the healing professions, there has accrued during the past decade a body of knowledge and practice which indicates this nihilism is unwarranted. This survey is based upon the author's beliefs in current community mental health theory and the value of preventive as well as curative group endeavors in improving the quality of life of the elderly in our society. In 1959 the suggestion was made that group endeavors on behalf of the elderly could be successful in a variety of intra- and extramural settings.[3]

This review surveys the literature of the extramural group therapies for older persons and records some of the significant progress and trends of the past decade. It also indicates some problems and prospects which lie ahead.

METHODOLOGY

The major review articles of: (1) the *International Journal of Group Psychotherapy*;[4-11] (2) *Progress in Neurology and Psychiatry*;[12-21] (3) *Yearbook of Neurology, Psychiatry and Neurosurgery*;[22-29] and (4) *Yearbook of Neurology and Neurosurgery*;[30-33] (5) *Yearbook of Psychiatry and Applied Mental Health*;[34-35] and (6) the *Index Medicus*[36] provided the gross clues to the original articles and other publications in the literature on extra-mural group approaches to the mental health and psychiatric problems of the elderly. The original articles were perused and form the basis of this communication.

Although there has been an explosive growth of the literature on group psychotherapy and of the geriatric population, these two develop-ments have remained generally quite apart and unrelated. Not only has the geriatric population in the past decade increased but those seeking mental health attention have likewise increased greatly. The group psy-chotherapy literature for the years 1964–1971 surveyed in the *International Journal of Group Psychotherapy* covers a total of 2623 references. In 1964 there were 170 references, and each of the last three years, 1969, 1970, 1971, totaled 418, 481, and 460 references respectively. There has been an enormous growth of interest and publication in the field of group psychotherapy, but alas, there has not been a comparable parallel increase or a relatively proportionate increase in the geriatric group therapies literature. "A search of the 1971 group psychotherapy literature located only two articles involving group methods with the aged."[37] However, some of the ingenuity and "the heart" expressed in the literature dealing with this approach afford compensations even though it is difficult to con-tradict the conclusion expressed by Liederman and Green:[38] "It is easy to overlook the similarity that exists between the psychologic needs of the elderly person and those of the younger age groups."

Goldfarb[39] has observed: "Over the past 20 years, there has been great interest in group therapy of old persons—The prevalence of group work with old people is not reflected by the number of reports in the literature."

COMMUNITY MENTAL HEALTH FOR THE ELDERLY

We are living in times when the major emphases are upon the preven-tion of hospitalization for the mentally ill of all ages; when "we were put-ting our money where our mouths were" we were actively supporting community mental health and community psychiatric approaches. How important a place do the elderly have in community, extramural treatment programs which in the 1960's were to be broad, flexible, and with equal opportunity availability to all? Unfortunately not very. And yet, in the light of the available evidence, this is unsound and unworthy of our cherished standards of offering freely our very best to all who may benefit. Perhaps if group workers become better acquainted with the efforts of their col-leagues they may emulate them to the benefit of our elderly.

GERIATRIC PATIENT-CARE EPISODES[40]

As of the beginning of 1966, 1,136,567 patients were resident in a public (state, county, Veterans' Administration) or private mental hospital, psychiatric inpatient service of a general hospital, or under active care in an outpatient clinic. During the following twelve months, 1,550,857 persons were admitted to these facilities. The sum of these two numbers has been called patient-care episodes and provides an index to the extent to which services are used by members of a given group. In 1966, 1,235 persons per 100,000 received care in a psychiatric service.

The rate of patient-care episodes for all services, specific for age, rises from 609 per 100,000 in the age group under 15 years to a maximum of 2,098 per 100,000 in the 35-44-year-old age group. From this peak the rate decreases to 1,547 per 100,000 for the 55-64 age group and then increases slightly to 1,652 per 100,000 for persons 65 years and over.

Considerable disparity exists in the patterns of use of specific types of facilities by the different age groups. The outpatient clinics provide services predominantly to persons under thirty-five years of age and the mental hospitals provide services predominantly to persons over thirty-five years of age. The patient-care episode rate for mental hospitals increases with advancing years, while that for outpatient clinics and psychiatric services in general hospitals decreases. In the age group sixty-five years and over the patient-care episode rate for mental hospitals is 1,222/100,000, for psychiatric units in general hospitals 297/100,000, and for outpatient clinics 134/100,000.

The high patient-care episode rate in mental hospitals for the sixty-five and older is accounted for by two factors: those who grew older in the hospital setting and the high admission rate for patients with mental disorders of the senium (brain syndromes with arteriosclerosis and senile brain disease).

Since 1955 the mental hospital patient population has declined at an annual accelerated rate of change. Patients in each age group contributed to the decrease at varying rates, with the 55-64-year-old age group the least rapid at 0.3 per cent per year and the 65 and over, who in 1966 constituted about 30 per cent of the entire resident population of state and county mental hospitals, at the rate of 1.1 per cent per year.

If one is dedicated to the notions of, wherever possible, preventing hospitalization and minimizing burdens and costs for patients, their families, and communities, then efforts to extend promising techniques and develop new ones to this end are in order.

A previous review[41] indicated how inpatient group therapy and activities were of considerable value. In the past decade many mental health professionals have demonstrated their willingness, ability, and success in applying themselves in these endeavors in behalf of the geriatric patient. It would appear consonant with the further development of community-focused efforts that community group therapeutic approaches be more fully developed and utilized for their therapeutic as well as for their preventive benefits.

AIMS, GOALS, AND DEFINITIONS

Group psychotherapy has been defined by Erika Chance[42] as a professionally planned set of relationships, involving the therapist and a number of patients, which aims at helping each of the patients to better social adjustment by means of a series of controlled mental processes.

Stein as reported by Goldfarb[43] indicates that group therapy "uses group methods and activities to encourage personal activity, sociability, and social integration of the individual member." Goldfarb himself goes on to state that "in general, group therapy supports, directs, and helps old persons with psychiatric problems to understand what their behavior does to them and to others and how these factors have come to be." It has the

> general aims to assist the old person toward having minimal complaints and being minimally complained about; to help him make and keep friends of both sexes and have sexual relationships where interest and capacity for these survive to help him relieve tensions of biological and cultural origins; and to help him work and play within the limits of his functional status and as determined by his past training, abilities, and self-concept in society.

Liederman and Green[44] define group therapy with the aged as a social and psychological process in which emotional reeducational and relearning experiences can occur. Goals may be to improve reality testing; aid socialization; foster an awareness of the relationship of emotional reactions to anxiety and defensive patterns of behavior; provide motivations for continued improvement and a source of new identifications and mutual support; and provide an opportunity for release of impounded anger.

Whether one holds the view that there are no goals in group therapy, as Hinckley and Herman[45] have declared, but instead there are as many objectives as there are members, or feels that there are various goals, nonetheless, "Any treatment regimen for aged patients must cope with certain factors inherent in or frequently associated with the aged human organism."[46]

Goldfarb's[47] caveat: "Group therapy, because of its diversity, can do many things for many people but not necessarily the same things for all the people helped. . . . Although group therapy is useful, its limitations must be recognized. Expectations are often excessive."

THE SETTING

The locus in which the group therapy occurs may influence the goals and aims of the therapy. For example, in a state mental hospital setting the focus may be "to increase the discharge rate, to decrease problems of patient management, to ameliorate disturbing behavior, to raise staff morale, to improve staff attitudes and conduct toward old and aged patients, to improve patients' adaptation to an institutional environment, to improve interpersonal relationships, and to decrease personal suffering."[48]

The community settings are apt to have a somewhat more flexible and adaptable patient-clientele, and perhaps can focus more upon an enrichment of life than the more narrowly defined treatment of illness. The distinctions may not always be sharply drawn but sometimes the preventive rather than the curative emphasis is apparent, as in the use of group therapy to assist in the preretirement and retirement problems of the relatively well. Encouragement of personal and social activity, amelioration of marital, family, and social frictions, and even the management of fear and anger have similarity to the group therapy of younger age groups, as has been indicated.[49]

The significance of the setting in which group psychotherapy is conducted has been carefully considered by Chance,[50] who suggests a division

> into those in which the therapy represents the only or primary contact between therapist and the patients, and those in which the therapist and/or his colleagues also have other responsibilities toward the patient. Whenever the therapist is a part of a system of service . . . he tends to have some responsibility not only for the group psychotherapy but also for the milieux in which he encounters the patient. . . . The group psychotherapist, despite every effort to clarify his function, may be identified with the institution, endowed with disciplinary powers, and expected to modify the patient's environment on his behalf. Instead of relating to him as a person, the patient tends to view him as a representative of the institution. Instead of ventilating personal material and connecting current experiences and feelings with previous important encounters, patients will ventilate feelings about the institution.

GROUPS IN COMMUNITY MENTAL HEALTH CENTERS

In 1970 Pattison[51] reported the results of a nation-wide survey on the use of group methods in community mental health centers for all types of patients. In brief, his reported survey represents 45 per cent of identifiable U.S. comprehensive community mental health centers, along with some additional data from other community health programs. He recognizes that his data cannot be considered definitive, but nonetheless they do reflect a broad sample of current community center practices.

Over-all he noted: "If a comprehensive community mental health center does not have an articulated treatment philosophy in regard to groups, it appears that group methods tend not to be employed in a systematic and coherent way and are used minimally." A second finding from the data raises the question "as to how far comprehensive community mental health center program concepts have moved from the treatment philosophy of intensive therapy directed toward major personality change . . . to a use of group methods aimed at maintenance or restoration of social function."

A third finding indicated that among the ten functional areas of comprehensive community mental health center programing as defined by the Community Mental Health Center Act (CMHC), the most frequent areas in which groups are used are outpatient services and in community consultation and education; they are least used in emergency and diagnostic services.

Another finding was that "group methods are not a generalized modality in CMHC. Only traditional intensive outpatient psychotherapy groups are used by a large majority of CMHC. The farther one moves from traditional mental health definitions of patient populations and of mental health professional roles, the less group methods are used. . . . CMHC services tend to cluster around more traditional services."

A fifth point of Pattison's is that:

> Mental health professionals rarely have systematic training in anything other than intensive small psychotherapy groups. However, such methods are obviously inappropriate in the conduct of many other types of groups used in CMHC programs. There appears to be a lack of any coherent conceptual system which would provide CMHC staff with a framework for using a variety of group techniques for different purposes and the training of CMHC personnel in a broad array of group methods so that they are in a position to make selective use of group methods according to the needs of the given client population.

Others have considered some of the obstacles minimizing group work efforts for the elderly in community settings. One of the more useful because it provides a framework for analysis is that of Louis Lowy.[52] In discussing some "roadblocks to group work practice with the aged," Lowy delineates as relevant and significant obstacles:

(1) Attitudes of community, agency, and worker toward the aged.

(2) Knowledge of group processes and use of this knowledge in relation to work with older people.

(3) Skills of the group worker, particularly with regard to diagnosis and treatment functions.

When community attitudes toward the aged reflect a youth and work orientation, they tend to lump the aged into "an homogeneous group of chronically ill, dependent people" indicated by such stereotypes of the elderly as: (1) having less capacity to adapt and change; (2) having lost normal drives and desires; and (3) being in a period of decline and depressed. It is not surprising, then, that many agencies and institutions develop programs and practices which reflect these community attitudes and biases. The worker himself may "still hold little belief in the creative potentialities of the older person and most caseworkers do not see the same challenge in work with the aged that they see in work with children and young families."

Among the roadblocks to group work with the elderly are those in relation to existing knowledge of group processes and the use of this knowledge. For instance, "many group services for older adults are carried on in large rather than small groups," which are, according to Lowy, more diagnostic and treatment oriented. He also believes "the task of working with older adults is a resocialization process," more likely in smaller groups.

Finally, Lowy turns to roadblocks in relation to the skills of the worker in diagnosis and treatment. He indicates that "many of our goals need to be assessed realistically in the light of the available resources to achieve them. Obviously some of our goals should be more modest." He concludes on a positive note:

> While there are many roadblocks to group work with older adults, there are also ways to identify them and . . . to overcome them. It is not an easy task, because it involves modifying attitudes and unfreezing the stereotypes which are part of our culture. It will be possible to produce changes only if old and young work together to whittle away the barriers. . . group work must be an active agent of change. . . .

Despite what obstacles there may be to group efforts in behalf of the elderly, there are obvious advantages to their development.

In November 1971, the Committee on Aging of the Group for the Advancement of Psychiatry[53] formulated guidelines for the establishment of services for the aged in community mental health centers: "Group psychotherapy should be available to the elderly in groups with patients of all ages as well as in groups for aged patients only." The inclusion of the elderly may be beneficial to all of the patients by increasing the range of life problems presented in the group and by exposing members to new adaptive styles. "On the other hand, a psychotherapy group exclusively for elderly patients may avoid possible domination of the group by younger and more verbal patients. It may also permit the therapist to fill some of the common needs of elderly patients, such as support for a sense of self-esteem and being cared about by others within the group."

Hopefully, as Chance indicated:[54]

The community mental center will not only . . . provide some opportunity for the same therapist to conduct concurrent therapies, but also provide for vertical staffing so that the same therapist may see a patient through from pre-admission to the post-hospitalization phase of treatment. Such vertical staffing would permit a much better integration of the experience of illness into the continuity of the patient's experience. . . . Such a continuity of experience represents an extremely important resource in group psychotherapy . . . and where the person of the therapist and the membership of the group can be kept relatively constant across techniques and milieux, the patient's experience of continuity will be enhanced.

COMMUNITY GROUP APPROACHES

In a truly comprehensive community mental health program for the elderly and the aged, a wide network of agents and agencies extend their skills, efforts, and facilities to them. In addition to the traditional psychiatric facilities providing inpatient services, there should ideally be not only the traditionally defined elements of a comprehensive mental health center but other community agencies—not narrowly defined as psychiatric, but rather perhaps more in the style and fashion of the neighborhood centers: community centers, Y's, churches, civic recreation departments, homes for the aged, settlement houses, and a whole host of community institutions devoting some measure of their efforts to group approaches to the elderly.

Some of these efforts will focus upon avoiding the pitfalls of the "storage bin" philosophy, of maintaining the aged—giving them the gift of life and at the same time destroying their dignity—when they become an ever-growing part of Michael Harrington's *The Other America*,[55] where they remain disengaged.

Euster[56] describes these members of the aged population who belong to *The Other America*:

They are primarily poor older persons who experience frequent episodes of illness and injury that interrupt and disrupt their family and community lives. As such episodes become more severe, these persons may require long-term residential care and treatment as well as specially planned arrangements related to housing, diet, medical care, and aftercare supervision. They are persons who must use limited retirement incomes to cover additional expenses for special arrangements necessitated by extended medical care. They are persons exploited by the false claims and promises of public and proprietary nursing and extended care institutions. Their limited resources diminish as hopes of restoration become more illusion than fact. They are persons whose recovery from illness commonly leaves some form of residual disablement and the subsequent need for a more structured form of living.

Hospitalization and institutionalization are rarely considered by medical and social service personnel as solutions to the varied physical, social, and psychological problems of older adults. By intuition and experience, one knows that such forms of treatment and care should be used only when outpatient and community services break down or are not available. The expense, the humiliation, and the frightening climate that persons face when they are placed in institutions have been documented. Dignity, pride, and autonomy are relinquished as older persons are transferred to cultures of dependency. Boredom, silence, ritual, and stripping of privacy are typical of institutions that spend considerable effort in proclaiming their good patient-to-staff ratios.

In a community mental health center there are various realities which necessitate the careful but flexible setting of realistic treatment goals, the choice of treatment modality, and the therapist. Among these are "the chronic nature of many of the problems encountered, the limitations of the various techniques, the staggering service needs coupled with perennial staff shortages. . . ."

GROUP APPROACHES IN COMMUNITY MENTAL HEALTH

There have been a number of attempts to improve the lot of the elderly which are not strictly classifiable as group psychotherapy.

As a background for a review of some of these, it is useful to note Scheidlinger's[57] classification of "group influence attempts that lie outside the more strictly clinical range of group psychotherapy." He indicates that "far-reaching therapeutic effects in the sickest of people can occur through group influence measures considerably removed from what one would commonly view as psychotherapy." Indeed, this is in keeping with current preventive psychiatric theory that when one strengthens the stability of family life, peer grouping, informal organizations, or the neighborhood as a whole, one is in effect promoting the effectiveness of vital psychosocial care-giving systems, and with community mental health theory that "an essential component of anyone's social and psychological functioning resides in a meaningful reciprocal relationship between him and at least one, if not a number, of relatively stable groups."

Scheidlinger's classification scheme includes "all programs in which small face-to-face groupings are utilized to promote socializations, better interpersonal relationships, improved role behavior and task performance, and rehabilitation. This classification system of group modalities is linked to patient needs and allows for interaction patterns on different depth levels." He used these guideposts: (1) the specific aims of a given practitioner for each group member and particular group; (2) the depth (regressive) level of group interaction; and (3) the techniques used by the group leader. He also used five major group influence attempts focused on:

(1) Activity-catharsis-mastery such as manual activity and work groups that foster reaching out, touching, and exploration of materials; occupational therapy that provides cathartic opportunity, tension channeling, and ego mastery.

(2) Cognitive-informational offers group educational models, including family life education, occupational or recreational skills.

(3) Interpersonal-socialization focuses upon group approaches designed to meet people's needs for security, a sense of belonging, and companionship.

(4) Relationship-experiential methods may contain a definite diagnostic and treatment intent; included are patient social clubs, social rehabilitation, halfway house programs, and social group work in medical and psychiatric settings.

(5) Uncovering-introspective efforts are group psychotherapy clinically defined.

PARTIAL HOSPITALIZATION

Day hospitals and day centers have been one of the more promising developments of recent psychiatric endeavor, yet their incorporation of group programs for the elderly has been laggard. A study[58] of patterns of utilization in partial hospitalization cited by Beigel and Feder[59] indicates that "For every inpatient psychiatric facility that provides a partial hospital program, there are four that do not, and for every patient cared for in a partial hospital, there appear to be more than 40 inpatients who are not. Furthermore, most partial hospital programs operate below capacity with approximately one-fifth having less than ten patients."

If we look more closely at this study we find few, or small percentages at best, of the patients beyond sixty-five years of age. The programs vary, quite understandably, according to philosophies of treatment, and it is only where the goal of treatment is social readjustment that group therapy has any prominence. Beigel and Feder stress the importance of developing two types of partial hospital programs: (1) the day hospital for short-term, intensive, crisis intervention; and (2) the day care center for long-term treatment of the chronic patient, emphasizing social and vocational rehabilitation. They go on to emphasize that "Criteria commonly used for determining suitability for admission to partial hospitals, such as diagnosis, prior hospitalization, family involvement, and suicidal ideation, are not significant in evaluating the patient's chance of complete or incomplete utilization of the partial hospital. The significant criterion is the acuteness or chronicity of the clinical state at the time the patient seeks help." If so, the latter criterion would make many an elderly patient eligible for group psychotherapeutic intervention. Indeed, the British experience would seem to bear this out.

The value of a day hospital program in diminishing hospital admissions and readmissions, and particularly in its effect on depression and loneliness, has been documented by Woodford-Williams[60] and J. C. Brocklehurst.[61] The latter's survey clearly indicates the need for developing nonhospital social day centers as complementary establishments to geriatric day hospitals. Shaw and Macmillan[62] have described a day center for the psychiatric elderly who are in one of the following categories: (1) for daytime care and attention while the responsible relative is at work; (2) old people, living alone and deteriorating mentally because of their isolation; and (3) home situations with emotional tension where the old person's future is in jeopardy.

Brocklehurst contends "it is common knowledge that the greatest scourge of old people is loneliness, and although it is not the task of the hospital service to treat loneliness, unless it is treated, a considerable burden of preventable psychiatric and physical disease is likely to follow." According to Woodford-Williams, "the day hospital clearly provides an inexpensive unit for the relief of mental depression, for the reintegration of the elderly into society, and for intensive rehabilitation that would not be practical on a normal out-patient basis." As indicated,[63] group psychotherapy has a definite place in the day center program.

HOMES FOR THE AGED

Many different group approaches are possible in a home for the aged. Although the health, illness, and declining faculties of the group are realistic obstacles, nonetheless when group programing is consistent with the total life of the resident it may yield worthwhile results. Its importance cannot be overestimated, for one of the most familiar settings for the aged is the home for the aged. At some of them imaginative group programs have been devised to improve the quality of life. The following three examples indicate a pre- and immediately subsequent to placement program for relatives and applicants on the waiting list, a resident program, and a program for "the outcasts" or "the disengaged."

There is a recognized need to help the families of the aged when a change of environment is contemplated for the old person. When Manaster[64] was working at the Park View Home for the Aged in Chicago, he devised a family therapy program focused upon treating these patients and their families *before* the change of environment and immediately thereafter. The basic objectives of the group meetings were to achieve: (1) an awareness on the part of the family of the reasons for the patient's behavior, and an understanding of what it means for the parent to be at the geriatric center; (2) an awareness by the relatives of their own feelings and reactions about having "put their parents away," and the manner in which these feelings (e.g., guilt) affected the relationships between themselves and their parents and the center; and (3) a clearer understanding and appreciation of the entire field of aging and the attendant problems, not only in relation to the aged parent, but also in relation to themselves and the community. The program was judged to be of definite value for the families and applicants.

An awareness of the coping necessary for a person admitted to a geriatric center—a life crisis—was reported by Bowers.[65] His data indicated "that psychiatric problems tended to cluster around the period of admission and early adjustment. . . ."

An excellent account of "a positive, patient-oriented therapeutic milieu program" in the community setting of a home for the aged has been detailed by Wolf,[66] who found that "when the aged person is exposed to a forcefully presented milieu program or group process, these patients are not only responsive, but productive as well." In his step-by-step account of the development of the program he provides a useful model for community agencies whose primary focus and orientation are not psychiatric. He sets forth an outline indicating how to develop that aspect of their program which will enhance their effectiveness as well as improve the quality of life for the aged.

Feil's[67] presentation of group work in a home for the aged focused upon "the outcasts—'the sitters'—the residents who cannot fit into the social milieu." Her intent was to remotivate them to more active living. She presents considerable detail of her techniques for helping specific groups of disengaged elderly prepare for entry into occupational therapy, physical therapy, sheltered workshops, and discussion groups, "groups whose primary goal is not socialization but individual rehabilitation." Her main goals in remotivation were: "1. to stimulate verbalization, 2. to increase interaction between group members, and 3. to promote a sense of worth so the individual can move toward some degree of independent action that will make him feel part of the community life. . . ."

Holzman and Sabel[68] set up a group visiting program in a home for the aged wherein specific staff recommended by the nursing and occupational therapy departments would visit groups of chronic brain syndrome patients twice a week for one-half hour. The patient group would consist of relatively emotionally stable residents plus residents newly admitted to the home. "The long-time residents were expected to help the newer residents to become better oriented and acclimatized to the home, and perhaps to establish new friendships with them."

The authors admit the lack of scientific evaluation of their program, but do report: "The tentative results from this service program indicate improved morale in both staff and patients. . . ." The nursing aides had a greater feeling of their own importance, were gratified that their recommendations were considered, and were learning about themselves, their patients, and their colleagues.

If the foregoing examples of group programs were more widely known, one suspects the following view of homes for the aged would be modified if not fully corrected:[69]

> It has been our experience that a home for the aged is usually conceptualized by the general public as a kind of warehouse where elderly people are stored until their death. Not only is this morbid concept held in varying degrees by the community, but also by emotionally involved children and relatives as well as by those entering the home. Unfortunately it may also be held by those who are responsible for the care of the aged, viz., the professional and sub-professional staff. In addition to their coping with this notion, the staff also has to adjust unconsciously to such complex emotional tasks as sustaining the dignity of the newly admitted patient, alleviating his depression and anxiety, and relieving the guilt of children and relatives which may be either self-imposed or transmitted to them. There are serious frustrations in accomplishing these tasks, and there are also the daily frustrations of seeing little or no improvement in patients, standing by helplessly while an older human being goes down hill often slowly and sometimes all too rapidly, as well as the ultimate powerless feeling when a patient dies. Many of these emotional problems in the staff exist at an unconscious level, and regrettably, their presence becomes clear to the observer when recriminations often arise between the different departments of a geriatric institution as to what the other department could or should have been doing to help the patient.

SOCIAL CLUBS

Social clubs are a community locus where group methods may vary widely, yet be quite effective in helping the elderly achieve fuller life returns. That the social club may provide through the group experience a socialization experience and a "bridge back to the wider community" for older patients who had spent ten to twenty years in a state mental hospital has been documented by Hawxhurst and Walzer,[70] who utilized task-centered group discussions along with excursions into the community. These workers feel that "The developing thrust of the 'Friendship Club' is in the direction of performing socially useful tasks which will bring a degree of social recognition and wider community acceptance. We believe the negative social identity of members will be modified as they come into meaningful contact with others."

A refreshing example of how to offset some of society's deprecatory image of the aged can be gleaned from a social worker's deliberate use of the established social work techniques of conflict, controversy, and confrontation in a Golden Age Club of a community center. Forman points out:[71]

> Social workers are often misguided by expedience, custom, and lack of time and, as a result, frequently find themselves planning and providing the facilities for and doing the thinking of the members of older adult

groups. Some of the needs of the aged—to belong, receive recognition, "retire" from the hectic pace of life, retain their cultural heritage, and the like—can be achieved in this fashion. The programs planned for them are informative, the facilities and services provided are important, the thinking done for them is valuable, yet in all these ways the same rejection of the aged is demonstrated that is deplored when it is practiced by society at large. Discussion is encouraged, but argument is shied away from; democracy is preached, but the emotion of controversy is avoided; social workers inform, but take little action. In sum, comfortable and secure activities are dealt with, all of which have some value, but few of which serve to dissolve the stereotype of the uselessness of the aged.

The agency felt that the club's emphasis on entertainment and recreation had prevented the group from dealing with: (1) opportunities for decision making; (2) dependency; and (3) involvement in the community.

Even though the group had demonstrated its ability to manage its own affairs, remain financially self-sufficient, and plan programs, a professional worker was engaged to work with them. He was to be the catalyst in helping the group examine its values, question its practices, and think out its goals. To do this effectively the worker would have to challenge the status quo. Because the group felt threatened by anger, conflict, and disagreement and the power structure preferred at least the semblance of an untroubled and secure atmosphere, this approach could not fail to create controversy and generate emotion. It was felt that a differentiated use of conflict—purposefully and selectively planned—could prove an effective means of helping the older adults move toward a healthier and more meaningful experience.

Forman reasoned:

Conflict, controversy, and confrontation, as social work techniques, have long been used effectively in work with groups, but have found only limited application in work with the aged. Social workers also are affected by the efforts of society to isolate older people from conflict situations. They see the diminution of family status, loss of work role, physical deterioration, and so forth, and try as they will, are conflicted. How can these "poor" old people be challenged? Is the worker prepared to deal with the continuing confrontation this role will create with the group's power structure? Are older people able to handle the tension and emotional by-products?

After describing what he did to accomplish his three aims, Forman concluded:

Conflict, controversy, and confrontation applied differentially are useful techniques in working with older adults. Healthy and productive conflict has an invigorating and stimulating effect on older people and can expedite group movement. Dealing with and resolving conflict creates satisfaction, a sense of achievement, and the reality of participating more fully in life. Each successfully resolved conflict increases the group's ability to deal with future conflicts. The behavior of individuals leads one to believe that group successes in this area are internalized by the members.

NEIGHBORHOOD REHABILITATION CENTER

A community setting in which group vocational guidance is integrated into the over-all program of rehabilitation of the aged has been documented by Rusalem[72] and his colleagues. They describe their work at a neighborhood rehabilitation center for the aged which developed its program "around the demonstrated interests and capacities of its older disabled persons." From their statistical and case material data they generalize: "There are large numbers of severely disabled older persons unable to use public transportation whose vocational potential will remain undeveloped unless special neighborhood programs are developed expressly for them." Such a program is feasible in diverse urban areas, but "must be structured with the special needs and capacities of older disabled persons clearly in mind."

The group appears large enough to justify the creation of such a program which operates most effectively when "it functions within a community framework which offers other agency services such as social casework, housing, custodial care, health, and recreation." Focusing upon a neighborhood enables a vocational rehabilitation facility to apply community action principles to case finding, reaching out to a population not ordinarily accessible to rehabilitation agencies.

> When neighborhood services are offered to the community, individual benefits include an improved sense of well being and worth, greater economic and personal comfort, more favorable family relationship, reduction in medical and psychological symptoms, and enhanced satisfaction with life.
>
> At the same time, the family and the community may benefit . . . finding reduced need for financial support, less dependence upon special protective services, better integration of the individual into the family and the community, and greater freedom from organized community helping activities.

An interesting approach to group therapy for the chronically ill and the geriatric patients has been described by three occupational therapists.[73] They have devised an assembly-line method which permits patients to participate regardless of ability. The essential features of this restoration therapy program as they describe it include "grading for individual needs, production of items for use in the hospital, a wide variety of media, provision for patient recognition and low cost." Through this group activity program the restoration of hand skills, work habits, endur-

the quality of their lives, whether they are well or sick, do work; the foregoing documents this incontrovertible fact.

REFERENCES

1. Department of Health, Education and Welfare, Older Americans Act, Public Law 89-73, HEW Indicators 41-56, 1965.
2. Martin Roth, "Recent Progress in Psychiatry of Old Age and its Bearing on Certain Problems of Psychiatry in Earlier Life," *Bio. Psychiat.*, 5:103-125, 1972.
3. Mathew Ross, "A Review of Some Recent Treatment Methods for Elderly Psychiatric Patients," *Arch. Gen. Psychiat.*, 1:578-592, 1959.
4. B. W. MacLennan and N. S. Felsenfield, "The Group Psychotherapy Literature 1964," *Int. J. Group Psychother.*, 15:251-269, 1965.
5. B. W. MacLennan, "The Group Psychotherapy Literature 1965," *Int. J. Group Psychother.*, 16:225-241, 1966.
6. B. W. MacLennan and N. Levy, "The Group Psychotherapy Literature 1966," *Int. J. Group Psychother.*, 17:378-398, 1967.
7. ———, "The Group Psychotherapy Literature 1967," *Int. J. Group Psychother.*, 18:375-401, 1968.
8. ———, "The Group Psychotherapy Literature 1968," *Int. J. Group Psychother.*, 19:382-408, 1969.
9. ———, "The Group Psychotherapy Literature 1969," *Int. J. Group Psychother.*, 20:380-411, 1970.
10. ———, "The Group Psychotherapy Literature 1970," *Int. J. Group Psychother.*, 21:345-380, 1971.
11. B. Lubin, A. W. Lubin, and C. W. Sargent, "The Group Psychotherapy Literature 1971," *Int. J. Group Psychother.*, 22:492-529, 1972.
12. R. J. Corsini, R. Daniels, and R. McFarland, "Group Psychotherapy," in E. A. Spiegel (ed.), *Progress in Neurology and Psychiatry* (New York: Grune & Stratton, 1960), 15:526-534.
13. R. L. McFarland, R. S. Daniels, and E. Solon, "Group Psychotherapy," in E. A. Spiegel (ed.), *Progress in Neurology and Psychiatry* (New York: Grune & Stratton, 1961), 16:527-538.
14. R. S. Daniels, R. L. McFarland, and E. Solon, "Group Psychotherapy," in E. A. Spiegel (ed.), *Progress in Neurology and Psychiatry* (New York: Grune & Stratton, 1962), 17:526-535.
15. R. L. McFarland, R. S. Daniels, and M. Lieberman, "Group Psychotherapy," in E. A. Spiegel (ed.), *Progress in Neurology and Psychiatry* (New York: Grune & Stratton, 1963), 18:622-630.
16. M. A. Lieberman, R. Daniels, and R. McFarland, "Group Psychotherapy," in E. A. Spiegel (ed.), *Progress in Neurology and Psychiatry* (New York: Grune & Stratton, 1964), 19:599-605.
17. R. S. Daniels and M. Lieberman, "Group Psychotherapy," in E. A. Spiegel (ed.), *Progress in Neurology and Psychiatry* (New York: Grune & Stratton, 1965), 20:717-722.
18. M. A. Lieberman, G. G. Meyer, and R. McFarland, "Group Psycho-

therapy," in E. A. Spiegel (ed.), *Progress in Neurology and Psychiatry* (New York: Grune & Stratton, 1966), 21:579-585.

19. G. G. Meyer, M. A. Lieberman, and J. Perlmutter, "Group Psychotherapy," in E. A. Spiegel (ed.), *Progress in Neurology and Psychiatry* (New York: Grune & Stratton, 1967), 22:501-508.

20. J. Perlmutter, M. A. Lieberman, and G. G. Meyer, "Group Psychotherapy," in E. A. Spiegel (ed.), *Progress in Neurology and Psychiatry* (New York: Grune & Stratton, 1968), 23:548-556.

21. G. G. Meyer, A. G. Burstein, A. Serrano, J. H. Gladfelter, and B. F. Beran, "Group Psychotherapy," in E. A. Spiegel (ed.), *Progress in Neurology and Psychiatry* (New York: Grune & Stratton, 1971), 26:515-528.

22. R. P. Mackay, S. B. Wortis, O. Sugar et al. (eds.), *Yearbook of Neurology, Psychiatry and Neurosurgery 1960-1968* (Chicago: Yearbook Medical Publishers, 1961), 584 pp.

23. ———, *Yearbook of Neurology, Psychiatry and Neurosurgery 1961-1962* (Chicago: Yearbook Medical Publishers, 1962), 600 pp.

24. ———, *Yearbook of Neurology, Psychiatry and Neurosurgery 1962-1963* (Chicago: Yearbook Medical Publishers, 1963), 631 pp.

25. ———, *Yearbook of Neurology, Psychiatry and Neurosurgery 1963-1964* (Chicago: Yearbook Medical Publishers, 1964), 608 pp.

26. ———, *Yearbook of Neurology, Psychiatry and Neurosurgery 1964-1965* (Chicago: Yearbook Medical Publishers, 1965), 734 pp.

27. ———, *Yearbook of Neurology, Psychiatry and Neurosurgery 1965-1966* (Chicago: Yearbook Medical Publishers, 1966), 734 pp.

28. ———, *Yearbook of Neurology, Psychiatry and Neurosurgery 1966-1967* (Chicago: Yearbook Medical Publishers, 1967), 757 pp.

29. ———, *Yearbook of Neurology, Psychiatry and Neurosurgery 1967-1968* (Chicago: Yearbook Medical Publishers, 1968), 684 pp.

30. R. N. DeJong, O. Sugar, et al. (eds.), *Yearbook of Neurology and Neurosurgery 1968-1969* (Chicago: Yearbook Medical Publishers, 1969), 510 pp.

31. ———, *Yearbook of Neurology and Neurosurgery 1969-1970* (Chicago: Yearbook Medical Publishers, 1970).

32. ———, *Yearbook of Neurology and Neurosurgery 1971* (Chicago: Yearbook Medical Publishers, 1970).

33. ———, *Yearbook of Neurology and Neurosurgery 1972* (Chicago: Yearbook Medical Publishers, 1971).

34. S. B. Wortis, et al. (ed.), *The Yearbook of Psychiatry and Applied Mental Health 1969-1970* (Chicago: Yearbook Medical Publishers, 1970), 415 pp.

35. D. Bond, et al. (ed.), *The Yearbook of Psychiatry and Applied Mental Health 1970-1971* (Chicago: Yearbook Medical Publishers, 1971), 558 pp.

36. *Index Medicus 1960-1973* (Washington, D.C.: Department of Health, Education and Welfare, National Library of Medicine, January, 1960), Vol. 1, No. 1.

37. Lubin, Lubin, and Sargent, "Group Psychotherapy Literature," *op. cit.*

38. P. C. Liederman and R. Green, "Geriatric Outpatient Group Therapy," *Comp. Psychiat.*, 6:51, 1965.

39. A. I. Goldfarb, *Group Therapy with the Old and Aged in Comprehensive*

Group Psychotherapy, edited by H. J. Kaplan and B. J. Sadock (Baltimore: Williams & Wilkins, 1971), pp. 623-642.

40. *Patients in State and County Mental Hospitals 1967*, Mental Health Facilities Report N.I.M.H.—Mental Health Statistics Series A, No. 2, 1969.
41. Ross, "Some Recent Treatment Methods," *op. cit.*
42. E. Chance, "Group Psychotherapy in Community Mental Health Programs," *Am. J. Orthopsychiat.*, 37:920-925, 1967.
43. Goldfarb, *Group Therapy with the Old*, *op. cit.*
44. Liederman and Green, "Geriatric Outpatient Group Therapy," *op. cit.*
45. R. G. Hinckley and L. Herman, *Group Treatment in Psychotherapy*, A *Report of Experience* (Minneapolis: University of Minnesota Press, 1951).
46. M. D. Bowers, *et al.*, "Brain Syndrome and Behavior in Geriatric Remotivation Groups," *J. Geront.*, 22:348-352, 1967.
47. Goldfarb, *Group Therapy with the Old*, *op. cit.*
48. *Ibid.*
49. Liederman and Green, "Geriatric Outpatient Group Therapy," *op. cit.*; Goldfarb, *Group Therapy with the Old*, *op. cit.*
50. Chance, "Group Psychotherapy," *op. cit.*
51. E. M. Pattison, "Group Psychotherapy and Group Methods in Community Mental Health," *Int. J. Group Psychother.*, 20:516-539, 1970.
52. L. Lowy, "Roadblocks in Group Work Practice with Older People: A Framework for Analysis," *Gerontologist*, 7:109-113, 1967.
53. *The Aged and Community Mental Health: A Guide to Program Development*, Publication #81, Group for the Advancement of Psychiatry, New York, N.Y., 1971.
54. Chance, "Group Psychotherapy," *op. cit.*
55. M. Harrington, *The Other America: Poverty in the United States* (New York: Macmillan, 1962), pp. 101-120.
56. G. L. Euster, "A System of Groups in Institutions for the Aged," *Social Casework*, 52:523-529, 1971.
57. S. Scheidlinger, "Therapeutic Group Approaches in Community Mental Health," *Social Work*, 13(2):87-95, 1968.
58. R. M. Glasscote, *et al.*, *Partial Hospitalization for the Mentally Ill—A Study of Programs and Problems* (Washington, D.C.: Joint Information Service, 1969).
59. A. Beigel and S. L. Feder, "Patterns of Utilization in Partial Hospitalization," *Am. J. Psychiat.*, 126:1267-1274, 1970.
60. E. Woodford-Williams, "Four Years Experience of a Day Hospital in Geriatric Practice," *Geront. Clin.* (Basel), 7:96-106, 1965; idem., "The Function and Structure of a Geriatric Department," *Geront. Clin.* (Basel), 9:199-205, 1967.
61. J. C. Brocklehurst, "The Work of a Geriatric Day Hospital," *Geront. Clin.* (Basel), 6:151-166, 1964.
62. P. Shaw and D. Macmillan, "Nuffield House: A Day Center for the Psychiatric Elderly," *Geront. Clin.*, 3:133-145, 1961.
63. Ross, "Some Recent Treatment Methods," *op. cit.*

64. A. Manaster, "The Family Group Therapy Program at Park View House for Aged," *J. Amer. Geriat. Soc.*, 15:302-306, 1967.
65. M. Bowers, "Clinical Aspects of Depression in a Home for the Aged," *J. Am. Geriat. Soc.*, 17:469-475, 1969.
66. A. S. Wolfe, "Participation of the Aged in the Group Process," *Ment. Hyg.*, 51:381-386, 1967.
67. N. Feil, "Group Therapy in a Home for the Aged," *Gerontologist*, 7:192-195, 1967.
68. S. Holzman and N. Sabel, "Improving the Morale of the Patients and Staff in a Geriatrics Institution by a Supervised Visiting Program," *Gerontologist*, 8:29-33, 1968.
69. *Ibid.*
70. D. Hawxhurst and H. Walzer, "Patients Helping Patients," *Ment. Hyg.*, 54:370-373, 1970.
71. M. Forman, "Conflict, Controversy, and Confrontation in Group Work with Older Adults," *Social Work*, 12:84, 1967.
72. H. Rusalem et al., "Neighborhood Rehab for the Aged," *Rehab. Rec.*, 7:28-31, 1966.
73. A. Gralewicz et al., "Restoration Therapy: An Approach to Group Therapy for the Chronically Ill," *Am. J. Occup. Ther.*, 41:294-299, 1968.
74. H. B. Peck, "Group Psychotherapy and Mental Health," *Int. J. Group Psychother.*, 1:301-310, 1951.
75. E. Hallowitz, "The Challenge to the Group Psychotherapist Created by a Society in Flux," *Int. J. Group Psychother.*, 20:423-434, 1970.
76. H. Levinson, "Use and Misuse of Groups," *Social Work*, 18:66-73, 1973.
77. S. Silverstein, "A New Venture in Group Work with Aged," *Social Casework*, 50:573-580, 1969.
78. J. Shapiro, "Single Room Occupancy: Community of the Alone," *Social Work*, 11:24-33, 1966.
79. R. W. Bateman and H. J. Stern, "Baltimore's Housing Court Clinic," *Social Work*, 6:43, 1961.
80. A. F. Panzetta, "The Concept of Community. The Short Circuit of the Mental Health Movement," *Arch. Gen. Psychiat.*, 25:291-297, 1971.

40

GROUP PSYCHOTHERAPY
WITH ALCOHOLICS

Ruth Fox

There is no chronic disease having more devastating effects on the individual, on the family, and on society than alcoholism. Because it is a type of abnormal behavior of extreme complexity, with physical, psychological, social, and spiritual overtones in a cause and effect relationship, it requires a multidiscipline approach to therapy which must vary a great deal depending upon the severity of the case and the stage of the disease. Hospitalization is often necessary to interrupt the pattern of addictive drinking. Medication such as tranquilizers, energizers, vitamins, or disulfiram (Antabuse), singly or in combination, may aid in maintaining the sobriety which is an essential prerequisite to the rehabilitative measures of psychosocial therapy. The spectacular success of the group approach of Alcoholics Anonymous, the shortage of trained personnel in the psychiatric field, the meager success of an orthodox psychoanalytic approach in alcoholism, and the growing public awareness of the enormity of the problem have led to the rapid growth of group therapy for alcoholics. A wide variety of groups have been used, some purely didactic and informative, some psychoanalytically oriented, some largely inspirational, and some using a combination of techniques (Armstrong and Gibbins, 1956; Brunner-Orne, 1958; Feibel, 1960; Gliedman *et al.*, 1956; Greenbaum, 1954; Pfeffer *et al.*, 1949; Thompson and Kolb, 1953; Vogel, 1957).

Groups vary in size from six to eight up to forty or fifty, while some lecture-type groups, followed by discussion, may total 200 or more. Good results have been claimed for each type of group.

My own groups consist of eight to ten persons of mixed sex with an age range from nineteen to sixty years (most being between twenty-five and forty-five years old) who meet once a week for one and one-half to two

Reprinted from the *International Journal of Group Psychotherapy*, Vol. 12, No. 1, January 1962, pp. 56-63. Amended by the author, September 1973.

hours in the evening. The groups are homogeneous in that all participating have a problem with alcohol, but heterogeneous in terms of underlying emotional pathology, which may range from near normal when abstinent, through character disorders and psychoneurosis, to mildly psychotic, schizophrenic, or depressive reaction. The admission of a homosexual of each sex has been found to stimulate discussion of deeper dynamics in the group provided there are at least one or two virile males and feminine women also present. Psychopaths and frank psychotics are generally excluded. There is a fairly wide variation in education, social background, and financial status, but all are of normal or superior intelligence. Some patients, especially in the early weeks, may be receiving tranquilizers, energizers, dietary supplements, and so on, and most are receiving disulfiram (Antabuse) for the first ten to twelve months (Fox, 1958). Some are attending Alcoholics Anonymous (A. A. *Today*, 1960) meetings as well, some are receiving one hour a week of individual psychotherapy, and occasionally a patient may be under deep analysis with me or some other analyst.

Several of the wives of my alcoholic patients (Fox, 1956) are attending group therapy sessions of their own, and many are also members of the Al-Anon Family Groups (1958), a fellowship for the families and friends of the alcoholic.

Most alcoholics are not well motivated for therapy and are merely submitting because they are severely threatened with the loss of something important to them: job and financial security, family and home, prestige, physical health, and so on. Very few wish to stop drinking. They tend to minimize or deny the extent or consequence of their involvement with alcohol; project the blame for their alcoholically induced problems on persons nearest to them, on adverse situations, or on society; build up an elaborate system of alibis and rationalizations; and react with hostility toward those who insist that they stop drinking. This defensive system may break down, however, after a particularly traumatizing experience with alcohol, so that the patient in his total physical, mental, social, and moral collapse may be at last receptive to proffered help and hope. Due to the campaign of education of the past three decades in America, however, and much longer in Holland and the Scandinavian countries, many alcoholics are now being reached at an earlier stage of their illness when rehabilitative measures can be most effective. Of over 4,000 alcoholics seen in my private practice in the past two decades, 80 per cent were employed (although they might be just losing a job), most were married and living with families, and all were trying to carry on as near normally as possible in spite of the considerable handicap of alcoholism. Only 3 per cent of the alcoholic population in the United States are the skid-row derelicts.

So helpful is group therapy to the alcoholic that it should be instituted as soon as possible, often on the very day of the first contact when resistance to the idea of this kind of help may be surprisingly low, perhaps because the alcoholic coming off a prolonged drinking bender is so beaten down and his defenses so shattered that he hasn't the will to resist. Even a few days after sobriety has been attained, the defenses characteristically used by these patients are again firmly entrenched and serve as powerful resistance to therapy of any sort.

We can only understand the tenacity of this resistance to therapy if we realize that total and permanent sobriety means an almost total change in an alcoholic's style of life, for the consequences of years of addictive drinking have infiltrated and encroached upon every area of his functioning. Having become physically dependent on alcohol, cessation of drinking causes severely painful withdrawal symptoms which can be obliterated at once with further drinking. Even after sobriety has been attained, the alcoholic is in a poor state of physical health, feeling ill, tired, irritable, depressed, and sleepless, and having a poor appetite most of the time. Since he has become psychologically dependent on alcohol as his chief source of pleasure as well as his chief prop in meeting the day-to-day problems of living, sobriety throws him into depression and panic. Alcohol as a social lubricant is denied him, so that he feels out of place in most social gatherings. Since drinking has been a substitute for intellectual and aesthetic pursuits, he finds himself with nothing to contribute, and his self-esteem is nil. He has also probably been indoctrinated with the many myths about alcohol, that it is somehow virile, sophisticated, and smart to drink heavily. He may equate not drinking at all with being weak, "square," and unmanly. It is a help to the alcoholic to let him know that we know just what he is up against in giving up alcohol. Unless he can envision a life without alcohol as better than one with it, he will not give it up. We have to try to develop a positive attitude and motivation, for the negative, purely punitive one has failed through the centuries.

Having been considered by his family and society as weak and immoral rather than ill, the alcoholic, in spite of an apparent superficial amiability, is apt to be bitter, angry, confused, wary, and suspicious. Rejected and isolated by society, he has withdrawn behind a defensive barrier; he is trapped, lonely, vengeful, and afraid. Alcohol has usurped most of his former interests; his social life is fast disappearing; he is being excluded from the warmth of his family; his confidence in himself has gone; and he either sees himself as an abject, hopeless failure or reacts with violent, hostile defiance. The advancing regression and helpless dependency caused by his addiction to alcohol are something the alcoholic is well aware of but cannot combat.

During the early sessions of a new group of alcoholics, most of the conversation centers around the common problem of drinking and its meaning to each patient. I believe the therapist should play a more than usually active role in these initial sessions, which must be didactic and informative as well as emotionally therapeutic. Patients must be taught all we know about the condition, its definition, cause, incidence, symptoms, differential diagnosis, epidemiology, treatment, and prevention. Patients must learn how alcoholic drinking differs from excessive social drinking, and they must learn to look on it as a specific illness with its specific phases, characteristics, effects, and consequences. The alcoholic must learn to recognize the compulsive nature and the characteristic progression of the disease. He should learn to recognize alcoholic behavior with, first, social dependence on alcohol, next, psychological dependence, and, finally, physiologic dependence. The alcoholic must learn also what he can do about his illness in order to recover. He must learn that total sobriety for life is the essential goal and that he can never drink safely again. He should be told about Alcoholics Anonymous, Antabuse, psychotherapy, medical rehabilitation, and so on, as aids to his group therapy program. This didactic part of the therapy can be greatly aided by books (Mann, 1958; Fox, 1955) and by films showing the physiological effect of alcohol on the body, as well as the psychological and social effects of alcoholism. Also, in this early phase, all kinds of help must be given to the patient: emotional, physical, vocational, spiritual, and at times even financial.

In these early phases, although there is important interaction beginning among the patients and there is a beginning awareness of the fact that alcoholic drinking is largely a symptom of an underlying personality maladjustment, the interchange does not go very deep, nor do the patients reveal too many of their deeper fears and anxieties. Though superficially friendly, they seem unable to show real warmth or tenderness, and most are too fearful of showing aggression to handle their basic problems of hostility, though sudden irritations, antipathies, and rivalries with the leader or other members do begin to show up. Gradually, too, tentative overtures of friendship and understanding become evident.

In the second phase of group therapy, which may run from one to four years, there is a working through of feelings, thoughts, behavior, and personality traits, a study of the functions of alcoholic drinking and any secondary gains therefrom, and analysis of resistance, types of defense mechanisms used, and the various transference maneuvers brought into play.

Though alcoholics show no typical personality pattern, alcohol being used to "solve" the most diverse problems, they do seem to share a certain constellation of traits which may have etiologic significance or may be a result of the molding process of their similar experience with the crisis of alcoholism. A battery of psychological tests on 300 alcoholics, done, of course, *after* addition was well advanced, showed a remarkably frequent occurrence of the following character traits: a low frustration tolerance and inability to endure anxiety or tension; a schizoid type of adjustment, with feelings of isolation, strong social fears, devaluated self-esteem, and undue sensitiveness; repressed or conscious feelings of omnipotence and grandiose ambitions with little ability to persevere; extreme narcissism and often exhibitionism; unaccountable and marked mood swings; a constant inner battle between passivity and aggression, with conscious or unconscious marked hostility and rebellion; a strong tendency to act out repetitively their conflicts and instinctual impulses, both aggressive and sexual, with or without the help of alcohol; a strong, archaic, punitive superego structure with harsh self-condemnation, sense of unworthiness, and guilt leading to masochistic, self-punitive behavior; strong dependent needs, frustration of which leads to depression and despair or to hostility, rage, and fantasies of revenge; and in almost all cases a sexual problem of immaturity, impotence, frigidity, promiscuity, latent or overt homosexuality, sadomasochistic level of fixation or regression, or confusion regarding the sexual role. The most usual defenses are regression, denial, introjection, projection, and rationalization. Insights regarding these mental mechanisms come slowly and often painfully.

Alcohol is for the alcoholic as well as for the nonalcoholic a social lubricant, a shared cultural activity, a means toward greater friendliness, intimacy, and closeness, a means of augmenting pleasurable sensations as well as a means of lessening anxiety, tension, depression, and pain. Because of some specific vulnerability of the alcoholic, alcohol has also come to mean much more than this to him. It serves first as a means of gratification of certain unacceptable aggressive or sexual desires with the sure punishment meted out by the relentless superego in the physical and mental anguish and remorse of the hangover, the disapproval and rejection by family and society, financial losses, and the social disgrace. Another function of alcohol can be revenge and retaliation against the persons who care about him but whom he wishes to punish. It also can serve to satisfy narcissistic needs, putting him in a state of exalted self-esteem, making him feel confident, worthy, witty, loved, sought after—all the feelings he lacks when sober. He has the illusion under alcohol that he has a right to unconditional and unqualified love, approval, and acclaim no matter what he does, and that his wants should be supplied without effort on his part. Alcohol allows him to shed the adult responsibilities of work, family, and society.

All the evidences of resistance one finds in a neurotic group are also found in the alcoholic group, in addition to the specific resistances against giving up alcohol. Persistent hostility can be a defense, with the mistaken idea that defiance represents strength while loving represents weakness.

Of all the devices to cover up awareness of painful reality the alcoholic uses especially that of denial that he is ill. In the state of early euphoria of sobriety he may deny that he has any personality difficulties at all, what Alcoholics Anonymous has called the "honeymoon stage." Projection of the blame for his plight is another favorite defense of the alcoholic, with the wife, the boss, or society seen as the denying one. Another oft-used device to protect himself from blame is rationalizing that the fault lies in the kind of work he does, or the place he lives, or his associates, or that his fine points aren't really appreciated. These and many other "dodges" need to be recognized and their purpose understood before they can be given up.

The multiple transferences which are elicited in the group must be recognized and understood as irrational relics from the past, inappropriate to the present, automatic, compulsive, irrelevant, and repetitive. Their quality of rigidity and the intensity and strong accompanying emotions of love, hate, bitterness, revenge, and ambivalence must be recognized as carryovers of conditioned responses built up in an unhappy childhood. The nature of transference reactions, their derivations, purpose, and characteristics must be explained to patients, who often become adept at recognizing them in their own and others' distortions (Wolf, 1950). The investment of other group members with the attributes and qualities of parental or sibling figures shows such extreme disparity from patient to patient that the illusory nature of these responses finally becomes apparent, clearing the way for an honest appraisal of the true qualities present in the individual being reacted to. Not only are the various group members the recipients of these transference feelings, but so is the leader. In the context of the transference, the leader often becomes the good father or mother, or the dominating, authoritative, and restricting parent of either sex. Flashes of memory from the past can illuminate dramatically the genesis of these transference feelings, leading to a loosening of their hold and their resolution. Confrontation of each member with his different and characteristic projection onto another member helps each one not only to see how subjective and inaccurate his investment of that person was, but how destructive to the development of a healthy relationship it can be. Since the transference maneuver can be considered as a current attempt to right an old wrong, into it goes all the bitterness of the old hurt, with all the old desire to dominate, exploit, own, control, punish, or destroy the object. Problems of sibling rivalry, competition with authority, separation anxiety, and many other emotions in the group are transferential in nature and gradually become recognized as such.

During this second phase, there will be analysis of conflicts on both the intrapsychic and the interpersonal level, ventilation and catharsis, communalization of problems, group identification and acceptance, reality testing of old and new concepts, with the abandonment of fantasy, an opportunity to try out new ways of relating to others as peers and as authority figures, the attainment of insights regarding neurotic behavior in general and in oneself in particular, the learning of one's uniqueness of needs as well as potential, and the gradual abandonment of the wholly narcissistic position for one of mutual interdependency.

To give a greater depth of feeling to the group therapy experience, psychodrama has been used and found to be quite effective. In psychodrama the patient is given a chance to discover his "spontaneous self." He has the opportunity to act out his conflicts, his dreams, his memories, his present life experiences, his fantasies. He can relive his past experiences as they were, or as he saw them, and relive them as he wished they had been, and he can enact future scenes or experience old scenes in a less distorted manner. Role playing, role reversal, the use of auxiliary egos or doubles, the "behind the back" technique, the enactment of fantasy, give real insight into the true feelings and attitudes of the patient and those close to him (Moreno, 1955, 1957).*

In an alcoholic approaching the terminal stage of treatment the same type of profound changes have occurred as are described by Wolf (1958) in neurotic patients. Not only has he accepted total and permanent sobriety without resentment, but he is continuing to free himself from the remnants of the neurotic restraints and strictures which crippled him before. Emerging from behind his rigid façade of compulsion, distrust, and hostility, he is developing a healthy self-interest and awareness of his own worth and needs, but at the same time he appreciates the needs of others in a democratic way. He is learning to scale down some of his inordinate demands on himself and others; to plan ahead and yet remain spontaneous, adaptable, and ready for new and challenging experiences; to postpone certain gratifications and to deny others entirely when necessary; to liberate and develop his formerly stunted creative powers; to appreciate the possibility and even at times the desirability of being different and to have the courage to be so; to accept the problem we all have with status in our society and to learn to be comfortable with both peers and authority figures; to have the courage to express a feeling of legitimate anger when it is necessary and wise; to develop a sense of values and ethics; and to find happiness and fulfillment with his wife, his children, his friends, and his co-workers. Usually, a member's leaving the group is discussed for several weeks before the decision is made. Though the group may miss him, his recovery gives them hope for themselves. Since maturity is not a goal but a road, it is hoped that the patient will continue his development as long as he lives.

Group analysis is enormously helpful in treating alcoholics, but by itself it is not enough, especially in the early stages of treatment. We must create a total therapeutic atmosphere in which the alcoholic can recover. This means more education of the public and the helping professions. It means more research into causes and into methods of treatment, with a team approach and a cross-fertilization from many disciplines. It will take the formation of many more local committees throughout the world by civic-minded citizens of good will to conquer the problem. And it will take money and government support to bring this great public health

---

* The Psychodrama Director in this study was Hannah Weiner of New York City.

problem under control. From the long-range, preventive point of view, however, we know that billions of dollars can be saved by solving this problem, to say nothing of its importance to the health and happiness of millions of persons.

BIBLIOGRAPHY

Al-Anon Family Groups (New York: Al-Anon Family Groups, 1958).

A. A. *Today* (New York: Cornwall Press, 1960).

Armstrong, J. J., and Gibbins, R. J., "A Psychotherapeutic Technique with Large Groups in the Treatment of Alcoholics," *Quart. J. Stud. Alcohol.*, 17:461, 1956.

Brunner-Orne, M., "Group Therapy of Alcoholics; International Conference," *Quart. J. Stud. Alcohol.*, 19:164, 1958.

Feibel, C., "The Archaic Personality Structure of Alcoholics and Its Implications for Group Therapy," *Int. J. Group Psychother.*, 10:39, 1960.

Fox, R., and Lyon, P., *Alcoholism, Its Scope, Cause and Treatment* (New York: Random House, 1955).

———, "The Alcoholic Spouse," in V. Eisenstein, ed., *Neurotic Interaction in Marriage* (New York: Basic Books, 1956).

———, "Treatment of Alcoholism; Antabuse as an Adjunct to Psychotherapy in Alcoholism," *N.Y. State J. Med.*, 58:1540, 1958.

Gliedman, L. H., Rosenthal, D., Frank, J., and Nash, H., "Group Therapy of Alcoholics with Concurrent Group Meetings of Their Wives," *Quart. J. Stud. Alcohol.*, 17:655, 1956.

Greenbaum, H., "Group Psychotherapy with Alcoholics in Conjunction with Antabuse Treatment," *Int. J. Group Psychother.*, 4:30, 1954.

Halpern, B., "Psychodrama in an Out-Patient Alcoholic Clinic," Paper presented at the National State Conference on Alcoholism, New Haven, Conn., 1951.

Mann, M., *New Primer on Alcoholism* (New York: Holt, Rinehart and Winston, 1958).

Moreno, J. L., "Discovery of Spontaneous Man," *Group Psychother.*, 8:103, 1955.

———, "Sociatry, The Social Atom and Death," in *Progress in Psychotherapy* (New York: Grune & Stratton, 1957).

Pfeffer, A. Z., Friedland, P., and Wortis, S. B., "Group Psychotherapy with Alcoholics," *Quart. J. Stud. Alcohol.*, 10:198, 1949.

Thompson, C. E., and Kolb, W. P., "Group Psychotherapy in Association with Alcoholics Anonymous," *Am. J. Psychiat.*, 110:29, 1953.

Vogel, S., "Some Aspects of Group Psychotherapy with Alcoholics," *Int. J. Group Psychother.*, 7:302, 1957.

Wolf, A., "Psychoanalysis of Groups," *Am. J. Psychother.*, 4:1, 1950.

———, "The Advanced and Terminal Phases in Group Psychotherapy," Paper presented at the Second Annual Institute, American Group Psychotherapy Association, January 22-25, 1958.

41

GROUP THERAPY OF ALCOHOLICS
WITH CONCURRENT GROUP MEETINGS
OF THEIR WIVES

Lester H. Gliedman
David Rosenthal
Jerome D. Frank
Helen T. Nash

The question of what can be done for the alcoholic has recently received increasing and well-deserved attention. The extent of alcoholism and the personal, familial, and community effects of this disease need no elaboration. The therapeutic challenge is a great one and only a beginning has been made toward meeting it. One of the more frequently employed ways of dealing with this illness has been by means of group therapy. The popularity of this form of treatment reflects not only the rising application of the group approach to many types of emotional illness but also the success of Alcoholics Anonymous. Not only has this lay organization transformed the outlook for many alcoholics from one of despair to one of hope, but it has demonstrated the therapeutic value of the group in their recovery.

To study the value of the group in a psychiatric setting, an exploratory project in this type of treatment of alcoholics has been in progress in the Outpatient Department of the Henry Phipps Psychiatric Clinic of the Johns Hopkins Hospital for the past 18 months. This project was limited to married male alcoholics whose wives would participate in concurrent but separately conducted discussion meetings.

Previous experience in the treatment of alcoholism had led us to believe that inclusion of the family in the recovery process of these patients

Reprinted from the *Quarterly Journal of Studies on Alcohol*, Vol. 17, No. 4, December 1956, pp. 655-670.

would be desirable. Where antisocial actions constitute the major part of the presenting picture of an illness, these are often directed against a specific target, i.e. a particular person, object, group, or relationship, because of an underlying emotional disturbance. In married alcoholics, the actions center on drinking behavior and the target is most often the wife. Therefore, both the alcoholic and his wife were included in this attempt to gain better understanding of the underlying emotional disturbance as well as the relationship between the alcoholic and the person who is most frequently the object and the stimulus of the drinking behavior.

Two other considerations prompted the decision to involve both the patients and their wives. (a) It was thought that this might attract couples with high motivation for therapy in both partners and that the wife's acceptance of some responsibility for the treatment would enhance the patient's motivation and help sustain him through a course of therapy. (b) It was felt that systematically obtained information from both partners might provide a check on the validity of information received from each.

The general plan was first to describe the patients and their marriages by several measures and next, after thus spelling out the task confronting therapy, to estimate how effectively this was met by group treatment.

PROCEDURE

Considerable difficulty was experienced in obtaining patients for this study. Of 45 couples contacted, only nine accepted treatment and appeared for processing. This points to a frequently made observation that alcoholic patients are often not motivated to accept psychiatrically or medically sponsored treatment, even when a departure from traditional approaches is offered. At any rate, the patients in the present study constitute a highly selected sample and the results must be considered in this light.

Each of the nine patients who kept appointments for treatment had some current, compelling reason for doing so—such as pressure from the wife, threatened loss of job, marked deterioration of financial status, or varying combinations of these. Though these circumstances may be thought of as forms of coercion, they at least pointed to the fact that these patients were accessible to external influence.

The Evaluation Process

The nine patients and their wives were evaluated before and after treatment by four measures: a drinking checklist, a symptom checklist, an adjective checklist, and a social ineffectiveness scale. Patients and wives were interviewed separately.

The drinking checklist consists of 29 items describing characteristics of pathological drinking which can be rated in terms of 4 degrees of severity, and was derived in part from Seliger[1] and in part from Jellinek.[2] Each patient and his wife separately completed this form as it pertained to the patient's current drinking.

The symptom checklist is a modification of the Cornell Index[3] and consists of 33 distressing symptoms of a psychological nature which are rated on a 4-point scale of severity. These symptoms can be grouped into several subscales: anxiety; depression; irritability; obsession-compulsion phobia; and paranoid-schizoid traits. Each patient and his wife rated the patient's symptoms on the basis of how the patient currently felt.

The adjective checklist, specially designed for this investigation, is made up of 52 adjectives that have been commonly applied to alcoholics. Five judges were able to divide these into two groups. One group implies something good, complimentary, rewarding, or satisfying. The other group implies something bad, critical, unrewarding, or dissatisfying. For example, adjectives such as mature, close, trusting, would fall in the former category, while bragging, nagging, and deceitful would be classified in the latter. Each patient was requested to select those adjectives which described him when sober and when intoxicated. He was asked also to describe his wife with these adjectives as she appeared to him when he was sober and when he was intoxicated. Each wife was requested to describe herself with these adjectives when her husband, the patient, was sober, and again when he was intoxicated. Likewise, she was asked to select those adjectives which she thought described her husband when he was sober and when he was intoxicated. By means of the adjectives selected, and the group in which they fell, it was possible to characterize the satisfaction or dissatisfaction associated with sobriety and intoxication, and the satisfaction or dissatisfaction associated with the marriage when the patient was sober or intoxicated.

The social ineffectiveness scale is made up of 15 categories of interpersonal ineffectiveness which were operationally defined and rated on a 5-point scale of severity, based on the inappropriateness and frequency of these behaviors as they occurred in relation to the various significant persons in the patient's current life. The categories are: overly independent; superficially social; extrapunitive; officious; impulsive; hyperreactive; overly systematic; overly dependent; withdrawn; intrapunitive; irresponsible; overcautious; constrained; unsystematic; sexually maladjusted. The rating of social ineffectiveness and its rationale are discussed by Parloff, Kelman, and Frank.[4] Husband and wife were rated on this scale following a structured psychiatric interview of each. This interview emphasized present as opposed to past interpersonal functioning.

As a result of these procedures, it was possible to estimate each patient's current drinking severity, psychological discomfort, interpersonal ineffectiveness, and satisfaction or dissatisfaction derived from sobriety and intoxication. For each wife, it was possible to estimate her present interpersonal ineffectiveness and her satisfaction or dissatisfaction when the patient was sober and intoxicated. For each couple, it was possible to describe the current satisfaction or dissatisfaction of the marriage when drinking occurred and when it did not. Since each of these measures was completed and scored before and after group therapy, the effects of treatment on each could be examined not only clinically but statistically as well.

Preparation for Therapy

Following completion of the initial evaluative procedures each patient and wife were oriented with regard to the forthcoming group sessions. The routine aspects of the program were stressed, such as frequency and duration of meetings; length of treatment; place; billing; procedure for cancellation of visits; absences; the fact that meetings would be recorded and the reasons for this; the purpose of the observer who would be present; and the confidentiality of the proceedings. All of the participants were informed that they need talk about themselves only as they saw fit, but that it would be through the medium of their experiences, especially current ones, that they could be helped and possibly help others. The patients were told that medications were available and would be employed as necessary, that is, to help them when they needed help. The role of the therapist, as both a member and leader of the group and as a resource person, was outlined. The parallels between the projected group sessions and their life situations were emphasized so that the rationale for group therapy would be more apparent. The patients were informed that their wives were to be involved in concurrent but separate discussion sessions to broaden the base for recovery by insuring that both marital partners would better understand the nature of the patient's alcoholism and have a share in its amelioration. This was also made explicit to the wives.

In addition, the patients and their wives were told that alcoholism was a disease in which the goal of treatment was total abstinence; that though the aim is to help the patient stop drinking, the term "illness" implies a certain progression of events which the patient may not be able at all times to control, any more than a person even with a well-regulated chronic disease can avoid periodic exacerbation; that there is little or no place for such things as condemnation and threats in the treatment of any sickness, medical or psychological; and that though it was preferable for the patients to attend the treatment sessions while sober, it was expected that this would not always be possible and, therefore, they should plan to be present regardless of condition. This last policy was adopted because it was strongly felt that sick patients should not be turned away at a time when their need for treatment was greatest. All were informed that individual therapy sessions were available if needed. The essence of the above information was mimeographed on sheets which were given to each patient and his wife and was repeated again in the early group sessions.

The last part of the interview was devoted to determining what were the most convenient times for the meetings. From this, two 1½-hour sessions per week were arranged for the patients and one weekly session for the wives. The particular nights and hours scheduled were those which the participants themselves selected, even though the administrative problems raised by this were considerable. It was planned to see the patients twice as often as their wives because of Greenbaum's[5] finding that group therapy with alcoholics was more effective at twice weekly than at weekly intervals and to differentiate between the programs for the patients and the wives. To categorize the participation of the wives as treatment and as identical with that of the patients seemed unwarranted and at the same time likely to increase the possibility of the wives being uncooperative. To help distinguish between the two programs, it was planned that the wives would have a nonphysician female leader.

Description of Therapy

The therapeutic orientation was analytic in a limited sense, stressing the need to keep anxiety with its known disastrous results from overwhelming these patients. Use was made of methods of controlling such tension in therapy as have been reported by Bordin.[6] To this end, the sessions were somewhat structured, although no prearranged topics were employed as discussion guides. The structuring developed out of the ongoing activity in each meeting. Direct requests by the patient for information and advice were more frequently satisfied than is usual in analytically oriented group psychotherapy. Interpersonal transactions of one patient with another were analyzed only rarely, while those described by a patient as going on between himself and persons outside the group, including his wife, usually were. This permitted the discussion of important psychological issues in a less anxiety-arousing context. Medication was used when the patients described situations which required it. The drugs employed were reserpine, dexedrine, mephenesin, antihistamines, and vitamins. These were used more frequently early in treatment and served as a further means of controlling tension in the patients and enabling them to stay in the treatment program.

As therapy progressed, the group therapist became impressed by these patients' preoccupation with the temporal present. They seemed especially insulated from their own past experiences and peculiarly unable to project into the future. They appeared to operate more in the "here and now" than other groups of patients. Because of this, a deliberate attempt was made to bring the past into the present by having patients review their previous alcoholic outbursts in detail, with the hope that this might function as a deterrent to current drinking. Likewise, attempts were made to rehearse for the future and to cultivate planfulness by discussion of impending life problems. An account of the temporal orientation in alcoholics has been presented elsewhere by Gliedman.[7]

An additional observation in the group therapy sessions was the hypersensitivity of the patients to depressive feelings and the rapidity with which they experienced them. Specifically, in the group interplay, one or more of the members involved, usually the relatively inactive ones who were less in the therapist's attention, silently recoiled from the proceedings. As time passed, it was apparent that these patients were feeling depressed, let down, inadequate, and hurt following such engagements. This came to our attention by the return of such members to subsequent meetings in an intoxicated state or through their reports of intoxication after these meetings. It was therefore necessary, in the later sessions, to take steps to support the less active participants in the meetings, and especially the silent ones, by rephrasing the matter being discussed to include the possibility of viewpoints other than those of the active participants, or by controlling monopolizers of the meetings. In short, the therapist intervened more frequently and was more supportive than with other patients.

The wives group functioned more like the usual analytically oriented therapy group. Though they were highly defensive and found a common rallying topic in criticism of their husbands, still much of the discussion tended to be about themselves. Such intimate topics as sexual frigidity were profitably discussed, and helpful interpersonal exchanges with other group members occurred. In contrast to the preoccupation of the patients with the temporal present, the wives were concerned with the future and the past. If they felt attacked, they did not react by silence and depressiveness, as their husbands tended to do, but instead retaliated actively and often overcommitted themselves in the expression of their attitudes. Therefore, an important consideration of the group leader was to keep the wives from such overcommitment by rephrasing their expressed points of view in such a way that a subsequent modification of attitude would not be construed as a loss of face. Frequent interventions of this sort were required. The marital relationship was discussed often, the wives usually maintaining that even when their husbands were sober the marriages were lacking in important aspects. Although initially the discussion sessions were not viewed by the wives as treatment, they tended to use the meetings not only to participate in the recovery of the husbands but as therapy for their own problems. This was an outgrowth of their inability to reconcile their constant criticism of their husbands with the many years they had endured the unhappy state of affairs.

A total of 32 sessions was planned for the patients and 16 for the wives. When these were completed, the program was stopped and each couple was studied again.

RESULTS

A total of 9 couples was processed initially. The patients' attendance ranged from 4 to 26 meetings; 4 attended 20 or more sessions. Two patients dropped out of treatment and their final processing was not possible. The attendance of the wives ranged from 1 to 15 meetings; 4 attended 12 or more sessions. One wife dropped out of the program and was not available for re-evaluation. Complete data are therefore available on 9 couples initially but only on 7 finally.

General Description of Subjects

All the patients tended to recognize alcoholism as their main problem. Table 1 itemizes some relevant characteristics of the nine patients and their wives prior to treatment. It makes clear that this is a seriously ill group of patients, currently ambulatory and employed, for whom heavy drinking had become, in a sense, a way of life. In recent years the drinking was becoming worse. They came to treatment only under duress, largely at the insistence of their wives. The wives appeared better organized than their husbands, had slightly more education, and were the main force

Table 41–1   General Characteristics of Nine Patients and Their Wives Prior to Treatment

	Patients	Wives
Age, years, average	41	40
Age range, years	27-54	27-54
Education level, grade	10	12
Duration of alcoholism, years		
16-20	4	—
10-15	2	—
5-9	2	—
3-4	1	—
Course of alcoholism during previous year		
Improving	0	—
Worsening	6	—
Fluctuating	3	—
Stationary	0	—
Previous hospitalization for mental complications of alcoholism	3	—
Previous hospitalization for physical complications of alcoholism	3	—
Reported physical complications of alcoholism	6	—
Arrests for intoxication	6	—
History of alcoholism in antecedents	6	1
Disturbing childhood experiences	6	0
History of other emotional illness	0	1
Previous psychotherapy	2	1
Previous Alcoholics Anonymous membership	4	—
Currently employed	7	6
Active desire to enter combined treatment program	0	7
Active pressure from wife to enter treatment program	5	—

holding the families together. Almost all of them held full-time or part-time jobs to insure a dependable source of income.

Table 2 lists some characteristics of the patients' marriages. In most instances the initiative for the marriage rested with the woman, who usually had desired marriage for reasons other than the man's attractiveness. The women seemed to have been aware of their prospective husbands' excessive drinking so that the marriages tended to be incidents in a drinking career that already had started. The course of the marriages was stormy and the patients' alcoholism became increasingly worse. Currently the marriages were battlegrounds, and the family life was so organized that everything tended to be viewed as having or not having an effect on the patients' drinking.

Table 41-2   General Characteristics of Marriages of the Nine Couples Prior to Treatment

Duration, years, average (and range)	14(1-35)
Excessive drinking of patients before marriage	7
Ulterior motivation of wives for marriage	6
Previous marriages of wives	3
Previous marriages of patients	0
Childless marriages	3
Sexual maladjustment	8
Separations during present marriages	9
Currently reported "happy" marriages	0
Total organization of family about alcoholism	9
Nondrinking (totally abstinent) wives	6

Initial Description of Patients on Scales

The seriousness of the patients' drinking was reflected on the drinking checklist. The wives' ratings agreed with those of the patients, except that the wives rated the patients as significantly more violent when intoxicated than the patients scored themselves ($P < .05$).

Though the patients did not appear so clinically, the symptom checklist revealed high scores in the areas indicative of depressiveness and irritability. The wives agreed with these findings but saw the patients as even more irritable than the patients saw themselves ($P < .05$) and also rated them as higher in the paranoid-schizoid spectrum of symptoms ($P < .05$) than the patients scored themselves.

Interpersonally, as indicated on the social ineffectiveness scale, the patients were rated as very ineffective. The wives also scored high on this scale but less than the patients in every instance. The wives consistently rated the patients as more ineffective than the interviews with the patients alone indicated. A translation of this scale into clinical terms reveals that the patients socialized in a very limited, impersonal fashion. They related to people in a stereotyped, shallow, cliché-ridden manner, with a paucity of the shared, deeper feelings, and often knew no way of participating in closer interpersonal relationships without alcohol. They were impulsive and labile, frequently finding themselves propelled into situations beyond their depth. In such states, they either overreacted or did not react at all. They were unreliable and unpredictable, excessive drinking being only one aspect of this trait. They were dependent and, at the same time, fought against those on whom they depended. Ambivalence characterized much of their behavior. Their sexual life was quite unsatisfactory.

The wives were highly opinionated, forceful, openly critical of their husbands, and given to manipulations of one sort or another presumably to control their husbands' drinking and to stabilize the family life. Though they were capable of closer interpersonal relationships, their husbands' drinking had narrowed this activity. There was a high degree of sexual frigidity which was acknowledged without great difficulty. They used sex as a bargaining weapon for the husbands' maintenance of sobriety. Nevertheless, they had good work records and ran their homes in an orderly, responsible manner. Where there were children, the wives reacted to the patients more as if they were uncontrollable offspring than marital partners. It is emphasized that this was the presenting picture at the start of treatment, when the patients' alcoholism had created such a crisis as to obscure most of the more positive aspects of the functioning of each marital partner.

In spite of the rather dismal picture reflected by the ineffectiveness scale, the adjectives selected by the patients to describe themselves in the sober and intoxicated states revealed that they received much more satisfaction from sobriety than from intoxication. Only two patients indicated the reverse. The wives, however, in contrast to their outspoken, positive characteristics as evaluated on the ineffectiveness scale, revealed ambivalence toward themselves on the adjective checklist both when their husbands were drinking and when they were sober. This ambivalence was greater, however, when the patient was intoxicated.

Seven of the patients described their wives with adjectives which implied that they were satisfied with their marital state when sober. This is just the opposite of the implications that might be drawn from the adjectives selected by the wives to describe the patients when sober. Six of the wives viewed their marital state as unsatisfactory. However, during the patients' intoxication each partner was markedly dissatisfied with the other, except one wife who described her husband in the intoxicated state in such a way as to imply that she was receiving some satisfactions from his drinking.

Description of the Patients Following Treatment

Because of the drop-outs, only seven couples could be evaluated after treatment. The two patients who discontinued treatment seemed to do so because of events in group therapy. One was a silent member; the other was repeatedly involved with a more active, more psychologically sophisticated patient but in such a manner as to be placed in a relatively inactive, passive role. Both might have remained in therapy had earlier cognizance been taken of the implications of their behavior on their status in the group. One, after a session in which he suffered what in retrospect was not just an exchange of views but an interpersonal defeat, though it did not seem so at the time, kept returning to the group meetings in an intoxicated state. Then, while drunk, he would reply to the patient with whom he was involved in the prior meeting. He finally left, presumably after obtaining a job which precluded his attendance. His wife, who continued to attend the wives' discussion sessions until their completion, reported that he was furious following his encounters in the group with this patient, but continued in treatment at her insistence for a total of ten sessions. According to her, he then stopped drinking and obtained a job so that he could announce this to the group as his reason for quitting and thereby show up the other patient whose alcoholism was unchecked. She stated that he remained sober and working until two months later, when she was re-evaluated, after which he resumed drinking excessively. The second drop-out was never actively involved in the group but obviously was reacting to it. Treating him as one would a silent patient in a neurotic group probably was important in his termination of treatment. Instead, attempts should have been made to elicit his participation, at least by acknowledging that though he was silent his unexpressed and possibly different feelings and attitudes were just as worthy of consideration as those of the more vocal group members.

The seven couples who could be evaluated before and after treatment showed several changes in each of the measures employed. On the drinking checklist, five of the seven patients improved. Two were totally abstinent, two reduced the frequency of their drinking by half or more, and one only slightly. One pretreatment monthy liquor bill of approximately $350 was decreased to $40. In general, the drinking expenditure of each patient was decreased and represented a realiable index of improvement. Though the wives generally acknowledged the patients' improved status with regard to less drinking and less expenditure for liquor, if a patient did any drinking at all she tended to rate the effects of this drinking at the time of final evaluation just as she did prior to treatment. The difference between the patients' pre- and post-treatment scores on the drinking checklist bordered on a level of acceptable statistical significance ($P > .05 < .10$). The difference between the preliminary and final scores of the wives' ratings was not statistically significant.

The symptom checklist scores showed moderate decreases in five of the seven patients. Two of the patients who showed improvement in their drinking behavior showed a small increase in psychological symptoms after treatment. On the subscales of this checklist, however, the patients as a group showed statistically significant decreases in depressiveness ($P < .05$) and irritability ($P < .01$). The wives agreed with this and also reported a statistically significant reduction in the patients' paranoid-schizoid symptoms ($P < .05$).

Other than the changes in drinking, there were only slight modifications in social ineffectiveness. Interpersonally, the patients and their wives continued to operate in a manner not much different from that which prevailed before the onset of the group program. More than half of the couples, however, showed improvement in sexual adjustment. More than half of the wives showed slight increases in intrapunitiveness—a reflection of the fact that they eventually came to see themselves as sharing to some degree the responsibility for the patients' excessive drinking.

Statistically significant changes on the adjective checklist revealed that sobriety became more satisfying to the patients ($P < .02$) than it was before treatment. The wives, however, tended to describe themselves in an ambivalent fashion, just as they did initially. In addition, the patients under the condition "sober" described their wives with significantly more of the satisfying adjectives than initially ($P < .01$) and the wives described the patients similarly ($P < .05$). This suggests an improved outlook with regard to marital status.

The above changes are not statistically related to the duration or intensity of the patients' alcoholism. They do bear a significant relationship to the initial descriptions of the patient when intoxicated. Those patients who did not improve or improved only slightly were the ones whose adjective checklist descriptions under the condition "intoxicated" showed the most disagreement with their wives' description of them under the same condition. The greater discrepancies resulted primarily from patients having selected adjectives denoting satisfaction to describe themselves during intoxication, while the wives selected the opposite. To a lesser degree, a minority of the wives initially selected some adjectives denoting satisfaction with their hunbands in the intoxicated state, while the patients selected the opposite adjectives in so describing themselves. Had both the patients and their wives selected adjectives indicative of satisfaction derived from the patients' intoxication, it is unlikely that they would have entered into treatment.

DISCUSSION

The four measures employed defined the challenge facing group therapy. They indicated that this was a chronic and severely alcoholic population, with marked symptoms of depressiveness and irritability; severe interpersonal ineffectiveness characterized by extreme, ambivalent behavior;

and much marital dissatisfaction. What did the group form of treatment have to offer?

The changes which took place fall into a certain hierarchy that is suggestive of the value of group therapy in this illness. The greatest changes were in the areas of marital milieu (satisfaction of patient and wife with each other) and personal morale (satisfaction with self). The next largest change was recorded in psychological symptoms, especially in irritability and depressiveness. Fewer, though important, changes took place in drinking behavior, and the least change occurred in social ineffectiveness. If the first three of these are accepted as components of what is known as self-esteem, it seems clear that the major contribution of the group program was in this area. It emphasized that despite the patients' facade to the contrary, this particular group of alcoholics was characterized by troubles in this area. As a group, they tended to be demoralized prior to therapy, most clearly demonstrated by those symptoms indicating depressiveness which were characteristic of all the patients. This is to be distinguished from the syndrome of depression. These patients are not clinically depressed. However, their tolerance for the feelings of depressiveness appears to be low. They seem to be highly sensitive to the experiences of defeat, failure, and inadequacy for which their psychological make-up, especially their propensity to live as if there were no yesterday or tomorrow, predisposes them. Such feelings are less likely to be cushioned by the knowledge of having effectively dealt with them in the past or by the expectations of having another opportunity in the future to manage better the events responsible for them. The depressiveness of the hang-over state may well represent these feelings in pure culture.

In any event, it is tempting to speculate that the need to cope with depressiveness, lowered morale, or feelings of damaged self-esteem in general, is one of the more important motivations for excessive drinking. It is with regard to these feelings that the group seems to make its special contribution in the treatment of alcoholism. The group can accomplish this for several reasons. Firstly, it provides a controlled milieu in which alcoholics may use one of their major interpersonal resources, superficial sociability, without having it threatened; or they can try to improve this technique of relating and to experiment with other techniques. The opportunity to socialize in a manner for which they are equipped is valuable in itself. It enables them to continue having esteem-enhancing experiences similar to those achieved in the past, yet at the same time they are made aware that these are not the maximum of which they are capable.

Secondly, in a group the patients can take treatment at their own pace. They can participate psychologically as desired or withdraw psychologically if needed while still being physically present. Again, this has the effect of decreasing the threatening aspects of treatment.

Thirdly, an all-alcoholic group fosters mutual identification and support, which ordinarily is difficult for these patients to achieve. Usually, they are so preoccupied with their own crises that they are insulated from many available healthful influences. In a group, they can be encouraged more readily or even pulled up by the bootstraps of a fellow alcoholic's successes.

Fourthly, the alcoholic's preoccupation with the temporal present is more readily modified in the group situation. The "here and now" orientation of a member may be expanded by the presence of other patients who share this orientation but not quite to the same degree. In a group, therefore, more can take place that falls within the optimal communication range of these patients while still affording the opportunity of a different and potentially healthier experience.

Finally, the group tends to dilute the transference reactions so that the strong, often esteem-damaging, drink-precipitating feelings for which these patients are notorious are more comfortably controlled and more likely to be faced. In other words, the group maximizes the conditions for the more optimal functioning of alcoholics in a treatment situation, while minimizing the occasions for realization of their worst potentialities. This enhances morale or self-esteem by creating a nonthreatening, supportive, socially rewarding, flexible, yet challenging atmosphere which is within the patient's range of capabilities, so that a desired goal, sobriety, is perceived as attainable.

The involvement of the wives added a very special value to this program. The patients and their wives were both implicated materially in the pathological drinking. In fact, the wives constituted the major pressure which forced the patients into treatment. It was almost as if the patients as a group had the pathological sign, while the wives experienced the suffering. Considered in this way, the family unit was the patient and properly the focus of the therapeutic effort.

There seemed to be other advantages in having concurrent groups for the patients and their wives. The procedure had the effect of emphasizing the marriage and other related psychological factors which play an important role in alcoholism, without requiring special therapeutic tactics to accomplish this. For immature individuals such as these couples, setting the proper therapeutic task, especially in a more or less automatic, nonverbal manner, was a major accomplishment. It enabled them to know what was expected and served as a constant frame of reference within which the therapy proceeded. The fact that the two groups did not meet together provided the needed privacy for consideration of the very conflict-laden marital situation. Again, with both members of the couple in the program, coming into treatment was less likely to be construed as an admission of guilt or to be used as a weapon than if only one of the pair were involved.

The use of the adjective checklist as a means of describing the marital status and observing the changes which occur in it proved quite fruitful. In the future it may be used to fit other situations where the family rather than one of its members is the treatment unit. It also seems potentially valuable as a means of penetrating the obscuring features of the alcoholic crises and estimating the healthful motivation some of the patients may have. In the present study, it revealed that sobriety was satisfying enough for several of the patients to want more of it, while intoxication was sufficiently dissatisfying to act as an important spur to change.

Not only this, but satisfactions obtained during intoxication were related to lack of improvement. These satisfactions from intoxication could be experienced either by the patient or by his wife. This finding corroborates a frequently expressed opinion that when either partner has a stake in the patient's drinking, the prognosis is less favorable. The value of the adjective checklist arises precisely from the fact that this information is not readily available when alcoholics are first seen. On the surface, alcoholics may look very much alike. In addition, they tend to elicit hostile reactions from those trying to help them because the nature of drunkenness is such that it usually is responded to as something offensive or immoral. Regardless of the reasons for this, the effect is to hide not only many of the healthier characteristics of these patients but the unhealthier ones as well. The checklist is an attempt to gain a better evaluation of these patients in spite of their pathological drinking and in spite of the prevailing attitudes on intoxication. It is in process of further exploration as a means of estimating motivation, but the small number of patients and the need for follow-up studies make additional generalization unwarranted at present.

The present investigation also serves to highlight another finding. Each of the patients entered treatment unwillingly. Traditionally, this has been considered antitherapeutic. Yet the changes obtained in this limited study would seem to indicate otherwise. It may be that the adverse effects are dissipated if the source of the pressure to enter therapy is also included in the treatment program. Implicit in the participation of the wives may be their tacit recognition of their own need to change. This may not only lessen many of the esteem-damaging implications perceived by the patients as associated with coming into treatment, but may also represent a constructive, hopeful attitude on the part of both.

SUMMARY

Nine married male alcoholics took part in a group therapy program that included parallel but separate group discussion meetings of their wives. The preparation for therapy and the nature of the specific group treatment offered have been described. The patients' initial status and their progress were described by four scales. These scales highlighted their deficient self-esteem, unsatisfactory marital state, depressiveness, and irritability. The group therapy program fostered healthful changes in these areas in addition to amelioration of the drinking behavior. The advantages of the group approach in the treatment of alcoholism and the values derived from concurrent group sessions of the patients' wives have been discussed. The need to interpret these findings on the basis of the essentially self-selected, unique population which made up this study cannot be too strongly emphasized.

REFERENCES

1. R. V. Seliger, *How to Help an Alcoholic* (Columbus, Ohio: School and College Service, 1951).
2. E. M. Jellinek, "Phases of Alcohol Addiction," *Quart. J. Stud. Alc.*, 13:673-684, 1952.
3. Cornell Index Manual, New York; Psychological Corporation; 1948.
4. M. B. Parloff, H. C. Kelman and J. D. Frank, "Comfort, Effectiveness and Self-awareness as Criteria of Improvement in Psychotherapy," *Am. J. Psychiat.*, 111:343-352, 1954.
5. H. Greenbaum, "Group Psychotherapy with Alcoholics in Conjunction with Antabuse Therapy," *Int. J. Group Psychother.*, 4:30-41, 1954.
6. E. S. Bordin, "Ambiguity, as a Therapeutic Variable," *J. Cons. Psychol.*, 19:9-15, 1955.
7. L. H. Gliedman, "Temporal Orientation and Chronic Alcoholism," *Maryland Rev. Alcsm.*, 2:1-2, 1955.

42

PRACTICAL ASPECTS OF GROUP WORK
WITH THE MENTALLY RETARDED

James E. Payne
Martha Williams

Group work with the mentally retarded may take place in two rather
different situations—all of the members of the group may be retarded or
the group may be mixed, with retarded and nonretarded members. Problems in working in both situations are presented below, along with some
implications for programing.

WORKING WITH ALL-RETARDED GROUPS

In 1961 the New York Association for the Help of Retarded Children
sponsored a conference on Social Group Work with the Mentally Retarded.
The apparent consensus of the papers presented at the conference[1] was that
in the initial stages of group formation, it was difficult for retardates to get
a sense of "group feeling," to form much group cohesion. Rather, the group
members tended to relate primarily to the group leader on an individual
basis. Helping the retardates move to an appreciation of the group and to
seeing themselves as group members was complicated by their being somewhat less verbal than normals and by the realistic need for the leader to be
somewhat more directive than he would be with other groups. Movement
in group process was generally slower at all stages, but the important conclusion was that progress was made, that retardates can effectively be
formed into groups, and that they can acquire and improve social skills
from experiences in group situations.

Other studies have substantiated this finding that retardates can be

Reprinted from *Group Process*, Vol. 4, No. 1, 1971, pp. 9-17.

helped by group experiences. After working for some time with groups of retarded teenagers, Gershenson and Schreiber[2] noted increased participation of members in the group; they more freely offered suggestions for programing, there was less dependence on the leader, and there was some movement toward subordinating individual needs to those of the group. Some of the factors that seemed to be associated with members' gains in social skills were prior experiences and the composition of the group. Retardates who had had previous experience in group or other positive social experiences made greater progress than those who had not; success was greater in groups in which members were more homogeneous in background, social class, religion, and ethnic group.

In another study, Scheer and Sharpe[3] noted the effects of age and institutionalization on the progress made by institutionalized delinquent retardates after several weeks of day camping. Their very important primary conclusion was that the benefits derived from a group experience are effective only to the extent that the retardates' total environment permits; improvements in group members' behavior diminished or disappeared when they returned to an institutional program that did not support these positive changes. Further, progress was greater for younger retardates who had spent less time in the institution. This latter finding might at first appear to contradict the finding of Gershenson and Schreiber that prior group experience facilitated progress; residence in an institution would appear to be a "group experience," but Scheer and Sharpe found that it inhibited progress. Depending on its program, an institution may be only a large collection of individuals, with little or no sense of group identity and with little of the benefits that can accrue to a well-structured group program.

Scheer and Sharpe concluded that programs that seek to modify retardates' social behavior must first make certain that the total environment—the milieu—will permit and foster positive change. If it is not so structured, then this must be the first goal for any program that hopes to achieve effective and lasting improvement of retardates' social skills.

ROLE OF THE GROUP LEADER

In any group situation, the role of the leader and his impact upon the group members play an important part in determining the outcome of the group experience. This seems to be even more important when the group members are retarded. As noted above, in the initial stages of group formation, retardates tend to be less verbal, to need more direction, and to move slowly in developing a sense of group identity. This implies much for the role of the leader. He must be more directive, but not too much so; striking a proper balance that neither overestimates nor underestimates retardates' dependency needs is one of the more difficult and most important tasks of the group leader. He must be able to tolerate less verbal activity and less participation, but he must persist in trying to involve members in activities and in communicating acceptance and a sense of enjoyment about the group. In short, as Gershenson[4] puts it, he must be "enthusiastically patient."

Of particular importance for the group leader is his continual awareness that programing is the *means* to his desired end. It is all too easy for social workers, vocational rehabilitation counselors, and other leaders of groups of retardates to overemphasize the importance of a particular discussion session or of participation in some particular activity, implying that the particular activity itself is the primary focus of importance. The leader's great task is to formulate his goals clearly for the group and for its individual members, and then to recognize that there are many programatic means by which these goals may be achieved.

WORKING WITH MIXED GROUPS OF RETARDED AND NORMAL

Frequently there are situations in which a mentally retarded person is a member of a group which is predominantly composed of nonretarded persons. In vocational rehabilitation or special class settings, these other members may have some other type of disability; in other instances, they may be normal. The common problem is how to structure and work with a group in which retardates are a deviant minority.

INTEGRATING RETARDATES INTO GROUPS

There has for some time been general agreement among those who work in the field of mental retardation that retardates, particularly the moderately and mildly retarded such as those in rehabilitation programs, should be integrated into the "mainstream" of community life as much as possible. While this is unobjectionable as stated, it is frequently not made clear just what "integration" of the mentally retarded means. Clearly, the mere physical proximity of retardates to normals is not integration; workers in the field have observed the scapegoating or ignoring of retardates by normals too often not to know that bringing a retardate into a group does not necessarily achieve integration. And neither does it necessarily lead to integration at some later time. The point that is missed by those who have failed with this approach is that integration is not just a goal; more importantly, it is a process—as Rosen[5] puts it, a "dynamic process in time." Thus integration of retardates into groups of nonretardates is something to be worked *on*, not toward, and it must be worked on continually if it is to be successful.

There are several obstacles that group leaders must deal with in this integration process. One of the more important of these is the stigma associated with retardation. Wright[6] and Rosen have dealt at length with the sources of prejudice against all handicapped persons, including the mentally retarded, and the impact that this prejudice has upon the handicapped individual himself. Greatly summarized, the major finding they report is that mildly retarded individuals form their self-image largely from the inferences they draw about the attitudes that nonretardates have toward them; that is, if a preponderance of the significant persons with whom the retardate has social contact devalue, or fear, or pity him, the retardate will perceive these attitudes, may accept them as valid, and thus come to devalue, fear, or pity himself. To the extent that this is true, the group leader has a double problem; he must deal not only with the explicit or overt stigma put upon the retardate by nonretarded group members but also with the implicit acceptance of these attitudes by the retardate himself. True integration of the retardate into a nonretarded group obviously requires the resolution of both aspects of this problem of stigma. Or, as Kolodny and Waldfogel[7] note, "planned exposure of the handicapped child to his normal peers on a regular and continuing basis should aim ideally not only at the modification of inappropriate attitudes on the part of the normal children toward him, but also at some revision of his attitudes toward . . . himself."

But this is not the only obstacle in the process of integrating regardates into groups with the nonretarded. Kolodny and Waldfogel also note that while the attitudes of others toward the retardate and of the retardate toward himself are of critical importance, this should not obscure the importance of the realities of the problem of mental retardation in relation to the purposes and activities of the group into which the retardate is being integrated. As an example of this problem, Kahn[8] has noted that it is quite unlikely that an orthopedically handicapped child could be successfully integrated into a basketball team. Other examples could be envisioned for other disabilities; the point is that retardates do have very real deficiencies in certain areas of performance, and to the extent that these areas are important for the functioning of the group, the reality of retardation becomes another obstacle to integration.

GUIDELINES FOR PRACTICE

Despite these obstacles, many who work with the mentally retarded have found it both desirable and worthwhile to work at integrating them into groups of nonretarded. Epstein[9] has listed some of the goals of integrated groups. These include: improving the self-image of the retardate; increasing his ability to socialize; presenting an opportunity for the retardate to learn social skills by exposure to (and imitation of) normal peers; and helping the nonretarded group members learn to accept persons who are different.

Several studies have reported the reactions of nonretarded group members to the retardate. Kahn[10] and Preininger[11] both found normals reacting toward retardates with derision, curiosity, and pity in the early formation period of the group experience. Later, as integration had progressed, these attitudes changed to indifference or toleration. Age seems to be one of the major factors in this attitude shift. Teenagers have been found by several writers[12] to be the most difficult age group in which to integrate a mentally retarded person. Children and adults, even, in some cases, adults in their early twenties, have been found to be less rejecting of retardates. Level of retardation is also an important factor. The mildly retarded have more often been successfully integrated into nonretarded groups. It has also been observed, however,[13] that IQ *per se* is of little value in predicting success of a retardate in an integrated group; general social functioning and prior experience in a variety of social situations were more valid predictors.

IMPLICATIONS FOR PROGRAMING

In discussing action implications of present patterns of services for the mentally retarded, Gunner Dybwad underscores the concept of *normalization* as extremely important for guiding planning in the MR field. In Dybwad's words:[14] "Normalization draws together a number of other lines of thought on social role, role perception, deviancy, and stigma that had their origin in sociology and social psychology. It implies programing on three distinct levels." These levels include:

(1) Helping retarded persons, within the limits of their capacities, learn to behave like typical persons of similar age and sex.

(2) Interpreting the retarded person to others so as to minimize differences and maximize similarities.

(3) Molding public attitudes so as to further the acceptance of deviancy in general; creating, in other words, greater public tolerance of individual differences.

These guides to programing are helpful for planning group services for retarded clients who are hopefully to be integrated into the community and jobs. Group leaders can provide an important service to the retarded by developing positive learning experiences, "normalizing" experiences, which will better equip these clients for social living. To do this effectively means that leaders should first of all share their own knowledge and experiences with each other. Successful strategies for improving the social skills of the retarded are often developed "in the field" through the creative efforts of individual practitioners. These successful programs need to be fully communicated to others. The literature provides many examples of such programs. For instance, Johnson[15] reports that Pero used a social orientation method of social training with retarded persons in an institutional setting to guide them toward release in the community. The orientation included lessons on occupational and social adjustment, human relations, improved daily living, personal growth and development, and school adjustment. The students "formed a code of ethical values helpful to everyday living."

Such examples are abundant in the literature, but often detailed descriptions of the content of such programs are not readily accessible to practitioners. The rapid dissemination of relevant literature to practitioners is a problem in all fields. Special staff personnel with education/training responsibilities should be given the task of culling, collecting, and rapidly disseminating good literature to field practitioners, as well as providing continuing educational experiences for those who wish to develop special skills. The usual ways of exchanging experiences in working with clients are through the literature, workshops or meetings, inservice training, consultation, and/or personal contact with colleagues. These ways, of course, have been utilized and will continue to be utilized as methods of communicating about group work programs devised for the retarded. All persons engaged in working with the retarded should be alert to these avenues of information and communication and should take full advantage of them. Increasing the effectiveness of and institutionalizing these channels of communication within organizations are major administrative tasks. Making use of the available channels is the responsibility of practitioners. Further, practitioners should make known their own successful group work programs to others through these same channels.

A second major task of the group leader is to diagnose adequately the social skill level of his clients. For each client one should ask: What are this person's past social experiences? What "gaps" in social learning need to be filled? What areas of learning have been neglected and how will this affect his ability to adjust in *this* program or in this *particular* situation? This means that the leader must diagnose the client's capacities and select the social situation to which the client can best adapt, grow, and contribute. The integration of retardates can best be achieved when their particular strengths are matched to the values and needs of the context into which they are placed. In one setting being a good fisherman and bowler may be very important in social acceptance. In another, dancing and "the social graces" may be more important. The social skills and capacities of retardates in rehabilitation programs should be improved with reference to the setting in which they must work and, on the other side of the coin, job settings should be selected with their special social skills in mind.

In rehabilitation programs, retardates already placed successfully in work situations can be of great help to newly placed co-workers. A type of group counseling stressing a partnership of successfully placed retardates helping to orient and support newly placed and perhaps younger retardates would be one kind of group approach that would yield benefits to both older clients and newer ones. Retardates can be a good source of feedback about various employing agencies. They can provide positive models to newer clients and they can also receive the follow-up services they need through such a group service.

Using more experienced retardates as "co-counselors" need not be limited to those working in the same employing organizations, however. Retardate co-counselors working with a vocational rehabilitation counselor could help orient newly placed retardates to the community in general by introducing them to recreation, social, and leisure time activities and health and other service resources. To summarize, working with groups of clients can help the leader in his diagnosis of each client's social skills. There is an opportunity to observe the client in relationship with others, specifically his peers of both the same and opposite sex. Forming clients into such small mutually supportive groups can provide the leader with insights into each client's social skills not always evident in a one-to-one counseling relationship. Further, he can learn much about job placement situations by listening carefully to the group discussions he hears. Peers have a way of sharing information and "getting to the heart of things" not always easily accomplished in usual one-to-one counseling sessions. Furthermore, peers are much more skillful in giving feedback to each other about "how to get along better" or "learning the ropes."

A third task for those who work with the retarded is to utilize needed group resources for clients in the community. Some resources simply need to be tapped. Many organizations such as Campfire Girls, Scouts, Boy's Clubs, city recreation departments, Y's, Jewish Centers, and other religious agencies, have provided group experiences to children, youth, and adult handicapped persons for years. Often all that is needed for these agencies to provide services is a request for such services. Fees, if necessary at all, can be paid by voluntary groups, the clients themselves, or through other special resources. Often clients who will not go to such agencies alone or on their own will go with an already established group of friends. Thus working with groups of clients who can plan to take advantage of community resources together is a productive approach.

A fourth area for group work is in the counseling and guidance process itself. The counseling of clients in groups should not be thought of as just a way to save time. Rather the group itself is a valuable counseling aid. For a retardate, entering into the community and beginning to work, especially after a period of institutionalization, can be something of a crisis; a failure can be devastating. A group can enter this experience together (not necessarily at the same work location, but in the same community at about the same time). Such groups can share experiences and be mutually supportive. This requires developing a group with esprit de corps and a common purpose. Each client can contribute to the success of the others and can give support to those who need it during "low periods." The leadership of such groups could be supplied by counselors who perhaps would require some special training in group counseling techniques. Group counseling could, of course, include the participation of employers and families of clients as well as others, perhaps even normal co-workers. The goals for such groups should determine patterns of participation and programing.

REFERENCES

1. M. Schreiber, "Social Group Work with the Mentally Retarded," *Proceedings* of a conference sponsored by the New York Association for the Help of Retarded Children, April 28, 1961.
2. S. Gershenson, and M. Schreiber, "Mentally Retarded Teenagers in a Social Group," *Children*, 10(3):104-108, 1963.
3. R. M. Scheer, and W. M. Sharpe, "Social Group Work in Day Camping with Institutionalized Delinquent Retardates," *Training School Bull.*, 60: 138-147, 1963.
4. S. Gershenson, "Social Group Work with Adolescent Retardates," *Proceedings* of a conference sponsored by the New York Association for the Help of Retarded Children, April 28, 1961.
5. A. Rosen, "Theoretical Concepts in the Behavioral Sciences Regarding Integration," Paper presented at a conference sponsored by the New York Association for the Help of Retarded Children, December 6, 1963.
6. B. Wright, *Physical Disability—A Psychological Approach* (New York: Harper & Row, 1960).
7. R. L. Kolodny, and S. Waldfogel, "Modifying Tensions Between the Handicapped and Their Normal Peers in Group Work with Children," *Child Welfare*, 46:30-37, 1967.
8. S. Kahn, "Integration of the MR in a Traditional Group Work Agency," Paper presented at a conference sponsored by the New York Association for the Help of Retarded Children, December 6, 1963.
9. I. Epstein, "An Agency Experience Involving Retarded Children in Normal Group Settings," Paper presented at a conference sponsored by the New York Association for the Help of Retarded Children, December 6, 1963.
10. Kahn, "Integration of the MR," *op. cit.*
11. D. R. Preininger, "Reactions of Normal Children to Retardates in Integrated Groups," *Social Work*, 13:75-77, 1968.
12. Epstein, "An Agency Experience," *op. cit.*; Kahn, "Integration of the MR," *op. cit.*; S. Rafel, "Integrating Groups of Retardates in a Community Center: The Experience of Bronx House," Paper presented at a conference sponsored by the New York Association for the Help of Retarded Children, December 6, 1963.

13. M. Schreiber, (ed.), "Integration of the Mentally Retarded in Community Group Service Agencies: A Look at Knowledge, Methods, and Gaps, *Proceedings* of a conference sponsored by the New York Association for the Help of Retarded Children, December 6, 1963.

14. G. Dybwad, "Action Implications, U.S.A. Today," in R. B. Kugel and W. Wolfensberger (eds.), *Changing Patterns in Residential Services for the Mentally Retarded* (Washington, D.C.: President's Committee on Mental Retardation, 1969), pp. 383-428.

15. G. O. Johnson, "Psychological Characteristics of the Mentally Retarded," in W. M. Cruickshank (ed.), *Psychology of Exceptional Children and Youth* (Englewood Cliffs, N.J.: Prentice-Hall, 1963), pp. 448-483.

43

GROUP THERAPY TECHNIQUES USED BY THE EX-ADDICT THERAPIST

Edward Kaufman

In the last ten years there has been a broadening in the role of para-professionals in the field of mental health. The area where the parapro-fessional has achieved the greatest success and prominence is in the treatment of drug addiction. Here the ex-addict paraprofessional is utilized as a primary therapist in every treatment approach from chemical to drug-free. The primary chemical approaches are Methadone maintenance (MM) and Cyclazocine blockade. The drug-free programs are generally either residential therapeutic communities (TC) or day centers and are modeled on the self-help or Synanon approach. Although the ex-addict is utilized by both chemical and drug-free approaches, the therapeutic tech-niques which are used by the ex-addict are most generally associated with drug-free programs.

Recently there was an emphasis on Methadone maintenance, particu-larly by government funding sources, that threatens the virtual extinction of the TC approach. This may be because MM has proven to be cheaper and because better validated statistics are available to document its success. In order to survive, the drug-free approaches must document their success statistically[1] and present their treatment methods for careful scrutiny.[2] This article will examine the techniques utilized by ex-addict therapists. The psychodynamics and psychopathology of the addict will be discussed in an attempt to understand how these techniques work. The possibility of a partnership between the professional and the ex-addict therapist will also be discussed.

This author supervised all the therapists who worked at Reality House during a four-year period. Reality House is a self-help day center for the treatment of addicts. It began in 1967 with a staff which left Exodus House.[3] These therapists were mainly ex-addicts and included graduates

Reprinted from *Group Process*, Vol. 5, No. 1, 1972, pp. 3-19.

of the Casriel Institute, Daytop Village, Exodus House, and Phoenix House, as well as Reality House. In addition, the author has evaluated the methods of other TC's through personal observation and review of the literature. The therapeutic style of a graduate of any of these programs generally enables one to predict from which program he graduated. Still, the individual's own personality makes a substantial and recognizable contribution to his therapeutic style. When a Phoenix House graduate became Director of Therapy at Reality House, a fusion took place between his style and the treatment principles of Reality House.

There are some principles which are in evidence in all TC's and some which are individualized depending on the personal style of their charismatic founders and leaders. All residential TC's require twenty-four hours a day of commitment and participation. The successful day centers function for an eight-hour day, five to six days a week, and offer back-up services in crises. All programs require total abstinence from drugs and utilize regular urinalysis to help ensure this. They all require a commitment to actively changing one's existence in society. Although threats of violence are frequent, no actual physical violence is permitted in any program. Most programs forbid any sexual activity between members, particularly during the first year in the program. All programs utilize stratified groups with many gradually progressing levels.

The programs differ significantly as to degree of confrontation, with many programs confronting brutally at every level of therapy. Generally those programs which confront brutally are also quite authoritarian. However, even in the most authoritarian programs there is a great deal of love and concern for the addict, and the community functions as a family which both loves its members and sets limits for them. Frequently, this is the first time in his life the addict has experienced these influences simultaneously.

The following techniques utilized by the drug-free approaches will be discussed: identification, "love and concern," confrontation, responsibility, acting "as if," reward and punishment, stratified vocational levels, TC as a family, and emphasis on the present. Many of these techniques are used by paraprofessionals working in MM programs as well as self-help therapeutic programs for nonaddicts. They are worthy of study as modalities which can be utilized by any self-help movement. As paraprofessionals strive toward developing their own therapeutic discipline, these therapeutic modalities may form the backbone of this new "profession."

IDENTIFICATION

As an addict matures through a program he identifies with varying kinds of therapists. In most programs the first therapist the addict meets is a recent graduate or advanced member of the program. This therapist is very much like the addict in attitude and language, yet he has "made it."

That is, he has stopped using drugs, even though he has come from an environment identical to the addict's. He may offer a highly emotional catharsis of his own struggle to give up drugs with which the addict can identify. He may share difficult experiences in his own life prior to giving up drugs. He demonstrates that he is not where he is through magic. Frequently the addict is quite "hungry" for an identification with a strong accepting male figure because his prior contacts with such individuals have been so limited. Because of the similarities between the addict and ex-addict and the relationship hunger of the former, these identifications are made quite rapidly. In later phases of a program the addict might identify with someone from his ghetto environment who has never been an addict.

This same kind of identification is very risky with the inexperienced ex-addict therapist and can rapidly develop into overidentification. The novice ex-addict is still struggling in the ghetto on a low salary. He may repeatedly share his sense of frustration in meeting his own reality in a way which prevents the addict from reacting properly to his more frustrating reality. They are still both used to immediate gratification. If the addict fails, the novice ex-addict is vulnerable to identification with the failure and may duplicate it either through his own overidentification or his sense of disappointment.

In the final phases of a program particularly like Odyssey, Exodus, and Reality House, the addict identifies with the professional therapist who may come from a totally different sociocultural environment. In addition, the addicts frequently identify with the charismatic leaders of their respective programs. Such leaders as Chuck Dederich of Synanon, Dave Deitch of Daytop, Pleasant Harris of Methadone Maintenance, and Amos Henix of Reality House are examples of very strong leaders who are readily identified with. Several programs utilize the "as if" concept (described below), in which the therapist is readily identified with as a model for the "as if" behavior.

"LOVE AND CONCERN"

Reality House considers "love and concern" a part of their basic concept. Here it is supposedly "given only as a reward for adult and giving behavior on the part of the members."[4] Since Reality House is a nonresidential treatment center, it may be necessary to give more of this kind of direct gratification in the initial phases of therapy to seduce the addict into therapy as well as to provide immediate gratification to replace the loss of drugs. Reality House is aware of the difficulties of providing this kind of gratification and it is gradually withdrawn when the individual becomes motivated and begins to maintain adaptive change in his personality. Synanon initially provided a prolonged period of "unconditional love" which was soon shortened to include only the time when the individual kicked "cold turkey." The giving of unconditional love is a controversy in all forms of therapy, including the drug-free programs. When this love was limited at Synanon, the original maternal figure and several of her followers left the program.[5]

Chessick[6] has noted the great need of the addict for unconditional love. He warned that these needs were "intense, insatiable and led to feelings of deep disappointment and despair because they could never be satisfied." He emphasized the addicts' need "to be close to a mother-like figure who would be able to satisfy their every need without even the necessity of their asking for it." Although drug-free approaches would not agree with so primitive a concept of the addicts' need for love, the difficulties of directly gratifying this need are always kept in mind. An attempt is made to deal with these difficulties by giving the love only in return for the addict's meaningful attempts to understand or change himself. Odyssey House has a cardinal prohibition against any meeting of demands based on a premise that this inhibits the individual from his own maturational growth.[7]

At times the love and concern are expressed by reassuring physical gestures such as handholding or embracing. The therapist sets the tone for this kind of interaction, but most of it goes on among members. At Reality House, this touching only takes place following significant insight or meaningful emotional interaction.[8] It does not have the rehearsed quality frequently attributed to encounter techniques. It is more compatible with the uses of touch as defined by Mintz.[9] These include touch as a natural part of any warm ongoing relationship, touching to convey a sense of being accepted, or to convey reality, or as a necessary modality when verbal communication is unavailable.

At Reality House the therapist attempts the difficult task of communicating to the member the feeling that although he is accepting him, he is simultaneously demanding more and more from him. The therapist may also express love and concern by listening carefully and paying attention to the member and not ridiculing the member's difficulties or productions. (The latter is not different from conventional precepts for establishing a therapeutic alliance.)

CONFRONTATION

The paradigm of confrontation is the "hair cut" as practiced at Synanon.[10] Here four or five significant figures "take apart" a member. In this type of meeting all of the individual's behavior is reviewed in a very brutal manner, although the interaction is totally verbal. There is an attempt to strip an individual of all of his sick patterns of behavior, with an attempt to put him back together by the end of the meeting. At some

TC's, the hair is actually shaved off. A further extreme of the "hair cut" is the "fireplace ritual" in which an individual who has broken a cardinal rule and has not reported it is ridiculed by the entire community into revealing his "offense." Daytop utilizes confrontation groups on a regular basis. Members confront each other with their behavior and its impact on others until, layer by layer, these defenses are removed. At Daytop, marathons are also utilized to break down defenses and lay individuals open to "the gut level of emotional truth."[11] Phoenix House utilizes several types of encounter confrontations. The floor encounter is leaderless, is utilized at an orientation phase, and emphasizes emotional catharsis. At this level, "the accuracy of the confrontation or interpretation is not important." The tutorial encounter is directed by a senior or staff member who unleashes his powerful force on each member in turn. "Behavior that is anti-social, amoral, self defeating or immature is considered stupid" and that attitude is expressed vividly and repeatedly. The stupid behavior and the rationalization and denial which follow are rapidly attacked and the member's facade of bravado, self-righteousness, or justification crumbles under the blistering scrutiny of the group. The only acceptable defense is honesty. After the encounter there is a social gathering to decompress affect and to administer emotional first aid.[12]

Although brutal confrontation is one of the most controversial of these techniques, it has some usefulness. It should not be used in nonresidential settings where the individual has to face the stress of the "street" immediately after having his defenses stripped. For this reason it has limited use in a day center such as Reality House. Such a rapid stripping of an individual's defenses can cause a psychotic disruption of a fragile ego.[13] These confrontations can also lead to a false superficial display of emotionality because of community pressures to do so which does not result in any meaningful change. When practiced in a closed community and in an atmosphere of love they can be quite effective. Confrontation may also be quite helpful when the addict is entering treatment, to sift out unmotivated addicts and to motivate those who are borderline in wanting help.

A very valuable form of confrontation is one which combines identification. This combination is used to strip away defenses gradually and identify with the feelings underlying these defenses. The first defenses which must be stripped away are those such as "I am an addict whose only problem is drugs" or "I use drugs because I am the helpless victim of an insane society." Ex-addicts are particularly adept at getting past these rationalizations to the underlying anxiety. As one ex-addict therapist states:

> It's like getting into the hole with the person and walking out with him. As he goes on explaining to you what the feelings are, you constantly reassure him that you know and understand what he's saying and

feeling. If you have any experiences within your life that are similar, you give up these experiences, you particularly identify with the person's fear, letting him know that you have felt fear, and how you have dealt with it. First you may help him recognize his fear by saying. . . . "Yeh, I can remember how afraid I was to be able to do that" and then he begins to feel his own fear. Once you can get to the fear, the other problems come pretty easily.[14]

The principle of getting to underlying feelings is a basic one of all workable psychotherapies, but is done quite effectively by ex-addicts. All of these programs strongly emphasize the expression of feelings. Program members are taught to express feelings by first identifying them and then are specifically trained in understanding and verbalizing their feelings.[15]

Another example of the use of identification to enhance the confrontation of defenses is in the area of homosexual problems. Most addicts who have been in prison have had a significant amount of homosexual experience which has been rationalized by the addict as coming out of convenience rather than need. However, the skillful ex-addict who has gained insight into his own homosexual experiences and fears in prison can readily recognize and tap the homosexual conflicts of the program member. The therapist might talk about his own confusion about being out of a heterosexual environment or how he felt when he first became aware that he was looking at another man's body in a shower. The therapist is particularly able to tap the power and dependency motivations of homosexual and pseudohomosexual behavior which are so overt in prison settings. In a prison setting much homosexual activity has as its primary motivation the control or subjugation of another male or is a means to being cared for or feeling loved.

RESPONSIBILITY

All self-help programs use "responsibility" as a crucial aspect of treatment. Reality House stresses the individual's accepting the responsibility for his own existence. Mr. Henix, the Director of Reality House, emphasizes that the individual must realize "that certain reality factors are there and can't be changed. So the only thing that he can do is to change himself and in that way change his relationship to outer realities." Odyssey House requests that the individual accept responsibility for himself and his actions and that residents assume sole responsibility for the rules which they have instituted.[16]

In general, all programs insist that the addict assume responsibility for a commitment to his own rehabilitation. Many programs will not accept an addict who is unwilling to at least begin to do this. Utilizing responsibility for self-improvement and to the maintenance and success of the program is utilized as a cornerstone for permanent change. It removes a "we–they" dichotomy from life. It constantly asks the individual what he has done to produce a situation and what he can do to change it, rather than blaming it for his plight.

ACTING "AS IF"

This is a concept which is utilized by most programs and was formulated by Casriel.[17] He states that after three to six months of acting "as if" they were the men they want to be, they will start actually to be those men. Reality House requires that even before an individual obtains any insight there are some areas in which he must perform "as if" he did. He is asked to abstain from alcohol, drug use, lateness, and grossly inappropriate and antisocial behavior. The individual is taught that to change his behavior he must first form an image of the kind of man he wants to be, and that with effort he can carry out his plan. The program member begins to abandon his self-destructive behavior and to look for positive ways to live. He acts "as if" he is the person he wants to be and eventually his feelings begin to mirror the desired attitudes. Each step that he makes in a positive direction is rewarded and acknowledged. As the time lengthens since the last negative act, the positive behavior is reinforced, particularly if he is surrounded by others in his group who are struggling in the same way.[18]

Odyssey House states this concept in "the rule of three . . . by first doing, I proved that it can be done. The second doing followed with ease, and the third slipped unnoticed. I had a habit of living."[19]

REWARD AND PUNISHMENT

Although the principle of reward and punishment is utilized in all therapies, it is a basic method of all ex-addict approaches and is used more directly than in most conventional approaches. Synanon emphasizes status and approval as basic rewards. Dederich explains this: "An addict, especially, will do more for approval than he will do for anything else. Amazingly so will most people. Every efficient organization from Uncle Sam's Army to the Salvation Army knows this."[20] At Synanon, the number of drug-free days is used as a status symbol, with yearly birthdays utilized for recognition of this. Any member can rise as high as his abilities will take him. The third level at Synanon carries with it such rewards as roles in policy making and personal use of the organization's cars. The fourth or the top stage belongs to the directors of Synanon. The punishment is generally administered through verbal confrontations similar to those described at Phoenix House. Another crucial punishment is depriving an individual of his status. At Reality House an attempt is made to have the individual see demotions in level as learning experiences and evidence that he is not really ready to function at a given level. However, the punishment aspect of such demotion can never be denied, particularly when promotions are utilized as rewards. In addition, "love and concern" is given as a reward whenever an individual is really working emotionally on changing himself. All programs use stratified therapies, with promotions and demotions as an important part of reward and punishment systems of change. Interestingly, most programs have four levels and require eighteen months for completion.

STRATIFIED VOCATIONAL LEVELS

This is a further elaboration of the graduated therapy level aspect of reward and punishment. This system is most clearly used at Exodus House and Reality House. At the first work level the individual's tolerance for a work situation is examined and a vocational plan is formulated. He can be evaluated for concrete skills outside of his verbal games as well as his ability to turn his verbal insights into behavior. At the second work level the trade is more important, but still secondary to behavioral analysis. Here there is greater emphasis on end products and relevance to career choice. In the final work phase the individual attends a vocational training program which qualifies him for his chosen career.[21]

THE TC AS A FAMILY

Synanon was founded on the family model and continues to recognize the need for strong paternal and maternal leaders. Reality House replaced its charismatic male founder, Leroy Looper, with an equally strong ex-addict, Amos Henix. Casriel spells out the paternalistic role of Dederich, who administers Synanon with "conditional love" which Dederich refers to as "the male principle." "Few senior members are eager to leave Synanon since they do not view it as an institution but as a loving, healthy, honest family relationship, for most, the first such relationship they have ever known."[22] New members are considered as helpless infants who must mature through oral, anal, and phallic phases. Sibling rivalry is generally not evident at first, but becomes more overt after three to six months in the program, when it is dealt with in groups.

It is probably more applicable to consider these ex-addict therapy centers as extended families than as TC's. Waldorf[23] presents a modification of Maxwell Jones' characteristics of a TC, which include: (1) better and thorough communication among all persons in the community, including patients and staff; (2) involving everyone in decision making so that all aims and achievements are mutual; (3) a therapeutic milieu which reflects the attitudes and beliefs of everyone; (4) establishing multiple leadership based more on charisma than specific authority. Where most ex-addict centers do not meet the criteria for a true TC is in the areas of shared decision making and shared attitudes. For the first three to six months, there is a very strong feeling that the member is a helpless baby and that only the staff know what is good for him. It is assumed that if the member were an adult, he would do things in just the way the staff is doing them for him. The staff enacts policy in a very authoritarian way, which is the antithesis of a TC. What preserves the TC is that the prominent authorities are mainly nonprofessionals who have suffered exactly what the member has. In his identification with the therapist the member feels that he is being told what is best for him and what he would do if he were not a "baby."

EMPHASIS ON THE PRESENT

Most programs emphasize the here and now. To discourage the use of the past as a rationalization for not changing, attempts are made to bury the past. As Mr. Henix states:[24]

> Occasionally, we look at the past for reference, but we don't allow a person to get lost in the past. We try to get the person to say how this affects them now, and to be able to find the thread that leads into his "here and now," and to realize that he has the choice of changing. That he is not fixed like a radiator or a light-bulb, but that he can realize whatever he wants to realize providing he's willing to do what he has to do now in order to change, knowing what his past was like.

Odyssey House also discourages the use of the past to avoid present responsibility. It may be explored when it is of clear relevance, but what is stressed is a "now what posture. This emphasizes what resources are present to cope effectively." The patient is challenged to begin today!

DISCUSSION

Therapeutic modalities such as confrontation, conditional love, identification, and stratified group therapy have been developed at Synanon and elaborated by other self-help organizations. However, all of these techniques were in existence prior to the founding of Synanon in 1958. Other aspects of the techniques of ex-addicts have been borrowed from existentialism, reality therapy, learning theory, the therapeutic community, transactional analysis, and psychoanalysis. As a group, the techniques described in this article warrant examination as a separate method of psychotherapy —as different and unique as any system of therapy. These methods can be utilized by paraprofessionals who have never been addicts, particularly if they share certain basic experiences with their clients (incarceration, poverty background, language, mode of emotional expression). The wide applicability of such paraprofessionals has been suggested by Grant,[25] who emphasizes the use of the product of a problem to treat a problem. Commonality of experience with the client, by itself, does not qualify an individual to be a therapist. These techniques are best learned gradually and under close supervision, preferably by both experienced paraprofessionals and professionals. Many programs have abrogated the use of professionals, particularly psychiatrists. It has been felt that they were not useful because of the lack of commonality of experience, presence of middle-class standards, and too intellectualized an approach. Such programs as Odyssey and Reality House have realized the worth of psychiatrists, particularly after all the "games" have been eliminated by the ex-addict. At advanced levels, psychiatrists have even utilized ego-reconstructive techniques.

The professional can play an important part in training, particularly if he is sensitive to the development of an amalgam of more classical techniques with those utilized by ex-addicts.

It is not enough to say that the psychiatrist or other professional who participates in an ex-addict program must deviate from the traditional analytic or even community psychiatric role. He will be tested immediately about his attitudes toward blacks, social class, money, violence, and even parking his car in the ghetto. He must be prepared to answer questions directly and honestly, rather than focus on the questioner and his motives. Just as the ex-addict therapist is successful through identification, and giving up love and concern, so must the professional be willing to talk openly of his own problems, feelings, and fantasies when appropriate. At the same time, he must maintain his professional objectivity so that he can use his skills for the benefit of the program.

This attitude also prevails at Odyssey House, where "acceptance and status are accorded by the patients to a professional on the basis of his functioning as a real, warm, capable person, and not on title per se. No one can, either patient or worker, demand respect, but each must earn it."[26]

Whether the ex-addict methods are more statistically effective than traditional methods remains to be proven.[27] In any case, their claimed and seeming success as well as changes in the social and cultural patterns of addiction requires a reevaluation of the theories of the character structure of the addict. The classical psychoanalytic view of addiction has been well summarized by Fenichel.[28] He states that drugs are used "to satisfy the archaic oral longing which is sexual longing, a need for security and a need for the maintenance of self-esteem simultaneously." Like the infant in his oral phase, "objects are nothing else for them but deliverers of supplies." Their "amorphous tension actually resembles the very earliest stage in libidinal development, before there is any organization at all, namely the oral orientation of the infant." Savitt, on the basis of his review of the literature and the psychoanalysis of four middle-class addicts, feels that viewing addiction as an oral fixation does not describe the primitive quality of addiction to intravenous heroin usage. He feels that addiction is preoral, stating that "the person who needs to inject the drug intravenously requires more rapid protection than those who utilize oral incorporation of need satisfying drugs. Unless tension is completely obliterated, he is left in a situation akin to the undifferentiated state of the neonate."[29]

Most of these theories were based on studies of middle-class addicts at a time when they were a rarity and at the same time that most addicts were a relatively homogeneous group of lower-class individuals from the urban ghetto. Currently there is a need for a more flexible approach to the evaluation of the character structure of the addict.

Within the past few years there has been an emergence of several new types of addicts. The new addict is frequently younger than in previous years. He may come from the armed forces in Vietnam, our leading preparatory schools and universities, and urban and rural middle-class areas across the country. The products of these different backgrounds are very different people with very different ego structures, causes of addiction, and needs for treatment.[30] Frequently, the price of their habit forces all of them into a similar life style of manipulation and extraction which can be mistaken for a common primitive ego structure. Addictive symptoms, not unlike hysterical symptoms, can be noted in many different categories. These symptoms range from a direct, relatively nonpsychopathologic expression of the social ills of the ghetto to a need for replenishment of bodily integrity in the schizophrenic. In a study of twelve college student heroin addicts done by this author, it was noted that the college group uniformly was composed of overt or borderline psychotics. Personnel studies of ghetto addicts reveal a much lower incidence of borderline and overt psychosis. This is compatible with a general rule about psychopathology, which is that the more a symptom deviates from an individual's cultural norms, the more pathologic the symptom is likely to be.

Preble[31] has recently noted the changing quality of assertiveness in the ghetto addict. He points out that the addict is no longer the helpless, "nodding" street corner hangout, but an assertive, aggressive individual who "hustles" for his drugs and the money to pay for them. He implies that the addict may be a healthier ghetto dweller than his counterpart who languishes on welfare with no attempt to change his environment.

One way to determine the effectiveness of the ex-addict techniques would be a thorough use of psychological tests and/or psychoanalytic interviews of "cured" ex-addicts to determine intrapsychic change. To date there has been a paucity of such studies. One common observation of ex-addicts is that they appear to have hypertrophied internal prohibitive measures against any drug or substance abuse. Even the occasional use of any drug or alcoholic beverage (and cigarette at Synanon by any member or even visitor) is severely criticized. These individuals who are supposed initially to have very weak superego or conscience mechanisms seem to have very harsh punitive restrictions against the abuse of any chemical. Frequently these harsh restrictions are placed by the individual against any antisocial activity on the part of himself or others. Very much like the member of Alcoholics Anonymous who forbids himself even a taste of alcohol, the conscience has been strengthened, but in a very rigid way which permits little or no flexibility. This rigid overreaction is suggestive of reaction formation, as was noted in a study of ex-addicts by Vaillant.[32]

There is also a question as to how much ego structure is changed as the addict becomes the ex-addict. Initially, much of the change is brought about through an emulative identification utilizing the "as if" technique. As the member practices the strengths gained in this way, they become a permanent part of his defensive system. Bess, Janus, and Rifkin[33] studied seventeen ex-addicts who were graduates of various programs. Their TAT's demonstrated major themes of denial of aggression and sexuality. Other characteristics demonstrated by ex-addicts in this study included a "rose colored glasses" syndrome, with the individual seeing himself as "popular, attractive, desirable, happy, secure and superior." These authors felt that a "personalized combination of hope and reality provides a new gratification and the strength that is needed to renounce drug use." It is likely that there is a continuum of change in adaptive ego and superego strength among addicts. Most of those who still require Methadone or a residential setting have had little intrapsychic change but have relied on denial and reaction formation. Those individuals who have matured in their social and vocational achievements without the aid of Methadone or continued involvement in a program have generally made the greatest gains in inner strengths. Some individuals continue to be involved in programs, but as directors or high executives. One should not consider an individual who functions at the highly responsible level necessary to lead such demanding programs as dependent on the program, or addicted to being an ex-addict. His work is no more an addiction than the work of any successful business or professional man.

Those techniques which are particularly valuable for the consideration of the professional therapist in his work with nonaddicts are many. They include those which tap underlying feelings such as confrontation, "game" elimination, and identification with these feelings. Encouraging individuals to act "as if" is a valuable tool for converting insight into behavioral change. It is preferable that the professional not utilize this technique until some insight has taken place. The giving of love and concern in the early phases of therapy is a technique which can be utilized with some regressed or unmotivated patients. The ex-addict approaches as well as other recent developments in therapy have helped break through the therapist's taboo against touching the patient. These approaches are also one more example of the applicability of reward and punishment and learning theory to all therapies. The drug-free TC's are among the best functioning examples of these communities and their methods; their structuring of authority is particularly worthy of examination by TC's not involved in drug problems.

Even if the professional therapist does not utilize these techniques directly in this treatment of nonaddicts, he should consider utilizing the ex-addict as a co-therapist whenever he deals with addicts. The ex-addict is able to remove the individual's games and tap his feelings in a way which makes the patient more available to the professional so that the latter can use his techniques. The ex-addict's methods are more valuable when the patient's illness is a direct expression of social forces than when it is a result of severe intrapsychic pathology. When the heroin addiction is a result of the social factors of the ghetto, it is a process that can be reversed by groups of individuals bred by the ghetto who are working mutually to overcome their addiction, particularly if that group is led by an individual who has come from that environment and has himself succeeded in overcoming his own addiction.

In his foreword, Casriel[34] makes a statement which captures the difficulties in evaluating these programs objectively as well as their potentially great impact on the professional therapist's techniques and life style. "While we were picking each other's brain, we stole each other's heart." All therapists, professional and paraprofessional, owe it to themselves to be exposed to the group techniques of ex-addicts in order to decide how much to let them into their brains and hearts.

REFERENCES

1. E. Kaufman, "Methadone and/or Ex-Addict Therapy: Are They a Cure for Heroin Addiction?," *Contemp. Drug Prob.*, 1:207-224, 1972.
2. E. Kaufman, "A Psychiatrist Views an Addict Self-Help Program," *Am. J. Psychiat.*, 128:846-851, 1972.
3. *Ibid.*
4. *Ibid.*
5. D. Casriel, *So Fair a House: The Story of Synanon* (Englewood Cliffs, N.J.: Prentice-Hall, 1963).
6. R. D. Chessick, "The 'Pharmacogenic Orgasm' in the Drug Addict," *Arch. Gen. Psychiat.*, 3:545-556, 1960.
7. J. Densen-Gerber, *The Odyssey House Method: A Comprehensive Program for the Prevention and Treatment of Drug Addiction*, undated descriptive brochure.
8. Kaufman, "A Psychiatrist Views," *op. cit.*
9. E. Mintz, "Touch and the Psychoanalytic Tradition," *Psychoanal. Rev.* 56:465-476, 1969.
10. Casriel, *So Fair a House, op. cit.*
11. J. Kalof, *A Study of Four Voluntary Treatment and Rehabilitation Programs for New York City's Narcotic Addicts* (New York: Community Services Society, 1967).

12. M. S. Rosenthal and D. V. Biase, "Phoenix Houses: Therapeutic Communities for Drug Addicts," *Hosp. and Comm. Psychiat.*, 20:26-30, 1969.
13. L. Blank, "The Uses and Abuses of Encounter Groups," *Group Proc.*, 4: 106-116, 1971.
14. Kaufman, "A Psychiatrist Views," *op. cit.*
15. D. Casriel, "A Modification of Adaptational Psychodynamic Theory in the Wake of Successful Treatment of the Drug Addict at Daytop Village," paper presented at American Psychiatric Association Meeting, Atlantic City, N.J., May 1966.
16. Densen-Gerber, *The Odyssey House Method*, *op. cit.*
17. Casriel, "A Modification," *op. cit.*
18. Kaufman, "A Psychiatrist Views," *op. cit.*
19. Densen-Gerber, *The Odyssey House Method*, *op. cit.*
20. Casriel, *So Fair a House*, *op. cit.*
21. Kaufman, "A Psychiatrist Views," *op. cit.*
22. Densen-Gerber, *The Odyssey House Method*, *op. cit.*
23. D. Waldorf, "Social Control in Therapeutic Communities for the Treatment of Drug Addicts," *Intern. J. the Addictions*, 6:29-44, 1971.
24. Densen-Gerber, *The Odyssey House Method*, *op. cit.*
25. D. Grant, Personal communication, 1972.
26. Denson-Gerber, *The Odyssey House Method*, *op. cit.*
27. Kaufman, "Methadone and/or Ex-Addict Therapy," *op. cit.*
28. Fenichel, Otto, *The Psychoanalytic Theory of Neurosis* (New York: W. W. Norton, 1945).
29. R. A. Savitt, "Psychoanalytical Studies in Addiction: Ego Structure in Narcotic Addiction," *Psychoanal. Quart.*, 32:43-57, 1963.
30. Kaufman, "Methadone and/or Ex-Addict Therapy," *op. cit.*
31. E. Preble and J. Casey, "Taking Care of Business—The Heroin User's Life on the Street," *Intern. J. the Addictions*, 4:1-24, 1969.
32. G. E. Vaillant, "A Twelve-year Follow-up of New York Narcotic Addicts: IV, Source Characteristics and Determinants of Abstinence," *Am. J. Psychiat.*, 123:537-584, 1966.
33. B. Bess, S. Janus, and A. Rifkin, "Factors in Successful Narcotics Renunciation," *Am. J. Psychiatry*, 128:861-865, 1972.
34. Casriel, *So Fair a House*, *op. cit.*

44

MULTIFAMILY PSYCHOSOCIAL GROUP TREATMENT WITH ADDICTS AND THEIR FAMILIES

Milton M. Berger

Since opening its doors in 1966, the program of the therapeutic community residence of the Quaker Committee on Social Rehabilitation, Inc., for female narcotic addicts has relied heavily on psychotherapeutic and educational group methods to accomplish its psychosocial goals. However, in recognizing the multifaceted problems which plague the drug addict, we have not neglected the biological rehabilitation also required by addicts whose bodies often reflect pathology in their teeth, liver, gastrointestinal, and genito-urinary systems.

In our attempts at total rehabilitation of addicted residents whose histories commonly reflected high school dropout, imprisonment, hustling, and disturbed child-parent relations, we soon realized the importance of a more active approach and the values of greater involvement with responsible members of residents' families.

Initially we attempted to seek out the one or more major types of family settings which spawn an addict member. Gradually we learned that all types of families could serve to bring up a future addict. Common familial factors tend to be: gross or more often subtle evidences of parental inconsistency; a breeding ground for disrespect for authorities so that the child learns that he can "get away with murder"; marked spoiling, over-giving, overprotection, overdomination, or neglect so that the future addict is rigidly driven to an attitude of "I want what I want when I want it"; and the lack of experience or interest in being willing to incorporate a frustration-tolerating self-image.

We started our multifamily groups to widen the network of constructive resources available to us and our residents and to catalyze and educate

Reprinted from *Group Process*, Vol. 5, No. 1, 1972, pp. 31-45.

family members into becoming protherapeutic allies in our difficult task. The format we developed was to arrange for a once-a-month evening meeting so that families could make long-range plans to attend, as some had to travel long distances in order to participate. All residents attend and an average of ten to eighteen relatives from four to eight families of the residents come voluntarily to each meeting. The meetings are conducted regularly by the psychiatric consultant, who has had much experience in group methods for developing potentials in individuals and families. The executive director and the counseling supervisor also attend every meeting while other members of the staff participate on a voluntary basis. Such staff have included houseparents, vocational education teachers, social work and rehabilitation counselors, psychologists, psychiatrists, and recreational and activity workers, as well as volunteers. Upon invitation visitors have come to these meetings from professional schools, other private and governmental drug treatment agencies, and from other addiction treatment centers considering the incorporation of our multifamily treatment model into their facilities.

GROUP STRUCTURE AND ATMOSPHERE

The monthly multifamily meeting consists, then, of approximately forty to fifty persons meeting from 8:45 P.M. to 10:15 P.M. in the largest room in our treatment center. The meeting is conducted in a style and tradition which incorporates what is best in a Quaker meeting and in an analytically oriented psychotherapy group. There is an awareness of the presence of the group leader as an authority without his being authoritarian. The psychotherapeutic method is flexibly applied in an educative fashion. The residents and their families can feel and accept the sense of the staff as united though allowing room for individual expression and differences. The seemingly unstructured structure may serve as a model for a family which is united though not rigid. Through open communication on all subjects, collusive attempts to undermine and by-pass authority can be exposed and worked through if the communicational atmosphere is one of "It's all right."

Most often we have used the oval or circular group structure traditional in family and group psychotherapy. However, forty people in a circle requires a large amount of space. When people speak softly or quietly it is difficult to hear them, especially if a room air conditioner is making noise. For diverse reasons then, we may alter the format so that we ask participants to shift their chairs into two concentric circles or we form the small family group within the large group.[1] We may do this not just for acoustic reasons but in order to focus in on the problems of interrelationships and communication between one resident and her family. Typically, members of the resident's family present and involved include two relatives, either both parents, or a parent and a sibling over eighteen, or a parent and a grandmother, or a mother and an aunt in a fatherless family. I ask for two other residents to come forward and sit with the family and with myself to serve as "advocates of truth." One is assigned to the side of the resident and one to the side of the other members of the family.

The entire group is reminded of our group code, i.e., we seek to elicit truth in order to examine what has transpired in the past and what goes on in the present. We do not wish to participate in blaming, finger pointing, or guilt provoking which serves to maintain and increase hostility, distrust, and distance among the family members. The two resident-peer advocates are directed to speak up and "pull the covers" whenever they hear the resident or the family expressing what is commonly referred to as "bullshit." Their presence and activity lends a touch of levity to an often too-serious and angry confrontation and also keeps the dialogue from straying too far from the focus of interest in the interaction. Through these attitudes and messages we work toward the development of a group atmosphere at these meetings which inherently states, "It's all right for us to be open here to discuss and express our feelings about anything and anyone."[2] This permissive attitude does not give individuals the right to scapegoat or hurt others sadistically under the rubric of being honest or "frank." It is up to the leader of such a group to attend to the sensitivities of all present and to "blow the whistle" on interaction or dialogue which seems to be getting out of hand or uncontrollable.

The multifamily meeting is not permitted to be a separate experience for our residents from the rest of our program. As family attitudes and values are expressed concerning giving, receiving, responsibility for self and others, trust, money, impulse control, frustration-tolerance, dependency-independency, parental rules, and so on, the discussion is moved toward a comparison of these with attitudes and values of other families and also the staff of our rehabilitation center. The values anchored in our approach often serve to reinforce the constructive values and requirements for maturation, responsibility, and privilege in the families of our residents. At other times the different values and practices between our community and other families serve to reinforce the resident's demand for her family to examine and alter their rigid, tyrannical positions which promote rebellion and acting out and stultify growth and continued self-examination.

SCREENING

Initially we permitted any blood, marital, or common-law relative to attend our multifamily meetings. We soon learned that some mothers and brothers and husbands came to the meeting and left supplies of marijuana, up and down pills, alcohol, or money with residents during or after the formal group meeting. They did this to please or appease the resident who is their addicted relative, thus perpetuating their initial pattern of collusion against authorities, rules, regulation, and structure. We tried to educate the families as to the destructiveness of this behavior in terms of the contract with us and the setting, and how disastrous it could be to their relative who was in our program as well as to others. This was not enough to stop the practice. It led us to establish the practice of setting up appointments with our social workers to screen carefully in advance those family members who seemed reliable, emotionally stable, and cooperative enough to attend the meetings. An attempt was made by some families to violate the general rule that participants had to be eighteen years or older. They presented us with the *fait accompli* of bringing younger brothers, sisters, cousins, and friends to the residence. We held ground on the policy of prior screening and age limit, although we accepted the potential value of having meetings for interested persons of all ages and did arrange for such special meetings on occasion. Family members such as dominating alcoholic mothers, common-law husbands, boyfriends who had in collusion with our resident managed to convince us that they were common-law husbands, but, in fact, were pimps or alcoholics, gave us problems on some occasions when their aggressive oppositional stance and attitudes provoked marked turbulence, hostility, and nearly disrupted the multifamily meetings because of the high level of tension produced.

THE WORK IN MULTIFAMILY MEETINGS

The work in multifamily meetings for the most part consists in interaction, discussion, identification, and examination of those conflicts, attitudes, covert alliances, and unconscious arrangements in families which have led to disruptive family patterns and possibly to drug usage. It is made clear that there is no one family pattern or attitude which always leads to drug addiction. However, it is also made clear that in all addicts there exist common problems in the areas of dependency, little or no impulse control, and poor frustration tolerance which accompanies an attitude of "I want what I want when I want it!" Also common is the problem of difficulty in respecting inner or outer authorities and controlling forces necessary for survival of self and others. We attempt, therefore, to build into our therapeutic community increased awareness and interest in one's real self as well as in the right and interests of others, especially those on whom addicts are dependent: to build an increased capacity to look at themselves and to develop an expanded observing ego while they are alone and experiencing primary-process or other thoughts which could lead to impulsive or compulsive acting out.

THE ACTUAL GROUP MEETING

Difficulties in getting started are a common pattern. It has been a continued source of surprise to experience families of addicts, who have traveled long distances on a weekday evening after a long day of work, coming together and sitting in a passive-dependent fashion most of the time. There is great resistance to initiating group discussion by spontaneous help or opinion seeking. There is a regression to passive waiting for leadership to come from the group leader, despite the urgency of the problem of having an addict in the family, despite the sense of confusion and guilt which is present in family members who wonder if they have in some way done harm or could have done more to prevent their relative from becoming addicted.

A common starting theme presented by me has been to state that "We don't know all the answers to drug addiction causes or its treatment. However, we do know that people turn to drugs to either move away from one feeling or another such as pain, anxiety, boredom, or isolation, or to move toward another type of feeling such as joy, happiness, peace, excitement, or satisfaction. Would any of our residents or their families like to add to this or ask any questions about it?" This usually gets the discussion and interaction going. A resident may say to her parent, "I couldn't stand your constant nagging. There was nothing I could do right as far as you were concerned. At least my drug friends accepted me as I was. I didn't have to prove anything to them. When I was with them there was fun and excitement and I felt okay." This then allows the whole multifamily group to examine the impact of the relationship between parent and child upon the child's self-image, self-concept, and degree of self-hate. Factors in family life which contribute to self-hate, to resignation from trying to grow constructively, are then examined. The unconscious and sometimes conscious basis of patterns of hurting oneself in order to hurt parents can then be seen in terms of its genesis and further development. The satisfactions felt by the addict as he is able to achieve a vindictive triumph over his parents can be explored in terms of the feelings of power and control it gives to the addict, who most often feels impotent and powerless in his relationship to his parents.

Patterns of nonverbal behavior which are communicated between family members and which are similar to those between the addict resident and our staff can be pointed out as expressions of transference.[3] Multifamily group participants find much excitement and enlightenment in learning how their nonverbal behaviors, of which they themselves are unaware, are in fact observed, interpreted, and reacted to by others. Another common pattern which emerges is that, despite the differences in family background, addicts universally do not have an adequate sense of caring for self.

In the multifamily meeting the repetitive self-defeating attitudes, roles, and games played by an addict and his family can be observed and explored. I refer to such games and roles as: copout, crisis-creator, the abused one, the martyr, the rejection-collector, the saint, the help-rejecting complainer, the victim, the Prima Donna, the manipulator, the guilt provoker, the compulsive helper, "I don't know," "I couldn't care less," "I can't help it," "It's not my fault," "But it's not easy," "divide and conquer."

An addict states: "I took drugs because it allowed me to feel open as if I were flowing and flying. I liked the feeling of freedom to fly with no resistance, no restraints, no constraints. I liked to just have feelings, to just have sensations and no thoughts to bother me. I liked not having to be serious." Such a statement provokes discussion from the entire group as to what life is about, and then leads into the issues of how parents create in their child the illusion that "life owes me a living and a loving" and that life is to be a place where they are always happy and all their wishes are to be satisfied or gratified immediately if not sooner. The pattern is experienced of parents who have suffered a great deal and experienced much deprivation in their own childhoods and therefore have attempted to give to their child things "to keep them happy" to make up for what they did not have.

At times we focus on learning ways of *feeling high—elated—joyful without drugs* by becoming more aware of what is really going on in ourselves and nature and life—that is to be enjoyed! All participants are invited to share ways of feeling great that they have learned about at any point in their lives. Examples of such peak moments experienced without drugs are: the view of an early morning sunrise, a swim in a cool lake, observing a planted seed come above ground as a small seedling in a flower pot on one's window sill, and stretching out all the way into total relaxation with an ah-ah sound.

Observing, exploring, and identifying patterns and systems of unconscious family "arrangements," as well as the responses of the family members to each other, can expedite insight, understanding, and motivation to change.[4] Typical repetitive, regulating patterns which are revealed are:

(1) Placate—"You're right" or "Yes, I'm wrong about that."

(2) Blame or provoke guilt—"But you made me do it that way" or "It's your fault because. . . ."

(3) Preach—"When I was a child. . . ." or "I can't understand how someone who's been given everything like you have, can sit there and say that."

(4) Change the subject to something irrelevant—"I'll get back to that but I want to point out that the other day. . . ."

(5) Withdrawal of one or more family member(s) into silence, resignation, and a "What's the use? It won't make any difference anyway" attitude.

(6) Denial—"It may have looked that way, but you just don't understand."

(7) Psychosomatic response—"Since I've been sitting here my heart is pounding like it's going to break" or "I'm getting a splitting headache now—you upset me when you say those things."

(8) Discounting—a family member used a dismissing type of head nod to the side and down or hand movement with palm down to indicate that what was being expressed by another family member is being "put down" or discounted.

(9) Being realistic—the family is open and truthful, and conscientiously attempts to recognize, accept, and resolve realistic conflicts of interest or problems while being congruent in communicating or relating.

CRISIS CREATING

Crisis creating is a common pattern in addicts and their families.[5] Identifying this pattern and describing its values is of great importance to addicts and their families. Here is an example of the value of crisis creating to one eighteen-year-old resident who had been an only child of parents who separated when she was six. Donna poignantly told the group as she sat with her father to her right and her mother and grandmother to her left, "Since I was thirteen the only time I have seen my parents together is when I awakened from an overdose and found myself in a hospital with both my parents at my bedside. I really enjoyed the concern and attention they were both paying to me. At the same time I felt that what I had to do to get it was worth it. I admit now that it would be nice if I could get it some other way."[6] The underlying motivation of creating crises to go beyond feeling dead, low, depressed, or alone can then be explored, as well as other alternatives and ways to feeling more alive and to having relationships with others. It can be pointed out to the addicts and their families that we know that crises and emergencies commonly bring families and other individuals together. However, there are other ways of communicating and relating which can bring about communion and better relationships, primarily that of truthful, confrontational communication such as we are experiencing in this group without blaming or guilt provoking.

RESIDENTS' EVALUATIONS

In response to a written questionnaire concerning the multifamily group meetings, the following are typical verbatim statements:

Question: What is your reaction to the monthly multifamily group meeting?

Answers: To be truthful, I was against Family Therapy at first. Because I didn't feel by bringing my problems of my relationship with my parents to Family Therapy would help me to find a solution to them, or help me to see them more clearly. My first repercussion toward Family Therapy was to secede, especially when they started questioning me about my relationship with my mother, and what I felt the reason was that lead me to drugs. But as I attended Family Therapy regularly, I found that once I was able to communicate and relate to my parents, I wasn't as nebulous as I had been.

I feel it helps the new girls get more in touch with their feelings towards their parents and understand both sides. As for the older girls, they seem to identify with each happening that goes on in family therapy.

. . . have help me out a great deal. Unfortunately my family don't come, but when I do go home I share to them my problem, and I explain to them they fault, so we can have a better understanding and relationship.

. . . it will bring the girls closer to their families. Also more communication with one another.

. . . the meetings have been a vital necessity in establishing relationship with the family. It's a good way to establish communications and understand the differences.

It should be more than once a month, at least twice. When my family first came they, they were so surprised that they received so much; from hearing other family talk.

. . . a chance to get a better relationship going with their family.

I feel that the family therapy that we have once a month is very good; even though everyone seems to sit there and not say a word until it is just about time to go.

. . . feel that this meeting can open up a lot of new doors for the parent resident relationship.

I feel that the family group therapy is the second most essential thing in the Committee's program. It allows parents to get a better understanding of exactly what's been going on with their children during their temporary period of withdrawal from self and family. It also allows parent and child to obtain different views of how they (the parent) should have handled a problem pertaining to the use of drug abuse.

The meeting is good for some girls.

At first it was only a night to be with my parents. My feelings have changed now, because I feel that these groups have really improved our relationship for the better.

Question: What has helped you to see your family life and relationship more clearly or differently?

Answers: I am able now to tell my parents exactly what is on my mind. They especially my mother is very over-protective. I always felt that if I told her or went against her program her feelings would be hurt . . . has made me realize that I have to live my own life and do not any longer need to be tied to my mother's apron strings.

My family and I have a good relationship already.

I see my family life a little clear now, Because I really see what they must have been going through by me being on drugs.

The duration of being away from them in the sense of not having them project rights or wrongs for me to function. Realizing I am the only one at this point who has to deliberate, and deal with upcoming situations.

I feel that the family therapy helped me, yet I feel that after we did bring things out in the open and stopped blaming each other that's when we really got together.

My family relationship is more clearer in many ways. We are aware of many feelings about each other than before. The understanding of one another is better; and, together we are learning to accept one another again.

I don't have immediate family here in New York, however, I have come to understand that it is not "I" alone with a problem, but a common problem. The feelings I have shared as well as the compassion has helped me to look at people in a warmer sense.

I still feel the same about my family. For we never really talked, and only once my mother came to family therapy.

In the past I have been blaming my father for all my mistakes, but I feel that I made the mistakes, and it is up to me to get myself together, and try to forgive him for his faults. Because we all are human, and we are entitled to make mistakes. And just by knowing this I feel that I have accomplished a great deal.

Just being clean has made me aware of my feelings and those of my family. I feel that I need to get closer to them in many things. Then I would be able to let them know how I feel about myself and about them. I don't have an understanding with my people so this ends our relationship before it gets a chance. I very much want to get closer to my husband because I feel very strongly that in the process of helping myself I can help him also.

I now understand that my parents are trying to help me not hurt me. I also feel they have become more trusting of me from listening to my views and the opinions of other people.

. . . our relationship at the present time has more trust, and a lot more understanding to every degree. I strongly feel now they see I'm a woman and not a drug addict as *I WAS*.

It helped me see that parents also have many problems and they also go through many changes. Because they also do not see things very clearly.

. . . that is the only time I really get to hear my parents true feeling, and they get to hear my true feelings. And by having Family Therapy you get a better understanding with your parents, and sometimes you may form a better relationship between them.

PARENTS' EVALUATIONS

Evaluation forms were mailed to all residents' family members able to attend meetings. It was learned that those who have come have attended an average of five multifamily meetings. Responses to these forms are reported below:

Question: What benefit have you gained from attending?

Answers: Seeing my daughter. Getting an insight to the different feelings of the girls in the way they deal with their environment.

A closeness to all of the girls and their problems. An appreciation of your program.

I would say that more insight was realized. And I am starting to examine myself instead of others.

I heard other family problems, which made me understand why my daughter acted rebellious.

Question: What would you like to hear discussed that you haven't brought up?

Answers: More interesting talks on human behavior.

The residents methods of fooling us when they are on drugs and how "they" think the families should stay on the alert when they complete the program. I think that family members of more of the residents should be encouraged to attend. Possible inducements might be—Don't use the same form letter notice all the time, Have something short but interesting before the meetings, like a residents craft exhibit, a visit to the class rooms, etc. Coffee and cake or cookies baked by the residents.

How many drug users make it and what feelings do they encounter while trying to make it.

CONCLUSION

Multifamily group therapy helps parents learn that we find almost universally in our residents an inability to live with frustration which pushes them to demand or manipulate others into immediate gratification of their needs, often by tyrannizing, threatening, or guilt provoking; an inability to postpone impulse gratification and to accept a regimen of structured behavior in which the rewards are not immediately visible; a lack of respect or trust in authorities who can be manipulated or are manipulative; and a low self-esteem and little healthy pride in accomplishment or effort. Our multifamily meetings have been an attempt to engage families to work with us rather than to collude with their addict relative against us.

The multifamily group approach serves to reinforce the impact of what residents gain in their regular group psychotherapy sessions through additional therapeutic interactions, stimulations, communications, transferential and cross-cultural experiences, and simple education in more mature everyday living.[7]

More specifically, participation in the large group of residents, some families, and staff members provides:

(1) A culturally significant opportunity for open acceptance and sense of belonging which counteracts self-isolating, self-separating, destructively defensive maneuvers which are common in addicts.

(2) A sense of a "home away from home." Although our addiction treatment residence is not really a biological family unit, it is a symbolic family which provides a more constant, accepting, and reality-oriented "family" experience than they had experienced in their own family unit. Respect develops for authority expressed and administered with FIRMTH (firm warmth).

(3) Another opportunity to face and accept the compulsive rationalizations, evasiveness, distortions, projections, and magical pseudosolutions used by themselves and other addicts to maintain dependency and avoid the responsibility of "growing up."

(4) An opportunity for reinforcement of an insight or feeling so that it is really brought home and can lead to a change in motivation, attitude, or behavior.

(5) Another experience to undermine the self-hating notion that "I am worthy only of disrespect" as significant others, strangers, peers, and staff openly accept that "in view of my actual past life, I, such as I am and was, did the best I could do *and now am accepted on faith with hope and trust that I can do better* for myself and others *if I want to* and *am willing to make a sincere effort to change."*

(6) An opportunity for each resident to realize that addicts who come from backgrounds that seemed far more ideal than their own also got involved with drugs and developed ways of escaping from reality and maturation similar to their own.

(7) An opportunity to learn that life isn't just fair and that we do not have the right to expect life to give us a living and a loving because we've suffered so.

(8) An opportunity to experience the kaleidoscopic variations of daily living and yet the similarities in the lives of everyone. This helps in undermining the feeling of pathological uniqueness in every neurotic and every addict.

(9) An opportunity for family members: *a*) to regain respect for their addicted relative because she is now committed to a program of self-help and to listen to their point of view; *b*) to understand more about the inner pressures which lead toward drug abuse; *c*) to develop new ways of communicating; *d*) to renew trust with some optimism, hope, and faith; and *e*) to be involved more actively in the rehabilitation of their relative.

Our experience leads us to the firm conclusion that there is a definite value in incorporating multifamily psychosocial group therapy meetings into the regularly scheduled total program of a drug addiction treatment center.[8] Such groups partially fulfill psychotherapeutic, social, and community needs of addicts and their families.

REFERENCES

1. H. Chertoff and M. M. Berger, "A Technique for Overcoming Resistance to Group Therapy in Psychotic Patients on a Community Mental Health Service," *Int. J. Group Psychother.*, 21:53-61, 1971.
2. M. M. Berger, "The Function of the Leader in Developing and Maintaining a Working Psychotherapy Group," in J. L. Moreno (ed.), *International Handbook of Group Psychotherapy* (New York: Philosophical Library, 1966).
3. M. M. Berger, "Nonverbal Communications in Group Psychotherapy," *Int. J. Group Psychother.*, 8:161-178, 1958.
4. M. M. Berger, "The Use of Videotape in the Integrated Treatment of Individuals, Couples, Families and Groups in Private Practice," in M. M. Berger (ed.), *Videotape Techniques in Psychiatric Training and Treatment* (New York: Brunner/Mazel, 1970), pp. 119-160.
5. M. M. Berger, "The Recognition and Management of Emergencies in Group Psychotherapy," *Group Proc.*, 3:61-75, 1972.
6. M. M. Berger, "Multifamily Therapy with Addicts," *The Antidote*, 3:5, April, 1970.
7. M. M. Berger and D. Mendell, "A Preliminary Report on Participation of Patients in More than One Psychotherapy Group Concurrently," *Int. J. Group Psychother.*, 13:210-216, 1967.
8. E. Leichter and G. Schulman, "Emerging Phenomena in Multifamily Group Treatment," *Int. J. Group Psychother.*, 18:69-79, 1968; idem., "Interplay of Group and Family Treatment Techniques in Multifamily Group Therapy," *Int. J. Group Psychother.*, 22:167-176, 1972.

45

ISSUES RAISED IN A GROUP SETTING BY PATIENTS RECOVERING FROM MYOCARDIAL INFARCTION

Carolyn Bascom Bilodeau
Thomas P. Hackett

The issues that five convalescent male heart patients most frequently raised during twelve weekly group meetings led by a psychiatric nurse concerned group process, current and future states of health, effects of illness on one's life, treatment of illness, the role of "patient" and its effect on the family, history of illness, and medical care after discharge. Participants stated that the meetings had significantly influenced their adjustment to and acceptance of myocardial infarction.

Recent studies have confirmed the common knowledge that a patient's emotional reactions to myocardial infarction continue long after hospitalization. The successful adjustment achieved by most patients in the hospital seems to be shaken when the patient faces the stresses of life following discharge. Worries about changes in physical activity and work capability (Adsett and Bruhn, 1968; Druss and Kornfeld, 1967; Hackett and Cassem, 1970; Nite and Willis, 1964; Roth, Berki, and Wolff, 1967; Willis and Dunsmore, 1967; Wynn, 1967), acceptance by the family (Adsett and Bruhn, 1968; Druss and Kornfeld, 1967; Hackett and Cassem, 1970), sexual adequacy (Adsett and Bruhn, 1968; Druss and Kornfeld, 1967), modifications in smoking and drinking habits (Adsett and Bruhn, 1968; Druss and Kornfeld, 1967; Hackett and Cassem, 1970; Roth, Berki, and Wolff, 1967; Willis and Dunsmore, 1967), and recurrent heart attack with possible death (Adsett and Bruhn, 1968; Druss and Kornfeld, 1967; Hackett

Reprinted from the *American Journal of Psychiatry*, Vol. 128, No. 1, July 1971, pp. 73-78. Copyright © 1971, the American Psychiatric Association.

and Cassem, 1970) may become overwhelming. Attempts to master these concerns through repression, denial, and other defensive measures are seldom successful.

In order to examine the psychological problems of coronary convalescence and to test the value of group meetings in resolving them, an approach was devised that used the techniques of small group therapy. These techniques provided the investigator (C.B.B.) with an organizational format already tested in a medical setting (Deutsch and Lippman, 1964; Linden, 1962; Schoenberg and Senescu, 1966) and allowed her to gather data from a number of patients simultaneously. At the time this project was started, the literature contained no study on the use of group therapy with patients recovering from myocardial infarction. Since then, Adsett and Bruhn have published findings that indicate an "improved psychosocial adaptation" in patients and their wives as a result of group therapy (Adsett and Bruhn, 1968).

This study was undertaken not only to gain information about the emotional component in coronary heart disease, but also to determine whether a group of postcoronary men would be willing to meet twelve times with a nurse as their leader. If such sessions proved valuable to the patients, it would be profitable to incorporate such meetings into a coronary convalescence program.

METHODS

Our sample consisted of English-speaking male patients under fifty-five years of age who were admitted to the coronary care unit on the ward medical service with their first myocardial infarction. To establish rapport with potential group members and to provide an orientation to group process, the nurse (C.B.B.) conducted five taped interviews with each patient during hospitalization. In the fourth interview she introduced the idea of a "heart club" where men could share their concerns and feelings about heart disease. The meetings would also provide nurses and doctors with coronary convalescence data.

Of the ten patients randomly selected, five could not attend because of distance or severity of illness. The five participants ranged in age from thirty-five to fifty-three. One was divorced; four were married. Their jobs involved strenuous physical activity frequently complicated by tension or pressure.

The nurse maintained biweekly telephone contact with each patient from day of discharge until the first group meeting. These calls maintained their interest and provided for expression of concerns and questions.

Weekly evening meetings lasted seventy-five minutes. With members' permission, sessions were taped.

Table 45–1   The 15 Most Frequently Expressed Issues

Issue	Per cent of All Issues Raised	Time Consumed Per cent	Rank
Leader	10.7	6.8	5
Group cohesiveness	7.7	4.2	10
Current state of physical health	7.3	5.0	8
Medical care after discharge	6.3	7.1	4
Work	5.7	8.5	2
Medications	5.1	6.0	6
Smoking	4.8	8.7	1
Current state of emotional health	4.5	2.3	14
Death	4.1	3.3	12
Attitude of others	3.5	3.5	11
Nature of illness	3.5	2.2	15
Nutrition	3.2	7.5	3
Illness and death of others	3.2	2.7	13
Family, home, friends	3.1	4.3	9
Finances	3.0	5.2	7

FINDINGS

Four members came regularly, and a fifth attended irregularly.

Analysis of Data

Thirty-four issues were identified from transcriptions of the taped sessions. Issues were introduced by members and generally reflected group concerns. Each meeting was analyzed to obtain: (1) the number of different times an issue was raised; (2) the amount of time spent on each issue; and (3) the number of different issues introduced. A Spearman rank order correlation coefficient applied to the total number of times each issue was expressed in the twelve meetings and the total amount of time spent on each issue showed a high positive correlation ($r = .85$) that is significant at less than the .01 level.

The fifteen most frequently expressed issues are listed in Table 1. Ten of these were raised in every meeting. These fifteen issues comprised 75.5 per cent of all issues expressed and consumed 77.3 per cent of the discussion time. "Leader" refers to all comments made concerning the group leader, including requests for her opinion on medical or social matters, comments on her appearance and role, and expressions of positive or negative feelings toward. "Group cohesiveness" refers to comments reflecting the growing bond of unity within the group. The following is an example: "We're charter members. When my grandchildren get older they might see a plaque listing the names of the charter members of the heart club up on the wall of the hospital lobby and say, 'There he is.' "

The number of different issues raised in each meeting dropped steadily from twenty-nine in the first meeting to nineteen in the twelfth meeting. This progressive decrease may indicate that some of the issues expressed at earlier meetings had been resolved.

To provide a broader view of the issues raised by group members, the thirty-four issues were grouped into seven general categories. The number of times that issues within each category were raised was totaled. Issues concerned with group process ranked first, indicating members' acceptance of and involvement in the weekly meetings. Second were issues concerned with current and future states of health.

Ranking third were issues concerned with effects of illness on one's life. The number of times issues in these first three categories were raised increased in the last six meetings. Ranking fourth were issues concerned with treatment of illness; issues concerned with the role of patient and its effect on the family ranked fifth. Ranking sixth were issues concerning history of illness; in last place were issues related to hospital care. The last four categories were raised more frequently in the first six meetings.

Commonly Raised Issues

1. *Nature of illness.* Competition was high as members graphically described and compared the severity, course, and symptoms of their heart attacks. Nearly 70 per cent of the times this issue was raised occurred in the first three meetings. A constant struggle to understand and accept the illness and its implications was obvious as members alternately voiced doubt and asserted belief in the diagnosis. "I still don't know what the hell kind of heart attack I had." "How bad was my heart attack. . . . Is it good, bad, medium, half-medium?" "I don't know what I've had yet, whether I had a heart attack or whether I ran out of wind." "Is his worse than mine, or is mine worse than his?"

2. *Medications.* Not only the name and type of medication, but also the color, number, and dosage of pills were compared. The greater the number of pills per day and/or the need for nitroglycerin, the further a member was "on the way out." A decrease in number indicated improvement. Members exhibited excellent knowledge of anticoagulants, but viewed tranquilizers as "crutches" on which no real man ought to depend. None recalled having had the importance of sedation explained or emphasized by his doctor.

3. *Nutrition.* Members discussed with considerable feeling the problems involved in adhering to diets, e.g., weight gain, watching others eating foods they were deprived of, and family vigilance. "My granddaughter, she's only a little thing, she looks at everything I eat during the day, and at night she tells the old lady everything I've eaten." Misconceptions and

questions concerning foods allowed on the diets were repeatedly raised even though members had received written diet instructions before discharge. Although members recognized the importance of weight control, four out of five found this task difficult and blamed having cut down or stopped smoking for their increased appetites.

4. *Medical care after discharge.* Each member was followed in the medical clinic by a house officer who cared for him in the hospital and was keenly aware of his doctor's response to his progress. The longer the time between appointments, the better the members felt they were.

5. *Smoking.* All members viewed smoking as a direct road to a second heart attack, and will power was stressed as an important factor in stopping. Three members stopped smoking completely, while two resumed smoking cigarettes, but less frequently than before their heart attacks.

6. *Work and activities.* Members varied in the degree of anxiety they experienced with increased activity and the return to work. Two were given less strenuous jobs, but were unhappy performing them. Two returned to their previous work; this violated one member's medical restrictions. The fifth member received a disability pension.

7. *Sex.* All members directly or indirectly admitted diminished libido and fear of death during intercourse, a fear that was shared by their spouses. "Your heart's weak yet, man . . . sex life alone can kill you right now." Two members who attempted intercourse and were impotent blamed tranquilizers. Two others stated that they were in no hurry to commence sexual activity, while the fifth was reluctant to ask his doctor because "he might say I have to wait a year." No member had discussed these concerns with his doctor, and no doctor had introduced the subject.

8. *Illness and death of others.* Patients were interested in comparing or finding differences in symptoms, course, treatment, and survival rate of others with the diagnosis of heart attack. Disregarding medical advice was held responsible for recurrent heart attacks and death in others. Identification with long-term survivors increased as the group members progressed in convalescence.

9. *Attitude of family.* From the third meeting on, members described being closely supervised by their families on activities, diet, smoking, medication, and naps. Aggravation, frustration, humiliation, and anger in reaction to this surveillance were vividly expressed. "When you get out of here with a heart attack, it's a pain in the ass to go home because everybody's on your back." At the same time, members interpreted their spouses' behavior as necessary for their continued well-being and as a manifestation of concern. They recommended a separate "heart club" for wives, but specifically stated that the two clubs should not hold joint meetings.

10. *Current states of health.* All members experienced increased body awareness. They repeatedly commented on the presence or absence of

symptoms and immediately associated them with a recurrent heart attack. "You know, as soon as you feel lousy you say, 'Oh, oh, it's the ticker.' " They described themselves as generally more grouchy and irritable with diminished tolerance for aggravation, tension, and noise.

11. *Future states of health.* Two members felt certain they would have second heart attacks—one because he found adhering to restrictions so difficult and the other because his tolerance for activity was low. One member denied concern about the future. Two admitted that fear of another coronary made them comply with the limitations of a cardiac regimen. The subject of death was raised in the form of direct comments or questions, veiled observations, and jokes. "For Christ's sake, she's talking to four mummies. She's getting us here every week to get all the information she can, and then she'll probably go to our funerals." Four of the five agreed that the thought of death came to mind frequently, and one of these found his sleep affected by these thoughts.

12. *Group process.* Although the group was presented to the patients as a club, the process of growing into and becoming a cohesive group was a dynamic and prominent feature. Members were generally talkative and assertive and grew in their ability to share with and give support to others. As they became comfortable in the group setting they used slang and profanity, joked and teased, and expressed feelings freely. "All right, John, you haven't said a word for five minutes. Get your name on this tape or you don't get credit for showing up." "I enjoy talking to you because I can get more information from you than anybody I know. We can sit down relaxed and talk to you." "If we didn't come in, the club wouldn't run. . . . Even if I have to come in on a stretcher they're going to bring me in on Tuesday nights."

Role of the Nurse

In the hospital and in telephone contacts, the nurse listened to the patient, provided information as he was able to assimilate it, and encouraged him to communicate with his doctor when necesssary. If the patient's spouse answered the telephone, the nurse talked with her about the patient and asked for her responses to his illness. Most frequently the spouse felt guilty that she was not doing enough, feared that her husband would have another heart attack, and was angry that he would not adhere to restrictions or demanded special attention. Occasionally the nurse suggested modifications in approach so that the patient would not feel so helpless and dependent.

In the group sessions the nurse was relatively nondirective and gave little interpretation to the material discussed. She attempted to create an atmosphere in which the members could interact easily with her and with other members.

Patient Reactions

All participants reacted positively to the hospital visits, telephone calls, and group meetings. They regarded the nurse's efforts in their behalf as evidence that the hospital was interested in them. They appreciated the opportunity to talk and commented on feeling better after doing so. The telephone calls were seen as a bridge between the security of the hospital and home, with its many sources of anxiety and frustration. Knowing that the nurse would call diminished members' feelings of helplessness and isolation.

Patients saw the nurse as someone they could "bother" even with "silly" questions. She helped them to avoid disturbing the doctor who was "busy" and often inaccessible; they trusted that she would advise them to contact the doctor when necessary. As medical appointments became more infrequent, members saw the club as the main place for them to ask questions, voice concerns, and find support.

The predominant feelings expressed were fear and anxiety. To cope with these and other feelings of aggravation, anger, dependency, sadness, inadequacy, and shame the members used various observable techniques: joking, changing the subject, displacement, projection, denial, rationalization, and identification. As the meetings progressed, the use of some of these mechanisms diminished, and members could express more of their feelings directly.

No patient experienced angina, dyspnea, or any other untoward physical or emotional symptom during these meetings. Rather, the meetings were described as the most relaxing time of the week, a time when members were accepted for just being themselves. Because of their positive response to the group, members requested continuation of the meetings. They were continued for twelve more weeks and thereafter on a monthly basis.

DISCUSSION

Our findings agreed with those of others that convalescence is a period riddled with emotional difficulties. Furthermore, many of the concerns and conflicts experienced by patients after discharge center around issues that could be resolved in part through explanations and clarification by the doctor. An uneven pattern of communication emerged in which some areas were meticulously covered, while others were hardly touched. Thus each patient knew a great deal about his cardiac and anticoagulant medication, yet had serious questions about the type of sexual activity that was permissible.

All were told they must be relaxed and get sufficient rest, but none had been encouraged to use tranquilizers and hypnotics to attain this state of mind should their own efforts fail. "Avoid overexertion" was advice that each remembered, but all were vexed with the question of what constitutes too much activity. Although each patient realized that he had had a myocardial infarction, there was a constant reassessment of the experience that ranged from considering it to have been mild, on the one hand, to lethal, on the other. These fluctuations were largely the function of the defense of denial, but they also betrayed a lack of information.

The following points, although obvious, emerged as suggestions for the discharge preparation of similar patients:

1. Patients will benefit from learning that the adjustment to a myocardial infarction is an ongoing process that continues long after hospitalization ends. Telling patients that during this period the majority of patients experience feelings of fear and depression might make these responses more endurable.

2. Anticipating the anxiety that occurs when the patient leaves the hospital, starts to increase his activities, and returns to work might reduce apprehension at these critical points. The use of tranquilizers should be advocated by the physician as an aid to relaxation. Specific sanction of the use of sedatives and hypnotics is necessary in order to overcome the moral stigma that is so often attached to their use.

3. Clear, written instructions on medications, diet, sex, activities, and the return to work, as well as discussions of these issues with both the patient and his spouse, should minimize conflicts at home after discharge.

4. Since so many pleasures are stripped from the patient recovering from myocardial infarction, it is well to remind him that many of the restrictions are temporary and that some substitutes are available.

CONCLUSIONS

Male patients recovering from myocardial infarctions joined and had positive feelings toward this group experience. The regularity and frequency of the meetings gave patients an opportunity to express fears before they blossomed. The nurse could review or reinforce old teaching and help patients find more effective ways of coping with frustration.

This study merely opens the door to an area that urgently requires investigation. Does the use of groups conducted by a nurse significantly affect the recovery process of coronary patients during three months of convalescence? If so, what type of group is apt to be most effective? What is the optimal size? Does the sex and profession of the leader make a difference? How long should group activity persist? Will patients cared for on the private service have a need for such a group?

Since coronary heart disease is one of the most serious threats to this nation's health and exacts an immeasurable economic toll, any remedial device deserves attention, particularly if it is as simple and inexpensive as the formation and maintenance of heart clubs.

BIBLIOGRAPHY

Adsett, C. A., and Bruhn, J. G., "Short-term Group Psychotherapy for Myocardial Patients and Their Wives," *Canad. Med. Assn. J.*, 99:577-584, 1968.

Deutsch, A. C., and Lippman, A., "Group Psychotherapy for Patients with Psychosomatic Illnesses," *Psychosom.*, 5:14-20, 1964.

Druss, R. G., and Kornfeld, D. S., "The Survivors of Cardiac Arrest," *JAMA*, 201:291-296, 1967.

Hackett, T. P., and Cassem, N. H., "Psychological Reactions to Life-threatening Illness: A Study of Acute Myocardial Infarction," in H. S. Abram, ed., *Psychological Aspects of Stress* (Springfield, Ill.: Charles C. Thomas, 1970), pp. 29-43.

Linden, M. E., "The Use of Group Psychotherapy in Psychosomatic Medicine," in J. H. Nodine and J. H. Moyer, eds., *Psychosomatic Medicine: The First Hahnemann Symposium* (Philadelphia: Lea & Febiger, 1962), pp. 757-758.

Nite, G., and Willis, F. N., *The Coronary Patient: Hospital Care and Rehabilitation* (New York: Macmillan, 1964), pp. 269-270.

Roth, O., Berki, A., and Wolff, G. D., "Long-range Observations in Fifty-three Young Patients with Myocardial Infarction," *Am. J. Cardiol.*, 19:331-338, 1967.

Schoenberg, B., and Senescu, R., "Group Psychotherapy for Patients with Chronic Multiple Somatic Complaints," *J. Chronic Dis.*, 19:649-657, 1966.

Willis, F. N., and Dunsmore, N. M., "Work Orientation, Health Attitudes, and Compliance with Therapeutic Advice," *Nurs. Res.*, 16:22-25, 1967.

Wynn, A., "Unwarranted Emotional Distress in Men with Ischaemic Heart Disease (IHD)," *Med. J. Aust.*, 2:847-851, 1967.

46

GROUP PSYCHOTHERAPY
FOR CHILDREN

Max Rosenbaum
Irvin A. Kraft

The theory conceptualized in group psychotherapy of children proposes to support the patient's ego growth while he learns to master the chaotic emotions within himself and achieve an adequate interaction with the external world. The family-like setting provides the background for corrective emotional experiences by the maintenance of a maximum of constancy and gratification and a minimum of frustration (Block, 1961; Scheidlinger, 1960). Patients in the group are aided in resolving their differences in a constructive fashion by the therapist, who guides (reacts) with "directness, protective restraint, and verbal clarification" (Scheidlinger, 1960).

The concept of group psychotherapy for children began to emerge when Witmer recognized the importance of a child's emotional adaptation to the school situation. In 1896 he established at the University of Pennsylvania the first psychoeducational clinic for emotionally disturbed children.

A therapeutic classroom differs from group psychotherapy, however, by its goal of education of the intellect. The teacher primarily concentrates on bolstering the child's ego by exploring conscious manifestations of his unconscious patterns rather than by utilizing the classroom group in a directed way to promote emotional health. Undoubtedly, therapeutic use of peer group occurs, but it is not group psychotherapy as defined here.

In 1934 Slavson (1947) began activity group therapy with latency-age

Reprinted from *Manual of Child Psychopathology*, ed. B. B. Wolman (New York: McGraw-Hill Book Company, 1972), pp. 935-950. Used with permission of McGraw-Hill Book Company, © 1972.

children. For the first time children were placed in a deliberately designed situation in which certain actions of the leader were predicated according to a theory of personality and behavior. This contrived group differed from other groups of children, such as a scout troop or swimming team, by its purpose as well as by the special restrictions enforced.

Instead of direct interpretation, controlled group play in a permissive environment afforded patients the opportunity to act out conflicts and emotions. Control resulted when specific limits and ground rules were declared. Slavson believed that relative control of impulsivity could be learned in the group psychotherapy setting. Recognizing that individuation of approach is essential in both group and individual psychotherapy, he noted that children communicate predominantly through motor activity. For a child, play activities issue from inner fantasies that seek expression and resolution. With a child's insight limited, action is his language; the therapist discerns meaning in behavior. Regardless of the approach used in therapy for an individual child, Slavson stressed that feelings of helplessness and dependency characteristic in most children must be recognized as well as the often extreme reaction to criticism, discipline, and punishment from adults.

The goal of group psychotherapy—the education and control of the emotions—is accomplished by various techniques designed to provide an aura of acceptance rather than rejection of feelings and of specific types of behavior. The therapist, as leader of the group, attempts to provide situations which encourage behavior that reveals information from which the emotional content can be extracted and translated intellectually. For example, after a child experiences an outburst of anger in a psychotherapy group, the therapist translates, "Anger is a difficult emotion to control." The child feels better. He gains experiential insight by the verbalization of the feeling and by realizing that retribution does not follow the admission of one's true feelings. Experiential insight may come through interaction with other group members, identification, rationalization, denial, catharsis, or identification with the aggressor. Defense mechanisms tend to be enacted and utilized within the psychotherapy group in an environment of impunity and safety.

Response to treatment can be measured in terms of each child's verbal or nonverbal behavior, activity level, and interrelationships with other children in the group as well as with the leader. Patients bring selected segments of their outside life to the treatment group, and learnings in the group are transmitted through behavior to their outside life. But the child's behavior in treatment is not the same as in his outside life.

Client-centered psychotherapy, Adlerian concepts, and classical psychoanalytic principles dominate the practice of group psychotherapy for children. The literature describes commonalities of assumptions in the work performed by a therapist, regardless of his orientation in theory. These commonalities include the existence of unconscious thinking, psychic determinism, infantile sexuality, the oedipal conflict, and a topological construct of mind. Overriding these factors, however, awareness of developmental vectors and forces always strongly influences the therapist's ultimate therapeutic patterns.

The child's ego is different from that of the adult in that it is still in the process of evolving. The balance between primitive impulses and restraint has not been established. Slavson (1964)(b) reported: "Whether impulses or restraining forces predominate, each person has worked out a relation between the two, which is the foundation of his character. This is not the situation with the young child."

Under such conditions of ego turmoil, methods and techniques used in adult psychotherapy cannot be applied to children without significant alterations and changes. The child needs freedom to act out feelings and to speak his mind, but the therapist clarifies the limits. In general, the motor acting out of small children in the group is accepted, since the adult therapist can intervene at any time. The therapist uses his theoretical information and his guided or supervised experiences to evolve an individualized treatment style which enables him to work well and comfortably with his patients. His choice of a framework of several conceptual schemes may coincide with recent trends of increasing ambivalence regarding the value of psychoanalytic theory. Enthusiasm for attempting techniques such as operant conditioning or behavior therapy is increasing. Caution dictates that ready simplification of approaches to treatment of children leads to many blind alleys.

As an example, the few studies in print seem to support the hypothesis of parental rejection as primary in children's problems in living, but this rejection is also related to the type of disturbance. Some children in treatment see parents as excessively psychologically controlling; others wish for greater parental control. The great variety of parental descriptions that may emerge complicates group treatment of children. Goldin (1969) summarizes the literature on parental behavior as reported by children. His review should prove helpful to those who wish to form children's groups.

GROUP FORMATION IN CHILDHOOD

Most naturalistic observations of our culture's childhood behavior indicate a trend toward group formation in the latency period, especially in its later years (Block, 1966; Boulanger, 1965; Coolidge and Grunebaum, 1964). In the field of psychoanalysis, Buxbaum (1945) introduces an intriguing formulation regarding group formation. She believes that two peak periods of group formation occur in the lives of children. The first is in the five- to seven-year age period; the second occurs during adolescence. Posing the question of the needs for which the child seeks and finds satisfaction in the group more than in any other social setting, she suggests that the childhood period of group formation occurs during the phallic phase, when the child is forced to give up his physical dependence on his mother. The child's close relationship with his mother undergoes severance gradually as he achieves independence in motility, expression, and body care. He no longer needs his mother for survival. His relationship to her changes from an anaclitic one to one of an object libidinal character. Rejection of his sexual wishes for her leaves him frustrated and drives him into transferring his feelings for her to other people. In the group, the young child finds support for his newfound physical independence from the mother. Feeling deserted, ousted from a protective atmosphere upon which he used to rely, he finds a welcome shelter in the group experience. The fear of separation from mother and home is overcome by transferring allegiance to the group leader. Transference becomes an essential and causative factor in childhood and adolescent group formation, serving as a principal motivating force in group formation and a principal cohesive force among group members.

Social scientists have attempted to understand childhood group processes from another viewpoint. Muzafer Sherif and Hadley Cantril (1947) proposed a sophisticated theory with a dynamic conception of the individual and his relationship to society which elaborates on the work of Cooley (1902, 1909, 1918). While dynamic and effective, Cooley's work was somewhat mystical. Although his work often is overlooked by group therapists, he stated that social process and control, basic to all group dynamics, are based on the intimate, face-to-face interactions which form the hallmark of the primary group. Cooley stated that the primary group has a psychological structure represented by close identification or intimacy. Later, George Herbert Mead (1934) defined the self process, but his formulations were incomplete because they were cognitive. Sherif (1948) borrowed the term *reference group* from social psychologist Herbert Hyman (1942) to designate the influence of the group upon the values and attitudes of the individual. While it developed that Sherif was referring to a different phenomenon than that which Hyman had described, both were interested in how groups affect people, according to each individual's distinctive relationship to the group (Turner, 1966). Sherif's major concern was how the individual acquires the attitudes and values of a group. Sociologists until that time had concentrated on the group's reaction to the individual (Thibaut and Kelley, 1959).

Since group formation occurs as a natural phenomenon in childhood development, the age and developmental stage of the child have influenced the growth of group psychotherapy techniques perhaps more than any other factor. Therapists group children by age and often by the nature of their presenting difficulties (Anthony, 1965; Kraft, 1967; Sobel and Geller, 1964). Children are grouped into five categories: preschool and early school age, late latency (ages nine to eleven), pubertal (ages twelve and thirteen), early adolescence (ages thirteen and fourteen), and middle through late adolescence (fourteen to seventeen). The most useful periods of group therapy are the second and fifth. This article concerns the first two or three categories. Just as developmental patterns lead to age divisions of group members, the settings in which therapists operate influence their procedures.

TREATMENT SETTINGS

Group psychotherapy of children occurs almost anywhere disturbed children are involved in some type of therapeutic procedure. The diagnostic category may or may not be important for the composition of the group, for authors vary in their experiences and their recommendations. Group therapy may occur in a state hospital (Sobel and Geller, 1964). Different forms of group therapy, such as puppetry, have been used in hospital wards. Hospitals not specifically oriented to psychiatric disturbances, such as a hospital for asthmatic children, also include group therapy as part of their total regimen of medical care of the child.

In residential treatment settings, group psychotherapy is used, especially in small units, depending on the treatment philosophy of the director. In larger units, the manpower problems tend to make the increased use of group methods a necessity. Another, more common site for group therapy is the day hospital. Psychoeducational settings lend themselves effectively to various kinds of group therapy.

Probably the most frequent setting for group therapy is the outpatient clinic. Through the years, group psychotherapy of children, independent of or concomitant with treatment of the parents, has been used even in the most orthodox child guidance center (Boulanger, 1965; Ganter, Yeakel, and Polansky, 1965; Novick, 1965; Slavson, 1964 (a)(b); Smolen and Lifton, 1966). A fifth setting in which group therapy is being used more often is the public school (Frey and Kolodny, 1966). Beard, Goertzel, and Pearce (1958) describe involvement of children in unusual settings, such as an adult prison.

COMPOSITION OF THE THERAPY GROUP

The child's developmental age and the therapist's setting strongly influence the selection of children for group psychotherapy. The group therapist, whether beginner or expert, must look at his patient population and decide what types of children to include in his therapeutic program. The diagnostic categories convey the entire spectrum of nomenclature. Work has been done with psychotic children by Sobel and Geller (1964) and Speers and Lansing (1964). Reports describe group psychotherapy with severe psychoneurosis, personality trait disorders, behavior disorders, retardation, school failures, school phobias, and delinquency.

A therapist involved in any therapeutic program decides what type of child he is going to treat on the basis of his own interests and by considering the availability of children for the specific procedure.

Examples of these various categories may help the less experienced group psychotherapist. Frey and Kolodny (1966) demonstrate social-group treatment methods in their care of the alienated child in a school environment. Their subjects had failed to find ways of relating to the school without excessive fear or anger. Boulanger (1965) excludes from his analytic psychodrama "children who are hyperactive, physically or intellectually defective, delinquent or predelinquent, prepsychotic, psychotic. . . ." He includes children with psychoneurotic character structure from birth, symptom formation, and inhibition. Sobel and Geller (1964) suggest that in their therapy in a hospital setting, the level of functional and behavioral integration of the child was the important factor. "Ability to get along in a structured setting was actually necessary for participation. . . ." Coolidge and Grunebaum (1964) demonstrated the effects of group psychotherapy in conjunction with other inabilities on a child with severe school-phobia symptomatology. Ginott (1961) suggests: "A therapeutic group must consist of children with dissimilar syndromes so that each child will have the opportunity to associate with personalities different from and complementary to his own." Speers and Lansing (1964) described their program with preschool psychotic children.

An intriguing sequence of techniques for kindergarten and latency children was described by Anthony (1965). He termed these the *small-table* and *small-room* methods:

> The circle, which constitutes the top of the table, is divided into five sectors, each of which is separated from the other by a low, removable wall. Between the walls lies the place or "territory" of the individual member. The walls end at the center of the table at a trough containing water. This is, therefore, common to all the members of the group. Each territory is equipped with a set of playthings, and each set has its own special color, making it distinguishable from other sets. The transactional processes in this nursery group are carried out on both the concrete and verbal level. On the concrete level, the children may scale the miniature walls with ladders or tunnel under them. They may borrow or lend their toy equipment, helping to construct their own themes or the themes of others.

He described the work with latency children in equally interesting fashion:

> With this method, a contract was made with the group whereby an activity period of their own choosing followed a period of talking. As I became more and more experienced with groups of this kind, I gradually

shortened the activity period, until now I have done away with it alto-gether, in favor of a group session in which activity occurs spontaneously, and is then generally interpreted in terms of defense. The group is treated in an analytic way, and the role of the therapist is strongly interpretative. The one cardinal rule is that all interpretations are, from the very begin-ning, directed towards the group, however personally directed the com-ments of the individual members may be. The group is allowed to develop classically, without a program and without an occupation, and is con-fronted with its own tensions and silences.

Gender has not played a major role, except that the frequency of children being brought to attention ranges from three or four boys to one girl. Thus, by availability, boys are more frequently seen in group psycho-therapy in the childhood age group as compared with the middle to late adolescent groups. There are reports of mixed groupings, but both the source of supply and proclivity by the leaders have led primarily to the use of separate gender groups.

Composition may be seen more as a function of the therapeutic out-look and concepts of the therapist, the setting, and the availability of patients than as the result of a particular theoretical position. Some investi-gators in state hospitals have found that even with a large number of children available (Sobel and Geller, 1964), the group membership is selected by the criteria of accessibility to insight and the character of the group. Therapists tend to group their children by their availability, such as including psychotic children in a group but excluding a delinquent or mildly disturbed child. This was true in the work done in the East Bay area, except there they found that they could use a "provocateur," or healthier child, with a group of psychotic children in a constructive way.

The composition of groups, therefore, can be of almost any kind if the therapist is flexible enough in his outlook. It seems that the degree of ego strength would be a major factor in forming a group as well as the degree of hyperactivity and the amount of disturbance created by impulse-ridden children. This hyperkinesis, which is thought to be a function of ego strength in the extreme, would be too disruptive to a group of late-latency children, who are involved primarily in school-performance prob-lems.

Intellectual Quotient

The intellectual level of a child often is predictive of his functioning in a therapy group for children, depending upon the age and IQ's of the other children. Therapists generally believe that children with average intelligence or above-average levels can function adequately in a group. The major problem rests with children who either are extremely brilliant or have IQ levels below 85. It is difficult for children with lower IQ levels to function adequately in a group because they do not understand what is going on and are often the butt of jokes injected by the brighter group members. It is cruel in most cases to expect a group of bright children to accommodate to the slow pace and often grossly immature development of a retardate, in spite of the fact that emotionally disturbed children often show significant immaturity. But the kind of immaturity shown by most disturbed children of normal intelligence differs from the emotional levels and slow development of disturbed retardates. Most investigators prefer to place retardates in groups which are homogeneous with reference to intellectual quotient.

Sternlicht (1965) strongly supports group therapy for children who are mentally retarded, taking issue with the assumption that insight is necessary for successful personality change. Neham (1951) views group therapy with children who are mentally retarded as mainly ego-supportive, and Stevenson and Knights (1962) see their group therapy as social reinforcement. Cowen (1962) stresses group play techniques in his work with the "exceptional" child. In general, therapists working with mentally defective patients stress the importance of careful screening for membership balance, even as they maintain it should be done with nondefectives.

Family Structure

A child's previous or present family structure influences his performance and production within a group, but his orientation to his peers tends to be paramount in importance. Since no attempt is made to replicate life in the therapy group, except in groups with two therapists of opposite sex, the family structure is not too important. The child is more involved with his peer relationships than he is in a direct way with his family, especially in the mid- to late-latency group and the preadolescent group. Thus the group tends to be ego supportive and helps the child reorient himself to his family and his peer group through his group work with his peers. This is the purpose for which the group is designed. Thus, the child may discuss his parents and may react to the therapist as if he were a parent, but his interaction in the group is determined predominantly by his peer-oriented discernment. He may treat his peers as if they were siblings, which would reflect the viewpoints in the family structure about children.

Other criteria for selection suggest that children who show a common social hunger, the need to be like their peers and to be accepted by them, should be included. Usually the therapist excludes the child who has never realized a primary relationship, as with his mother, since individual psychotherapy could help the child more. For his preschool groups, Ginott (1961) rejects children with murderous attitudes toward siblings, sociopathic children, children with perverse sexual experiences, habitual thieves, and extremely aggressive children. The children he usually selects are effeminate boys, shy and withdrawn children, and children with phobic reactions and primary behavior disorders. For groups composed of latency-age children, therapists tend to exclude incorrigible or psychopathic children, homicidal children, and overt sexually deviant children. The severely threatened, ritualistic, socially peculiar children who cannot establish effective communications at any useful level with the group members fail to do well in these groups.

PSYCHOTHERAPY TECHNIQUES

The techniques of group psychotherapy of children vary according to the propensities of the therapist, the facilities available to him, and the age of the patients involved. A survey of the literature indicates that many variations occur within the limits of nonexploitation of the patient. A sense of balance must be provided by the therapist. There is a delicate balance between that which is ethical and that which is not acceptable as appropriate technique.

In a field where few guidelines exist and little work has been done compared with the volume of work done with adults, it seems dangerous to let people go on their own. But what standards do we have to go by? Perhaps the best safeguard is the professional competency and integrity of the therapist himself. The setting in which he works, usually an institution, may act as a safeguard in protection for the children. Few articles have been published describing the private practice patterns used by solo practitioners in their treatment of children. Most of the literature cites work in institutional settings, perhaps because group therapy for children requires a physical plant to accommodate children with different emotional conditions.

We still face the question of the lack of standardization of techniques. Certain characteristics of techniques are generic, however. Children are grouped with some commonality. Children who have syndromes that seem incompatible with those of the other children are excluded, as pointed out by Boulanger (1965) in his article on analytic psychodrama of children.

Other basic techniques include those imitative of individual interviews, activity interviews, group psychotherapy with an analytic framework (Kraft, 1967) to activity group therapy, which is the most commonly fostered sponsored group therapy technique (Scheidlinger, 1960). Most group psychotherapy of children, up to the adolescent group, includes some involvement of play. In interview-type group psychotherapy, the boys and girls need some type of play period or feeding situation at the end of the session.

Many therapists agree that the general pattern of talking does not relieve enough of the tensions, so that at the end or at some point of the therapy, kinesics or active play becomes necessary. In our culture, at most levels of involvement, food is also considered part of social intercourse. Since groups at play often involve a snack or other type of feeding at some point, this is often found as part of a group therapy procedure with children. Eating can be a very useful psychological adjunct for the therapist. As Slavson (1964)(a) pointed out: "Some group therapists who placate their patients by various means, rationalize it as playing out the 'good parent role.' " Feeding the patients fulfills the needs of the therapist. Children eating together participate in social interaction in a situation which is present in school life (eating lunch at school) and in home life. We assume that many families tend to aggregate around the transmittal of food from the parents to the children.

Dream Interpretation

Few reports on the use of dreams in group therapy of children appear in the literature. Certainly in the younger age group, dreams may be reported spontaneously, but they usually are not elicited or interpreted by the therapist in a direct way. Dreams can help, however, by being used as a focus for discussion of all the group members simply by having the child who narrates the dream seek comments from the other group members on similar dreams that they have had. "What do you think Johnny might be saying by his night thinking?" as dreams are often termed. In one case, we found that we could use both dreams and responses to Rorschach cards in the same way. The children tended to have fantasies and comment on each other's productions in their forty-five minutes or so of interview group therapy in a late-latency group. This might be hard to do with children of preschool level or of the oedipal period.

Free Association

Free association is used in the sense of translating play. This certainly would occur in children who play together under the aegis of the therapist. The use of free association and other devices to obtain unconscious material is not clearly defined in the literature. The assumption is made that unconscious material is pertinent and involved in the treatment process, although it is not necessarily pointed out to the children. Usually the techniques involve ego-oriented interpretations, providing the opportunity for expression of strong, basic emotions. "It's all right to let your angry feelings out, so long as you know what to do with them," or "When parents do something like that, children may feel sad."

Time Factors in Therapy

Frequency of group meetings may vary from daily to once a week. The frequency of meetings is determined to a great extent by the time flexibility of therapists and the availability of patients, which depends upon the setting, transportation, and other variables. Few studies exist that show comparisons between matched groups with multifrequency meetings versus meetings once a week or less frequently. In actuality, the therapist who is going to work with children considers the frequency primarily on the basis of the mechanisms and involvements of his setting rather than by any theoretical consideration of what would seem to be the best number of times to meet. This same question remains unsettled in adult group therapy and in individual psychotherapy.

The duration of a session varies also. In most of the prescriptions for group psychotherapy of children, the duration of a session is partly a function of mechanics and proclivities of the therapist and partly determined by the availability of the children and other factors. Once again, no scientific study has compared the various possible time intervals in a controlled way. The amount of time per session usually is determined by the child's concentration span and the type of group psychotherapy involved. With psychotic children, such as those reported by Speers and Lansing (1968), a session might continue for hours. Smolen and Lifton (1966) reported on brief sessions.

The question of the length of therapy is answered in view of the situation. In group psychotherapy to prepare children for individual or residential treatment, Ganter, Yeakel, and Polansky (1965) used it for three years with positive results. Duration of treatment is a function of the continued availability of the child, the parents' commitment to bring the child to the setting if it is nonresidential, and other factors. Since group psychotherapy usually is not considered the only treatment for children, depending upon the diagnostic category, other factors may determine discharge and treatment rather than the group psychotherapy itself. Some groups are set up on a time-limited basis. Burdon and Neely (1966) used a short-term group therapy approach in their work with boys aged seven to twelve who showed repeated school failure. The therapy, limited to from three to five months, with involvement of child, mother, and father in mandatory group therapy, was held once a week for ninety minutes. The families studied were Caucasian and culturally homogeneous, mostly "blue-collar" and office workers. The entire treatment program with intact family structure was organized around the concept of family responsibility and involvement.

Instrumentation in Psychotherapy

Instrumentation in the life sciences and in psychotherapy is increasing. Schwitzgebel (1968) reviewed about fifty electromechanical devices used for psychotherapeutic purposes. In time, we will apply these techniques to groups of children. Skinner (1938, 1953) emphasized the function of contingent consequences in shaping and maintaining behavior. A logical outgrowth was the designing of an apparatus for more precise environmental control and response measurement. Simple mechanical devices have been devised for prompting the behavior of preverbal children (Biddleston, 1953). Quarti and Renaud (1962) invented an apparatus for the treatment of chronic constipation. Thus, technology finally is moving into psychotherapy and, more specifically, behavior therapy.

The implications for treating children in groups become clearer as therapists speak of ignoring the person (intrapsychically speaking) and altering the relevant environment via mechanical means. Schwitzgebel (1968) suggests:

> An unhappy mother might be taught to love her incontinent child in order to modify his behavior, but the mutual frustration might be avoided by the use of a toilet-training device which functions somewhat independently of the mother's knowledge or mood. The improvement of psychotherapeutic endeavors can likely be hastened by the invention of better social mouse traps.

Behavioral Techniques

The need for shortcuts, as well as public pressure on psychotherapists to produce results, will lead to increasing instrumentation and a behavioral mechanistic approach to child therapy. After all, children rarely have friends at the bar of justice. The unhappy adult's complaints bring children to the attention of therapists. It is reasonable to assume that psychotherapists who practice in the decade ahead will be heavily pressured by a culture which insists on teaching children to conform. Intensive psychotherapy is increasingly challenged as new "gimmicks" are brought to the field of psychotherapy. It is unfortunate that behavior therapists are unaware of much psychoanalytic experience. For example, long before behavior therapists used the technique, Eissler (1949), who was psychoanalytically trained, gave money at times to juvenile delinquents in treatment. He was aware of the dangers in such an approach. Currently, therapists who use the technique seem less aware.

Desensitization techniques, originally used by Wolpe (1958) and Lazarus (1961) and later by Paul and Shannon (1966) in work with college students aged nineteen to twenty-four, lend themselves readily to work with children. For years, experienced clinicians have used behavioral techniques selectively. Toussieng and Schechter (1967) use group therapy for children until introspection becomes more tolerable; then they use individual psychotherapy. Using group therapy selectively, they note that schizoid children with fears of social contact do poorly in groups until they have gained more social confidence in individual psychotherapy, at which time group therapy is helpful in developing better social skills. In residential treatment settings, the child is provided with an environment which can accept his assaults without retaliation. Here the child often joins a group and interacts and then may withdraw while he works through some areas without pressure. Clement and Milne (1967) used play therapy groups with eleven third-grade boys. They applied a behavioral model with children who were referred by their teachers because of shy, withdrawn behavior. They used operant conditioning techniques, including brass to-kens which could be used to buy other tokens, trinkets, and candy. Again, they were apparently unaware of the early work done by pioneers in child therapy who used reward mechanisms. While their study is well designed and makes a contribution to research in child therapy, their results are not significant.

Stimulated by the work of Paul and Shannon (1966), Kondas (1967) in Czechoslovakia worked with groups of twenty-three children using group desensitization as a method for reducing stage fright. His results were generally positive, but his goals were limited. Among behavior thera-pists, Clement and Milne (1967) may be considered the strongest expo-nents of operant conditioning. Often, behavior therapists use simple rein-forcement techniques, such as letting the child talk into a tape recorder. Schwitzgebel and Kolb (1964) describe this in detail in their work with adolescent delinquents. Occasionally, investigators in allied fields become enthusiastic about working with groups of children and adolescents. They may or may not have positive results, but there is rarely a theoretical rationale behind the work. An example of this is in the report of Laeder and Francis (1968), in which they provided group therapy for stutterers in junior-senior high school in a rural setting. They noted the isolation of students in rural settings and praised the idea of workshops in rural settings.

Psychodrama has been used for children of all ages. Boulanger (1965) reports on a most fascinating use of this form of therapy in a technique he terms *group analytic psychodrama*. He suggests: "Psychodrama offers the unique possibility of meeting the therapeutic needs of the latency child by using action for a symbolic dramatization of his conflicts." He uses a plot which is enacted by the patients and co-therapists.

Personality of Therapist

No studies on the personality patterns of therapists are known or have been reported. A few reports delineate the role of the gender of the thera-pists. Some people assume that if there is female and male, the children react as if the therapists were creating duplications of the mother-father initial role relationships to the children. The gender of the therapist often is immaterial except in working with delinquent or incorrigible boys who have tremendous acting out problems. It would be difficult for most women to handle these situations without the help of some forceful agent, presumably the male therapist or co-therapist.

FAMILY THERAPY

Family therapy in its multiple variations includes children in a group therapy situation. Environmental factors determine frequency, numbers in the group, and the format used. Wilmer, Marks, and Pogue (1966) began an experiment in group therapy at San Quentin Prison in 1964. They included thirteen inmates in group treatment with their wives and their thirty-five children, aged two to seventeen years, who met monthly at the prison. The children's group was largely oriented around game playing and was devoted to helping the children work through feelings about fantasy fathers who ostensibly had deserted them.

The rationale was based on the work of Anna Freud and her associate, Burlingham, in their study (1944) of fatherless children in England during World War II. They noticed the children's intense and persistent attachment to a fantasy father. In the case of the fantasy father, the child replaced the long lost or missing father with an omnipotent father, endowed with all the desired elements of the benign parent. Or the child went to the opposite extreme and imagined the father as hating, rejecting, and cruel.

Wilmer and his colleagues met with the entire family for thirty to forty minutes and then divided the participants into three groups: husbands and wives, children under nine years of age, and children over nine years of age. While Wilmer's sample may be considered atypical, his findings may be relevant for therapy with disordered family settings, such as hard-core poverty settings. He found that initial separation of the participants, with the children meeting in a group separate from the parents, reinforced the children's separation anxiety as well as the parents' suspicion about what the youngsters were saying about the mothers and fathers. Finally, the families met together, and then at the children's request the children met alone. A female psychiatric nurse and a male correctional officer led the children's group.

Much rewarding work remains to be done in correlating family therapy, parents' groups, and children's groups. Most therapists agree that concomitant therapy with the parents is helpful. Some therapists believe that parental psychotherapy, such as a mothers' group, will be sufficient and more than adjunctive to remedying the problems with preschool through latency-age children. Multiple impact therapy can serve as both a diagnostic instrument and an intake device in family therapy. In these circumstances, one often sees clearly how the child patient can serve as the emotional radar of the family (Ganter, Yeakel, and Polansky, 1965; Macgregor, 1964; Speers and Lansing, 1964).

CONCLUSIONS

For group therapy of children, the decade ahead should reflect the moves toward a mechanistic approach to psychotherapy. The literature reveals a paucity of clear thinking concerning therapy of children. We may anticipate more contributions from social psychologists and academic contributors, which should be welcomed by struggling clinicians. Rosenbaum

(1965, 1969) has called attention to the confusion exhibited by clinicians as they plunge ahead without studying the ethical and philosophical issues involved in psychotherapy. The current emphasis on immediate consumption and instant gratification, the antithesis of the much-vaunted Puritan ethic, which stressed the saving of money, the postponement of desires, and the pursuit of long-range goals, is bound to be reflected in treatment goals in work with children. It is critical that issues be studied by clinicians, who often enter community settings, particularly hard-core poverty areas, with minimal awareness of the social structure that is being disturbed (Heacock, 1966).

Another intriguing aspect is the extremely broad extension of group therapy into social areas. A significant aid to clinicians is the work of Makarenko (1936), a Soviet educator, who was hostile to psychological concepts and believed they were of little help to him. A brief summary of his work is germane. After the Bolshevik Revolution and World War I, the Russians were faced with the problem of seven million war orphans, called "wild boys," roaming the countryside in packs. Makarenko set himself to the task of reclaiming these children. He became disillusioned in attempting to find help in the work of educators preceding him and became so bitter that he developed a profound antagonism toward any educational procedure which stressed psychology. His hero was Maxim Gorki, and he founded a colony for youngsters named the Gorki Colony. His aim was to develop a consciousness of the primacy of the group participatory leadership rather than supervisory leadership. He finally developed the concept of the collective, a concept found in the Israeli kibbutzim. When we consider that he worked with children from shattered family groups, in which there was destruction of traditional values, his work shows relevance for today's workers in community mental health. While the reader may disagree with the uses made of his concepts in the Soviet culture, his experiences and conclusions are important (Makarenko, 1936, 1953, 1954, 1955). To Soviet parents, he is what Spock is to American parents.

What can practicing clinicians look forward to in the decade ahead as they contemplate group therapy with children? The trend is toward a pragmatic view. However, theoretical positions overlap. Clinicians find their way to heaven only to find that someone else has been there before them, but the newcomer did not know about the previous voyage. Greater commonalities among the findings of different schools emerge more consistently than the advocates care to recognize.

In a specific review of the psychotherapy of phobias, a term used with roughly the same meaning by psychotherapists of many orientations— behavior therapists, psychoanalysts, school-phobia workers, and logotherapists—Andrews (1966) found that the psychotherapists were consistent in recognizing the underlying problem with school phobias. All the different schools noted the subtle collusion of work among family members, including the child, to prevent loss and separation. Thus, Fenichel (1945) noted that a common factor in all phobias is the regression to childhood, and this represents the psychoanalytic view. In describing a patient, Lazarus (1964), a devoted exponent of behavior therapy, states: "Overprotective and anxious parents provided abundant opportunity for the acquisition of neurotic habits (phobias)." A major disagreement among practitioners is exemplified by Haley (1963) and Fry (1962), who consider symptoms as tactics in human relationships, and by the behavior therapists who reject the idea that there is any purposive element in neurotic symptoms (Wolpe, 1958).

There are many indications for the use of group psychotherapy as a treatment modality. Some indications can be described as situational, when the therapist works in a reformatory setting in which group psychotherapy seems to have reached the adolescents better than individual treatment. Economics indicate therapy groups, since more patients can be reached simultaneously. Perhaps more appropriate would be the necessity to use a treatment procedure that will best help the child for a given age, developmental stage, and type of problem. In the younger age group, the child's social hunger and his potential need for peer acceptance help determine his suitability for group therapy. Criteria for unsuitability are controversial.

The results of group psychotherapy with children are difficult to evaluate. Favorable results were reported in one study of nondirective play therapy and another of delinquents in which control groups were used. Evaluating the results of group psychotherapy of children proves as difficult as assessing individual psychotherapy of children. Since few studies have been controlled for time as well as for other factors, including follow-up evaluations (Novick, 1965), one can say that group therapy does not supplant or replace individual therapy. It is a tool with which the therapist might become familiar by using it under supervision. In crowded child psychiatric clinics, for example, various group techniques help relieve pressures at intake, diagnosis, and treatment levels. Impressionistically, certain results can be indicated. Group psychotherapy helps children feel unconditionally accepted by the therapist and the group members.

Failures can be seen as part of each child's development. Complexes of feelings and ideation gain expression. Feelings of guilt, anxiety, inferiority, and insecurity find relief. Group psychotherapy of children is still young and undeveloped in its full potential for study and treatment.

BIBLIOGRAPHY

Aichorn, A., *Wayward Youth* (New York: Viking, 1935).
Andrews, J. D. W., "Psychotherapy of Phobias," *Psychol. Bull.*, 66:445-480, 1966.

Anker, J. M., and Walsh, R. P., "Group Psychotherapy: A Special Activity Program and Group Structure in the Treatment of Chronic Schizophrenics," *J. Consult. Psychol.*, 25:475-481, 1961.

Anthony, E. J., "Age and Syndrome in Group Psychotherapy," in A. L. Kodis and C. Wineck, eds., *Topical Problems of Psychotherapy* (New York: S. Karger, 1965) 5:80-89.

Astrachan, M., "Group Psychotherapy with Mentally Retarded Female Adolescents and Adults," *Am. J. Ment. Def.*, 60:152-156, 1955.

Beard, J. H., Goertzel, V., and Pearce, A. J., "The Effectiveness of Activity Group Therapy with Chronically Regressed Adult Schizophrenics," *Int. J. Psychoanal.*, 8:123-136, 1958.

Berschling, C., and Homann, J., "A Proposal for the Establishment of a Group Psychotherapy Program for Adolescents," *Psychiat. Comm.*, 8(1): 17-36, 1966.

Biddleston, R. J., Time and activity clock device, Patent No. 2,629, *U.S. Patent Gazette*, 186, 1953.

Block, S. L., "Multi-leadership as a Teaching and Therapeutic Tool in Group Psychotherapy," *Comp. Psychiat.*, 2(4):211-218, 1961.

———, "Some Notes on Transference in Group Psychotherapy," *Comp. Psychiat.*, 7(1):31-38, 1966.

Boulanger, J. B., "Group Psychoanalytic Therapy in Child Psychiatry," *Canad. Psychiat. Assn. J.*, 6:272-275, 1961.

———, "Group Analytic Psychodrama in Child Psychiatry," *Canad. Psychiat. Assn. J.*,10:427-241, 1965.

Burdon, Arthur P., and Neely, James H., "Chronic School Failure in Boys: A Short-term Group Therapy and Education Approach," *Am. J. Psychiat.*, 122:1211-1219, 1966.

Buxbaum, E., "Transference and Group Formation in Children and Adolescents," in *The Psychoanalytic Study of the Child*, Vol. 1 (New York: International Universities Press, 1945), pp. 351-365.

———, *Your Child Makes Sense* (New York: International Universities Press, 1949).

Case, M. E., "The Forgotten Ones: An Exploratory Project in the Use of Group Activities for the Therapy of Deteriorated Psychotic Patients," *Smith College Studies in Social Work*, 21:199-231, 1951.

Clement, P. W., and Milne, D. C., "Group Play Therapy and Tangible Reinforcers Used to Modify the Behavior of Eight Year Old Boys," *Beh. Res. and Ther.*, 5:301-312, 1967.

Cooley, C., *Human Nature and the Social Order* (New York: Scribner's, 1902).

———, *Social Organization* (New York: Scribner's, 1909).

———, *Social Process* (New York: Scribner's, 1918).

Coolidge, J. C., and Grunebaum, M. G., "Individual and Group Therapy of a Latency Age Child," *Int. J. Group Psychother.*, 14:84-96, 1964.

Cowen, E. L., "Psychotherapy and Play Techniques with the Exceptional Child and Youth," in W. M. Cruickshank, ed., *Psychology of Exceptional Children and Youth* (Englewood Cliffs, N.J.: Prentice-Hall, 1962).

Durkin, H. E., *The Group in Depth* (New York: International Universities Press, 1965).

Eissler, K., ed. *Searchlights on Delinquency* (New York: International Universities Press, 1949).

Epstein, N., "Activity Group Therapy," *Int. J. Group Psychother.*, 10:180-194, 1960.

Fenichel, O., *Psychoanalytic Theory of Neurosis* (New York: Norton, 1945).

Freud, A., and Burlingham, D. T., *Infants Without Families* (New York: International Universities Press, 1944).

Frey, L. A., and Kolodny, R. L., "Group Treatment for the Alienated Child in the School," *Int. J. Group Psychother.*, 16:321-337, 1966.

Fry, W. F., "The Marital Context of an Anxiety Syndrome," *Fam. Proc.*, 1:245-252, 1962.

Ganter, G., Yeakel, M., and Polansky, N. A., "Intermediary Group Treatment of Inaccessible Children," *Am. J. Orthopsychiat.*, 35:739-746, 1965.

Ginott, H., *Group Psychotherapy with Children* (New York: McGraw-Hill, 1961).

Goldin, P. C., "A Review of Children's Reports of Parent Behaviors," *Psychol. Bull.*, 71:222-236, 1969.

Gratton, L., and Rizzo, A. E., "Group Therapy with Young Psychotic Children," *Int. J. Group Psychother.*, 19:63-71, 1969.

Haley, J., *Strategies of Psychotherapy* (New York: Grune & Stratton, 1963).

Heacock, D. R., "Modifications of the Standard Techniques for Out-patient Group Psychotherapy with Delinquent Boys," *J. N. M. A.*, 58:44-47, 1966.

Heinicke, C. M., and Goldman, A., "Research on Psychotherapy with Children: A Review and Suggestions for Further Study," *Am. J. Orthopsychiat.*, 30:483-494, 1960.

Hyman, H., "The Psychology of Status," *Arch. Psychol.*, 269, 1942.

Kondas, O., "Reduction of Examination Anxiety and 'Stage Fright' by Group Desensitization and Relaxation," *Beh. Res. and Ther.*, 5:275-281, 1967.

Kraft, Irvin A., "Group Therapy," in A. M. Freedman and H. I. Kaplan, eds., *Comprehensive Textbook of Psychiatry* (Baltimore: Williams & Wilkins, 1967), pp. 1463-1468.

Laeder, R., and Francis, W. C., "Stuttering Workshops: Group Therapy in a Rural High School Setting," *J. Sp. Hear. Dis.*, 33:38-41, 1968.

Lazarus, A. A., "Group Therapy of Phobic Disorders by Systematic Desensitization," *J. Abnorm. Soc. Psychol.*, 63:504-510, 1961.

———, "Behavior Therapy with Identical Twins," *Beh. Res. and Ther.*, 2:313-320, 1969.

Macgregor, R., *Multiple Impact Therapy with Families* (New York: McGraw-Hill, 1964).

Makarenko, A. S., *The Road to Life* (tr. by Stephen Garry), Vol. 1 (London: Stanley Nott, 1936).

———, *Learning to Live* (Moscow: Foreign Languages Publishing House, 1953).

———, *A Book for Parents* (Moscow: Foreign Languages Publishing House, 1954).

————, *The Road of Life: An Epic of Education* (Moscow: Foreign Languages Publishing House, 1955).

Matis, E. E., "Psychotherapeutic Tools for Parents," *J. Sp. Hear. Dis.*, 26:164-170, 1961.

Mead, G. H., *Mind, Self and Society* (Chicago: University of Chicago Press, 1934).

Moe, M., "Group Psychotherapy with Parents of Psychotic and Neurotic Children," *Acta Psychother. Psychosom.*, 8:134 and 146, 1960.

Mullan, H., and Rosenbaum, M., *Group Psychotherapy* (New York: Free Press, 1962).

Neham, S., "Psychotherapy in Relation to Mental Deficiency," *Am. J. Ment. Def.*, 55:557-572, 1951.

Novick, J. I., "Comparison Between Short-term Group and Individual Psychotherapy in Effecting Change in Nondesirable Behavior in Children," *Int. J. Group Psychother.*, 15:366-373, 1965.

Paul, G. L., and Shannon, D. T., "Treatment of Anxiety Through Systematic Desensitization in Therapy Groups," *J. Abnorm. Psychol.*, 71:125-135, 1966.

Quarti, C., and Renaud, J., "A New Treatment of Constipation by Conditioning: A Preliminary Report," *La Clinique*, 57:577-583, 1962.

Rosenbaum, M., "Group Psychotherapy," in B. B. Wolman, ed., *Handbook of Clinical Psychology* (New York: McGraw-Hill, 1965).

————, "Current Controversies in Psychoanalytic Group Psychotherapy and What They Mask," in L. Eron and R. Callahan, eds., *The Relation of Theory to Practice in Psychotherapy* (Chicago: Aldine, 1969).

Sager, C. J., "Combined Individual and Group Psychoanalysis, Symposium. 1959: 2. Concurrent Individual and Group Analytic Psychotherapy," *Am. J. Orthopsychiat.*, 30:225-241, 1960.

Scheidlinger, S., "Experimental Group Treatment of Severely Deprived Latency-aged Children," *Am. J. Orthopsychiat.*, 30:356-368, 1960.

Schwartz, M., "Analytic Group Psychotherapy," *Int. J. Group Psychother.*, 10:195-212, 1960.

Schwitzgebel, R. L., "Survey of Electromechanical Devices for Behavior Modification," *Psychol. Bull.*, 70:444-450, 1968.

————, and Kolb, D. A., "Inducing Behavior Change in Adolescent Delinquents," *Beh. Res. and Ther.*, 1:297-304, 1964.

Sherif, M., *An Outline of Social Psychology* (New York: Harper & Row, 1948).

————, "Superordinate Goals in the Reduction of Intergroup Conflict," *Am. J. Sociol.*, 63:349-358, 1958.

————, and Cantril, H., *The Psychology of Ego-involvements* (New York: Wiley, 1947).

Sherif, M., Harvey, O. J., White, B. J., Hood, W. R., and Sherif, C. W., *Intergroup Conflict and Cooperation: The Robbers Cave Experiment* (Norman, Okla.: Institute of Group Relations, 1961).

Sherif, M., and Sherif, C. W., *Groups in Harmony and Tension* (New York: Harper & Row, 1953).

Skinner, B. F., *The Behavior of Organisms* (New York: Appleton-Century-Crofts, 1938).

———, *Science and Human Behavior* (New York: Macmillan, 1953).

Slavson, S. R., ed., *The Practice of Group Therapy* (New York: International Universities Press, 1947).

———, ed., *The Fields of Group Psychotherapy* (New York: International Universities Press, 1956).

———, "The Scope and Aims of the Evaluation Study," *Int. J. Group Psychother.*, 10:176-179, 1960.

———, *A Textbook in Analytic Group Psychotherapy* (New York: International Universities Press, 1964). (a)

———, "Para-analytic Group Psychotherapy: A Treatment of Choice for Adolescents," *Pathways in Child Guidance*, 6:1-15, 1964. (b)

Smolen, E. M., and Lifton, N., "A Special Treatment Program for Schizophrenic Children in a Child Guidance Clinic," *Am. J. Orthopsychiat.*, 36:7736-7742, 1966.

Sobel, D., and Geller, J. J., "A Type of Group Psychotherapy in the Children's Unit of a Mental Hospital," *Psychiat. Quart.*, 38:262-270, 1964.

Speers, R. W., and Lansing, C., "Group Psychotherapy with Preschool Psychotic Children and Collateral Group Therapy of Their Parents: A Preliminary Report of the First Two Years," *Am. J. Orthopsychiat.*, 34:659-666, 1964.

———, "Some Genetic-dynamic Considerations in Childhood Symbiotic Psychosis," *J. Am. Acad. Child Psychiat.*, 7:329-349, 1968.

Sternlicht, M., "Psychotherapeutic Techniques Useful with the Mentally Retarded: A Review and Critique," *Psychiat. Quart.*, 39:84-90, 1965.

Stevenson, H. W., and Knights, R. M., "Social Reinforcement with Normal and Retarded Children as a Function of Pretraining," *Am. J. Ment. Def.*, 66:866-871, 1962.

Thibaut, J., and Kelley, H., *The Social Psychology of Groups* (New York: Wiley, 1959).

Toussieng, P. W., and Schechter, M. D., "Treatment of Emotional Problems in Childhood," *J. Okla. State Med. Assn.*, 198-205, 1967.

Turner, R. H., "The Contributions of Muzafer Sherif to Sociology," Paper read at the American Psychological Association meeting, New York, September 4, 1966.

Wilmer, H. A., Marks, I., and Pogue, E., "Group Treatment of Prisoners and their Families," *Ment. Hyg.*, 50(3):380-389, 1966.

Wolpe, J., *Psychotherapy by Reciprocal Inhibition* (Stanford, Calif.: Stanford University Press, 1958).

47

GROUP THERAPY AND
DRUG THERAPY

R. A. Sandison

The purpose of this paper is to examine some of the common ground between those psychiatrists whose approach to the patient is drug oriented and those who are concerned with group dynamics. At present, there is some evidence that the two groups are becoming more polarized. Those who rely on drugs incline to the medical model and toward an organic view of mental illness, endowing such conditions as schizophrenia and manic-depressive illness with the quality of chronicity. The widespread use of long-acting fluphenazines for the former, and of long-term lithium treatment for the latter, reflects this philosophy. The psychotherapist, on the other hand, may shun diagnostic labels and think of his patients as "people." He is consequently distrustful of drugs and looks for the possibility of radical change in those whom he is trying to help. Certain assumptions also tend to be made about the kinds of patients these two groups of psychiatrists are supposed to help. The organic psychiatrist leans more toward psychosis, and if he enters the field of neurosis and personality disorder, he thinks in terms of drugs and behavior therapy. On the other hand, both group therapists and individual therapists lean in the direction of neurosis, following the classical dictum of Freud that psychotics are too narcissistic to respond to a dynamic approach.

It is worth noting another anomaly at this point. When the group therapist changes his hat, so to speak, and becomes a T-group trainer, he is then supposed to exclude those who are "looking for therapy" through sensitivity training, while any psychotic manifestations during or after such training are regarded as undesirable and to be avoided.

All psychiatrists, however, would do well to note certain current trends which have, in addition, particular relevance for group psychotherapists. It is, for example, by no means certain that the classical concepts concerning the nature and prognosis in the major psychoses hold good when these conditions are studied in their natural environments. Just as the biologists have found that animals studied in the wild behave very differently from those in the laboratory or in zoos, so, until recently, almost the whole of our data about psychotics was derived from studying them in those zoos or laboratories called mental hospitals. Community studies on schizophrenics, such as those by Leff and Wing[1] and Hirsch and his associates[2] show big differences between the behavior of patients in the community and those in hospital. Another important series of trends concerns the concept of mental illness, and particularly psychosis, itself. Laing and associates[3] have examined schizophrenic behavior in the light of family interaction and social pressures. Szasz[4] has brought into question institutional concepts of madness as being based on earlier, and now discarded, mythologies, a theme which echoes similar sentiments expressed on this side of the Atlantic by Gordon Rattray Taylor[5] and Alex Comfort.[6] Finally, psychoanalysis itself is emerging from the fetters of the oedipus complex, and in the process, psychotics are being seen as no more than a special case. Among the French School, Deleuze and Guattari[7] appear to be leaders in a movement which sees the unconscious less as a stage in the theatre, and more as a factory for production. In this connection, a recent review of their book[8] states: "Psychotics are now emerging from the humanitarian ghetto which deprived their discourse of meaning; the affinities between normality and psychosis as its full realisation may one day seem closer than those between normality and neurosis, which may eventually appear as the only true mental illness."

The implications of these changes are considerable. Psychotics may perhaps turn out to be just as, or more, amenable to group therapy as neurotics, and classical polarization between drugs and psychotherapy may turn out to have been based on false assumptions. It will, therefore, be worthwhile examining the propositions that group psychotherapy can substantially benefit psychotics, and that drug therapy does not exclude a psychodynamic approach, but is rather complementary to it.

MODE OF ACTION OF DRUGS AND THE PLACEBO RESPONSE

Ancient chemical methods of treatment were directed toward the expelling of real or suspected causal agents of disease from the body. Out of sympathetic magic and the empirical use of galenicals homeopathic medicine arose. Findlay dates the commencement of modern chemotherapeutics from the discovery of arsphenamine by Ehrlich and Hata in 1910. The great advances in this field did not occur until the introduction of prontosil rubrum by Domagk in 1935, rapidly to be followed by sulphonamides, antibiotics, and other specifics. In psychiatry, as we know, the first approach to a specific remedy was the use by Delay in 1952 of chlorpromazine for schizophrenia, insulin having proved to be nonspecific and later to be nonactive in the treatment of this condition.

The so-called drug era in psychiatry has been promoted by the philosophy that psychiatric patients are ill people with symptoms, that they will get better when those symptoms disappear, and that the search must go on for those drugs which will relieve the symptoms. From an early date, however, it was evident that psychotropic drugs and psychiatric illnesses did not behave in the same causal way as illness and drugs do in general medicine. Presumably penicillin will cure pneumonia, provided the causal organism is sensitive, equally well in any country or culture in the world, whereas not only is proof lacking concerning the efficacy of most drugs used in psychiatric practice, but their beneficial effect varies from one country to another, and even between different wards of the same hospital. Patients are not only known to respond better to certain drugs, such as the benzodiazapines, when prescribed by an optimistic physician, but many psychiatric patients improve for a time on inert tablets, the so-called placebo response.

It is also known that schizophrenics may relapse despite being on regular medication with long-acting injections of fluphenazine. At the same time it is known that many inpatients in psychiatric hospitals, and a high proportion of outpatients, do not take their medication, often without deleterious effects. The power of the tablet, or of the injection, must therefore reside to some extent in the doctor, while the good results reported with long-acting fluphenazines for schizophrenics in the community overlook the fact that these are the patients having regular reassuring contact with so-called Modecate Clinics,[9] or being visited regularly by community nurses. This is not to say that drugs do not contribute effectively to the care of psychiatric patients, but as I have tried to show in a recent paper,[10] depressed patients may be denied the psychotherapy they need because doctors have too great an emotional investment in the power of antidepressant drugs.

THE HALLUCINOGENIC DRUG ERA

It is perhaps not without significance that coincidental with the advent of those drugs, such as phenothiazines, which control and suppress symptoms, there arose an esoteric movement which rested on the use of mind-expanding, fantasy-creating hallucinogenic drugs such as L.S.D. (Lysergic acid diethylamide). Those who practiced psychotherapy assisted by L.S.D. in the 1950's and 1960's were rewarded not only by much insight into the nature of neurosis, character, and personality disorders and many cures resulting not from the suppression of symptoms, but also by the mind-revealing possibilities of L.S.D. which facilitated personal growth when assisted by a competent therapist.

Observations on naturally occurring hallucinogens suggested that not only was their use confined to a chosen few, but that group activity was closely connected with their use. These observations fit in with our knowledge of the use of powerful drugs, amulets, or charms in many societies until recently. Such was the power attributed to the remedy that responsibility for its use was divided among the group who gathered round the afflicted person. In some countries the group is also employed to ward off the evil god held responsible for the disease.[11] The secrets of the apothecaries and others were closely guarded, and there was frequent rivalry between the medical man and the priest as to who had the more effective remedy. In the years before homeopathy was practiced the principle of treatment was, according to Culpeper:[12] "All diseases are cured by their contraries, but all parts of the body maintained by their likes." Thus the more serious diseases were held to be curable only by remedies of an obscure nature which were expensive and difficult to prepare and which had to be administered by a person of undoubted authority supported by the utterances of the group with which he himself was identified, e.g., by the prayers or incantations of the people.

The Anglo-Saxons do not appear to have recognized group influences so greatly as more primitive peoples in relation to drug taking. According to Wasson and Wasson,[13] the American Indians eating the hallucinogenic mushrooms do so in a group and do not themselves expect a curative effect; they only ask a question and expect a prophetic answer. Thus they frequently take the mushrooms for advice when someone is ill. This ritual has something in common with the Chinese casting of hexagrams mentioned in the *I Ching*,[14] in that the particular time at which the experiment is carried out is important, a group of people must be present, and a definite question must be asked. As to how the answer is given, it is clear that the primitives believe that the gods speak to them through the mushroom. We might say in the language of contemporary psychology that the archetypes are raised into consciousness as hallucinations or ideas which can be communicated to others. The Wassons reproduce a sixteenth century Mexican drawing in which there are three mushrooms on one side, a man eating them in the center, and a god behind him who is speaking through the mushroom. This, in passing, is exactly what one feels about the action of L.S.D.—that it compels the unconscious to speak and that the archetypes appear in consciousness in the form of images, thoughts, feelings, and sensations which are strange and unusual but which are nevertheless part of the subject concerned.

It is likely that in ancient times the use of drugs was attended by a group, and that the individuals taking part had to expend some effort, mental or physical or both, if the value of the substance was to be realized.

Dale[15] points out that the curative value of drugs in the sixteenth to eighteenth centuries was proportionate to their rarity, value, or difficulty of preparation, and this must be an indication of the psychological power inherent in the preparations. One can therefore see the necessity for the group being present, dissolving the magical power of the drug lest it should prove too dangerous for the patient. In ancient legends the more effective drugs were also dangerous to life. Now these same drugs or their modern equivalents have become debased, sold in vast quantities over the counters of drugstores, or worse, dispensed for next to nothing on the doctor's prescription, demanding from the patient no effort for their collection or preparation and no contribution from him on either a psychic or social level while under their influence.

In retrospect, deep insulin treatment for schizophrenia and L.S.D. treatment for neurosis both relied heavily on group influences for their benefits. Research by Ackman, Harris, and Oldham[16] and by Leyton[17] showed that the insulin did little pharmacologically for the patients, while we believe that the best results with L.S.D. patients were achieved when several patients were treated in one center, where they could meet and mix freely. In such centers they met together in the mornings, separated as each individual faced himself under the L.S.D., and met again to share the experience with one another later in the day. Perhaps even better results were obtained when the patients spent all their treatment time together as a group, which Spencer[18] did with adults, and which the author also did with a group of adolescent girls.

Some of the fantasies experienced by a group of patients undergoing deep insulin treatment are worth recording, since they have relevance to some current work, reported below, which I am carrying out with a group of psychotics. As there are very few reports of psychological material from deep insulin patients, I make no apology for the following inclusions, although the material is now several years old.

One of the best examples of this, in my experience, concerns a young girl who at the beginning of the insulin treatment had a childish fantasy during recovery that she was playing with a ball. Within a few days the fantasy extended to the doctor, and she had an idea on waking that she was playing tennis with him. Finally all the patients were drawn into this game, the patient thinking that she was throwing the ball around to each one in turn. This coincided with clinical improvement. The critical psychological phase for a patient undergoing deep insulin treatment is during the period of recovery from the coma, and one not infrequently finds patients who are afraid of dying during this period and who experience a great struggle to come to consciousness again. There are other patients who object to being brought out of the coma, preferring to remain out of touch with the realities of life, and this is usually associated with a bad prognosis.

Many patients describe the insulin experience as unpleasant, like dying. One of my patients cried out loudly and screamed against death, but at the end of the struggle she saw an urgent need to live and a great impulse came over her to eat, and she stuffed quantities of food into her mouth almost to the point of choking. Another patient, on waking from coma every day, would think she was dead; this went on for weeks without any change, and the patient said "Now I take it for granted that I am dead." Another patient thought she had had a serious operation during treatment; that she was dead and the process of restoration to life was too hard to go through. The interest of these death experiences lies in the fact that they are not entirely individual, for sooner or later the patient becomes concerned about the other members of the group. I had one patient who insisted on being brought round from the coma before any of the other patients because she felt that she could then watch over them and assist in their recovery. Another patient was convinced that I was giving insulin to the other patients to make them die, and on one occasion actually tried to prevent me from giving the injection. Another patient in the course of a group meeting expressed much the same idea, saying: "Why do you put them in a coma? You must be hurting them."

There are psychological reasons for believing that the overcoming of the death experience and of the state of regression induced by insulin are factors of great importance in the patient's recovery. It is well known that both animals and human beings under the influence of danger tend to congregate into groups, and that this has the effect of diminishing the individual fear of death. There is therefore every reason to believe that the gathering of patients undergoing insulin treatment into a group is most desirable. One further example can be given of the need for a group. A female patient, twenty-eight years of age, married and with a child, had a schizophrenic breakdown in which she thought she was being hypnotized. She was confused, aggressive, and restless. As she was so disturbed, insulin treatment was carried out in a single room. She became progressively more regressed, incontinent, and degraded. She later explained that she believed there were three dragons on one arm and three on the other which were trying to make her completely insane. Her remedy was to retreat into infancy so that she became childish and incontinent, and she actually believed herself to be taking refuge in the womb. As soon as she was transferred to the insulin room she started to recover. She had a fantasy that on recovery from treatment the bedclothes became like a tunnel and that she was born over the end of the bed. We could not help being impressed by this change after the patient was removed from the isolation of the single room.

Jung, analyzing the different forms of rebirth, considers that the rebirth or transmutation experiences of groups sharing a common experience are a form of identification with a group, and that this is something entirely different from experiencing the rebirth in oneself. These insulin experiences seem to be both; there is evidence that the transmutation experience is personal and that the group is required both for its completion and its performance.

Another female patient, after thirty-four comas, had an idea that those undergoing insulin treatment could not endure legal marriage and that they either had to experience natural unions or else remain virgins. This patient, herself married, felt after the next coma that she was no longer married, that the group and her husband were mutually exclusive. She said it was like being married to the group instead of to him. In the thirty-sixth coma this notion was developed, and she feared that the treatment had turned her into a harlot. We have in this experience the chief feature of the initiation rites—namely, subjection to those in authority, pain and discomfort of the treatment, segregation in the hospital, emergence into the group, and acceptance of the patient when he is better as a more adult and balanced individual. One may conclude that these results can be obtained only through giving the drug, in this case insulin, to the patients as a group. The phenomena can quite easily be demonstrated and worked out by anybody who cares to look for them, and it seems unfortunate that studies on the effects of insulin treatment have not included any commentary on these important psychological factors. Whether insulin is the only method of bringing out these phenomena remains to be seen. Leyton[19] has reported on the treatment results in two identical groups, one of which received distilled water injections and the other insulin. The results in the two groups were similar. Furthermore, she adds in a personal communication, some of the patients in the placebo group thought they had been in a coma after the injections.

REPORT ON THERAPY WITH A GROUP OF PSYCHOTICS USING SOME ENCOUNTER GROUP TECHNIQUES

From the time of Pinel there have been reports which suggest that confrontation between psychotics in a group can have beneficial results. It is now generally accepted that the good results achieved in the treatment of schizophrenia by deep insulin were not only due to the patients spending much time as a small group with staff whom they knew and trusted, but also to the close physical contact the staff had with the patients.

Banerji[20] led a small school of Indian psychotherapists who believed that the problem for the schizophrenic lay in his inability to trust others, and in his consequent feelings of isolation and rejection by social groups. He designed exercises, perhaps the forerunner of current encounter group techniques, to improve trust. For example, he would range the patients together in two opposing lines, whereupon one group advanced on the other, shouting as they did so, with the object of taking one of the other group into their midst, which was resisted. In another exercise patients walked on a broad plank a foot or so from the ground, the sides of which were then folded down to make a narrow plank, thus compelling the patient to accept a steadying hand from the other patients.

With these ideas in mind, it occurred to me that there was scope for an experimental group for psychotics, although experience had shown that such patients could not tolerate the tensions of the conventional therapy group.

The setting for this group was the Psychiatric Day Centre in Southampton, England, which is currently caring for about fifty patients. The majority of them are suffering from neurotic and personality disorders, though in general we do not apply diagnostic labels to this group of people. Those attending this Day Centre are cared for by a multidisciplinary team consisting of doctors, social workers, occupational therapists, and nurses, together with an art therapist and one or two part-time specialists.

We observed at the beginning of 1973 that there was a group of patients, some seven or eight in number, at the Day Centre who stood out as manifesting psychotic symptoms. This was a rather unusually large number for this particular unit. The therapy for the majority of patients consists of fairly intensive group and individual psychotherapy, the group therapy being partly conducted on formal lines, and partly of a looser and more spontaneous nature. It, therefore, seemed reasonable to put the psychotic patients into a group, and we thought that in a very small way we might try to repeat the conditions of deep insulin treatment. It was therefore decided that this group of patients should meet formally with four members of staff for thirty to forty-five minutes each day, and that in between times these members of staff would take some special responsibility for this particular group of patients. The group started meeting on February 6, 1973, and has continued for three months. This report is the result of these first three months of the life of the group, and is perhaps significant since insulin treatment generally lasted for about the same period of time.

The following is a brief account of the patients who attended the group:

(1) Miss W. R., aged 22. Her first admission to hospital was in 1967 with an acute schizophrenic illness. She thought she was receiving radio messages which influenced her mind. She was admitted again in 1969 and a further admission was in September 1972. She was discharged to the Day Centre in January 1973.

(2) Miss A. R., aged 28. Her first admission was in April 1970 with a diagnosis of schizophrenia, when she had feelings of influence, visual hallucinations, and thought that television programs referred to her. She was again admitted to hospital in July 1970 and on a third occasion in

August 1970. Her fourth admission lasted from January to July 1972, again with a diagnosis of schizophrenia, when she thought that she was a Lamb of God and that her mind was being controlled. She has attended the Day Centre since 1972.

(3) Mr. R. H., aged 26. He had four hospital admissions starting in 1965 with a diagnosis of schizophrenia. His fifth admission was from October 1972 to January 1973, when he thought that he was controlled by his girlfriend's father, although he had no girlfriend. He came to the Centre in January 1973.

(4) Mr. D. O'M., aged 32. He had three admissions to hospital between 1970 and 1972 with a diagnosis of schizophrenia. He thought he was persecuted by the neighbors and had persistent auditory hallucinations. He came to the Day Centre in January 1973.

(5) Mr. R. B., aged 35. His first admission was in 1970 and a diagnosis was made of a schizophrenic illness of uncertain duration, perhaps about seven years, although the patient's view was that he had been ill since childhood. He believed that he was in contact with God and spirits, that a spaceship would take him to another planet, and that the world would blow up. He had further admissions to hospital in 1971 and 1972. In January 1973 he relapsed and came to the Day Centre as an alternative to admission, when he was totally involved in his fantasies and unable to engage in any activity at home.

(6) Mr. R. G., aged 26. He came to the Day Centre in March 1973 and was, therefore, a late entrant to the Group, and should not perhaps be included in the present series. His talk was very disjointed and his answers were off the point. He thought that his thoughts were repeated inside his head.

(7) Mr. P. B., aged 36. His illness is probably of several years' duration. He was first seen in 1971 and given outpatient treatment. By 1972 there was a fully developed schizophrenic psychosis. He believed the doctors had changed their identity, and he slept with a coil around his bed to keep out "earth vibrations." He attended the Day Centre from January 1973.

(8) Miss H. J. A., aged 35. She was first admitted in 1972 with a diagnosis of depression with an immature personality, but her subsequent investigation at the Day Centre showed a well-developed underlying psychotic process.

(9) Miss H. B., aged 17. She had had three admissions to mental hospitals in 1971, and was admitted again to hospital in December 1972 until February 1973. She started attending the Day Centre from hospital in January 1973. The diagnosis of psychosis was less clear in her case. She had persistent visual hallucinations following an incident at seven years of age when her sister was severely burned in a fire, and following forced sexual intercourse with an older boy when she was fourteen.

(10) Miss V. N., aged 18. First admission 1971 with insidious history of withdrawal, loss of interest, hallucinations, and bizarre delusions. Diagnosis was schizophrenia. Second admission December 1971 to Febru-

ary 1972. Started attending the Day Centre from hospital in January 1973. Diagnosis—still schizophrenia.

After each meeting of the group, the staff met together and recorded things which had happened, so we have a complete record of the events of the group. The following is a very brief account of some of the things which took place during the three months. The first thing that the staff noticed was the extent to which the patients were prepared to talk about themselves and their problems, and the extent to which they were prepared to recognize their feelings and emotions. For example, at early meetings, H.J. started to talk about her childhood and revealed material which had not been recorded previously. V.N., probably the most disturbed member of the group at that time, started to talk about her mental disturbance and her hallucinations. At the third meeting the patients spent nearly all the time talking about religion, and it was clear that the meeting was a curious mixture of psychosis and reality, but as everybody seemed to accept this as being quite reasonable, relatively little anxiety was created. The group showed an early interest in R.H. who said very little, but often spent much of the group time laughing, sometimes quite loudly. The patients often asked him why he did this, but he was not really able to give adequate replies. Sometimes H.J. felt herself laughing in a kind of rapport with him.

From the beginning it had been suggested that the patients and staff sit on cushions on the floor, which is the general pattern of groups at the Centre. R.B. had always sat apart from the others, usually on a chair, but during the first week he joined the rest of the group, saying "I think I might as well join you." It was noticeable that this move helped the patients to talk more about their psychotic experiences. For example, W.R. talked about her voices, and said she thought she had extrasensory perception. During the second week the patients felt some further trust developing, and patients such as R.B. and D.O'M. talked a lot about their problems. R.B. spoke extensively about his religious delusions and his notions that the government was trying to control this planet and other planets. These revelations tended to cause much greater anxiety in the group, and the patients found it more difficult to attend; some had to leave before the end of the meeting.

At about this time the patients started to talk more symbolically, perhaps as a kind of defense against direct revelation. At the start of one meeting they began talking about searching for treasures in the earth. W.R. made the point that the things of childhood were lost forever, and looking back was like searching for buried treasure in one's life. R.B. at about this time said that once a year he had to go to church to get instructions, and this day came up. He was very tense during this period and was asked afterwards whether he had been to church and whether he got these instructions. He said he had been there but had failed to get them because the church was changed as the other people were. Because of the anxiety in the group, the staff felt that this was the moment, at the end of the first fortnight, to introduce some simple trust exercises. These were started on February 21, when all the patients were present, except for V.N. At the beginning of this meeting I reminded the group that we had talked about ways of fostering trust, and I said that I felt we might find ways of showing trust in each other rather than just talking about it. One of the staff then suggested that we should form a close circle and link hands, and there was an immediate response.

We then asked them how they felt. P.B. said that he had never been able to trust therapy but could trust people. D.O.'M. said that he had never been able to trust anyone in his life before, but now felt that he could. W.R. and H.J.A. said that it was very helpful. H.B. said she felt secure, quite different from how she felt on her own. W.R. agreed with her and H.J.A. said she felt peaceful. P.B. said he felt a lot of power and force running round the group. When questioned about this he said it ran from his right hand to his right wrist and arm and out through his left arm, rather as if he were a battery. D.O.'M. said he felt the power but he seemed extremely anxious. Then R.B. was asked how he felt and he said "very uneasy," but appeared quite out of touch with his feelings and saying inappropriate things. He said he had shaken hands with lots of people but they had all let him down. He thought the doctors were praying for magical healing powers. We then asked him if he would feel safer in the center of the group, and as he assented, we put him there and made a circle round him. He then said that he felt like a wet frog.

P.B. had earlier described R.B. as a "theogist" who could move mountains with his will. When he was in the center of the group he said he reminded him of someone on children's television. H.J.A. said she saw R.B. as an object of affection. When he was asked to sit back in the circle, W.R. said to H.J.A., "Perhaps that's why you don't want to sit in the middle because you shy away from affection." We then asked if anyone else would like to go in the middle, but this created some anxiety. The group was then asked to decide how we should close the meeting and, fairly spontaneously, everybody got into a hug in the center.

The same kind of exercise was repeated on the following day, and on February 23 we asked them whether they felt like a group. When I asked them what they saw in common with each other, immediately W.R., D.O.'M., and H.J.A. said that they heard voices. At the end of this meeting H.B., who hadn't said anything through the meeting, said she didn't want to go, as there was something she wanted to talk about. She then commenced talking about her mother, and R.H. joined in by making one of his rare statements, saying that his mother was like that, too, namely that she told lies all the time. H.B. then got extremely angry and started attacking me, saying that she wanted to kill me. Then followed a prolonged abreaction from H.B.—most of the other patients had left, but it was of great interest that R.H. remained throughout and offered assistance at one point. Eventually H.B. calmed down, but we thought that this abreaction was a turning point for her, although she remained very disturbed for some two weeks afterward. It was following this event that she felt safe enough to reveal a great many things in her own life which had not come out before, particularly with regard to the fire, her sexual experiences, and family interaction. Some of these were revealed in the group and some to the staff in individual sessions. She exhibited a great need for close physical contact with the staff, and in several of the subsequent sessions she sat clinging closely to one of the staff, not always the same member.

Space does not permit the introduction of much further anecdotal material, but it may be helpful at this point to mention one or two general happenings during the life of the group. For example, it was noted that the patients did talk about feelings and that they were quite sensitive to the feelings of other patients. P.B., who is certainly one of the more psychotic members of the group, showed considerable sensitivity, saying that there were certain things which he felt he should not talk about at this stage to the other group members for fear of upsetting their feelings. In this we felt that he was correctly judging the situation. In general, the patients exhibited less neurotic behavior than the other patients at the Centre, and this was reflected in their behavior in the group—not only were they more spontaneous and less inhibited about some topics, but they lacked characteristic indecisiveness. For example, when our group was invited to sit in a circle and join hands, they did so immediately, and this was commented on by one of the other groups, who said that they had taken two and a half months to reach a similar decision. We noticed also that it was not difficult to get warm reactions in the group, and that the psychotic material had been shared.

It was also much easier for this group to accept a new patient, and it seemed clear that the group had enabled the patients to form relationships with each other. There was sometimes a rather light-hearted feeling in the group, and we wondered whether this was necessary to psychotics to help them loosen up their feelings. We noted that, in isolation, a psychotic often seemed flat, but in the group they showed a much greater intensity of feeling and warmth, and the staff felt that it was a very comfortable group to be in. It was also not a dependency group in the sense that the patients were less dependent on the staff than a neurotic group, and seemed to be more dependent on each other, contrary to our expectations. As the group went on, the psychotic material seemed to get less, and we thought that this material was often used by them as a defense mechanism.

It might be useful at this point to say what has happened to the patients in terms of social adjustment during the three months of the group. D.O.'M. has gone back to work, after a great improvement in his social relationships and reestablishing contact with his neighbor, whom he felt had persecuted him so much in the past. W.R. is currently looking for a job and has moved into a local hostel in Southampton, a big step for her. R.B., perhaps one of the most disturbed members of the group, is seen by members of the staff outside the group as having made the biggest improvement of all in terms of ability to communicate and make social relationships. V.N., who had been a rather long-staying patient in a disturbed ward of the hospital, and who attended as a day patient there, came to the group for about the first six weeks, improved very greatly, and was discharged home at the end of that time. As she lived a considerable distance from the Day Centre she was not able to continue attending the group, which was most unfortunate. Right at the end of the three-month period she had to be readmitted to the hospital.

P.B. is now looking for a job and has greatly improved, though it is felt that he still has much to communicate to the group, which would help him. H.J.A. is talking in terms of a job, but again has much to communicate and much to work through, which could be helpful. A.R. has attended rather irregularly and is generally felt to be a person who has gained the least from the group, and indeed appears to be relatively unchanged. R.H. has also attended irregularly. He is dominated by a very powerful and possessive mother who decides what he is going to do, and who is almost certainly unconsciously keeping him in a state of illness. There has been a good deal of improvement, particularly in his ability to achieve rapport with other people. He established considerable rapport with H.J.A. and also with one of the therapists, mostly at a nonverbal level. Again we feel that if he had been able to attend more regularly, and if he can attend in the future, further improvement could be expected. H.B. started to communicate more and to improve after the abreaction and left the group about two weeks before the end of the three months, as she felt that she no longer required its support and needed to look for a job. I think that we can confidently predict that her improvement will continue. R.G. joined the group late and cannot therefore be properly included in the series, as it is too early to consider improvement.

In summary, it would appear that the three-month exposure of the group of psychotic patients to fairly intensive group therapy, which included some encounter group techniques, has produced results similar to those which might have been expected in the days when such patients commonly received insulin therapy. We have also observed that, under these conditions of group therapy, the psychotic patients behaved very differently from their textbook expectations, thus supporting the previous assertion that psychosis may be made a special case from normality. Perhaps the feelings of this particular group are best summed up by something which was said by W.R. at the next to last meeting. She asked if anybody could remember the first time they found they were attractive to anyone. She remembered walking past a brewery, a man whistled, and she thought, "Hooray, I'm a woman!"

REFERENCES

1. J. P. Leff and J. K. Wing, "Trial of Maintenance Therapy in Schizophrenia," *Brit. Med. J.*, 3:599-604, 1971.
2. S. R. Hirsch, R. Gaind, P. D. Rohde, B. C. Stevens, and J. K. Wing, "Outpatient Maintenance of Chronic Schizophrenia Patients with Long-acting Fluphenazine: Double-blind Placebo Trial," *Brit. Med. J.*, 1:633-637, 1973.
3. R. D. Laing, *The Divided Self* (London: Tavistock, 1960); *idem.* and A. Esterson, *Sanity, Madness and the Family* (London: Tavistock, 1964).
4. T. S. Szasz, *The Manufacture of Madness* (New York: Harper & Row, 1970).
5. G. R. Taylor, *The Angel Makers: A Study in the Psychological Origins of Historical Change* [1750-1850] (London: Tavistock, 1964).
6. A. Comfort, *The Anxiety Makers: Some Curious Preoccupations of the Medical Profession* (London: Nelson, 1967).
7. G. Deleuze and F. Guatteri, *Capitalisme et Schizophrène* (Paris: Minuet, 1973).
8. *London Times Literary Supplement*, 1973, p. 295.
9. H. Freeman, "Long-Acting Tranquillisers in Schizophrenia," *Psychol. Neurol.*, 2:3, 1971.
10. R. A. Sandison, "Depression: Illness, Social Disease or Natural State?," *Lancet*, 1:1227, 1972.
11. T. J. Pettigrew, *On Superstitions Connected with the History and Practice of Medicine and Surgery* (London: Churchill, 1844).
12. N. Culpeper, *The Physician's Library* (London: 1653), p. 267.
13. V. P. Wasson and G. Wasson, *Mushrooms, Russia and History* (New York: Pantheon Books, 1957).
14. James Legge, trans., *I Ching* (New York: Dover Publications, 1963).
15. H. Dale, "Medicinal Treatment: Its Aims and Results," *Brit. Med. J.*, 2:423, 1957.
16. B. Ackman, A. Harris, and A. J. Oldham, "Insulin Treatment of Schizophrenics," *Lancet*, 1:607-611, 1957.
17. S. Leyton, "Glucose and Insulin in Schizophrenia," *Lancet*, 1:1253, 1958.
18. A. M. Spencer, "Permissive Group Therapy with Lysergic Acid Diethylamide," *Brit. J. Psychiat.*, 109:37-45, 1963.
19. Leyton, "Glucose and Insulin," *op. cit.*
20. S. N. Banerji, "Schizophrenia," *J. Indian Med. Assn.*, 25:402-404, 1955.

48

RECURRENT PROBLEMS IN THE MANAGEMENT OF TREATMENT GROUPS

Erika Chance

Psychotherapy is defined as the use of the professionally planned relationship to help the individual patient resolve inner conflicts and modify habitual coping patterns in the direction of better adaptation and increased effectiveness. Groups can be, and are, used in many therapeutic ways. Those designed for the purpose of psychotherapy must represent a *network* of professionally planned relationships so that *each* individual patient may experience reduction of inner tensions and conflict and modification of maladaptive defensive patterns.

In the very planning of the group, the therapist's organizational capacity is challenged. In addition, his notions of how much or how little control a good therapist should have over his patients is liable to be tested severely. The wealth of clinical material presented requires talent for abstracting the common elements or the contrasting features in the life experiences of six or more patients. Spontaneity—when tempered by quick thinking—is at a premium. The high visibility of the group therapist's work to both patients and colleagues requires a great deal of inner security.

Perhaps the greatest professional hazard of good group psychotherapy lies in the paradox that increased demands on the therapist's control must go hand-in-hand with a greater capacity for self-examination and open acknowledgment of the larger number of learning problems which this technique involves.[1]

These learning problems fall into three broad areas: First, the therapist who wants to treat six patients simultaneously needs far more control over the milieu in which the group is to operate than in individual therapy. Second, he needs to have control of group processes in order to facilitate the network of therapeutic interaction in the group. Third, the simultane-

Reprinted from the *International Journal of Social Psychiatry*, Vol. 17, No. 3, 1971, pp. 210-216.

ous demands of patients and his own high visibility present a stress which requires far more control over his own responses than is needed in the privacy of the individual hour.

PROBLEMS IN CONTROL OVER THE MILIEU

Even the simple and earthy problem of finding a room in which the group can meet regularly without interruptions holds many a pitfall. It is surprising how hard it is for clinic, school, hospital, or agency staff to remember that "Do Not Disturb" sign on the conference room. Such "forgetting" may well be related to communication problems between the therapist and his colleagues.[2] In any institution where the addition of group therapy to the range of helping techniques represents (as it should) a new and different way of relating to patients, mixed feelings on the part of colleagues and administration should be expected. Curiosity, fear, skepticism, and even hostility can be dealt with if the group therapist will create some regular opportunities for discussion with his colleagues. There, he can elaborate on the varied use of groups in the treatment plan:

(1) Diagnostic or orientation
(2) Preliminary to individual therapy for those patients who are too threatened by the intimacy of the one-to-one situation
(3) Concurrent with individual therapy (possibly with a colleague as the individual therapist)
(4) Exclusive group psychotherapy
(5) Group therapy as an aid to termination

As colleagues and administrators learn about the different applications of this technique in the service of a series of individual patients, so fears that group therapy is a massive means of disposition, that it threatens the principle of confidentiality and other cherished standards of professional work, are allayed. For the group therapist the work of creating a benign milieu for the treatment group will pay off in practical terms in more and better referrals for his special endeavors and in more adequate space provisions. The support of colleagues and administration will help in reducing the stress of exposure to the simultaneous demands of six or more patients. He will be less apt to join his patients in negative transference to the institution[3] if his own relationship with it is secure.

PROBLEMS IN CONTROL OVER GROUP PROCESS

Learning problems in this area are not confined to the prevention of disasters. Regular staffing of patients whose treatment plan includes group psychotherapy will help us all to answer a crucial question in the field: "Which treatment modality fits the needs of which patients best?" A detailed work-up of each patient considered for group psychotherapy will do much to resolve those learning problems for the therapist which occur in the course of conducting the treatment group.

On Understanding Each Patient

Detailed assessment of each patient will help the therapist to follow more accurately and to facilitate more appropriately those psychotherapeutic processes of which the patient stands in greatest need. Among six different people in spontaneous interaction it is hard to determine the exact level of rapport, the quality of transference, the degree of ventilation, insight, and the extent of reality testing which is operant for each. Unless the therapist has the case material at his fingertips, he will be left far behind in understanding the meaning of a patient's communication on the three levels at which it is stimulated by the group: As a message to the therapist, as a communication to the patient-peers, and also as a means of self-representation.

Devices for Selection, Balancing, and Control of the Group Process

One easy device to help the therapist bear in mind commonalities and differences among a series of patients consists in tabulating the known facts as follows:

> A. *Biosocial aspects:* Sex, age, socioeconomic status, I.Q., appearance, estimated ego strength
> B. *Defenses:* Interpersonal, intrapsychic
> C. *Family history:* Important persons

Selection so that there is reasonable homogeneity under heading A will facilitate rapport and empathy among the patients. Similarity in socioeconomic status and a relatively narrow age range will make it easier for patients to use each others' ventilation vicariously. Common factors in life experiences with significant persons will facilitate personal and vicarious insight for members of the group. Working through and reality testing of common central problems will be greatly aided if group members have different ways of coping with problems which are in themselves basically similar. Thus, moderate heterogeneity under heading B is desirable. If, however, the range of styles is too wide, patients may be unable to borrow each other's coping patterns. For example, the inclusion of a hyperaggressive dominant woman in a group in which all other patients are passive or withdrawn is likely to freeze members of the group in their habitual style of defense.

Most important in screening data about patients selected for group psychotherapy is the need to make sure that they have comparable ego strength. In a group of psychoneurotics the therapist can devote himself to facilitating ventilation and uncovering sexual and aggressive conflicts.

When a psychotic patient with weak ego structure is added to the group, the therapist tends to find himself uncovering material for psychoneurotic members while he hopes that the psychotic patient will not hear him. When he endorses defenses which distance, isolate, and concretize emotional experiences for the psychotic patient, he is forced to tell the psychoneurotic members of the group not to listen.

Disruptions of Therapy: Crisis or Treatment Opportunity?

1. *Change in membership.* When the composition of the group is found to be imbalanced by any of the above criteria, two corrective measures are possible. First is the addition of a new patient. Where a patient is likely to become an isolate because of very different sociobiological characteristics (culture, race, economic status), it may help to give him company. The addition of a new and carefully selected patient may also help where the range of characteristic defenses is too wide, as in the group of five passive women with one extremely dominant and hostile one, cited above. It may help to add another aggressive patient to match the first one in such a situation.

In a group where one patient has been included accidentally whose ego strength is markedly less than that of the other patients, it is more probable that the therapist will eventually have to resort to the second alternative: the removal of that patient. Either crisis can be used to great profit if the therapist will take it as an occasion to encourage patients to review their expectations from the group, their experiences in it, their perception of the therapist, and so on.

2. *Absenteeism and late arrivals.* These can be used in similar ways. If the defaulter is brought up-to-date by one of his peers, the therapist can use this as a means of checking how patients have felt about the group experience. Where late-coming is chronic, the patients who attend punctiliously may begin to call the defaulter to order. The therapist can reserve his intervention to a gentle probing among all the group members as to occasional reluctance to attend the group, possible methods of fortifying oneself just before the session, curiously repetitive transportation difficulties, and other forms of resistance. In short, such disruptions of attendance can be put to use in facilitating work on resistance to therapy.

3. *The absent therapist.* The therapist's vacation or his termination of a therapy is often a painful experience for the participants in individual treatment. Since group psychotherapy makes it easier for the patient to express aggressive and hostile feelings, the problems become correspondingly more acute. The announcement of the therapist's impending departure is often met initially by an apparent deafness. Depressive silences are frequently followed by attempts to work through feelings of desertion with stories of death, illness, separation from loved ones, and catastrophes which left the patient helpless. The alert therapist will help the patients to

work through these displacements and will support them in bringing out their anger and disappointment, first in the context of the displaced experience, and then in relation to himself. Such acceptance of the patients' rage will prevent competitive acting out ("I'll go on vacation before you"). It will do much to help the patient assume an active and independent stance in relation to the experience of therapy. With outpatients it is helpful to allow about six to eight weeks for working through problems of termination. With inpatients and children's groups, because of reduced anxiety tolerance and shorter time perspective, four weeks appear to be about optimal.

It is obvious that "baby-sitting arrangements" during a therapist's vacation or inclusion of the incoming therapist in the final sessions prior to termination by the outgoing therapist are contraindicated if the goal includes helping the patient to uncover, work through, and cope with the loss of an important relationship. These maneuvers are often "guilt protectors" for the therapist, or even the outcome of fear of the patients' anger and disappointment.

Control over Processes Within the Group Psychotherapist

1. *Criteria for optimal intervention.* If the therapy group is to serve its purpose, then interaction among the patients is the primary therapeutic agent. When patients are so selected and worked up that the chances of mutual rapport, personal and vicarious ventilation, insight, and reality testing have been maximized, then one of the problems for the therapist consists in not obstructing these processes. Any one intervention should bear critical scrutiny from three points of view:

(a) Was the intervention necessary? Or could one of the patients have made the same kind of comment? If the therapist preempts a formulation which could have been made by one of the patients, he has hindered rather than helped group process and autonomous growth. What internal pressures may have led him to do so?

(b) Was the intervention appropriate? It is always difficult to make a formulation which will be relevant to six or more patients. Yet, even when the therapist addresses only one of the members of a group, the rest will think, "here but for the grace of God, go I."

(c) Was the intervention economic, simple, and brief? The language of the patient is often very far removed from the clinical, shorthand, and intellectual qualifiers which are second nature to most of us. Can we afford to think aloud in the therapy group?

In summary, the basic question underlying these criteria for intervention in group psychotherapy is: "Whose group is it?"

2. *Resistance.* The core of this concept is the patient's inability to let unconscious feelings and ideas come to consciousness. In the group, even more than in individual therapy, the young therapist is apt to lose sight of

this definition and to consider resistance primarily as a negative interpersonal response to himself and to the help he has to offer. When a group repeatedly confronts the therapist with spurts of talk followed by long, heavy silences, it is hard for him to remember that the patients may have difficulties in dealing with themes such as homosexuality and death, and that if they refuse to talk, it is only because they have projected the inner fears of these experiences onto him. The important intrapsychic conflict experienced by the patient is obliterated for the therapist by his own feeling of impotence in the interpersonal struggle with six "recalcitrant" patients. Their willingness to talk, to ventilate, becomes a direct measure of his own effectiveness. As his anxiety rises, so he pressures the patient increasingly. As the external pressure by the therapist mounts, the opportunity for the patients to look inward and examine their inability to verbalize decreases. Work on intrapsychic resistance, originally displaced by transference processes onto the therapist, has been transformed into a real interpersonal power struggle by the therapist insisting on response to him. In this kind of crisis the therapist appears to forget that the interpersonal response of compliance can represent resistance at least as well as the more negative behaviors of absenteeism or refusal to talk.

3. *Negative Transference and Countertransference to the Institution.* The psychotherapy group facilitates ventilation of hostile feelings toward the therapist. At the same time the stress of accepting the hostile feelings of six or more patients at once is much greater than in an individual hour. Small wonder, then, that many a therapist will offer the patient a target other than himself. Complaints about doctors will not be met by the gentle query: "Me too, perhaps?" but rather by the suggestions that of course the departments of dentistry, radiology, and even the adjacent O.B.G.Y.N. Department are not respectful of the patient's feelings. In inpatients' settings, griping about the ward personnel is a common early stage of psychotherapy groups. The therapist here has the choice of linking the patients' discontent to their poor expectations from all helping figures, of remaining neutral, or of joining in the attack on the colleagues outside the treatment room. Support for ventilation of hostility on professional helping figures other than oneself can serve a number of defensive purposes for the therapist under stress. First, it serves to displace the patient's hostility from the therapist to more distant targets. Second, the therapist may unconsciously wish to split the transference. Let colleagues or other departments bear the brunt of the negative transference. He, then, will become the good father, the target of positive transference. Third, and perhaps most important, the therapist in relation to the institution he serves and vis-à-vis his colleagues has many unmet expectations of nurturance, support, and help. The patient's expression of anger against these targets may offer him the kind of personal gratification which is better found outside the treatment room. Insofar as institutions, clinics, and agencies func-

tion as professional helpers to groups of patients, leadership of a treatment group means for some therapists the arena in which they, in rivalry with the host institution, can demonstrate that they can establish better rapport and give more effective help.

4. *Are Learning and Leading Compatible?* In summary, group therapy makes for more stringent demands on the therapist's coping capacities than individual therapy. The pressures include: Problems in control over the milieu in which the group is to function; problems in understanding the meaning of each patient's communication, in abstracting commonalities and differences; and problems in enhancing the basic therapeutic processes of rapport, ventilation, insight, and reality testing for six or more patients simultaneously. The technique represents a model in which the external pressures on the therapist are so high that he may find it more difficult to look inward to cope with the most important pressure of all— the threat to his own feeling of adequacy. Given these stresses, it becomes of primary importance to offer the group therapist regular consultation in which he can begin to define these problems and to look upon the role of leadership in a psychotherapeutic group as a concentrated learning opportunity rather than as a challenge to demonstrate his own effectiveness.

REFERENCES

1. E. Chance, "Training in Analytic Group Psychotherapy: Observations on Some Learning Problems in the Dimension of Power," *Int. J. Group Psychother.*, 15:3, 1965.
2. E. Chance, "Group Psychotherapy in Community Mental Health Programs," *Am. J. Orthopsychiat.*, 37:5, 1967.
3. N. Reider, "A Type of Transference to an Institution," *Bull. Menn. Clin.*, 1953; S. L. Safirstein, "Institutional Transference," *Psychiat. Quart.*, 41:3, 1967.

49

NOTES ON HELP-REJECTING
COMPLAINERS

Milton M. Berger
Max Rosenbaum

In this paper, experiences with help-rejecting complainers (HRC) are reviewed in order to: a) offer a clinical definition of this syndrome; b) present some differences and similarities between the classic sadomasochist and the HRC, while offering a rationale for the understanding of some of the underlying motivations and processes used by such patients; c) present general observations and specific clinical illustrations to delineate the pattern further so that it becomes more recognizable; and d) offer some suggestions concerning techniques for working through the process of help-rejecting complaining during combined individual and group psychotherapy.

DEFINITION

An HRC is a patient who, sometimes through nonverbal[1] but more often through verbal communication is driven to make demands on, as well as to manipulate* and govern† others. As a result, the therapist and the peer group members direct toward the HRC their hopefully helpful attention, concern, care, interpretations, and advice. The interpretations

Reprinted from the *International Journal of Group Psychotherapy*, Vol. 17, No. 3, July 1967, pp. 357-370.

* According to *Webster's Seventh International Dictionary* (Springfield, Mass.: G. & C. Merriam Co., 1963), to manipulate is "to control, or play upon by artful, unfair or insidious means, especially to one's own advantage; (2) to change by unfair or artful means so as to serve one's own purpose." A synonym for manipulate is "handle." Handle implies directing an acquired skill to the accomplishment of immediate ends. Manipulate implies adroit handling and often suggests the use of craft or of fraud.

† To govern is "to control, direct or strongly influence the actions of others." One of the archaic definitions of govern is "manipulate" (*Webster's*).

and advice may be based on professional training as well as life experience and frequently include suggestions for alleviating and changing the HRC's condition. *The HRC then rejects the help given to him.* His despairing condition is communicated ostensibly as being one of hopeless* failure to "make it" in life because of events and forces beyond his control. He communicates a quality of helplessness despite his excessive and repeatedly intellectualized wish for life to be different. Meanwhile, he sucks and sucks and demands and demands and sucks and sucks some more. At first the group members make repeated and varied efforts to reach out to the HRC, but gradually they become annoyed, frustrated, and angry with his behavior. When finally they feel that somehow they have been "sucked in" or "taken in," they may turn on the HRC with anger or rejection; they may even tell him that they wish he would leave the group because he "holds them back" from their own ongoing changing and living. This occurs when the group members feel that the HRC is a destructive alchemist who turns whatever they give him, both quantitatively and qualitatively, out of their individual and group resources into an abyss of waste.

The most recent elaboration of the concept of the HRC was presented by Frank and his associates. They emphasized the need for descriptive, humanistic, process diagnoses, which are of more practical value than standard, symptomatic, diagnostic classification of the neuroses. Frank and his colleagues stated that:[2]

> The pattern of the HRC is characterized by behavior suggesting that the patients fear they will be ignored unless they maintain a continuing claim for attention. They do this by repeatedly presenting a complaint or problem, while at the same time implicitly or explicitly rejecting any advice or help offered. This pattern occurs with very little stimulation, other than what is implied in the therapeutic situation itself. Its effects are to cause other patients or the doctor to offer advice, and to impede or break the continuity of the group. The would-be help givers soon become frustrated and annoyed.

Since this original description, the term "help-rejecting complainers" has often been used by therapists[3] but, to our knowledge, it has not been clearly delineated.

SOME DIFFERENCES AND SIMILARITIES BETWEEN SADOMASOCHISTS AND HRC'S

It is important to be aware of the differences between the classic sadomasochistic pattern and that of the HRC. We perceive the latter type of individual along the dimension of social interaction, since exclusive pre-

---

* Obviously, the patient is not hopeless; otherwise he would not be coming. However, his latent motivation appears to be to destroy the therapist and the group members.

occupation with the intrapsychic function does not capture the subtle nuance of the behavior of the HRC. Fenichel, in his extensive description of character disorders, has delineated rather carefully the various types of masochistic traits. He suggests:[4]

> Sadism initially develops from the instinctive greediness with which the incorporation aims of the pregenital impulses are prosecuted, representing a way of striving for instinctive aims rather than an original instinctual aim in itself. Another root of sadism is the negative instinctual aim of getting rid ("spitting away") of painful stimuli. Both greediness and hate become condensed when the destruction or the damage of an object turns into an instinctual aim of its own, the completion of which produces a kind of erogenous pleasure.
>
> All pregenital impulses, in their aims of incorporation, seem to possess a certain destructive component. Unknown constitutional factors, and above all, experiences of frustration, greatly increase this destructive element. In addition to oral and anal sadism other erogenous zones may serve as sources of sadism. It is often the specific repression of this component of infantile sexuality that later leads to conflicts and thus to neuroses.
>
> Masochism, the direction of the destructive component in sexuality against the individual's own ego, is the counterpart to sadism. It is of special theoretical importance since its manifest aim of self-destruction seems to contradict the pleasure principle. The problem is whether this is due to a genuine self-destructive instinct operative "beyond the pleasure principle" or whether this contradiction is only an apparent one, the masochistic phenomena being reducible to changes in the direction of sadistic drives, necessitated by the environment. . . . In principle, these elaborations can be understood in the following ways:
>
> 1. They may represent a turning of sadistic impulses against the ego.
>
> 2. They may represent a necessary evil in so far as experience has brought the conviction that pleasure can only be attained by bearing a certain amount of pain; thus enduring this pain becomes an unfortunate but unavoidable intermediary aim. The masochistic act may represent a "lesser evil": by a self-destructive act one unconsciously pays a small price to avert a greater dreaded evil. This is the psychology of "sacrifice." A greater hurt is averted by voluntarily submitting the ego to an earlier and lesser one.
>
> 3. The mechanism generally used to master traumatic experiences may complicate a person's sexuality; when something unpleasant is expected, it may be anticipated actively to a controllable degree and at a known time.
>
> 4. Experiences may inhibit activity and provoke a regression toward receptive behavior. Many masochistic phenomena appear in analysis as a strengthening of a passive-receptive giving oneself up for the sake of the pleasure of regaining participation in omnipotence. One's own smallness can be enjoyed if it serves as a way of feeling that one participates in somebody else's greatness.

We believe that Fenichel does not capture in his definition what we have observed clinically, which is that there is a tremendously manipulative quality in the HRC as well as an effort to defeat the culture. In his statement, Fenichel notes the "unknown constitutional factors" at work. In addition to the acquisitiveness, there appears to be a very low threshold for frustration. While it is of theoretical interest, it is extraneous to our description whether there is a primacy of what Fenichel calls "instinct greediness" or a primacy of "manipulation." Current research in ego-psychology would appear to point to the second possibility.

While acknowledging that the line between the classically defined "sadomasochist" and the HRC is not always clear, we believe that the HRC represents a larger clinical entity.*

GENERAL OBSERVATIONS

Our experience with HRC's leads us to believe that as a group they were subject, rather early in life, to severe deprivation and/or abandonment. For example, some have had psychotic or schizophrenogenic-type mothers; some were born out of wedlock and did not know their actual mothers or fathers and were raised in orphanages without adequate surrogate mothering or fathering; some lost their real fathers through death within the first three years of their lives, or the father left the mother and rarely contacted the family during the child's formative years. Those reared in a family culture embittered toward middle-class norms (e.g., welfare culture) may perceive the therapist as embodying middle-class values.

There seems to be a strong defect in the pleasure apparatus, in the capacity to experience joy or pleasure. For some HRC's, this is related to the fact that they were so severely criticized in childhood that they could take no joy in their actual accomplishments. The perfectionistic demands made on them were so great that what they did accomplish was never good enough.

The patient may cling ferociously to his pattern of help-rejecting complaining in order to avoid facing his essential emptiness. It is important to note the frequency with which depressive trends accompany HRC's. Often help-rejecting complaining emerges acutely as the patient begins to change and experiences genuine despair, a time which may be accompanied by thoughts of suicide.

A common demand of the HRC is that the therapist give him more or do more for him so that he can trust someone and thus believe that he himself is significant because he is given to and cared for. Yet, at the same

* We relate the help-rejecting syndrome not only to sadomasochism, which is usually considered to have sexual components, but also to oral dependency, i.e., pre-genital conflicts.

time, there is a specific propensity in HRC's to trust nothing and no one. As a result, the therapist is constantly tested to elicit how much he will give quantitatively and qualitatively, and how much he will take!

It is important for the HRC that he cause a great sense of frustration in fellow group members as part of creating a moment of significance. At such times the HRC may feel alive and important as a "crisis creator."

Clinically, HRC's frequently may tell the therapist or the group: "You just don't understand me. But how could you? After all, you don't have the background I do." HRC's find it difficult to give up this pattern because for them help-rejecting complaints may be their only claim to significance.

One patient (M.), a twenty-eight-year-old secretary whose history indicated profound emotional absenteeism on the part of her parents as well as extreme criticism and demands for perfection by them, smiled proudly as she informed her therapist: "My dentist wants me to come to the dental clinic so that he can show my teeth to his students. He says I have positively the worst case of this kind that he has ever seen." It is important that the therapist not deny the distorted idea of uniqueness held by the HRC; rather, it is vital to educate him to the fact that he can still be "unique" as a person without suffering in some way.

We ask the HRC to risk giving up what he believes to be his identity when he gives up his help-rejecting complaints. In this sense he is similar to the patient with homosexual problems who experiences his total identity as "I am a homosexual," or the patient who paints and believes his whole identity is wrapped up in "I am an artist." It is important for the therapist to help the HRC to develop a concept of his own identity which goes beyond the distorted perception he has of himself, whether it be that of a failure despite his efforts, a homosexual, or an artist.

Group members frequently feel better when a member who is an HRC is absent. This brings up the sensitive and difficult matter of whether or not to ask an HRC to leave a group whose growth he is holding back. What is the responsibility of the therapist to the other members as well as to the HRC? The HRC is also involved in the important question of selection of members for a psychotherapy group. Should a therapist knowingly place an HRC in a group? And what about placing two in the same group? Would it be advisable to place HRC's in a homogeneous group of HRC's? Would a group of such patients be deadlocked in bitter competition for the therapist's attention? These latter questions may be more apparent than real because it has been our experience that we do not make the complete diagnosis of the HRC syndrome until some time after the patient has already been placed in a group.

There is paradoxical truth in the statement often made by HRC's to their group: "You don't understand me." It happens this way. The HRC has a capacity to stir up in others feelings of annoyance, irritation, helplessness, hopelessness, futility, and confusion. Then, quite often, the feeling of not comprehending the HRC occurs in the therapist and/or group members. One or more group members may, in fact, state: "We don't understand how you can remain such a blind, stubborn fool! It is confusing to have you here, ostensibly asking for help but then making mincemeat out of any help we offer you." The HRC usually counters with: "You see, I knew I was right about your not understanding me! You just told me you don't." Here we see how the HRC drives others to a state of confusion. Thus he is able to justify his feelings of being abused and misunderstood even by those who are mutually with him in the therapeutic encounter and are supposed to be trying to be sincere with him and with one another. The HRC concludes: "If this is the way it is here with you, you can imagine what it is for me outside of the group." The pattern, and the hopelessness too, are then perpetuated as a basis for the HRC to feel he has a valid right to complain and whine.

The HRC repeatedly communicates in his body positionings, attitude, and words: "Here I am. I can't help myself." He frequently feels angry inside during therapeutic sessions as he looks at the therapist and thinks: "Why don't you stimulate me to talk. *You* know how to do it." There is the constant request for oral magic.

Therapists who are quick to invest themselves with the HRC are easily frustrated. Clinically, a clue to recognition is the feeling of becoming unduly fatigued as a session progresses. The therapist is often taken in by the notion that the HRC really wants to "change" to a new way of living, which is the therapist's wish, when actually the HRC may only want to be with someone who will feed him. The therapist believes: "I'll lend him a crutch, give him help and aid and support," but then he finds that the HRC will not give up the crutch. He makes the crutch a part of his body and fights tenaciously to maintain the dependent relationship.

HRC's often feel the world owes them a living and a loving because they have suffered so. Feeling unique because of how, and how much, they suffer, there is a need to maintain the image of "poor, pitiful Pearl." If something positive happens in their lives, they may never share it openly with the group or may allow it to slip out only months after the fact. They have to maintain that there is a reality basis for their continuous whining. Frequently there exists a deep-seated feeling of not wanting to give satisfaction to others. To make a change in one's self which others would enjoy, even if it would be good for oneself, would mean gratifying others. There is a perverse process here of "reaming" oneself in order to "ream" others.

CLINICAL ILLUSTRATIONS

Told by a group member that he had seemed more spirited and alive in the past month, Fred, a thirty-five-year-old divorced accountant who has aspirations to fulfill himself as an artist and who has repeatedly stated that his parents trained him to be a misfit, immediately replied: "I wouldn't want you to be taken in by the way you see me now. You see me for a few moments in the week and don't realize I may be drowning the rest of the week. Sometimes the people on shore don't realize a man is drowning; they just assume he's playfully waving his hands." Fred continued, "People have always seemed to be or feel more optimistic about me than the facts warrant." HRC's frequently have a very low self-image. They manage, *somehow*, to belittle any compliment or "reaching out" to them by others. They "take the starch out of" a significant moment in which someone is indicating that he could actually care for and be truly concerned for them.

Two years ago the same patient, Fred, came to therapy with suicidal intentions. These thoughts were precipitated when his wife locked him out of their apartment and insisted that she had to get a legal separation and perhaps a divorce. On one occasion Fred informed a group member who was present for her first group session that her stated problems seemed rather trivial and that he could not understand what she was making such a fuss about. He followed this up with the statement that: "It seems like such a waste to me listening to you when my problems involve life and death and yours seem so superficial." The therapist proceeded to elicit from the new patient, Frances, the fact that, while her problems seemed trivial to Fred, in her they led to depression, severe migraine headaches, and almost every morning on awakening, a feeling of: "Oh, my God, another day. How will I ever get up and face it!" Later, in the same group session, the new patient commented to Fred that he seemed to her to be a person of intelligence and real substance and she could not quite understand why, with his appearance of adequacy, he had to maintain that he was a naked, helpless, vulnerable little child who could hardly believe that he could make it in life.

Another group member, Harriet, commented to the therapist in an individual session: "Fred makes me feel guilty when I'm with him, even when I speak to him. It's as if he keeps asking for something, wanting something, and no matter what I say or do or give, it's wiped out immediately by his attitude that any suggestions I make are stupid and show I don't really understand him or his problems or his needs!" She went on to remark that in an earlier group meeting Fred expressed the feeling that when suggestions were given to him, he felt as if he were being exposed to "bear-sticking" or "pig-sticking." She concluded her statement about Fred by saying, "I experience Fred as just one big whine!"

The song, "Nobody Knows the Trouble I've Seen, But Jesus," applies to most HRC's. (One of the authors of this paper, M. R., occasionally finds himself humming this during a group session, thus focusing the group's attention on the process going on.)

At a different meeting of his group, Fred stated: "When I was living with my wife and children and working to earn a living, I consistently felt that I was giving, giving, giving." He said he felt everything came out of his emotional hide and he received nothing in return. Underneath he was "always angry, angry, angry. Now I want to be given, given, given." On one occasion following a group meeting, Fred sent a note to his therapist stating:

> Verbal help is not enough. It requires more commitment on the part of the one extending the help. Here, indeed, actions speak louder than words. The helper may have to, initially at least, do more for the person to be helped than he would like. Let us assume that I must get a job. Ideally, I ought to go out, look for one, apply for it, and go to work. From a practical standpoint, this may be such a disturbing, demoralizing, and depressing contingency that the helper may need to provide me with leads and perhaps even with the initial job.
>
> To argue that this may defeat the very purpose of the help proffered is unrealistic. A man whose breathing has stopped does not benefit from advice on how to draw in breath and how to expel it. Temporarily, artificial respiration must be applied externally until the victim is able to take over himself. One telephone number or social introduction is worth hours of lecture on the virtues and rewards of self-reliance and self-help to the lonely, isolated person.*
>
> I would guess that the would-be helper often is biased in the direction of underestimating the magnitude and scope of the problems faced by the person needing help. He may react with irritation that his suggestions are rejected or met with skepticism. This may be because the problems faced by the one needing help are not unique and are shared even by those who have "solved" these problems for themselves. The helper does not want his applecart upset by the doubts or disbelief of the one crying for help.

Fred continued to express his negative attitude as extending to the entire world. He said, "This need to be dependent takes over! It is overpowering!" Later, at the same session, Fred said, when speaking of his problems in fulfilling himself as an artist, "I don't like to be taught. I don't like to be put under the restraints of teaching. I don't like to experiment." This last statement certainly adds another dimension to our understanding of the difficulties in working with such patients.

When Fred became aware that there was something in himself, i.e., an unconscious, neurotic need, which drove him to continue to be an HRC, he suddenly felt more hopeful. He was able to give up some of his feeling of being a helpless, hapless, hopeless victim of a malevolent, nonchanging fate. He now focused his energies on combating what he spoke of as "the infernal machine inside of me" which operated to keep him helpless,

---

* This would indicate that the HRC desires primarily "situational therapy," i.e., therapy in which the world is changed or altered for his benefit.

needing, and inadequate. He suddenly saw the possibility that he could be more than that "needing self," that he did not have to remain completely identified with that "needing self."

Another case of an HRC is Betty, a married woman in her mid-thirties. She has one older sister who is married, has a family, and seems to have accepted life in a resigned fashion rather than as an experience to be enjoyed. Betty's parents own a small service-type business. They live in the same building where the business is located. Betty's father has always bitterly resented his status in life, and for some years he has been active in left-wing political activities. During Betty's formative years she was heavily indoctrinated with the notion of labor's exploitation, which has left a marked imprint upon her. Betty's mother works with the father and appears to be the dominant force in the family structure. When Betty was twenty she married, apparently in large part in order to leave the home environment of her parents. At that time she was an extremely passive person, very hungry for affection and quite willing to overlook any type of indignity. Her husband, an almost classic psychopath, would claim to work but managed to finance the marriage by borrowing money, gambling, and sometimes through outright fraud. He would leave home early in the morning, as if he were going to work, and return for his evening meal. Betty became aware that he was not working when outraged tradespeople complained about unpaid bills. Eventually, after much urging from her parents, sister, and brother-in-law, she filed for an annulment.

Betty entered into analysis shortly after her annulment. Apparently her experience was largely a supportive one, and when her analyst moved to an area about one hour's travel from New York City, he actively discouraged Betty from continuing treatment. He appeared to have been "worn out" by her.

When Betty came to her second therapist, she was passive, tearful, and preoccupied with complaints about her fate. She was first seen individually and then in a group. She was unable to relate to the group, however, since she felt that she needed more individual attention. She constantly provoked the group and finally alienated the other members. At this point she was returned to individual treatment and thus was apparently successful in gaining the attention she claimed that she needed. Some time later, she met Stan, a man who had been married previously. Stan was a bright, rather insecure man, suffering from a variety of psychosomatic ailments. He felt that he had been manipulated in his first marriage by a very aggressive and dominating wife who was quite similar to his own mother. The marriage of Betty and Stan, which was entered into against the analyst's advice, proved to be one long series of arguments. Betty became pregnant "accidentally," had an abortion, and continued to be bitter toward Stan. As in her first marriage, she complained but made no effort to improve her situation. Finally, she became pregnant again and decided to have the child in order to "stabilize the marriage." Her husband made no provision for hospital care, and she finally gave birth in the public ward of a hospital even though Stan came from a wealthy family and had access to emergency funds.

Betty spent the next two years in a continual vendetta with her husband and finally arrived at a divorce. During the last few months of her marriage, she met another man, James, an attorney who had been married before. A rather infantile individual, he came from a family in which the father dominated the mother. James was the father of two children. The divorce he had obtained from his wife was a Mexican decree and subject to contest, which he used as a weapon against Betty after they married. Shortly before their marriage, a malignancy was discovered in James which was brought under control by major surgery and cobalt treatment.

From the minute of Betty's marriage to James, their "idyllic relationship," which had been questioned by the analyst, turned into one long series of complaints. Suddenly James was no longer the devoted husband and "new father" of her child but a monster who had forcefully removed her from the cultural stimulation of New York City and plunged her into the intellectual abyss of suburbia. Every analytic session was an uninterrupted series of complaints, and there was no mention of any positive contribution that James could make to a marriage. James consented to enter analysis, but apparently the more matter-of-fact he became about her demands, the more frenzied she grew. Through all this, she continued to profess deep love for him, as well as excellent sexual compatability with him.

At this point in her analysis, Betty claimed that she wished she was the passive, "nothing" person she "used to be." According to her, her self-assertiveness had led to nothing but unhappiness. During her marital tensions with her third husband, she was referred to another analyst for consultation. The analyst met with her and her husband and felt that her demands were so strong that she could not be gratified. She identified completely with her children. Every rejection they experienced was perceived as her own. Her strongest theme was that of complaint. She was like one large boil. Her pattern of behavior appeared to be the product of her social experiences and her indoctrination in Marxism. She fantasied herself as the exploited laborer. Although she enjoyed the pleasures of surburban living, she seemed unable to accept her social position. She ridiculed the aspirations of the "bourgeois" and yet aspired to enroll her children in a private school. She found suburbia an intellectual desert and yet avoided any people who might prove stimulating. While ostensibly looking for a strong man to replace her father, whom she did not respect, she rejected any such man. It was most important for her to feel "short-changed."

SUGGESTIONS CONCERNING TECHNIQUE

Clinically, it is sometimes of help to state to the HRC: "You are trying to defeat me and the group, but we refuse to be defeated. We believe there is more to you than just the failure, the inadequate one, the one who doesn't quite make it," or "You can still be unique without maintaining your need to fail to live successfully!"

Perhaps some of the frustration and annoyance and even anger which is experienced by the therapist working with an HRC is that the therapist's neurotic image of omnipotence is deflated by such a patient. Perhaps it is just that his healthy needs to be successful as a therapist are frustrated, particularly since there is a huge investment of his energy and time with the HRC. The compulsively neurotic needs of the HRC patient directly and powerfully affront the *raison d'être* of the therapist and group. It is important for the therapist to be aware whether his unhealthy omnipotency need or his healthy need for satisfaction is being frustrated. He must develop ways of dealing with his own responses.

It is sometimes of value to say to the HRC: "I think you are more afraid of swimming to the raft you cry out for than of remaining where you are. You apparently enjoy the state of drowning." The therapist or a group member may point out that the HRC bathes himself in a sea of self-pity rather than getting truly disgusted with being the way he is, that if he were really disgusted he might try to change despite his cowering and his fear, that he might find that he could risk taking a leap over the abyss of his life if he abandoned his self-pity.

If the establishment of personal intimacy and trust is the *sine qua non* of successful therapy, then the therapist must develop ways of bridging the gap between such patients and himself. Sometimes this is accomplished indirectly, and it is always a slow process. The therapist should not allow the group to scapegoat the HRC, nor, however, should he permit an HRC to scapegoat, totally frustrate, or bog down the group. Eventually, a meaningful bond based on mutual respect may develop, with a just acknowledgment of the degree of responsibility of each person for what is going on in his life: inside himself, in his group, and in the world. The HRC has to give up feeling sorry for himself, give up feeling that he is a helpless victim of a malevolent family, world, and fate. It is important that he develop a sense of compassion for himself as opposed to self-pity. Finally, we attempt to foster the growth of the HRC as his own good father and his own good mother.

CONCLUSION

HRC's appear to have a lack of belief in the possibility of an authentic human experience.

Since the HRC perceives the world as object-related, all people are originally rejected as people. The first effort of the HRC, as defined earlier in this paper, is to manipulate people as objects on a giant chessboard. This means that, in treatment, the HRC must first unlearn previous patterns of response, which are generally deep-seated.

We have found that diagnosing a patient as an HRC generally occurs during the ongoing group process. The group precipitates his more blatant mechanisms, while the mechanisms are more masked in individual sessions.

The HRC essentially relates on a primitive social level. What he perceives to be his own needs precludes his perception of a total social field. Because of the primitive quality of the HRC's pattern of responses, the therapist for the HRC must look forward to a long-term engagement. We believe that the commitment to therapeutic work with an HRC is from three to ten years' duration, even with combined therapy. Much of this time may be expended on the patient's learning of new social roles. Possibly, we are engaged in developing compensatory mechanisms for a human being who is constitutionally underdeveloped.

Last, we wish to note the following:

1. We are involved with individuals in whom there is an ongoing process of learning and relearning. Therefore, all the principles and experimentation in the field of learning theory are applicable, including the primitive learned response, the unlearning of this primitive response, and the new learning experience.

2. The HRC seems to engage in a pattern of "tunnel" vision in which there is no incidental light entering upon the visual field. The HRC fits himself with blinders so that he does not have to be cognizant of peripheral experiences which might distract him from his immediate purpose: primitive gratification.

3. It may be that deprivation of early physical contact with peers and/or parents, deprivation of fulfillment of early intimacy needs, and deprivation of certain social and sensory affectionate experiences produce the *anlage* for the development of the HRC.

4. It may be that we have to develop new and better ways of reaching these patients and establishing meaningful contacts with them, so that the HRC's can give up their old patterns and risk trying new patterns.

5. It is most important, however, that we do not lose sight of the individual differences in people which may lead to their having had to become HRC's. Our task is to help them acknowledge and then risk giving up the "arrangement" of their early family life.

REFERENCES

1. M. Berger, "Nonverbal Communications in Group Psychotherapy," *Int. J. Group Psychother.*, 8:161-178, 1958.
2. J. D. Frank, *et al.*, "Behavioral Patterns in Early Meetings of Therapeutic Groups," *Am. J. Psychiat.*, 108:771-778, 1952.
3. S. Brody, "Syndrome of the Treatment-Rejecting Patient," *Psychoanalyt. Rev.*, 51:75-84, 1964.
4. O. Fenichel, *The Psychoanalytic Theory of Neurosis* (New York: W. W. Norton, 1945), pp. 73-74.

50

BEHAVIORAL METHODS IN GROUP
AND FAMILY THERAPY

Robert Paul Liberman

The work of behaviorally oriented clinicians with groups and families is distinguishable from other approaches by its emphasis on specifying problems and goals in concrete, behavioral terms; on measuring change in behavior from the problematic to the desirable; and on using principles of learning and conditioning to facilitate behavioral change. Specification of the problem leads naturally to an elaboration of therapeutic goals, and should be a mutual, collaborative effort between the therapist and the patients. The development of a simple but reliable recording or measurement system for monitoring the targeted behavior provides an opportunity to evaluate therapeutic progress that the therapist and clients should frequently review so as to make decisions about changing goals and interventions. Principles of learning, such as positive and negative reinforcement, modeling, shaping, extinction, punishment, satiation, time-out from reinforcement, stimulus control, and counterconditioning, form the basis for formulating treatment tactics and strategies.

A thorough understanding of behavioral principles permits the therapist to make educated guesses (or experimental analyses in the case of research) about the environmental influences that maintain the problem behavior and make it difficult for the patient to function more adaptively. The most important feature of behavior therapy, however, is its inextricable bond with empirical values. As in other sciences, the science of human behavior relies utterly on measurement. The implication for clinicians is that they should not use a technique for its own sake, but only for its effective impact on behavior. Lindsley's (1956) aphorism sums up the empirical creed: "Pinpoint, record, consequate (reinforce), and if at first you don't change the behavior, try, try again."

Reprinted from *Seminars in Psychiatry*, Vol. 4, No. 2, May 1972, pp. 145-156. Used with permission of Grune & Stratton, Inc. and the author.

The initial clinical studies using behavioral technology were of individual cases. This afforded the clinicians a simpler, more reductionistic arena within which to apply the basic principles of learning that had been developed in experimental laboratories using individual animals. In the pioneering compendium of behavior modification edited by Ullmann and Krasner (1965), forty-five of fifty studies were single-case designs. Working with single cases gave behavior therapists confidence that the interventions derived from laboratory studies were effective in a wide variety of clinical settings and in many types of behavioral disorder. Since the time of that publication, many studies have appeared that employed the behavioral approach with families and groups. This article will provide a comprehensive picture of the variety of efforts now being made by behavior modifiers in groups and with couples and families. More detailed information can be obtained by consulting the bibliography.

BEHAVIORAL METHODS IN GROUP THERAPY

The arena of group therapy makes eminently good sense therapeutically from the perspective of behavioral or learning principles. If we assume that psychotherapy is a learning process, then group therapy affords some natural advantages over individual therapy for learning new behaviors and attitudes. Much of our learning occurs through the process of imitation, also called modeling, or identification. In the group situation, each individual has a variety of models to imitate and hence the potentially assimilable repertoire is much greater than in individual therapy. It is also known that imitation occurs more rapidly and thoroughly when the models have features in common with the imitator; thus, having peers present as well as a therapist facilitates observational learning.

Behavior increases and is strengthened as it is reinforced by the social environment. There are many sources of reinforcement in the group (co-members and therapist), and some may be more effective than others. One does not have to rely upon the quixotic mixture of transference–countertransference to produce change in an individual. The stimulus situation in group therapy is closer to naturally occurring social situations than that in individual treatment. Generalization of what is learned in group therapy should occur more readily in real-life situations. There also is the opportunity to structure the group therapy situation so that it closely simulates the problematic situations of a patient, using various members of the group in role-playing or behavioral rehearsal scenes.

There are two general categories of behavioral approaches to group therapy. First, there are those clinicians who have infused behavioral specification, recording, and technology into conventional or nondirective group formats. Behavioral techniques are superimposed upon the ongoing group dynamics. Many of these clinicians were trained in the analytic, nondirective modes of doing therapy and developed expertise in behavior modification at a later stage of their careers. The second type of approach involves the structuring of the group format in ways that maximize the directed input of behavioral techniques, with little or no encouragement of group process. The differences between the approaches narrow down to the degree to which the leader is directive in structuring what happens in the group.

BEHAVIORAL METHODS IN NONDIRECTIVE GROUP THERAPY

A variety of behavioral methods have been used in conventional group therapy settings in which there is no interference with the spontaneous group interaction. Dinoff and his associates (1960) used verbal prompting and reinforcement to increase personal and group-centered references made by group therapy patients. Whenever the desired responses were expressed by patients, the therapist rewarded them by verbal approval. Heckel, Wiggins, and Salzberg (1962) effectively eliminated silences in a therapy group of chronic psychotics by surreptitiously introducing a noxious noise whenever the group fell silent for more than ten seconds. The noise was turned off as soon as a group member broke the silence. This procedure is an example of negative reinforcement; the group avoided the aversive stimulus by increasing their talk. Shapiro and Birk (1967) showed how systematic, preplanned use of approval and attention from the therapist can serve effectively as a therapeutic tactic in dealing with patients' problems, such as monopolizing the group's attention, distancing maneuvers, and lack of assertiveness.

In a controlled study of two matched therapy groups of nonpsychotic outpatients, Liberman (1970a, 1971a) found that an experimental group led by a therapist who systematically reinforced intermember expressions of cohesiveness and solidarity experienced faster symptomatic improvement than a comparison group led by a therapist in a more intuitive, psychodynamic fashion. The patients in the experimental group also showed significantly greater cohesiveness and changes on personality tests that assessed dimensions of interpersonal competence and comfort. In both groups, whether or not the therapist was aware of the contingencies of reinforcement, a lawful positive relationship was evident between the group members' expression of cohesiveness and the therapist's activity (prompting and acknowledging). The causal direction of this correlation, from therapist to patients, is documented in Figure 1, which shows the response of the group members to a change in the contingencies of reinforcement by the experimental therapist. Midway during the nine-month course of therapy, the therapist switches from reinforcing cohesiveness to reinforcing positive self-references made by individual patients. The patients respond to this switch by decreasing their cohesive behavior and increasing their talking positively about themselves. After four sessions, the therapist resumes the initial contingency and the patients return to a high level of cohesiveness.

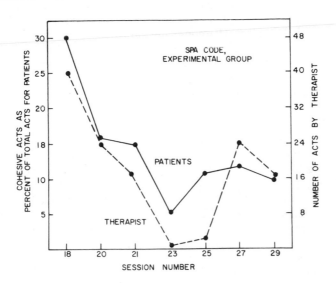

Fig. 50–1   Effect on patients' behavior of change in therapist's reinforcement of cohesiveness.

Since the focus of Liberman's study was on intermember expressions of cohesiveness, it is of interest to speculate as to how reinforcing a dimension of group dynamics could affect individual patients. A case synopsis of one of the patients from the experimental group illustrates how cohesiveness may generate other beneficial changes in an individual's behavioral repertoire.

Miss Lily was a 28-yr-old, single, Catholic nurse who was referred for group therapy after discharge from her second hospitalization. The patient had periods of intense anxiety, panic, and impaired reality testing during the previous 4 yr and made one suicide gesture. She had 2 yr of individual psychotherapy and was diagnosed as a borderline character with depressive and hysterical features. She wanted group therapy to help relieve her anxieties and also to give her feedback on how she "comes across to others." She was greatly concerned over her attractiveness to men and her difficulty in maintaining a man's interest in her.

She was a very active participant in the group and often took the role of a supportive cotherapist toward other patients, particularly in encouraging them to talk openly about their feelings. Miss Lily expressed more cohesive acts per session than any other member of the group, and she received much reinforcement from the therapist for this behavior. Also, however, she was high in expressing other emotions, such as negative feelings; she expressed more hostility to the therapist than any other member. As she was reinforced for showing solidarity and concern for others in the group, and as concomitantly she poignantly described her feelings of rejection and loss in her relationships with men and in giving up for adoption an illegitimately conceived baby, she also had insight into her dependency and helplessness. Her complaints about needing someone to care for her markedly decreased. She terminated her individual therapy and kept a stable nursing position for the entire year of the group, something she had not previously been able to do.

Miss Lily reported gradual improvement in her target or chief complaints with the average decreasing from 9.3 ("bothers me very much") to 3.8 ("bothers me a little") at termination of the group. At follow-up 1 yr later, she reported even greater reduction in her symptomatic and interpersonal complaints. She had a more responsible nursing position and was planning to marry a man whom she had known for 8 mo. Personality tests (MMPI, ICL, TAT) revealed a major increase in dominance across all levels. In her public presentation (MMPI) she changed from being frequently angry, irritable, and critical of others to liking responsibility, and being forceful and often respected and admired by others. On the level of self-description (ICL), she became more self-confident, assertive, and independent. On the TAT, her fantasy of herself changed from being dependent, wanting to be cared for, and very anxious to win approval to a projection of being warm, sociable, affectionate, and understanding. She showed greater self-actualization (ICL/ideal self ICL) and on sociometric ratings gradually moved her own self-description closer to the way she was assessed by her fellow group members—toward greater dominance and love.

Operant conditioning methods have been applied to children's play therapy groups (Clement, Fazzone, and Goldstein, 1970).

Second- and third-grade boys who were referred to the clinic by their teachers because of shy, withdrawn behavior were randomly placed in groups of four, which met once a week for 20 consecutive sessions. In the behavior modification group, the boys received tokens for social approach behavior with each other during spontaneous play. The presentation of the tokens was paired with praise from the therapist and the tokens were exchanged for small toys and candy after the session. A comparison group of boys was given verbal praise for socializing and playing together, but did not receive tokens. The boys in the token group changed more than the comparison and no-treatment control groups and they continued to be better adjusted at a 1-yr, posttherapy follow-up.

Modeling or learning through imitation also has been used effectively to increase the social skills of withdrawn children (O'Connor, 1969).

Nursery school children who displayed marked social withdrawal were shown a film depicting increasingly more active social interactions between children with positive consequences ensuing in each scene. The film contained a narrative sound track that emphasized the appropriate behavior of the models. Children exposed to a control film containing no social interaction displayed no change in withdrawn behavior whereas those who viewed sociable models increased their level of social interaction in the school playroom to that of nonisolate, normal children.

The data from these studies indicate quite convincingly that the therapist has a strong influence on group behavior. It would seem crucial for all group therapists to understand and systematically use their influence in directing group members toward behavior that will be of therapeutic value. If a therapist is aware of his reinforcing potency, it should lead him to a sense of greater responsibility for formulating goals for his patients and for the group as a whole.* The goals preferably should be formulated in behavioral terms—that is, in a way that makes the goals visible and observable—so that he can maximize his effectiveness and assess his progress. This view of the therapist as being able directly to affect the development of group and individual behavior strips away the defensive excuse that it is up to the patient to improve, and properly puts more of the burden for patients' therapeutic progress on the leader.

Different behavioral techniques were used in a clinical investigation by Liberman (1972b) in an attempt to increase social interaction among four chronic schizophrenics. The patients studied were four hospitalized chronic schizophrenic women, each institutionalized for over fifteen years at Saint Elizabeth's Hospital in Washington, D.C. Reliable, quantitative records were made of their social conversation during fifty-minute meetings. During the base line period conventional interchanges occurred at a rate of one per minute (average of six sessions). Contingent reinforcement for conversation among the women was introduced, using tokens that could be exchanged for candy, cake, cigarettes, and jewelry. The tokens were distributed at the end of each session. At each session during the

---

* Truly nondirective psychotherapy (without a goal) is about as possible and as useful as nondirective surgery. This does not mean patients should be forced to work toward behavioral goals not of their choice, by the coercive use of arbitrary vs. natural reinforcers. In the earliest clinical paper on this subject fully and frankly advocating the systematic explicit use of reinforcement and behavioral shaping in group therapy (Shapiro and Birk, 1967), it was stated: "Therapy without manipulation is a mirage which disappears on close scrutiny. Therapists who staunchly take the position that one should never directly influence patients are, we feel, simply saying that one form of manipulation (overt, explicit, and planned) is not as proper as another (covert, implicit, and unplanned). It seems to us that as long as therapists put themselves in the position of judging what is sick and what is healthy, desirable and undesirable, appropriate and inappropriate, then they are in the business of manipulation. . . . From our experimental knowledge of behavior, it is clear that a therapist who comes into the same room with any patient or group of patients and speaks, nods, looks, smiles, or frowns (or doesn't do any of these things!) is manipulating behavior, whether he recognizes it or not."

contingent reinforcement phase, one patient was provided with a "bug-in-the-ear" device (a remote control communication system) through which verbal reinforcement was given for her conversational behavior. At the end of the session, the verbal reinforcements were converted to bonus tokens that she had earned.

A noncontingent reinforcement phase was next introduced, with the patients receiving their tokens before the session and the bug-in-the-ear used to reinforce silence. This was done to assess the causal influence of the contingency vs. the tokens per se. A final phase returned the patients to reinforcement contingent upon their social conversation. Using the same design, another series of sessions was run, using a game that the patients played which elicited conversation and social interchange.

Contingent token reinforcement increased participation in an open-ended conversation by ten times over the base line and noncontingent reinforcement phases. Although the game situation alone produced a high rate of conversation, introduction of contingent reinforcement doubled the rate of the base line. There was evidence that simply raising the rate of conversation also produced changes in the content or quality of the conversation, making the patients' talk more closely approximate that of normals. Application of the findings of this research is now being made in the therapeutic community meetings of an entire ward of chronic schizophrenic patients.

BEHAVIORAL METHODS IN DIRECTIVE GROUP THERAPY

The group therapy formats that will be described have been structured according to the nature of the behavioral method being applied. Spontaneous and free-flowing group process and interaction are discouraged and the therapist takes a more task-oriented educational role with his group. However, as in any work group, group dynamics such as cohesiveness do implicitly develop and enhance the learning that goes on at a more explicit level.

Desensitization

Systematic desensitization, one of the first of the behavioral therapies, is used for patients with avoidance problems based upon fear or anxiety. Phobias are the prime targets of desensitization. The desensitization process consists of learning deep muscle relaxation; developing a hierarchy of scenes and situations graded from those that elicit minimal to maximal anxiety (each hierarchy is a separate dimension so that a person feeling a fear of heights and of public speaking would have two hierarchies constructed); and pairing the imagining of the scenes, in a stepwise, systematic fashion, with deep muscle relaxation. When the patient can imagine a scene that produces little anxiety in real life while remaining relaxed, he then progresses to the next scene in the hierarchy, which evokes somewhat greater anxiety in real life. Since the experience of profound relaxation is incompatible with anxiety, the individual's anxiety is counterconditioned or extinguished (desensitized). More complete descriptions of clinical and experimental aspects of desensitization are given by Paul (1969) and Wolpe (1969).

Desensitization has been applied in group settings for patients with various anxiety reactions. A group of individuals with a similar problem are taken through the steps of the desensitization program simultaneously. Patients with fears of traveling (Lazarus, 1961), public speaking (Paul, 1966), examinations (Ihli and Garlington, 1969), and socializing have been successfully treated in group settings with a substantial saving of therapists' time. Liberman (1971b) has produced an automated, self-desensitization program on record.

The use of desensitization in groups appears to be as effective as individual desensitization, and in several controlled studies was more effective than conventional psychotherapy. The group situation can be engineered so that patients with different avoidance problems can be treated at the same time. This is done by providing each person with an index card or paper on which his individualized hierarchy is written. After the group has been taught to master deep muscle relaxation together, the therapist cues their moving through their hierarchies by saying, "Now, picture the next scene on your list as vividly as you can while remaining deeply relaxed." Each person moves at his own pace, so that some individuals will complete their desensitization before others.

Assertive Training

Assertive training is a generic term covering any structured group situation that facilitates the acquisition of emotionally expressive behaviors. Behavioral goals can include learning how to stand up for oneself, saying "no" to people who are exploiting you, and expressing affection, anger, tenderness, or sadness. There has been little empirical work published describing the effects of assertive training, but theoretically any affective dimension of behavior can be taught (Alberti and Emmons, 1970; Serber, 1972; Wolpe, 1969). The behaviorist position assumes that once the appropriate overt expressions of emotions are learned, the inward or subjective feelings will be experienced.

The process of assertive training involves a series of steps: identify the problems in expressing feelings and specify the "where, when, how, what, and with whom" of the problem; target the goals of training, which usually consist of new behaviors, to rectify deficits in performance or modulate excessive or overly intense emotional expressiveness; simulate the problem situation, using the group members to role play or rehearse the relevant scenes (usually scenes that have occurred in the recent past or are likely to occur in the near future); use modeling and shaping (reinforcing successive approximations) to modify gradually the client's expressive behaviors (elements of the total gestalt are added one by one, such as facial expression, vocal tone and loudness, posture, accessory body movements, eye contact [nonverbals], and speech content); have the group give feedback to the individual on his improving performance (positive feedback for improvements rather than confrontation for failure is emphasized); and give the individual assignments to practice the behaviors learned in the group setting in his real-life situations, and then use group approval to reinforce successes.

Assertive training has become a keystone of treatment at the Oxnard Day Treatment Center, a comprehensive community mental health center (Liberman, 1972a). Almost all patients referred to the center have major deficits in their repertoires of emotional expressiveness. Many of them are passive and withdrawn and reluctant to stand up for their rights. They fail to generate reinforcers from their families and work settings but instead allow the world to operate on them. Some patients are deficient in expressing affection or anger or sadness. The expression of these emotions, with convincing nonverbal correlates, is the goal of assertive training.

The training is carried out in small groups of four to ten patients, with two staff members as leaders. The patients participate in an average of five weekly group sessions, since the center emphasizes short-term treatment. Each patient is given a "report card," which lists the targeted goals for his "homework" between training sessions. The start of each session is set aside for feedback from the patients on their progress. When a goal has been achieved in the community (when the training has generalized), a new goal is selected. Examples of specific goals that were set in a recent group include: expressing enthusiasm and desire for help to a vocational rehabilitation counselor, expressing affection to husband, asking a girl for a date, requesting that husband allow wife to drive the car, telling roommate to bathe more often, confronting subordinate at work with poor performance, and selling oneself at a job interview. Data are now being collected on the outcome of the assertive training groups, with preliminary results showing that over 75 per cent of the targeted goals are achieved in natural settings.

Using similar behavioral techniques (specification of problem behavior and therapeutic goals and reinforcement of desired behavior by a preprogrammed therapist), Lewinsohn, Weinstein, and Shaw (1969) have effectively treated isolated and asocial depressed patients in groups. Structured interpersonal exercises, similar to those employed in sensitivity and encounter groups, were used to facilitate interpersonal communication. The object of the group process was to increase the level of positive reinforcement that each member received from others in the group. In a family service agency, time-limited (eight-week) behavioral groups were established and clients were taught behavioral assessment of their problems and problem-solving skills. Behavioral rehearsal was used to improve or build new emotional expressiveness, and the clients were helped to develop a plan for modifying their own behavior in their real-life settings. Social reinforcement by the leaders for progress was soon imitated by the group members, and strong, protreatment norms were established. Follow-up at one and six months revealed that in almost all cases the members had either maintained or gone beyond the gains made at the time of termination (Lawrence and Sundel).

Assertive training is a general label that currently includes many different approaches that have in common only their dependence upon behavioral and learning principles. These approaches will be more specifically formulated and evaluated during the next five to ten years, but they already promise to be a major movement for generating change through groups. One potentially revolutionary application of this approach, which has already begun, is the training of deprived minority group members in adaptive skills so that they can advance both socially and occupationally.

BEHAVIORAL METHODS IN FAMILY THERAPY

Family therapy provides a potentially effective setting for behavior modification because the interpersonal milieu that undergoes change is the day-to-day, face-to-face encounters that an individual experiences with the most important people in his life: his spouse and members of his immediate family. When any form of family therapy is successful it is because the therapist is able to guide the members of the family into changing their modes of dealing with each other. In behavioral or learning terms, we can translate "ways of dealing with each other" into consequences of behavior or contingencies of reinforcement. Since the family is a system of interlocking, reciprocal behaviors, family therapy proceeds best when each of the members learns how to change his or her responsiveness to the others. Family therapy should be a learning experience for all the members involved. A pioneer in the scientific and behavioral analysis of deviant behavior in families has been Patterson (1968, 1969, 1971). He and his colleagues have developed a treatment approach that takes place in the home. Moving the treatment focus from the clinic to the home represents an important departure, since behavior change will be more likely to generalize and survive if it occurs in a natural setting.

Base line observations of family interactions are made for at least two weeks, with a focus on the ways in which parents maintain deviant behavior in their children by inadvertently reinforcing it. The parents are required to work with a programed manual containing illustrations of principles of reinforcement, extinction, and methods of specifying and recording behavior. They are helped to specify in their child the problem behavior they wish to modify and the goals toward which they wish to work. In some cases the child is given the same opportunity to alter parental behavior. The parents are then asked to record the frequency of these behaviors during a particular hour of the day or sampled throughout the day. They also must record the consequences that the desired and undesired behaviors engender in themselves. In the final phase, the parents are taught, through demonstration and supervised practice, to change their reinforcement contingencies from maladaptive to adaptive behaviors. Another method they are taught is called time-out from reinforcement, which consists of putting the child in isolation for a brief period contingent upon severe misbehavior (e.g., tantrums or aggression). This serves as a punishment and removes the child from a situation in which he might inadvertently be reinforced for his acting up. In this step-by-step fashion, family problems are modified one at a time. When indicated, similar reinforcement practices are also introduced in the school and peer group settings.

Results with eleven families indicate that significant changes in deviant behaviors occurred in ten. Significant change was defined as a reduction in frequency of the targeted problem behavior of 50 per cent or more from the base line. Other investigators have used instructions, demonstrations, and videotape-guided feedback on performance to teach new repertoires of child management to parents (Bernal, 1969; Hawkins *et al.*, 1967; O'Leary, O'Leary, and Becker, 1967; Wahler, 1969). Most of the reports consist of detailed research on single cases, with uniformly promising and efficient results.

The therapist who has a solid therapeutic alliance and positive relationship with a family in treatment can use himself as a lever to generate change in the family system of reinforcement contingencies. Liberman (1970b) has pointed out that the therapist using a behavioral approach asks, "Which interpersonal transactions between the therapist and family members and among family members can serve to alter the problem behavior in a more adaptive direction?" The therapist acts as a reinforcer to help the family or couple change their ways of dealing with each other. A helpful way to conceptualize these tactics is to view them as behavioral change experiments in which the therapist and family together reprogram the contingencies of reinforcement operating in the family system. The behavioral change experiments consist of family members responding positively to each other contingent on new and more desired and reciprocal ways of behaving. A brief case vignette will illustrate this approach. The therapist was a psychiatric nurse* and the author was a consultant to her.

---

* The author acknowledges the contribution of Nancy Sanders, R.N., who was the therapist for Mrs. G.

Total professional time was under twenty hours.

Mrs. G., a 27-yr-old mother of three young children, had been in psychotherapy with a psychiatrist and later with a psychiatric social worker at a mental health center for 4 yr. She complained of frequent, severe depressions during which she felt suicidal and occasionally hysterically out of control. Antidepressant medication and other tranquilizers were used but were ineffective. Before deciding to hospitalize the patient, the current therapist referred her to the Day Treatment Center, where the author is a consultant.

A family session, consisting of the patient, her husband, and her parents, plus a detailed history-taking effort, led to a behavioral analysis of the problem. Mrs. G.'s husband, a taciturn, conscientious, hard-working man, spent little time talking with her, except when she seemed depressed. At these times, he became exquisitely sensitive to her, even responding with solicitude and concern to her nonverbal signals of unhappiness and moodiness. To compound the reinforcement that Mrs. G. received for her depressions and expressed helplessness, her parents immediately would come to her side whenever she intimated a need for them. Mrs. G. spoke with her parents on the phone several times a day and saw them at least daily. Her parents would take off from their jobs to rush to her side when she called in crisis saying, "I can't go on by myself." The elicitors of her depressions were mainly recurrent bouts of pyelonephritis and cystitis, which were painful and debilitating. But the primary element in the depression was the bountiful and constant social reinforcement Mrs. G. received from her husband and parents for the sick role.

A behavior modification approach to family therapy was formulated and implemented by a nurse at the Day Treatment Center. Mrs. G., her husband, and her parents participated in framing the details of the program and agreed to carry it out. Mrs. G.'s parents were instructed completely to ignore her complaints (she agreed to this and urged them to follow through, after understanding the rationale), and were reassured that, by so doing, they would be assisting her growth toward a position of strength and confidence. They were also told to converse with their daughter at least once a day, and to focus on reality issues and on her successful coping efforts at home. Their conversations on the phone and personally were to terminate as soon as she began complaining about symptoms or helplessness. Mr. G. was instructed to do the same but in addition was provided with a more tangible means of reinforcing his wife's adaptive behavior. The behavioral analysis revealed that the chain of complaining and depressive behaviors lasting most of the evening began at the moment that Mr. G. returned home from work. A frown, downcast look, or tearful eyes cued Mr. G. that something was wrong and then began the spiral of his reinforcing her depression with concern (or impatience and annoyance), her showing even more depressive features, his reinforcement, etc.

We decided to reverse the chain at its beginning by having Mr. G. reinforce any nondepressive behavior shown at the time of his arrival with the giving of a poker chip to his wife. She would have to return the poker chip to him if she exhibited any depressive behavior that evening. She could exchange the poker chips earned thereby in the following manner: individual "therapy" chats with her nurse-therapist at the Day Treatment Center during which Mrs. G. was free to discuss anything, including her complaints, one chip for 15 min; complaining time with husband, one chip for 15 min; lunch out with mother, five chips; and evening out with husbc d for dinner and show, ten chips.

Mrs. G. accumulated chips quickly; rarely an evening passed without her earning and keeping a chip. She initially spent her chips for complaint sessions with her therapist and, less often, with her husband. These occurred three times the first week, twice the second week, and only once the third week. She then began spending her chips for "fun" outings. The spiral was reversed and she continued receiving social reinforcement from husband, parents, and people at the Day Treatment Center for her improved verbal and task-oriented behavior. During the fifth week of the program, she travelled 100 miles by herself to a university medical center for a diagnostic work-up of her renal disease, an accomplishment that was new to her and that netted much additional recognition of her functional capacity. Now, 2 mo later, Mrs. G. is no longer coming to the mental health center. Her husband, however, who was the critical agent for change, continues to visit the nurse-therapist at increasing intervals for booster sessions to keep his reinforcement flowing contingent upon his wife's adaptive behavior.

By taking advantage of a group setting, behavioral interventions with families can be promoted by teaching parents in groups the principles of behavior that they need to understand and use in becoming effective managers of their children's maladaptive behavior. The training can be carried out in large or small groups (Liberman, 1971c, 1972b). At the Oxnard Mental Health Center, we have been working with groups of four to ten patients for a ten-session module. The first session is devoted to teaching the parents how to specify and pinpoint problems and goals. They learn to translate their initially vague and general problem descriptions into behaviorally specific descriptions that are countable. During the first two sessions they receive didactic instruction in basic behavioral principles such as reinforcement, extinction, shaping, schedules of reinforcement, and punishment. These principles are graphically illustrated with films and case studies, many of them carried out by parents from previous groups. The parents learn to count behaviors and to graph their frequency. A simple but lucid programed text on behavior modification is used, with assignments given each week (Patterson and Gullion, 1971). Behavioral interventions are formulated for use with their children at home. Each parent carries out at least three intervention programs during the ten sessions; one intervention is aimed at modifying a problem of their own behavior (e.g., overeating, coming home late from work, inadequate meal preparation, procrastination over housework).

It should be pointed out that behavioral principles are purposely imbedded in the framework of the course. The parents must make a $10 deposit at the first session, which is refunded if they attend all sessions. Each evening's session begins with a quiz covering their reading assignment. Parents receive ten minutes of the group leader's undivided time and attention only if they bring in their graphs with the data clearly up-to-date. No data means that they must listen to the others without direct consultation with the leader. Finally, the parents are rewarded for their task behavior at the end of the session with a fifteen-minute period of unstructured conversation and discussion. Refreshments are provided intermittently to reinforce attendance and promote cohesiveness.

CONCLUSIONS

The behavioral approach to group and family therapy, with its more systematic and specific guidelines, makes it less likely that a therapist will adventitiously reinforce or model contradictory behavior patterns. The behavioral approach, consistently applied, is a fast and effective means of modifying maladaptive behavior in family and group systems. Although the technology of the behavioral clinician, based on empirical laws of learning, is important in treatment, his relationship with the family or group also contributes to the outcome. A therapist who does not have a positive alliance with his group or family does not possess reinforcing or modeling properties. His role as an educator and lever for initiating changes in the group or family reinforcement contingencies depends partly on his capacity to show empathy, warmth, and concern for those with whom he is working.

Working behaviorally with families and groups leads to a total systems view of the problems and suffering of individuals. Behaviorally oriented therapists cannot afford to restrict themselves to the therapy sessions. Much effort involves collaboration and involvement with other systems impinging on the individual or family, such as schools, rehabilitation services, and the home. Home visits particularly have become a crucial step in successfully intervening with families.

Hopefully, further clinical and research progress made by behavior therapists will challenge all family and group therapists, regardless of their theoretical leanings, to specify more clearly their interventions, their goals, and their empirical results. Only when this happens can we develop a compendium of techniques with known and predictable effects for a wide variety of clinical problems.

BIBLIOGRAPHY

Alberti, R. E., and Emmons, M. L., *Your Perfect Right* (San Luis Obispo, Calif.: Impact, 1970).

Bernal, M. E., "Behavioral Feedback in the Modification of Brat Behaviors," *J. Nerv. Ment. Dis.*, 148:375, 1969.

Clement, P. W., Fazzone, R. A., and Goldstein, B., "Tangible Reinforcers and Child Group Therapy," *J. Am. Acad. Child Psychiat.*, 9:409.

Dinoff, M., *et al.*, "Conditioning the Verbal Behavior of a Psychiatric Population in a Group-therapy Situation," *J. Clin. Psychol.*, 16:371, 1960.

Hawkins, R. P., *et al.*, "Behavior Therapy in the Home: Amelioration of Problem Parent-child Relationships with the Parent in a Therapeutic Role," *J. Exceptional Child Psychol.*, 4:99, 1967.

Heckel, R. W., Wiggins, S. K., and Salzberg, H. D., "Conditioning Against Silences in Group Therapy," *J. Clin. Psychol.*, 18:216, 1962.

Ihli, K. L., and Garlington, W. J., "A Comparison of Group vs. Individual Desensitization of Test Anxiety," *Behav. Res. Ther.*, 7:207, 1969.

Lawrence, H., and Sundel, M., "A Behavior Modification Approach to Group Work with Adults," Unpublished manuscript available from authors at School of Social Work, Michigan University.

Lazarus, A. A., "Group Therapy of Phobic Disorders by Systematic Desensitization," *J. Abnorm. Soc. Psychol.*, 63:504, 1961.

Lewinsohn, P. M., Weinstein, M. S., and Shaw, D. A., "Depression: A Clinical-research Approach," in R. D. Rubin and C. M. Franks, eds., *Advances in Behavior Therapy*, Vol. II (New York: Academic, 1969), p. 231.

Liberman, R. P., "A Behavioral Approach to Group Dynamics," *Behav. Ther.*, 1:141, 1968. (a)

———, "Behavioral Approaches to Family and Couple Therapy," *Amer. J. Orthopsychiat.*, 40:106, 1970. (b)

———, "Reinforcement of Cohesiveness in Group Therapy: Behavioral and Personality Changes," *Arch. Gen. Psychiat.*, 25:168, 1971. (a)

———, *Self-desensitization of Test Anxiety by a Recorded Program* (Newark, N.J.: Testing Studies Institute, 1971). (b)

———, "Teaching Parents to be Therapists for their Children," paper presented at the 23rd Annual Meeting of the American Association of Psychiatric Services for Children, Beverly Hills, November 19-21, 1971. (c)

———, "Behavior Modification in a Community Mental Health Center," in R. Rubin *et al.*, eds., *Advances in Behavior Therapy*, Vol. IV (New York: Academic, 1972). (a)

———, "Reinforcement of Social Interaction in a Group of Chronic Mental Patients," in R. Rubin *et al.*, eds., *Advances in Behavior Therapy*, Vol. III (New York: Academic, 1972). (b)

Lindsley, O. R., "Training Parents and Teachers to Precisely Manage Childrens' Behavior," Unpublished.

Martin, D., "Teaching Child Management Techniques to Parents: A New Approach," paper presented to the 23rd Annual Meeting of the American Association of Psychiatric Services for Children, Beverly Hills, November 19-21, 1971.

O'Connor, R. D., "Modification of Social Withdrawal through Symbolic Modeling," *J. Appl. Behav. Analysis*, 2:15, 1969.

O'Leary, J. D., O'Leary, S., and Becker, W. C., "Modification of a Deviant Sibling Interaction Pattern in the Home," *Behav. Res. Ther.*, 5:113, 1967.

Patterson, G. R., "Behavioral Techniques Based on Social Learning," in C. M. Franks, ed., *Behavior Therapy: Appraisal and Status* (New York: McGraw-Hill, 1969), chap. 9.

––––––, and Gullion, M. E., *Living With Children* (Champaign, Ill.: Research Press, 1971).

Patterson, G. R., Ray, R. S., and Shaw, D. A., "Direct Intervention in Families of Deviant Children," *Oregon Res. Institute Bull.*, 8:1, 1968.

Paul, G. L., *Insight vs. Desensitization in Psychotherapy* (Stanford: Stanford University Press, 1966).

––––––, "Outcome of Systematic Desensitization," in C. M. Franks, ed., *Behavior Therapy: Appraisal and Status* (New York: McGraw-Hill, 1969), chaps. 2, 3.

––––––, and Shannon, D. T., "Treatment of Anxiety through Systematic Desensitization in Therapy Groups," *J. Abnorm. Psychol.*, 71:124, 1966.

Serber, M., "Systematization of Assertive Training," in R. Rubin *et al.*, eds., *Advances in Behavior Therapy*, Vol. 4 (New York: Academic, 1972).

Shapiro, D., and Birk, L., "Group Therapy in Experimental Perspective," *Int. J. Group Psychother.*, 17:211, 1967.

Wahler, R. G., "Oppositional Children: A Quest for Parental Reinforcement Control," *J. Appl. Behav. Analysis*, 2:159, 1969.

Wolpe, J., *The Practice of Behavior Therapy* (New York: Pergamon, 1969).

Ullmann, L. P., and Krasner, L., eds., *Case Studies in Behavior Modification* (New York: Holt, Rinehart, 1965).

51

PREPARING LOWER-CLASS PATIENTS FOR GROUP PSYCHOTHERAPY: DEVELOPMENT AND EVALUATION OF A ROLE INDUCTION FILM

Hans H. Strupp
Anne L. Bloxom

Among the more serious impediments to progress in psychotherapy are those related to the patient's preconceptions or expectations and their alignment with the realities of the psychotherapeutic experience. Obstacles include not only lack of information but: a) poor motivation stemming from apathy or feelings of helplessness; b) defensive inhibitions and the threat of self-examination; and c) misconceptions such as viewing one's emotional problems as physical ailments, attributing the cause of one's troubles to external circumstances, and seeking an authoritarian relationship with an expert who henceforth assumes responsibility for the outcome. These tendencies, while present throughout the population, are most prevalent among the lower socioeconomic classes. Thus, psychotherapy and the lower-class patient have traditionally been a poor match.*

To produce a better alignment between the patient's feelings, attitudes, and expectations about psychotherapy, and the experiences he actually faces as a patient, one might expose the patient to a role induction interview (RII) prior to psychotherapy in which the patient is told what he needs to know.† Such an interview might be conducted either by the

Reprinted from the *Journal of Consulting and Clinical Psychology*, Vol. 41, No. 3, 1973, pp. 373-384, with some revisions. © 1973, American Psychological Association. Reprinted by permission.

* An extensive, topic-coded bibliography providing the basis for the foregoing discussion can be found in Strupp and Bloxom, 1971.

† Credit for the pioneer effort in this area belongs to Martin T. Orne.

therapist himself (Orne and Wender, 1968) or by another trained individual (Hoehn-Saric *et al.*, 1964). Another approach consists of vicarious therapy pretraining in which prospective patients listen to a tape recording illustrating "good" patient behavior in group therapy prior to the beginning of actual group therapy (Truax, 1966).

To determine whether a role induction interview has a favorable effect on the course and outcome of psychotherapy with clinic patients, Hoehn-Saric and associates (1964) compared two groups of neurotic outpatients in individual psychotherapy. The study reported benefits for the experimental group which had received the RII, including better in-therapy behavior and attendance, a more favorable therapeutic relationship, and superior outcome ratings of improvement and social effectiveness.

Yalom and associates (1967) examined the effects of a role induction interview on the early course of group psychotherapy for sixty middle-class outpatients treated by psychiatric residents. They found that the RII increased the development of interpersonal interaction within the group sessions and tended to strengthen the patient's faith in group therapy as a form of treatment. No outcome measures were employed in this study.

An attempt to isolate key factors in the effectiveness of patient preparation was made by Sloane and associates (1970), who examined the effects of various induction procedures on the therapeutic outcomes of thirty-six relatively sophisticated clients treated on an individual basis by psychiatric residents. An anticipatory socialization interview prior to therapy resulted in significantly higher pre- to posttherapy change scores in therapists' ratings on an index of total social, sexual, and work adjustment, but no significant benefits were reflected in symptom change or attendance.

A vicarious training procedure (VTP) developed by Truax (1966) also produced encouraging results. He reported that VTP had major therapeutic benefits for outpatients, modest therapeutic benefit for hospitalized mental patients, and no therapeutic benefit on institutionalized juvenile delinquents. (See also Truax, Shapiro, and Wargo, 1968; Truax, Wargo, and Volksdorf, 1970; Truax, Wargo, Carkhuff, Kodman, and Moles, 1966.)

A related approach to patient training, reported by Warren and Rice (1972), utilized the extratherapy techniques of "stabilizing" (encouraging the patient to discuss and introduce in therapy any concerns with his therapy or therapist) and "structuring" (teaching the patient how to participate productively in the therapy process) at four points within a time-limited, client-centered therapy program. The combined techniques were effective in reducing attrition, improving in-therapy process, and thus achieving greater constructive personality change through therapy.

Since role induction procedures have clearly emerged as promising techniques meriting further research, it seemed desirable to explore whether a role induction instrument could be developed which would combine the advantages of an individual interview with mass administration. Thus, the purpose of this study was: a) to develop such an instrument, and b) to assess its value under field conditions.

DEVELOPMENT OF ROLE INDUCTION FILM

The anticipatory socialization interview (Orne and Wender, 1968) serves three major purposes: a) to establish a rational basis for the patient to accept psychotherapy as a means of helping him deal with his problem, recognizing that talking is not seen by most patients as a treatment modality; b) to clarify the role of patient and therapist in the course of treatment; and c) to provide a general outline of the course of therapy and its vicissitudes, with particular emphasis on clarification of the patient's negative and hostile feelings. In addition, we wished to convey specific points of information to create more positive and realistic attitudes concerning psychotherapy. Thus the role induction should prepare the patient:* a) to express personal feelings to a mental health professional; b) to recognize that talking about troublesome feelings can be useful; c) to understand that change requires work that he must do himself; d) to accept the knowledge that some of his difficulties are self-inflicted, through inadequate thinking and defensive attitudes; e) to understand that some physical ailments can be, in part at least, caused by psychological stresses; f) to realize that there are adaptive and maladaptive ways of expressing anger, hostility, resentment, and aggression; g) to accept peers as potential allies and friends instead of enemies; h) to expect no miracles and understand that personality change takes time; i) to accept the knowledge that medication provides no solution to problems in living; j) to learn that difficulties in living are common, and that they can be dealt with more effectively by talking about them than by hiding them; and k) to expect that there are no "cures" for life's difficulties—only more or less adequate ways of dealing with them.

A documentary film was selected as the most effective vehicle for creating positive attitudes toward mental health services in the prospective patient population. After extensive preliminary work, including the study of actual interview data, the film entitled *Turning Point* was produced (black and white, 16 mm., running time thirty-two minutes).* Its potential advantages included direct appeal to a wide audience, particularly members of the lower-income group who are seen as the prime target audience; dramatic impact; and realistic presentation of the nature and

* Some of the points are noted by Riessman, Cohen, and Pearl (1964).
* Herschel N. Pollard contributed valuable assistance as writer and production coordinator.

extent of benefits from mental health services, especially from group psychotherapy.

The film is a dramatic story dealing with the life of a truck driver. Tom Sievier is a man in his early thirties whose major problem, as depicted in the film, is a volatile temper which leads to open conflict with authority figures, notably his boss, as well as with co-workers and his family. Following a violent verbal interchange with the boss, he gets fired from his job. Prospects for help from a mental health clinic, where he is seen in a preliminary interview by a social worker, impress Tom as dim. His pattern of uncontrolled aggressiveness leads to dismissal from several other jobs, and Tom's wife and children leave him after one of his provocations. He reaches a state of despondency, turns to alcohol, and eventually contemplates suicide. Recalling a friendly interaction with a patient whom he had encountered at the clinic, he returns and joins a therapy group. A series of scenes showing the therapy group in action demonstrate how, in the context of this experience, Tom gains some understanding of his own contribution to the difficulties in his life. The film ends as Tom succeeds in applying these insights: He regains his original job and works out a more satisfactory relationship with his wife.

EVALUATION OF ROLE INDUCTION FILM

Method

To assess the merits of the newly developed role induction film in a setting similar to the field conditions under which such an instrument would ordinarily be used, a series of therapy groups composed of typical members of the target population was initiated and a systematic comparison made of the effects of varying induction procedures upon the course and outcome of group psychotherapy.

Patients. A total of 122 patients was selected from twelve community agencies. Emphasis was placed on lower-income clients who were in need of psychological counseling to reach their rehabilitation objectives, yet had minimal motivation to seek and accept mental health services. The sample population proved to be well balanced by sex and by race, containing similar proportions of males and females and of blacks and whites. The average age was twenty-nine. Although patients ranged from seventeen to sixty-five years of age, the majority were young adults in their twenties or thirties. The educational level ranged from fourth grade through college, with the average years of education falling at 10.8.

Therapists. Four therapists were selected on the basis of their extensive experience in group psychotherapy, particularly with patients similar to those constituting the target population. Three were male clinical psychologists holding the Ph.D. degree; one was a female psychiatric nurse with comparable training and experience. All were actively working as therapists, considered highly competent by their peers, and were paid a regular professional fee for their participation in the project.

Design. It was stipulated that each psychotherapist would treat three groups of patients for twelve weekly sessions, each group initially being composed of approximately ten individuals. Each group was introduced to group psychotherapy by one of the following procedures (the order of the induction procedures was varied across therapists):

1. *Group F* viewed *Turning Point,* the role induction film developed as part of this project. Patients were simply informed that they were to see a motion picture; no further instructions were given.

2. *Group I* received a *role induction interview* patterned after the Anticipatory Socialization Interview developed by Orne as adapted by the investigators at the Henry Phipps Psychiatric Clinic. All interviews were conducted by an experienced psychiatrist who met with designated groups at their first scheduled meeting. Patients were encouraged to ask questions about group psychotherapy and relevant concerns.

3. *Group N* viewed a *neutral (control) film* dealing with early marriage. This condition was included to equalize the interest and attention devoted to prospective patients receiving the foregoing procedures. It occupied a comparable amount of time but contained no information relevant to the induction process. Instructions paralleled those of the role induction film.

Procedure. To evaluate the effectiveness of the role induction procedures in as natural a setting as possible, the study included two phases: the therapy phase and the research phase. Separate personnel were employed in each phase. By administering the research instruments outside the therapy setting we hoped to obtain more open and honest responses and to avoid interference with the therapeutic process.

The *therapy phase* consisted of a free twelve-week group therapy program for any community agency's clients who were in need of such services but who, for reasons of inadequate resources or lack of interest, had not received therapeutic aid. The therapy program was incorporated into the agency's setting, with clients maintaining their primary contact with the agency. Each therapy session lasted one to one and one-half hours and was conducted in accordance with the therapist's preferred style. Therapeutic techniques may be characterized as broadly eclectic.

The *research phase* included ten data-collection sessions spaced throughout the program. Appropriate sets of ratings were presented to clients in booklet form and they were paid $1.00 for each completed booklet. It was emphasized that only research personnel would have access to the rating information. Therapists completed separate ratings at comparable intervals.

Assessments were made before and after the induction session, before session 1, and following sessions 1, 3, 5, 7, 9, 11, and 12. Therapists and patients were unaware of the design and purpose of the study.

Research Instruments. A battery of tests and rating instruments was developed specifically for this project. Published scales were used whenever possible. Some instruments were modified for group psychotherapy and the wording simplified for lower-class patients. Assessment forms included Personnel Tests for Industry: Verbal Test A (Wesman, 1952); Psychotherapy Expectancy Inventory, Revised (Berzins, Friedman, and Seidman, 1969); Self Disclosure Scale, Revised (Jourard, 1964) Discomfort Scale (Hoehn-Saric *et al.*, 1964); Marlowe-Crowne Social Desirability Scale (Crowne and Marlowe, 1960); ratings of motivation, knowledge of therapy, and expected improvement; Target Symptoms (Battle *et al.*, 1966); ratings of process, satisfaction, and improvement in therapy; Therapy Behavior Scale (Hoehn-Saric *et al.*, 1964); patient's attractiveness for psychotherapy; severity of disturbance; and prognosis in therapy.

Results*

Statistical Procedures. A least-squares analysis of variance was employed to isolate main effects for the three role induction conditions, the four therapists, and repeated measures over time, as well as to examine for interactions of these variables. Results discussed here are primarily those derived from examination of the role induction condition main effects and condition by repeated measures interactions. Correlations were calculated by the Pearson Product-Moment method. The 5 per cent level of confidence was the criterion of significance.

Preinduction Comparability of Patients. There were no initial induction group differences in social desirability, severity of disturbance, symptom discomfort, target symptom severity, prognosis in therapy, attractiveness for psychotherapy, self-disclosure, expectation of playing an active role in therapy, motivation to begin therapy, or quality and outcome of the screening interview. In addition, the three groups were considered well matched in terms of sex, race, age, and education.

Patients' Attitudes Toward Induction. Patients who received either of the role induction procedures enjoyed their initial role induction meeting more than those in the neutral condition, and they considered the session as more helpful in preparing them to benefit from the group sessions to follow. Their attitudes were apparently based on more than the possible "entertainment value" of the induction procedure, since significant positive correlations were found between these items and other measures of positive expectations (willingness to begin the treatment program, anticipated

---

* See Strupp and Bloxom (1971) for further details of procedure; a transcript of the role induction interview and the question-and-answer session that followed; the complete text, source, and schedule of administration of all research measures; and a more exhaustive report of the results from the evaluation study.

satisfaction with the first therapy session, estimated global improvement, and realistic expectations of improvement): subsequent measures of in-therapy behavior and satisfaction; and posttherapy measures of outcome (gain in self-understanding, global improvement, and the therapist's satisfaction with the patient's progress in therapy).

It is also important to note that patients who were in greatest need of help, as evidenced by therapists' ratings of severity of disturbance, tended to experience the most positive reaction to the role induction procedures.

Motivation to Begin Group Sessions. Therapists' ratings of motivational factors showed pre- to postinduction changes in the direction of increased motivation for patients who had either viewed the role induction film or participated in the role induction interview. Patients in the neutral group showed consistent decrements in all ratings of motivation to begin therapy. The film procedure equaled or surpassed the interview in bringing about these motivational changes in patients—changes which must have been exhibited in the patients' overt behavior, which provided the basis for the therapists' ratings. The therapists, it will be remembered, were unaware of the scheduling, content, or purpose of the role induction meetings.

Knowledge of Therapy and Patient-Therapist Roles. Both role induction procedures effected a favorable change in the patient's understanding of the therapy process and his role in it, while patients in the neutral condition showed either negligible or unfavorable changes in this area. A specific component of this favorable change was the increased expectancy of playing an active role in the therapy process (initiating and continuing discussion). At the same time, the therapist tended to be seen as functioning more clearly in a guiding role. Those in the neutral condition showed no change in expectancies concerning their participation; rather, there were marked increments in their expectancy that the therapist would offer direct suggestions and answers to their problems.

Therapist Ratings of Patient Attractiveness. There were no group differences in rated attractiveness following the screening interview. After the first therapy session, patients in the film and interview groups were rated as more attractive than those in the neutral group. The level of attractiveness had risen comparably for the two induction groups, while remaining unchanged for the neutral group.

Estimated Posttherapy Improvement. In ratings made after the induction, both therapists and patients expected a significantly greater improvement for patients who had participated in one of the role induction procedures. The film was most effective in raising the patients' expectations, although the two role induction procedures appeared to have similar effects in terms of therapists' ratings. Patients in the neutral condition showed a lower expectancy of improvement, both in terms of therapists' and self-ratings.

Symptom Discomfort. A twenty-five-item Discomfort Scale was completed by the patients prior to their induction session and a week later (before their first therapy session). All patients showed a significant drop in the total discomfort score as well as subscale scores for somatic symptoms, anxiety, and depression following the induction. (The improvement related to the number of symptoms reported as well as to their severity.) This increased comfort was manifested in the patients' subsequent behavior, since changes in the severity of disturbance ratings made by the therapists following the screening interview and again after the first therapy session closely paralleled the discomfort ratings of the patients. While entering a therapeutic program produced a significant decrease in the discomfort reported by patients and in the level of disturbance rated by therapists, the specific content of the induction procedures was not sufficiently powerful to produce any *differential* changes among groups.*

Patients' Satisfaction with Therapy Sessions. While there was a slight tendency for all patients to report a higher level of satisfaction by the end of the therapy program, patients in the two role induction groups reported significantly greater satisfaction than those in the neutral group at every point in time.

Patients' Progress in Therapy and Perceived Improvement. Comparable self-ratings of satisfaction with progress in therapy showed the film induction group as reporting the greatest satisfaction, the interview group occupying an intermediate level, and the neutral group ranking third. When *changes* in the patients' levels of satisfaction over time were examined, it was found that the ratings of patients in the neutral group tended to fluctuate around their initial level, while patients in the film and interview induction groups became more satisfied with their progress as the therapy program continued. This increase in satisfaction was most pronounced during the first half of the therapy program for patients who had viewed the induction film, while it did not appear until the latter half of the therapy program for patients who had participated in the induction interview.

Patients assessed how they "get along with others" at comparable points throughout the therapy program. Although the induction conditions appeared to have no demonstrable effect on the *level* of satisfaction reported by patients, there was a significant difference among groups in their change scores on this item. By session 11, patients who had participated in the film or interview induction procedures showed a significant increase in satisfaction with their interpersonal relations, while patients in the neutral condition remained relatively unchanged. Again, this increase in

* Posttherapy ratings on the Discomfort Scale and Severity of Disturbance measures indicated that this postinduction improvement was maintained throughout the therapy program, though no further improvement was evident. Posttherapy ratings continued to reveal no significant induction group differences.

satisfaction appeared early in the therapy program for patients in the film induction group and later in the program for those in the interview group.

Therapist Ratings of Patients' In-Therapy Behavior. Therapists were asked to rate each patient's in-therapy behavior (on a five-point scale) following session 1 and again at the end of the therapy program. During session 1, patients who had viewed the induction film exhibited the most "appropriate" behavior; patients who had participated in the induction interview received intermediate ratings; the behavior of patients in the neutral procedure was considered least appropriate ($p = .001$). Posttherapy ratings of the patients' behavior throughout all therapy sessions revealed two points of interest: a) the *level* of appropriateness was greater for all patients, indicating that they were learning more appropriate in-therapy behavior as the sessions progressed. There was a slight tendency for patients with the poorest initial ratings to show the greatest improvement; b) the ranked order of the three role induction groups, from session 1 ratings, remained unchanged, and the difference among groups was still statistically significant ($p = .01$).

Some more specific aspects of patients' in-therapy behavior were measured by the Therapy Behavior Scale (descriptions of sixteen desirable and fifteen undesirable behaviors which a patient might exhibit during his therapy sessions). At all points in the therapy program there were sizable induction condition effects, with patients who had participated in the film or interview procedures exhibiting more desirable behavior than those in the neutral condition. The effects of the induction conditions were greatest at session 1 ($p = .001$) and gradually diminished as the therapy program progressed to session 11 ($p = .06$). The interview group showed greatest benefits early in therapy; by session 6 the scores for the interview and film groups had merged.

Attendance. There were no statistically significant differences among patients from the three role induction groups on any of the attendance indices. This may have been partly a function of the nature of patient recruitment and of the over-all structure of the therapy program. Only 6 per cent of the patient population reported as a reason for termination that they did not wish to continue therapy, while 35 per cent terminated because they had left their parent agency.

Therapist Ratings of Patient Attractiveness. While the preinduction ratings revealed no differences among patients, the postinduction ratings showed a significant difference among groups resulting from an increase in attractiveness for patients in the film and interview groups and no change for patients in the neutral group; posttherapy ratings revealed a decrease in attractiveness for all patients regardless of induction condition, but there were still significant group differences in *level* of attractiveness which favored the patients in the two role induction groups.

It appears that the role induction training enhanced the patients' attractiveness to their therapist. This effect was most marked early in therapy, but was still present (relative to the neutral group) in the post-therapy ratings. The induction film and interview procedures seemed equally effective in this respect.

Patient Ratings of Posttherapy Improvement. Although all groups reported substantial improvement, significant induction group differences were reflected in posttherapy ratings of global improvement, improvement in specific target symptoms, and self-understanding achieved through therapy. All group differences favored the two role induction conditions over the neutral condition, with the role induction film appearing somewhat more effective than the interview procedure.

Therapist Ratings of Posttherapy Improvement. There were no statistically significant differences among the three treatment conditions in similar ratings of posttherapy improvement completed by the therapists. When the therapists' evaluations were compared with the patients' self-ratings, it was seen that the self-ratings generally reflected higher levels of improvement.

Figure 1 presents the per cent of patients rated as "Improved," "No Change," or "Worse" by themselves and their therapists, for each of the three role induction conditions. As in the mean levels of improvement, there were significant induction group differences in the patient ratings but not in the therapist ratings, and greater improvement was reported by patients than by therapists. However, this generalization does not hold for patients in the neutral condition. Here patient and therapist ratings of

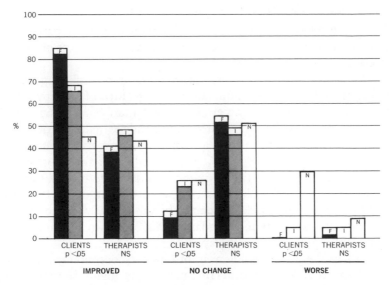

Figure 51–1.   Posttherapy global improvement: comparison of patient and therapist ratings.

"Improved" were comparable, but 30 per cent of the patients rated themselves as "Worse" compared to only 7 per cent who were so regarded by their therapists.

Patients' Satisfaction with the Treatment Program. It will be recalled that patients in the induction film and interview groups reported greater satisfaction with their therapy sessions than those in the neutral group. Following the last session, patients were asked whether they would recommend the group meetings to a friend. Of the patients in the induction film group, 85 per cent said they would recommend the group therapy sessions, compared to 77 per cent of the interview group and only 63 per cent of the neutral group.

Patients in the two role induction conditions consistently reported greater satisfaction and benefit from therapy. In a direct posttherapy rating of the helpfulness of the induction procedure, it was evident that patients viewed some role induction as more helpful than none; the induction film was considered, in retrospect, as the most helpful procedure.

Discussion

Consistent evidence was presented that a role induction procedure facilitated a favorable therapy experience for lower-class patients. Participation in either of the role induction procedures was clearly more beneficial than the neutral procedure. The interview seemed to be superior in conveying a detailed knowledge of the process of group therapy, whereas the film was superior over a wider range of measures.

Measures Not Reflecting Role-Induction Benefits

While the majority of instruments completed by both patients and therapists showed the foregoing differential effects, certain areas of measurement yielded inconclusive results.

1. *Attendance.* Although earlier research produced conflicting evidence concerning the effects of role induction on attendance of therapy sessions (Hoehn-Saric et al., 1964; Sloane et al., 1970; Yalom et al., 1967), in the present study, none of the various attendance indices reflected differential induction effects. Failure to attend a session was primarily a function of termination. (There was only a 10% absence rate over the entire therapy program for "active" clients.) The majority of patients terminating from the therapy program did so because they were discharged by the parent agency. Only seven patients left therapy, because they were not satisfied with the groups. In addition, attendance was found to be unrelated to satisfaction or improvement in therapy.

Patients in the present study were of lower socioeconomic status with minimal motivation for psychotherapy; many were highly resistant to discussions about "mental health" and had rejected repeated attempts to guide them toward therapy. This fact, coupled with the findings of Frank,

Gliedman, Imber, Nash, and Stone (1957) that lower-class patients exhibit a dropout rate double that of middle-class patients and that the dropout rate for group therapy is three times that for individual therapy strongly suggests that attendance in this study was relatively encouraging.

2. *Therapists' Ratings of Outcome.* While patients' self-ratings of therapy outcome showed clear-cut differences favoring the role induction procedures, therapists' ratings failed to do so. A possible explanation for these discrepancies is that patients and therapists were using different base lines for judging improvement. Perhaps patients compared their post-therapy state with their entire recent history before entering therapy, whereas therapists compared the patients' posttherapy performance only with their performance in the early therapy sessions. It is important to note that patients showed a great deal of change immediately following their induction session, and these changes were more marked and broader in scope for patients in the induction film and interview conditions. On some measures, such as appropriate in-therapy behavior, patients in the two role induction conditions were able to begin their first therapy session at a very high level, while patients in the neutral condition began at a lower level which gradually increased. On other measures, such as symptom discomfort, all patients showed a significant positive change immediately after their induction session, and maintained this level throughout therapy. If the therapists used patient behavior in the first therapy session as part of the base line from which they judged subsequent improvement (as they surely must have in the absence of any other extensive data), it becomes obvious that much of the gain experienced by the patients would be lost in the therapists' improvement scores, and this loss would be greater for patients in the induction film and interview groups. This could explain the patient-therapist discrepancies in both degree of improvement and differences between conditions. Other possibilities are that therapists were more cautious in their assessments (using a broader spectrum of patients as a standard), and that patients' ratings were inflated by placebo effects and the desire to please the researchers.

The only previous investigation of a role induction technique in which comparable ratings by therapists were employed (Hoehn-Saric *et al.*, 1964) showed statistically significant differences in the predicted direction. Since there were numerous differences between the two studies, the divergent findings are difficult to interpret. However, possible factors include: a) therapists' level of experience (ratings in the Hoehn-Saric study were made by psychiatric residents, whereas in the present one more experienced therapists were used); and b) time of final evaluation (Hoehn-Saric assessed improvement for all patients at the time of termination irrespective of when it occurred, whereas in the present study only patients in attendance at the end of the program were assessed).

Relation to Other Role Induction Studies. Three major studies employing a role induction interview as preparation for psychotherapy have been reported in the literature (Hoehn-Saric *et al.*, 1964; Sloane *et al.*, 1970; and Yalom *et al.*, 1967). Direct comparisons are difficult because each study varied considerably in terms of the specific content of the induction interview; furthermore, there were differences relating to patients (level of sophistication) and therapists (experience level) as well as major variables and measuring instruments. Despite the numerous divergences, all studies found a role induction technique to have significant beneficial effects on one or more of the major variables investigated.

It is interesting to note that when the four relevant studies (including the present one) are ranked with respect to a) magnitude of effects attributable to the role induction procedure, and b) patients' level of sophistication about psychotherapy, there emerges a direct inverse relationship, the least sophisticated patients showing the greatest response to role induction. To stress the importance of the patient variable in the outcome of these studies does not, of course, rule out the influence of other factors, such as content of the induction interviews, therapists' level of experience, and assessment techniques. Bergin (1971) documents the relevance of the latter two factors and concludes that nearly three times as many studies involving experienced therapists yield positive results as do those employing unexperienced therapists, and that separate outcome factors often emerge as a function of the rater and of the assessment instrument.

Implications. Why does a role induction procedure work and how does it achieve beneficial results? Since studies designed to isolate the components have met with little success (Imber *et al.*, 1970; Sloane *et al.*, 1970), it may be more profitable to think in terms of a learning experience leading to more favorable therapy process. The content of the role induction interview or film covers a wide range of relevant information. Consequently, a patient who accepts this information is equipped with more realistic expectations concerning the process of therapy, his role vis-à-vis the therapist and other patients, the meaning of improvement, and the steps he must take to benefit from the experience. These changed expectations produce complementary changes in attitudes, motivations, and behavior which make him more attractive to the therapist and in other respects enhance his likelihood of success. Coupled with the symptomatic relief a patient typically experiences upon entering therapy, the foregoing factors may potentiate a favorable therapy outcome.

The primary contribution of a role induction procedure is: a) to provide accurate information concerning the process of therapy; b) to dispel misconceptions and prejudice which are abundant in all strata of the population, but particularly among unsophisticated persons; c) to enhance the prospective patient's motivation for psychotherapeutic change; and, perhaps most important, d) to pave the way for a more realistic view concerning emotional problems in living and their resolution. The latter entails an acceptance of the position that the individual must take a more active role in mastering his problems, assume greater responsibility for himself and his place in the world, and oppose the tendency for dependency and passivity. These lessons obviously cannot be learned in a single session or by viewing a film. Nevertheless, the motion picture developed for this purpose appears to be an excellent vehicle for initiating the process.* A filmed instrument has the added advantages of efficiency, mass administration, standardization of procedure, and wide audience appeal for lower socioeconomic groups; moreover, viewing a film in familiar surroundings arouses little anxiety in the reluctant or defensive patient, and may pave the way for a more relaxed face-to-face encounter with mental health professionals.

BIBLIOGRAPHY

1. Battle, C. C., Imber, S. D., Hoehn-Saric, R., Nash, E. H., and Frank, J. D., "Target Complaints as Criteria of Improvement," *Am. J. Psychother.*, 20:184-192, 1966.
2. Bergin, A. E., "The Evaluation of Therapeutic Outcomes," in A. E. Bergin and S. L. Garfield, eds., *Handbook of Psychotherapy and Behavior Change: An Empirical Analysis* (New York: Wiley, 1971), pp. 217-270.
3. Berzins, J. I., Friedman, W. H., and Seidman, E., "Relationship of the A-B Variable to Patient Symptomatology and Psychotherapy Expectancies," *J. Abnorm. Psychol.*, 74:119-125, 1969.
4. Crowne, D. P., and Marlowe, D., "A New Scale of Social Desirability Independent of Psychopathology," *J. Consult. Psychol.*, 24:349-354, 1960.
5. Frank, J. D., Gliedman, L. H., Imber, S. D., Nash, E. H., and Stone, A. R., "Why Patients Leave Psychotherapy," *AMA Arch. Neurol. Psychiat.*, 77:283-299, 1957.
6. Frank, J. D., Nash, E. H., Stone, A. R., and Imber, S. D., "Immediate and Long-term Symptomatic Course of Psychiatric Outpatients," *Am. J. Psychiat.*, 120:429-439, 1963.
7. Hoehn-Saric, R., Frank, J. D., Imber, S. D., Nash, E. H., Stone, A. R., and Battle, C. C., "Systematic Preparation of Patients for Psychotherapy: I. Effects on Therapy Behavior and Outcome," *J. Psychiat. Res.*, 2:267-281, 1964.
8. Imber, S. D., Pande, S. K., Frank, J. D., Hoehn-Saric, R., Stone, A. R., and Wargo, D. G., "Time-focused Role Induction," *J. Nerv. Ment. Dis.*, 150: 27-30, 1970.
9. Jourard, S. M., *The Transparent Self* (Princeton: Van Nostrand, 1964).
10. Orne, M. T., and Wender, P. H., "Anticipatory Socialization for Psychotherapy: Method and Rationale," *Am. J. Psychiat.*, 124:1202-1212, 1968.
11. Riessman, F., Cohen, J., and Pearl, A., *Mental Health of the Poor: New*

---

* Copies of the induction film, *Turning Point*, are available from the senior author for purchase or rental.

Treatment Approaches for Low Income People (New York: Free Press, 1964).

12. Sloane, R. B., Cristol, A. H., Pepernik, M. C., and Staples, F. R., "Role Preparation and Expectation of Improvement in Psychotherapy," *J. Nerv. Ment. Dis.*, 150:18-26, 1970.

13. Stone, A. R., Frank, J. D., Nash, E. H., and Imber, S. D., "An Intensive Five-year Follow-up Study of Treated Psychiatric Outpatients," *J. Nerv. Ment. Dis.*, 133:410-422, 1961.

14. Strupp, H. H., and Bloxom, A. L., "Preparing the Lower-class Patient for Psychotherapy: Development and Evaluation of a Role Induction Procedure," Final Report: Research and Demonstration Grant No. 15-P-55164, Social and Rehabilitation Service of the Department of Health, Education and Welfare, September 1971 (Available from Interlibrary Loan, Joint University Libraries, Vanderbilt University, Nashville, Tennessee, 37240).

15. Truax, C. B., "Counseling and Psychotherapy: Process and Outcome," Final Report: V.R.A. Research and Demonstration Grant No. 906-P, University of Arkansas, Arkansas Rehabilitation Research and Training Center, June 1966.

16. ———, Shapiro, J. G., and Wargo, D. G., "The Effects of Alternate Sessions and Vicarious Therapy Pretraining on Group Psychotherapy," *Int. J. Group Psychother.*, 18:186-198, 1968.

17. Truax, C. B., Wargo, D. G., and Volksdorf, N. R., "Antecedents to Outcome in Group Counseling with Institutionalized Juvenile Delinquents: Effects of Therapeutic Conditions, Patient Self-exploration, Alternate Sessions, and Vicarious Therapy Pretraining," *J. Abnorm. Psychol.*, 76:235-242, 1970.

18. Truax, C. B., Wargo, D. G., Carkhuff, R. R., Kodman, F., and Moles, E. A., "Changes in Self-concepts During Group Psychotherapy as a Function of Alternate Sessions and Vicarious Therapy Pretraining in Institutionalized Juvenile Delinquents," *J. Consult. Psychol.*, 30:309-314, 1966.

19. Warren, N. C., and Rice, L. N., "Structuring and Stabilizing of Psychotherapy for Low-prognosis Clients," *J. Consult. Clin. Psychol.*, 39:173-181, 1972.

20. Wesman, A. G., *Personnel Tests for Industry: Verbal Test A* (New York: The Psychological Corporation, 1952).

21. Yalom, I. D., Houts, P. S., Newell, G., and Rand, K. H., "Preparation of Patients for Group Therapy," *Arch. Gen. Psychiat.*, 17:416-427, 1967.

Part 5

TRAINING

THE PAPERS that are included in this section suggest the development of training concepts in group psychotherapy. Perhaps one of the more interesting aspects of the papers that follow is their consistent neglect of any consideration of the principles of social psychology and group dynamics in the training of individuals as group therapists. Although Warkentin, in his paper on group therapy, recognizes the importance of continual group experience for the therapist in order for him to recognize his "ordinariness as a person," there is no comment about any principles of group composition which may aid the therapist in his work. Warkentin has added to his original paper from today's viewpoint. Recognition of the values that are embodied in the training of group therapists is pointed to by Beukenkamp. This is not discussed in any great detail, but can be found amplified from the perspective of the philosopher in Part 6 (see Friedman, "Dialogue and the 'Essential We' ").

The remaining paper in this section consists of the findings of Aaron Stein in his survey of practices in the field of group psychotherapy. Again there is little acknowledgment of the importance of the contributions of social psychology to the training of the group psychotherapist. For example, Stein does not report any group psychotherapists as being aware of the distinctive difference between the closed dyadic group experience that exists between therapist and patient in individual psychotherapy and the more open group experience in group psychotherapy (see Rosenbaum, "The Challenge of Group Psychoanalysis," article in Part 3). Stein is more comfortable with the "medical model," and this emphasis is reflected in his description of training.

52

THE UTILIZATION
OF A THERAPY GROUP
IN TEACHING PSYCHOTHERAPY

Samuel B. Hadden

The amount of teaching time allotted to psychiatry in most medical schools is not sufficient to give the student more than a sketchy appreciation of the nature of mental illness, its symptomatology and classification. The average internship does not include much training in the management of mental illness, and as a result most physicians enter the practice of medicine incapable of rendering adequate psychiatric service to their patients. Major psychotic disturbances are referred to psychiatric centers, but the neuroses, not fully understood, are often mismanaged.

Students and physicians ought to be better acquainted with psychotherapeutic procedures; at least they should be more familiar with the results obtained by psychotherapeutic techniques so that they may treat patients more satisfactorily, or refer them for early specialized treatment, rather than continue the mismanagement so common today. There is little doubt that psychiatric teaching has improved greatly in the last ten years, but newer methods must be tried in order to use the allotted time more efficiently. The utilization of a therapy group in a teaching program offers this promise.

Shortly after we began the use of the group method in the treatment of psychoneurotic patients at the Presbyterian and Philadelphia General Hospitals, interns attended as guests, and they were very much pleased with the understanding of psychopathology and psychotherapeutic methods which they acquired. Some attended regularly and indicated that the sessions had proved an excellent way of learning the fundamentals of psychotherapy. In an early communication on the group method [1] I stated:

Reprinted from the *American Journal of Psychiatry*, Vol. 103, No. 5, March 1947, pp. 644-648.

"Although the group clinic has not been a part of the formal instruction in psychiatry of any class of students, the interns, residents and others who attended have been enthusiastic about its possibilities. At this time when there is need for the rapid training of psychiatrists in the management of the neuroses, the group method ought to be considered in such a program." Additional experience has strongly confirmed this belief.

From the beginning those interested in psychiatry who came to the sessions were very enthusiastic despite the fact that they simply sat in on the sessions as observers, had no contact with patients and little opportunity to discuss what they observed. About three years ago we were requested by Dr. Gammon, director of the department of neurology, to take over the treatment of psychoneurotic patients in the neurological outpatient department of the Hospital of the University of Pennsylvania. Here students were assigned to observe, and many were stimulated to greater interest. When the neurological outpatient service assumed responsibility for the treatment of discharged service men with neuroses, a special clinic was organized for their treatment on a group basis. Student volunteers were requested, and seniors were assigned to take histories of the men referred. This first group functioned during their senior year, and students attended the group sessions regularly. All reported favorably on their experiences.

With the reopening of the fall term in September, 1944, volunteer senior students began to attend the clinic. They took histories, conducted follow-up interviews, attended the group sessions, and participated in discussions on the mechanisms of the therapy sessions. With few exceptions the volunteers were regular in attendance and their interest was most gratifying.

Each patient referred to the clinic was assigned to a student who took his history, did the indicated examinations, and arranged conferences with his patient each week before or after the period devoted to group discussion. The students participating were mainly seniors in the army or navy medical program and were accepted by the recently discharged neurotic veterans for what they were—sincere, earnest students soon to become a part of army or navy medicine.

Patients enrolled in the clinic were either discharged veterans or men rejected for military service because of neuroses. They were referred by the Veterans' Bureau, the Red Cross, and other agencies. New patients were accepted at any session. Meetings were held once a week and lasted from one hour to an hour and a half. Before the discussion period each week I tried to see as many patients and students as possible and discuss specific problems or answer questions. Because I had no teaching assistants it was impossible to give as much supervision as was desirable, and I could not become personally acquainted with the problems of every patient or lend much assistance to the students in the handling of their patients. Despite the lack of adequate supervision the students acquired some knowledge of dynamics and acceptable psychotherapeutic procedures, and the patients improved.

At each weekly meeting, after the students had spent twenty to forty minutes with their assigned patients, the student-physicians and patients assembled and a group session was held. The patients were encouraged to do most of the talking, but the students were directed to participate and to ask questions and make comments when the discussion lagged or when they saw an opportunity to direct attention to the specific problems or needs of a patient under their care.

In the early sessions we presented fundamental psychodynamic principles in simple language and helped the patient and student to understand how disturbance of body function may be produced by emotion.[1] At later meetings mental mechanisms such as repression, sublimation, rationalization, projection, introjection, and regression were plainly described and were illustrated by common examples to draw the patient into the discussion and have him indicate his awareness of the working of these mechanisms in himself. It was a surprise to students and physicians alike to discover how readily patients recognized and spoke of their own use of rationalization, projection, and similar mechanisms.

After patients acquired a reasonable appreciation of simple psychodynamics, brief histories were presented for discussion. These cases were selected to show the role of rejection, overprotection, and other experiences in the production of neurotic traits. We have found this very valuable because it is an effective method of vicarious catharsis and patients identify themselves with the experiences of the persons under discussion. As various features of the cases were analyzed by the group, insight into the workings of their own minds as well as that of the person whose case was discussed was effectively obtained. During such presentations patients divulged their problems and life histories very freely and rapidly acquired an objective attitude toward themselves and their difficulties.

The effectiveness of the therapy sessions was heightened for the patients by the presence of the students. Patients in attendance understood that the sessions were part of the training of the students, consequently comments made by the therapist or students were accepted by the patients as being authentic. During the first year of our experimental use of the group, students were selected in turn to direct at least one session. This gave them valuable experience in presenting their views, but as they were not sufficiently advanced to guide the discussion into proper channels the practice was discontinued in the last year.

It is not the purpose of this paper to present the dynamics of group therapy but to indicate its usefulness as a means of teaching students. By attendance at therapy sessions students have had the opportunity of observing the development of a patient's history as well as the explanation of his symptoms. They have watched the uncovering of repressed experiences, with resulting abreaction during the discussions. They have also had the opportunity of dealing with patients as they began to understand their acquisition of neurotic patterns of behavior and gradually recognize their visceral symptoms as emotionally determined. During discussion of patients' difficulties students have been able to observe rationalization, projection, and other mechanisms utilized by patients in attempts to protect themselves in the discussion before the group. They have seen how patients were assisted to recognize their use of these mechanisms in such a way that no additional psychic trauma was effected. In the group they have watched feelings of resentment and flagrant hostilities manifested by patients and have observed the handling of these situations by the therapist with the aid of the group. Discussion of the situations after the termination of the sessions has helped students to understand what they have witnessed. They have acquired an appreciation of methods used in dealing with the patients during the therapeutic process. The acquisition of insight by patients has been demonstrated to the group, first in its intellectual aspects, and frequently full emotional insight has been observed in patients under their care.

The benefits to students in attendance have been considerable. Before participation in the group sessions few of the students had any appreciation of what could be accomplished for neurotic complaints, and to have them realize that such symptoms as pain, cardiac palpitation, nausea, vomiting, syncope, giddiness, uncontrollable anger, and irritability could be improved by psychotherapeutic manipulations was a revelation to many. The attitude of hopelessness in dealing with neurotic symptoms has been dissipated. Most of the students are now able to understand that neurotic symptoms are real and not imaginary. It was interesting to observe the students as they interviewed their patients and felt it necessary to give them some kind of medicine, even though it be a placebo. However, since no medication was administered to any of the patients, students have come to know that these crutches are seldom of value in dealing with the neurotic.

One of the most beneficial effects to these volunteer students has been the awakening of a real interest in psychiatry. Several have admitted that prior to their experience with the group they had little regard for psychiatry, but have since decided that it is a hopeful as well as an interesting branch of medicine. About one third of those who attended sessions during the two-year operation of the veterans' clinic have decided upon psychiatry as their specialty, and many have already begun their career in army or navy psychiatry.

Comments of some of the students are of interest. One of the most frequent remarks was that this was the first opportunity they had had to work with the neurotic patient on such an intimate and prolonged basis.

These students have emphasized the fact that although they heard much about "treating the patient as an individual," they had no practice in doing so and no occasion to observe the handling of patients' emotional problems. Several expressed the feeling that after they had handled a patient in the group they felt it was as much an improvement in teaching the treatment of neuroses as going to the patient's bedside was an improvement in the teaching of clinical medicine. It was common for students to express surprise at the ease with which the neurotic patient was helped to accept his illness as an understandable entity, and how this understanding created hope in the patient. Many were surprised when I asserted that the symptoms of the neurotic were real, and some entered into lengthy disagreement with the viewpoint as to how pain could possibly be established by neurotic mechanisms unless on an imaginary basis. It was an interesting experience for me to observe the skepticism with which many of the students regarded any assurance of improvement in these patients. They were all so thoroughly impressed with the organic side of medicine that it was difficult for them to accept functional disturbance on any basis other than a conscious or near-conscious level. Several expressed amazement that such symptoms as tachycardia, breathlessness, epigastric pain, and digestive disturbance could be influenced by psychotherapy. Many were disturbed when their patients were not given some kind of prescription for their symptoms, and some were surprised when patients returned after they had not been given any medication. As the course ended most of them were enthusiastic, and some were quite critical of the great emphasis placed on the psychoses and of the failure to recognize and handle neurotics properly in other departments.

It may be illuminating to quote from a few of the students' reports. One stated that as he proceeded through medical school he felt the "art of medicine was a thing of the past." He had developed such an intense reliance upon "scientific methods" that he was considerably prejudiced, and it was as "a very skeptical senior" that he "volunteered to attend the Tuesday evening sessions." Of the first session he reported:

> I left the class with a realization that something must be done about the one-sided view I held. My first encounter was with a veteran who had served three years overseas. He seemed acutely ill mentally, and I was completely at a loss as to what course to follow, so I urged him to keep talking. I kept trying to remember what we had been told in our third year—"permit the patient to talk and ask leading questions to direct the conversation along the path you desire."

The student permitted the patient to talk, and suddenly he realized "the patient had apparent confidence in me, despite the fact he knew I was a student doctor" and he, the patient, was anxious to be helped. This experience was unique to the student-doctor because he somehow had a fixed idea that neurotics *liked to stay sick*. Incidentally, this particular patient had a very intense anxiety neurosis with many visceral components, and the student expressed further amazement that marked improvement of these symptoms was eventually effected without medication.

Another student wrote:

> At the end of our lecture courses I had a rough idea of what a neurosis was, but not much more than that. I had the impression that the psychoses, rather than the neuroses, made up the bulk of psychiatric practice.

To this student it was surprising to observe patients—such as he had seen in medical dispensary—with common complaints on a neurotic basis, resistant to all medication, respond to psychotherapeutic measures in the group.

One of the first physicians in regular attendance at the group sessions was an intern at the Philadelphia General Hospital. He had attended regularly during his senior year in medical school and continued attendance as an intern. He is now an army captain doing psychiatric work, and recently wrote me that up until his senior year in medical school—when he first attended the group sessions—he had no appreciation of any curative procedures for the psychoneurotic disturbances. He stated: "As you know, the treatment of the 'neurotic' individual in medical dispensaries was to give them a pat on the back and a bottle of elixir of phenobarbital." He further remarked:

> Observing a group of patients over a period of several sessions impressed upon me far more of the psychodynamics than I had been able to grasp anywhere else—despite the fact that my interest had always been in psychiatry. . . . Some of my most vivid recollections of group pyschotherapy have to do with the hate, fear, explosive antagonism, guilt and sorrow that would unfold like a drama during an evening's session. Having witnessed the handling of these reactions has helped me infinitely in coping with similar situations that I am now meeting.

Other students have commented as follows:

> The group experience teaches in the same way that clinics and ward work teach in medicine. It provides practical experience by dealing with and handling patients—something books and lectures cannot provide. I have learned to believe that every person who is sick has some degree of psychoneurotic overlay, and that handling this is an important factor in speeding recovery.

Another in reporting his experience said: "It caused me to revolt against the physician who damns the neurotic and prescribes bromides."

In presenting suggestions for improvement of the group method of instruction every student favored its expansion and recommended:

1. Additional instruction which should include more guidance of the student's individual session with his patient.

2. Better training in history taking prior to participation in the group procedure.

3. Holding of sessions more often than once a week.

4. More discussion and instruction after each group session, that students may receive a clearer explanation of the subtleties of the comments made by patients.

All the opinions of students were obtained shortly before or after their graduation, and all were secured after the termination of their contact with the group.

In addition to the remarks of these undergraduate students, naval officers in attendance have been very enthusiastic in their comments about the value of the course as a method of instructing them in handling psychoneurotic problems in the services. These men attended for rather brief periods and, as those who have had experience with group therapy realize, in order to understand its effectiveness it is usually necessary to attend many sessions to observe the group interaction and appreciate its benefits to the patients.

Although this experience with the group as a teaching medium has been rather brief, and the views expressed by the students must be evaluated in the light of their lack of experience and their immaturity, I personally believe that the method is valuable for teaching sound psychotherapeutic procedures to students and physicians, and for making them more proficient in the handling of psychosomatic disorders. For a long time there has been rather general agreement that it is very difficult to teach students psychotherapeutic methods because of the intimate patient-physician relationship which is disturbed by the presence of another individual. In the group method the student can see and observe all of the potent psychodynamic mechanisms employed to effect improvement in the emotionally disturbed. Rapport and transference can be satisfactorily established, and every psychotherapeutic measure seems to be increased in effect in an active group. I have gained much from the group discussions and have learned how to handle individual patients far better after noting behavior in a group.

In discussing with students in attendance the benefits they derived from participation in the group project, it surprised me to learn that many of them stated they had received invaluable assistance in effecting a better personal adjustment in their own lives. Many reported that they had become aware of the genesis of undesirable personal characteristics which they possessed and were able to direct curative measures. Several were enthusiastic about this phase of the project and believed it was the only experience through which they had personally benefited in their whole medical school course. When we realize the harmful effect of personality maladjustment in the physician, we can fully appreciate the value of this group training to the medical student.

In conclusion, I believe that group sessions, with adequate supervision, can be used to teach psychotherapy just as satisfactorily as clinical medicine is taught. It gives students the opportunity to interview, examine and discuss cases with their chiefs, and then observe the technique and result. They become participants in a dynamic psychotherapeutic relationship. Group therapy permits the gaining of experience under supervision, and makes the training of therapists shorter and more effective. It gives to all students a better understanding of the value of psychotherapeutic mechanisms, and for many it develops insight into some of their own personality difficulties and gives remedial assistance.

REFERENCE

1. S. B. Hadden, "Group Psychotherapy: A Superior Method of Treating Larger Numbers of Neurotic Patients," *Am. J. Psychiat.*, 101:68-7, July 1944; "Treatment of the neuroses by class technic." *Annals Int. Med.*, 16:33-37, January 1942.

53

THE TRAINING OF THE GROUP PSYCHOTHERAPIST

Aaron Stein

Although ten years have elapsed since my original article appeared in the first edition of this book, the basic principles concerning the training of the group psychotherapist described then are essentially valid today. The increased utilization of sensitivity or laboratory training has raised many questions about the use of this method for training in group psychotherapy. Questions also have been raised about the place of family and marital therapy and the newer, more active group approaches in training for group psychotherapy. All of these issues will be considered in this article.

A working definition of group psychotherapy indicating the important elements involved follows: Group psychotherapy is a method of treating mental and emotional illness in which the therapist fosters the establishment of relationships (with the therapist and among the patients) in the group, and, by encouraging the development of interaction among the patients in the group (both in relation to each other and the therapist), he facilitates verbal (and nonverbal) communication in the group.

This definition of group psychotherapy obviously is medically oriented. It refers to the treatment of mental and emotional illness and indicates that the presence of such illness has been established or diagnosed. It also states that the treatment involves a relationship with a therapist and that, through this relationship, interaction and spontaneous verbal expression of the factors entering into the mental and emotional illness occurs in the group. Defining it in this way differentiates group psychotherapy from other group therapeutic methods, such as group counseling and guidance, and from various other group activities that are therapeutic, such as social activities, artistic activities, and occupational activities performed in groups.

It also differentiates group psychotherapy from "nontherapeutic" discussion groups allegedly set up to promote personal growth or to teach group dynamics. Recent experiences with the adverse consequences resulting from active pressure methods in the "nontherapeutic" group approaches has underlined the necessity of clearly distinguishing between therapeutic and nontherapeutic approaches and utilizing appropriate safeguards in the latter (Stein, 1971).

MATERIAL OBTAINED FROM PERSONAL EXPERIENCE IN TRAINING GROUP PSYCHOTHERAPISTS

The writer's own experience in training group psychotherapists has comprised three distinct activities connected with training three different groups of students. The first group consisted of psychologists and social workers connected with a social agency. The second was composed of psychiatric residents in two voluntary mental hospitals. The third group was composed of graduate psychiatrists in the psychiatric outpatient department of a general hospital.

Psychologists and Social Workers

The training of the psychologists and social workers will be described first. This occurred in connection with the writer's serving as consultant in group psychotherapy to a private social agency that had set up a group psychotherapy project* for the treatment of young adolescents, both male and female, ranging in age from twelve to fifteen, who had been referred because of delinquent behavior. They were treated with combined activity and interview group psychotherapy by the social workers and psychologists belonging to the project. The work in supervising and training these group psychotherapists continued for ten years.

The instruction in group psychotherapy with this group was accomplished in two ways: (1) through supervision of the group psychotherapy; and (2) through regular meetings of a workshop or case study seminar. In the supervisory sessions, the group therapists met on a regular basis, once a week, with experienced group psychotherapists, and every phase of their work with the group was gone into.

In addition, every two weeks a seminar or workshop was held which all of the group psychotherapists and their supervisors attended. At these seminars the work was divided into two parts. In the first part, one of the group therapists read a session from his group, with the entire group participating in a discussion concerning the material from this group session. The second part of the seminar usually was devoted to a discussion of the principles and techniques of group psychotherapy, utilizing questions and problems brought up by the group therapists. However, this

* The Group Psychotherapy Project of the Girls' and Boys' Service League, New York, N.Y.

discussion sooner or later centered around the group psychotherapists' anxiety and countertransference difficulties (although these were not labeled as such) in relation to their role as therapist. The point that needed to be clarified most often was their specific function as a group therapist.

Several characteristics of this group should be mentioned. First, they were all relatively young and, with one or two exceptions, had not had too much experience in their respective fields. Because of their lack of knowledge and experience in dealing with various types of psychiatric patients, many of them became quite anxious if some of the adolescents showed possible psychotic symptoms or showed such symptoms as a moderately severe depression. The second point was their lack of experience in individual psychotherapy. While many of them had been exposed to much didactic and theoretical material concerning the psychodynamics of interpersonal relationships and of psychotherapy, their lack of actual experience in the one-to-one relationship in individual psychotherapy handicapped them greatly and often prevented them from seeing what was going on in the group.

The third and most important difficulty that was encountered was getting them to use the group and the group method in performing the group psychotherapy. Only their experience in doing group psychotherapy and having repeatedly pointed out to them in their supervision and seminars the way in which a group could be used enabled them finally to understand what was meant by using the group method in performing group psychotherapy.

Psychiatric Residents

Next, the experience obtained in the training of the psychiatric residents in a voluntary mental hospital will be described.* The psychiatric residents were first-, second-, and third-year residents in psychiatry receiving their psychiatric training at this hospital.

Briefly, the training of the residents in group psychotherapy was as follows: The first-year residents were given a series of about twelve didactic lectures in which the basic points concerning group psychotherapy were covered. Following this they attended a weekly continuous case seminar or workshop, in which a second-year resident reported his experience in selecting and preparing patients for a group, setting up the group, and doing the group psychotherapy. The material from the group sessions was followed at these meetings for the rest of the year so that the residents could follow a group from its inception well into the group psychotherapy.

In addition, each first-year resident who wished to do so could act as a recorder-observer for a second-year resident who was conducting a group. The recorder-observer was instructed not to participate in the group ses-

* The Hillside Hospital, Glen Oaks, N.Y., a voluntary mental hospital of some 280 beds with an approved three-year psychiatric residency training program.

sions. He took notes, and later he and the group therapist went over the notes for each session with a supervisor who was skilled in group psychotherapy. This was a particularly valuable and most instructive experience for the first-year residents.

In the second year, the resident began to do group psychotherapy by himself under the supervision of an experienced group psychotherapist, and had as a recorder-observer a new first-year resident. The second-year residents were not required to attend the didactic lectures of the continuous case seminars that were given to the first-year residents, but most of them chose to do so and contributed greatly to the variety and spontaneity of the discussion.

In the third year, the residents, who by now had had one year of experience in group psychotherapy with inpatients, used group psychotherapy in the outpatient department. This continued throughout the third year. Thus, at the end of the three years of their psychiatric residency, the residents in the group psychotherapy program had had three years of experience, the first year as a recorder-observer, the second year as a group therapist with inpatients, and the third year as a group therapist with outpatients.

The same kind of training program in group psychotherapy for psychiatric residents was set up in 1955 in the psychiatric department of a general hospital, The Mount Sinai Hospital in New York City, which several years ago became the hospital center of The Mount Sinai School of Medicine of the City University of New York. This training program is continuing with some modifications from the one described above.

These are as follows: The first-year resident receives an intensive six-week course in therapeutic group approaches and group psychotherapy with inpatients. He then begins to participate in the large community work meetings and other therapeutic community groups and in small psychotherapy groups with inpatients, first as an observer and then as leader of such groups. In the small inpatient groups, in many instances, the first-year resident has a nurse and an activities therapist as co-therapists. He (or she) is supervised by an experienced group therapist who also helps him and the other members of the team to become aware of and deal with patient-staff and patient-patient interaction and other group dynamics occurring on the inpatient unit. In addition, the first-year resident attends a biweekly seminar (held for five months) covering group dynamics and group therapeutic approaches, including the therapeutic community and group psychotherapy with inpatients, illustrated by discussion of typical group sessions reported by the residents.

The rest of the training program in group psychotherapy at Mount Sinai Medical Center consists in training in group psychotherapy with outpatients for the second-year residents (similar to the procedure described for third-year residents at Hillside). The second-year resident treats one or two outpatient groups (including aftercare patients) under the supervision of an experienced group therapist and attends a five-month-long service seminar covering the principles and techniques of outpatient group psychotherapy, illustrated by typical sessions presented by the residents.

In the third year at Mount Sinai, the residents either continue with their outpatient groups or work with special groups—addicts, alcoholics, psychosomatic patients, adolescents—or with groups in community centers as part of the community medicine and community psychiatry program. Again, at the end of the three years of the psychiatric residency, the resident will have had three years of group psychotherapy training with inpatients, outpatients, and special groups of patients.

Now to point out some of the difficulties encountered in this type of training program. Two of them are exactly like the difficulties that were encountered with the psychologists and social workers, and are related entirely to lack of experience and knowledge of the residents. This manifested itself, especially in the first-year residents, in anxiety and in all kinds of countertransference attitudes which they clearly demonstrated in their questions and discussions in the continuous case seminars. Similar difficulties were noted in relation to their lack of experience in individual psychotherapy.

At Hillside and at Mount Sinai, the residents receive intensive training in clinical psychiatry and in individual psychotherapy. Because of this, they were in a much better position when it came to beginning group psychotherapy than were the psychologists and social workers mentioned previously. The results were clearly evident. The residents in their second year with one year of training in individual psychotherapy, and with intensive training in clinical psychiatry as well, were much less anxious, much more knowledgeable, and consequently more adept and more secure in their approach in group psychotherapy.

However, the psychiatric residents, just as the psychologists and social workers, had a great deal of difficulty at first in understanding the concept of using a group and a group method in performing group psychotherapy. In some ways this difficulty was aggravated by the emphasis they had received in their first year on the utilization of individual psychotherapy. The idea of letting the patients in the group express and interact and work out the problems that were brought up was quite difficult for the residents to grasp. They would deal with the individual patients in the group instead of the group as a whole and would let themselves be drawn into participating in the group when the group would have functioned best on its own.

This was helped to some extent by having the first-year residents attend as recorder-observers in the group psychotherapy led by a second-year resident, and then attend the supervisory session with the group leader. By the time the resident in his second year began to do group psychotherapy, he had some idea of how to use the group and the group method in performing group psychotherapy. However, it was chiefly their own experience in performing group psychotherapy in the second and third years which was most effective in helping them understand how to use the group and the group method properly in doing group psychotherapy.

One more point might be mentioned. At various times it was proposed that the residents participate as patients in a psychotherapeutic group composed entirely of residents. There are several reports describing group psychotherapy with residents (Hadden, 1956). Good results have been claimed both therapeutically and for training. This was opposed by the senior medical staff because it was felt the residents had enough anxiety and other difficulties to cope with, especially including marked tendencies to identify with the patients in the hospital. It was thought that it might lead to further complications in an already complicated situation if residents were put into a psychotherapeutic group as patients. Also, in the discussions and in the continuous case seminars, no attempt was made (and this was adhered to deliberately) to do any therapy for the very obvious difficulties shown by the residents. All discussions were centered upon the work at hand, and whatever therapeutic effects that emerged (and there were many) were arrived at in this indirect fashion, not as a result of direct therapeutic management.

The use of sensitivity training groups as part of training in group psychotherapy has become a widespread practice in recent years, and has been described as part of the training for psychiatric residents, nurses, psychologists, social workers, and so on. This will be discussed later in this paper. At Mount Sinai, a weekly staff group meeting which is a modified type of sensitivity training meeting and which uses some group psychotherapeutic techniques has been used for a few years as a method of dealing with staff tensions. It does appear to be useful for dealing with staff tensions and also appears to have some value for training in group dynamics. Work with this type of group is continuing and will be reported at some future time (Weitzner, Pun, and Stein, 1972).

Graduate Psychiatrists

Now to come to the third group—the graduate psychiatrists who were trained in group psychotherapy. These were members of the attending staff of the Psychiatric Outpatient Department of The Mount Sinai Hospital in New York City. All of them had completed their psychiatric residencies and their psychiatric training. Work with the group was begun in 1955 and is continuing. In the beginning all those involved were somewhat older men, all of whom had been analyzed and some of whom had had analytic training. All had had many years experience with individual psychotherapy of a psychoanalytically oriented type. They had joined the staff of this particular clinic at the hospital upon learning that it was going to become a Group Psychotherapy Clinic, and thereby showed their interest in learning group psychotherapy. This was, then, a relatively experienced group of mature psychiatrists, psychoanalytically oriented, who at this stage in their work undertook training in group psychotherapy.

Since none of them had any previous training or experience in group psychotherapy, a training program was begun with a series of twenty-four didactic lectures in which the basic elements of group psychotherapy were covered. Because they were experienced individual psychotherapists, they were permitted upon completion of these basic lectures to begin to select patients for a group, to prepare them, and then to begin to do group psychotherapy.

The instruction with respect to performing group psychotherapy then proceeded in two ways. First, each one of the psychiatrists met once a week with the chief of the clinic (the writer) to receive individual instruction and supervision in such matters as selection of patients, structuring of the group, preparation of the patients, the first session, the various phases of group psychotherapy, and so on. Concurrently with this individual supervision, a continuous case seminar was held in which all the members of the clinic, the chief of the service, and various other people, including some experienced group psychotherapists, participated. Here one of the men presented material from his group and then various aspects and problems relating to the material were discussed. During the first year of the clinic, when most of the men in the clinic were new, one group was followed straight through. In addition, once a month, one of the other therapists would present material from his group so that each one had the opportunity to present. The discussions were quite active and spontaneous, and many points relating to techniques, dynamics, and so on, were raised and thoroughly discussed.

In the following years the training program has varied somewhat. Several new members have joined the clinic staff, including some younger men who had completed their training in psychiatry but whose experience was not as extensive as those previously mentioned. For these newcomers, the didactic lectures and the individual instruction and supervision were continued. For the more experienced men, weekly conferences or seminars were held, covering a large variety of topics relating to the technique and dynamics of group psychotherapy. There has been a continuing effort to understand the functioning of the group, with the idea of establishing valid criteria for using group psychotherapy as a selective form of treatment.

As would be expected because of their initial interest, this group was quite enthusiastic about the work. A very interesting result of this was that all of them, after a year or two of experience at the clinic, set up psychotherapeutic groups in their private practice.

Now to point out some of the difficulties involved. First, all of these experienced psychiatrists and psychotherapists showed anxiety, of course, when they first began to do group psychotherapy. However, their anxiety was not as much related to lack of knowledge and experience as had been true with the two previous groups of trainees that were mentioned. Instead, it was the experience of being exposed to the group in a fashion so different from what goes on in individual therapy that was anxiety-provoking to all of them.

Second, their previous concentration on individual psychotherapy of a psychoanalytic type made it difficult at first for them to work freely in this new psychotherapeutic technique. They tended to carry the attitudes and ideas they had accumulated in their individual psychotherapy experience into their work as group psychotherapists. Very frequently it was found that they were all treating the patients in the group as individuals and not utilizing the group and the group method in performing group psycho-therapy, the same difficulty that was encountered in training the less experienced psychologists, social workers, and psychiatric residents.

Again this difficulty in using the group and the group method in performing group psychotherapy was overcome by having them perform group psychotherapy by themselves under adequate supervision. However, it must be said that the resistance of this experienced group to utilizing the group and the group method in performing group psychotherapy was more persistent and more difficult to deal with in certain ways than that encountered with the fresher, younger, and less experienced trainees previously mentioned.

Before completing the description of the training experience with the graduate psychiatrists, two points might be mentioned. The training program at first did not include having the younger group psychothera-pists act as a recorder-observer for the more experienced group therapists. However, particularly as younger men enter the program, they are required as part of their training to participate as a recorder-observer in group psychotherapy conducted by more experienced group psychotherapists.

The second point to be mentioned about this group is that here again there was no attempt to include as part of their training participation as a patient in a psychotherapeutic group. The reasons were somewhat similar to those previously stated for the psychiatric residents—the orientation of the senior medical staff and a definite feeling on the part of all concerned that such participation was not an essential part of training for group psychotherapy.

REVIEW OF THE LITERATURE ON THE TRAINING
OF THE GROUP PSYCHOTHERAPIST

The original article on the training of the group psychotherapist covered the literature quite thoroughly through 1962, and this older literature will be summarized here. Since 1963, the literature on training has become quite large; only representative reports will be listed here. Complete listing of all the group psychotherapy literature, with special sections devoted to training, is given each year in the *International Journal of Group Psychotherapy*. For example, Rosenthal *et al.* (1963) covered the group therapy literature for 1963; they list nine articles devoted to training. In 1964, MacLennan and her co-workers took over the surveys of the group therapy literature which appear each year in the *International Journal of Group Psychotherapy* (MacLennan *et al.*, 1964) and set up a separate section of these annual surveys which is devoted to articles on training. MacLennan continued to list the articles on training in group psychotherapy in these special "Training" sections of the annual surveys from 1964 through 1970.

The review of the older literature will be summarized here: the views of Hulse (1958) and of Slavson (1947) that only experienced psychotherapists with adequate knowledge of basic psychopathology should undertake group psychotherapy, since it is much more difficult than individual psychotherapy, summarizes the feeling of several writers.

Detailed accounts of methods of training group psychotherapists are described in several articles. Boenheim (1959) describes the three-year training program in group psychotherapy at the Columbus State Hospital in Columbus, Ohio. Ross *et al.* (1958) describe how training in group psychotherapy was integrated with psychiatric training in the three-year psychiatric residency program at the University of Cincinnati. The most carefully thought-out and detailed plan for training of the group psychotherapist is given by Mullan (1959) in the second part of a symposium on "Training in Group Psychotherapy."

Several reports deal with a specific aspect of training—the supervision of the trainee in the performance of group psychotherapy. Geller (1954) accomplished this by means of "unstructured" supervisory seminars, with excellent results. Grotjahn (1955), as soon as he had established a good relationship with the student, entered the students' groups as an interested observer. Spotnitz (1958) used a group psychotherapeutic technique to help group psychotherapists learn how to deal with their resistance to the impact of intensive emotional reactions from severely disturbed patients in groups.

A number of reports deal with the use of group psychotherapy and group psychotherapeutic techniques in teaching and training in psychiatry, social work, psychology, and related fields, as well as for training in group psychotherapy. Hadden (1956) has reviewed this literature and divided it into two main techniques. The first, to which Hadden and his co-workers (Peltz *et al.*, 1955) are among the chief contributors, consists in having the student attend group sessions as an observer-recorder or an "auxiliary therapist." As already noted, Ross (1958) and Boenheim (1959) utilized this technique in training for group psychotherapy, as do several others, including this writer, in association with Miller and Wender.

In the second of the techniques mentioned by Hadden, the students —either in an actual psychotherapeutic group or in a group in which group psychotherapeutic techniques are used—through an examination of their own behavior and reactions in the group, learn not only group psychotherapy, but psychiatry, psychotherapy, and other related matters as well. In reports already noted, Geller, Ross, and also Patton (1954) used this method for teaching and training group psychotherapy. The efficacy of this method in the training of medical students in psychiatry was independently confirmed in two reports by Ganzarain and his co-workers (1955, 1959).

The use of a group psychotherapeutic technique in teaching indicates that treatment to a greater or lesser degree is being carried on at the same time. There is a group of workers who emphasize that the therapeutic effects obtained in using group psychotherapeutic techniques in teaching are the most important factors in helping students to learn. Not only are resistance and defensive inhibitions (true blocks to learning) lessened, but increased awareness of their own reactions enables the students to see and understand what is occurring in patients. These views are cited by Hadden (1956); Semrad (1951, 1957) and Berman (1953a, 1953b) also used these techniques.

Obviously, a logical development of such views would lead to the conclusion that a group psychotherapeutic experience is a necessary part of the training of the group psychotherapist, and several authors have stated this. The clearest and most emphatic statement to this effect is the one already cited by Mullan (1959).

PRESENT-DAY VIEWS CONCERNING THE TRAINING OF THE GROUP PSYCHOTHERAPIST

In the original article, the results of a questionnaire sent to thirty workers with extensive experience in the training of group psychotherapists were described and discussed, including the question of participation in a psychotherapeutic group as part of training in group psychotherapy. These will not be repeated here since they are essentially the same as those to be described below.

The most important finding in the results of the original questionnaire was the essential agreement, except for the question of a personal group psychotherapeutic experience, as to what constituted good training in group psychotherapy. This foreshadowed an important development as regards the training of the group psychotherapist. This was the appearance of the "training guide" entitled *Guidelines for the Training of Group Psychotherapists: A Model Suggested by the American Group Psychotherapy Association*, which was issued in 1970 (it will be referred to here as the AGPA Training Guide, Inc., 1970).

This guide, the culmination of years of work by the authors of the guide, the Board of Directors, and, especially, the members of the Standards and Ethics Committee of the American Group Psychotherapy Association, was the first clear-cut statement—one might say, the first "official" statement—as to what were considered the basic requirements for adequate training in group psychotherapy.

The essential elements in the guide are the following.

*Professional Requirements before Entering Training Program
(in Group Psychotherapy)*

(1) Candidates must fulfill the requirements for degrees in their professions (M.D., Ph.D., and M.S.W.) and have certain minimal professional experience in their field—one to two years.

(2) They must have completed 200 hours of doing supervised individual psychotherapy before *entering* the training program, and must have completed a total of 400 hours of doing individual psychotherapy with adequate supervision before *completing* the training program.

(3) A personal psychotherapeutic experience is strongly recommended.

Educational Requirement

To be obtained before or during group psychotherapy training:

(1) Basic Physiology, endocrinology, and neurology.
(2) Normal human development, genetic, psychosexual, and so on.
(3) Psychopathology and clinical diagnosis.
(4) Family dynamics, group behavior and culture.
(5) Survey of schools of psychotherapy.
(6) Seminar in research in group psychotherapy.

Training Program, Minimum Two Years

(1) Didactic courses in group psychotherapy—90 hours.
(2) Continuous group case seminar—60 hours.
(3) Clinical experience—3 therapy groups—60 hours a week with each, under qualified supervision.
(4) Participation as a member in a group psychotherapy or group training experience, with qualified leadership for a minimum of 60 hours.

Additional specialized training for group psychotherapy with children and adolescents.

In preparing the present revision of this article, it was felt it would again be useful to obtain the current views on the training of group psychotherapists by submitting a questionnaire to a representative group of workers experienced in this field. A questionnaire was prepared and distributed to obtain the views of this experienced group of workers as regards: (1) the validity of the AGPA Training Guide at the present time; and (2) the need or desirability for including family therapy, marital therapy, and the newer active group approaches in the training of the group psychotherapist.

The questionnaire was sent to sixty-two members of the American Group Psychotherapy Association who, like those in the original article, "are recognized authorities in group psychotherapy and all of whom have been, and for the most part still are, active for many years in the training of group psychotherapists." An attempt was made to include workers who were active in the fields of family and marital therapy and in some of the newer group approaches. The professions of those to whom the questionnaire was sent included psychiatrists, psychologists, social workers, and educators.

Some thirty of the sixty-two workers responded, somewhat less than 50 per cent. The data obtained can best be summarized under the four headings used in the questionnaire, as follows:*

(1) *Guidelines for the Training of the Group Therapist—American Group Psychotherapy Association.*

Question: A copy of this guideline is enclosed for your convenience. Do you feel it adequately represents present-day views on training?

Question: Do you agree with the requirement for participation as a member in a "group psychotherapy or group training experience?"

(2) *Question:* In view of the increasing use of family therapy, do you feel training in this should be required as part of the training of the group psychotherapist?

* The valuable assistance of those who replied to the questionnaire is gratefully acknowledged; many spent a great deal of time and effort on the replies and their thoughts and comments were most helpful. Because of an error the names of all the respondents were not properly identified. The names of those who replied and were correctly identified are: James Anthony, M.D.; Marvin L. Aronson, Ph.D.; Boris M. Astrachan, M.D.; Reuven Bar-Levan, M.D.; Stanley L. Block, M.D.; Helen E. Durkin, Ph.D.; Theodore M. Feldberg, M.D.; Jay W. Fidler, M.D.; S. H. Foulkes, M.D.; Edrita Fried, Ph.D.; Robert L. Goulding, M.D.; Sidney Levin, M.D.; Robert Mac-Gregor, Ph.D.; Beryce W. MacLennan, Ph.D.; Elizabeth E. Mintz, Ph.D.; Hugh Mullan, M.D.; E. Mansell Pattison, M.D.; William E. Powles, M.D.; Max Rosenbaum, Ph.D.; Donald A. Shaskan, M.D.; Max Sugar, M.D.; Irwin D. Yalom, M.D. The author extends his most sincere apologies to those respondents whose names, in error, were not identified on the questionnaire and, therefore, were not listed here.

(3) *Question:* In view of the widespread interest in and utilization of new group approaches, both therapeutic and nontherapeutic, should some training in any of the methods listed below be included in the training of the group psychotherapist?

Laboratory Training or Sensitivity Training
Encounter Groups
Marathon Groups
Psychodrama and Role-Playing
Utilization of Transactional Analysis in Groups
Group Desensitization and Behavior Therapy

(4) *Question:* Are there any other group approaches or techniques you feel would be useful for the group psychotherapist in training?

To summarize the results of the answers to the questionnaire:

(1) Most people felt that the intensive type of training program outlined in the AGPA Training Guide and requiring about two or three years to complete was the most desirable type of training for the group psychotherapist.

(2) *All* felt that a personal group psychotherapy and group training experience should be part of the training.

(3) Most felt a basic psychodynamic or psychoanalytic approach was still the most valuable one for training.

(4) Most workers felt some training in family and marital therapy should be included.

(5) In addition, most workers felt training in family therapy could be used to fulfill in part the requirement for training in group psychotherapy.

(6) The general feeling of most of the respondents concerning the newer active group approaches was that the group psychotherapist in training should be made familiar with those by means of a seminar, including theoretical concepts, but actual training or participation need not be required.

Of interest, and perhaps indicative of future trends, was the thinking of several workers that training programs should be set up for professionals other than mental health professionals and for nonprofessionals to enable them to do therapy in groups.

GROUP EXPERIENCES AS PART OF TRAINING IN GROUP PSYCHOTHERAPY

As was clearly indicated in the original article, some personal group experience was considered essential by most workers. Ten years later, at the present writing, *all* of those who responded felt that a personal group psychotherapy experience *and* a group training experience were essential for training in group psychotherapy. This is in agreement with the requirement for a group therapy experience listed in the AGPA Training Guide.

In the original article, the following comments were made concerning a *personal group psychotherapy experience for the trainee*: "No clear-cut data is available concerning the question of the trainee's participation as a patient in a psychotherapeutic group. While many workers who have had the experience regard it as valuable, there have not been any reports in the literature describing such an experience or such a group in any detail."

The more recent views of some of those who feel a personal group psychotherapy experience is valuable is summarized below:

M. M. Berger (1969) is a strong advocate of the experiential approach to training, and states that a group psychotherapy and group training experience are essential for and most useful in group psychotherapy training. He did not find any disturbances resulting from the inclusion of trainees in such groups, and feels that if disturbances do occur in the members of such groups "in my opinion it is due to faulty leadership or excessive sickness in a group member rather than an inherent fault in providing an intimate, trusting training in therapy group experience to the working members of an institution."

Sadock and his co-workers (1968, 1969) have utilized group psychotherapy for years as part of the training of psychiatric residents. They recommend it enthusiastically and feel it has educational and personal therapeutic benefits as well as providing an excellent basis for future group psychotherapy training. They mention that the residents go through a rebellious phase, but that the dropout rate is less than 10 per cent. They specifically state (Sadock and Kaplan, 1969): "At no time, however, did the group process precipitate or aggravate emotional problems." They felt it helped identify personal difficulties in a member who could then be referred for individual therapy.

Gottschalk and Pattison (1969) also stated that no objective studies are available to indicate clearly the usefulness of personal group psychotherapy or group training experiences for group psychotherapy trainees, but they feel that more research on this should be undertaken.

Kamin (1966), describing a group psychotherapy experience as part of the group psychotherapy training of third-year psychiatric residents, found it to be of considerable value. However, it imposed "severe emotional demands," and some of the participants at times found it jeopardized social relationships and made working together more difficult; those who were "badly shaken up" were propelled into individual therapy.

Astrachan and Redlich (1969) reported their work with a group training experience along the "study group" lines of the Rice-Tavistaok type, in which the leader functions as an "ambiguous leader" by limiting his interventions to comments on the group's behavior. They found it most useful in helping the residents learn the more unconscious aspects of group interaction, and, while the group interaction caused some emotional disturbances in the members, it did not cause any excessive or psychotic reactions.

Grotjahn (1969) states that a group psychotherapy experience facilitates working out of a "family transference" and "allows insight into the group therapeutic process in general."

Sherman and Hildreth (1970) and Lakin, Lieberman, and Whitaker (1969) also found a personal group psychotherapy experience very useful as part of group psychotherapy training.

Difficulties arise when residents and others who work closely with each other are in a psychotherapy group together. The points Yalom (1970) makes about a residents' training group apply here:

> Groups of mental health professionals, and especially psychiatric residents who will continue to work together throughout their training, are extremely difficult groups to lead. The pace is slow, intellectualization is common, and self-disclosure and risk taking minimal. The neophyte therapist realizes that his chief professional instrument is his own person and generally is doubly threatened by requests for self-disclosure: not only his personal competence but his professional competence is at stake. In training programs the group leader is often placed in a double role in the student groups: he is both teacher-evaluator and T-group leader. Generally, this compounds the problem and forces undue attention to authority issues. Eventually the group's problem with the leader must be resolved around the issue of trust.

Horowitz (1963, 1967), one of the workers who uses, with good results, an unstructured group training experience as part of a course in group dynamics for first-year psychiatric residents, states that "many of the issues which are raised resemble those in a therapeutic group." He states he did not find this particularly disturbing to the residents. However, an unpublished report from the same institution describes severe disturbances in several members of a residents' training group.*

Zinberg and Friedman (1967), workers who have had extensive experience with teaching and training in groups which use group psychotherapeutic techniques, describe many of the problems which arise in using such groups. These include increased anxiety and other emotional disturbances resulting from the group interactions, blocks to learning from stimulation of affect-laden material, increased defensiveness and fear of exposure from those working closely together, and acting out in extragroup relations. Kaplan (1967) concurs with Zinberg and Friedman in the difficulties encountered in training groups, and cautions that this makes clarification of goals necessary to differentiate a training group from a therapy group.

Redlich and Astrachan (1969), who strongly advocate group dynamics

---

* Personal communication.

training, state clearly that "quite frequently a number of participants, a few individuals whom we have observed became temporarily so upset we had reason to call their behavior psychotic."

I. L. Berger (1967, 1969), discussing resistances to learning in group dynamics programs, points out the difficulties involved in clarifying goals and boundaries between what is educational and therapeutic, the stirring up of anxieties as a result of disrupting defenses, and the difficulty in controlling regressive reactions, when short-term intense experiential groups are used for training. More specifically, he found blocks in learning related to unresolved problems in initial dependency, and increased defensiveness about exposing themselves—their status and roles—in the group leading to resistance in learning about group psychotherapy, an "avoidance of discussion of their professional group experience."

Some comments made in the original article may be useful here: "However, the whole question needs to be further evaluated. Slavson* raised an important point when he questioned how effective such a therapeutic experience can be when it is undertaken in connection with training. The same question can be raised about the so-called individual training analysis. It is a very common experience for analysts who have completed their training analysis to find it necessary some years later to undergo an additional analysis. In part, this may be, as Freud (1937) pointed out, in relation to needs engendered by doing analysis, but some of the need may stem from the fact that the original training analysis could not be as therapeutically effective as an analysis conducted under different circumstances. Here, Mullan's idea, cited above, as to the circumstances of a personal group psychotherapy experience is important.

Turning now to a *personal group training experience*, this differs from a personal group psychotherapy experience and refers to the trainee having a personal experience in a sensitivity or laboratory training group. These are also called "group process groups," "group dynamics training groups," and so on. All of the respondents to the recent questionnaire felt that this type of experience was essential for the group psychotherapy trainee.

The recent literature amply supports this view. According to the annual reviews of the group therapy literature previously cited, many articles are published each year describing the use of a sensitivity training experience in training for group psychotherapy. Yalom (1970) feels that a T-group experience is most valuable and may offer many types of learning (of dynamics of groups) not elsewhere available, including being "able to learn at an emotional level what he may previously have known intellectually." As noted previously, he stresses that there are many difficulties involved in use of T-groups with those who work together closely. A representative group of workers who find a personal group training expe-

* Personal communication.

rience essential in group psychotherapy training are: Astrachan and Redlich (1969), M. M. Berger (1969), Horowitz (1963, 1967), Lakin, Lieberman, and Whitaker (1969), Kaplan (1967), Redlich and Astrachan (1969), Sherman and Hildreth (1970), and Zinberg and Friedman (1967). All feel that a personal group training experience clarifies areas involving peer, family, and authority relationships, offers a firsthand group experience, and provides a clear and most useful understanding of the relationships and interactions in a group.

There is considerable evidence of difficulties in connection with such sensitivity training group experiences. These have been noted previously in the discussion of problems arising with use of a personal group experience for group psychotherapy trainees. Of special interest in this connection are the articles of I. L. Berger (1969), Gottschalk and Pattison (1969), Kamin (1966), Kaplan (1967), and Stein (1971). The section on groups (1969) in the *American Journal of Psychiatry* contains several articles discussing the problems arising in sensitivity training groups.

The recent group therapy literature continues to discuss the usefulness of experiential—group psychotherapy and group training—methods versus more didactic or educational methods in teaching group psychotherapy. The articles of I. L. Berger (1967, 1969), M. M. Berger (1969), and Kaplan (1967) address themselves to this issue. The Symposium on "Approaches to Training through the Small Group" (1967), which includes several of the above articles, discusses the experiential-didactic issue at length.

SUMMARY AND CONCLUSIONS

Material concerning the training of the group psychotherapist has been presented from three sources: (1) the writer's personal experience with three different groups of trainees of varying background and experience; (2) the experience of others, again with students of varying background and experience, as presented in the literature; and (3) the views of experienced group psychotherapists working in different settings and with students of various types. The somewhat surprising and rather reassuring finding is that the experience of all concerned leads to a more or less complete agreement on what is essential in the basic training of the group psychotherapist. These basic requirements are essentially the same as those suggested in the AGPA Training Guide.

Now, to summarize these requirements:

1. The group psychotherapist, in addition to some basic knowledge in such areas as sociology and anthropology, should have acquired a thorough knowledge of normal human development—genetic, psychosexual, and so on; of basic physiology, neurology, and endocrinology; of psychopathology

and psychodynamics; of family dynamics, group behavior and culture; and of the different schools and techniques in group psychotherapy and group approaches. He should also have had a well-rounded experience with a wide variety of psychiatric cases and should be well versed in psychiatric diagnosis. Such training would require a period of two, or more likely three, years to complete, and some of this should be acquired before beginning group psychotherapy training.

2. The group psychotherapist should have had a well-supervised and adequate experience in individual psychotherapy, preferably preceding his group psychotherapy by at least one year.

3. A personal analysis or psychotherapeutic experience is considered essential by most observers, to avoid personal areas of conflicts leading to blind spots in the therapist, and also to help him become aware of the nature of emotional reactions. Analytic training or its equivalent with regard to the dynamics and technique of individual analytic psychotherapy was felt to be highly desirable (or even absolutely necessary by some) for the group psychotherapy trainee.

4. Participation by the group psychotherapist trainee in a psychotherapeutic group is considered necessary by most observers in helping the trainee further work out personal problems, especially those connected with difficulties in relation to peers and authority figures. It was also felt that such personal participation in a group as a patient gives the trainee a firsthand knowledge of group psychotherapy. A few felt that such an experience was neither necessary nor desirable and raised some question as to its effectiveness.

5. Participation in a personal group training experience was considered essential for the trainee in group psychotherapy by *all* the workers who responded. This view is concurred in—with the utilization of appropriate safeguards and a clear-cut relationship to the didactic program—by the present writer.

The passage of ten years and the experience gained in training large numbers of group psychotherapists has entirely confirmed the wisdom of including the basic requirements described above. Additional training is considered necessary to work in specialized ones, with children, adolescents, and families. These are important facts to be considered in planning training group therapeutic approaches for professionals other than those in the mental health field, and for nonprofessionals.

Thus, to return to the definition of group psychotherapy, the group psychotherapist needs to know something of the factors leading to mental and emotional illness and their treatment, especially the type that utilizes a group and a group method to facilitate communication in the group, both verbal and nonverbal, through the establishment of relationships and interactions with the therapist and among the members. Adequate training for group psychotherapists should fulfill these needs.

BIBLIOGRAPHY

AGPA Training Guide, *Guidelines for the Training of Group Psychotherapists: A Model Suggested by the American Group Psychotherapy Association* (New York: American Group Psychotherapy Association, 1970).

Astrachan, B. M., and Redlich, F. C., "Leadership Ambiguity and Its Effect on Residents' Study Groups," *Int. J. Group Psychother.*, 19:487-494, 1969.

Berger, I. L., "Group Psychotherapy Training Institutes: Group Process, Therapy or Resistance to Learning," *Int. J. Group Psychother.*, 17:503-512, 1967.

———, "Resistance to the Learning Process in Group Dynamics Programs," *Am. J. Psychiat.*, 126:850-857, 1969.

Berger, M. M., "Experiential and Didactic Aspects of Training in Therapeutic Group Approaches," *Am. J. Psychiat.*, 126:845-850, 1969.

Berman, L., "A Group Psychotherapeutic Technique for Training in Clinical Psychology," *Am. J. Orthopsychiat.*, 23:322-327, 1953. (a)

———, "Mental Hygiene for Educators: Report on an Experiment Using A Combined Seminar and Group Psychotherapy Approach," *Psychoanalyt. Rev.*, 40:319-332, 1953. (b)

Boenheim, C., "Clinical Experience with Group Psychotherapy," Lecture given at Third Annual Institute, American Group Psychotherapy Association, Inc., New York, N.Y., January 1959.

Freud, S., "Analysis Terminable and Interminable" (1937), in *Collected Papers*, Vol. V (London: Hogarth Press, 1950), pp. 316-357.

Ganzarain, R., *et al.*, "Group Psychotherapy in the Psychiatric Training of Medical Students," *Int. J. Group Psychother.*, 8:137-153, 1958.

———, "Study of the Effectiveness of Group Psychotherapy in the Training of Medical Students," *Int. J. Group Psychother.*, 9:475-487, 1959.

Geller, J. J., "An Experience in Group Psychotherapy as a Teaching Device," *Group Psychother.*, 7:130-138, 1954.

Gottschalk, L., and Pattison, E. M., "Psychiatric Perspective on T-Groups and the Laboratory Movement: An Overview," *Am. J. Psychiat.*, 126:823-839, 1969.

Grotjahn, M., "Special Problems of Supervision in Group Psychotherapy," *Group Psychother.*, 3:309-315, 1951.

———, "Problems and Techniques of Supervision," *Psychiat.*, 5:9-15, 1955.

———, "Analytic Group Therapy with Psychotherapists," *Int. J. Group Psychother.*, 19:326-333, 1969.

Groups, Special Section on "Groups," *Am. J. Psychiat.*, 126:823-877, 1969.

Hadden, S. B., "The Utilization of a Therapy Group in Teaching Psychotherapy," *Am. J. Psychiat.*, 103:644-648, 1947.

———, "Training," in S. R. Slavson, ed., *The Fields of Group Psychotherapy* (New York: International Universities Press, 1956), pp. 302-316.

Horowitz, L., "Transference in Training Groups and Therapy Groups," *Int. J. Group Psychother.*, 14:202-213, 1963.

———, "Training Groups for Psychiatric Residents," *Int. J. Group Psychother.*, 17:421-435, 1967.

Hulse, W. C., "Training for Group Psychotherapy in the U.S.A. and Abroad," *Int. J. Group Psychother.*, 8:257-264, 1958.

Kamin, I., "The Resident as Patient in Group Psychotherapy," *Int. J. Group Psychother.*, 16:313-320, 1966.

Kaplan, S. R., "Therapy Groups and Training Groups: Similarities and Differences," *Int. J. Group Psychother.*, 17:473-504, 1967.

Lakin, M., Lieberman, M. A., and Whitaker, D. S., "Issues in Training Group Psychotherapists," *Int. J. Group Psychother.*, 19:307-325, 1969.

MacLennan, B., and Felsenfeld, N. S., "The Group Psychotherapy Literature 1964," *Int. J. Group Psychother.*, 15:251-264, 1964.

Miller, J. S. A., Kwalwasser, S., and Stein, A., "Observations Concerning the Use of Group Psychotherapy in a Voluntary Hospital," *Int. J. Group Psychother.*, 4:86-94, 1954.

Mullan, H., in C. Beukenkamp, H. Mullan, N. Papanek, F. Tate, and M. Berger, "Training in Group Psychotherapy: A Symposium," *Am. J. Psychother.*, 12:493-507, 1959.

Patton, J. D., "The Group as a Training Device and Treatment Method in a Private Psychiatric Hospital," *Int. J. Group Psychother.*, 4:419-428, 1954.

Peltz, W. L., Steel, E. H., Hadden, S. B., Schwab, M. L., and Nichols, F., "Group Therapeutic Experience as a Method of Teaching Psychiatry to Medical Students," *Int. J. Group Psychother.*, 5:270-279, 1955.

Redlich, F. C., and Astrachan, B. A., "Group Dynamics Training," *Am. J. Psychiat.*, 125:1501-1508, 1969.

Rosenthal, L. Schamess, G., and Leibowitz, M., "The Group Psychotherapy Literature 1963," *Int. J. Group Psychother.*, 14:227-246, 1963.

Ross, W. D., *et al.*, "Integrating Training in Group Psychotherapy with Psychiatric Residency Training," *Int. J. Group Psychother.*, 8:323-328, 1958.

Sadock, B., and Kaplan, H. J., "Group Psychotherapy with Psychiatric Residents," *Int. J. Group Psychother.*, 19:475-486, 1969.

———, and Friedman, A., "Integrated Group Psychotherapy Training and Psychiatric Residency," *Arch. Gen. Psychiat.*, 18:276-279, 1968.

Semrad, E. V., and Arsenian, J., "The Use of Group Processes in Teaching Group Dynamics," *Am. J. Psychiat.*, 108:358-363, 1951.

———, and Standish, C., "Experiences with Small Groups in Teaching Group Psychology," *Group Psychother.*, 10:191, 1957.

Sherman, R. W., and Hildreth, A. M., "A Resident Group Process Training Seminar," *Am. J. Psychiat.*, 127:372-375, 1970.

Slavson, S. W., "Qualification and Training of Group Therapists," *Ment. Hyg.*, 31:386-396, 1947.

Spotnitz, H., "Resistance Reinforcement in Affect Training of Analytic Group Psychotherapists," *Int. J. Group Psychother.*, 8:395-402, 1958.

Stein, A., "Psychiatric Complications of Encounter Groups," Paper presented at the NYDB-APA Divisional Meeting, New York City, November 1971.

Symposium on "Approaches to Training through the Small Group," *Int. J. Group Psychother.*, 17:419-512, 1967.

Weitzner, D., Pun, M., and Stein, A., "The Staff Group Meeting," Paper presented at Grand Rounds at the Department of Psychiatry, The Mount Sinai Hospital, May 1972.

Wender, L., Stein, A., "The Utilization of Group Psychotherapy in Teaching Psychotherapy," *Int. J. Group Psychother.*, 3:326-329, 1953.

Yalom, I. D., "Concluding Remarks: Training and Research," in I. D. Yalom, *The Theory and Practice of Group Psychotherapy* (New York: Basic Books, 1970), pp. 374-379.

Zinberg, H. E., and Friedman, I. J., "Problems in Working with Dynamic Groups," *Int. J. Group Psychother.*, 17:447-456, 1967.

54

AN EXPERIENCE IN TEACHING PSYCHOTHERAPY BY MEANS OF GROUP THERAPY

John Warkentin

In a school setting, the psychotherapist is definitely a hybrid creature. His function is not clearly that of a physician, who heals sick patients with the single purpose of making them healthy. Neither is he a traditional teacher, who helps the student acquire information and certain standardized skills. The therapist in a school combines some functions of both the teacher and the physician. The proper mixture of these functions is difficult to determine.

This paper reports an experiment which was intended to clarify the extent to which it is possible for a teacher to contribute to the emotional growth of students. The teacher cannot avoid contributing to the affective learning of students. His very position before a class makes the teacher a recapitulation of other parental figures, whose attitudes are inadvertently learned by students; yet the social responsibility for such affective learning may not always be consciously acknowledged by the teacher. Students are even more likely to be quite unaware of the unacknowledged therapeutic parent-child relationship. All concerned will readily deal openly with intellectual needs, but often remain silent regarding evident emotional needs. In the present experiment this was changed to place conscious emphasis on feelings, attitudes, and motivation. The purpose was to determine the value of directly therapeutic approach by the teacher.

This experiment was conducted twice, once for two years with grade school teachers, and then for eight years with medical students. In both cases our effort was to help groups go through a growing experience which would make the members free to use their own person therapeutically.

Reprinted from *Progressive Education*, May, 1955, pp. 79-82.

Group psychotherapy was begun with some of the same attitudes as those which prevail in a teacher's college, where classroom procedures are acted out by the teachers in training. At times there was a competitive element similar to that of the mock trials held in a law school. As opportunity arose, we discussed openly the need for an emotional experience, such as might be expected of theological students before they enter the ministry. The quality of any such "corrective emotional experiences" undertaken with student groups was always modified by the fact that nobody present acknowledged a need for treatment. When pathology was discussed by a group member, this was not taken as evidence of illness, but rather as "growing pains." This emphasis decreased the shame and fear, and increased the expectation of achieving greater stature as a whole person.

GRADE SCHOOL TEACHERS

The experiment with teachers was done in a grade school with 800 pupils. The principal agreed to have a psychotherapist be at the school from 3 to 4 P.M. every Wednesday, to talk with the teachers about personality problems in children and adults. Attendance was voluntary, but most of the teachers consistently came to every meeting. The principal usually attended, but he exercised no authority.

At first the therapist did all the talking, giving some lectures on psychodynamics, psychosexual development, and interpersonal relationships. From the first he explained that he was talking to get the group acquainted with his thinking and feeling, and that he would stop lecturing as soon as more discussion developed. After about three months, very little lecturing was necessary.

At first the group discussions dealt with problem children, with the teachers asking the therapist what to do about them. The therapist never gave advice in so many words, but commented on the attitude of the teacher as she described the problem child. The therapist also offered guesses as to how the teacher might cause problem behavior in her children. Some teachers were extremely hesitant to acknowledge feelings of resentment or even revenge concerning difficult pupils. The "anesthesia" of group participation and support gradually helped some of these rigid teachers to be more spontaneous in giving expression to their emotions. By the end of the first year the therapist did much less leading, and was often a participant in discussions between the teachers. The issues considered branched out from problem children to such other subjects as relationships to parents, relationships between teachers, and functions of the principal. In one respect the therapist remained alert to his responsibility as leader, and this was to prevent the development of excessive anxiety. For example, when one teacher spoke of unusual sexual feeling, the therapist suggested that the group seemed large for this, and that some members present might be uncomfortable if such material were discussed. In a similar manner the therapist tried to protect teachers who were not well liked against too much aggression from the rest of the group. This also occurred in terms of the principal, who was repeatedly criticized.

During the second year, the group took over much of the therapeutic function. The original leader remained an active participant, expressing his own feelings as he had opportunity, or helping to clarify the expressions in the group. Sometimes he even discussed the psychodynamics operating at the time to assist with conscious insight. The leader never quite became an ordinary member of the group. As occasion arose, he pointed out the wisdom of not giving direct advice, or the danger of gossiping about therapeutic confidences, the value of silence in answer to some questions, and the use of fantasy in developing feeling relationships.

After two years, the results were gratifying, particularly the increased enthusiasm of the teachers for their work with children and each other. A kindergarten teacher spoke of being happier with visits by parents. She had felt free for the first time to have mothers stay all day with their children when they started school in the fall. Another teacher spoke of feeling "less trapped" by her pupils. Several referred to having discovered the principal as a person, and that this had enriched their teaching eperience. There were also negative comments, such as that the therapist had failed to do enough factual teaching. Several teachers spoke of not attending regularly because they did not like him, or doubted his sincerity, or considered him too impractical. However, most comments were positive. Several teachers felt themselves to have grown as people in both their professional and private living.

An additional outcome was a special treatment procedure initiated by the teachers for problem children. This pertained only to pupils who were conspicuous in the classroom because of unusual shyness, asocial behavior, or other evidences of marked emotional disturbance. Some teachers had asked the therapist to take the most difficult children for individual treatment, but he had refused. He explained that he was there to help the teachers meet their problems, not to remove them. As a result, the teacher with a behavior problem would ask another teacher to have lunch with the problem child a number of times, so that the "strange" teacher became the therapist. In this way the therapeutic function was isolated from the teaching function. This isolation helped to intensify the therapeutic relationship in these special cases. Transcripts of some of these interviews were written out, and later presented to the group for comment. In this way the school did not export its emotional problems, but worked through them within its own framework. The teachers continued this kind of work for some years after the end of our experiment. The success of this program was taken as further indication of the emotional growth of the teachers participating.

MEDICAL STUDENTS

Our grade school work served as preliminary experience for a more pretentious effort in teaching psychotherapy to medical students. This was undertaken in a medical school which had no previous active department of psychiatry. It was arranged that each student would get 300 hours of work in psychiatry during his four years. About one-fourth of this time was devoted to group psychotherapy.

During the first three months in the fall, the entire freshman class met every Monday at 9 A.M. for an hour of introductory lecture on interpersonal relationships. In December the class was divided into groups of 12 to 15 students, with a staff member assigned to meet with each group for an hour every week through the rest of the freshman and sophomore years. The instructor introduced himself as offering no direct teaching, but willing to share his knowledge and feelings with the group. He explained that the students would not be graded. Attendance was voluntary, but whenever somebody was absent repeatedly, the others usually took this up with him.

The initial response of medical students to this division into groups and to the free discussion varied from outright hostility to tentative acceptance. Each year some of the freshmen objected that they did not want to discuss personal problems in public. Some even asked sarcastically whether the instructor (group leader, therapist) considered them all to be mentally sick. The instructor would then explain that the extent to which members of the group became "patients" was not predetermined, but each would get out of the group as much or as little as he wanted. He also indicated that the group itself had complete control over how it functioned. In the earlier sessions, students expressed various fears, such as of becoming too upset or that members of the group would gossip if intimate material was revealed. They stated that it would be easier to see the instructor alone. They complained that a student could not expect much help from his colleagues since they "were all in the same boat," and that the instructor should be more directive in getting the group started. Some of this early discussion was met by the instructor with complete silence, some with further questions or with explanations. The instructor spoke quite freely about his own life, of experiences with previous groups, and sometimes about private patients in such a way that they could not be identified. The students were told that all the instructors had been psychotherapeutic patients, and questions regarding that experience were answered as openly as seemed appropriate.

By the end of the freshman year, most of the groups had gone through some rather warm exchanges of feeling, including open expressions of hostility toward the instructor and authority generally. Other issues discussed were complaints about various courses in the school, attitudes toward academic achievement, questions regarding sex and marriage, and the difficulties in being free with each other in the group. In contrast to the work with teachers, the instructor did not try to control the anxiety level in these medical student groups. Consequently there were disturbing occasions of much anger or affection, as members of a group overcame the usual barriers between them.

When the group met as sophomores after the summer vacation, there was usually a strengthening of group feeling. The basis for this increment is not clear, but it was as if the interval of three months had served to integrate the group experiences of the freshman year. Much of the interpersonal irritation had disappeared, and the group was more ready to spend the second year working, each member to get help for himself, or to offer help to his colleagues in the group. During the weekly hour of the sophomore year it was not uncommon for some student to announce that he needed some help. At such times the other members of the group withheld their own therapeutic need in order to function as multiple therapists to the man who had made himself a "patient." It was a measure of the therapeutic capacity of the group that such a patient often toook up fundamental problems, such as self-esteem, identification, fears of self-destruction, and moral values. It was rare for the same student to be a patient in two consecutive weekly sessions. On occasion the group offered to help some member, by pointing out his lack of adjustment in some area, or his lack of growth. This was often done with such gentleness and intuitive skill that it amazed the instructor. A characteristic experience toward the end of the sophomore year, and therefore the end of the group, was the need of the students to discover inadequacies in the instructor, and to be able to help him grow. Another aspect was an increasing freedom to express positive feelings, and a desire for some kind of social meeting with wives and girl friends at a party. This was usually held in the home of the instructor.

In the eight years of this program, it has been the opinion of the staff that about 75% of the medical students profited personally and professionally, and were positively oriented toward the whole area of psychotherapy. In their later work with patients, students repeatedly referred to their group experiences to provide a basis for evaluating difficult relationships. A minority of the students showed little or no benefit, but even some of these men later were found to be utilizing their psychotherapeutic teaching in practice. The staff received many grateful remarks from men who felt that the group therapy sessions had been a major integrating factor in their education. A third year student said, "I used to think I'd start living after I got through school; now I want to learn to live before I get through." One man came to the surprising realization that his honesty was primarily a fear of getting caught if he were dishonest, and he was seeking a sense of personal integrity within himself. Another had expected to be successfully married if he once got his M.D., but decided that presentation of this degree to a girl would be a rather inconsequential aspect of building a satisfying marriage.

Certain sociological factors were worth noting, since psychotherapy is somewhat "off center" from the conventional focus of an educational setting. This was of particular concern in the medical school, where the faculty raised questions. There were comments that group therapy might be anti-educational, since it emphasizes motivation and feeling, rather than logic and factual learning. Some of the faculty thought that the medical students were becoming too uninhibited in their critical evaluation of medical teaching. A few parents also came to the Dean to complain about the new thinking their sons were learning in the group meetings. The staff took these comments seriously, and discussed them in the groups.

DISCUSSION

The experiment described leads to the conclusion that a psychotherapist can perform a significant function in an educational program. By force of tradition, the American school places a heavy emphasis on learning facts and reporting these accurately in tests. When the student has achieved a standard level of intellectual and mechanical skill, he is rewarded with a degree. The teacher's responsibility for the student's emotional growth is minimized. For 12 to 20 years of his early life the curriculum impresses on the student the overwhelming importance of performing successfully in competition with others. There is little open encouragement of affective growth. Perhaps our culture is now producing the psychotherapist as a counteremphasis, to acknowledge that meditation, love, fear, and dreams also constitute a legitimate area of systematic growth. *Progressive Education* is to be congratulated on devoting an entire issue to exploring the affective factors in education.

In the preliminary work with teachers, the therapist was primarily helping the group to permit themselves to consider their feelings about their work and themselves. There was a loosening of rigid teaching attitudes. Teachers were helped to take their feelings seriously as related to children, co-workers, and parents. The developing respect in the teacher for herself as a person then in turn resulted in more concern for the emotional development of her pupils. However, the changes seen in the teachers were not of a deep personality re-integration. The therapist had simply helped the teacher to use more adequately and with less fear some capacities already present.

With the medical student groups, the therapist functioned with less hesitancy. His manner encouraged "explosions" of feeling as these developed. He often gave his own free-associations, even though these might disturb the group. The result was a much more tumultuous experience than had occurred with the teachers. However, the group repeatedly had the experience of coming through interpersonal conflict to a new affection and respect for each other. In the case of some students, the therapist also saw signs of rather profound intrapersonal growth. The final outcome was judged to be the emergence of capacities which seemed new to the student.

In both parts of this experiment, the therapist felt considerable surprise that such work was possible within conventional school hours. This preliminary success leads to many other questions regarding the affective dimension in education. For example, the relationship between the work of the therapist, as described above, and that of the regular teacher who feels responsible to present more than her subject matter, remains largely undefined. What has been possible to demonstrate is that interaction in a group offers an approach to emotional growth in a school setting.

SUMMARY

Group psychotherapy with grade school teachers and medical students, conducted one hour per week for two school years, was possible with very satisfactory results. The response of the groups was positive and encouraging. In both experiments, follow-up contacts made two and three years later indicated that growth which was encouraged by the group sessions was continuing. It was found that a prerequisite for teaching psychotherapy in this way was a relatively permissive atmosphere. Given such a setting, group therapy was found to be a powerful method of developing the therapeutic capacity of teachers and students.

ADDITIONAL AUTHOR'S NOTE (1961)

Since the publication of the paper, the group with whom I am associated in the practice of psychotherapy has continued to work together. We have become convinced that the teaching of treatment by means of group experience is a valuable adjunct in the education of the "psychotherapist" at all levels, from the relatively untrained status of the grade school teacher to the fully accredited psychotherapist with many years experience. It seems to me now that the tendency toward the "hardening of the categories" (in Esther Menaker's phrase) is likely to be inevitable for the full-time psychotherapist, unless he is repeatedly challenged both professionally and personally in group experiences with colleagues. Such training for the experienced therapist by means of an on-going group experience was well described by Dr. Carl Whitaker. He points out that the resistances to further growth found in the mature therapist are likely to be so great that only group psychotherapy in some form can bring enough pressure on him to once again learn humbly about human nature. After the therapist has graduated from his own personal therapy, he is likely to find few experiences that can regress him enough to make further growth possible. Patients so effectively assign status to us in our function as therapists that we very much need the group experience with colleagues in which we are accepted as ordinary people with much room to learn and to grow.

AUTHOR'S COMMENTS FOR REVISED EDITION

The experiments which are reported in the foregoing paper were done from 1945 to 1953. At that time group psychotherapy was in its infancy and of uncertain reputation. *Teaching* by means of affective group encounters was very rare. By now there has been a tremendous development of many types of groups. The spectrum of involvement goes from intense marathons in the nude to other groups in which part of the hour is devoted to formal lecturing and the remainder is discussion.

All such involvements in groups have in them the potential for both intellectual learning and emotional maturation. Our early experiments reflect this, although the dynamics were not so clear to us then. The degree to which a group is "training" depends on the person of the leader. This is conspicuously evident in the way group supervision of trainees is now done; it can be very didactic, or it can be so personal as to approach being psychotherapy. We differentiate the two types of emphasis according to the anxiety level in the group. It is high whenever the character structure of participants is challenged. Anxiety is relatively low when insight or intellectual learning is promoted. We have learned to limit anxiety systematically when our primary purpose is training rather than personal growth.

To do good training, the group leader must clearly structure the action so that the group does not flounder from one extreme to the other, from overwhelming affective involvement to intellectual sterility. This is being done very effectively in training institutions such as Georgia State University. Undergraduate classes there in the Psychology of Adjustment utilize limited group involvement in conjunction with brief bursts of lecturing, role-playing, and person-to-group encounters. The graduate classes in clinical psychology can tolerate more affective involvement and benefit from less didactic intervention.* In general, technical supervision for young psychotherapists in training has progressed from conventional individual critique sessions. Supervisees are now often trained more effectively in various forms of group seminars, where they share their interview experience with each other and reenact problem situations. As they develop into professional persons, training continues in therapy groups in which they are participants, and the emphasis is increasingly on their intrapersonal maturation (gut learning) along with continued disciplined professionalism. The primary purpose remains that of professional training. The

* Personal communication from Dr. Elizabeth Valerius.

maintaining of lively involvement by both the supervisor-teacher and the trainees depends on the emotional impact of their relating. The joyful adventure for the teacher is to facilitate both aspects of the students' growth.

In the many years since 1953, my greatest professional interest has continued to be the training of students in "psychotherapy." This was my purpose in editing a new journal, VOICES, *The Art and Science of Psychotherapy*, which used very little of the professional lingo and addressed itself to the development of all students of human nature. The level of educational status of "trainees" does not seem important to me. Obviously those in a psychology graduate program are more challenging, and even more so are those of postdoctoral maturity. However, working with groups of public school teachers or others of less than doctoral training remains a top priority challenge in our society. For this reason the preceding chapter of work with teachers and medical students seems to me worthy of republication once again.

Keeping the senior psychotherapist-teacher alive has become an increasing concern to me. It is necessary for the senior therapist to have the joy of seeing both professional and personal growth in those whom he is training. This is often most readily seen in the exciting experiences of trainees at the graduate level. Yet this alone is not enough to keep an older therapist lively and creative. The resistances to further growth found in the mature therapist are likely to be so great that he suffers "hardening of the categories." He needs an ongoing patienthood to support his growing personhood. Only his experiences as a patient in group psychotherapy can regress him enough to open up new capacities. Only a humbling group experience can bring enough pressure on older therapists so that we once again discover the magnitude of our ignorance and the wonder of almost infinite human capacity.

Part 6

THE CURRENT SCENE: GROUPS FOR THERAPY AND GROWTH

IN THIS SECTION we have included papers which deal with current conflicts as well as provocative themes in contemporary group psychotherapy.

The paper by Friedman relates the values that are to be found in the positive existentialism of Martin Buber. They have particular relevance to workers in the field of group psychotherapy, since Buber's concern is with the authenticity of human experience. Buber emphasizes the importance of the meeting between individuals as they grow toward fuller awareness of their responsibilities toward one another and to the community and life relationships. This paper has been included because it points to the importance for all group therapists of organizing and exploring a philosophical basis for the work in which they are engaged. The impersonalization that so often characterizes psychoanalytic treatment is rejected by many contemporary therapists, and the importance of the here and now experience is emphasized. This has been noted earlier and is stressed again in the paper by Beukenkamp.

These papers by Beukenkamp and Friedman essentially deny the somewhat inflexible orientation of those psychoanalysts who view the group experience primarily within the familial framework. The group therapist's awareness of his subjective involvement, as well as his conceptualization of the group therapy experience as essentially interpersonal, appears to be increasingly stressed in contemporary psychotherapy. Many therapists who practice individual psychotherapy exclusively criticize this emphasis on the importance of the here and now orientation, which is certainly apparent when individuals are in a therapy group. The here and now orientation has been criticized as being so reality oriented that it denies the intrapsychic mechanisms of the individual patient. The answer of many contemporary psychotherapists who support experiential or existential psychotherapy which embodies a here and now approach is that their therapeutic approach constantly brings to the attention of the patient his belonging to the human community and his responsibilities in all life relationships, and that his intrapsychic functioning is repeatedly reflected and demonstrated in his interaction with others.

Bell's paper summarizes work in the field of family group therapy. He approaches the family from a modeling point of view and tries to reconcile small group theory, from social psychology, with psychotherapy of the family. He proposes a definition of the family in terms of social psychological theories. This is quite dissimilar from a psychoanalytic approach. He has also brought his article up-to-date.

The current popularity of encounter groups has obscured the dangers and risks involved when participants are exposed to these techniques. The article by Stone and Tieger describes the need for adequate screening of participants in such an experience.

Since the advent of family therapy, there have been many innovative approaches. The article by Speck and Rueveni describes the concept of network therapy of the social network of a schizophrenic family. In this process a variety of sensitivity training techniques were introduced.

The article by Jones covers the therapeutic community as a change system, as well as the function of a process consultant.

The next-to-last article is a suggested reading list for people who are interested in sensitivity, growth, and encounter groups as well as transactional and gestalt therapy groups. The list covers the basic approaches.

The plethora of techniques used with groups is often confusing to the student and practitioner. It becomes difficult to differentiate between the scientific and the charismatic approach. The *Guidelines* set forth by the American Psychological Association should help clarify the issues that are often beclouded as one studies the current scene.

There is no certainty about previously expressed convictions. George Homans' early book, *The Human Group*, represented for many readers the earlier functionalist paradigm of Talcott Parsons, who created the social relations department at Harvard. Since then, Homans served as chairman of the sociology department at Harvard, and this department separated from the social relations grouping at that university and then joined again. At the last report, Homans is the strongest advocate of B. F. Skinner's ideas within American sociology and has become an advocate of behaviorism.*

---

* Homans, G. C., "The Sociological Relevance of Behaviorism," in R. L. Burgess and D. Bushell, Jr., eds., *Behavioral Sociology* (New York: Columbia University Press, 1969), pp. 1–24.

55

DIALOGUE AND THE "ESSENTIAL WE"

The Bases of Values in the Philosophy of Martin Buber

Maurice Friedman

The bases of values in Martin Buber's thought are his philosophy ot dialogue and his philosophical anthropology, or the study of the problem of man. On this twofold foundation he establishes such basic value categories as the distinction between "I-Thou" and "I-It" relationships and that between "dialogue" and "monologue," the responsibility of the whole person to meet and respond to what addresses him in the "lived concrete," the primacy of the dialogical over the psychological, confirmation and "imagining the real," genuine speech and the "essential We," the distinction between "existential guilt" and neurotic guilt-feelings. These categories can help illuminate the value problems that arise in group psychotherapy and that are central to the goal and direction of such therapy.

"I-THOU" AND "I-IT"

Martin Buber's philosophy of dialogue is best known through its classic presentation in his little book *I and Thou*. In this book Buber makes his now famous distinction between the two relationships or basic attitudes that constitute human existence: the "I-Thou" and the "I-It." What distinguishes these relationships is not the object of the relation, but the nature of the relationship itself and the difference between the "I" that enters into the one relationship and the "I" that enters into the other. The "I-Thou" relation is direct, mutual, present. In it the other person is related to in his uniqueness and for himself, and not in terms of his relations to other things. In an "I-Thou" relation my partner reveals himself

Reprinted from *The American Journal of Psychoanalysis*, Vol. XX, No. 1, 1960, pp. 26-34.

to me directly, as just the person he is. I do not seek for his meaning by enregistering him in one or another general category. In the "I-It" relationship, on the other hand, the other is my object and not my partner. I observe him and use him; I establish his relation to this or that general category. I know him with the same detachment that I know any object, or I see him purely in emotional terms, but, in either case, not as a really independent person standing over against me. Hence this relationship is never really direct or mutual or truly present. In the "I-Thou" relation emotion and reason, intuition and sensation are included in the wholeness of the person responding to what he meets. The "I" of the "I-It" relationship, in contrast, is always partial, and it is just as much "I-It" if it is emotional as if it is rational, if it is subjective as if it is objective.

Both "I-Thou" and "I-It" are necessary for human existence. "I-it" again and again provides the base for ordered civilization, for technical accomplishment, for scientific advance. Yet "I-It" is not sufficient for human existence even on the barest terms. Without the "I-Thou" relation, the biological human individual would not become a person, a self, an "I" at all. He begins with the "I-Thou" in his relation to his mother and family and only later develops the separating relationship of "I-It." As long as the "I-Thou" and the "I-It" remain in healthy alternation, ever new material from the realms of the physical, the biological, the psychological, and the social is brought into the "I-Thou" relation and given new, present meaning. When "I-It" becomes predominant and prevents the return to the Thou, however, man loses authentic existence and ultimately falls into pathological self-contradiction. Thus, Buber's "I-Thou" philosophy is both descriptive *and* normative, fact and value. The normative comes in in the difference between mere existence and authentic existence, between being human at all and being more fully human, between holding the fragments of the self together sufficiently to get by and bringing the conflicting parts of oneself into an active unity, between having partial, disparate relations with others and having fuller, more responsible ones.

THE LIFE OF DIALOGUE

In *Between Man and Man*, Buber expresses his basic distinction in terms of the contrast between "dialogue" and "monologue." Dialogue may be silent and monologue spoken. What really matters in genuine dialogue is my acceptance of the "otherness" of the other person, my willingness to listen to him and respond to his address. In monologue, in contrast, I only allow the other to exist as a content of my experience. Not only do I see him primarily in terms of his social class, his color, his religion, his IQ, or character neurosis, I do not even leave myself open to him as a person at all.

Values as a living human reality only exist in the "life of dialogue," in the direct, reciprocal relation between man and man, for in it alone are we able to know and respond to the other in his uniqueness. It is only when I "really have to do" with the other that I can really be responsible to him. "The idea of responsibility is to be brought back from the province of specialized ethics, of an 'ought' that swings free in the air, into that of lived life. Genuine responsibility exists only where there is real responding." [1] Responsibility, to Buber, means the response of the whole person to what addresses him in the "lived concrete"—his full concrete situation. No abstract code is valid in advance of particular situations. None has universal validity, because value does not exist in the universal at all, but in the particular, the concrete, the "interhuman." This does not mean that moral codes are of no use if they are recognized as what they are—abstractions, generalizations, rules of thumb that may be helpful in pointing us back to the concrete values that men have discovered in real meeting. But they cannot take the place of our discovering for ourselves, each time anew, what is the right direction in a particular situation. The movement of values, therefore, is from the concrete situation and the deep-seated attitudes which one brings to that situation to the response and decision that produce the moral action.

> No responsible person remains a stranger to norms. But the command inherent in a genuine norm never becomes a maxim and the fulfillment of it never a habit. Any command that a great character takes to himself in the course of his development . . . remains latent in a basic layer of his substance until it reveals itself to him in a concrete way . . . whenever a situation arises which demands of him a solution of which till then he had perhaps no idea.[2]

The "ought" which arises in the concrete situation is not the pure "I-Thou," but what Buber calls the *quantum satis*—the sufficient amount of what one can do in that hour and in that situation. Just because real values arise in the concrete situation and in terms of the particular person confronted with that situation, the "ought" must include and be based on the real concrete person and all the limitations and resources that he brings with him into the situation.

But this can never be done by advance assessment, no matter how thorough one's knowledge of oneself or another, for, except in general terms and over-all predictions, one's resources are only known in the situation itself. One's potentialities do not simply inhere in one as a part of one's make-up, but are called out of one in response to what meets and demands one in this hour.

> What is possible in a certain hour and what is impossible cannot be adequately ascertained by any foreknowledge. . . . One must start at any given time from the nature of the situation in so far as it is at all recognizable. But one does not learn the measure and limit of what is attainable

in a desired direction otherwise than through going in this direction. The forces of the soul allow themselves to be measured only through one's using them. . . .[3]

PHILOSOPHICAL ANTHROPOLOGY

Buber's philosophy of dialogue has found its most thoroughgoing philosophical base in the philosophical anthropology which Buber has developed in his later years. Philosophical anthropology is concerned with the uniqueness of man, what makes man a problem to himself.

In "What Is Man?" Buber establishes the focus of the problem of man in the "interhuman," the "sphere of the between." Man, essentially, is neither a self-sufficient, primarily isolated individual, such as Freud saw man, nor an organic collectivity. The fundamental fact of human existence is man with man, the genuine dialogue between man and man. The psychological, the psychic stream of happenings within each man, is only the accompaniment of the dialogical. It is not itself the reality and goal of human existence. "All real living is meeting." Individuation is not the goal, only the indispensable way to the goal. This point is absolutely central to Buber's thought and it cannot be emphasized too strongly. Many psychotherapists and psychologists, such as Erich Fromm and Carl Rogers, who today recognize the essential importance of mutual relations between men still see these relations largely as the function of the individual's becoming and the means to that end. As long as dialogue is entered *merely* as a means to the end of health, maturity, integration, self-expression, creativity, "peace of mind," "positive thinking," and richness of experience, it will not even produce those things, for it will no longer be true dialogue and will afford no real meeting with the other.

DISTANCE AND RELATION

Through contrasting man with the rest of nature, Buber derives a twofold principle of human life consisting of two basic movements: "the primal setting at a distance" and "entering into relation." The first movement is the presupposition for the second, for we can only enter into relation with being that has been set at a distance from us and, thereby, become an independent opposite. Only man can perform this act of setting at a distance because only man has a "world" (*Welt*)—an unbroken continuum which includes not only all that he and other men know and experience, but all that is knowable now and in the future—while an animal only has an environment or realm (*Unwelt*). "Only the view of what is over against me in the world in its full presence, with which I have set myself, present in my whole person, in relation—only this view gives me the world truly as whole and one."

Distance given, man is able to enter into relation with other beings ("I-Thou") or to enlarge, develop, accentuate, and shape the distance itself, turning what is over against him into his object ("I-It"). An animal cannot see its companions apart from their common life, nor ascribe to the enemy any existence beyond his hostility. Man sets man at a distance and makes him independent. He is, therefore, able to enter into relation, in his own individual status, with those like himself.

CONFIRMATION AND "IMAGINING THE REAL"

The basis of man's life with man is . . . the wish of every man to be confirmed as what he is, even as what he can become, by men; and the innate capacity in man to confirm his fellow men in this way. . . . Actual humanity exists only where this capacity unfolds.[4]

This mutual confirmation of men is most fully realized in what Buber calls "making present," an event which happens partially wherever men come together, but in its essential structure only rarely. Making the other present means to "imagine the real," to imagine quite concretely what another man is wishing, feeling, perceiving, and thinking. The particular pain I inflict on another surges up in myself until, paradoxically, we are embraced in a common situation. It is through this making present that we grasp another as a self, an event which is only complete when he knows himself made present by me. This knowledge induces the process of his inmost self-becoming, "for the inmost growth of the self is not accomplished, as people like to suppose today, in man's relation to himself." An animal does not need confirmation because it is unquestionably what it is. A man needs confirmation because he exists as a self, at once separate and in relation, with unique potentialities that can only be realized if he is confirmed in his uniqueness.[5]

Buber describes "imagining the real" as a "bold swinging" into the life of "the particular real person who confronts me, whom I can attempt to make present to myself just in this way, and not otherwise, in his wholeness, unity, and uniqueness." [6] "Imagining the real" is crucial for genuine ethical responsibility, in which one's response is not to subjective interest or to an objective moral code, but to the person one meets. It is also essential for friendship and love, in which each member of the relationship is made present by the other in his concrete wholeness and uniqueness. But imagining the real is also essential for all the helping relationships—pastor and congregant, teacher and student, therapist and patient. If we overlook the real "otherness" of the other person, we shall not be able to help him, for we shall see him in our own image or in terms of our ready-made categories and not as he really is in his concrete uniqueness. But if we allow him to be different and still accept and confirm him, then we shall have helped him realize himself as he could not without us.

"HEALING THROUGH MEETING" AND ONE-SIDED "INCLUSION"

In friendship and love, "inclusion," or experiencing the other side, is mutual. In the helping relationships, however, it is necessarily one-sided. The patient cannot equally well experience the relationship from the side of the therapist or the pupil from the side of the teacher without destroying or fundamentally altering the relationship. This does not mean that the therapist, for example, is reduced to treating his patient as an object, an It. The one-sided inclusion of therapy is still an "I-Thou" relation founded on mutuality, trust, and partnership in a common situation, and it is only in this relation that real therapy can take place. If "all real living is meeting," all true healing also takes place through meeting. If the psychotherapist is satisfied to "analyze" the patient, "i.e. to bring to light unknown factors from his microcosm, and to set to some conscious work in life the energies which have been transformed by such an emergence, then he may be successful in some repair work. At best he may help a soul which is diffused and poor in structure to collect and order itself to some extent. But the real matter, the regeneration of an atrophied personal center, will not be achieved. This can only be done by one who grasps the buried latent unity of the suffering soul with the great glance of the doctor: and this can only be attained in the person-to-person attitude of a partner, not by the consideration and examination of an object." [7] But a common situation does not mean one which each enters from the same or even a similar position. In psychotherapy the difference in position is not only that of personal stance, but of role and function, a difference determined by the very difference of purpose which led each to enter the relationship. If the goal is a common one—the healing of the patient—the relationship to that goal differs radically as between therapist and patient, and the healing that takes place depends as much upon the recognition of that difference as upon the mutuality of meeting and trust.

> . . . the specific "healing" relation would come to an end the moment the patient thought of, and succeeded in practising "inclusion" and experiencing the event from the doctor's pole as well. Healing, like educating, is only possible to the one who lives over against the other, and yet is detached.[8]

This excludes neither Erich Fromm's conviction that the therapist at the same time heals himself in some measure through his own response to the patient, nor Carl Rogers' feeling of the equal worth and value of the client (which leads Rogers, mistakenly in my opinion, to stress the full mutuality of the client-therapist relationship), nor Trigant Burrow's and Hans Syz's emphasis on an "inclusive therapy" in which, particularly in group therapy, the therapist aids the patients by allowing them to see some of the social and personal distortions in himself.[9] But it does preclude accepting the therapist's *feeling* of mutuality as equivalent to the actual existence of full mutuality in the situation *between* therapist and patient. The scientific impersonalism that characterized the orthodox conception of the psycho-analyst is rightly rejected by many present-day therapists. But this should not lead us to a sentimental blurring of the essential distinction between therapy and other, less structured types of "I-Thou" relations. In the latter, as Buber puts it, there are "no normative limitations of mutuality," but in the former the very nature of the relationship makes full mutuality impossible.

THE ESSENTIAL WE

The relation between man and man takes place not only in the "I-Thou" relation of direct meeting, but also in the "We" of community. As the "primitive Thou" precedes the consciousness of individual separateness, whereas the "essential Thou" follows and grows out of this consciousness, so the "primitive We" precedes true individuality and independence, whereas the "essential We" only comes about when independent people have come together in essential relation and directness. The essential We includes the Thou potentially, for "only men who are capable of truly saying *Thou* to one another can truly say *We* with one another." This We is not of secondary or merely instrumental importance; it is basic to existence, and as such it is itself a prime source of value. "One should follow the common," Buber quotes Heracleitus, i.e., join with others in building a common world of speech and a common order of being.

> Man has always had his experiences as I, his experiences with others and with himself; but it is as We, ever again as We, that he has constructed and developed a world out of his experiences.

Thus amid the changes of world image, "the human cosmos is preserved, guarded by its moulder, the human speech-with-meaning, the common logos." [10]

The importance for group psychotherapy of Buber's concept of the common world as built by the common speech-with-meaning can hardly be overestimated. Speech, from this point of view, is no mere function or tool, but is itself of the stuff of reality, able to create or destroy it. "Man has always thought his thoughts as I . . . but as We he has ever raised them into being itself, in just that mode of existence that I call 'the between.'" Speech may be falsehood and conventionality, but it is also the great pledge of truth. Whether he takes refuge in individualism or collectivism, the man who flees answering for the genuineness of his existence is marked by the fact that he can no longer really listen to the voice of another. The other is now only his object that he observes. Only if real listening as well as real talking takes place will the full possibility of healing be present in group psychotherapy, for only thus, and not through any mere *feeling* of group unity, will the full potentiality of the group as a group be realized. "He who existentially knows no Thou will never succeed in knowing a We." [11] One *should* follow the common, and that means that lived speech, "speech-with-meaning," is itself a value. Values are not just the content, the building blocks of speech. They exist, in the realest sense, in the "between," in the dialogue between man and man.

It is not only the fate of groups that depends upon the common "speech-with-meaning." If man does not recover the genuineness of existence as We, he may cease to exist at all.

> In our age, in which the true meaning of every word is encompassed by delusion and falsehood and the original intention of the human glance is stifled by tenacious mistrust, it is of decisive importance to find again the genuineness of speech and existence as We. . . . Man will not persist in existence if he does not learn anew to persist in it as a genuine We.[12]

GUILT AND GUILT-FEELINGS

The centrality of man's existence as We is basic to Buber's distinction between "groundless" neurotic guilt—a subjective feeling within a person, usually unconscious and repressed—and "existential guilt"—an ontic, interhuman reality in which the person dwells in the truest sense of the term. The analyst must see the illness of the patient as an illness of his relations with the world. "A soul is never sick alone," writes Buber, "but always through a betweenness, a situation between it and another existing being." True guilt does not reside in the human person but in his failure to respond to the legitimate claim and address of the world. Similarly, the repression of guilt and the neuroses which result from this repression are not merely psychological phenomena but events between men.[13] Existential guilt is "guilt that a person has taken on himself as a person and in a personal situation," an objective dialogical guilt that transcends the realm of inner feelings and of the self's relation to itself. Existential guilt is the corollary of the answerability and responsibility of the self in the concrete dialogical situation. It is failure to respond and, by the same token, failure to authenticate one's existence. "Existential guilt occurs when someone injures an order of the human world whose foundations he knows and recognizes as those of his own existence and of all common human existence." [14] This "order of the human world" is not an objective absolute existing apart from man: it is the interhuman itself, the genuine We, the common logos and cosmos. What it means to injure this common order is known to every man who has experienced real guilt, but also to every group therapist who has had to discover the direction his group must take for real therapy, and in so doing, like Alexander Wolf, distinguish between constructive and destructive group trends and constellations.[15] The therapist may lead the man who suffers from existential guilt to the place where he himself can walk the road of illuminating that guilt, persevering in his identification of himself as the person who took on that guilt, and, in so far as his situation makes possible, restoring "the order of being injured by him through the relation of an active devotion to the world." [16] "In a decisive hour, together with the patient entrusted to him and trusting in him," the therapist "has left the closed room of psychological treatment in which the analyst rules by means of his systematic and methodological superiority and has stepped forth with him into the air of the world where self is exposed to self. There, in the closed room where one probed and treated the isolated psyche according to the inclination of the self-encapsulated patient, the patient was referred to ever-deeper levels of his inwardness as to his proper world; here outside, in the immediacy of one human standing over against another, the encapsulation must and can be broken through, and a transformed, healed relationship must and can be opened to the person who is sick in his relations to otherness—to the world of the other which he cannot remove into his soul." [17]

REFERENCES

1. M. Buber, "Dialogue," in *Between Man and Man*, trans. Ronald Gregor Smith (Boston: Beacon Paperback, 1955), p. 16.
2. M. Buber, "The Education of Character," *op. cit.*, p. 114.
3. M. Buber, *Pointing the Way: Collected Essays*, ed. and trans. Maurice S. Friedman (New York: Harper & Bros.; London: Routledge & Kegan Paul; 1957), p. 206.
4. M. Buber, "Distance and Relation," trans. Ronald Gregor Smith, *Psychiat.*, Vol. XX, No. 2, May 1957, p. 102.
5. *Ibid.*, p. 104.
6. M. Buber, "Elements of the Interhuman," trans. Ronald Gregor Smith, *Psychiat.*, Vol. XX, No. 2, May 1957, p. 110.
7. M. Buber, *I and Thou*, trans. Ronald Gregor Smith (New York: Charles Scribner's Sons, 1958), 2nd revised edition with new postscript by author, p. 132 ff.
8. *Ibid.*, p. 133.
9. Erich Fromm's statement is from a personal conversation I had with him in which he indicated his full acceptance of the principle of "healing through meeting." That of Rogers is from a dialogue I moderated between him and Martin Buber at the University of Michigan in March 1957, the transcript of which has been privately circulated by Dr. Rogers but not printed. In this dialogue the difference between the two men becomes apparent, not only in this point, but in Rogers' belief that man is basically good, Buber's that he is polar, with his strongest capability of good being coupled with his strongest potentiality of evil; Rogers' emphasis on unqualified acceptance

as opposed to Buber's emphasis on a confirmation which, while it accepts the other as a person, may also wrestle with him against himself; Rogers' emphasis on subjective becoming and dialogue as a means to that becoming, Buber's emphasis on dialogue with the becoming of the self only an aspect of dialogue rather than its goal. Buber could not accept Rogers' statement that he treats neurotics, schizophrenics, and paranoiacs the same and that he has full mutuality with them as a description of the situation but only of Rogers' feeling about the situation. For a description of the approach of Burrow and Syz, cf. Hans Syz, "An Experiment in Inclusive Psychotherapy," Exp. Psychopathol., 1957, pp. 129-169.

10. M. Buber, "What is Common to All," trans. Maurice S. Friedman, The Review of Metaphysics, Vol. XI, No. 3, March 1958, p. 377.
11. Ibid., p. 378.
12. Cf. 10 above, p. 378.
13. Cf. 3 above, p. 95 ff.
14. M. Buber, "Guilt and Guilt Feelings," trans. Maurice S. Friedman, Psychiat., Vol. XX, No. 2, May 1957, p. 117.
15. Alexander Wolf, "The Psychoanalysis of Groups," Am. J. Psychother., Vol. III, No. 4, October 1949, Vol. IV, No. 1, January 1950. [Also reprinted as Chapter 23 in the present volume.]
16. Cf. 14 above, p. 22.
17. Cf. 3 above, p. 96 ff.

56

BEYOND TRANSFERENCE BEHAVIOR

Cornelius Beukenkamp

The term transference, introduced by psychoanalysis, refers to the behavior of the patient toward the therapist. It is the reproduction of the repressed and forgotten experiences of early childhood. This reproduction not only takes the form of the reactions but also appears in the dreams. Freud limited the term to displacements occurring during the therapeutic psychoanalysis. Jung held that the patient must find a relationship to a living present object in his strivings for adaptation.

Generally, therapists see transference as coming from any of the various segments of the psychic structure. For example, there is superego transference, ego transference, ego-ideal transference, and id transference.

Usually, when the patient no longer shows evidence of transference behavior, this then, is felt to be a manifestation of the resolvement in a beneficial manner.

This paper does not find any disagreement with these long established tenets. However, when attending clinical meetings, how often do we not hear wide differences in interpretations concerning the same segment of behavior. In fact, many erudite discussions have ended without any understanding being reached.

And later on with reflection, we have seen that the other interpretations given carried considerable validation as well. This experience, along with a decade of group psychotherapy experience, brought about the following thoughts: Perhaps human behavior cannot be divided so arbitrarily by placing it upon a single dimensional plane. Further, since the usual therapy setting includes only one plane, the interpretations by the therapist must be obviously unidimensional in their orientation. When others hear clinical material by report, they may render valid interpretations which ap-

Reprinted from the *American Journal of Psychotherapy*, Vol. X, No. 3, July 1956, pp. 467-470.

pear in conflict with those presented since the observer may be speaking from a different plane. In the past, these differences were always attributed to the different theoretical formulations held by each. This no doubt does play an important part. Nonetheless, it might be, simply as suggested, a different vantage point from which to observe the multiplicity of levels involved. For, if we return to the basic concept of transference-behavior, we realize that it is predicated upon an understanding of a projectional system of recall. The patient in such a setting is the donor. It is he who decides what we shall see or listen to. It is he and not ourselves who permits us to see into which of his levels the type of inadequacy he cares to have revealed. And, when I speak of levels, I mean not psychosexual levels but levels of interaction. Levels of interaction refer to the concept of multidimensional behavior.[1] This concept sees three levels in operation. The first, is that of the child-parent configuration (Primary Polarity); the second, the sibling-to-sibling and family member to society feelings (Secondary Polarity); and finally, a self-limited and prepropagational, antioriginal familial directed enterprise closely resembling normal adolescence, labeled Tertiary Polarity.[2]

This then, may be a cogent reason why so many observers disagree when attempting to understand a patient's behavior in therapy. That is, the interpretations given may appear to be in conflict only because they are speaking from one of these dimensions and thus fail to take in a most vital realization that man is not, in his normal life, a single psychic dimensional organism. He is born into a group, develops as a part of the group, his adjustment is to the group, and even in his death his departure is felt as a loss to his group. So then, is it not obvious that when we are attempting to evaluate human behavior one must think in a multidimensional way bearing in mind that the family configuration with its ramifications is the prototype of social structure.

If then, we are not outflanked by the patient's need to control his environment and ourselves, as a part of it, he has the possibility of then engaging in multiple interactions. This is essential if ever he is to leave behind him his symbiotic level of behavior. Not to do so may be the etiology of the formation of the iatrogenetic neurosis or "transference neurosis."

These considerations are based upon seeing therapy conceptualized as an interpersonal process—one in which the ego emphasis should be on growth and repair. The growth and repair is designed to give the ego strength so that it can separate itself in its symbiotic struggle—free itself from the cravings of its orality and of equal import, cease in its excessive identifications. This kind of therapy should, therefore, attempt with proper timing to become an experiential occurrence. If this occurs, within multiple meaningful relationships approximating normal family life, the ego will then engage in behavior, after repair, which may be called "beyond transference behavior."

It is not necessary or even at times advisable to place every patient into a group therapy program; nor is it wise for every therapist to do so in order to practice multidimensional therapy. We state these values for we feel that not every patient is suited in terms of his psychopathology; and not every therapist's personality, from a talent-interest viewpoint, is predisposed for such undertakings.

The therapist using individual treatment is undoubtedly familiar with the shiftings of identities projected upon him [multiphasic behavior[3]]. He, the individual therapist, can use these shifting identities of the one-to-one relationship in such a way that multidimensional therapy becomes possible. For example, if he emphasizes the patient's expressed interest in the mentioned third parties and drives away from the circumscribed and overly introspective concern of the patient's ego, so common in this setting, he can then create a specialized form of group configuration. This type of special creative pursuit by the therapist will aid his patient in releasing him from his parasitic dependencies, excessive orality, and resistant symbiotic identifications.

Naturally, those using combined therapy (individual and group) have this above-mentioned opportunity structured before them.

This multidimensional therapeutic approach is further enhanced if the therapist uses an objective appraisal of his subjective involvement with his patients. By this is meant an active participation with those present in the therapy setting, as if he was observing not the patient alone, but instead, himself together with his patient in action.

Suggestions offered to aid therapists both to reach and understand "beyond-transference behavior" are as follows: Strive to have the reliving process of therapy approximate as closely as possible human multiple psychology. This you can do by taking into consideration that the single human being is normally found in a multiple human setting. In other words, emphasize "the other people" in his life when he, the patient, refers to them in his communications. This will bring about not only the desirable clinical results already mentioned but reveal the two types of "beyond-transference behavior." First, that which is new experiential behavior within a given single configuration or polarity, i.e. behavior not based upon a reliving process. Second, that behavior which is not based upon recall and possesses the emotion present in the family feelings or the feelings of belonging to a multiple human structure.

REFERENCES

1. C. Beukenkamp, "The Multidimensional Orientation in Analytic Group Therapy," *Am. J. Psychother.*, IX:477-483, 1955.

2. C. Beukenkamp, "Further Developments of the Transference Life Concept in Therapeutic Groups," *Hillside Hosp. J.*, V:441-448, 1956.
3. C. Beukenkamp, "The Multidimensional Orientation in Analytic Group Therapy," *loc. cit.*

57

RECENT ADVANCES IN FAMILY GROUP THERAPY

John Elderkin Bell

When I first spoke in Scotland on family group therapy in 1955, it might have been said that the therapy had progressed through much of a first developmental phase, the advancement of the idea and somewhat random pioneering exploration. Experience in working with whole families had allayed my initial anxieties lest I precipitate a damaging emotional crisis, and had modified a somewhat unfavorable attitude to parents developed in the traditional child guidance setting. It had also proved that the patterns established in the first five years of life are often less resistant to change than had been thought. It demonstrated the therapeutic value of factors not previously much considered, such as freedom in communication and active group participation within the family. It had also proved that behavior of children and adults is more responsive to current social influences than many personality theories would indicate.

It had been demonstrated that many disturbances among older children and adolescents could be alleviated by therapeutic efforts that consistently involved both the parents and all children over nine years of age. The sequence through which family therapy progresses had been defined, permitting refinements in technique. The role of the therapist was becoming more deliberate. Sufficient control over the treatment had been attained to suggest that family therapy was feasible, economical and widely applicable (21).*

By this time others had also initiated new approaches to dealing with the family for both research and therapeutic purposes. Primarily these investigators (Dreikurs (37-39); Adelaide Johnson (64); Ackerman (1-13,

Reprinted from *Journal of Child Psychology and Psychiatry*, 1962, pp. 1-15. Pergamon Press. Amended by J. E. Bell, September 1973.

* All numbers in parentheses refer to the bibliography at the end of this article.

19); Bowen and his group (23-26, 29, 42)) applied observations of various family members to the understanding of disturbed individuals, and permitted extension of theories about personality development and pathology in individuals. For example, Brodey (29), a spokesman for the last group which had experimented with hospitalization of total families of which one member was schizophrenic, detailed how the narcissism of parents led to their dealing with their schizophrenic child as an externalized projection of their own ungratified needs, preventing them from facing realistically and helpfully the child's own unmet needs. As a consequence the child reacted with schizophrenic responses.

A CRITICISM

Theories such as these, extending systems developed to explain pathological processes within individuals, may prove less efficient for understanding family processes than those which start from a social psychological orientation. We have to ask whether or not the narcissism of the parent of a schizophrenic or of any disturbed child is different in quantity or quality from that of the normal parent. If so, there should be some method of defining the distinctions and determining the extent of the narcissism. It is doubtful, however, that this can be accomplished. Social group theory would suggest that we are dealing here with a phenomenon that is virtually universal rather than distinctive for these types of family.

One might propose that all individuals in their social relations, whether parents, children, friends, are constantly engaged in a balancing act, juggling the self-wishes against the imposed demands from other individuals. Out of this elemental action in the social group emerges the variety of roles possible within the group. As a consequence, the child and parents will function in certain ways, which will differ from parent to parent and from child to child. Each will attempt to induce the others to accomplish what he is unable to accomplish himself. Each will interpret the needs of others in the light of his own ungratified needs. These simply represent two among many mechanisms through which social interaction is accomplished, and which are not necessarily pathological.

AN EXTENDED PERSPECTIVE

The point of view on family process to be developed here has been anticipated in the publications of Spiegel and Norman Bell (95-99). They follow the philosophic position of Dewey and approach the family from a transactional point of view. They postulate that the events involving the family occur within a total system of interdependent sub-systems, any one of which—for example, the individual, the family, the community, the value system—may become temporarily a focus of observation. The "world" being observed must include the observer and his observing. Within the field encompassing the interconnected sub-systems, a component system, such as the individual, can be isolated and studied as an entity. But this is an heuristic device that will involve some distortion or sacrifice of precision and predictability.

With others, they composed a multi-disciplinary team to develop the relationships among three levels of systematic concept formation, namely, the intrapsychic, the interpersonal relations in the family, and the culture. In the first, they used the theory of psychodynamics from psychoanalysis; in the second, the concepts of social role and role-conflict resolution; in the third, culture-value orientations.

They especially emphasized the cultural and social role aspects of family differences, in marked contrast to the individual-orientated perspective of some of the therapists mentioned above. They dealt with such phenomena as the presence of an emotionally disturbed child in families from Irish, Italian or early American families. In such families they reported acceleration of attempts to assimilate new cultural values. Undue rapidity of these efforts resulted in intrapsychic conflict in the parents, which intruded into the social relations between the parents and the children, leading to selection of a child as a scapegoat to accomplish a pathological stabilization of the parents' role-conflicts. Here is a demonstration of differences of explanation that emerge from different foci of observation. The definition of "family" determines the theory that will eventuate.

THREE DEFINITIONS OF FAMILY

Basically three definitions of the family have been reflected in theory and practice:

(1) The first is based on the family as seen through the eyes of a child, or as reconstructed by an adult patient. The family appears as a beneficent or a malicious influence, determining alternately the growth of healthy and pathological personality reactions. In the major writings upon which our clinical practice of psychotherapy with both children and adults was founded, the basic idea of the family turned around an individual seen genetically in polar relationship with other family members, particularly the parents. To the observer, the members of the family interacting with the individual were given form primarily by the manner in which they appeared to this individual. Any amplification of the picture provided by therapeutic interviews with a mother, or occasionally a father, or a home visit, still did not modify the orientation toward the child, but simply expanded the information available for understanding him and his reports and fantasies about his family.

(2) The second definition uses a sociological approach. This leads to theories concerning communication in the family, group attitudes and

ideals, family group decisions, and family group activities. This point of view de-emphasizes the individual and focuses on the interactive aspects of the family; this is the direction of some theories relating to family group therapy, and will be explored in detail later.

(3) Thirdly, we observe the cultural approach, emphasizing the family as an institution in both its nuclear and extended aspects; this leads especially to theories concerning the culture and the community as a source of values, norms, standards of behavior, roles, generalizations about fathers, mothers, children, the style of the family, and sociocultural factors in the development of pathological conditions.

These three modes of defining the family are not necessarily compatible in the present stage of theoretical development. Eventually we may be able to arrive at a single theory which will deal simultaneously with the phenomena of family behavior as seen from these three perspectives. For the moment it may be more productive to isolate the relationships within these three modes of observation and to organize our theories accordingly.

FAMILY GROUP THEORY

Family group theory represents an application of small group theory from social psychology to the natural group of the family. The therapy which led to the development of the theory and which is also, in its later stages, an outgrowth of theory, is an effort to apply knowledge of the operation of small groups to the production of change in the family unit. The aim is to answer a series of questions.

The Family as a Group

The first question concerns the nature of the family as a group. To understand the processes in family therapy, it is necessary to attend to three social units:

(1) The first is the single collective unit composed of the parents and children. This unit is founded on and developed from the organic base of a biological relationship. This is a given. Even an artificial, or adoptive, family is modeled on the biological family. This unit is commonly referred to as the nuclear family. Family group therapy consists normally of treatment of this collective group as a unit.

(2) Secondly, we must recognize that within the single collective unit of the family, there are a series of subgroups, not static in composition, but forming, expanding, contracting, dissolving. These subgroupings help to explain the dynamic processes in family life. Whereas the collective unit of the family has identity as a concept and as a structured entity, the subgroups within it are characterized more by their functional aims and action than by any defined structure as social units. These subgroups may be discerned when we observe two individuals in a family teaming up together

for some mutual purpose that excludes the rest of the family members. Such teams are constantly being formed, dissolved, or expanded, as when a team opens its group to include one or more additional members. In reverse, a larger subgroup may shove a member out and close ranks against him. The process of family life may be described, then, as a sequence of emerging subgroupings within the collective unitary nuclear group. The unitary group may be regarded as an assumed system of subgroups which may be separately identified at any point in time. In point of fact, despite the physical contiguity of its members, the family may seldom appear as a single group, particularly when observed over a span of time. While not forgetting that the overall family is a group with recognizable boundaries, one is usually made aware of the subunits.

(3) Thirdly, as will be amplified later, it seems valuable to acknowledge that the group therapy situation involves a third group, composed of the family members plus the therapist. In regarding the family as a collective unit, we consider it in isolation from the observer. Similarly, when we identify subgroupings within the unit, we deduce structure and describe behavior as though they existed apart from the social process of observation. The resultant over-simplifications are partially corrected through focusing on the total social group in the therapy situation, which, of course, in its dynamic progress involves subgroupings comparable to those in 2 above. In contrast to the first two natural groupings, the total therapy group is constructed, encouraging us to apply extensive published findings about such groups (compare reference 60).

Processes of Group Formation

Having identified the above three social units, we encounter a second question: how may we define the processes of group formation in the family? As with all human relationships, we may think of those in the family as beginning when the aims of an individual confront those of others in his situation. "Aims" is used here as a general term encompassing the meanings of the words "instinct," "drive," "motive" and "goal." Two consequences may follow:

(1) First, when the individual's aims are complementary to those of others, he receives their support for his goal-seeking activity. Action then ensues.

(2) Secondly, when the individual's aims are non-congruent with those of others, an ambiguous situation is created which the respective individuals, singly or in small groups, seek appropriate ways of resolving. There is an oscillation of action and reaction, moving individuals together and apart. These actions I have called *transitive actions,* for want of a better overall term to cover all the specific transitive verbs such as "love" and "hate" that describe the process. I have avoided terminology sometimes used for this purpose, such as "interaction," "inter-relationships,"

because it carries too much emphasis on the subject and the object, and too little on the process between them. Under conditions which we cannot fully specify, these processes eventuate in the resolution of the conflict by the use of either new or habitual patterns of behavior.

Applied specifically to the family, we may define the processes of group formation as *action processes leading to the accommodation of complementary or conflicting demands of individuals who are contiguous by reason of specific biological relationships or of selection after the pattern of these relationships.*

Such action processes are observed within the manifold relationship possibles in the various combinations of family members. The processes may be further specified in terms of their *purposes*, that is in terms of their motivational origins; the *media* in which they are couched, whether verbal or nonverbal, i.e., as processes of communication; and the *mechanisms* observed as the family members maneuver in the attempt to reconcile their conflicting aims through such action processes as decision, evaluation, and revision. They may be further described by the *form* of the structure of interrelationships observed at any point of time, especially by specification of such polarities as dominance-submission, independence-dependence, leading-following, or through such mutual correspondences as loving, hating and fearing.

Some common-sense observations about the family permit us to elaborate our understanding of these action processes. Normally the family goes through a longer and more varied history of group action than any other small group in our society. It is distinguished from other groups by some particular characteristics of its relational possibilities.

For one thing, it is composed of individuals at different age-levels, developing at different maturational rates, and with disparate age-valuations. The psychological characteristics of particular ages produce dissimilar requirements for change and possibilities for action. At particular periods, new processes of interaction are demanded with great speed. For instance, parents of a first-born child are often amazed at the rapidity with which they have to revise their ways of handling him in view of the sudden and dramatic shifts in behavior that take place overnight. A pattern is no sooner established than the child's maturation requires a new schedule or a new method of handling. This, it seems to me, is part of what is implied in the statement that "children keep you young." Their maturation requires flexible reactions from their parents.

No maturational process is more telling in its effects than the growth of language. As the development of language progresses from communication with the simple signs available to the young child to the complicated symbolic language of the adult, new possibilities for action and demands for changes in family relations continually emerge. We shall see how inability or failure to accommodate to such demands may be related to the breakdown of the family and the precipitation of psycho-pathological behavior.

Other agents (of a dynamic and changing nature) which help to define the action potentialities of the family group are found in the biological or genetic make-up of the individuals; yet others are found in the community and cultural pressures on the individuals and the group. We are not overlooking the importance of these when we concentrate on the family as a social group, but rather simplifying our own analysis of the nature of the family. We acknowledge the need to revise our points of view to take into account these other components of family interaction.

As stated in our definition, the action process of the family leads to mutual accommodation, which consolidates complementary aims and reconciles the conflicting demands of individuals, thus leading to the structuring of the formerly ambiguous and inchoate operational field (forming of groups). This process includes action within the whole unit or between subgroups of the larger unit. The group units are being revised constantly as other action steps are needed. Thus we describe the forming, remaking and dissolving of the family group(s).

Health and Pathology in the Family

Next we must consider the question of health and pathology in the family. We are speaking here of social health and illness, especially the latter, which may subsume a broad range of social problems shown in one or more family members. We recognize that health and pathology are value-judgments applied to the behavior of the family group or individual members by those inside or outside the family. In dynamic terms, the judgment that behavior is pathological is a demand for change in present behavior, whether or not this is possible. Health, in similar terms, represents behavior which is socially supportable and sanctioned within the family group, outside it, or both. Behavior may be called healthy or pathological as though it were clearly one or the other, which is never actually the case, since the judgment is always related to the personal standards of the judge, none of which occur universally.

To speak of the healthy and efficient family implies then some broad concurrence on the characteristics of such a family. Among those that might secure such broad agreement are the following:

(a) It shows, by the mutual satisfaction of its members and by action in concert, that complementary aims exist and are supporting the functions and structure of the group as a group.

(b) It has available multiple methods for accommodating the mutually incompatible demands of its individual members. It demonstrates from day to day a variety of patterns by which it faces and handles the conflicts between individuals and factions within it.

(c) It has means of repeatedly evaluating the consequences of its achievements of accommodation.

(d) It chooses to operate flexibly, so that new methods of accommodation may be discovered and taken up when radical shifts are required.

In contrast, we believe that the family that produces a disturbed individual has not been able yet to achieve the above action patterns.

THE SYMPTOM AS COMMUNICATION

In attempting to explain the development of pathological behavior from the family group point of view, we have found it necessary to differentiate the conditions within which acute symptoms are developed and those within which chronicity is produced. It would appear that when symptoms develop suddenly, we have especially an effort on the part of an individual to bring about a change within the family group. In this light, the acute symptom may be regarded as a sign about a person's needs, his desires and anticipation for the other, and his resulting goals. Thus, among other concepts the symptom may be thought of as an attempted communication expressed in such a manner and intensity as to effect disturbance in the group. Often signs learned in early life are used because of their simplicity, even though they may have lost their historical sign-value and be now less efficient in most situations than more complicated symbolic language. The use of a more primitive sign language suggests the breakdown of more complex communication, and ineffectiveness in more mature language. This inadequacy may be the result of defects in the symbols formerly available, as when the symbols are too ambiguous, when their meaning to speaker and listener is not equivalent, when the intended recipient is not attending, when, having heard, he fails to respond or mobilizes powerful counter-communications in protest against what he hears.

In practice, the acute symptom is commonly expressive and/or motoric rather than verbal, in accordance with the observation that nonverbal communication generally takes precedence over verbal communication in the family. In a group with such a long history of development, where the earlier nonverbal language was a required form of communication, a brief gesture often speaks a whole paragraph. Analysis of the communication system in the family leads to the following observations:

(1) Frequently the nonverbal is the preferred language, especially when there are young children, but also with older children and adults.

(2) For the most part, the verbal and nonverbal are interchangeable as modes of communication; this is a basis for family group therapy, where the nonverbal must for a great part be translated into the verbal.

(3) Sometimes the nonverbal represents a breakdown of the verbal method of communication. The latter may then be restored only when there is especial support and sanction for expressing content verbally.

(4) Sometimes the nonverbal represents that which has not attained consciousness and cannot therefore be expressed verbally. Support may lead to the development of insight, awareness of the meaning of the behavior, and the ability ultimately to verbalize; but expression cannot be attained until insight is present.

(5) Sometimes the nonverbal and the verbal are mutually contradictory or inconsistent.

(6) Sometimes nonverbal language tends to be used for private communication within the family group in preference to the more public verbal communication. Particular words and verbal expressions may also develop a private symbolic value within the family and be used in intimate ways, even though the outward form is public.

Returning to consideration of the acute symptom, if the crisis it represents is not resolved, then the symptom processes are incorporated into the patterns of family action, and groups are formed on the basis of the existence of the symptom action; such groups may include or exclude the individual with the symptom. The symptom then is perpetuated as a role, partly developed, partly assigned. Such a role may retain to a certain extent some of its communicative purpose, but it tends to lose this aim as it is reinforced by the pressures of the family group and thus becomes habitual. Here we have, then, the development of chronicity. An illustration may help to clarify this. In one family, a small boy had been traumatized when his mother forced him out of the family car and told him to walk a short distance home because he had been misbehaving; his acute response was the development of car-sickness. Had this been effective in telling his parents of his anxiety that he might be ejected from the car, the symptom would have accomplished its communicative purpose. Instead, the family reorganized its life around the car-sickness, avoiding occasions for the boy to ride in the car, but also insuring, in effect, that the car-sickness would persist when riding was necessary. In family therapy, when the family could recognize and attend to the communicative intent in the car-sickness, they heard his memory of the early trauma, and about the anxiety that had persisted for the ensuing eight years.

The chronic symptom becomes a way of interrelating—a mode of action—and attains the usefulness of the familiar as the family works out its purposes. It is perpetuated because it has become integrated into an established web of family interactions and its persistence is necessary to the continuation of this structure. Within this pattern the value of the symptom to the respective family members may vary; it would not serve the same purposes for the patient who carried the symptom as for any other. Though each may use it in his own way, the family significance is primarily its functional necessity to a stabilized mode of interaction. No one may consciously wish it to persist, although an unconscious need for the pathology may be demonstrated by the emergence of symptomatic behavior in one or more other family members when the patient begins to improve. The symptomatic mode of action seems to be forced on another family member in order to preserve the overall pattern of the family process.

CONCOMITANTS OF CHRONICITY

When chronic symptomatology is deeply entrenched in the behavior patterns of an individual, we may often observe one or more associated conditions or situations in the family.

(1) There may be a limitation or reduction in the range of methods of accommodation to conflicts between the family members, for instance, progressive limiting of the action patterns permitted in the family. Patterns of behavior become stereotyped; the manners of relating become fixed and unresponsive to modifying influences. The stereotypes may be represented in the rigid structuring of subgroups within the family; in the constriction of the expressed goals toward which individuals, subgroups, and the family as a whole direct themselves; and in the inflexibility of their choice of action patterns.

(2) There is a diminution of symbolic communication and an increase in the use of simple signs. Thus the messages which can be transmitted are impoverished quantitatively and qualitatively. There is also reduced reception of messages through failures in listening, hearing, and in the visual perception of gestures and facial expressions.

A particular form of impoverished communication, the contradictory or ambiguous message, has been described especially by Jackson, Bateson, Haley, Weakland, *et al*. Reporting on their research on family communication in schizophrenia (16-18, 56, 104, 105) they discriminate two levels in the exchange of messages that leads to the defining of relationships. The first is the simple message conveyed by the words. The second is the qualification of the message conveyed by the mode of speech and the accompanying motoric elements—movement, gesture, facial expression and tone of voice. Sometimes the qualifications are congruent with the message; in other instances they are incongruent.

The authors trace the schizophrenic problem in part to a particular form of contradictory communication which they call "double-bind"; this is defined as a situation in which one member of the family imposes mutually inconsistent requirements on another, thus preventing movement in any direction. This complete stifling of decision or action forces the individual out of direct communication and into incongruent responses.

(3) There is a breakdown in the evaluation process through which individuals attain and revise their perceptions of others, their awareness of their own methods of responding to others, and their aims, both personal and mutual. Consequently, they act in such a way as to perpetuate the pathological behavior and as though it were impossible to revise. Verbally

they may protest their distress at the behavior of the sick family member, while at the same time perpetuating, without insight, the conditions that result in the pathology.

(4) The family values "change" insufficiently or excessively. Change is an aim of families in varying degrees. This difference is reflected in the extent of the development of family lore which provides traditional patterns of interaction. For a family to be effective as a group, a balance seems to be necessary between the aim of preserving tradition and achievement of change. If the clinging to old ways is too strong, as in immigrant groups, the family will face disruption, both because of the conflict in values with the culture and the internal rigidity of the family; if, on the other hand, change is overvalued, advantage cannot be taken of the economy of stable patterns.

FAMILY THERAPY AS A MECHANISM FOR CHANGE

Let us now consider some points of view about how family group therapy produces change in face of such pathology. We do not know if the processes are fundamentally different when the symptoms are acute and have produced a crisis in the family, or when they are chronic and integrated into the family interaction. We suggest that, in the latter case, some crisis must be precipitated, perhaps by the pressure of community reaction, or perhaps by some change in the state of the person who has been carrying a pathological role in the family.

The initiation of change through family therapy begins with the referral, which is itself a request for change, but characteristically for change in an *individual*. The first problem in family therapy is to translate this request for change in the individual into one for change in the *family* where it may be assumed change is needed. Such an assumption would not be foreign to the thinking of family members in most instances. The therapist supports this point of view when he insists on seeing the family as a group rather than as a series of individuals in isolation.

When the motivation for family change is established, the therapist forms a group with the family in which he attempts to play a planned, controlled, and communicated role. At the beginning it appears that he establishes with each individual a subgroup, each of which demonstrates to the whole some new possibilities of action for each of the family members. As an outsider, he calls into play actions embodying patterns that the individual uses in his public life beyond the family. These patterns have been potentially available for use within the family, but have been crowded out or never permitted among the customary stereotyped actions there. During this phase of the therapy, the therapist models the behavior that elicits new patterns beyond those ordinarily seen. This modeling sets the pattern by which family members later seek from others behavior that is beyond their stereotypes. Thus, in later stages of the treatment the family members function somewhat as the therapist does at the beginning, but more essentially as individuals acting in ways beyond their conventional patterns.

At all stages the therapist must ensure the participation of each member of the family. Since the participation will be primarily on a verbal level, there are certain requirements as to age, ability to conceptualize abstractly, and knowledge of language that require a particular level of maturity from each of the family members. Also, each must have engaged in enough extrafamily life to develop patterns of behavior beyond those used in the family. These patterns are important because they are potentially available to expand the modes of interaction within the family. It has been found that nine years of age is about the lower limit for the average child to participate, according to the method I have developed. It may be feasible, by using other modes of communication, to work with family groups that include younger children, although many who have tried to include those who are younger have confirmed the validity of setting the criterion for minimal age at approximately nine.

In order to promote participation, the therapist must develop and maintain the clearest possible definition and presentation of his own functions. As with all groups that are constructed, there is an initial stage of common exploration of the respective roles of individuals and the sanctioned modes of communication. The speed with which this may be accomplished depends on the therapist's clarity about his own role, and his ability to communicate to the other members of the conference the ways in which he will and will not take part. Thus, the orientation of the parents and the children is especially important.

Equally important are:

(1) The therapist's clear awareness of the formal responsibilities he will undertake.

(2) His defining of the manner in which he will accomplish them.

(3) The relationship between what he says and what he communicates nonverbally, which determines the extent to which he can make his role explicit. The less ambiguity there is in the role of the therapist, the more rapidly the group will structure itself into a functioning conference.

In the initial states of treatment, when the therapist is establishing working relationships with each individual participant in the family, the members begin to perceive that there are new possibilities of action being revealed, and that these may be incorporated experimentally into their joint action. Normally this begins in two-person subgroups in the family (parent-child, husband-wife). These two-person subgroups are consequently enlarged, combined, grouped, and regrouped toward an inclusion of as many family members as is optimal for the action to be accomplished.

The therapist's over-all activity may be described, then, as an effort to promote social interaction through communication within the family unit, permitting it thereby to experience, appraise, define, and reorder its relational processes. The therapist builds social action on the basis of his own methods of participation. He conducts relationships—now with one, now with two, now with all—in the presence of the others. He disrupts unsatisfactory patterns of relationships as he encourages individuals to reaffirm old intentions that have been frustrated. He calls up new intentions. He stimulates the family to clarify its goals, to choose more appropriate group goals for the whole family and more suitable personal goals for use in life outside the family's direct involvement. He demonstrates, through the ways individuals relate to him, that within the family there may be: a) increased fluidity in communication; b) greater flexibility in roles and functions; and c) greater discipline in the choice and forms of relationships.

He promotes thereby new evaluations within the family of the potentialities and skills of the individual members. He encourages the family members to reassess the past, if they bring it up in relation to present difficulties during the course of the treatment. They may then begin to reexamine responsibility for earlier difficulties, the meaning of symptomatic behavior, and the family climate within which it grew. The therapist prevents any family members from evading the implications of their relationships with him and others. He demonstrates forms of relationships that can be transferred to other interactions in the family. This leads the family to the conviction that change is possible and desirable, and may bring about a greater measure of behavior the family would interpret as positive.

In accomplishing the changes in the therapy, the therapist places more emphasis on interaction than on the content of the actions and verbalizations of any individual. In a sense, his focus is on what is happening between individuals rather than on what is happening to a single person. His attention floats at the center among the family members, rather than on internal processes within an individual. He watches for the behavior that is called up in others when an individual acts in his own way; he does not require explanation of an individual's action so much as response to it, and experiencing of it. When the family is freely engaging in interaction, the therapist's own participation becomes observational and reflective. When the interaction shows evidences of being blocked, he intervenes to free the action and communication. Thus he is extremely active in ongoing evaluation of the social processes in the family, and in continual readiness to intervene and conduct therapeutically oriented participation of family members in the total group process.

Family group therapy is, then, a treatment method which depends on the presence and control of the therapist. He uses his own personal and social skills to help the family attain what it has shown itself unable to reach at the beginning of treatment, the ability to live for its own total welfare as defined by its own values, for the welfare of each of its family members, and ultimately for the betterment of the community.

SUMMARY

The history of the author's development of family group therapy and of some studies of the family has been reviewed briefly. Various definitions of *family* were discovered and a proposal was advanced to define family in terms of social psychological theories of small group behavior. From the perspective of such a definition, formulations were attempted relative to the development of the family group, its stability, its action processes, its health, and its pathology. In light of these conceptions, a brief analysis was undertaken of the processes involved in family group therapy as a mechanism for the promotion of interactional change.

REFERENCES

1. Ackerman, N. W. (1951) Group Dynamics 1. "Social role" and total personality. *Amer. J. Orthopsychiat.* 21:1-17.
2. Ackerman, N. W. (1954) Interpersonal disturbances in the family: Some unsolved problems in psychotherapy. *Psychiatry* 17:359-368.
3. Ackerman, N. W. (1956) Psychoanalytic principles in a mental health clinic for the pre-school child and his family. *Psychiatry* 19:63-76.
4. Ackerman, N. W. (1957) A changing conception of personality: a personal viewpoint. *Amer. J. Psychoanal.* 17:78-86.
5. Ackerman, N. W. (1957) An orientation to psychiatric research on the family. *Marriage Fam. Living* 19:68-74.
6. Ackerman, N. W. (1958) *Psychodynamics of family life.* Basic Books, New York.
7. Ackerman, N. W. (1958) Toward an integrative therapy of the family. *Amer. J. Psychiat.* 114:727-733.
8. Ackerman, N. W., and Behrens, M. L. (1955) Child and family psychopathy: problems of correlation. In *Psychopathology of childhood.* Hoch, P. H., and Zubin, J. (Eds.), Grune and Stratton, New York, pp. 177-196.
9. Ackerman, N. W., and Behrens, M. L. (1956) A study of family diagnosis. *Amer. J. Orthopsychiat.* 26:66-78.
10. Ackerman, N. W., and Behrens, M. L. (1956) The family group and family therapy: the practical application of family diagnosis. *Int. J. Sociometry* 1:52-54.
11. Ackerman, N. W., and Behrens, M. L. (1957) The family group and family therapy. Part II. The practical application of family diagnosis. *Int. J. Sociometry* 1:82-95.
12. Ackerman, N. W., and Neubauer, P. B. (1948) Failures in the psychotherapy of children. In Hoch, P. H. (Ed.), *Failures in psychiatric treatment.* Grune and Stratton, New York.

13. Ackerman, N. W., and Sobel, R. (1952) Family diagnosis: an approach to the study of the preschool child. *Amer. J. Orthopsychiat.* 20:744-752.
14. Alanen, Y. (1958) The mother of schizophrenic patients. *Acta psychiat. neurol. scand.* 33:Suppl. 124.
15. Barrabee, P. (1957) The family as the unit of treatment in mental health therapy. *Marriage Fam. Living* 19:182-186.
16. Bateson, G. (1958) *Cultural problems posed by a study of schizophrenic process.* Presented at the American Psychiatric Association, Conference on Schizophrenia, Honolulu.
17. Bateson, G. (1958) *The group dynamics of schizophrenia.* Presented at the Institute on Chronic Schizophrenia and Hospital Treatment Programs, Osawatomie State Hospital, Osawatomie.
18. Bateson, G., Jackson, D. D., Haley, J., and Weakland, J. (1956) Toward a theory of schizophrenia. *Behav. Sci.* 1:251-264.
19. Behrens, M. L., and Ackerman, N. W. (1956) The home visit as an aid in family diagnosis and therapy. *Soc. Casewk.* 37:11-19.
20. Bell, J. E. (1953) Family group therapy as a treatment method. *Amer. Psychologist* 8:515 (T). Also privately published.
21. Bell, J. E. (1961) Family group therapy: a new method of treatment for older children, adolescents, and their parents. *Publ. Hlth. Monogr. 64.*
22. Beatman, F. (1957) Family interaction: its significance for diagnosis and treatment. *Soc. Casewk.* 38:111-118.
23. Bowen, M. (1960) A family concept of schizophrenia. In Jackson, D. D. (Ed.), *The etiology of schizophrenia.* Basic Books, New York.
24. Bowen, M. (1957) *Family participation in schizophrenia.* Presented at the annual meeting of the American Psychiatric Association, Chicago, May 15.
25. Bowen, M., Dysinger, R. H., and Basamania, B. (1959) Role of the father in families with a schizophrenic patient. *Amer. J. Psychiat.* 115:1017-1021.
26. Bowen, M., Dysinger, R. H., Brodey, W. M., and Basamania, B. (1957) *Study and treatment of five hospitalized family groups each with a psychotic member.* Read in the sessions on Current Familial Studies at the annual meeting of the American Orthopsychiatric Association, Chicago, March 8.
27. Bowlby, J. (1949) The study and reduction of group tensions in the family. *Human Relations* 2:123-128.
28. Brady, J. P. (1958) Language in schizophrenia: review of several approaches to the problem. *Amer. J. Psychiat.* 12:473-487.
29. Brodey, W. M., and Hayden, M. (1957) Intrateam reactions: their relation to the conflicts of the family in treatment. *Amer. J. Orthopsychiat.* 27:349-355.
30. Burgum, M. (1942) The father gets worse: a child guidance problem. *Amer. J. Orthopsychiat.* 12:474-485.
31. Chance, E. (1959) *Families in treatment.* Basic Books, New York.
32. Clausen, J. A., and Yarrow, M. R. (1955) Mental illness and the family. *J. soc. Issues* 11:3-5.
33. Clausen, J. A., Yarrow, M. R., Deasy, L. C., and Schwartz, C. G. (1955)

The impact of mental illness: research formulation. *J. soc. Issues*, 11:6-11.

34. Cleveland, E. J., and Longaker, W. D. (1957) Neurotic patterns in the family. In Leighton, A. H., Clausen, J. A., and Wilson, R. N. (Eds.), *Explorations in social psychiatry*. Basic Books, New York.

35. Deutsch, M. (1958) A research approach to family diagnosis and treatment. *Marriage Fam. Living* 20:140-145.

36. Dicks, H. V. (1955) The predicament of the family in the modern world. *Lancet* 1:295-297.

37. Dreikurs, R. (1949) Counseling for family adjustment. *Individual Psychol. Bull.* 7:119-137.

38. Dreikurs, R. (1949) Psychotherapy through child guidance. *Nervous Child* 8:311-328.

39. Dreikurs, R. (1951) Family group therapy in the Chicago Community Child Guidance Center. *Ment. Hyg.* 35:291-301.

40. Dublin, T. D., and Fraenkel, M. (1949) Preventive medical services for the family. In *The family as the unit of health*. Milbank Memorial Fund, New York.

41. Dunn, H. L. (1956) Public health begins in the family. *Pub. Health Rep.* 71:1002-1010.

42. Dysinger, R. H. (1957) The "action dialogue" in an intense relationship: A study of a schizophrenic girl and her mother. Presented at the annual meeting of the American Psychiatric Association, Chicago, May 15.

43. Fibush, E. (1957) The evaluation of marital interaction in the treatment of one partner. *Soc. Casewk.* 38:303-307.

44. Fisher, S., and Mendell, D. (1956) The communication of neurotic patterns over two and three generations. *Psychiatry* 19:41-46.

45. Fleck, S. *et al.* (1957) The intrafamilial environment of the schizophrenic patient. II. Interaction between hospital staff and families. *Psychiatry* 20:343-350.

46. Fleck, S., Freedman, D. X., Cornelison, A., Terry, D., and Lidz, T.: *Intrafamilial environment of the schizophrenic patient—V. The understanding of symptomatology through the study of family interaction*. Read at the annual meeting of the American Psychiatric Association, May, 1957.

47. Foote, N., and Cottrell, L. S. (1955) *Identity and interpersonal competence: New directions in family research*. Univ. Chicago Press, Chicago.

48. Foster, R. (1956) A point of view on marriage counseling. *J. couns. Psychol.* 3:212-215.

49. Galdston, I. (1958) The American family in crisis. *Ment. Hyg.* 42:229-236.

50. Gerard, D. L., and Seigel, J. (1950) The family background of schizophrenia. *Psychiat. Quart.* 24:47-73.

51. Glasmann, R., Lipton, H., and Dunstan, P. L. (1959) Group discussions with a hospitalized schizophrenic and his family. *Int. J. group Psychother.* 9:204-212.

52. Goolishian, H. A. (Univ. Texas, Medical Branch, Galveston). Personal communication.

53. Green, R. (1948) Treatment of parent-child relationships. *Amer. J. Orthopsychiat.* 18:442-446.

54. Griffiths, W. (1954) Changing family health patterns: A review of recent research. *J. Home Econ.* 46:13-16.
55. Groves, E., and Groves, C. (1946) *Dynamic mental hygiene: With special emphasis on family counseling.* Stackpole, Harrisburg, Pa.
56. Haley, J. (1959) Control in psychoanalytic psychotherapy. *Progr. Psychotherapy* 4:48-65.
57. Hall, B. H., and Wheeler, W. (1957) The patient and his relatives: initial joint interview. *Social Work* 2:75-80.
58. Hallowitz, D., et al. (1957) The treatment process with both parents together. *Amer. J. Orthopsychiat.* 27:587-607.
59. Halpert, H. P. (1958) Activities of the National Institute of Mental Health which affect American families. *Marriage Fam. Living* 20:261-269.
60. Hearn, G. (1957) The process of group development. *Autonomous Groups Bull.* 13:1-7.
61. Henry, J. (1951) Family structure and the transmission of neurotic behavior. *Amer. J. Orthopsychiat.* 21:800-818.
62. Henry, J., and Warson, S. (1951) Family structure and psychic development. *Amer. J. Orthopsychiat.* 21:59-73.
63. Jackson, D. D. (1951) The question of family homeostasis. *Psychoanal. Quart.* 31:79-90.
64. Johnson, A. M., and Szurek, S. A. (1952) The genesis of antisocial acting out in children and adults. *Psychoanal. Quart.* 21:323-343.
65. Kluckhohn, F. R. (1958) Variations in the basic values of family systems. *Soc. Casewk.* 39:63-72.
66. Koos, E. L. (1946) *Families in trouble.* King's Crown Press, New York.
67. Lewin, K. (1947) Group discussion and social change. In Newcomb, T. M., and Hartley, E. L. (Eds.), *Readings in social psychology.* Holt, New York, pp. 330-334.
68. Lidz, T. (1958) Schizophrenia and the family. *Psychiatry* 21:21-27.
69. Lidz, T., Cornelison, A. R., Fleck, S., and Terry, D. (1957) The intrafamilial environment of schizophrenic patients. I. The father. *Psychiatry* 20:329-342.
70. Lidz, T., Cornelison, A. R., Fleck, S., and Terry, D. (1957) The intrafamilial environment of schizophrenic patients. II. Marital schism and marital skew. *Amer. J. Psychiat.* 114:241-248.
71. Lidz, R. W., and Lidz, T. (1949) The family environment of schizophrenic patients. *Amer. J. Psychiat.* 106:332-345.
72. Lidz, T., Parker, B., and Cornelison, A. (1956) The role of the father in the family environment of the schizophrenic patient. *Amer. J. Psychiat.* 113:126-132.
73. Liebman, S. (Ed.). (1959) *Emotional forces in the family.* Lippincott, New York.
74. Lippmann, H. (1954) Emotional factors in family breakdown. *Amer. J. Orthopsychiat.* 24:445-453.
75. Mangus, A. (1957) Integration of theory, research, and family counselling practice. *Marriage Fam. Living* 19:81-88.
76. McKnight, W. K. (1948) Care of patient's family in a private mental hospital. *Ment. Health Bull.*, Penna. Dept. Welfare, 25:6.

77. Midelfort, C. (1957) *The family in psychotherapy*. McGraw-Hill, New York.
78. Milbank Memorial Fund. (1949) *The family as the unit of health*. Milbank Memorial Fund, New York.
79. Mitchell, C. (1956) The place of counseling in a family agency. *J. Jewish Communal Service* 32:356-367.
80. Mittelmann, B. (1948) The concurrent analysis of married couples. *Psychoanal. Quart.* 17:182-197.
81. Mittelmann, B. (1952) Simultaneous treatment of both parents and their child. In Bychowski, G., and Despert, J. L. (Eds.), *Specialized techniques in psychotherapy*. Basic Books, New York.
82. Mudd, E. (1951) *The practice of marriage counselling*. Association, New York.
83. Mudd, E. *et al.* (Ed.) (1958) *Marriage counselling*. Association, New York.
84. Parsons, T., Bales, R. F., *et al.* (1955) *Family socialization and interaction process*. The Free Press, Glencoe, Ill.
85. Pollak, O. (1956) *Integrating sociological and psychoanalytic concepts: An exploration in child psychotherapy*. Russell Sage Foundation, New York.
86. Reichard, S., and Tillman, G. (1950) Patterns of parent-child relationships in schizophrenia. *Psychiatry* 13:247-257.
87. Richardson, H. B. (1945) *Patients have families*. The Commonwealth Fund, New York.
88. Ruesch, J. (1953) Synopsis of the theory of human communication. *Psychiatry* 16:215-243.
89. Ruesch, J. (1954) Psychiatry and the challenge of communication. *Psychiatry* 17:1-18.
90. Ruesch, J. (1955) Non-verbal language and therapy. *Psychiatry* 18:323-330.
91. Ruesch, J. (1957) *Disturbed communication*. Norton, New York.
92. Ruesch, J., and Bateson, G. (1951) *Communication—the social matrix of psychiatry*. Norton, New York.
93. Ryckoff, I. M., Day, J., and Wynne, L. C. (1958) *The maintenance of stereotyped roles in the families of schizophrenics*. Read at the American Psychiatric Association Meetings, San Francisco, May.
94. Schwartz, C. G. (1957) Perspectives on deviance: Wives' definitions of their husbands' mental illness. *Psychiatry* 20:275-291.
95. Spiegel, J. P. (1954) New perspectives in the study of the family. *Marriage Fam. Living* 16:4-12.
96. Spiegel, J. P. (1956) A model for relationships among systems. In Grinker, R. R. (Ed.), *Toward a unified theory of human behavior*. Basic Books, New York.
97. Spiegel, J. P. (1957) Interpersonal influences within the family. In *Group Processes, 3rd Conf*. Macy Foundation.
98. Spiegel, J. P. (1957) The resolution of the role conflict within the family. *Psychiatry* 20:1-16.

99. Spiegel, J. P., and Kluckhohn, F. R. (1954) Integration and conflict in family behavior. *Group for the Advancement of Psychiatry*. Report No. 27. Topeka, Kansas.
100. Stroup, A., and Glasser, P. (1959) The orientation and focus of marriage counseling. *Marriage Fam. Living* 21:20-24.
101. Szurek, S. *et al*. (1942) Collaborative psychiatric therapy of parent-child problems. *Amer. J. Orthopsychiat.* 12:511-516.
102. Tietze, T. (1949) A study of the mothers of schizophrenic patients. *Psychiatry* 12:55-65.
103. Van Amerongen, S. (1954) Initial psychiatric family studies. *Amer. J. Orthopsychiat.* 24:73-83.
104. Weakland, J. H. (1960) The "double-bind" hypothesis of schizophrenia and three-party interaction. In Jackson, D. D. (Ed.), *The etiology of schizophrenia*. Basic Books, New York.
105. Weakland, J. H., and Jackson, D. D. (1958) Patient and therapist observations on the circumstances of a schizophrenic episode. *Arch. Neurol. Psychiat.* 79:554-574.
106. Wertheim, E. S. (1958) Family casework in the interest of children. *Soc. Casewk.* 39:2-3.
107. Wertheim, E. S. (1959) A joint interview technique with mother and child. *Children* 6:23-29.
108. Wynne, I. D., Ryckoff, I. M., Day, J., and Hirsh, S. E. (1958) Pseudo-mutuality in the family relations of schizophrenics. *Psychiatry* 21:205-220.

ADDITIONAL BIBLIOGRAPHY

Ackerman, N. W. (Ed.). (1970) *Family process*. Basic Books, New York.
Ackerman, N. W. (1967) *Treating the troubled family*. Basic Books, New York.
Bell, J. E. (1973) *Family therapy*. Jason Aronson, New York.
Bell, J. E. (1973) *Involving the family in hospital treatment*. Jason Aronson, New York.
Bowen, M. (1961) Family psychotherapy. *Am. J. Orthopsychiat.* 31:40-60.
Brodey, W. M. (1959) Some family operations and schizophrenia. *Arch. Gen. Psychiat.* (Chicago) 1:379-402.
Dreikurs, R. (1948) *The challenge of parenthood*. Duell, Sloan and Pearce, New York.
Dreikurs, R. (1950) Technique and dynamics of multiple psychotherapy. *Psychiat. Quart.* 24:788-799.
Dysinger, R. H. (1961) The family as the unit of study and treatment. *Amer. J. Orthopsychiat.* 31:61-68.
Erickson, G. D., and Hogan, T. P. (1972) *Family therapy: An introduction to theory and technique*. Brooks/Cole, Monterey, Calif.
Glick, I. D., and Haley, J. (1971) *Family therapy and research: An annotated bibliography of articles and books, 1950-1970*. Grune & Stratton, New York.

Haley, J., and Glick, I. D. (1965) *Psychiatry and the family: An annotated bibliography of articles published 1960-1964.* Family Process, Palo Alto, Calif.

Haley, J., and Hoffman, L. (Eds.). (1967) *Techniques of family therapy.* Basic Books, New York.

Hill, J. A., and Hill, R. (1967) *International bibliography of research in marriage and the family, 1900-1964.* University of Minnesota Press, Minneapolis. (regularly updated)

Howells, J. G. (Ed.). (1968) *Theory and practice of family psychiatry.* Oliver and Boyd, Edinburgh.

Jackson, D. D. (Ed.). (1968) *Communication, family, and marriage. Human communication, vol. 1.* Science and Behavior Books, Palo Alto, Calif.

Jackson, D. D. (Ed.). (1968) *Therapy, communication, and change. Human communication, vol. 2.* Science and Behavior Books, Palo Alto, Calif.

Mahrer, A. R., and Pearson, L. (Eds.). (1971) *Creative developments in psychotherapy: I.* Press of Case Western Reserve University, Cleveland.

National Clearinghouse for Mental Health Information. (1965) *Family therapy: A selected, annotated bibliography.* National Institute of Mental Health, Chevy Chase, Md.

Olson, D. H. (1970) Marital and family therapy: Integrative review and critique. *J. Marriage and the Family* 32:501-538 (includes 8 pages of references).

Spiegel, J. P., and Bell, N. W. (1959) The family of the psychiatric patient. In Arieti, S. (Ed.), *American Handbook of Psychiatry.* Vol. 1. Basic Books, New York.

58

SCREENING FOR T-GROUPS: THE MYTH OF HEALTHY CANDIDATES

Walter N. Stone
Murray E. Tieger

The authors screened 105 applicants for attendance at a week-long T-group conducted by nonprofessionals. The psychological evaluation and screening procedures included a written application, psychological tests, and a small group experience. Fifteen applicants were not permitted to attend the T-group; six additional applicants chose not to attend. The authors describe the diagnostic groupings of those who were rejected and present vignettes of several applicants. They also discuss the need for screening procedures for any group experience and the current lack of established guidelines for such screening.

A widespread and urgent searching for psychological freedom and an equally insistent interest in increasing self-awareness have been channeled into activities that have been called the social phenomenon of the past two decades, a phenomenon that is central to what is known as the human potential movement. These activities range from nude marathons to seminars on group process and are grouped together under the label "sensitivity training."

Industries, school systems, departments of professional training, and church organizations are among those that have utilized such training methods to help individuals within their systems to increase their competence in interpersonal situations, to develop leadership skills, and to broaden self-awareness. Concomitantly, there are quite intense pressures to attend some type of training in order to be "in," considered for promotion, or given additional responsibilities.

As T-groups are praised as avenues for attaining these lofty goals, an antithetical response is also being expressed. Birnbaum[1] warned against

Reprinted from the *American Journal of Psychiatry*, Vol. 127, No. 11, May 1971, pp. 1485-1490.

the revelation of intimate personal information that is so highly charged that "it makes continuing work relationships very difficult if not impossible." More specific fears were expressed in a *Wall Street Journal* article[2] subtitled "Sessions can produce breakdowns"; an even more critical report warned against "useless, dangerous, corrupt and even fatal groups."[3] Despite these and other warnings,[4] the incidence and consequences of serious mental disturbances in T-groups is difficult to ascertain. One article[5] estimated that less than 1 per cent of participants become psychologically disturbed and that in almost all these cases there "was a history of prior disturbance." A comparable incidence was reported by Ross and others[6] following a survey of all psychiatrists in a metropolitan area in which numerous organizations sponsored sensitivity training.

At the other extreme, Gottschalk[7] reported his direct observations of thirty-two participants during a laboratory at Bethel, Maine. Gottschalk stated that eleven of his group evidenced "obviously acute pathological emotional reactions." In a more controlled study of a group of college students who attended a T-group, group psychotherapy, or a psychology class, Reddy[8] utilized self-rating scales and reported that, as a group, those students participating in the T-group had a significant increase in scores that indicated exacerbation of pathological signs, whereas the others had a nonsignificant decrease in their scores.

Differing criteria for diagnosing adverse reactions make direct comparison of data from one study to another invalid. In addition, the wide variation in leadership skills, intensity and duration of the laboratory experience, and the psychological vulnerability and motivation of the applicants suggest that each organization needs to evaluate its own program as to the probable source of any psychological decompensation, and then to institute appropriate corrective measures.

In response to several instances of psychological decompensation associated with T-group experiences, we were engaged as consultants to an organization of churches that was in the process of developing an extensive leadership program and was sponsoring a variety of structured and unstructured group experiences. Our work in screening for T-groups as one portion of our ongoing consultation and program development is the basis for this paper.

METHOD

All applicants for the one-week T-groups were evaluated in a three-part screening program. The groups were advertised as having dual goals of personal growth and leadership development. The applicants, who came from several sources and had a variety of motivations, included: (1) clergymen who wanted to use what they learned in their churches and some clergymen who were directly asked to attend by church authorities; (2) lay members who either volunteered or were asked to attend by their ministers in order to work more effectively in such church activities as coordinating religious classes and women's organizations; (3) clergymen's wives who primarily wanted self-learning or felt left out after their husbands had T-group experience; and (4) other parish members and a few unaffiliated people who had become acquainted with the programs.

The screening procedures were devised to help evaluate the motivation and psychological strengths of the applicants and to assess their usual coping mechanisms in stressful situations. The methods employed were the following:

1. Each applicant completed a formal written application that requested information on motivation; a brief medical history, including data on psychological and psychosomatic illness; and a personal life history.

2. A series of psychological tests was administered, including the Minnesota Multiphasic Personality Inventory (MMPI), sentence completion, and early memories.

3. The applicant participated in a one-and-a-half-hour small group experience co-led by one of the authors and one of the T-group trainers. During this meeting, the leaders explicitly announced that the two major goals of the session were evaluation by its leaders of the psychological readiness of applicants and providing an experience that would help the applicants to decide whether they wanted to participate in a T-group. Several days after this screening, a conference was held to evaluate and approve or disapprove the applicants' requests to attend the T-group.

RESULTS

During the three years of this study, 105 applicants were seen for full evaluation in the program outlined above. There were fourteen small group screening meetings for six different sensitivity laboratories. Of these 105, twenty-three were screened out by psychological evaluation, by themselves, or by administrative decision.

Fifteen of the twenty-three people were told by the screening committee that, on the basis of the screening information, they either *should not* attend the week-long sensitivity training session or might better attain their objectives by other means. Four of these were not accepted because of evident difficulties with reality testing, although none could be clinically diagnosed as psychotic. Paranoid thinking either appeared directly in the small group sessions or was revealed in vignettes from recent life experiences. In addition, all four showed marked evidence of severe psychopathology on the written evaluation.

The following example describes an applicant who demonstrated problems of reality testing and was asked not to attend:

Case 1. Ruth, a 38-year-old married woman, initiated part of the early discussion in the screening group by introducing the idea that the women in the group would be turned down before the men because of the men's leadership function. She further commented in a hostile fashion that the leaders would inflexibly screen out a fixed proportion of candidates and that women would be turned down on the basis of their sex. She did not accept assurances that there were no such criteria or quotas. She indicated in the group that she wanted attention and interest from men but was sure that she would not get it. When confronted by other members in the group with her provocativeness, Ruth said she was just teasing.

The responses from the written psychological material indicated Ruth utilized defenses of projection as well as externalization of responsibility. She wanted others to share with her, to satisfy what she described as a "mind like a sponge," but she was guarded and evasive about herself. She anticipated rejection and seemed to be hurt easily. The material reflected several loose associations and evident non sequiturs. The clinical impression was of an aggressive, demanding, antagonistic paranoid personality, with significant potential for psychotic decompensation.

Marked acute and/or chronic neurotic reactions manifested by either intense anxiety or depression were evident in eight of the fifteen applicants. Often it was difficult to separate acute reactions in an applicant's current life situation and an ongoing characterological pattern with relatively ineffective adaptational mechanisms. An example follows.

Case 2. Helen, a 24-year-old married woman, stated in her application that her minister had suggested that she attend a T-group to help her work out some problems he had noted in her interpersonal relationships. In the screening group, Helen related in a childlike fashion, demanding attention either verbally or nonverbally. She was anxious and smiled frequently when others were reacting to stress within the group. She was aware that she irritated people and they became angry with her, but she had not considered what she did to evoke these reactions.

Helen's responses to the written tests reflected a masochistic pseudo-femininity in which her needs to be loved and admired at any cost were prominent. Somewhat overidentified with her child, Helen hinted that she utilized sexuality to humble or control men. She seemed to fear and yet expect rejection and was quite insecure even about her sexual prowess. She described her need to "hug men" and be "straightforward" about sex.

In an individual interview Helen revealed concerns about the emptiness in her life, and repeatedly said that she finally had something worthwhile to do in caring for her 11-month-old son. She reported important marital problems, especially both partners' struggles to separate from their parents. She had somatic complaints of a chronic headache and vague intermittent stomach pains for which she had been treated, although no ulcer had been demonstrated radiologically. She seemed to be quite labile, depressed, anxious, and unable to step back and evaluate herself except in response to environmental stimuli. When she was told she could not attend a week-long T-group at the present time, Helen looked sad and cried. When she was asked what her feelings were, she could only state rather pathetically, "I always cry when I go to the doctor's office."

Some applicants with other personality disorders and difficulties in impulse control were not allowed to attend. For example, two men were not accepted because of active homosexual behavior. We made the judgment that under the intense relationships and interactions of a T-group experience, which would include members of their own and nearby churches, these men might reveal their homosexuality; this would make continuing working relationships in their parishes very difficult. In addition, one woman with severe intermittently active ulcerative colitis, who became the focus of rather intense affect in the screening group, was not allowed to attend because of concern over exacerbation of her colitis.

Several strategies were tried in communicating the decision to defer attendance in the T-group. As a general approach, we suggested to the applicants who were not accepted that they seemed to be experiencing considerable current tension and anxiety. We offered the opportunity to talk about any acute situations that might be currently operative, but firmly suggested that they wait for a year before reapplying for a week-long T-group. While informing two clergymen of our decision that they not attend the T-group at that time, we explored the possibility of their receiving psychiatric treatment. Both were anxious and depressed. We suggested that an alternative to the learning they wanted from the group might be found in psychotherapy. Both seemed relieved at the opportunity not to attend a T-group and they subsequently began individual psychotherapy.

In addition to these fifteen who were told they could not attend the T-group, six applicants "self-screened." They would not have been excluded for psychological reasons, but their initial motivation often seemed vague and ambivalent.

> *Case 3.* A married couple, Esther and Ted, utilized the group experience to reevaluate their motivation. Esther had been asked to apply by her minister, one of the T-group leaders, for whom she worked as a secretary, and Ted apparently then decided he wanted to go because Esther was going. In the screening group Esther said she had applied because she felt "my minister and boss would not lead me astray," but they both expressed perplexity at why they had thought of attending a T-group.

Finally, two applicants were asked not to attend for administrative reasons, i.e., both were wives of clergymen who were members of the small staff of the T-group.

In our follow-up study, two applicants whom we had evaluated and accepted experienced disruptive psychological reactions while attending the laboratory. One, a minister who appeared to interact warmly in the screening group, showed significant pathology on the written portions of the evaluation. During the T-group he became suspicious and then overtly psychotic. He was removed from the T-group and received immediate psychiatric attention. Later it was revealed that fifteen years previously he had a three-month psychiatric hospitalization. The second applicant was permitted to attend primarily upon the strong recommendation of her psychotherapist. In the group, she became progressively agitated and anxious and was unable to sleep. She was removed from the group for a one-day period but was allowed to return and to attend a closing two-hour didactic session.

We were able to obtain partial outcome data from the first group for which we screened. This was a large regional meeting in which forty-one of seventy-five participants came from other areas and had not undergone any screening. Four of the forty-one unscreened participants left the laboratory prematurely. Two women had severe anxiety-hysterical reactions with screaming and uncontrolled crying. Two men made a homosexual liaison and left after the first day. Of the screened group, only the woman described previously withdrew temporarily from the meetings and returned for the final session.

DISCUSSION

A great number of very important issues are raised in undertaking the process of screening and evaluating people for such high-stress situations as those in a T-group. Few guidelines are available, but anecdotal experiences of many T-group leaders and psychiatrists, who have seen serious psychological disruption during or immediately following these intense experiences, attest to the need for such procedures. We were aware that the leaders of these groups had limited formal background in psychological theory, and although many were talented and sensitive people, they often felt at a loss and were made anxious themselves with too much revelation of primitive impulses or intrapsychic pathology.

Although our initial aims had been limited primarily to screening out psychotic or prepsychotic applicants, or those who were so intensely anxious that they would not be able to learn from the T-group or might disrupt the group process, our experience indicated a need to broaden these guidelines. The possibility of exacerbation of a psychosomatic illness seemed to be a very real reason for screening out. Applicants who had a history of difficulty in impulse control might be pressured into acting destructively or into revealing highly personal material in a setting where confidentiality was difficult to maintain. For their self-protection, these applicants were not permitted to attend.

The screening process for those applicants who responded affirmatively to the questions about previous therapy or counseling did not significantly differ from those who had not received treatment, and final judgment was reserved for the screening committee. People who were currently in therapy were told privately that they should discuss the prospective laboratory experience with their therapists, and if any questions arose about the nature of the laboratory, the therapists could contact one of us for detailed information. In the course of our study it became apparent that many psychiatrists were uninformed about T-groups. They hoped that their patients might benefit from the laboratory but had not considered some of the potential risks.

The small screening group was equally important in providing information to be used in evaluation and in providing the applicants with the impact of an unstructured group before they committed themselves to a week-long experience. The brief group meeting seemed to us to provide an ample experience for an applicant to reevaluate his motivation. If withdrawal was stimulated primarily by anxiety evoked in the session, it is possible that some people who might have utilized the T-group were scared away unnecessarily, but they may also have subjectively felt real psychological danger.

One unexpected positive effect of the screening was the leaders' response. Some of the leaders who participated in the screening process felt much more confidence in their leadership roles. They knew the participants and could better anticipate initial responses in the group, and they felt reassured that the likelihood of potential disruptive reactions had been lessened.

Lakin[9] has written about the ethical considerations involved in T-group training. He noted, with serious concern, that trainers often lack awareness of their own limitations, that there is often little or no screening, and that there are few investigations of the effects of these groups. Certainly we would emphasize that any organization that assumes the responsibility for sponsoring such training programs needs to recognize that many reluctant applicants are pressured to apply to T-groups. These pressures arise not only from the nonprofessional community, but also from therapists of all disciplines. Thus, an independent assessment team has the task of helping applicants evaluate their own motivation as well as minimizing the chance for psychological decompensation.

No screen is fine enough or discriminating enough to preclude all potential disruptions. Our screening, which required judgments with relatively incomplete information, was based upon an evaluation of each individual's strengths and weaknesses and may have used too fine a mesh. Thus, it is possible that some of the applicants we asked not to attend might have made it through the T-group, since group support can help people over the rough spots and provide a productive experience for the individual. Perhaps the necessity for screening will diminish with increased leader competence, but at this time it does not appear that screening can be totally circumvented by any responsible organization purporting to have the applicant's best interests at heart.

In summary, we have described our experiences with screening applicants for an intensive week-long sensitivity laboratory. Evaluation consisted of a written application, psychological tests, and a one-and-one-half-hour small group session. Of the 105 applicants, fifteen were told they could not attend for psychological reasons: four for problems with reality testing, including paranoid thinking; eight for severe symptomatic neurotic problems; two for overt homosexuality; and one with intermittently active chronic ulcerative colitis. In addition, six applicants "self-screened" by choosing not to attend the T-group. The screening apparently enabled these applicants to reevaluate their motivation for attending or aroused enough anxiety to alter their initial plans to attend.

REFERENCES

1. M. Birnbaum, "Sense About Sensitivity Training," *Saturday Review*, 52: 82-97, November 15, 1969.
2. R. E. Calame, "The Truth Hurts: Some Companies see More Harm than Good in Sensitivity Training," *Wall Street Journal*, 49:14-15, July 14, 1970.
3. E. L. Shostrom, "Group Therapy: Let the Buyer Beware," *Psychol. Today*, 2:36-40, 1969.
4. R. Crawshaw, "How Sensitive is Sensitivity Training?" *Am. J. Psychiat.*, 126:868-873, 1969; J. L. Kuehn and F. N. Crinella, "Sensitivity Training: Interpersonal 'Overkill' and Other Problems," *Am. J. Psychiat.*, 126:840-845, 1969; S. S. Jaffe and D. T. Scherl, "Acute Psychosis Precipitated by T-group Experiences," *Arch. Gen. Psychiat.*, 21:443-448, 1969; F. C. Redlich and B. Astrachan, "Group Dynamics Training," *Am. J. Psychiat.*, 125:1501-1507, 1969.
5. "What is Sensitivity Training?" *NTL Institute News and Reports*, 2:2, April 1968.
6. W. D. Ross, M. Kligfeld, and R. M. Whitman, "Psychiatrists, Patients and Sensitivity Groups," Paper presented at the 123rd annual meeting of the American Psychiatric Association, San Francisco, Calif., May 11-15, 1970.
7. L. A. Gottschalk, "Psychoanalytic Notes on T-groups at the Human Relations Laboratory, Bethel, Maine," *Compr. Psychiat.*, 7:472-487, 1966.
8. W. B. Reddy, "Sensitivity Training or Group Psychotherapy: The Need for Adequate Screening," *Int. J. Group Psychother.*, 20:366-371, 1970.
9. M. Lakin, "Some Ethical Issues in Sensitivity Training," *Am. Psychol.*, 24:923-928, 1969.

DISCUSSION BY IVAN B. GENDZEL

Drs. Stone and Tieger refer in their presentation to Crawshaw's paper[1] and to Kuehn and Crinella's paper,[2] both of which clearly warn, as have many others, of the potential harmful effects of T-groups. Kuehn and Crinella specifically state: "Certain high achievers who have evidenced solid and public proof that they are well defended and not excessively suggestible might profit from a well controlled small group experience in developing leadership skills. However, certain other individuals should be systematically excluded." These include psychotic individuals, characterologic neurotics, hysterics, and individuals in crisis.

Stone and Tieger have described their methods of screening individuals for T-groups and their criteria for exclusion. They have presented this well and deserve our commendation in putting forth one model for screening or evaluation.

Their evaluation consisted of a written application, written psychological tests, and, perhaps most importantly, one-and-one-half-hour small group sessions. They felt they had to reject 14 per cent of the applicants. They also stressed why they felt that the three separate parts of the evaluation were important and how they neatly complemented each other. I should think that small group sessions would perhaps be most valuable in suggesting what the applicant's subsequent behavior in the group might be. Perhaps equally important is that it allows the applicant to experience for himself to a small degree what might subsequently happen, thereby giving him further information with which to make the decision for himself.

I agree heartily with the idea of initial screening for T-groups. I believe this serves two major points. Stone and Tieger have certainly emphasized the importance of removing those who might personally be harmed by the experience or who might interfere with the satisfactory functioning of the group. I would suggest that equally important in this screening process is a chance for the applicant to explore further his motivation for attending the group experience, and for the leader and applicant to discuss their expectations of each other. The authors mention the additional unexpected positive effect of the leaders' feeling reassured that the likelihood of serious difficulty in the group has been lessened.

My experience has included screening several hundred people for twenty-four-hour marathon group meetings[3] and others for weekly outpatient therapy groups for individuals or couples. In addition, I have had some limited experience in meeting with unscreened groups. My rate of rejection, particularly for the marathon groups, was almost nil. However, preliminary meetings did afford an opportunity to discuss the motivations and expectations of the applicants, to delineate this more clearly, and to have the group more prepared and eager when the meetings began. This was noticeably lacking in the unscreened groups and I personally was aware also of being more reserved and hesitant.

The entire issue of enlightened, voluntary consent is probably central to this whole matter. The initial screening can help to provide information to the participants so that they know better what they are deciding about and can thereby lessen the likelihood of detrimental experiences. The other important consideration should be the option any participant has to leave the group (and subsequently return if he wants) if and when he feels that he cannot handle what happens. Given these two basic criteria, the casualty rate from group experiences can be significantly lessened.

REFERENCES

1. R. Crawshaw, "How Sensitive is Sensitivity Training?" *Am. J. Psychiat.*, 126:868-873, 1969.
2. J. L. Kuehn and F. M. Crinella, "Sensitivity Training: Interpersonal 'Overkill' and Other Problems," *Am. J. Psychiat.*, 126:840-845, 1969.
3. I. B. Gendzel, "Marathon Group Therapy and Nonverbal Methods," *Am. J. Psychiat.*, 127:62-66, 1970.

59

NETWORK THERAPY—
A DEVELOPING CONCEPT

Ross V. Speck
Uri Rueveni

A social network is defined as that group of persons who maintain an ongoing significance in each other's lives by fulfilling specific human needs.[1] In working with the social network of a family containing a labeled schizophrenic person, we have sought to assemble all members of the kinship system, all friends of the family, and wherever possible friends of kin of the family, plus the neighbors of the nuclear "schizophrenic" family. Experience with about a dozen such social networks would indicate that the typical lower middle class or middle class white urban "schizophrenic" family has the potential to assemble about forty persons for network meetings.

Previous papers by Speck,[2] Speck and Olans,[3] and Speck and Morong[4] have reported our experiences in treating the social networks of several schizophrenic families. The treatment of four additional social networks in the first six months of 1968 has added further experience, particularly in supplying new concepts and methods.

Perhaps psychiatrists have been "hung up" in dealing with single patients, dyads, the nuclear family, or small groups for reasons similar to runners a few years ago who did not believe it was possible to do the four-minute mile. We have been working on the hypothesis that pathology and schizophrenia involve higher social levels than the nuclear family. We subscribe to a multigenerational transmission process as outlined by Hill,[5] Bowen,[6] Laing and Esterton,[7] and others. We believe that significant pathology is present in the kinship system of the schizophrenic, in their friends and in their neighbors. We believe that "madness" is basically a failure in communication and that "mad" modes of communication are

Reprinted from *Family Process*, Vol. 8, No. 2, September 1969, pp. 92-101, with the permission of the copyright owner.

maintained in the entire system around the labeled "schizophrenic person" and his family. We begin with the hypothesis that the social network of the schizophrenic family is the main mediator between madness in the culture and madness in the nuclear labeled family. Our goals are to increase the communication within the social network and in particular between individual members of the schizophrenic family and their kin, friends, and neighbors.

We conceptualize this process, modified after Bott,[8] as tightening the bonds between members of the social network of the nuclear schizophrenic family, loosening the double binds in significant dyads or triads, and tightening the network of relationships within the whole social field. Social networks are composed of persons. The relationships between these persons, in some degrees extremely loose, in others nonexistent, make up the web of interconnected relationships within the social network. By simply gathering the network together in one place at one time with the purpose of forming a tighter organization of relationships, potent therapeutic potentials are set in motion. The assembly of the tribe in crisis situations with an expectation that something is about to happen probably had its origins in prehistoric man. Tribal meetings for healing purposes are well known in many widely varying cultures.

Recently, sociologists such as Sussman and Burchinal[9] have rediscovered that even in our own culture of nuclear families the extended family kinship system still plays a significant role in the adaptation of nuclear families, sometimes over a period of many years. The extended family kinship system still is overtly acknowledged throughout the entire Eastern Hemisphere as the primary supplier of emotional, physical, and economic stability to the younger generations. It has been hypothesized that decreased rates of mental illness and juvenile delinquency result when a person has a large social network which is actively functioning and intervening in his life. By convening the social network of the schizophrenic family we are reconstituting a forgotten, covert, and often hidden group of persons and relationships. The purpose is to make the entire group as intimately involved as possible in each other's lives and to supply a strong sense of tribe support, reassurance, and solidarity.

THE PRESENTING NETWORK PROBLEM

The A family had been treated by conventional family therapy for a few sessions in the past with little success because JoAnn, the twenty-six-year-old daughter and labeled "schizophrenic person," had refused to attend any of the sessions. The rest of the family lacked sufficient motivation to continue the family therapy or to involve JoAnn sufficiently in the process. Mr. A was an alcoholic and a bright, unsuccessful professional. Mrs. A worked and provided most of the financial support for the family.

JoAnn was a single, unemployed, housebound young woman who had only left the home on one or two occasions at night to walk the dog during the past five years. She had never been employed. Verna, her twenty-four-year-old sister, was in graduate school, doing well with her studies, but somewhat shy and timid. It was the family's fond hope that she would someday become a psychiatrist. John, the sixteen-year-old brother, had dropped out of school at the age of twelve and was living a hippie-like existence in a nearby large city.

JoAnn had had several bouts of individual psychiatric therapy beginning in her early childhood and occurring sporadically over a ten-year period. Mrs. A and Verna consulted us because of JoAnn's repeated suicidal threats, her refusal to work or leave the house, Mr. A's alcoholism, the strong symbiotic dependency openly admitted between Mrs. A and JoAnn, and John's incipient schizophrenic withdrawal. Verna was complaining that she would never be able to escape the family and that she would eventually become their financial support and their healer. She felt trapped and did not even feel that she would be able to leave town and pursue a career in medicine. She developed a notion that she was being groomed to be a psychiatric healer for her family. Verna put the pressure on her mother to seek help to try and change the family. The network was suggested as the most rational approach to produce change in such a rigidly malfunctioning family system. Our assessment of the situation was that Verna's motivation was insufficient to overcome the deep family resistances to any approach to treatment, including family treatment.

GOALS AND RATIONALE

We seek a therapeutic approach which will be effective in modifying the strategy of a schizophrenic patient; provide a broad enough matrix to enable emotional encounters on a variety of levels by the network members; tighten the interpersonal relationship bonds between network members; and provide a therapeutic climate for change. Specifically our approach seeks to: (1) create conditions for a climate of trust and openness among all network members; (2) facilitate and increase interpersonal relationships between the network members themselves as well as between the immediate family members and the network members; (3) focus on the consequences of the patient's behavior within the network setting for the purpose of enabling the patient to begin to modify and possibly cope differently with his destructive strategies; and (4) alter the relationships between tribe members in order to change the state of the network as a whole, increasing communications and human relationships, strengthening bonds between people, and removing pathological double binds.

PROCEDURES

Six four-hour evening sessions were conducted. The meetings were held in the home of the "schizophrenic" family and responsibility for the arrangement of space as well as invitation of immediate family members, relatives, neighbors, and friends was delegated to the family.

Along with the fact that we are dealing with crisis situations where few alternatives aside from hospitalization present themselves, our experience is that there is no particular difficulty in assembling the tribe. When crisis referral is received by one of us we indicate to the referring person, who is usually a member of the nuclear family, that our preference would be to do a tribe treatment, and that the family is to get on the phone and call all of the persons who are significant in their lives. The invited persons are told that they are assembling for a tribe meeting in order to help the crisis in the nuclear family. They are also told that there will be a team of professionals present who will structure the meetings and treat the tribe. Recently we have suggested that invited members of the social network be told that they should expect to attend for a minimum of six evenings. Each meeting is held for about four hours on a successive weekly basis.

In the network sessions we are more prone to talk the "not" language of schizophrenia. We are apt to ask the assembled group what they should tell the schizophrenic family *not* to do. It is only in the later phases of the network meeting that we turn to a more secondary process type of advice giving by the assembled network to the family. It is possible that one of the problems in schizophrenia is a locking of a failed dialectic[10] (in other words, a strong polarity of black versus white is present with no possibility of any synthesis into shades of gray). The task of the group is to get the family inside the dialectic. This structure fits into our theoretical position of remaining at a metalevel to wherever the group is at any given time. The metalevel is the level which forces the polarity to resolution and synthesis. We negate the bind and force it to go to the synthesis.

Presession

During the presession, which was about a half an hour to fifty minutes before the main session began, group members began to assemble in the house. The therapists arrived early, observed the arrival of network members, and installed the tape recorder. They chatted with the immediate family members as well as other network group members, primarily focusing on the latest news related to the family. Attention was paid to gossip and generally interesting comments or observations which could be utilized later on in the main session. We have found that these presessions are extremely useful and colorful, providing a great deal of information which is quite helpful in conducting the six sessions.

Main Session

When the entire network was present, the tribe members were asked to assemble into two concentric groups which we called the "inner group" and the "outer group." This structure was used to intensify interpersonal relationships among the network members as well as to facilitate and sensitize the group members to each other and to the "schizophrenic" family. At the end of each of the main sessions, a postmeeting reaction sheet was given to each group member to write, very briefly, his feeling about how the session went that evening, the strong points, the weak points, and any other additional comment he might have. Those sheets were not signed but were collected, and the contents of the group reactions were copied on large sheets of paper and brought in to the next meeting to be hung on the walls and read to the group. This provided a wealth of material for the group members to interact with.

A Typical Network Meeting

The authors of this paper have been operating recently as a co-therapy team. In addition we have invited two to four other professionals to act as consultants to us. Their role is essentially a training one in network or tribe therapy, but because of the large numbers of persons assembled and the multiplicity of interpersonal events which occur at any one time, it is an advantage to have another group of professionals who can make observations and report these to the team heads so that we can "huddle" at times to plot strategy or change our approach in the operation of the network meetings. Our team members fan out through the living room area of the home, talking to various persons in the network and picking up network gossip or news. We are constantly informed about the state of the network, from both the conscious and unconscious point of view, by our team members, who act as network information gatherers. The network members are told at the beginning that this is not similar to most conventional psychotherapies, that we are dealing with the tribe, that there are no secrets or collusions which will be treated in a confidential manner. We explain that confidences will be violated routinely and that our purpose is to make all communication in the network as overt as possible. Before a social network session begins there is a great air of tension and expectancy in the room. We routinely tape record from the moment we enter the home. Tensions in the group tend to rise and fall. It is exceedingly noisy. It is quite easy to observe when the entire tribe has assembled, and at this point we begin our formal meeting. In first sessions we give a ten- or fifteen-minute talk on the purposes of the network assembly and the goals of the group. In subsequent network meetings we have a network news time in which we bring everyone in the network up-to-date on all the things which have been happening and all the things which have been said. We purposefully violate all confidences which have been revealed in one-to-one relationships. This tends to heighten the tension among network members.

The network is told that they have assembled to help the family. We then set up an inner group and an outer group with the purpose of sensitizing the entire assembled network to the expression of feeling and intimacy in the large group. We have found that by using an inner and an outer group a type of dialectic is set up in which a polarity of feelings occurs. Splitting the tribe into two concentric groups with different assigned tasks produces an increase in group tension which is desirable in the process of tightening the network. The two critical and competitive groups generate increasing tension which leads to deeper interpersonal involvement and tribe commitment. When the tension between the two groups becomes unbearable, cohesiveness of the whole tribe is facilitated. We have called this process the synthesis.

The inner group starts first and tends to get intimate and strip itself of conventional social defenses. The outer group tends to be very critical of the inner group. The inner-and-outer group technique increases the speed of total group (network) involvement. This we regard as important in the rapid polarization of affects which must occur if a six-session treatment of a social network is to be successful. Once a strong polarity has occurred, the therapists work on bringing about a synthesis so that the two groups unite into one group with strong and cohesive feelings. When this has occurred, hopefully early in the network therapy, the therapists again set up a polarity and a dialectic so that a new movement toward synthesis must occur. With each polarization there tends to be a movement deeper into the material which is dealt with. When the outer group says that the inner group is superficial, a negation dialectic is set up so that it provokes the inner group to try harder. The interaction between inner group and outer group makes the outer group try harder in turn. This forces all persons to try to heal each other.

Postsession

Following the main session, the tribe members remained for coffee and usually met in small groups to discuss whatever was important to them. These meetings usually took from a half an hour to an hour after the therapists left the group. Again we felt that these postsessions provided the group members with a chance to interact on a very informal basis, feel each other out, and even talk about the therapists who had just left.

RESULTS

Results of network therapy, as in any other type of psychotherapy, are extremely difficult to measure. That changes occur throughout the network, that individuals change jobs, tighten significant relationships, and become more aware of themselves and others, we have no doubt. The primary goal of our therapy with this particular network was accomplished —the loosening of the symbiosis between JoAnn and her mother. JoAnn, who did not want the network meetings and tried to terminate them, improved rapidly. Prior to the meetings, she only left the house on rare occasions. By the third meeting, JoAnn was employed by a network member. By the sixth meeting she was determined to move to her own apartment (a move which she has since made). For the first time in her life she is interested in dating. She is currently a very valuable assistant therapist in another network being treated by the authors.

At the sixth network meeting an evaluation questionnaire was administered. The responses revealed that seventeen network members felt the network therapy was either a phenomenal or good success. Seven felt it was fairly successful. No one felt that the network therapy was unsuccessful. Seventeen members wished to continue the network meetings after the therapists had finished their task. Two months later, an average of twenty persons were still attending weekly meetings in different members' homes. (These meetings were conducted by the tribe, without the attendance of any professional persons.)

At the sixth session network members felt, according to their answers on the questionnaire, that the strongest points in the network sessions were:

(1) "The cooperative communal spirit and desire to help."
(2) "Group can be instrumental in helping to change people."
(3) "People really caring for each other."
(4) "Creation of an atmosphere in which honesty is indispensable."
(5) "Unique experience. I appreciated seeing the therapists are more warmly human."
(6) "Increased ability to communicate."

Network members felt that JoAnn changed in the following respects:

(1) "JoAnn will talk in front of many people."
(2) "JoAnn works now. That's a good sign."
(3) "JoAnn was encouraged to go out of her home to work."
(4) "JoAnn enjoys now more being with people."
(5) "JoAnn discovered she has many friends."
(6) "JoAnn has been confronted with reality and has been forced to start accepting it."

(7) "JoAnn is more animated, more lively."
(8) "JoAnn improved socially."
(9) "JoAnn finds pleasure in communicating with others, has a more hopeful outlook of life."

Network members felt that JoAnn's father:

(1) "Seems more competent and relaxed."
(2) "Is alive and more communicative."
(3) "Like the cowardly lion of oz, has been given courage."
(4) "Has become a man."
(5) "Breaks down certain inhibitions."

Network members felt that JoAnn's mother:

(1) "Is more satisfied—finally came to grips with the problem."
(2) "Has gained much self-confidence."
(3) "Sees that her situation can change."

Network members felt that the following had happened to themselves:

(1) "Made us realize how many problems we all humans share."
(2) "Appreciate family relationships more now."
(3) "Enabled me to be less inhibited in expressing feelings."
(4) "I don't have to keep everything inside now."
(5) "I can see myself more clearly, my 'hangups' are clearer."
(6) "I saw my own difficulties mirrored in the father. It helped me tremendously."
(7) "These experiences helped me to express myself more openly."
(8) "I have been encouraged to communicate."
(9) "Helped me to discover a whole new set of compassionate human beings."

SUMMARY

In this paper we have discussed the concept of network therapy of the social network of a "schizophrenic family." Forty network members attended, consisting of the immediate and extended kin, neighbors, and friends of the "schizophrenic family." In order to accelerate the network process a variety of sensitivity training techniques were introduced. The network therapy appeared successful in modifying the relationships in the schizophrenic family, in tightening their social network (meetings are still continuing without the attendance of professionals), and in providing a viable social structure for continuing encouragement, support, employment, and avoidance of hospitalization.

REFERENCES

1. R. Speck and E. Morong, "Home-centered Treatment of the Social Network of Schizophrenic Families: Two Approaches," Paper presented at annual meeting of the American Psychiatric Association, Boston, May 1967.
2. R. Speck, "Psychotherapy of the Social Network of a Schizophrenic Family," *Fam. Proc.*, 6:208-214, 1967; idem., "Psychotherapy of Family Social Networks," Paper presented at the Family Therapy Symposium, Medical College of Virginia, Richmond, May 1967; idem., "The Politics and Psychotherapy of Mini- and Micro-Groups," Paper presented at Congress on Dialectics of Liberation, London, July 1967.
3. R. Speck and J. Olans, "The Social Network of the Family of a Schizophrenic: Implications for Social and Preventive Psychiatry," Paper presented at the annual meeting of the American Orthopsychiatric Association, Chicago, March, 1967.
4. Speck and Morong, "Home-centered Treatment," *op. cit.*
5. L. Hill, *Psychotherapeutic Intervention in Schizophrenia* (Chicago: University of Chicago Press, 1955).
6. M. Bowen, "A Family Concept of Schizophrenia," in Don D. Jackson (ed.), *The Etiology of Schizophrenia* (New York: Basic Books, 1960), 346-372.
7. R. Laing and A. Esterton, *Sanity, Madness and the Family* (London: Tavistock Publications, 1964).
8. E. Bott, *Family and Social Network* (London, Tavistock Publications, 1957).
9. M. Sussman and L. Burchinal, "Kin Family Network," *Marriage and Family Living*, 24:320-332, 1962.
10. V. Gioscia, personal communication, 1968.

60

THE THERAPEUTIC COMMUNITY
AS A CHANGE SYSTEM

Maxwell Jones

The "therapeutic community" has become a familiar term in psychiatric literature and practice. For me it has been a stepping stone to the much wider field of systems theory. I now spend much of my time as a process consultant[1] or interventionist[2] in the school system. A social system within the field of psychiatry has much in common with a school or any other unit in society. The core activities of any system are: (1) to achieve its objectives; (2) to maintain its internal environment; and (3) to adapt to, and maintain control over, the relevant external environment.[3] A process consultant looks at a social system with a view to making the individuals in that organization aware of the nature of communication, decision making, problem solving, and decision implementation within the system. He is a facilitator rather than an educator. His inputs reflect what he perceives in the fields of interpersonal interaction and conflict, and this "feedback" may or may not affect the organization's development or growth. Helping people to help themselves depends on their readiness or resistance to change.

This raises the basic question: Why change? An open system (where communications are free, decision making shared, interpersonal interaction uninhibited, leadership determined by free choice, and learning as a social process valued) may suit certain circumstances but not others.

Many people, although they grumble consistently about "them" (the people with power—administrators, professors, and so on), resist a change which implies greater sharing of responsibility and authority. The right to grumble with one's intimates is a cherished lunchtime occupation. Projecting the problems within the system onto "them" absolves the individual of all blame and maintains a pleasing fantasy that, given the opportunity, the individual or individuals could do much better. But these "little Napoleons" often by-pass an opportunity for change to a more open system, even when it presents itself. This is not surprising when one remembers that virtually everyone plays a passive recipient role in most homes, just as most do in the school system and in higher education and industry.

There are an increasing number of models for change to a more open system. These are to be found in industry, schools, colleges (including seminaries), prisons, churches, hospitals, mental health clinics, and so on. Such movements are to be found throughout history, e.g., Plato's Republic, Early Christianity, the Renaissance, the French Revolution, and Communism. In more recent times, linked to the concepts of organizational development and learning, Henderson Hospital (1947 to date) was such a model.[4]

The purpose of this paper is to examine the advantages and disadvantages of an open system. My opinions are based primarily on my experience in hospital and mental health clinic therapeutic communities over the past three decades, and more recently in several schools at the elementary, junior-high, and high-school levels.

LEVELS OF COMMUNICATION

Our middle-class cultural norms pressure us to say the right thing at the right time (expediency), to be polite rather than rude (hide some, or most, "gut level" feelings), and to respect our seniors or betters (although youth has largely repudiated this even in the classroom). The whole of our "success" system is built on the premise of conformity, knowing one's place in the pecking order, and basically being "two-faced" or living by a double standard. To deviate from the norms of society is to risk disfavor from the system and possible loss of career opportunity.

Individuals, groups, and sometimes whole systems claim to communicate at both cognitive and feeling levels, but this is only relative and usually limited to a specific goal. Thus a group or a small system, such as a mental health clinic with twenty professional personnel, may set aside a full day to look at its communication system. With the help of a process consultant, they may find an initial "risk taker" who shares his feeling of frustration with the group. This may encourage freer communication and facilitate group process (or learning), as compared with the more private communications with one's intimates which tend to reinforce the feeling of frustration rather than lead to problem solving. In the favorable climate of a workshop, free communication of feeling may appear to be sanctioned and even rewarded. But even for most professionals this openness represents a risk and runs counter to most previous experience and training. The relatively artificial situation of the workshop may bear little relationship to the everyday working conditions. We are looking at a process which at this point has only a potential for permanent change.

Will the group members who hold the formal power and authority in the group react negatively or even punitively to the "risk takers" in the ordinary work situation the next day? Will their peers exploit their openness and use it to their own advantage?

Resistance to change is an inherent quality of our society. The familiar is in some senses more comfortable (even if uncomfortable!) than the unknown. At this point the motivation to achieve the goal of more open communication in the system will determine the outcome, assuming that everyone in the system has a voice in decision making. Let us examine this assumption further.

DECISION MAKING AND CONSENSUS

In the traditional pyramidal organization structure, the top administration is responsible for major decision making. This may suit the majority of employees, who have only known passive dependent roles in their lives and have no great desire to share responsibility and authority. At the same time they are free to criticize the administration with those peers whom they trust. Such a stalemate may persist indefinitely and may represent a stable system, if the goals of the system are achieved by competent management.

If we return to our simple example of a one-day workshop involving twenty professionals working in a mental health clinic, some beginnings have been made in testing out the desirability and effectiveness of open communication at cognitive and feeling levels. Let us assume that no reprisals were experienced by the "risk takers" and several unresolved problems were shared by the whole team. Is the team prepared to embark on the long process of problem solving, decision making, and decision implementation? The process consultant does not see his role as primarily one of change agent. His function is to help the system to help itself by opening up communication, helping the client system to diagnose their problems, and motivating them to resolve these problems.

By the end of the one-day workshop, several problems may have emerged and been discussed. How significant this interaction is will depend on the amount of involvement and internal commitment achieved by each member of the team:[5]

> Internal commitment means the course of action or choice that has been internalized by each member so that he experiences a high degree of ownership and has a feeling of responsibility about the choice and its implications. Internal commitment means that the individual has reached the point where he is acting on the choice because it fulfills his own needs and sense of responsibility, as well as those of the system.
>
> The individual who is internally committed is acting primarily under

the influence of his own forces and not induced forces. The individual (or any unity) feels a minimal degree of dependence upon others for action. It implies that he has obtained and processed valid information and that he has made an informed and free choice. Under these conditions there is a high probability that the individual's commitment will remain strong over time (even with reduction of external rewards) or under stress, or when the course of action is challenged by others. It also implies that the individual is continually open to reexamination of his position because he believes in taking action based on valid information.

My use of the term "consensus"[6] implies that the internal commitment of all members of the team has some common goal which has been arrived at by a process of group interaction and learning. It implies a sophisticated stage of evolution by the team, whose members are prepared to modify personal preferences and goals to some optimal goal with which every group member can identify.

To reach such a level of decision making would take months or years of group interaction, decision making, and learning. Does the team wish to embark on such a long and painful process of learning?

In my experience, such a decision must be made by the team as a whole. If there are divergent factions, some favoring the step and others opposed to it, then no action should be initiated. If an administrator using (or abusing) his authority makes a unilateral decision to proceed, then the process of learning is jeopardized from the start. Internal commitment (by each group member), consensus, and learning as a social process are interdependent. In brief, shared decision making and consensus imply that the team has identified a common goal and will work together for its completion. Even if their efforts fail, they share the blame and will be motivated to learn from the experience. The same applies to success, which will help the whole system to grow.

The question of priorities is of fundamental importance. If the team decides to develop its communications and problem-solving skills, they must set aside time for such team interaction. Their willingness to do this is one measure of their motivation. Thus our mental health team, at the completion of their initial workshop, would have to decide to hold regularly scheduled meetings if they were to continue the process of learning. They would also have to decide if they wanted to continue with a process consultant or facilitator or use their own internal resources.

Social learning means that group interaction around common problems results in modification of individual attitudes and beliefs. This may be at a cognitive level, in which case the individual will be articulate about the change process. A particular example of this would be the interaction between psychoanalyst and his subject when an interpretation of unconscious material by the analyst may lead to insight. More usually this process applies to concrete "here and now" situations in which information sharing causes the subject to reevaluate his attitude in the light of other inputs and perspectives.

Or the change of attitude may be related to interaction at a feeling level, with the process of change only partly understood or totally outside consciousness. This applies to much of our personality growth. For instance, the growth of a social conscience in children between the ages of seven and nine is not a conscious learning experience which the children can explain.

In other words, we are implying that growth or maturation is a natural process which can be facilitated by a system which enhances this growth potential. If this is true, then by experimentally modifying school systems, we may learn more about the optimal conditions for growth. This brings us back to our original question: Why change? There is as yet no certainty about the optimal school system, if social learning is one of its major goals. The evidence suggests that some schools run on traditional subject-oriented lines compare favorably with other schools favoring open communication, shared decision making, and problem solving.[7] It seems that some children need firm direction and a dependent relationship to their teacher. They memorize subject matter and may grow into confident adults without much exposure to problem solving of "here and now" difficulties.

By contrast, other children seem to thrive in a "free" or "open" environment where their potential interests are fostered, and they can express feelings openly.

It is hard to devise tests which measure growth adequately, because no two educators can agree as to what exactly constitutes growth. Is it preparation for life in a highly competitive society leading to material success? Can it be defined as development of the individual's potential so that he experiences a feeling of self-fulfillment? Even when the criteria are limited to measuring the ability to recall subject matter (basically the purpose of school examinations), neither system can claim significant success over the other.

It would seem that much research is needed before we can outline clearly what the goals of an educational system should be. In the meantime the "progressive liberals" will continue in their conviction that traditional schools are "bad" and that open systems, if applied generally, would herald a new era of understanding and growth. Nor should such convictions be discouraged. The model for change created by A. S. Neill[8] has as yet no sound experimental data on which to base its effectiveness, but his ideas have provoked much discussion and stimulated whole systems to change, e.g., the "free" elementary schools in the United Kingdom and the United States.[9] The same could be said about the original model of a therapeutic community,[10] which a strong social science research team[11] failed to prove "effective" to the large body of psychiatric opinion; nevertheless this early model of a social system for change has had a profound influence on psychiatric thought and practice. In brief, social learning as a concept is favored by many, but much study and research is needed before it can be assumed to have a high priority in educational, hospital, and other systems. So the question—why change?—can be given only a qualified answer.

This brings us to the most important function of a process consultant: to help any system to see where it is at and where it wants to go. But to arrive at even tentative answers to these basic questions may require many time-consuming meetings, learning of new group skills, the emergence of potential leaders, redistribution of responsibility and authority with more sharing, and an overhaul of the decision-making process with at least an awareness of the significance of consensus, and of social systems generally.

Given such an organizational development, then change, if subscribed to by the team, will be an integral part of a learning process and may well imply growth for the entire system.

REFERENCES

1. E. H. Schein, *Process Consultation: Its Role in Organization Development* (Addison-Wesley Series on Organization Development, 1969).
2. C. Argyris, *Intervention Theory and Method* (Reading: Addison-Wesley, 1970).
3. *Ibid.*
4. M. Jones, *The Therapeutic Community* (New York: Basic Books, 1953); idem, *Beyond the Therapeutic Community* (New Haven, Conn.: Yale University Press, 1968).
5. Argyris, *Intervention Theory, op. cit.*
6. Jones, *Beyond the Therapeutic Community, op. cit.*
7. N. Mills, "Free Versus Directed Schools," *IRCD Bull.*, 7(4):September 1971.
8. A. S. Neill, *Summerhill* (London: Victor Gollancz, 1964).
9. C. Silberman, *Crisis in the Classroom* (New York: Vintage Books, 1971).
10. Jones, *The Therapeutic Community, op. cit.*
11. R. Rapoport, *Community as Doctor* (London: Tavistock, 1960).

61

A SELECTED LIST OF READINGS COVERING ENCOUNTER GROUPS, SENSITIVITY GROUPS, TRANSACTIONAL ANALYSIS, GESTALT THERAPY, AND GROWTH GROUPS

Max Rosenbaum

I have selected a list of readings which I believe to be long on theory and short on testimonial. Many of the people who work with groups have failed to present a systematic statement of the principles that guide their work. The articles and books that are listed should help the reader get some overview of a theory. In some cases this has been impossible because the proponent of a particular therapy approach has presented his theory in the form of a testimonial. I have aimed for intellectual rigor in my choice of readings.

BIBLIOGRAPHY

American Psychiatric Association Task Force, *Encounter Groups and Psychiatry* (New York: American Psychiatric Association, 1970).

Amir, Y., "Contact Hypothesis in Ethnic Relations, *Psychol. Bull.*, 71:319-342, 1969.

Argyris, C. T., *Interpersonal Competence and Organizational Effectiveness* (Homewood, Ill.: Dorsey Press, 1962).

———, "Groups for Organizational Effectiveness," *Harvard Bus. Rev.*, 42(2): 60-74, 1964.

———, "Explorations in Interpersonal Competence," *J. Appl. Beh. Sci.*, 1 (1):58-83, 1965.

———, "On the Future of Laboratory Education," *J. Appl. Beh. Sci.*, 3(2): 163-183, 1967.

Back, K. W., "Influence through Social Communication," *J. Abnorm. Psychol.*, 46:9-23, 1951.

———, *Sensitivity Training and the Search for Salvation* (New York: Russell Sage Foundation, 1972).

Bales, R. F., *Personality and Interpersonal Behavior* (New York: Holt, Rinehart and Winston, 1970).

———, Hare, P. A., and Borgatta, E. F., eds., *Small Groups: Studies in Social Interaction* (rev. ed.; New York: Alfred A. Knopf, 1965).

Bass, B. M., "Mood Changes During a Management Training Laboratory," *J. Appl. Psychol.* 46(5):361-364, 1962.

Batchelder, R. L., and Hardy, J. M., *Using Sensitivity Training and Laboratory Method: an Organizational Case Study in the Development of Human Resources* (New York: Association Press, 1968).

Bates, A. P., and Cloyd, J. S., "Toward the Development of Operations for Defining Group Norms and Member Roles," *Sociometry*, 19:26-39, 1956.

Bennis, W. G., *et al.*, "Note on Some Problems of Measurement and Prediction in a Training Group," *Group Psychother.*, 10:328-341, 1957.

Bennis, W. G., Benne, K. D., and Chin, R., eds., *The Planning of Change: Readings in the Applied Behavioral Sciences* (New York: Holt, Rinehart and Winston, 1962).

Bennis, W. G., and Shepard, H. A., "A Theory of Group Development," *Hum. Relat.*, 9(4):415-437, 1956.

Bergin, A. E., and Harfield, S., eds., *Handbook of Psychotherapy and Behavior Change* (New York: Wiley, 1971).

Berne, E., *Transactional Analysis in Psychotherapy* (New York: Grove Press, 1961).

———, *Games People Play* (New York: Grove Press, 1964).

———, *Principles of Group Treatment* (New York: Oxford University Press, 1966).

Bion, W. R., *Experiences in Groups* (New York: Basic Books, 1961).

Blake, R. R., and Mouton, J. S., *Managing Intergroup Conflict in Industry* (Houston, Texas: Gulf, 1965).

Bradford, L. P., Gibb, J. R., and Benne, K. D., eds., *T-group Theory and Laboratory Method: Innovation in Re-education* (New York: Wiley, 1964).

Buchanan, P., "Evaluating the Effectiveness of Laboratory T-group Training in Industry," in E. A. Fleishman, ed., *Studies in Personnel and Industrial Psychology* (Homewood, Ill.: Dorsey Press, 1967), 237-250.

Bunker, D., "Individual Applications of Laboratory Training," *J. Appl. Beh. Sci.*, 1:131-148, 1965.

Burke, R. L., and Bennis, W. G., "Changes in Perception of Self and Others during Human Relations Training," *Hum. Relat.*, 14(2):165-182, 1961.

Campbell, J. P., and Dunnette, M. D., "Effectiveness of T-group Experiences in Managerial Training and Development," *Psychol. Bull.* 70:73-104, 1968.

Cantril, H., "A Transactional Inquiry Concerning Mind," in J. Scher, ed., *Theories of the Mind* (New York: Free Press, 1962).

Clark, J. V., "Some Troublesome Dichotomies in Human Relations Training," *Hum. Relat. Training News*, 6(1):3-6, 1962.

————, and Clark, F. C., "Notes on the Conduct of Married Couples Groups," *Hum. Relat. Training News*, 12(3):2-12, 1968.

COPED (Cooperative Project for Educational Development), Final Report, Contract OEG 3-8-08069-43 (010). Project No. 8-0069. (Washington, D.C.: U.S. Office of Education) Vol. 1: *Research Outcomes*, 1970.

Cottle, T. J., "Encounter in Color," *Psychol. Today*, 1(7): 22-27, 40-41, 1969.

Craig, R. L., and Bittel, L. R., *Training and Development Handbook* (New York: McGraw-Hill, 1967).

Culbert, S. A., *The Interpersonal Process of Self Disclosure: It Takes Two to See One*. Explorations in Applied Behavioral Science, Vol. 3 (New York: Renaissance, 1967).

Egan, G., ed., *Encounter Groups: Basic Readings* (Monterey, Calif.: Brooks-Cole, 1971).

Enneis, J., "The Dynamics of Group and Action Processes in Therapy," *Group Psychother.*, 4:17-22, 1951.

Fagan, J., "The Tasks of the Therapist," in J. Fagan and I. L. Shepert, eds., *Gestalt Therapy Now: Theory, Techniques, Applications* (Palo Alto, Calif.: Science and Behavior Books, 1970).

Fleishman, E. A., Harris, E. F., and Burtt, H. E., *Leadership and Supervision in Industry*, Bureau of Educational Research Monograph No. 33 (Columbus, Ohio: The Ohio State University, 1955).

Framo, J. L., "Symptoms from a Family Transactional Viewpoint," in C. J. Sager and H. S. Kaplan, eds., *Progress in Group and Family Therapy* (New York: Brunner-Mazel, 1972).

Frank, J., *Persuasion and Healing* (Baltimore: Johns Hopkins Press, 1961).

————, "Training & Therapy," in L. P. Bradford, J. R. Gibb, and K. D. Benne, eds., *T-Group Theory and Laboratory Method* (New York: Wiley, 1964), pp. 442-451.

Gibb, J. R., "Climate for Trust Formation," in L. P. Bradford, J. R. Gibb, and K. D. Benne, eds., *T-group Theory and Laboratory Method* (New York: Wiley, 1964), pp. 279-309.

————, "The Effects of Human Relations Training," in A. E. Bergin and S. Garfield, eds., *Handbook of Psychotherapy and Behavior Change* (New York: Wiley, 1971), pp. 829-862.

Goldberg, C., *Encounter: Group Sensitivity Training Experience* (New York: Science House, 1970).

Golembiewski, R. T., *The Small Group* (Chicago: University of Chicago Press, 1962).

————, *Organizing Men and Power: Patterns of Behavior and Line-staff Models* (Chicago: Rand McNally, 1967).

————, and Blumberg, A., eds., *Sensitivity Training and the Laboratory Approach* (Itasca, Illinois: Peacock, 1970).

Gottschalk, L. A., and Pattison, E. M., "Psychiatric Perspectives on T-groups and the Laboratory Movement: An Overview," *Am. J. Psychiat.*, 126: 823-839, 1969.

Goulding, R., "New Directions in Transactional Analysis: Creating an Environment for Redecision and Change," in C. J. Sager and H. S. Kaplan, eds.,

Progress in Group and Family Therapy (New York: Brunner-Mazel, 1972), pp. 105-134.

Greening, T. C., "Sensitivity Training: Cult or Contribution?" *Personnel*, 41: 18-25, 1964.

Grinker, R. R., "A Transactional Model for Psychotherapy" and "A Demonstration of the Transactional Model," in M. I. Stein, ed., *Contemporary Psychotherapies* (New York: Free Press, 1961), pp. 190-227.

————, et al., *Psychiatric Social Work: A Transactional Case Book* (New York: Basic Books, 1961).

Harrison, R., "The Impact of the Laboratory on Perception of Others by the Experimental Group," in C. Argyris, *Interpersonal Competence and Organizational Effectiveness* (Homewood, Ill.: Irwin, 1962).

————, "Cognitive Change and Participation in a Sensitivity Training Laboratory," *J. Consult. Psychol.*, 30(3):517-520.

————, and Lubin, B., "Personal Style, Group Composition and Learning," *J. Appl. Beh. Sci.*, 1(3):286-301, 1965.

Hills, C., and Stone, R. B., *Conduct Your Own Awareness Sessions* (New York: Signet Books, 1970).

Hobbs, N., "Sources of Gain in Psychotherapy," *Amer. Psychol.*, 17(11):741-747, 1962.

Horwitz, M., "Hostility and its Management in Classroom Groups," in N. L. Gage and W. W. Charters, Jr., eds., *Readings in the Social Psychology of Education* (Boston: Allyn & Bacon, 1963), pp. 196-211.

House, R. J., "T-group Education and Leadership Effectiveness: A Review of the Empirical Literature and a Critical Evaluation," *Pers. Psychol.*, 20: 1-32, 1967.

Jaffe, S. J., and Sherl, D. J., "Acute Psychosis Precipitated by T-group Experience," *Arch. Gen. Psychiat.*, 21:443-449, 1969.

Jourard, S. M., *The Transparent Self: Self Disclosure and Well-being* (Princeton: Van Nostrand, 1964).

Kahn, R., "Aspiration and Fulfillment: Themes for Studies of Group Relations," Unpublished manuscript, University of Michigan, 1963.

Kaplan, H. I., et al., *Sensitivity through Encounter and Marathon* (New York: Dutton, 1972).

Kassajian, H. H., "Social Character and Sensitivity Training," *J. Appl. Behav. Sci.*, 1:433-440, 1965.

Kelman, H. C., "The Role of the Group in the Induction of Therapeutic Change," *Int. J. Group Psychother.*, 13:399-432, 1963.

————, and Parloff, M. B., "Interrelations Among Three Criteria of Improvement in Group Therapy: Comfort, Effectiveness and Self-awareness," *J. Abnorm. Soc. Psychol.*, 54:281-288, 1957.

Kilpatrick, F. P., *Explorations in Transactional Psychology* (New York: New York University Press, 1961).

Koegler, R., and Brill, Q., *Treatment of Psychiatric Outpatients* (New York: Appleton-Century-Crofts, 1967).

Laing, R., *The Politics of Experience* (New York: Pantheon Press, 1967).

Lieberman, M. A., Yalom, I. D., and Miles, M. B., *Encounter Groups: First Facts* (New York: Basic Books, 1973).

Lohman, K., *et al.*, "Some Perceptual Changes During Sensitivity Training," *J. Ed. Res.*, 53:28-31, 1959.

Luft, J., *Group Processes: An Introduction to Group Dynamics* (Palo Alto, Calif.: National Press, 1963).

Luke, R. A., Jr., "The Internal Normative Structure of Sensitivity Training Groups," *J. Appl. Beh. Sci.*, 8(4):421-437, 1972.

Miles, M. B., *Learning to Work in Groups* (New York: Teachers College Press, 1959).

———, "Human Relations Training: Processes and Outcomes," *J. Couns. Psychol.*, 7:301-306, 1960.

———, "On Temporary Systems," in M. B. Miles, ed., *Innovation in Education* (New York: Teachers' College Press, 1964), pp. 437-490.

———, "Changes During and Following Laboratory Training: A Clinical Experimental Study," *J. Appl. Beh. Sci.*, 1:215-242, 1965.

———, "The Development of Innovative Climates in Educational Organizations," Educational Policy Research Center, Stanford Research Institute, Menlo Park, Calif., Research Note EPRC-6747-10, 1969.

Mill, C. R., "A Theory for the Group Dynamics Laboratory Milieu," *Adult Leadership*, 11:133-160, 1962.

Moscow, D., "T-group Training in the Netherlands: An Evaluation and Cross-cultural Comparison," *J. Appl. Beh. Sci.*, 7(4):427-448, 1971.

Mowrer, O. H., *The New Group Therapy* (Princeton: Van Nostrand, 1964).

Myers, G., Myers, M., Goldberg, A., and Welch, D., "Effects of Feedback on Interpersonal Sensitivity in Laboratory Training Groups," *J. Appl. Beh. Sci.*, Vol. 5, No. 2.

Oshry, B. I., and Harrison, R., "Transfer from Here-and-now to There-and-then: Changes in Organizational Problem Diagnosis Stemming from T-group Training," *J. Appl. Beh. Sci.*, 2(11):185-198, 1966.

Person, R. W., "Relationship Between Psychotherapy with Institutionalized Boys and Subsequent Community Adjustment," *J. Consult. Psychol.*, 31:137-141, 1967.

Pfeiffer, J. W., and Jones, J. B., *A Handbook of Structured Exercises for Human Relations Training*, Vols. I-III (Iowa City: University Associates Press, 1969).

"*Philosophers and Kings: Studies in Leadership*," Daedulus, Vol. 97, No. 3 (Summer 1968): entire issue.

Psathas, G., and Hardert, R., "Trainer Interventions and Normative Patterns in the T-group," *J. Appl. Beh. Sci.*, 2 (2):149-169, 1966.

Reich, C. A., *The Greening of America* (New York: Random House, 1970).

Rice, A. K., *Learning for Leadership* (New York: Humanities Press, 1964).

Roberts, J., "Self-disclosure and Personal Change in Encounter Groups," Ph.D. dissertation, University of Chicago, 1971.

Rogers, C. R., "The Process of the Basic Encounter Group," in J. F. Bugental, ed., *Challenges of Humanistic Psychology* (New York: McGraw-Hill, 1967).

———, *Carl Rogers on Encounter Groups* (New York: Harper & Row, 1970).

Rosenthal, B., "The Nature and Development of the Encounter Group Movement," in L. Blank, G. Gottsegen, and M. Gottsegen, eds., *Encounter: Confrontation in Self and Interpersonal Awareness* (New York: Macmillan, 1971), pp. 435-468.

"Roundup of Current Research," *Trans-Action,* 8(4):4.

Rubin, I., "The Reduction of Prejudice through Laboratory Training," *J. Appl. Beh. Sci.,* 3:29-49, 1967.

Sata, L. S., and Derbyshire, R. C., "Group Process, T-Groups and Sensitivity Training: A Demonstration of the Living Laboratory." Mimeographed. College Park, Maryland: Psychiatric Institute, University of Maryland, 1967.

Sattler, J., "Racial 'Experimenter Effects' in Experimentation, Testing, Interviewing, and Psychotherapy," *Psychol. Bull.,* 73:137-160, 1970.

Schein, E. H., and Bennis, W. G., *Personal and Organizational Change through Group Methods: The Laboratory Approach* (New York: Wiley, 1965).

Schutz, W. C., "What Makes Groups Productive?" *Hum. Relat.,* 8(4):429-437, 1955.

——, *FIRO* (New York: Holt, Rinehart and Winston, 1958).

——, *The Interpersonal Underworld* (Palo Alto, Calif.: Science and Behavior Books, 1966).

——, *Joy* (New York: Grove Press, 1967).

——, "Not Encounter and Certainly Not the Facts" in L. W. Pfeiffer and J. E. Jones, eds., *The 1974 Annual Handbook for Group Facilitators,* (La Jolla, Calif.: University Associates Publishers, 1974) pp. 1-7.

——, and Allen, V., "The Effects of a T-group Laboratory on Interpersonal Behavior," *J. Appl. Beh. Sci.,* 2:265-286, 1966.

Seashore, C., "What is Sensitivity Training?" *NTL Institute News and Reports,* April 1968. Reprinted by Public Service Administration News: *Management Forum,* Vol. 18, No. 2, Section 2, June 1968.

Shaevitz, M. H., and Barr, D. J., "Encounter Groups in a Small College: A Case Study." Mimeographed. La Jolla, Calif.: University of California at San Diego.

Shepard, H. A., and Bennis, W. G., "A Theory of Training by Group Methods," *Hum. Relat.,* 4(4):403-414, 1956.

Shlein, J. M., Mosak, J. J., and Dreikurs, R., "Effect of Time Limits: A Comparison of Two Psychotherapies," *J. Couns. Psychol.,* 9:31-34, 1962.

Stock-Whitaker, D., "A Survey of Research on T-groups," in L. P. Bradford, K. D. Benne, and J. R. Gibb, eds., *T-group and Laboratory Method* (New York: Wiley, 1964), pp. 395-441.

Shore, M. F., and Masimo, J. L., "Comprehensive Vocationally Oriented Psychotherapy for Adolescent Delinquent Boys: A Follow-up Study," *Am. J. Orthopsychiat.,* 36:609-615, 1966.

Solomon, L., and Berzon, B., *New Perspectives on Encounter Groups* (San Francisco: Jossey-Bass, 1972).

Spiegel, J., *Transactions: The Interplay between Individual, Family and Society* (New York: Science House, 1971).

Stevens, B., *Don't Push the River: It Flows by Itself* (Moab, Utah: Real People Press, 1970).

Tannenbaum, R., Wechsler, I. R., and Massarik, F., *Leadership and Organization* (New York: McGraw-Hill, 1961).

Thelen, H., and Dickerman, W., "Stereotypes and the Growth of Groups," *Educational Leadership*, February 1949, pp. 309-316.

Thomas, D., and Smith, T., "T-grouping: The White Collar Hippie Movement," *National Association of Secondary School Principals Bulletin*, February 1968, pp. 1-9.

Watson, G., *Manual of Structured Exercises* (Newark, N.J.: Newark State College Laboratory of Applied Behavioral Science, 1971).

Wechsler, I. R., Massarik, F., and Tannenbaum, R., "The Self in Process: A Sensitivity Training Emphasis," in I. Wechsler and E. Schein, eds., *Issues in Sensitivity Training* (Washington, D.C.: National Training Laboratories, 1962), pp. 33-46.

Williams, R. M., Jr., *Strangers Next Door* (Englewood Cliffs, N.J.: Prentice-Hall, 1964).

Wilner, A. R., "The Theory and Strategy of Charismatic Leadership," *Daedalus*, Summer 1968.

Yalom, I., Houts, P., Newell, G., and Rand, K., "Preparation of Patients for Group Therapy," *Arch. Gen. Psychiat.*, 12:416-427, 1967.

62

GUIDELINES FOR PSYCHOLOGISTS CONDUCTING GROWTH GROUPS

American Psychological Association

The following guidelines are presented for the information and guidance of psychologists who conduct growth or encounter groups. They are not intended to substitute for or to supplant ethical practices for psychologists specified elsewhere.

The development of these guidelines was prompted by the concern of several units within the American Psychological Association that there be a set of operating principles for the use of psychologists active in such groups. The guidelines do not presume to specify or endorse any professional procedure or technique used in a group, but only to aid psychologists who offer groups to present themselves in a manner that is ethically sound and protective of the participant.

The present statement attempts to accommodate those suggestions from various psychologists in response to the draft statement published by the Board of Professional Affairs in the *APA Monitor* of December 1971 (Vol. 2, No. 12, p. 3). It is to be expected that these guidelines will be subject to modification as they are put to use, and also in the light of the evolution of new knowledge and practices in the utilization of growth groups.

1. Entering into a growth group experience should be on a voluntary basis; any form of coercion to participate is to be avoided.

2. The following information should be made available in writing to all prospective participants:

Reprinted from the *American Psychologist*, 28(10):933, October 1973. © 1973, American Psychological Association. Reprinted with permission.

Approved for publication by the Board of Directors of the American Psychological Association on February 15, 1973. An ad hoc committee consisting of Donald H. Clark, Wilbert Edgerton, and John J. McMillan (Chair), the Board of Professional Affairs, and the Board of Directors were successively responsible for development of the statement in its final form.

(a) An explicit statement of the purpose of the group;

(b) Types of techniques that may be employed;

(c) The education, training, and experience of the leader or leaders;

(d) The fee and any additional expense that may be incurred;

(e) A statement as to whether or not a follow-up service is included in the fee;

(f) Goals of the group experience and techniques to be used;

(g) Amounts and kinds of responsibility to be assumed by the leader and by the participants. For example: (i) the degree to which a participant is free not to follow suggestions and prescriptions of the group leader and other group members; (ii) any restrictions on a participant's freedom to leave the group at any time; and,

(h) Issues of confidentiality.

3. A screening interview should be conducted by the group leader prior to the acceptance of any participant. It is the responsibility of the leader to screen out those individuals for whom he or she judges the group experience to be inappropriate. Should an interview not be possible, then other measures should be used to achieve the same results.

At the time of the screening interview, or at some other time prior to the beginning of the group, opportunity should be provided for leader-participant exploration of the terms of the contract as described in the information statement. This is to assure mutual understanding of the contract.

4. It is recognized that growth groups may be used for both educational and psychotherapeutic purposes. If the purpose is primarily educational, the leader assumes the usual professional and ethical obligations of an educator. If the purpose is therapeutic, the leader assumes the same professional and ethical responsibilities he or she would assume in individual or group psychotherapy, including before and after consultation with any other therapist who may be professionally involved with the participant. In both cases, the leader's own education, training, and experience should be commensurate with these responsibilities.

5. It is recognized that growth groups may be used for responsible research or exploration of human potential and may therefore involve the use of innovative and unusual techniques. While such professional exploration must be protected and encouraged, the welfare of the participant is of paramount importance. Therefore, when an experience is clearly identified as "experimental," the leader should: a) make full disclosure of techniques to be used; b) delineate the respective responsibilities of the leader and participant during the contract discussion phase prior to the official beginning of the group experience; and c) evaluate and make public his or her findings.

AN EXHORTATION

GROUP PROCESS ANALYSIS:
PAST IS PROLOGUE

Eugene L. Hartley

Just as the publication of the volume of *Readings in Social Psychology*, prepared for the committee on the teaching of social psychology of the Society for the Psychological Study of Social Issues,[1] provided a base for the coalescence of the concerns of sociologists and psychologists interested in this field, so we may expect the present volume to contribute to the desired integration of the scientific and therapeutic approaches. The questions and challenges raised in the Introduction to the present series of papers must be confronted, along with many others. The reliance in this collection on the Western European tradition, and particularly on the English language publications, can be noted and understood, but still be deplored. Such sociocentrism cannot long be permitted to endure. In the "one world" of intellectual endeavor there must be no such barriers. It should be highly enlightening to see an analysis of readers' fantasies about the contents of a revised edition five or ten years hence.

The student of personality and the student of social psychology work at somewhat different levels of abstraction. The former attempts to identify and account for those aspects of the individual which characterize his activities in *all* his undertakings; the latter emphasizes the analysis of those aspects of the individual's behavior which derive from his membership in a structured society. Normally, the student of personality can be expected to offer but little to the examination of the *variable* responses of the individual as he plays his several roles in the course of a day. On the other hand, the social psychologist, with his point of departure the complexly structured society, will make only a limited contribution to the understanding of the internal integration of the affective responses of the individual which defines his joys and sorrows, satisfactions and discomforts. The merging of the two emphases makes it possible to establish continuity between the two levels of study so that we can see the transformation of such "personality" attributes as needs and cognitive styles into concrete, manifest behavior; and conversely, it can account more adequately for the growing distress of an individual who is successfully fulfilling the requirements of a high status constellation of middle-class roles. The emergent synthesis is not easy to achieve, for we are each ego-involved in the disciplines in which we have been trained; we have our frames of reference which contribute to our selective perceptions of the available data, our ego ideals which provide us with models, our didactic experiences which have confirmed us in our approaches. However, the need is great, and with the superordinate goal requiring endeavors beyond that available within either group, we can confidently expect a coalition. New reference groups must be formed and cathected, new norms must emerge.

The hand of tradition seems to lie more heavily on the practitioner than on the academician; therefore it is the practitioner who must make the more strenuous efforts. It would be well for him to remember that Freud's analysis of groups derived primarily from his observations of the church and the army. He was well aware of the restrictions this imposed on his formulations and qualified his delineation of a psychological group by noting that this only held for groups having a leader. Today, of course, we would restrict it to groups with authoritarian leadership. Freud noted further that the conscience was the most common derivative from the ego, but that there were many other splits. Apparently the superego residual of the Oedipus complex is not the end of the development of internalized norms and self-regulating mechanisms. Later cathexes are also integrated. "Normally," wrote Freud, "the superego is constantly becoming more and more remote from the original parents, becoming, as it were, more impersonal."[2] The analysis of groups as representing the family paradigm seems far less rigid in Freud's writing than in that of many of his followers.

The academician is far more ready to adopt new perspectives. The scientist has often been described as a faddist who embraces with enthusiasm new theories, new techniques, new terminologies. He will have difficulty, nonetheless, in accepting a formulation that suggests that the entire study of group process represents *merely* the elaboration of superego psychology. Perhaps it would be worth while searching for new terms in the more esoteric languages so that we may proceed with appropriate definitions unbeclouded by the connotations deriving from common usage. The "mask" significance of persona, and the "indivisible" root of individ-

ual, both belie current conceptual significances. As we study group processes within the individual as well as in the interpersonal units, new
dimensions should emerge, and we must be wary of having our understanding impaired by the channeling effects of inexact language.

Perhaps as a start we might address ourselves to the question of the
extent to which group therapy really involves the *group* process rather
than simply the concurrent analyses of the plural psychologies of a number of individuals. There is a tremendous difference between the functional interrelationships of individuals interacting to achieve a goal in
common and a similar setting of individuals with common goals. The commonly cited illustration of a team whose members must win or lose together well illustrates the group with a goal in common. The ordinary college class shows none of the same sort of interdependence inasmuch as
one student may, at the end of the term, get an A and his neighbor an F. Let
the college instructor, however, announce a surprise quiz, and the class becomes a well-knit group of interdependent individuals whose success or
failure in protesting the threat will blanket all equally. Note the great difference in reaction to events on the national and international scene, at
the threat of thermonuclear war, between, on the one hand, the person who
perceives his survival as a goal in common with that of potential enemies
and thinks in terms of the interdependence of mankind and, on the other,
the person who sees survival as a common goal but without a feeling for
any interdependence. Where does the group of the group therapist fit in?
Is it perceived by the participants as one in which their personal success,
their cure, depends on the progress of their neighbors? Or do they have a
sympathetic feeling for their fellow sufferers but essentially believe they
are autonomous units? Either way, the group setting adds new dimensions
to the therapy for the individual; but for the development of a sound and
integrated theory we must know and understand what is transpiring in
group process terms.

Let us approach another illustrative problem from the perspective of
the practitioner. One of the first questions raised by the novice is, "How
large should a group be?" What really *is* the optimal number of patients
who may be formed into a group? For psychoanalytic group therapy, a
very common answer, empirically derived, is "about eight to ten." The
practitioner may be satisfied—he knows how to proceed; but the scientist
would still want to know, "Why?" Let us consider the matter very briefly.
What is the effect of size on a group? If we expect every individual to interact with each other individual, how many interactional bonds or units
would there be in groups of different sizes? With two individuals, there is
one bond between them; with three, two bonds; with four, six; with five,
ten. The general formula, from elementary probability theory, would be
the one for predicting the number of combinations taken two at a time

from differently sized groups. If n equals the number of people in the group, the formula is: $n(n-1)/2$. Using this formula we can see that the interactional bonds within groups of various sizes increase as follows:

Number of people in group	Number of interactional bonds
6	15
7	21
8	28
9	36
10	45
11	55
12	66
13	78
14	91
15	105

Is the limit set at, let us say, eight because the therapist would have trouble keeping track of more than 28 interactional units? Or is it the patients who are so limited? With whose social perception span are we dealing? If the emphasis is on the patients' ability to maintain control over relationships, would we not expect this to be a variable depending on the kind and degree of the patients' pathology? If it is the therapist who is the limiting factor, would we not expect this factor to change as a function of experience? Are smaller groups less effective because they do not provide support or because they do not provide enough challenge and opportunity? To what extent ought the size of the group be varied during the progress of therapy in order to provide for increased therapeutic opportunities as the patients improve? Perhaps the decision about group size is primarily a matter of "practicality," the limit to the consumer's willingness to dilute his relationship to the therapist and still pay his fees; but might not this be related to the size of the family from which the patient comes? The relationship of group size to group processes is still a very real problem. Some laboratory studies of this problem have been undertaken, primarily with problem solving groups; are the results comparable to the findings (or observations) in therapy groups? The study of even small groups show consistent tendencies toward the development of scapegoating and supportive coalitions. Are such tendencies inherent in the group process, and how are they best integrated into the therapeutic theory and practice?

As we look forward to the continuing reciprocal enrichment of the studies and practice in the group process field, let us not overlook the need to retain our orientation toward the continued elaboration of the researches into the nature of motivation, of perception, and of the learning processes. Laboratory studies of traditional topics, as well as of such integrative concepts as coping and creativity, are making huge strides. For these tool concepts, unlike the advances in pharmacology, we do not have "detail men." We must do our own studying and appraising.

However, new knowledge does not come only from the laboratories. Clinicians in recent years have often noted that the pattern of presenting problems of patients coming for psychotherapy is manifesting a marked change. The classical symptomatology is far less frequently encountered now than formerly. Now patients are at a loss in their searching for identity, for meaning in life, far more often than before. But what new patterns of disorder will emerge tomorrow? Our age is characterized by a rate of acceleration in technological and social change hitherto unknown. The increasing tempo of this rate of change is bound to have profound effects on the human personality and its modes of adaptation —over and above the stresses of the threats of war and thermonuclear destruction. Whether cures will be found in surgery, pharmacology, psychotherapy, or milieu therapy, we can be fairly confident that there will be new forms of psychopathology to which we will have to address ourselves, new modes of adjustment to new kinds of problems which we will have to analyze.

If we are to meet the challenge of our field and our times, we must follow the precept of Gordon Allport to health workers and "develop skill as an *oculist*, training himself to look *at* his spectacles and not merely *through* them, and training himself to look both *at* and *through* the spectacles of the client with whom he deals."[3] Of both the scientist and the practitioner, the future demands no less.

ADDITIONAL COMMENTS: FOOTNOTE, ONE DECADE LATER

In the decade that has elapsed since the publication of the original edition of this volume, concern with groups, group psychotherapy, and group processes has increased phenomenally. An illustrative index may be derived from the entries in the Psychological Abstracts. From 1963 to 1972, the total number of items abstracted increased 290 per cent. Within those totals, the number of publication subjects indexed under Psychotherapy/ group increased 426 per cent. In 1963 the group psychotherapy entries were 0.9 per cent of the total number of items; in 1972 they were 1.3 per cent. The growth of the field has outstripped the more general increase in professional concern with the human condition.

	1963	1972	Increase
Total no. of items	8,381	24,325	290%
No. of entries Psychotherapy/group	74	315	426%
Entries: Total no. items	0.9%	1.3%	

The 1960's saw the continuation and development of the trends identified in the original edition. New elements appeared. For example, the efforts toward achieving greater objectivity-accuracy-efficiency in theory and practice led to the integration of the neo-Behaviorists (Behavioralists) into the field. In the original edition, it may be noted, John B. Watson was given only one passing mention, and Skinner and Wolpe were not referred to at all. During the decade, along with the development of the general emphasis on behavior theory and behavior modifications, practitioners of group psychotherapy have seen the rise of group desensitization and contingency management procedures as new approaches which have to be encompassed. Other theoretical innovations have been introduced, such as transactional analysis, and technological developments have been exploited, for example, videotape recording and review, and use of audio cassettes. New patient populations have been identified for attention and new problem foci have come to the fore. Such developments are, however, phenotypes.

A new genotypic trend has emerged during the decade and will require attention in the future. Objective data are not readily available, and it is difficult to achieve proper perspective. We shall try, however, to offer a series of suggestions which may stimulate the development of more systematic and sophisticated hypotheses. During the 1960's, "groupish" became a fad. Many trends contributed to the flight to the group as an alternative to more solitary forms of reaction. Perhaps most important among the causes were the continuing failure to alleviate the dehumanization of our industrialization and the increased deterioration of our urban centers past the threshold for toleration. The progressive dysfunction in the cities leading to increased depersonalization, anonymity, and alienation exacerbated the needs for social integration, social acceptance, and self-enhancement. The political disillusionment for many as the growing "peace movement" in the United States failed in its efforts to halt the armed violence in Southeast Asia led to a withdrawal and rejection of organized activities within the establishment framework, and to resurgence of a utopianism through small group bohemianism. Disaffection on college and university campuses through the 1960's was another contributing component. Combining the influences from the larger community with the specialized problems in the educational establishment, youth populations found ripe targets for their rejection of traditionalism, the value of expert knowledge and systematic study, and the validity of conventional regulatory forms and procedures in the social realm.

Group psychotherapists had been moving forward with therapy groups as the students of group process had been developing T-groups. Sensitivity groups and marathon groups were also developing under professional guidance. Suddenly, however, there were a multitude of communes and rap groups, awareness groups and personal exploration groups, confrontation groups, radical therapy leaderless groups, and marathon workshops in esoteric (erotic) subjects. Revitalized serious interest in Zen, Yoga, Sufism, and other Eastern studies and belief systems ran parallel to exploitation of superficial gleanings from these approaches. The success of self-directed groups, such as those among alcoholics, in which leadership was supplied by those who had experienced the problems and had leadership training, led to emulation by others who were involved in their problems but had not added the ingredient of specialized training. In short, a rising tide of antiintellectualism engulfed the group movement and encouraged the development of similarly named and superficially similar appearing groups in the community.

Attempts to differentiate qualified professionals from charlatans, to protect the community and susceptible individuals from the dangers inhering in some of the group activities, to develop appropriate procedures and training facilities, and to identify meaningful standards and credentialing devices were begun and are still under way. The social dynamics underlying the controversies that have arisen are all too familiar, and the extension of public understanding is meeting well-known obstacles. However, whereas a decade ago group psychotherapists were a comparatively small band of professionals exploring a new frontier despite the suspicions of many professional colleagues, they now are a somewhat larger group of accepted professional specialists who are trying to continue the development as they confront the excesses of popular imitation and dilution of their contributions.

Perhaps the best symbol of the "arrival" of group psychotherapy is the publication of the leaflet, "Facts About: Group Therapy,"[4] by the National Institute of Mental Health in 1972. What the comparable landmark will be a decade hence is hard to foretell. It is the fervent hope of many, however, that defenses against the shoddiness and dangers of so many of the faddish groupish activities will not blind responsible professionals among students of group process and psychotherapy to the possibilities of significant constructive insights emerging from the unorthodox. Such contributions as may be gleaned will need identification, clarification, and evaluation under controlled conditions, in the same fashion as we are seeing evaluated hypotheses arising from the orthodox. The dangers are very real, but the past provides the basis for optimism about the future.

REFERENCES

1. T. Newcomb, and E. L. Hartley, eds., *Readings in Social Psychology* (New York: Holt, Rinehart and Winston, 1947).
2. S. Freud, *New Introductory Lectures on Psychoanalysis* (New York: Carlton House, 1933), p. 92.
3. Second Dorothy B. Nyswander Lecture, Berkeley, California, May 23, 1958.
4. "Facts About: Group Therapy," DHEW Publication No. (HSM) 79-9155, National Institute of Mental Health, 1972.

NAME INDEX

SUBJECT INDEX